UTAH

W.C. McRAE & JUDY JEWELL

Contents

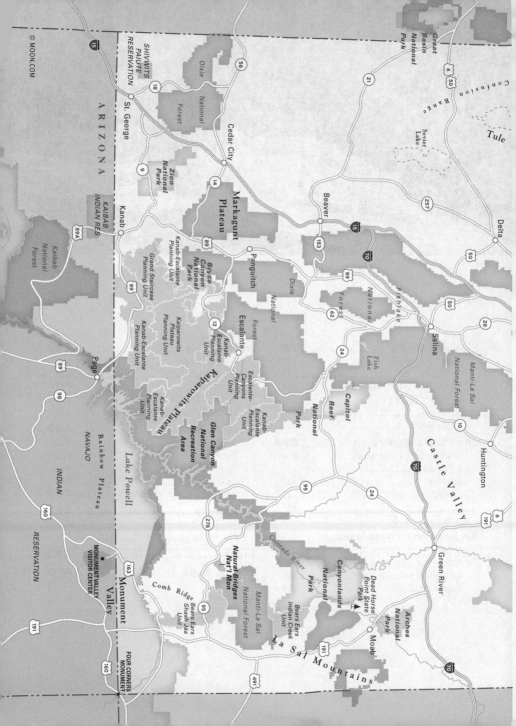

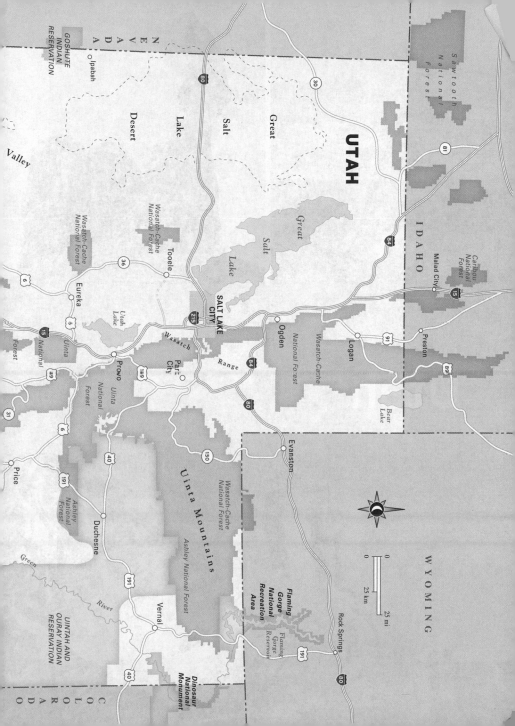

DISCOVER
Utah

The story goes that in 1847, when the trail-weary Mormon leader Brigham Young surveyed the Salt Lake Valley from Emigration Canyon high in the Wasatch Range, he declared, "This is the place." Since the founding of Salt Lake City and the settlement of Utah, many other people have taken a look at this dramatic landscape and agreed: "Yes, this *is* the place."

Few places on earth combine such spectacular terrain and unusual history. The state hosts the majestic splendor of the Wasatch Range, the colorful canyon lands of the Colorado Plateau, and the remote deserts and arid mountain ranges of the Great Basin. This region beckoned as the "Promised Land" to members of the struggling Church of Jesus Christ of Latter-day Saints in the 1840s—a place where those faithful to the Book of Mormon could survive and prosper in a land of their own. Today, this once insular state has put out the welcome mat—Utah's extravagant scenery and superlative recreational opportunities lure sightseers, mountain bikers, hikers, and skiers from around the world, many of whom stay on to make this beguiling state their home.

Utah presents some curious statistics: Although it ranks 31st among states in population, it is the 9th most urban state in the nation, a startling fact when

---

Clockwise from top left: Bryce Canyon vista; Balanced Rock; Alta Ski Area; Wolfe Ranch petroglyphs; Island in the Sky District of Canyonlands; flowers in Arches National Park.

you consider how utterly vacant—though dramatically beautiful—much of the landscape is. The unyielding deserts, craggy mountains, and imposing slickrock formations that cover much of the state aren't really fit for human habitation, and the majority of citizens live in a few large cities in the sprawling Wasatch Front metropolitan area.

About 60 percent of the people living in Utah are practicing Mormons. To outsiders, the social homogeneity of smaller towns far from Salt Lake City, Park City, and Moab can seem off-putting, but the strong religious and cultural bonds that tie families and communities together in Utah are themselves noteworthy and increasingly rare in the fast-paced modern world. The uniformity of the population stands in stark contrast to the diversity of the landscape and the abundance of opportunities for outdoor recreation.

From incredibly varied canyon country, remote and rugged mountain ranges, and glistening salt flats to ancient Native American rock art and cliff dwellings, fossilized dinosaur footprints, and old mining towns, the many fascinating sights and experiences of Utah are waiting to be discovered.

Clockwise from top left: view from Angels Landing; The Narrows in Zion National Park; Coyote Gulch; desert flora.

2 **Float in the Great Salt Lake**: The best place to get a sense of the continent's largest salt-water lake is **Antelope Island State Park** (page 88), where you can hike, view wildlife, or even take a dip in the briny water.

3 **Ski and Snowboard in the Wasatch Range:** Go upscale at **Deer Valley** (page 137), get deep in powder at **Alta** (page 126), or snowboard with the locals at **Brighton** (page 118). End the day with dinner and drinks in Park City.

>>>

10 TOP EXPERIENCES

1 Take in the Views at Arches and Canyonlands: From the postcard-perfect vista at Delicate Arch (page 390) to Mesa Arch (page 403) poised on a dramatic cliff-top and endlessly photographable Windows Section (page 390), there's plenty of natural beauty for lasting memories.

4 **Hike among the Hoodoos:** Bryce Canyon's pink and gold **hoodoos** are magnificent viewed from a distance, but you can also explore the pillars up-close (page 249).

<<<

5 **Explore the Slot Canyons:** Hike through the narrow rock channels carved deep into massive sandstone formations (page 315).

>>>

6 **Tour Temple Square:** Whether or not you're one of the faithful, this complex is a place to gain a greater understanding of the Church of Jesus Christ of Latter-Day Saints... or your own genealogy (page 34).

<<<

7 **Get Prehistoric:** Utah is littered with dinosaur fossils and dino tracks. The Dinosaur Quarry at **Dinosaur National Monument** (page 198) is a good place to see a wall of bones. In Salt Lake City, the **Utah Museum of Natural History** (page 43) has great exhibits, including the skeleton of a recently discovered new dinosaur species.

8 **Uncover Ancient Mysteries:** Head off the beaten path to Nine Mile Canyon (page 211) or Hovenweep National Monument (page 425) or Canyonlands' Great Gallery (page 417) to see some of the best examples of long-ago cultures.

>>>

9 **Bike Utah:** The **Slickrock Trail** in **Moab** gets all the love when it comes to destination-mountain biking, but Utah offers an abundance of alternative off-road biking adventures (page 29).

10 **Sky-gazing:** Whether painted with fiery sunsets or glowing with countless stars, these are some of the most gorgeous skies you'll ever see (page 251 and page 291).

<<<

Planning Your Trip

Where to Go

Salt Lake City

Salt Lake City is the state capital, home to a **major university** and seat of a major religion—a rare combination of attributes that makes for a certain amount of civic gravitas and self-focus. But to visitors, Salt Lake City presents a near-unique natural and built environment, where all-season, big-as-all-outdoors **recreation** co-exists with the sophisticated comforts of **urban living.** And as one of the fastest-growing metropolitan areas in the nation, Salt Lake City's population is increasingly diverse and cosmopolitan. The former rail hub of **Ogden,** along with its nearby ski resorts and nearby **Antelope Island State Park,** a wild and beautiful getaway in the Great Salt Lake, draw visitors beyond city limits.

Park City and the Wasatch Range

In the Wasatch Range, superb snow conditions and friendly ski resorts combine to offer some of the best skiing in North America. Each resort has its own distinct character, from folksy yet ski-crazy **Alta** to plush **Deer Valley** or the sprawling **Park City** resort. In Park City itself, upscale amenities, fine dining, and events such as the **Sundance Film Festival** compete with the slopes for the attention of skiers and boarders. During summer, the mountain passes and ski areas offer hiking and mountain biking.

Provo and Central Utah

Provo, home to **Brigham Young University,** is a good base for exploring the dramatic Wasatch peaks that rise directly behind the city. An

The historic Egyptian Theatre in Park City hosts the annual Sundance Film Festival.

especially nice back road is the **Alpine Scenic Loop,** which climbs up to 7,500 feet. Along the way you'll pass **Sundance Resort,** noted for its skiing and good restaurants, and **Timpanogos Cave National Monument,** open in summer for tours with park rangers.

Dinosaur Country

Vernal and **Price** have good dinosaur museums; visit dig sites at the remote **Cleveland-Lloyd Dinosaur Quarry** and see more than 1,000 bones exposed in the quarry at scenic **Dinosaur National Monument.**

Beyond dinosaurs, the lofty **Uinta Mountains** are noted for their trout-rich streams and lakes. The **Green River** cuts a mighty canyon through these mountains, exposing deep red cliffs. Called the **Flaming Gorge,** the canyon now contains a reservoir that's the center of a national recreation area. This region also has excellent ancient Native American rock art and important archaeological sites.

Zion and Bryce

Zion National Park presents stunning contrasts, with barren, towering rock walls deeply incised by steep canyons containing a verdant oasis of cottonwood trees and wildflowers. Zion is so awe-inspiring that the early Mormons named it for their vision of heaven.

Bryce Canyon National Park is famed for its red and pink hoodoos, delicate fingers of stone rising from a steep mountainside. Nearby, **Cedar Breaks National Monument** has similar formations without the crowds.

The Escalante Region

A large section of the **Escalante Canyons National Monument** preserves the dry washes and slot canyons trenched by the Escalante River and its tributaries. Long-distance hikers descend into the deep, narrow river channels here to experience the near-mystical harmony of flowing water and stone. The nearby **Grand Staircase** region monuments preserve rock arches, jutting promontories, slot canyons and fossil-rich formations that are best explored on rugged backroad adventures.

Arches and Canyonlands

In vast **Canyonlands National Park,** the Colorado River begins to tunnel its mighty—and soon to be grand—canyon through an otherworldly landscape of red sandstone. The beauty is more mystical at **Arches National Park,** where hundreds of delicate rock arches provide windows into the solid rock. High-spirited **Moab** is the recreational mecca of southeastern Utah, known for its mountain bike lifestyle and comfortable, sophisticated dining and lodging.

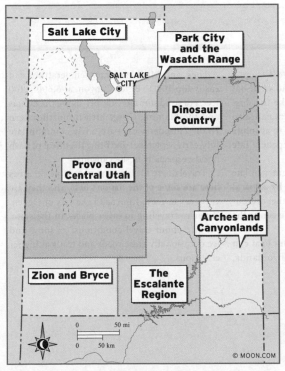

Salt Lake City

Park City and the Wasatch Range

SALT LAKE CITY

Dinosaur Country

Provo and Central Utah

Arches and Canyonlands

Zion and Bryce

The Escalante Region

0   50 mi

0   50 km

© MOON.COM

Bryce Canyon vista

When to Go

Spring (Apr.-early June) and **fall** (Sept.-Oct.) are the most pleasant times to visit, but the same spring showers that make the desert country shine with wildflowers can also dampen trails and turn dirt roads to absolute muck. Arm yourself with insect repellent late spring-midsummer.

Aspens turn gold in the high country in late September-early October, followed by colorful displays of oaks, cottonwoods, and other deciduous plants in lower canyons lower. This can be the best time to travel in Utah.

Except in the mountains, **summer** heat can rapidly drain your energy. In Canyonlands, Arches, and Moab, summer temperatures can easily top 100°F. Bryce Canyon, at 6,600-9,100 feet, is a good summertime bet, as are the Uintas and the Flaming Gorge area in northeastern Utah. Thunderstorms are fairly common late July-early September and bring the threat of flash floods, especially in slot canyons.

Travel doesn't let up in **winter**—the ski areas here are some of the nation's best, and they are very easy to get to from Salt Lake City or Ogden. If you're traveling to other places in the state, inquire about travel conditions, as snow and ice occasionally close roads and trails at higher elevations.

The Best of Utah

Utah's top sights form a ring within the state, making it easy to take a 10-day loop road trip that connects the state's most alluring attractions. Think of this as a sampler of Utah's varied destinations.

Day 1

Arrive in **Salt Lake City.** Take in the Mormon historic sites at **Temple Square,** wander through the historic neighborhoods along South Temple Street, and, depending on the weather, attend a free evening concert at the Mormon Assembly Hall, the tabernacle, or Gallivan Center. Spend the night at Hotel Monaco—or Little America, if you're on a budget (look for specials online).

Day 2

Drive north on I-15. Just south of Ogden, head west along a 7-mile (11.3 km) causeway to **Antelope Island State Park** to dip your toes into the Great Salt Lake and look for wildlife, including the island's bison herd. Have lunch on 25th Street, lined with historic storefronts now housing shops and cafés, in **Ogden.** After lunch, continue north to the verdant Cache Valley, where **Logan** is home to Utah State University and, in summer, the Utah Festival Opera. Try some delicious Aggie ice cream, made by the university's dairy school, and spend the night at the Best Western Weston Inn.

Day 3

Return south toward Salt Lake City on I-15, but this time skip the big city and turn east onto I-80 to **Park City,** Utah's top ski resort and film festival center. The old town area of Park City is a long and narrow street that remains from the town's beginnings as a mining camp. From right downtown, ride the Town Lift for a mountain hike, then wander along Main Street to shop the

Salt Lake Temple

Funky pianos are scattered around downtown Salt Lake City.

South Window in Arches National Park

boutiques and pick out a restaurant for dinner. For real fun, head a block off Main to High West, a distillery with good food and a Western vibe. Spend the night in style at Marriott's Summit Watch Resort, or save a few bucks at the Park City Hostel.

Day 4

Today, you'll put quite a few miles on the car. Drive from Park City to Provo on U.S. 189, through the very scenic **Provo Canyon.** Continue south on U.S. 6, first to Price and then to the town of Green River. After a brief drive along I-70, turn south onto U.S. 191 to Moab.

Day 5

You're in the midst of national parks, so start exploring. **Arches** is just a few miles away, so you'll have time to hike to **Delicate Arch,** explore the **Devils Garden,** and stop at every scenic viewpoint along the way.

Day 6

From Moab, drive south on U.S. 191.

Unfortunately, time doesn't allow for exploration of all the far-flung districts of **Canyonlands,** but at least pull off the road 40 miles (64 km) south of Moab at the road to Needles District and drive 10 miles (16 km) to **Newspaper Rock Historical Monument.** Continue south to Bluff, a tiny town along the San Juan River, where you can stay at the Recapture Lodge.

Day 7

From Bluff, drive to Mexican Hat and drop into the **Navajo Reservation.** As you continue on, the dramatic spires of **Monument Valley** soon fill the skyline. Snap some photos before traveling southwest to Arizona via U.S. 163 and picking up to Kanab.

Day 8

Two national parks in one day? No problem! From Kanab, get an early start and drive U.S. 89 and then Highway 9 to **Zion,** where you'll drop off the car and ride the shuttle bus along the Virgin River Parkway. Hop off and on, taking short hikes in the mighty Zion Canyon.

Stop for lunch at the Zion Park Lodge, then backtrack to U.S. 89 and continue north. Make the turn onto Highway 12 for **Bryce Canyon.** Check into the Lodge at Bryce Canyon, then catch a free afternoon shuttle along the parkway. Be sure to catch the sunset over the park's mysterious pink and orange hoodoos.

Day 9
From Bryce Canyon, continue east along Highway 12 to **Escalante** and hike the easy, mostly level hike to **Lower Calf Creek**

Falls, or try some more intense canyoneering through the **Dry Fork of Coyote Gulch.** Enjoy great food and comfortable lodging at Boulder Mountain Lodge, in Boulder, or rough it in one of the simple cabins at Escalante Outfitters.

Day 10
Return to **Salt Lake City** by following Highway 24 to Salina, then U.S. 50 to I-15, which will get you to the Utah state capital in time for dinner at the Red Iguana.

National Park Road Trip

Despite their proximity, visiting all of Utah's national parks is a bit complicated because of the rugged terrain and lack of roads. You must plan on a lot of driving, but it's worth it to see each park's unique sights, from Arches' colorful rock fins to Bryce Canyon's towering hoodoos to the desert hiking trails of Canyonlands' Needles District. The roads between the parks are also unbelievably scenic, so get into a road-trip frame of mind, cue up some good music, and head out to explore.

Day 1
Start in Moab and head a few miles north to

Island in the Sky District

view of the Colorado River from Dead Horse Point State Park

Ancient History

A lot of history is preserved in Utah's ancient rocks. **Dinosaur footprints and bones** abound, as do traces of the **Fremont** and **Ancestral Puebloan** people who lived here centuries ago.

JURASSIC UTAH

About 145-200 million years ago, dinosaurs laid down footprints (and their dead bodies) in sand and mud. Today, you can see their fossilized bones and footprints.

- **Utah Museum of Natural History:** Amid all the dinosaur bones in this Salt Lake City museum is a good video exhibit featuring paleontologists espousing theories about the formation of the Cleveland-Lloyd Dinosaur Quarry.

- **St. George Dinosaur Discovery Site at Johnson Farm:** This is one of the world's best dinosaur-tracks sites. Recently discovered tracks show early Jurassic dinosaurs running amok across the former lake beds here.

- **USU Eastern Prehistoric Museum:** The locally dug fossils here include the Utahraptor (remember *Jurassic Park?*). After the museum, in downtown Price, drive east from Huntington to the Cleveland-Lloyd Dinosaur Quarry and visit the excavation site.

- **Utah Field House of Natural History State Park Museum:** View a well-done introductory video and a great collection of dinosaur bones and fossilized plants and mammals. Head north from this Vernal museum to the northern edge of Red Fleet State Park and take a 3-mile (4.8 km) round-trip hike to see dinosaur tracks.

- **Dinosaur National Monument:** The monument's Quarry Exhibit Hall is built around a cliff face that has been excavated to expose about 1,500 dinosaur bones, including those of the stegosaurus. It's a short drive east of Vernal.

- **Big Water Visitor Center:** At the southern edge of the Kaiparowits Plateau, east of Kanab, this spiral-shaped building is home to bones from a 75-million-year-old, 30-foot-long duck-billed dinosaur.

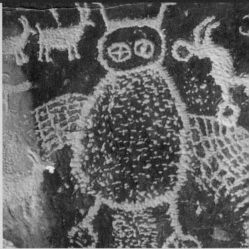
petroglyph in Nine Mile Canyon

PICTOGRAPHS AND PETROGLYPHS

Searching out pictographs (drawings painted on rock) and petroglyphs (images carved into stone) will lead you far off the beaten path and deep into canyons that were once central for Utah's ancient inhabitants.

- **Nine Mile Canyon:** Drive the now-paved road from Price to Utah's largest concentration of excellent rock-art panels and ancient grain caches tucked into the cliffs.

- **Sego Canyon:** North of Moab on I-80, Sego Canyon is a vast gallery of prehistoric art, where you'll find hundreds of etched images.

- **Fremont Petroglyphs:** Petroglyphs of horned mountain sheep and humans in feathered headdresses are easily viewed from a parking area along Highway 24 in Capitol Reef National Park.

- **BLM Newspaper Rock:** This showcase of rock art sits a few miles west of U.S. 191 on the entrance road for Canyonlands' Needles District.

- **Great Gallery:** In Canyonlands' remote Horseshoe Canyon Unit, human-size images of ghost spirits cover the walls in what was clearly a sacred place.

Arches National Park. Visit a few sites along the park road and hike to the famed **Delicate Arch.** Settle into your previously reserved campsite at **Devils Garden** and take an evening stroll down the **Devils Garden Trail.**

Day 2

Devote Day 2 to exploring **Canyonlands' Island in the Sky District,** taking in the astonishing vista points (particularly Grand View Point, perched high above the Colorado River) and saving time for a hike to the cliff edge. Camp at nearby **Dead Horse Point State Park** and explore the mountain biking there.

Day 3

Head into Moab for an early breakfast, and head south on U.S. 191. Pull off U.S. 191 south of Moab 40 miles (64 km) and drive toward the **Needles District** of Canyonlands. It's 38 miles (61 km) to the park gate (which will add considerably to the 115-mile (185-km) straight shot down 191), but good hiking awaits. If you're short on time just follow the park access road for 10 miles (16

km) from the highway to **BLM Newspaper Rock Historical Monument,** one of Utah's finest and most accessible petroglyph sites. Head back to U.S. 191, drive south to just past Blanding and head east on UT 95 across Cedar Mesa to the campground at **Natural Bridges National Monument.**

Day 4

From Natural Bridges, it's a pretty 100-mile (161-km) easy drive north on Highway 95 to Hanksville and west 28 miles (45 km) on Highway 24 to **Capitol Reef,** one of the National Park Service's unsung heroes, with scenery to match the other Utah parks but fewer visitors, a grassy campground, and a fruit orchard.

Day 5

From Capitol Reef, follow Highway 12 south to **Escalante Canyons National Monument.** The 61-mile (98-km) trip between Torrey and Escalante is one of the most scenic routes in all of Utah—don't plan to drive this in an hour. Take in all the scenery and sights, including a visit to

Explore Bryce Canyon on foot.

Utah's national parks seem custom-made for active kids, and all of the major parks have special activities for school-age visitors. Plenty of other attractions in this famously family-friendly state are fun for both kids and adults.

- **Utah Museum of Natural History:** Not only are the dinosaur skeletons impressive, so are the other highlights at this Salt Lake City museum, which include recently excavated finds from the Range Creek archaeological site (a remote site near the town of Price).

- **Homestead Crater:** Just a few miles from trendy Park City, you can swim or snorkel in the Crater, a warm 60-foot-deep spring-fed pond located in a cavern deep in the bowels of a 55-foot-high, cone-shaped limestone hill.

- **Thanksgiving Point:** Although some may see this sprawling park and education center north of Provo as the commercialization of family friendliness, it is a pretty awesome place to visit, with an excellent paleontology museum, a petting zoo, formal gardens, golf, entertainment venues, and plenty of places to eat.

- **Snow Canyon State Park:** The red rocks at this park north of St. George particularly invite scrambling. The 1.5-mile (2.4 km) round-trip Hidden Piñon Trail is good for kids who are just starting to hike.

- **St. George Dinosaur Discovery Site at Johnson Farm:** Check out some truly impressive dinosaur tracks, including some made by swimming dinosaurs.

Snow Canyon State Park

- **Hole 'n the Rock:** One man's 5,000-square-foot dream home, hollowed out from the base of a sandstone monolith south of Moab, is a full-blown roadside attraction, simultaneously tacky and touching.

- **River Rafting:** A half-day trip down the Colorado River near Moab may very well be the high point of a Utah vacation for the whole family. Outfitters are used to having everyone from toddlers to great-grandparents in their boats, although rafters must weigh more than 40 pounds.

the prehistoric ruins at **Anasazi State Park** and a hike across slickrock up the dramatic **Lower Calf Creek Falls Trail** to a waterfall.

Day 6
Explore more of the Escalante River canyons. Drive 12.5 miles (20.1 km) southeast on Highway 12 and turn onto the dirt Hole-in-the-Rock Road to traipse around **Devil's Garden.** You

can also visit the slot canyons of **Dry Fork of Coyote Gulch,** 26 bumpy miles (42 km) south of Highway 12.

Day 7
From Escalante, continue west 42 miles (68 km) on Highway 12 to **Bryce Canyon.** Spend the day riding the park shuttle to vista points and exploring hoodoos from trailheads along the road.

Days 8-9

Get up in time to see the rising sun light up the hoodoos, then drive west on Highway 12 to U.S. 89, and south from there to Highway 9. At Highway 9, turn west and enter **Zion National Park** via the dramatic **Zion-Mount Carmel Highway** (Bryce to Zion is 84 miles/135 km). Settle into your campsite (reserve in advance), then ride the park shuttle for a quick overview of Zion Canyon.

Salt Lake City Weekend

This getaway captures the best of Salt Lake City's sights, pleasures, and outdoor activities.

Friday

3PM: GO GRAND

Make your way in to the city from the airport and check into the **Grand America Hotel,** by far the city's most luxurious hotel (though the website often offers surprisingly affordable specials).

4PM: UTAH'S TOP GARDEN

Go to the University line of TRAX light rail, which has a stop just one block from your hotel, jump on the train to the University of Utah Medical Center stop, and catch a shuttle to **Red Butte Garden and Arboretum** to stretch your legs and learn about Utah's unique plant life.

6PM: MEDITERRANEAN, UTAH-STYLE

Take TRAX back downtown and head to **Martine Café** for tapas and drinks.

8PM: A STREAM RUNS THROUGH IT

Walk up Main Street to the **City Creek Center.** Check out the shops and the myriad of streams, falls, and other waterworks that run through the mall.

The Utah Museum of Contemporary Art is a hub for visual art, film, and spoken word.

- **Biking:** Moab gets all the press, and serious mountain bikers must visit, but **Red Canyon** (just outside Bryce) and the **San Rafael Swell** (northeast of Capitol Reef) have good biking without the hype. The mountain biking trails that lie in northeastern Utah near Vernal are also good. In southern Utah, the area around **Snow Canyon State Park** has good road rides. Avoid this area in the summer and ride the **Alpine Scenic Loop** or back roads around **Logan.**

- **Canyoneering:** Trek through the Virgin River on the **Narrows** hike, or plan ahead for the more challenging **Subway,** accessible via the less-traveled Kolob Terrace area of Zion.

- **Day Hiking:** The day hikes in Zion are plentiful and varied. Those in **Zion Canyon** are all easily accessible via the park shuttle bus, but you can lose the crowds by taking a day to drive outside the canyon and explore the **Kolob Terrace** area.

- **Fishing: Strawberry Reservoir,** near Heber City, is Utah's top trout fishery. Nearby, the **Provo River** is a lovely place to fly-fish.

- **Horseback Riding:** You can saddle up at **Zion** or **Bryce** National Parks. Across the Colorado River from Arches National Park, **Sorrel River Ranch** offers trail rides through dramatic red-rock landscapes.

- **Rafting:** The **Colorado River** offers sensational river rafting via outfitters in Moab. Find more solitude by floating through **Desolation and Gray Canyons** on the **Green River;** arrange to be flown in to Sand Wash and paddle 95 scenic miles (153 km) downstream to the town of Green River.

- **Rock Climbing:** One of the nation's "crack" climbing hotspots is just east of Canyonlands' Needles District, at **Indian Creek.**

- **Skiing:** Two Utah resorts are limited to skiers:

Enjoy Bryce Canyon on horseback.

go upscale at **Deer Valley** or join the rough- and ready-crowd at **Alta,** with slower lifts but plenty of character; pay a few bucks more for a pass at Alta and ski over to the bowls at **Snowbird.** Cross-country skiers can enjoy the quiet (and cheap) season at **Bryce,** when snow makes the hoodoos especially lovely. If you're just taking a break from a downhill-ski vacation, head over to Heber City, where **Soldier Hollow** has more than 20 miles (32 miles) of groomed trails.

- **Snowboarding:** Boarders go to **Brighton,** Utah's first ski resort, for the excellent terrain parks, easy backcountry access, and nighttime hours.

- **Stand-up Paddling:** The **Pineview Reservoir,** east of Ogden, is a good place to practice paddleboarding. Rentals are available in nearby Huntsville.

9PM: GENERATION X

Sip a craft cocktail at **Bar X,** where you'll glimpse a side of Salt Lake City that you probably didn't know existed: the hipsterati. If beer's your thing, head next door to **Beer Bar.**

Saturday
9AM: COFFEE AND TOAST

Grab a Green Bike and pedal over to the 9th and 9th neighborhood for coffee and toast (avocado toast if you must, or peanut butter on mocha bread) at **Publik Kitchen.**

10AM: TEMPLE SQUARE

To Latter-day Saints (LDS) believers, **Temple Square** is the equivalent of the Vatican or Mecca. Check out the visitors centers, listen to the organ in the tabernacle, view the temple (from the outside), research your family, and tour the gardens.

1PM: MEXICAN ON NORTH TEMPLE

Take a break from LDS holy sites with something wholly different: an excellent Mexican lunch at the **Red Iguana,** a longtime favorite for supremely tasty tacos and seven different kinds of mole.

2PM: ART NOUVEAU

View cutting-edge paintings and sculptures inspired by Utah landscapes and experiences at the **Utah Museum of Contemporary Art.**

4PM: SCULPTURE GARDEN

As a prelude to a rest before dinner, stop by one of Salt Lake City's (SLC's) truly unique sights, **Gilgal Gardens.** Here you'll see a series of engravings and statues designed and carved by an LDS bishop, including a Mormon version of the Sphinx.

7PM: UTAH HAUTE CUISINE

For one of the best meals in Utah, in one of the most stylish dining rooms in the city, take a seat at classy **Bambara,** in the Hotel Monaco.

10PM: DON'T ASK; PARTY

Check out the local music scene at **Urban Lounge,** an easygoing place with shows just about every night.

Sunday
9AM: HIKE THE CANYON

Take a stroll up **City Creek Canyon,** behind the state capitol, a paved path that winds up a beautiful narrow valley past willows and cascading pools to viewpoints over the city.

11AM: LAST BEST BREAKFAST

Drive to the mouth of Emigrant Canyon to **Ruth's Diner** for a hearty brunch in a dining room beside a rushing stream.

1PM: ANCIENT HISTORY

Before catching your plane back home, stop by the **Utah Museum of Natural History,** in a dramatic structure near the University of Utah. One of the top exhibits is the incredible cache of dinosaur bones from the Cleveland-Lloyd Dinosaur Quarry.

3PM: ONE LAST PINT

It's time to head to the airport, but there's time for one last brew at **Squatters Pub Brewery,** Utah's oldest brewpub. While you quaff your Provo Girl Pilsner, decide which of Salt Lake City's sights you'll visit on your next trip.

Deep Powder Without Deep Pockets

With lift ticket prices inching higher every year, it's nice to know that there are ways to make a ski trip more affordable. Here's one key: ski high, sleep low. And the other? If you are flying into Salt Lake City, take advantage of its great location and reduce your carbon footprint by taking the city bus and shuttles to the resorts.

Little Cottonwood Canyon

From downtown Salt Lake City, take the TRAX light rail south to the 7200 South Midvale-Fort Union station and transfer to bus 990, which travels up Little Cottonwood Canyon to **Snowbird** and **Alta.**

Big Cottonwood Canyon

From downtown Salt Lake City, take the TRAX light rail south to the 7200 South Midvale-Fort Union station. Transfer to bus 960 and head up Big Cottonwood Canyon to **Solitude** or **Brighton.**

Park City

Shuttle vans run from SLC to Park City. From downtown Park City, just catch the Town Lift to ski **Park City Mountain Resort.** Free city buses run to **Deer Valley** and the **Canyons area of Park City Resort.**

Sundance

Although Robert Redford's showcase **Sundance Resort** is a spendy place to stay, lift-ticket prices are a relative bargain. Not surprisingly, public transportation won't get you to this out-of-the-way resort, so you'll need a

Alta Ski Area

Moab may be the center of mountain biking in southern Utah, but it's by no means the only place that offers great trails and a vibrant infrastructure of bike rental shops and tour operators. Top mountain biking trails and destinations include:

- **Slickrock Bike Trail.** This is the trail that put Moab on the map, with 12 miles of trails on often steep sandstone outcrops. Be warned: this is not the place to learn slickrock biking skills; if you're not totally confident, check out other local trails that will prime you to conquer this world-famous route.

- **MOAB Brand Trails.** This series of interconnected trails north of Moab are great for slickrock beginners, with plenty of loop options to keep the ride interesting.

- **Gemini Bridges Trail.** Accessed from the Island in the Sky highway, this trail is one of the most scenic in the Moab area and makes only moderate demands in terms of skill and endurance. If you take a shuttle to the trailhead, most of the ride is downhill.

- **Historic Union Pacific Rail Trail.** This 28-mile paved trail runs from Park City (where it offers a handy alternative to driving) north to Echo Reservoir. Cruise it on a road bike or take a mountain bike to explore the single-track trails that loop off the main route.

The historic Union Pacific Rail Trail runs over 30 miles in and around Park City.

- **Vernal.** Find over 35 miles of bike trails at McCoy Flat, about 10 miles west of town. And that's just for starters; more trails are north of town near Red Fleet Reservoir.

rental car (or follow the lead of many guests and hire a limousine service).

Ogden

It's easy to get from Salt Lake City to Ogden via public transportation. Once you're there, Ogden operates a shuttle service from the downtown hotels to the **Snowbasin, Powder Mountain,** and **Nordic Valley** ski areas. All of these resorts offer half-day or night-skiing lift tickets, which cost less than a full day ticket.

Salt Lake City

In 1847, the Mormon prophet Brigham Young proclaimed this site the right place for a new settlement. Today, many residents and visitors still agree. Modern Salt Lake City offers an appealing mix of cultural activities, historic sites, varied architecture, engaging shopping, sophisticated hotels, and elegant restaurants. About 190,000 people live in the city, making it by far the largest and most important urban center in Utah, while more than one million people reside nearby in the city's sprawling suburbs.

Salt Lake City enjoys a physical setting of great visual drama. The city lies on the broad valley floor and terraces once occupied by prehistoric Lake Bonneville. Great Salt Lake, the largest remnant of that ancient inland sea, lies just northwest of the city. The Wasatch Range

Highlights

Look for ★ to find recommended
sights, activities, dining, and lodging.

★ **Temple Square Historical Tour:** Take a free 40-minute tour of this epicenter of Mormon faith, offering museums, public gardens, and eye-popping architecture. Whether you're a believer or not, you'll enjoy the spectacle (page 34).

★ **State Capitol:** Modeled on the U.S. Capitol, Utah's seat of government is grandly scaled and brimming with granite and marble. From the steps, views of the city and the Wasatch peaks are breathtaking (page 41).

★ **Red Butte Garden and Arboretum:** This oasis of green in arid Salt Lake City covers 30 acres. Two hundred acres of adjacent woodlands are laced with trails for hiking and jogging (page 43).

★ **Liberty Park:** This lovely park, with playgrounds, a lake, and lots of manicured lawns, is beloved for its Tracy Aviary, a bird zoo with falconry events (page 44).

★ **City Creek Canyon:** The most accessible hiking and cycling path in Salt Lake City starts right downtown and winds up along a rushing stream running past wooded glens. Enjoy an island of nature amid the city's urban sprawl (page 53).

★ **Union Station Museums:** This cavernous relic of Odgen's railroading past now serves as home to interesting museums and collections (page 78).

★ **Antelope Island State Park:** Hike or bike to explore the curious natural history of the largest island in the Great Salt Lake (page 88).

★ **Golden Spike Visitor Center:** The first transcontinental rail lines were joined at this

remote site in 1869; the visitors center and replica steam trains re-create the epoch-making event (page 94).

★ **American West Heritage Center:** This living-history museum showcases the Logan area's rich past from Native American culture to homestead farming (page 98).

★ **Benson Grist Mill:** This perfectly-preserved grain mill from the 1850s offers a fascinating glimpse into agrarian, frontier life (page 107).

rises immediately to the east; these rugged mountains, including many peaks exceeding 11,000 feet, are cut by steep canyons, which have streams that provide the area's drinking and irrigation water. Just minutes from downtown you can be skiing on some of the world's best powder in winter or hiking among wildflowers in summer. On the other side of the valley, to the west, Lewiston Peak (10,626 feet) crowns the Oquirrh (OH-ker) Mountains.

Salt Lake City's strong sense of focus and purposefulness comes from a near-unique combination of attributes. It's a state capital, a major university center, the largest city for hundreds of miles, and the seat of a wealthy and powerful worldwide religion.

The early Mormons' pride in their City of Zion is clearly seen in the old residential districts with their beautiful Victorian mansions, as well as the downtown area's ornate storefronts and civic structures. Few cities in the West retain such a wealth of period architecture.

PLANNING YOUR TIME

To see the sights in Salt Lake City requires at least three full days. Because the city is easily the most sophisticated place to stay and eat for hundreds of miles around (with the possible exception of Park City), it's also a comfortable and convenient hub for exploring the scenery and recreation of northern Utah.

You could easily spend a day visiting just the Latter-day Saints's museums, religious and historic sites, and administrative buildings that front Temple Square. Many people budget time to perform ancestry research while here—the church has extensive genealogical records and allows visitors to research family records free of charge.

A second day in Salt Lake City can be divided between visits to the state capitol and the nearby Pioneer Memorial Museum, plus a stop by the Utah Museum of Contemporary Art. Add in a picnic at Liberty Park and a

visit to the Tracy Aviary, a bird zoo with live falconry displays, and you'll have a full and varied day. A number of hiking trails begin right in the city: City Creek Canyon and Red Butte Garden and Arboretum, for example, are within reach of almost any downtown hotel.

Day-trip options include Antelope Island State Park, a good destination for hiking and mountain biking (plan to spend half a day exploring this island in Great Salt Lake), and Park City, a historic mining camp now turned glittering world-class ski resort. Ogden's museums and old city center can also be visited as a side trip from Salt Lake City, but if you're heading as far as Logan to attend one of its many music and theatrical festivals, it's worth spending the night. Depending on the season, skiing or hiking in the Wasatch Mountains directly behind the city should definitely be a part of every traveler's itinerary.

HISTORY

Salt Lake City began as a dream—a utopia in which the persecuted Latter-day Saints would have the freedom to create a Kingdom of God on Earth. Their prophet, Brigham Young, led the first group of 143 men, 3 women, and 2 children to the valley of Great Salt Lake in July 1847. The bleak valley, covered with sagebrush and inhabited mainly by lizards, could best be described as the land nobody wanted.

The pioneers set to work digging irrigation canals, planting crops, constructing a small fort, and laying out a city as nearly 2,000 more immigrants arrived that first summer. Tanneries, flour mills, blacksmith shops, stores, and other enterprises developed under church direction. Beautiful residential neighborhoods sprang up, reflecting both the pride of craftsmanship and the sense of stability encouraged by the church. Workers began to raise the temple, the tabernacle, and the other religious structures that still dominate the area around Temple Square. Colonization

Previous: skyline of Salt Lake City; Antelope Island State Park; historic greenhouse at the public Liberty Park.

Salt Lake City and Vicinity

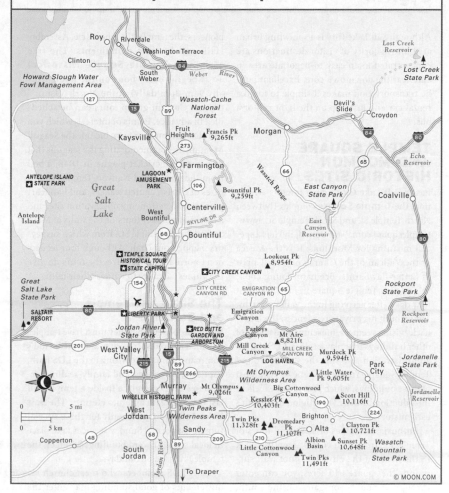

Roy
Riverdale
Washington Terrace
Clinton
Howard Slough Water
Fowl Management Area
South
Weber
Weber River
84
127
15
89
Kaysville
Fruit
Heights
Francis Pk
9,265ft
Morgan
Wasatch-Cache
National
Forest
273
Devil's
Slide
Croydon
Lost Creek
Reservoir
Lost Creek
State Park
84
80
Echo
Reservoir
ANTELOPE ISLAND
STATE PARK
Great
Salt
Lake
Farmington
Bountiful Pk
9,259ft
LAGOON
AMUSEMENT
PARK
106
Wasatch Range
66
65
East Canyon
State Park
Coalville
Antelope
Island
West
Bountiful
Centerville
SKYLINE DR
East
Canyon
Reservoir
68
Bountiful
80
TEMPLE SQUARE
HISTORICAL TOUR
STATE CAPITOL
Lookout Pk
8,954ft
Great
Salt Lake
State Park
154
CITY CREEK CANYON
CITY CREEK
CANYON RD
EMIGRATION
CANYON RD
65
Rockport
State Park
Rockport
Reservoir
SALTAIR
RESORT
80
LIBERTY PARK
Emigration
Canyon
Jordan River
State Park
West Valley
City
RED BUTTE
GARDEN AND
ARBORETUM
Parleys
Canyon
Mt Aire
8,821ft
Mill Creek
Canyon
MILL CREEK
CANYON RD
Murdock Pk
9,594ft
Park
City
Jordanelle
State Park
201
154
215
89
266
215
LOG HAVEN
Mt Olympus
Wilderness Area
Little Water
Pk 9,605ft
Jordanelle
Reservoir
Murray
WHEELER HISTORIC FARM
Mt Olympus
9,026ft
Big Cottonwood
Canyon
190
Scott Hill
10,116ft
West
Jordan
Twin Peaks
Wilderness Area
Kessler Pk
10,403ft
Brighton
224
0   5 mi
0   5 km
Copperton
48
68
Sandy
209
Twin Pks
11,328ft
Dromedary
Pk
11,107ft
Alta
210
Clayton Pk
10,721ft
South
Jordan
89
Little Cottonwood
Canyon
Albion
Basin
Sunset Pk
10,648ft
Wasatch
Mountain
State Park
Twin Pks
11,491ft
To Draper
© MOON.COM

of the surrounding country proceeded at a rapid pace.

As the Mormons' earthly City of Zion, Salt Lake City came close to its goal of being a community devoted to God. Nearly all aspects of political, economic, and family life came under the influence of the church during the first 20 years.

The isolation that had shielded Salt Lake City from outside influence began to fade around 1870, but the city remained conservative and inward-looking until the 1970s, when its superlative access to recreation began to attract an influx of young non-Mormons drawn to skiing, hiking, and other outdoor activities. With business booming, Salt Lake City soon became one of the leading cities of the American West. As a measure of the city's new prestige, Salt Lake City hosted the 2002 Winter Olympics.

Sights

Although Salt Lake City is a sprawling urban area, the majority of visitor destinations are concentrated in an easy-to-negotiate area in and near the downtown core. Excellent public transportation makes it simple to forgo a rental car and just hop on the light rail or a bus.

TEMPLE SQUARE AND MORMON HISTORIC SITES

Easily Salt Lake City's most famous attraction, the **Temple Square** complex (between North Temple St. and South Temple St., www.templesquare.com, 9am-9pm daily) has a special meaning for Mormons: It is the Mecca or the Vatican of the Church of Jesus Christ of Latter-day Saints. Brigham Young chose this site for Temple Square in July 1847, just four days after arriving in the valley. Nearby, Young built his private residences; the tabernacle, visitors centers, museums, and a host of other buildings that play a role in LDS church administration also line the streets around Temple Square. You're welcome to visit most of these buildings, which provide an excellent introduction to the LDS religion and Utah's early history.

Enthusiastic guides offer several tours of Temple Square, which covers an entire block in the heart of the city. A 15-foot wall surrounds the square's 10 acres; you can enter through wrought-iron gates on the south, west, and north sides. All tours, exhibits, and concerts are free. Foreign-language tours are also available—ask at the North Visitors' Center. Smoking is prohibited on the grounds.

TOP EXPERIENCE

★ Temple Square Historical Tour

Guides greet you at the gates of the square and offer an introduction to Salt Lake City's

pioneers, the temple, the tabernacle, Assembly Hall, and historic monuments. The free 45-minute **Temple Square Historical Tour** begins every hour on the hour (usually 9am-8pm daily) at the North Visitors' Center. Custom group tours can be scheduled in advance. Points of interest, which you can also visit on your own, include the Seagull Monument, commemorating the seagulls that devoured the cricket plague in 1848; a bell from the abandoned Nauvoo Temple; sculptures of Christ, church leaders, and handcart pioneers; an astronomy observation site; and a meridian marker (outside the walls at Main St. and South Temple St.) from which surveyors mapped out Utah. Although tour leaders don't normally proselytize, the tours do give the guides a chance to witness their faith.

The Salt Lake Temple and Gardens

Mormons believe that they must have temples in which to hold sacred rites and fulfill God's commandments. According to the LDS faith, baptisms, marriages, and family-sealing ceremonies that take place inside a temple will last beyond death and into eternity. The **Salt Lake Temple** is used only for these special functions; normal Sunday services take place in local stake or ward buildings—in fact, the temple is closed on Sundays.

Only LDS members who meet church requirements of good standing may enter the sacred temple itself; others can learn about temple activities and see photos of interior rooms at the South Visitors' Center. Non-Mormons are not allowed to enter the temple or its grounds. However, you can get a good look at the temple's east facade from the Main Street gates.

The plan for Salt Lake City's temple came as a vision to Brigham Young when he still lived in Illinois. Later, Young's concept became a reality with help from church architect

Temple Square

Truman O. Angell; construction began in 1853. Workers chiseled granite blocks from Little Cottonwood Canyon, 20 miles (32 km) southeast of the city, then hauled them with oxen and later by railroad for final shaping at the temple site. The temple dedication took place on April 6, 1893—40 years to the day after work began.

The foundation alone required 7,478 tons of stone. The tallest of the six slender spires stands 210 feet tall and is topped by a glittering statue of the angel Moroni with a trumpet in hand. The 12.5-foot statue is made of hammered copper covered with gold leaf.

East of the temple are acres of manicured **gardens** with reflecting pools and fountains. This is a very serene vantage point to take in the temple's gothic beauty.

The Tabernacle

Pioneers labored from 1863 to 1867 to construct this unique dome-shaped building. Brigham Young envisioned **The Tabernacle** as a meeting hall capable of holding thousands of people in an interior free of obstructing structural supports. His design, drawn by bridge-builder Henry Grow, took shape in massive latticed wooden beams resting on

44 supports of red sandstone. Because Utah lacked many common building supplies, the workers often had to make substitutions. Wooden pegs and rawhide strips hold the structure together. The large organ pipes resemble metal, balcony pillars appear to be marble, and the benches look like oak, yet all are pinewood painted to simulate these materials.

The tabernacle has become known for its phenomenal acoustics, a result of its smooth arched ceiling, and its massive pipe organ is regarded as one of the finest ever built. From 700 pipes when constructed in 1867, the organ has grown to about 12,000 pipes, five manuals, and one pedal keyboard. Daily **recitals** (noon and 2pm Mon.-Sat., 2pm Sun.) demonstrate the instrument's capabilities. The renowned **Mormon Tabernacle Choir,** 360 voices strong, is heard on the Sunday-morning national radio show *Music and the Spoken Word.* Visitors can attend choir rehearsals at 7:30pm Thursday or the broadcast performance at 9:30am Sunday (be seated by 9:15am); both are free. If attending performances in the Tabernacle is an important part of your itinerary, confirm your dates with the calendar at www.templesquare.com, as the choir is sometimes on tour; during certain times of the year, performances are held at the nearby Conference Center.

Assembly Hall

Thrifty craftspeople built this smaller Gothic Revival structure in 1877-1882 using granite left over from the temple construction. The truncated spires, reaching as high as 130 feet, once functioned as chimneys. Inside the **Assembly Hall** there's seating for 1,500 people and a choir of 100. The baroque-style organ, installed in 1983, has 3,500 pipes and three manuals; of particular note are the organ's horizontal pipes, called trumpets. The Salt Lake Stake Congregation once met here; now the building serves as a concert hall and hosts church functions.

North Visitors' Center

Wander around on your own or ask the ever-present tour guides for help. Exhibits at the **North Visitors' Center** focus on the life and ministry of Jesus Christ and the importance of ancient and modern prophets, including those from the Bible and from the Book of Mormon. An interesting scale model shows Jerusalem as it may have looked at the time of Christ. A spiraling ramp leads to the upper level, where *Christus,* an 11-foot replica of a sculpture by Bertel Thorvaldsen, stands in a circular room with a wall mural depicting the universe.

South Visitors' Center

Two exhibits at the **South Visitors' Center** cover the building of the Salt Lake Temple and "Strengthening the Family." Exhibits on the main level include paintings of prophets and church history, a baptismal font supported by 12 life-size oxen (representing the 12 tribes of Israel) as used in temples, photos of the Salt Lake Temple interior, and a scale model of Solomon's Temple. Head downstairs to see replicas of the metal plates inscribed with the Book of Mormon that Mormons believe were revealed to Joseph Smith in 1823. Ancient plates of Old World civilizations and stone boxes from the Americas are exhibited to support the claim that the plates are genuine.

Church History Museum

Brigham Young encouraged the preservation of church history, especially when he saw that Salt Lake City's pioneering era was drawing to a close. The **Church History Museum** (45 N. West Temple St., 801/240-4615, 9am-9pm Mon.-Fri., 9am-5pm Sat. and holidays, closed Sun., New Year's Day, Easter, Thanksgiving, and Christmas, free) houses a collection of church artifacts that includes the plow that cut the first furrows in Great Salt Lake Valley. Perhaps the most striking piece is the gilded 11.5-foot statue of Moroni that crowned a Washington DC chapel from 1933 to 1976.

1: Salt Lake Temple; **2:** The Tabernacle; **3:** Abravanel Hall is home to the Utah Symphony.

1

2

3

Step outside to see the 1847 log cabin, one of only two surviving from Salt Lake City's beginnings. The interior has been furnished as it might have been during the first winter here.

Family History Library

The **Family History Library** (35 N. West Temple St., 801/240-2331, 8am-5pm Mon., 8am-9pm Tues.-Fri., 9am-5pm Sat., closed most federal holidays, free) houses the largest collection of genealogical information in the world. Library workers have made extensive travels to many countries to microfilm documents and books. The LDS Church has gone to this effort to enable members to trace their ancestors, who can then be baptized by proxy. In this way, according to Mormon belief, the ancestors will be sealed in the family and the church for eternity. However, the spirits for whom these baptisms are performed have a choice of accepting or rejecting the baptism.

The library is open to the public. If you'd like to research your family tree, bring what information you have and get the library's booklet *A Guide to Research*. A brief slide presentation explains what types of records are kept and how to get started. Staff will answer questions. In most cases the files won't have information about living people for privacy reasons.

If you are new to genealogical investigation, you may want to start your research at the **FamilySearch Center** (15 E. South Temple St., 801/240-4085, 9am-5pm Mon.-Fri., closed most federal holidays), on the main floor in the Joseph Smith Memorial Building. The center has individual computer stations with access to family history resources, and staff is available to help you free of charge.

Brigham Young Monument

The **Brigham Young Monument,** standing in the middle of Main Street near North Temple Street, celebrates the first 50 years of settlement in Salt Lake City. Unveiled on July 24, 1897, it portrays Brigham Young in bronze atop a granite pedestal with figures below representing a Native American, a fur trapper, and a pioneer family. A plaque lists the names of the first 148 Mormon pioneers. The statue is also the originating point for the city's street-numbering system.

Joseph Smith Memorial Building

Built of white terra-cotta brick in modern Italian Renaissance style, the **Joseph Smith Memorial Building** (15 E. South Temple St., 9am-9pm Mon.-Sat.) opened in 1911 as the first-class Hotel Utah, built for church and business leaders. However, in 1987 the LDS Church, which owned the hotel, converted it into an office building and a memorial to LDS founding father Joseph Smith. The opulent lobby, with its massive marble columns, chandeliers, and stained-glass ceiling, remains intact; you definitely should walk through the lobby and admire the grand architecture. The 10th floor offers observation areas, the formal **Roof Restaurant** (801/539-1911), and the less formal **Garden Restaurant** (801/539-1911).

LDS Office Building

Day-to-day administration of the massive LDS Church organization is centered in the 28-story tower of the **LDS Office Building** (50 E. North Temple St., 801/240-2190), east of Temple Square. Such a volume of correspondence takes place that the building has its own zip code. The big attraction is a visit to the 26th-floor observation deck (open 9am-11am and 1pm-4pm Mon.-Fri., free). You'll see Temple Square and the whole city spread out below like a map.

Beehive House

The former house of Brigham Young, **Beehive House** (67 E. South Temple St., 801/240-2671, tours every 30 minutes 9am-8:30pm daily, last tour begins 8pm, free) was built in 1854 and occupied by Young and his family until his death in 1877. The adobe-and-brick structure stood out as one of the most ornate houses in early Salt Lake City. Free tours lasting 30 minutes take visitors through

Downtown Salt Lake City

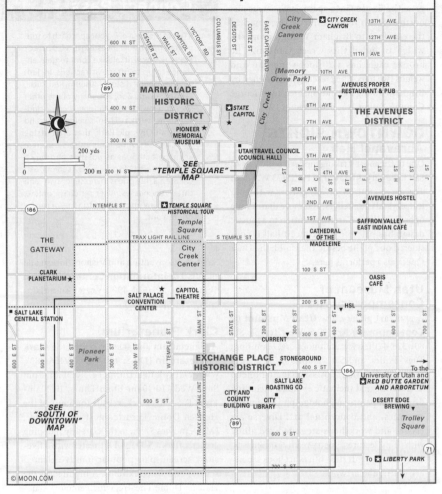

City Creek Canyon

☒ CITY CREEK CANYON

13TH AVE

12TH AVE

11TH AVE

(Memory Grove Park)

10TH AVE

9TH AVE — AVENUES PROPER RESTAURANT & PUB ▼

600 N ST

500 N ST

400 N ST

300 N ST

89

MARMALADE HISTORIC DISTRICT

☒ STATE CAPITOL ★

8TH AVE

7TH AVE

THE AVENUES DISTRICT

6TH AVE

PIONEER ★ MEMORIAL MUSEUM

UTAH TRAVEL COUNCIL (COUNCIL HALL)

5TH AVE

0   200 yds

0   200 m

200 N ST

SEE "TEMPLE SQUARE" MAP

4TH AVE

A ST

B ST

C ST

D ST

E ST

F ST

G ST

H ST

I ST

J ST

3RD AVE

186

N TEMPLE ST

☒ TEMPLE SQUARE HISTORICAL TOUR

2ND AVE

AVENUES HOSTEL

1ST AVE

SAFFRON VALLEY EAST INDIAN CAFÉ ▼

Temple Square

TRAX LIGHT RAIL LINE

S TEMPLE ST

CATHEDRAL ■ OF THE MADELEINE

THE GATEWAY

City Creek Center

CLARK PLANETARIUM ★

100 S ST

OASIS CAFÉ

★ CAPITOL THEATRE ■

SALT PALACE CONVENTION CENTER

200 S ST

HSL

■ SALT LAKE CENTRAL STATION

MAIN ST

STATE ST

200 E ST

300 E ST

400 E ST

500 E ST

600 E ST

700 E ST

300 S ST

600 E ST

500 E ST

400 E ST

300 E ST

200 W ST

W TEMPLE ST

CURRENT ▼

Pioneer Park

EXCHANGE PLACE HISTORIC DISTRICT

STONEGROUND

400 S ST

186

To the University of Utah and ☒ RED BUTTE GARDEN AND ARBORETUM

SALT LAKE ROASTING CO ▼

TRAX LIGHT RAIL LINE

500 S ST

CITY AND COUNTY BUILDING ■

CITY LIBRARY

DESERT EDGE BREWING ▼

Trolley Square

SEE "SOUTH OF DOWNTOWN" MAP

89

600 S ST

71

700 S ST

To ☒ LIBERTY PARK ▼

© MOON.COM

the house and tell of family life within its walls. The interior has been meticulously restored with many original furnishings. A beehive symbol, representing industry, caps the house and appears in decorative motifs inside. Brigham Young had about 27 wives but only one at a time stayed in this house; other wives and children lived next door in the Lion House. Downstairs in the main house, Young's children gathered in the sitting room for evenings of prayer, talks, and music. Upstairs, he entertained guests and dignitaries in a lavish reception room called the Long Hall.

The **Lion House** (63 E. South Temple St.), next door, was built of stuccoed adobe in 1855-1856; a stone lion guards the entrance. Brigham Young used it as a supplementary dwelling for his many wives and children. Today, the pantry and basement of the building are open to the public as the Lion House restaurant.

Eagle Gate

A modern replacement for the original 1859 gate, the **Eagle Gate** spans State Street just north of South Temple Street. It once marked the entrance to Brigham Young's property, which included City Creek Canyon. The bronze eagle has a 20-foot wingspan and weighs two tons. The present gate, designed by Brigham Young's grandson, architect George Cannon Young, was dedicated in 1963.

DOWNTOWN SIGHTS

Abravanel Hall

One of the most striking modern buildings in Salt Lake City, **Abravanel Hall** (123 W. South Temple St., 801/355-2787) glitters with gold leaf, crystal chandeliers, and more than a mile of brass railing. Careful attention to acoustic design has paid off: The concert hall is considered one of the best in the world; the Utah Opera also performs here.

Utah Museum of Contemporary Art

A civic art gallery, the **Utah Museum of Contemporary Art** (20 S. West Temple St., 801/328-4201, www.utahmoca.org, 11am-6pm Tues.-Thurs. and Sat., 11am-9pm Fri., suggested $5 donation) hosts a changing lineup of traveling and thematic exhibits, including displays of painting, photography, sculpture, ceramics, and conceptual art. Diverse art classes and workshops are scheduled along with films, lectures, poetry readings, concerts, and theater. A gift shop offers art books, posters, crafts, and artwork.

Salt Palace Convention Center

The enormous **Salt Palace Convention Center** (along West Temple St., between 200 South and South Temple St., 801/534-4777) is one of the largest convention centers in the West, with 515,000 square feet of exhibit space and 164,000 square feet of meeting space, including a 45,000-square-foot ballroom and 66 meeting rooms. Even in the sprawling scale of downtown Salt Lake City, this is a big building. The center houses the

Salt Lake City Connect Pass

If "all of the above" is your approach to trip-planning, consider investing in a **Connect Pass** (www.visitsaltlake.com) to gain entrance to up to fifteen attractions, including the Natural History Museum, Red Butte, Garden, Hogle Zoo, and many of the other sites and museums mentioned here, including some, such as Thanksgiving Point and the Utah Olympic Park, that are outside Salt Lake City. Ambitious visitors can cram as many activities as possible and buy a one-day pass ($36 adults, $32 seniors, $30 children 3-12); prices increase for two- and three-day passes. After purchase online, passes show up on a smartphone, or can be printed out.

Salt Lake Convention and Visitors Bureau and the **Visitor Information Center** (90 S. West Temple St., 801/534-4900, www.visitsaltlake.com, 9am-5pm daily).

Clark Planetarium

A planetarium and science center, the **Clark Planetarium** (110 S. 400 W., 801/456-7827, www.clarkplanetarium.org, 10:30am-7pm Sun.-Wed., 10:30am-10pm Thurs. 10:30am-11pm Fri.-Sat., check website for hours of the Hansen Dome Theatre, most exhibits free, IMAX movies $7-9), in the Gateway shopping center, offers a 3-D IMAX theater with a five-story screen, plus popular family-oriented science and space exhibits. A highlight is the Hansen Dome Theatre, which employs state-of-the-art technology to project a star show on a 360-degree 55-foot dome. Also in the Star Theatre are *Cosmic Light Shows*, which combine computer animation, special effects, and a 12,000-watt digital surround-sound system.

The Leonardo

A contemporary museum of science and culture, **The Leonardo** (209 E. 500 S., 801/531-9800, www.theleonardo.org, 10am-5pm daily, general admission $13 adults, $10 seniors, students, and military, $9 children 3-12; tickets to special exhibitions may be extra) is housed in the former Salt Lake City Public Library. The Leo, as it's called, has permanent exhibits on science, technology, engineering, art, and math but is largely known for hosting traveling exhibits such as the *Dead Sea Scrolls*, *Mummies of the World*, and the *Bodies* exhibition.

CAPITOL HILL
★ State Capitol

Utah's granite **State Capitol** (300 North and State St., 801/538-3000, http://utahstatecapitol.utah.gov, 7am-8pm Mon.-Thurs., 7am-6pm Fri., 8am-6pm Sat.-Sun.) occupies a prominent spot on a hill just north of downtown. The architectural style may look familiar: The building was patterned after the national capitol. The interior, with its Ionic columns, is made of polished marble from Georgia. Murals depict early explorers and pioneers; smaller paintings and statues show all of the territorial and state governors along with prominent Utah figures of the past. The Gold Room, used for receiving dignitaries, provides a formal setting graced by chandeliers, wall tapestries, elegant furniture, and cherubs on the ceiling. Enter the chambers of the House of Representatives, Senate, and Supreme Court from the mezzanine. Photo exhibits of the state's scenic and historic spots, mining, agriculture, and beehive memorabilia line hallways on the ground floor.

Forty acres of manicured parks and monuments surround the capitol. From the steps leading to the building, you can look out over Salt Lake City and straight down State Street, which runs south about 28 miles (45 km) without a curve. From near the Mormon Battalion Monument, east of the capitol, steps lead down into a small canyon and **Memory Grove,** another war memorial, and a series of streamside parks.

You're welcome to tour the capitol on your own during open hours; tour brochures are available from the visitors center just inside the east doors. Free **guided tours**

(information and Wednesday evening reservations 801/538-1800) are also available, departing every hour 9am-4pm Monday-Friday, except on state holidays, with additional tours (by reservation only) at 6pm and 7pm on Wednesday evenings. Meet in front of the large map on the first floor. Annual legislative sessions begin in January and last about 45 days.

Council Hall

The venerable **Council Hall** lies across the street from the capitol. Dedicated in 1866, the brick building served as the city hall and a meeting place for the territorial and early state legislatures. Council Hall used to stand downtown before being moved here in 1963.

It is now the home of the **Utah Office of Tourism** (www.visitutah.com). Drop in to see the staff of the **Salt Lake City Welcome Center** (801/538-1030, 8am-5pm Mon.-Fri., 10am-5pm Sat.-Sun.) on the main floor for information on sights, services, and events in the state.

UNIVERSITY OF UTAH AND VICINITY
Gilgal Gardens

On the way to the university from downtown is one of the oddest of Salt Lake City's public parks. The **Gilgal Gardens** (749 E. 500 S., http://gilgalgarden.org, 8am-8pm daily Apr.-Sept., 9am-5pm daily Oct.-Mar., free) is a colossally weird sculpture garden created by an LDS bishop whose spiritual quest led him to create stone-carved monuments and engrave stones with biblical and other religious verses.

Thomas Child began Gilgal Gardens in 1945, and work on the gardens and its sculptures continued until his death in 1963. The carvings and statues reflect a curious mix of Mormon, Old Testament, and Egyptian influences: A sphinx has the face of LDS founder Joseph Smith, while other sculpture vignettes represent Nebuchadnezzar's dream and a monument to the masonry trade. In all, there are 13 carved stone sculptures plus

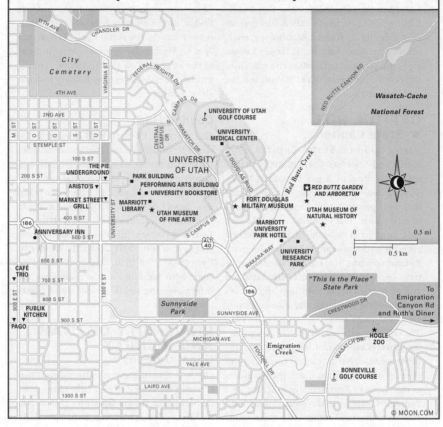

University of Utah and Vicinity

(Map labels:) 11TH AVE · CHANDLER DR · City Cemetery · VIRGINIA ST · FEDERAL HEIGHTS DR · 4TH AVE · 2ND AVE · M ST · L ST · K ST · S ST · U ST · S TEMPLE ST · CAMPUS DR · CENTRAL CAMPUS DR · WASATCH DR · N CAMPUS DR · UNIVERSITY OF UTAH GOLF COURSE · UNIVERSITY MEDICAL CENTER · RED BUTTE CANYON RD · Wasatch-Cache National Forest · 100 S ST · 200 S ST · THE PIE UNDERGROUND · UNIVERSITY OF UTAH · PARK BUILDING · ARISTO'S · PERFORMING ARTS BUILDING · UNIVERSITY BOOKSTORE · Red Butte Creek · RED BUTTE GARDEN AND ARBORETUM · MARKET STREET GRILL · MARRIOTT LIBRARY · UTAH MUSEUM OF FINE ARTS · FORT DOUGLAS MILITARY MUSEUM · UNIVERSITY ST · FT DOUGLAS BLVD · UTAH MUSEUM OF NATURAL HISTORY · 400 S ST · 186 · ANNIVERSARY INN · 500 S ST · ALT 40 · S CAMPUS DR · MARRIOTT UNIVERSITY PARK HOTEL · 600 S ST · CAFÉ TRIO · 700 S ST · 1300 E ST · 800 S ST · 186 · WAKARA WAY · UNIVERSITY RESEARCH PARK · 0 0.5 mi · 0 0.5 km · "This Is the Place" State Park · PUBLIK KITCHEN · 900 S ST · PAGO · 900 E ST · Sunnyside Park · SUNNYSIDE AVE · CRESTWOOD DR · To Emigration Canyon Rd and Ruth's Diner · MICHIGAN AVE · Emigration Creek · FOOTHILL DR · WASATCH DR · HOGLE ZOO · YALE AVE · BONNEVILLE GOLF COURSE · LAIRD AVE · 1300 S ST · © MOON.COM

innumerable flagstones with etched quotations within a garden setting. It's all very strange and oddly moving, and if you're attracted by people's curious spiritual journeys, you should make this one of your SLC stops—there's no other garden quite like this one.

University of Utah

Mormon pioneers established a university in their short-lived town of Nauvoo, Illinois, and they brought its books with them to Utah. The University of Deseret opened in 1850, just two-and-a-half years after the first colonists reached the Salt Lake Valley. It was renamed the **University of Utah** (201 Presidents Circle, 801/581-7200) in 1892 and now sprawls across a 1,500-acre campus.

About 28,000 students study in a wide range of fields—there are some 16 colleges and schools in all. The adjacent Research Park is a partnership of the university and private enterprise involving many students and faculty. Visitors are welcome at cultural and sporting events, libraries, the bookstore, the movie theater, and Olpin Union food services. Most recreational facilities are reserved for students. For a campus map, a list of scheduled events, and other information, drop by the **Park Building** (801/581-6515), at the top of President's Circle, or the **Olpin Union**

(801/581-5888), just north of Central Campus Drive. On-campus parking is available at metered spaces around the grounds and in pay lots next to the Olpin Union and the Marriott Library; free parking can be found off campus on residential streets.

Utah Museum of Natural History

The impressive **Utah Museum of Natural History** (301 Wakara Way, 801/581-6927, http://nhmu.utah.edu, 10am-5pm Thurs.-Tues., 10am-9pm Wed., $15 adults, $13 ages 13-24 and over age 64, $10 ages 3-12, free under age 3) has a large and varied collection of geology, biology, and anthropology exhibits. Visitors are greeted by expansive views from five-story windows and a series of exhibits that make great use of audiovisual technology and projected images. The exhibits touch on the state's early Native American history and feature eye-catching dioramas of various ecosystems. Young children can study insects and crawl "underground" in the *Our Backyard* exhibit, but easily the most impressive displays here are the skeletons of ancient creatures that once lived in Utah. In addition to a gift shop, the museum has a café open during all museum hours.

Utah Museum of Fine Arts

The ambitious **Utah Museum of Fine Arts** (410 Campus Center Dr., 801/581-7332, www.umfa.utah.edu, 10am-5pm Tues. and Thurs.-Sun., 10am-9pm Wed., $13 adults, $10 ages 6-18, seniors, and non-U of U students with ID) displays a little of everything, from 5,000-year-old Egyptian art to works by contemporary artists. Permanent exhibitions include art of China, India, Southeast Asia, Europe, Africa, the pre-Columbian Americas, and the early American West. Three large galleries host visiting exhibitions; there's also a pleasant café. Limited free parking is available in university parking lot 11.

★ Red Butte Garden and Arboretum

Utah's largest botanical garden, the **Red Butte Garden and Arboretum** (300 Wakara Way, 801/581-4747, www.redbuttegarden.org, 9am-9pm May-Aug., 9am-7:30pm Apr. and Sept., 9am-5pm Oct.-Feb., $14 adults, $12 seniors, $7 ages 3-17, free access to hiking trails in the natural area) offers 30 acres of floral displays, ponds, waterfalls, and 4 miles (6.4 km) of mountain nature trails in a 200-acre natural area. The garden visitors center features botanical gifts and books, and the Courtyard Garden is an excellent place for a family picnic.

To reach the garden from I-15, take the 600 South exit, which will take you east, then turn north and go two blocks to 400 South, and head east past where 400 South merges into 500 South. After rising up a hill, take the left onto Wakara Way and continue east to the Red Butte Garden and Arboretum exit.

Fort Douglas Military Museum

At the **Fort Douglas Military Museum** (32 Potter St., 801/581-2151, www.fortdouglas.org, noon-5pm Tues.-Sat., free, grounds dawn-dusk daily), artifacts and historical photos take visitors back to the days of the Nauvoo Legion, the Mormon Battalion, and U.S. Army life in pioneer Utah. In late 1862, Colonel Patrick Connor marched to this site with his California-Nevada volunteers and built Camp Douglas. Officially the post defended the mail route and kept the local Native Americans in check. Connor also felt it necessary to keep an eye (and cannons) on the Mormons, whom he and other federal officials distrusted.

The museum's exhibits show the histories of Fort Douglas and other military bases in Utah. A World War I room includes photos of German POWs once interned here. Other exhibits illustrate the big military buildup during World War II, when Utah even had a naval base.

The museum building, officers' row, and some of the other structures at Fort Douglas date from the 1870s and 1880s and are built in an architectural style termed Quartermaster Victorian. Pick up a walking-tour leaflet of the fort at the museum. Turn north onto Wasatch Drive from 500 South and travel 0.5 mile to the fort.

This Is the Place Heritage Park

It is believed that Brigham Young gazed on the Salt Lake Valley for the first time from this spot, now known as **This Is the Place Heritage Park** (2601 Sunnyside Ave., 801/582-1847, www.thisistheplace.org, park and visitors center 10am-5pm, $13 adults, $11 seniors, $9 children 3-11), southeast of the University of Utah near the mouth of Emigration Canyon. He then spoke the famous words "This is the right place. Drive on." Exactly 100 years later, on July 24, 1947, a crowd gathered to dedicate the massive *This Is the Place* monument. Twelve-foot bronze statues of Brigham Young flanked by Heber C. Kimball and Wilford Woodruff stand atop a central pylon. The park has a pleasant picnic area, and the monument honors not only the Mormon pioneers, but also the Catholic missionaries from Spain, fur trappers and traders, government explorers, and California immigrants who contributed to the founding of an empire in "the top of the mountains." A visitors center displays a mural depicting major events during the migration of the "Saints" from Nauvoo, Illinois, to their promised land. An eight-minute narration recounts the journey; foreign-language narration can also be requested.

The main attraction here, on the grounds near the monument, is a family-oriented recreation of a Utah pioneer village. Springtime here is known as "baby animal season." During the summer it comes alive with farming and crafts demonstrations and wagon and pony rides. In addition, three mini trains make loops around the park. Most of the two dozen buildings that were moved here are originals, some of the first in the valley. Some notable structures include Brigham Young's forest farmhouse, the 1847 Levi Riter cabin,

and the Charles Rich house, designed in the 1850s for polygamous family living.

Although the park is open on Sundays, activities are limited and admission fees are lower ($7 adults, $5 seniors, $4 children).

Hogle Zoo

Utah's state zoo, **Hogle Zoo** (2600 E. Sunnyside Ave., 801/584-1700, www.hoglezoo. org, 9am-6pm daily Mar.-Oct., 10am-5pm daily Nov.-Feb., $19 adults, $17 seniors, $15 children ages 3-12, winter fees $2 lower), an especially popular spot with the kids, is on the eastern edge of town and across from This Is the Place Heritage Park. Children like to ride the miniature train (spring-fall, $2) and see the *African Safari* exhibit. Many of the large-animal enclosures have natural settings; the elephants and rhinos have newly redesigned habitats. The *Rocky Shores* exhibit is home to arctic North American animals such as polar bears, sea lions, grizzly bears, and bald eagles. Two endangered red pandas are important (and spectacularly cute) new additions to the *Asian Highlands* exhibit.

SOUTH OF DOWNTOWN
★ Liberty Park

The large **Liberty Park** (bounded by 900 South, 1300 South, 500 East, and 700 East), southeast of downtown, is the jewel of the city's public park system and contains abundant recreational facilities in addition to an excellent aviary, an arts center, and 80 acres of grass and shady boulevards. A fun addition to the park is a conceptual "map" of northern Utah that re-creates the rivers, lakes, and mountains as a series of fountains and wading pools.

The Children's Garden—a playground, amusement park, snack bar, and large pond with rental boats (all spring-fall)—sits in the southeast corner of the park. The tennis center on the west side of the park offers 16 lighted courts and instruction; an outdoor swimming

---

1: Red Butte Garden and Arboretum; 2: City Creek Center; 3: Bar X and Beer Bar

pool adjacent to the tennis center is open in summer.

TRACY AVIARY

Birds have taken over the southwest corner of Liberty Park. **Tracy Aviary** (589 E. 1300 S., 801/596-8500, www.tracyaviary.org, 9am-5pm daily, open until 8pm on Mon. June-Aug., $12 adults, $10 students, seniors, and military, $8 ages 3-12) houses more than 400 individual birds of 135 species and offers shows with trained free-flying birds such as falcons. Birds on display include majestic golden and bald eagles, showy flamingos and peacocks, the hyacinthine macaw (the world's largest parrot), the golden pheasant of China, and hundreds of other feathered friends. Emus from Australia prance across fields, while ducks, geese, swans, and other waterfowl keep to the ponds. You'll also get to meet Utah's only native vulture, the turkey vulture.

Bird shows can change from season to season, so call or check the website to verify what's happening.

THE CHASE MILL

Just north of the aviary entrance, the Chase Mill was built by Isaac Chase in 1852 and is one of the oldest buildings in the valley. Free flour from the mill saved many families during the famine of 1856-1857. The mill is open daily as a historic monument. Formal gardens are north of the mill.

Chase's adobe house, built 1853-1854, farther to the north, has been restored. Go inside to see exhibits of the **Chase Home Museum of Utah Folk Art** (801/245-7285, 11am-4pm Tues. and Thurs.-Sat., 11am-8pm Wed., Memorial Day.-Labor Day., 11am-4pm Tues.-Fri. Labor Day-Memorial Day, free) sponsored by the Utah Arts Council. On display is contemporary Utah folk art, including quilts, rugs, woodcarvings, international art, and Native American works.

Entertainment and Events

Salt Lake City offers a wide variety of high-quality arts and cultural institutions; classical and religious music venues are particularly noteworthy. Jazz, blues, and alternative music clubs and dance bars are also numerous. In short, there's a lot more going on here than you might think.

Local publications are the best places to check for information on what's happening. The *City Weekly* (www.cityweekly.net) is the largest and most comprehensive free newspaper, with lots of arts and entertainment coverage. The daily papers, the *Deseret News* (www.deseretnews.com) and the *Salt Lake Tribune* (www.sltrib.com), both have listings in their Friday Weekend and Sunday Art and Entertainment sections. The Salt Lake Convention and Visitors Bureau website (www.visitsaltlake.com) also has lengthy listings of events and entertainment options.

NIGHTLIFE

Utah's liquor laws no longer require you to join a bar's private club just to have a drink. The best way to check out the club scene is to pick up a copy of *City Weekly,* a free and widely available news and entertainment weekly. If you're just looking for a beer and a chance to chat with the locals, try one of the brewpubs.

Bars

In the category of high-spirited, only-in-Salt-Lake fun, try out **Twist** (32 Exchange Place, 801/322-3200, www.twistslc.com, nightly), with Tuesday night karaoke and live music Wed.-Sat. Another good stop to go for drinks and good times right downtown is **Bar X** (155 E. 200 S., 801/355-2287), one of SLC's oldest and most characterful bars. Right next door, sister establishment **Beer Bar** (161 E. 200 S.,

Salt Lake City for Kids

DISCOVERY GATEWAY

Celebrate the power of play at Discovery Gateway (Gateway complex, 444 W. 100 S., 801/456-5437, www.discoverygateway.org, 10am-6pm Mon.-Thurs., 10am-7pm Fri.-Sat., noon-6pm Sun., $12.50 Mon.-Sat., $10 Sun.), where engaging interactive activities inspire learning in children and are often fun for the whole family. Kids get to put on plays, host the morning TV news, make short animated films, and engage in many other activities. They can also take part in a mock Life Flight, or rescue operation, in an authentic life-size helicopter.

LAGOON AMUSEMENT PARK AND PIONEER VILLAGE

History, recreation, and thrilling rides come together at the attractively landscaped Lagoon Amusement Park and Pioneer Village (375 Lagoon Dr., Farmington, 801/451-8000, www.lagoonpark.com), 16 miles (26 km) north of Salt Lake City. Lagoon traces its own history back to 1887, when bathers came to Lake Park on the shores of Great Salt Lake, 2 miles (3.2 km) west of its present location. The vast Lagoon Amusement Park area includes roller-coaster rides, a giant Ferris wheel, and other midway favorites. There are also musical performances and miniature golf. Lagoon A Beach provides thrilling waterslides and landscaped pools.

Pioneer Village brings the past to life with authentic 19th-century buildings, stagecoach and steam train rides, a Ute museum, a carriage museum, a gun collection, and many other exhibits. Wild West shoot-outs take place several times daily. Food booths are scattered throughout the park, or you can dine at the Gaslight Restaurant near the Opera House.

The complex is open 11am-10pm Sunday-Thursday, 11am-11pm Friday, and 10am-11pm Saturday June-late August or whenever the local school year begins. The complex is also open Saturday-Sunday early April-May and September-October, and there are other open days; check the website for the rather complex off-season schedule. An all-day ride pass is $59 from 48 inches tall to 65 years old, $53 for seniors, and $42 for those under 48 inches tall. The all-day pass includes Lagoon A Beach privileges, but be prepared to pay extra for special rides (although plenty of rides are included in the day pass). Parking is $10. Take I-15 to the Lagoon exit and follow the signs.

WHEELER HISTORIC FARM

Kids will enjoy a visit to the Wheeler Historic Farm (6351 S. 900 E., Murray, 385/268-1755, https://slco.org/wheeler-farm/, dawn-dusk daily, free admission) to experience the rural life of milking cows, gathering eggs, churning butter, and feeding animals. Hayrides in warmer weather and sleigh rides in winter take visitors around the farm. Henry and Sariah Wheeler started the farm in 1886 and developed it into a prosperous dairy and ice-making operation. Tour guides take you through the Wheelers' restored Victorian house, built 1896-1898, the first in the county to have an indoor bathroom (tour $4 adults, $2 children 3-12). The Rosebud Country Store sells crafts and snacks.

The Salt Lake County Recreation Department operates the farm and offers special programs for both youngsters and adults. There's no admission charged to visit the farm, but you'll pay for individual activities.

801/355-3618) has a wall full of taps, more beer in bottles, good food, and board games.

If you just want to dance, SLC offers a number of options. Area 51 (451 S. 400 W., 801/534-0819) has theme nights (College Night, Alterna-Mash, Fetish, and more). The vast multiple-floor Hotel/Club Elevate complex (155 W. 200 S., 801/478-4310) has enough dance floors and bar areas to fill an entire night's worth of fun.

If you're into the speakeasy cocktail scene, check out the underground bar at The Rest, beneath the Bodega (331 S. Main St., 801/532-4042, www.bodega331.com/therest). This is a popular (and very dark) spot for inventive cocktails and good Mexican food, so make a reservation if you don't want to be disappointed.

Live Music

The **Tavernacle Social Club** (201 E. 300 S., 801/519-8900, www.tavernacle.com) is a hipper-than-thou piano bar with an updated lounge act that features dueling pianos, sing-alongs, and karaoke Sunday-Tuesday.

To catch the flavor of local and regional bands, check out **Urban Lounge** (241 S. 500 E., 801/746-0557, www.theurbanloungeslc.com).

Blues jams and jazz bands are featured at **Gracie's Gastropub** (326 S. W. Temple, 801/819-7565, www.graciesslc.com). The food is also good here, so it's worth coming in and making an evening of it.

Touring national acts stop at **The Depot** (in the Gateway Center at 400 S. West Temple St., 801/355-5522, www.depotslc.com), a nightclub in the cavernous Union Station; it's also a good spot for meeting friends when there's no live band. Big names such as the Decemberists or Jason Mraz play **The State Room** (638 S. State St., 801/596-3560, www.thestateroom.com), a more intimate venue.

Gay and Lesbian

Salt Lake City isn't known for its vibrant gay scene, but there are a growing number of gay clubs. A good place to start the evening is **Club Try-Angles** (251 W. 900 S., 801/364-3203, 4pm-1am Mon.-Fri., 6pm-1am Sat., 2pm-1am Sun), with a pleasant patio for drinks and sunning. The **Sun Trapp** (102 S. 600 W., 385/235-6786, noon-2am daily) is known for its friendly, laid-back atmosphere.

THE ARTS

Most of Salt Lake City's top-flight music and arts performances take place in a handful of venues, themselves world-class facilities worthy of a visit. When you know the dates of your visit, contact the Salt Lake County Center for the Arts (801/355-2787, https://artsaltlake.org), which handles information and ticketing for most of the city's arts

offerings, to find out what's going on while you're here.

One of the city's main performance spaces is the **Capitol Theatre** (50 W. 200 S., 801/534-6364), a glittering vaudeville house from the turn of the 20th century that has been refurbished into an elegant concert hall. **Abravanel Hall** (123 W. South Temple St., between the Salt Palace and Temple Square, 801/533-5626) has fantastic acoustics and is home to the Utah Symphony and other classical music performances. The **Rose Wagner Performing Arts Center** (138 W. 300 S., 801/323-6800) has three performance spaces and is home to several local dance and theater troupes.

A new performing arts center, the **Eccles Theater** (131 S. Main St., 385/468-1010, https://artsaltlake.org/venue/eccles-theater) opened in the heart of downtown in 2016. This state-of-the-art theater holds the 2,500-seat Delta Performance Hall to host touring Broadway shows and other popular entertainment events, plus an intimate black box theater, a six-story grand lobby, and an outdoor plaza and galleria.

In **Temple Square** (800/537-9703), the Mormon tabernacle and the Assembly Hall host various classical and religious concerts, including performances by the famed Mormon Tabernacle Choir.

Theater

Pioneer Theatre Company (801/581-6961, www.pioneertheatre.org), one of Salt Lake City's premier theater troupes, offers a seven-show season running September-May. The company performs a mix of contemporary plays, classics, and musicals, plus the new Play-by-Play new play reading series. Although the company operates from the University of Utah's **Pioneer Memorial Theatre** (300 South and University St.), it is not part of the university itself. The Pioneer Memorial Theatre is also the site of University of Utah student productions and the Young People's Theatre, which produces plays for children.

The city's cutting-edge theater group is the **Salt Lake Acting Company** (168 W. 500 N., 801/363-7522, www.saltlakeactingcompany. org). This well-established troupe doesn't shy away from controversy: Its excellent production of Tony Kushner's *Angels in America* raised eyebrows and stirred strong reactions. Besides presenting new works from around the world, the company is also committed to staging plays by local playwrights; there are performances year-round.

The **Grand Theatre** (1575 S. State St., 801/957-3459 or 801/957-3263, http:// grandtheatrecompany.com), on the Salt Lake City Community College campus, is home to an October-April program of theatrical performances (mostly musicals) by both student and semiprofessional troupes.

For something more spoofy, the **Off Broadway Theatre** (272 S. Main St., 801/355-4628, http://theobt.org) is the place for improv competitions, Broadway comedies, and topical farces. At the **Desert Star Playhouse** (4861 S. State St., 801/266-7600, www.desertstar.biz), you'll find musical comedy revues and cabaret-style comedy skits, such as *My Big Fat Utah Wedding* or *Indiana Bones: Raiders of the Wall Mart.*

Classical Music and Dance

From its modest beginnings in 1940, the **Utah Symphony** (tickets 801/533-6683, www. utahsymphony.org) has grown to be one of the best-regarded orchestras in the West. Each season, the symphony performs in the glittering **Abravanel Hall** (123 W. South Temple St.) in Salt Lake City and travels to Snowbird, Deer Valley, Ogden, Provo, Logan, and other cities.

The **Utah Opera Company** (tickets 801/533-6683, www.utahopera.org), founded in 1978, stages four operas during its October-May season at the **Capitol Theatre** (50 W. 200 S.).

Another center for classical music and performance is the **University of Utah** (801/581-6772, www.utah.edu/arts). The university's symphony orchestra, chamber orchestra, jazz ensembles, opera, bands, and ballet, dance, and choral groups present regular concerts and performances on and off campus; the season runs September-May.

Ballet West (801/869-6900, https:// balletwest.org) began in Salt Lake City in 1963 as the Utah Civic Ballet, but as the group gained fame and began traveling widely, it chose its present name to reflect its regional status. This versatile group's repertoire includes classical and contemporary works. Most Utah performances take place September-May at the **Capitol Theatre** (50 W. 200 S.).

The professional **Ririe-Woodbury Dance Company** (801/297-4241, www. ririewoodbury.com) has one of the most active dance programs in the United States. The varied repertoire includes mixed media, eye-catching choreography, and humor. The group also shares its expertise by teaching production and dance skills to students and professionals. Ririe-Woodbury Dance Company is based at the Rose Wagner Performing Arts Center, as is the **Repertory Dance Theatre** (801/534-1000, www.rdtutah.org), a professional company focusing on classical American and contemporary dance.

Concert Series and Music Festivals

The **Madeleine Arts and Humanities Program** is held in the historic **Cathedral of the Madeleine** (331 E. South Temple St., 801/328-8941, www.utcotm.org, all events free). This series of choral, organ, and chamber music concerts takes place on Sunday evenings throughout the spring and early summer. Lectures, theatrical performances, and dance concerts are also held.

In June, the **Gina Bachauer Piano Competitions** (801/297-4250, www. bachauer.com) take over Salt Lake City. Competitions are divided into three categories based on age, and the three competitions are part of a four-year cycle of events that occur during the month of June. Dozens of young pianists from around the world take part in a two-week-long series of performances both as solos (early in the competition) and with the Utah Symphony (only the finalists). The winners compete for recording contracts and thousands of dollars in cash. It's a good chance to enjoy the musicianship of tomorrow's rising piano stars and to savor the thrill of musical competition.

TEMPLE SQUARE CONCERT SERIES

The concert series at **Temple Square** (801/240-3323, www.templesquare.com) presents hundreds of performances a year for the public; all are free. The LDS Church sponsors the varied musical fare to provide a common meeting ground of great music for Mormons and non-Mormons alike. You might hear chamber music, a symphony, operatic selections, religious choral works, piano solos, organ works, a brass band, or a percussion ensemble.

The renowned 360-voice **Mormon Tabernacle Choir** sings at 9:30am Sunday morning (you must be seated by 9:15am and remain seated during the entire performance). You can also hear the choir rehearse 8pm-9:30pm Thursday evening (you can come and go during the rehearsals). The Mormon Youth Symphony rehearses in the tabernacle 8pm-9:30pm Wednesday evening, and the Youth Chorus rehearses 8pm-9:30pm Tuesday evening.

In June-August and December, rehearsals and broadcasts are held across the street in the Conference Center, which can accommodate the larger summer and Christmas season crowds. Broadcasts are also held in the Conference Center during LDS semiannual General Conferences, which take place on the first Sunday of October and April. Admission on these two Sundays is available only to Conference ticket holders. Occasionally, when the choir is on tour, a youth choir, youth symphony, or other group replaces it.

The Temple Square Concert Series presents complimentary hour-long concerts featuring local and international artists at 7:30pm every Friday and Saturday evening in the Assembly Hall. Tickets are not required, but attendees must be age eight and older. June-August, the Temple Square Concert Series presents Concerts in the Park, held in the Brigham Young Historic Park (southeast corner of State St. and 2nd Ave.). These outdoor concerts begin at 7:30pm on Tuesday and Friday evenings June-August.

Organists demonstrate the sounds and versatility of the tabernacle's famous instrument in 30-minute **organ recitals** (noon and 2pm Mon.-Sat., 2pm Sun.).

SUMMER CONCERTS AND FESTIVALS

Salt Lake City is filled with free music concerts in summer, when local parks and public spaces become makeshift concert halls. Check local media or the visitors center for details on the following ongoing concert series.

Gallivan Center Concerts and Films features free noontime concerts on weekdays in summer, plus such free events as big band dance nights and al fresco movie nights at the downtown Gallivan Center (Main St. and 200 South, 801/535-6110, www.thegallivancenter.com/events.htm). The Utah Symphony (801/533-5626, www.utahsymphony.org) also offers an extensive summer series of concerts at Wasatch Front ski areas, a short drive from downtown Salt Lake City.

Cinema

First-run multiplexes are spread around downtown Salt Lake City; check the daily newspapers for listings. The city is lucky to have the **Salt Lake Film Society** (http://saltlakefilmsociety.org), which sponsors a "year-round film festival" with art and foreign films at the **Broadway Centre** (111 E. 300 S., 801/321-0310) and the **Tower Theatre** (876 E. 900 S., 801/328-1645).

Brewvies (677 S. 200 W., 801/355-5500, www.brewvies.com) is a brewpub-cinema combo where you can buy an ale and a burger and watch a first-run or cult favorite film.

For a selection of major-release first-run

movies in the downtown area, check out what's playing at the Megaplex 12 at the Gateway (165 S. Rio Grande St., 801/325-7500).

FESTIVALS AND EVENTS

Concerts, festivals, shows, rodeos, and other special events happen here nearly every day in summer, and the Salt Lake Convention and Visitors Bureau (90 S. West Temple St., 801/534-4900, www.visitsaltlake.com) can tell you what's going on. Also check the visitors bureau's Salt Lake Visitors Guide for some of the best-known annual happenings.

The first weekends of April and October see the annual General Conference of the Church of Jesus Christ of Latter-day Saints, held at Temple Square. The church president, believed to be a prophet of God, and other church leaders give guidance to members throughout the world; hotel rooms are in short supply at this time.

A large celebration of multiculturalism comes the third weekend of May, when the grounds of the Salt Lake City and County Building (State St. and 400 South) erupt with the Living Traditions Festival (http:// livingtraditionsfestival.com). Enjoy dances, food, and entertainment of the many different cultures that make up the Utah mosaic.

The Utah Arts Festival (801/322-2428, http://uaf.org) takes place the last weekend in June and includes lots of music, dance,

readings, art demonstrations, craft sales, and food booths. The event is held at Library Square (200 E. 400 S.).

The summer's single largest festival is in July. The Days of '47 Celebration (801/257-7959, www.daysof47.com) commemorates the arrival of Mormon pioneers here on July 24, 1847. The city celebrates with the huge 24th of July Pioneer Parade in the heart of downtown (the day is a state holiday), a marathon, lots of fireworks, and the year's biggest rodeo, held at the Delta Center.

Check out high-quality crafts, food trucks, and music at the mid-August Craft Lake City DIY Festival (Gallivan Center, 801/906-8521, https://craftlakecity.com). In addition to the shopping, festival goers can participate in workshops (many fill up; sign up online in advance).

The Greek Festival (Hellenic Center, 300 S. 300 W., 801/328-9681) in September celebrates Greek culture with food, music, folk dancing, and tours of the historic Holy Trinity Greek Orthodox Cathedral. The festival is held the weekend after Labor Day. The Utah State Fair (North Temple St. and 1000 West, 801/538-8441, www. utahstatefair.com), held at the state fairgrounds in September, is a celebration of the state's agricultural heritage and features rodeos, livestock shows and judging, arts and crafts exhibits, musical entertainment, and a midway carnival.

Shopping

SHOPPING MALLS

City Creek Center

The 700,000-square-foot City Creek Center (50 S. Main St., www.shopcitycreekcenter. com), built in part with funding provided by the LDS Church, stands at the very center of downtown Salt Lake City. Opened in 2012, it's one of the nation's largest mixed-use downtown redevelopment projects, with more than 100 stores and restaurants,

including Nordstrom, Macy's, and Tiffany & Co. The structure's design is notable: The indoor-outdoor space features a retractable roof, a 140-foot sky bridge over Main Street, a 1,200-foot-long re-creation of the historic City Creek, two 18-foot waterfalls, and some amazing fountains.

The Gateway

Just west of downtown, on the site of the

former rail yards, **The Gateway** (bounded by 400 West, 600 West, 200 South, and North Temple St., http://shopthegateway.com) was built in the run-up to the 2002 Winter Olympics as a destination boutique shopping mall, entertainment center, and condo development. The shops, restaurants, and entertainment venues line a winding pedestrian street that represents a developer's idea of Ye Olde Worlde. Here you'll find chain stores such as Abercrombie & Fitch or The Walking Company, a game arcade, the Megaplex 12 cinema (801/325-7500) and an impressive selection of restaurants and bars.

Trolley Square

Salt Lake City's most unusual shopping center was created when developers cleverly converted the city's old trolley barn. Railroad magnate E. H. Harriman built the barn in 1908 as a center for the city's extensive trolley system. The vehicles stopped rolling in 1945, but their memory lives on in **Trolley Square** (500 South and 700 East, 801/521-9877, www.trolleysquare.com). Inside you'll see several trolleys, a large stained-glass dome, salvaged sections of old mansions and churches, and many antiques. More than 100 shops and restaurants call this gigantic barn home.

BOOKS

Weller Book Works (607 Trolley Square, 801/328-2586, www.wellerbookworks.com, 11am-8pm Mon.-Thurs., 10am-9pm Fri.-Sat., noon-5pm Sun.), which had been in operation since 1925 as Sam Weller's Zion Book Store in the heart of downtown, is now in the Trolley Square shopping center just east of downtown. It's still a great store with a mix of new, used, and rare books covering many topics. The **University of Utah's bookstore** (270 S. 1500 E., 801/581-6326, 7:30am-6pm Mon.-Fri.) has a varied selection on many subjects.

OUTDOOR EQUIPMENT

If you suddenly realize you need a new tent pole, some zip-off pants, or any other gear for hiking, camping, bicycling, skiing, river-running, rock climbing, or travel, swing by **REI** (3285 E. 3300 S., 801/486-2100, 10am-9pm Mon.-Fri., 9am-7pm Sat., 11am-6pm Sun., www.rei.com). Gear can also be rented here, and the book section is a good place to look for regional outdoor guides. Topo maps cover the most popular hiking areas of Utah.

Utah Ski and Golf (134 W. 600 S., 801/355-9088, www.utahskigolf.com) rents golf clubs in summer and ski equipment when the snow falls. Another all-sport rental outfit is **Wasatch Touring** (702 E. 100 S., 801/359-9361).

Sports and Recreation

In Salt Lake City, a glimpse at the horizon and the craggy snow-covered Wasatch Mountains tells you that outdoor recreation is very close at hand. Even on a short visit to the Salt Lake area, you'll want to get outdoors and enjoy a hike or a bike ride up a mountain canyon. You won't be alone: The city's newest immigrants, young professionals, are as attracted to the city's right-out-the-back-door access to the great outdoors as to the region's vibrant economy.

PARKS

Salt Lake City has lovely parks, many of which have facilities for recreation. The U.S. Forest Service manages **Mill Creek** and **Big and Little Cottonwood Canyons** (entrance via E. 3800 S./E. Mill Creek Rd., east of Wasatch Blvd.) as part of the Wasatch National Forest. Located just east of the city, these canyons provide easy access to hiking and biking trail systems and to popular fishing streams.

For more information, visit

Uinta-Wasatch-Cache National Forest's Public Lands Information Center in the REI store (3285 E. 3300 S., 801/466-6411). For information about the city's park system, contact the Parks and Recreation office (801/972-7800, www.slcgov.com/cityparks); for county park information, call 801/468-2560 (www.slco.org/recreation).

★ City Creek Canyon

In the city itself, a pleasant and relaxing route for a stroll or a jog follows **City Creek Canyon,** a shady stream-filled ravine just east of the state capitol. The narrow road that runs up the canyon extends more than five miles (8 km), and gains over 750 feet in elevation, from its beginning at Memory Grove, just northeast of the intersection of East North Temple Street and State Street, to Rotary Park at the top of the canyon. Since pioneer days, people have obtained precious water from City Creek and enjoyed its diverse vegetation, wildlife, and scenery. Because City Creek is still part of the city's water supply, regulations exclude dogs, horses, and overnight camping.

Hikers and runners may travel on the road every day. In summer (Memorial Day-Sept. 30), bicyclists may enter only on odd-numbered days. Motorized vehicles are allowed on holidays and on even-numbered days during summer; a gate at the bottom controls entry. No motorized vehicles are allowed the rest of the year, but bicycles can use the road daily (except for a brief pause for deer-hunting season), weather permitting. A $3 charge applies if you drive through to the trailhead at the upper end (no reservation needed).

Reach the entrance to City Creek Canyon via Bonneville Boulevard, a one-way road. From downtown Salt Lake City, head east on North Temple Street, which becomes 2nd Avenue after crossing State Street, then turn left (north) and go 1.3 miles (2.1 km) on B Street, which becomes Bonneville Boulevard after 11th Avenue, to City Creek Canyon Road. Returning from the canyon, you have to turn right onto Bonneville Boulevard to the state capitol. Bicyclists and pedestrians may approach City Creek Canyon from either direction.

HIKING

A popular hiking destination from the trailhead at road's end (elev. 6,050 feet) is **City Creek Meadows,** 4 miles (6.4 km) away and 2,000 feet higher. After 1.5 miles (2.4 km), you'll pass Cottonwood Gulch on the left; a side trail leads up the gulch to an old mining area. After another 0.5 mile (0.8 km) on the main trail, a spring off to the right in a small meadow is the last reliable source of drinking water. During the next mile, the trail grows steeper and winds through aspen groves and then passes two shallow ponds. The trail becomes indistinct here, but you can continue one mile northeast to the meadows (elev. 8,000 feet); maps and compass will help. For splendid views of the Wasatch Range, climb north 0.5 mile (0.8 km) from the meadows up the ridge to where Davis, Salt Lake, and Morgan Counties meet. Hikers also enjoy shorter strolls from the trailhead along the gentle lower section of trail.

PICNICS

The big attraction for many visitors is a stop at one of the picnic areas along the road. Picnickers can reserve sites (801/483-6705). Sites are sometimes available on a first-come, first-served basis; midweek is best. Picnic permits cost $3 and up, depending on the size of the group.

Liberty Park

There are abundant reasons to spend time at **Liberty Park** (bounded by 900 South, 1300 South, 500 East, and 700 East, 801/538-2062), southeast of downtown, including the Tracy Aviary, the children's play area, and the acres of shade and lawn. The park also affords plenty of opportunity for recreation. The tennis center on the west side offers 16 lighted courts. The outdoor swimming pool adjacent to the tennis center is open in summer. During the sweltering Salt Lake summer, the shady boulevards provide a cool environment for jogging. You'll find horseshoe pits to the north of the park's historic Chase House.

Mill Creek Canyon

Great mountain biking, plentiful picnic areas, and many hiking possibilities lie along Mill Creek, just outside Salt Lake City. You can bring your dog along, too—this is one of the few canyons where pets are welcome. In fact, odd-numbered days are designated leash-free days in Mill Creek Canyon. Obey the posted regulations when you begin your hike. Bicycles are allowed in Mill Creek Canyon only on even-numbered days, the days when dogs must be leashed. A $3 fee is collected as you exit the canyon. Reach Mill Creek Canyon Road from 3800 Wasatch Boulevard.

HIKING

Salt Lake Overlook on Desolation Trail is a good hiking destination for families. The trail climbs 1,200 vertical feet in 2 miles (3.2 km) for views of the Salt Lake Valley. Begin from the lower end of Box Elder Picnic Area (elev. 5,760 feet) on the south side of the road. Energetic hikers can continue on Desolation Trail beyond the overlook to higher country near the timberline and go all the way to Desolation Lake (19 miles/31 km). The trail runs near the ridgeline separating Mill and Big Cottonwood Canyons, connecting with many trails from both canyons. Much of this high country lies in the Mount Olympus Wilderness. See the 7.5-minute topo maps for Mt. Aire and Park City West.

Alexander Basin Trail winds to a beautiful wooded glacial bowl below Gobblers Knob; the trailhead (elev. 7,080 feet) is on the south side of the road, 8 miles (12.9 km) up Mill Creek Canyon, 0.8 mile (1.3 km) beyond Clover Springs Picnic Area. The moderately difficult trail begins by paralleling the road northwest for a few hundred feet, then turns southwest through switchbacks for one mile to the beginning of Alexander Basin (elev. 8,400 feet). The trail to Bowman and Porter Forks turns right here, but continue straight 0.5 mile (0.8 km) for the meadows of the upper basin (elev. 9,000 feet). The limestone rock here contains many fossils, mostly shellfish. From the basin it's possible to rock-scramble to the summit of Gobblers Knob (elev. 10,246 feet). The name comes from an attempt by mine owners to raise turkeys after their ore played out; the venture ended when bobcats ate all the birds. See the 7.5-minute topo map for Mt. Aire.

MOUNTAIN BIKING

Bikers should follow Alexander Basin Trail to the end of the Mill Creek Canyon road, then set out on the Big Water Trail. The Great Western Trail (a 3,000-mile ridgetop trail stretching from Canada to Mexico) intersects Big Water at 1.5 miles (2.4 km). Bikers can turn off Big Water Trail and follow the Great Western Trail to the ridgetop divide overlooking the Park City Mountain Resort. Here, the route turns south and follows the Wasatch Crest Trail along the ridge and around the head of the upper Mill Creek basin. To avoid conflicts with hikers, Big Water, Little Water, and the Great Western Trail are closed to mountain bikes on odd-numbered days.

PICNICS

Picnic sites are free and available on a first-come, first-served basis; most lack water. The first one, **Church Fork Picnic Area,** is 3 miles (4.8 km) in at an elevation of 5,700 feet; **Big Water Picnic Area** is the last, 8.8 miles (14.1 km) up at an elevation of 7,500 feet.

Red Butte Garden

The 4 miles (6.4 km) of trails outside **Red Butte Garden** (300 Wakara Way, 801/581-4747, www.redbuttegarden.org, irregular hours and days, year-round, $12 adults, $10 seniors, $7 ages 3-17, free access to hiking trails in the natural area), east of the University of Utah, are a quiet place for a walk or a run. The hiking trails wind through wildflower meadows and past old sandstone quarries. You don't need to pay the admission to the gardens to hike the trails.

Sugarhouse Park

Mormon pioneers manufactured beet sugar at **Sugarhouse Park** (1300 East and 2100 South, 801/467-1721), on the southeast edge of Salt Lake City, beginning in 1851; the venture later proved unprofitable and was abandoned. Today, expanses of rolling grassland in the 113-acre park are ideal for picnics, strolling, and running. The park has a playground and fields for baseball, soccer, and football. In winter, the hills provide good sledding and tubing. A lake attracts seagulls and other birds for bird-watching. Sweet scents rise from the Memorial Rose Garden in the northeast corner.

WINTER SPORTS

Skiing has always been Utah's biggest recreational draw, and as host of the 2002 Winter Olympics, the Salt Lake City area drew the attention of international skiing and winter sports lovers. Summer visitors will find lots to like after the snow melts: Most ski areas remain open for warm-weather recreation, including mountain biking, hiking, trail rides, tennis, and plain old relaxing.

Downhill Skiing

Utah's "Greatest Snow on Earth" is close at hand. Within an hour's drive from Salt Lake City, you can be at one of seven downhill areas in the Wasatch Range, each with its own character and distinctive skiing terrain. The snow season runs from about mid-November to April or May. Be sure to pick up the free *Utah Ski* magazine from **Ski Utah** (2749 Parleys Way #310, Salt Lake City, UT 84109, 801/534-1779 or 800/754-8824); it's also available at most tourism offices in Utah. Alternatively, check out the website (www.skiutah.com). The planner lists most Utah resorts and has diagrams of the lifts and runs, lift-ticket rates, and detailed information on lodging.

Salt Lake City-area ski resorts are grouped quite close together. Although they are in different drainages, Solitude and Brighton ski areas in Big Cottonwood Canyon and Snowbird and Alta ski areas in Little

Cottonwood Canyon, all share the high country of the Wasatch Divide with Park City and Deer Valley ski areas. There is no easy or quick route among the three different valleys, however, and traffic and parking can be a real hassle. Luckily, there are plenty of options for convenient public transportation from Salt Lake City to the ski areas and among the resorts themselves.

Alternatively, you can ski between the various ski areas with **Ski Utah Interconnect** (801/534-1907, www.skiutah.com/explore/the-interconnect-tour, $395 per day), which provides a guide service for backcountry touring among Wasatch Front ski areas. Skiers should be experienced and in good physical condition because of the high elevations (around 10,000 feet) and the need for some walking and traversing. Touring is with downhill equipment. Tours depart daily from Deer Valley Resort or Snowbird Ski and Summer Resort and go through Park City Mountain Resort, Solitude Mountain Resort, Brighton Resort, and Alta Ski Area. The rates include the guide's services, lunch, and all lift tickets.

TRANSPORTATION

Salt Lake City's public bus system, the **UTA** (801/743-3882, www.rideuta.com), has regularly scheduled service to the four resorts on the west side of the Wasatch Range: Solitude, Brighton, Snowbird, and Alta. You can get on the buses downtown, where they connect with the TRAX light rail; at the University of Utah; or at the bottoms of the canyons. A couple of early-morning buses run up to the ski areas every day; return buses depart the ski areas around 5pm.

From the airport, **Canyon Transportation** (800/255-1841, http://canyontransport.com, $39 one-way, $76 round-trip) runs regular shuttles up Big and Little Cottonwood Canyons, with stops at Alta, Solitude, and Brighton. Runs to Park City are $45 one-way and $78 round-trip. **Alta Shuttle** (801/274-0225 or 866/274-0225, www.altashuttle.com, any trip $38 one-way) runs shuttles to and from the airport and Alta and Snowbird resorts in Little Cottonwood Canyon, and the Park City resorts.

Cross-Country Skiing

During heavy snowfalls, Salt Lake City parks and streets become impromptu cross-country ski trails, and any snowed-under Forest Service road in the Wasatch Range is fair game for cross-country skiers. The Mill Creek Canyon road is a favorite. If you don't mind cutting a trail or skiing ungroomed snow, ask at ski-rental shops for hints on where the backcountry snow is good.

Otherwise, there are numerous organized cross-country ski areas in the Salt Lake City area. The Mountain Dell Golf Course in Parley's Canyon (off I-80 toward Park City) is a favorite place to make tracks. There are cross-country facilities at Alta and Solitude ski resorts as well as at the White Pine Touring Center in Park City.

GOLF

Salt Lake City claims to have the highest number of golf courses per capita in the nation, with more than a dozen in the metro area. There's a course for every level of expertise, from city-owned nine-hole courses for beginners to championship-level courses like the 27-hole private **Stonebridge Golf Club** (4415 Links Dr., West Valley City, 801/957-9000, www.golfstonebridgeutah.com) and the 36-hole par 71 or 72 public **Mountain Dell Golf Course** (I-80 exit 134, 801/582-3812, www.slcgov.com), each offering challenging terrain and incredible mountain views. Other courses include **Bonneville** (954 Connor St., 801/583-9513, 18 holes, par 72), east of downtown; **University** (University of Utah campus, 100 S. 1900 E., 801/581-6511, 9 holes, par 33); **Forest Dale** (2375 S. 900 E., 801/483-5420, 9 holes, par 36), near Sugarhouse Park; **Nibley Park** (2730 S. 700 E., 801/483-5418, 9 holes, par 34); **Glendale** (1603 W. 2100 S., 801/974-2403, 18 holes, par 72); and **Rose Park** (1386 N. Redwood Rd., 801/596-5030, 18 holes, par 72), northwest of downtown.

ROCK CLIMBING

The Front (1470 S. 400 W., 801/466-7625, https://frontslc.com) is SLC's largest climbing gym, offering instruction, equipment rental, and a massive rock gym with 15,000 square feet of rope climbing on walls up to 70 feet high, and 10,000 square feet of bouldering. Day passes are available ($22 adults, $15 under age 13); there are also yoga classes, a weight room and cardio equipment at the complex.

SWIMMING

Two of the best and most central outdoor public pools are at **Liberty Park** (1300 S. 700 E.) and **Fairmont Park** (2361 S. 900 E.). Serious lap swimmers should check out the **Salt Lake City Sports Complex** (near the University of Utah, 645 S. Guardsman Way, 801/583-9713); it has a 25-meter indoor pool and a lovely 50-meter outdoor pool with great views of the mountains.

For an even bigger splash, try **Seven Peaks Waterpark** (1200 W. 1700 S., 801/377-4386, www.sevenpeaks.com, $25 adults, $20 under 48 inches tall), a water-sports theme park that features waterslides and a wave pool. The children's area has waterfalls, geysers, a "dinosaur beach," and a small wave pool.

SPECTATOR SPORTS

University of Utah (1825 E. South Campus Dr., 801/581-8849) athletic teams (the Utes) compete in football, basketball, baseball, softball, tennis, track and field, gymnastics, swimming, golf, skiing, and other sports.

Baseball

The **Salt Lake Bees** (801/325-233, www.milb. com/salt-lake) are the AAA affiliate of baseball's Los Angeles Angels. Games are played at the impressive Smiths' Ballpark (77 West 1300 South, Apr.-Sept.); it's hard to imagine a more astonishing backdrop to a game of baseball than the craggy Wasatch Front.

Basketball

Utah professional sports fans love their **Utah**

Jazz, who are usually strong contenders in the NBA's Western Division. The team plays at the Vivint Smart Home Arena (300 West and South Temple St.). Tickets are hard to come by at the last minute, but it's worth a call to the team's box office (801/325-2000) to inquire. Otherwise, you'll need to rely on scalpers or online sources such as Craigslist or StubHub.

Soccer

Real Salt Lake (801/727-2700, www. realsaltlake.com) is the city's Major League Soccer team, which plays at Rio Tinto Stadium (State St. between 9000 South and 9400 South), south of Salt Lake City in the suburb of Sandy. The women's team, the **Utah Royals FC** (https://www.rsl.com/utahroyalsfc), started up in 2018 and also plays at Rio Tinto.

Ice Hockey,

The **Utah Grizzlies** (3200 Decker Lake Dr., West Valley City, 801/988-7825, www. utahgrizzlies.com) are Salt Lake City's ECHL League ice hockey team. They take the ice at Maverik Center in West Valley City.

Food

Travelers will be pleased with the quality of food in Salt Lake City. If you've been traveling around the more remote areas of the state, the abundance of restaurants serving international cuisine will be a real treat. The city has become a hotbed of local and seasonal cooking, and many fine dining restaurants boast adventurous young chefs cooking with locavore directives.

Despite Mormon nondrinking culture, brewpubs caught on in Salt Lake City and are often the most convenient places to enjoy good food and drink. Note that by law all draft beer in Utah is 3.2 percent alcohol. Beer with higher alcohol content is considered hard alcohol and is sold only by the bottle. However, these bottles are now available at brewpubs, so if you'd rather have high-octane beer (outside Utah, known as regular beer), just order bottled beer.

The free *Salt Lake Visitors Guide* lists dining establishments. Dinner reservations are advisable at more expensive restaurants. Also note that most restaurants are closed on Sunday; if you're going to be in Salt Lake over the weekend, ascertain that your hotel has a restaurant, or you may be wandering the streets looking for an eating establishment that's open.

TEMPLE SQUARE AND DOWNTOWN
American

For moderately priced food with a side of history, try **The Lion House** (63 E. South Temple St., 801/539-3257, 11am-8pm Mon.-Sat., $8-18). Built in 1856, this was one of Brigham Young's homes, where his 27 wives and 56 children spent most of their time. High-quality cafeteria-style meals are available for lunch and dinner in the basement dining room, formerly the household pantry.

Some of the best views in the city are from the top of the 10-story Joseph Smith Memorial Building (15 E. South Temple St., www.templesquare.com/), the former Hotel Utah, where you'll find two excellent restaurants. The **Garden Restaurant** (801/539-3170, 11am-9pm Mon.-Thurs., 11am-10pm Fri.-Sat., $13-20) offers unparalleled views of downtown Salt Lake City. What's more, the restaurant is reasonably priced, offering sandwiches and salads for lunch and steaks, seafood, and continental dishes at dinner. With even better views onto Temple Square, the **Roof Restaurant** (801/539-1911, 5pm-9pm Mon.-Thurs., 5pm-10pm Fri.-Sat., $42 adults, $18 ages 11-17, $9 ages 4-6) offers an upscale buffet with prime rib, salmon, ham, shrimp, salads, desserts, and all the trimmings. The dessert buffet is a sweet wonder. Reservations are recommended; no alcohol is served at either restaurant.

If fast food is more your style, then at least try the local purveyor: **Crown Burgers** (downtown at 377 E. 200 S., 801/532-1155; 118 N. 300 W., www.crown-burgers.com, 10am-10:30pm Mon.-Sat., $5-8), with many outlets throughout the Salt Lake area, is the local favorite for char-grilled burgers and good fries. For that special Utah touch, ask for fry sauce with your french fries—it's a local condiment that's remarkably like Thousand Island dressing without relish.

Fine Dining

★ **The Copper Onion** (111 E. Broadway, 801/355-3282, http://thecopperonion.com, 11:30am-3pm and 5pm-10pm Mon.-Thurs., 11:30am-3pm and 5pm-11pm Fri., 10:30am-3pm and 5pm-11pm Sat., 10:30am-3pm and 5pm-10pm Sun., $13-33) always gets a mention when people talk about the best restaurant in Salt Lake City. Emphasizing full-flavored New American cooking, The Copper Onion offers a choice of small and large plates, with such delights as mussels with creamy black pepper sauce and lamb carnitas with pumpkin seed mole. For the quality, the prices are very reasonable.

★ **Bambara** (202 S. Main St., 801/363-5454, http://bambara-slc.com, 7am-10am, 11:30am-2:30pm, and 5:30pm-10pm Mon.-Thurs., 7am-10am, 11am-2pm, and 5:30pm-10:30pm Fri., 8am-2pm and 5:30pm-10pm Sat.-Sun., $29-46), in the Hotel Monaco, is another exciting fixture in the Salt Lake dining scene. The menu emphasizes the freshest and most flavorful local meat and produce, with preparations in a wide-awake New American style that's equal parts tradition and innovation. This is easily one of the most beautiful dining rooms in the city.

Mexican and Southwestern

Right downtown, **Blue Iguana** (165 S. West Temple St., 801/533-8900, www.blueiguanarestaurant.net, 11am-9pm Mon.-Thurs., 11am-10pm Fri.-Sat., 4pm-9pm Sun., $6-15) offers fairly standard Mexican cooking in a lively basement dining room with outdoor dining in a sweet courtyard. In addition to tacos and burritos, you'll find seven different moles and good margaritas.

At **Alamexo** (268 S. State St., 801/779-4747, www.alamexo.com, 11:30am-2pm and 5pm-10pm Mon.-Fri., 5pm-10pm Sat., $17-30), traditional Mexican cooking gets reinvigorated with the freshest of ingredients and unusual juxtapositions of flavors. In this airy, brightly painted dining room, you'll find roasted pulled duck tacos with yellow pepper and habanero cream salsa, and achiote and bitter orange-marinated pork shoulder baked in banana leaf. On Sundays, or if you're in the 9th and 9th neighborhood, visit **Alamexo Cantina** (1059 E. 900 S. 801/658-5859, 3pm-10pm Mon.-Sat., 3pm-9pm Sun.).

Asian

Salt Lake City has a number of excellent Asian restaurants; the scene changes quickly—ask the locals for the latest Thai or Vietnamese sensation. For the best and freshest sushi, go to **Takashi** (18 W. Market St., 801/519-9595, 11:30am-2pm and 5:30pm-10pm Mon.-Thurs., 11:30am-2pm and 5:30pm-11pm Fri., 5pm-11pm Sat., rolls $6-16), though the non-seafood dishes are also excellent (try the Asian ribs).

For Chinese food, go to **J. Wong's Thai & Chinese Bistro** (163 W. 200 S., 801/350-0888, jwongs.com, 11am-3pm and 5pm-10pm Mon.-Fri., noon-3pm and 5pm-10pm Sat., 4pm-9pm Sun., $12-28). You'll find an upscale dining room, beautifully prepared regional Chinese food (from dad's side of the family) and a good selection of Thai dishes inspired by the owners' trips to their mom's homeland. If you're the stay-at-home sort, J. Wong's does a steady take-out business and delivers to local hotels.

1: The Lion House restaurant; 2: Caffé Molise; 3: Valter's Osteria

Breakfast

If your idea of breakfast is excellent pastries and baked goods, head straight to **Eva's Bakery** (155 S. Main St., 801/355-3942, http://evasbakeryslc.com, 7am-6pm Mon.-Sat., 9am-3pm Sun.) for marvelous pastries, artisanal breads, soups, and sandwiches.

If waffles with a side of fries sounds good for breakfast, join the line at **Bruges Waffle and Frites** (336 W. Broadway, 801/363-4444, www.brugeswaffles.com, 9am-9pm Mon.-Thurs., 9am-10pm Fri.-Sat., 9am-2pm Sun., waffles from $6-12), a tiny eatery with tables out front and excellent waffles with a big choice of toppings. For a hearty lunch or dinner, try the Flemish stew and frites.

French

★ **Martine Cafe** (22 E. 100 S., 801/363-9328, www.martinecafe.com, 11:30am-2pm Mon., 11:30am-2pm and 5pm-9:30pm. Tues.-Fri., 5pm-9:30pm Sat.) offers delicious food and cocktails in atmospheric but informal surroundings. The antique high-ceilinged dining room is coolly elegant, and the cooking and presentation spans international cuisines prepared with French finesse. You have a choice of ordering small-plates-style ($7-24), à la carte ($16-39), or a prix-fixe four-course menu ($40) featuring delicacies such as house-made gnocchi with wild mushroom ragù.

Italian

Caffé Molise (55 W. 100 S., 801/364-8833, www.caffemolise.com, 11:30am-9pm Mon.-Thurs., 11:30am-10pm Fri.-Sat., 11:30am-9pm Sun., $16-35), offers a bistro atmosphere with lots of outside seating and tasty midpriced Italian specialties, including pasta, grilled chicken, and beef dishes.

Dig out your dress-up travel outfit for a visit to ★ **Valter's Osteria** (173 Broadway, 801/521-4583, http://valtersosteria.com, 5:30pm-10pm Mon.-Sat., $16-35), where the charming Valter and his attentive wait staff make every diner feel like a special friend. Valter's interpretations of his grandmother's Italian cooking can't be beat; try the sampler

of ravioli and gnocchi; the house-made pasta is flavorful and delicate. Note that Broadway is the same as 300 South.

Middle Eastern

Convenient to downtown, **Cedars of Lebanon** (152 E. 200 S., 801/364-4096, www.cedarsoflebanonrestaurant.com, 11:30am-2:30pm and 5pm-10pm Mon.-Thurs., 11:30am-2:30pm and 5pm-11pm Fri., 5pm-11pm Sat., 5pm-9pm Sun., $15-23) has Mediterranean flavors from Lebanon, Morocco, Armenia, Greece, and Israel, along with many vegetarian items. Belly dancers enliven the scene on Friday-Saturday evenings, and a visit to the hookah lounge can be part of the experience.

Pizza

Convenient to downtown, and offering Neapolitan-style wood-oven-baked pies, **Settebello Pizzeria** (260 S. 200 W., 801/322-3556, http://settebello.net, 11am-10pm Mon.-Thurs., 11am-11pm Fri.-Sat., noon-9pm Sun., $8-13) makes Neapolitan-style pizza that many consider the best in Utah—or in many states around.

Tucked in the Gallivan Center complex at the heart of downtown, **From Scratch** (62 E. Gallivan Ave., 801/961-9000, www.fromscratchslc.com, 11am-2pm and 4pm-9pm Mon.-Thurs., 11am-2pm and 4pm-10pm Fri., 4pm-10pm Sat., $15-16) takes its name seriously. The restaurant mills its own flour from local wheat and pretty much everything else that is on the menu (or goes into the food from scratch) is handmade. The pizzas are baked in a wood-fired oven but at lower temperatures than typical, resulting in a crisp but chewy slice. They also offers burgers and salads.

Steak and Seafood

The **Market Street Grill** (48 Market St., 801/322-4668, https://marketstreetgrill.com, 6:30am-2pm and 5pm-9pm Mon.-Thurs., 6:30am-2pm and 5pm-9:30pm Fri., 8am-3pm and 4pm-9:30pm Sat., 9am-3pm and 4pm-9pm Sun., $20-37), is a long-time SLC favorite featuring fresh seafood, steak, prime rib, chops, chicken, and pasta. Adjacent is an oyster bar. Three-course early bird specials ($20-$26) are available before 7pm. Market Street Grill is also a popular spot for a stylish breakfast.

The New Yorker (60 W. Market St., 801/363-0166, https://newyorkerslc.com, 5:30pm-9pm Mon.-Thurs., 5:30pm-10pm Fri.-Sat., $22-60) is yet another fine-dining house in a historic storefront. Here the emphasis is on excellently prepared certified Angus beef and fresh American lamb. If you're not up to a full meal, there's also a café (4pm-9:30pm Mon.-Thurs., 4:30pm-11pm Fri., 5:30pm-11pm Sat.). Or just go to the oyster bar and fill up on bivalves. The atmosphere is lively; the spot is in Salt Lake's financial district, so expect an audience of stockbrokers and businesspeople.

Vegetarian

Known not just for its healthy, plant-based meals, but also for its innovative cocktails, **Zest Kitchen & Bar** (275 S. 200 W., 801/433-0589, www.zestslc.com, 11am-10pm Mon.-Thurs., 11am-11pm Fri., 10am-11pm Sat., 10am-9pm Sun, $13-15, age 21 and up) is the place to go if you want a little bit of gin in your green smoothie. Besides "farm-to-glass" cocktails, the gluten- and soy-free menu features small plates for sharing such as a pile of shaved Brussels sprouts with a spicy almond sauce and entrees that include mac and (vegan) cheese or a jackfruit pizza. So much for staid old SLC.

Brewpubs

The state's oldest brewpub is **Squatters Pub Brewery** (147 W. Broadway, 801/363-2739, www.squatters.com, 11am-midnight Mon.-Thurs., 11am-1am Fri., 10am-1am Sat., 10am-midnight Sun., $10-22). In addition to fine beers and ales, the pub serves sandwiches, burgers, and other light entrées in a handsome old warehouse. In summer, there's seating on the back deck.

Very popular and kind of a scene, the ★ **Red Rock Brewing Company** (254 S. 200 W., 801/521-7446, www.redrockbrewing.com, 11am-11pm Mon.-Thurs., 11am-midnight Fri.-Sat., 10:30am-11pm Sun., $9-24) offers steaks, pasta, salads, and sandwiches, including an excellent variation on the hamburger, baked in a wood-fired oven inside a bread pocket. There's often a wait to get in the door, but the food and brews are worth it.

In addition to proper brewpubs (with beer made on the premises), there are also taphouses, and downtown the best is the **Beerhive** (128 S. Main St., 801/364-4268, noon-1am Mon.-Sat., noon-10pm Sun.). This handsome old storefront offers more than two-dozen regional microbrews on draft and more than 200 in bottles. You'll be able to taste beers from all around the state in one sitting. The Beerhive is within walking distance of most downtown hotels (cocktails available too).

Delis and Groceries
Siegfried's Delicatessen (20 W. 200 S., 801/355-3891, www.siegfriedsdelicatessen.com, 9am-6pm Mon.-Wed., 9am-9pm Thurs.-Sat.) has a great selection of charcuterie, cold cuts, breads, pastries, and cheeses. The deli also serves homemade German dishes for both lunch and dinner, with nothing that costs more than $10.

SOUTH OF DOWNTOWN
American
An excellent option for barbecue and soul food is **Sugarhouse Barbecue Co.** (880 E. 2100 S., 801/463-4800, www.sugarhousebbq.com, 11:30am-9pm Mon.-Thurs., 11:30am-10pm Fri.-Sat., noon-8pm Sun., $8-15), with Memphis-style slow-smoked ribs and Carolina pulled pork.

Fine Dining
A log cabin in the woods might seem like a perfect Utah destination, and at historic **Log Haven** (6451 E. Millcreek Canyon Rd., 801/272-8255, www.log-haven.com, 5:30pm-9pm daily, $27-45), that cabin also serves remarkably good food. Built in the 1920s, the

restaurant is splendidly rustic yet upscale, with ample outdoor seating in good weather. Though probably best thought of as a steak house, the menu offers a wide selection of New American dishes, including game, fresh seafood, and pasta. Log Haven is 4 miles (6.4 km) east of Salt Lake City in Mill Creek Canyon. **Table X** (1457 E. 3350 S., 801/528-3712, http://tablexrestaurant.com, 5pm-10pm Wed.-Sun., $20-40), with its serious farm-to-table aesthetic, three-chef collaboration, and beautifully reclaimed old building, is a quintessentially modern restaurant. Your steak can be from a cow (grass-fed and local) or a trumpet mushroom (with a lovely sauce topping it). If everything on the not-too-long menu looks good, go for the $55 tasting menu.

Asian

Salt Lake City has more Asian restaurants than you might expect. **Oh Mai** (850 S. State St., 801/575-8888, 11am-5pm Mon.-Sat., $5-8) specializes in delicious Vietnamese *bahn mi* sandwiches and pho. If you're looking for the same menu, but for dinner, head south (3425 S. State St., 801/467-6882, 11am-9pm Mon.-Sat.).

Breakfast

A pleasant place for a traditional breakfast is the **Park Cafe** (604 E. 1300 S., 801/487-1670, http://theparkcafeslc.com, 7am-3pm daily, $5-8). The Park is directly across from Liberty Park, which makes a great before- or after-breakfast destination.

In the same neighborhood, **Pig and a Jelly Jar** (401 E. 900 S., 385/202-7366, www.pigandajellyjar.com, 7:30am-3:30pm Mon.-Wed., 7:30am-9pm Thurs.-Sun., $8-13) takes the house-made charcuterie craze to the breakfast table. Everything here is made from scratch in-house, including all the pork sausages, bacon, ham, and other porky bits. At lunch and dinner, you'll find soups, salads, and sandwiches.

The Bagel Project (779 S. 500 E., 801/906-0698, https://bagelproject.com, 6:30am-2pm Mon.-Fri., 7:30am-2pm Sat.-Sun.) is the love child of a displaced East Coaster who found he needed to make his own bagels in SLC. Come here for excellent bagels, bialys, sandwiches and Mandel bread.

If you're looking for breakfast with a view, head to the lodges and resorts up nearby Wasatch Front canyons. The **Silver Fork Lodge** (11 miles/17.7 km up Big Cottonwood Canyon, 801/533-9977, www.silverforklodge.com, 8am-9pm daily, $7-14) is a favorite destination for a scenic brunch, perhaps followed by a hike.

French

For classic French cuisine when budget is no issue, **La Caille Restaurant** (9565 Wasatch Blvd., near Little Cottonwood Canyon, 801/942-1751, www.lacaille.com, 5pm-9pm Mon.-Fri., 10am-2pm and 5pm-9pm Sat., 10am-3pm and 4pm-8pm Sun., $39-56) offers superb pastry, crepes, seafood, and meat dishes in an 18th-century rural French atmosphere. Vineyards, gardens, ponds, and manicured lawns surround the re-created French château—it's hard to believe it's in Utah. Antique furnishings grace the dining rooms and halls. Dress is semiformal, and reservations are advised. The Sunday brunch ($30-38) is where to head if you feel like putting on the ritz.

Middle Eastern and Indian

For updated Middle Eastern cooking, try the very popular ★ **Mazza** (912 E. 900 S., 801/521-4572, www.mazzacafe.com, 11am-3pm and 5pm-10pm Mon.-Sat., $8-25), in the hip 9th and 9th neighborhood. Here you'll find an excellent Lebanese menu that goes far beyond the usual kebabs. There's another branch a few blocks southeast (1515 S. 1500 E., 801/484-9259).

Vegetarian

Even a meat-loving place like SLC offers a selection of dining options for vegans. **Vertical Diner** (234 W. 900 S., 801/322-3790, www.sagescafe.com, 9am-10pm Sun.-Thurs., 9am-11pm Fri.-Sat., $12-15) serves satisfying organic vegetarian cuisine, while the wine list emphasizes organic wines.

Brewpubs

Convenient to the many hotels south of downtown, the **Proper Burger Company and Proper Brewing** (865 Main St., 801/906-8604, www.properburgerslc.com, 11am-10pm Sun.-Thurs., 11am-11pm Fri.-Sat., $5-10), is pretty much what it sounds like—a casual spot for burgers and excellent craft beers.

Epic Brewing (825 S. State St., 801/906-0123, https://epicbrewing.com, 11am-10pm Mon.-Thurs., 10am-11pm Fri.-Sat., 11am-7pm Sun.) has been brewing great beers in Salt Lake City since 2008, but because of Utah's liquor laws, the "taproom" here pours full-strength beers from bottles, not taps. (Go figure.) It's also a requirement that food must be ordered along with beer; there's a serviceable menu of sandwiches from which to choose.

Even farther from downtown is **Bohemian Brewery** (94 E. 7200 S., Midvale, 14 miles/22.5 km south of central SLC, 801/566-5474, www.bohemianbrewery.com, 11am-11pm Mon.-Fri., 10am-11pm Sat., 10am-10pm Sun.). This excellent brewery features Czech-style lagers and is worth the drive if you like Central European food and brews.

EAST OF DOWNTOWN
American

Despite Mormon restrictions on caffeine, there are now plenty of fine coffeehouses in Salt Lake City. Look no farther than **Salt Lake Roasting Co.** (820 E. 400 S., 801/363-7572, www.roasting.com, 6:30am-9pm Mon.- Sat.), which offers a wide selection of coffees and pastries, a vaguely alternative atmosphere, and a pleasant outdoor patio in good weather. You'll find a second location at Library Square (210 E. 400 S., 9am-8pm Mon.-Thurs., 9am-6pm Fri.-Sat., 1pm-5pm Sun.).

American food doesn't have to be fustily traditional: at stylish ★ **HSL** (200 S. 418 E., 801/539-9999, http://hslrestaurant.com,

11:30am-2:30pm and 5pm-9pm Thurs.-Fri., 10am-2:30pm and 5pm-10pm Sat., 10am-2:30pm and 5pm-9pm Sun., 5pm-9pm Mon.-Wed., $16-32), the rib eye is served with morels, cauliflower puree, braised red cabbage and bacon; the halibut may feature turmeric and carrot hummus.

Fine Dining

A top spot for locavore cuisine is ★ **Pago** (878 S. 900 E., 801/532-0777, www.pagoslc.com, 5pm-10pm Mon.-Fri., 10am-2:30pm and 5pm-10pm Sat.-Sun., $19-32), where the best of local produce, mushrooms, fish, and meat are cooked with Mediterranean flair; try the roast chicken with figs, baked shallots, and balsamic vinegar.

Breakfast

For one of Salt Lake's favorite breakfasts, drive (or ride your bike) a couple of miles east of the city to **Ruth's Diner** (4160 Emigration Canyon, 801/582-5807, www.ruthsdiner.com, 8am-10pm daily summer, 8am-9pm Sun.-Thurs., 8am-10pm Fri.-Sat. winter, $8-15). The restaurant's namesake was a cabaret singer in the 1920s who opened her own restaurant in 1930. Ruth's has been in continuous operation ever since (the ads used to read "70 years in business . . . boy am I tired!"). Now open nearly 90 years, Ruth's is full of atmosphere and overlooks a rushing stream. It's a great place to go for an old-fashioned breakfast or a hearty lunch. Live music is featured at Sunday brunch.

Top a slice of toast with avocado, gravy, hash or peanut butter at **Publik Kitchen** (931 E. 900 S., 385/229-4205, www.publikcoffee.com, 7am-3:30pm Mon.-Fri., 8am-4:30pm Sat.-Sun. $5-10). Publik is primarily a coffee roaster, so the brew is good; visit their main coffee shop just south of downtown at 975 W. Temple (801/355-3161, 7am-6pm Mon.-Fri., 8am-6pm Sat.-Sun.

Greek

The city's best Greek food by far is served at ★ **Aristo's** (224 S. 1300 E., 801/581-0888, www.aristosslc.com, 11am-9pm Mon.-Wed., 11am-10pm Thurs.-Sat., meze $5-11, main courses $17-30), a swanky dining room up by the university. The flavors and quality are outstanding, and while the main courses are not cheap (but the lamb chops are worth it), it's easy to put together a meal of small plates, "street eats," and meze dishes.

Indian
Saffron Valley East India Café (26 E St., 801/203-3325, www.saffronvalley. com, 11am-3pm and 5pm-10pm Tues.-Sat., 11am-3pm and 5pm-9pm Sun., $12-19) offers an especially large selection of streetfood starters, dosas, salads, and other small plates, including unusual dishes such as Bombay (vegetarian) sloppy joes and crispy chicken poppers, in addition to more classic dishes from India and southeast Asia. The food here is sophisticated and unusual, far removed from the gloppy stew that often passes for Indian food. Head to the Sugarhouse neighborhood to find Saffron Bistro (479 E. 2100 S., 801/203-3754, 11am-3pm and 5pm-10pm Tues.-Sat., 11am-4pm and 5pm-9pm Sun., $8-19), which combines café, chai house, and market.

Italian and Mediterranean
Café Trio (680 S. 900 E., 801/533-8746, www.triodining.com, 11am-9:30pm Mon.-Thurs., 11am-10pm Fri., 10am-10pm Sat., 10am-9pm Sun. May.-Sept., $12-29), serves lovingly prepared Italian food set in a hip but casual dining room between downtown and the university. Try charred beets with avocado mousse and a sprinkling of granola, or the house-made ricotta gnocchi with spring pea puree.

Although the atmosphere at the second-floor **Stoneground** (249 E. 400 S., 801/364-1368, www.stonegroundslc.com, 11:30am-2:30pm and 5pm-9pm Mon., 11:30am-2:30pm and 5pm-10pm Tues.-Fri., 5pm-10pm Sat., 5pm-9pm Sun.) is industrial, windows at this Italian restaurant and pizzeria look out onto a gorgeous view of the Wasatch

Front and the patio is cooled by misters when the sun beats down. The thin-crust pizzas are excellent ($15-17), and pasta dishes and main courses are flavorful and full of character ($18-40).

Pizza
The Pie Underground (1320 E. 200 S., 801/582-5700, www.thepie.com, 11am-1am Mon.-Thurs., 11am-3am Fri.-Sat., noon-11pm Sun, slices $3-5), downstairs from the University Pharmacy, offers New York-style hand-thrown pizza.

Vegetarian
Oasis Café (151 S. 500 E., 801/322-0404, www.oasiscafeslc.com, 7am-9pm Mon.-Thurs., 7am-10pm Fri., 8am-10pm Sat., 8am-9pm Sun., $16-24) serves an ambitious all-organic menu that borrows tastes and preparations from around the world; while most dishes are vegetarian, fresh fish and some organic meats are also served.

Seafood
Located in a snappily repurposed auto shop just east of city center, ★ **Current Fish and Oyster** (279 E., 300 S., 801/326-3474, www.currentfishandoyster.com, 11am-10pm Mon.-Fri., 4pm-10pm Sat., 4pm-9pm Sun., $15-38) offers innovative preparations of fresh seafood in a stylish dining room, or in good weather, on a gardenlike front patio. Current is operated by some of Salt Lake City's top restaurateurs; service, setting, and food are all tip-top here.

Brewpubs
Desert Edge Brewery (273 Trolley Sq., 801/521-8917, www.desertedgebrewery.com, 11am-11pm Mon.-Fri., 11:30am-11pm Sat., noon-10pm Sun., $9-13), in Trolley Square, is also known simply as The Pub. The inexpensive menu offers sandwiches, pasta, Mexican

---

1: Rico Cocina Y Tequila Bar; **2:** Squatters Pub Brewery; **3:** Publik Kitchen; **4:** Current Fish and Oyster

dishes, and salads all day; some of the ales are cask-conditioned. The atmosphere is retro industrial chic, and there's a second-floor outdoor veranda.

The **Avenues Proper Restaurant and Publick House** (376 8th Ave., www.avenuesproper.com, 11am-10pm Tues.-Thurs., 11am-midnight Fri., 10am-midnight Sat., 10am-9pm Sun., $13-26) is Utah's smallest craft brewery, and from its location in the Avenues offers some of the best pub dining in the state. The food aspires to Food Network quality, with such dishes as duck fat popcorn with fennel pollen, Parisian gnocchi comes with grilled kale pesto, fresh corn, and heirloom tomatoes. Weekend nights are busy; get a reservation.

WEST OF DOWNTOWN
Italian and Mediterranean
Not far from downtown, ★ **Cucina Toscana** (307 W. Pierpoint Ave., next to Tony Caputo's Market, 801/328-3463, http://toscanaslc.com, 5:30pm-10pm Mon.-Sat., $15-43) offers high-quality grilled meats, salads, and pasta in a coolly elegant dining room. Reservations are a must, as Cucina Toscana is frequently jammed—for the best service, try to avoid peak dining hours.

Even though **Tin Angel Café** (365 W. 400 S., 801/328-4155, www.thetinangel.com, 11am-3pm and 5pm-9pm Mon.-Thurs., 11am-3pm and 5pm-10pm Fri., 10am-3pm and 5pm-10pm Sat., $13-24) offers small plates and tapas, the excellent preparations are largely Italian. In addition to a selection of tempting salads and pasta, bravura main courses include chicken confit with fennel/apple pilaf, and prosciutto-wrapped beef tenderloin with mashed horseradish cauliflower.

Mexican and Southwestern
★ **Red Iguana** (736 W. North Temple St., 801/322-1489, http://rediguana.com, 11am-10pm Mon.-Thurs., 11am-11pm Fri., 10am-11pm Sat., 10am-9pm Sun., $10-17) is one of the city's favorite Mexican restaurants; it offers excellent south-of-the-border cooking with a specialty in Mayan and regional foods. Best of all, flavors are crisp, fresh, and earthy. The Red Iguana is very popular, so arrive early—especially at lunch—to avoid the lines. There's also a second location (866 W. South Temple St., 801/214-6050) with the same hours and a lesser branch in the City Creek Center food court (28 S. State St., 801/214-6350, 7:30am-9pm Mon.-Fri., 10am-10pm Sat.).

Rico Cocina Y Tequila Bar (545 W. 700 S., 801/983-6692, http://fridabistro.com, 11:30am-3pm and 5pm-9pm Mon.-Fri.., 5pm-9pm Sat., $12-17) is the evolution of an upscale Mexican restaurant (the erstwhile Frida Bistro) toward simpler, more affordable fare. The tamales, fresh-cooked pinto beans, and handmade tortillas are joined by more sophisticated dishes, such as tiger shrimp with chipotle cream sauce or seared salmon with saffron cream and avocado.

Fine Dining
At first glance, ★ **Pallet** (237 S. 400 W., 801/935-4431, http://eatpallet.com, 5pm-9pm Mon.-Thurs., 5pm-10pm Fri.-Sat., $19-32) may seem a hipster cliche. But who cares—the locally sourced food is both delicious and ingenious. In this handsome refitted industrial space, expect to find such dishes as bison served over hominy and cornbread or roasted pork belly with carrots, radish, and plum jam. Don't skip dessert; seasonal fruits are put to good use in crumbles and ice cream.

Delis and Markets
A good place to stop for provisions is ★ **Tony Caputo's Market and Deli** (314 W. 300 S., 801/531-8669, http://caputosdeli.com, 9am-7pm Mon.-Sat., 10am-5pm Sun.), with great sandwiches, Italian-style sausage and cheese, loads of olives and other Mediterranean temptations, and a park nearby where you can have an impromptu picnic. Next door, **Carlucci's Bakery** (314 W. 300 S., 801/366-4484, www.carluccisbakery.com, 7:30am-5:30pm Mon.-Sat.) offers European-style breads and pastries.

In summer, the **Salt Lake Farmers Market** (300 S. 300 W., 8am-2pm Sat. June-Oct.) takes over Pioneer Park. The market offers a wide variety of international fare and to-go eating options, along with a selection of fresh fruits, vegetables, and baked goods. An arts and crafts market sets up adjacent to the farmers' booths.

Accommodations

Salt Lake City has the best selection of accommodations in Utah. Unless your budget is very tight, you may want to avoid the cheapest motels along West Temple Street or State Street. Many of these older motor court units have become residential lodgings, and the owners don't put much effort into upkeep. However, you should have a pleasant stay at all of the following accommodations.

There are several major lodging centers. Downtown Salt Lake City has the advantage of being close to Temple Square, Vivint Arena, the Salt Palace, and most other visitor attractions. South of downtown near 600 South and West Temple Street is a clutch of hotels and motels, including several business-oriented hotels. While these lodgings are only six blocks from the center of the city at Temple Square, keep in mind that blocks are very long in SLC (six blocks per mile). Another cluster of hotels and motels is west along North Temple Street, the primary surface street leading to the airport; these are convenient via the TRAX light rail line between downtown Salt Lake City and the airport. If your trip involves visiting the university, there are a couple of good lodging options near the campus.

Room rates can be rather high, although quality is good. The prices listed below are standard rack rates. You can frequently beat these prices by checking the hotel's website for specials. Also, because of hotel overbuilding for the 2002 Olympics—63 new hotels were built in the Salt Lake area after the city won the Olympic nod—you can often find real deals at internet booking sites if there's not a convention in town. Prices can vary by much as $100 per night within the same week, so the following prices are only guidelines.

If you have trouble locating a room, consider using the city's free reservation service (877/752-4386, www.visitsaltlake.com).

TEMPLE SQUARE AND DOWNTOWN

Parking is tight in downtown SLC; expect to pay about $10-15 on top of room costs if you're parking a car at a downtown hotel. Note that pricing at these hotels is particularly dependent on convention traffic; if there's not much going on, it's pretty easy to find a room at SLC's finest for well less than $200.

$100-150

The first of SLC's historic older hotels to be refurbished into a natty upscale lodging was the ★ **Peery Hotel** (110 W. 300 S., 801/521-4300, www.peeryhotel.com, $109-185). Its 1910 vintage style is preserved in the comfortable lobby, while the guest rooms are updated and nicely furnished. A restaurant is on the premises, and many others are within a short walk.

Overlooking Temple Square is the **Salt Lake Plaza Hotel** (122 W. South Temple St., 801/521-0130 or 800/366-3684, http://plaza-hotel.com, $117-130), which offers a pool and an on-site restaurant in addition to its great location.

$150-200

Some of Salt Lake's grandest heritage homes sit on Capitol Hill, just below the state capitol. Surely one of the most eye-catching is the red sandstone mansion now called the **Inn on the Hill** (225 N. State St., 801/328-1466, http://inn-on-the-hill.com, $145-245). Built in 1906 by a local captain of industry, the inn has 13 guest rooms decorated with period detail, but all with modern amenities such as private baths. Practically every room has broad views over Salt Lake City. Full gourmet breakfasts are included.

One of SLC's most popular convention hotels, the **Hilton Salt Lake City Center** (255 S. West Temple St., 801/328-2000, www1.hilton.com, $187-497) is a huge complex with an indoor pool, two fine-dining restaurants, a bar, fitness facilities, and valet laundry. When there's no convention in town, it's also a supremely comfortable (and often surprisingly affordable) spot for travelers; when convention crowds are in town, prices can double or triple!

Over $200

The **Salt Lake City Marriott Downtown at City Creek** (75 S. West Temple St., 801/531-0800 or 800/228-9290, www.marriott.com, $300-400) is directly across from the Salt Palace Convention Center. At this high-quality hotel, there's an indoor-outdoor pool, a sauna, a fitness center, a good restaurant, and a lounge. Weekend rates are often deeply discounted.

One block west of the temple is the **Radisson Salt Lake City Hotel Downtown** (215 W. South Temple St., 801/531-7500 or 888/201-1718, www.radisson.com, $222-523). At this modern 15-story hotel, you'll find a pool, a restaurant, and conference, business, and exercise facilities.

The ★ **Hotel Monaco** (15 W. 200 S., 801/595-0000 or 877/294-9710, www.monaco-saltlakecity.com, $224-301) occupies a grandly renovated historic office building in a convenient spot in the middle of downtown; on the main floor is **Bambara,** one of the most sophisticated restaurants in Utah. Guest rooms are sumptuously furnished with real élan: This is no anonymous business hotel in beige and mauve. Expect wild colors and contrasting fabrics, lots of flowers, and excellent service. Facilities include an on-site fitness center, meeting rooms, and concierge and valet services. Pets are welcome, and are even invited to the nightly wine reception. If you want to splurge on a hotel in Salt Lake, make it this one.

The ★ **Salt Lake City Marriott City Center** (220 S. State St., 801/961-8700, www.marriott.com, $220-249) sits above Gallivan Plaza, an urban park and festival space. A luxury-level business hotel, the Marriott has

the Peery Hotel

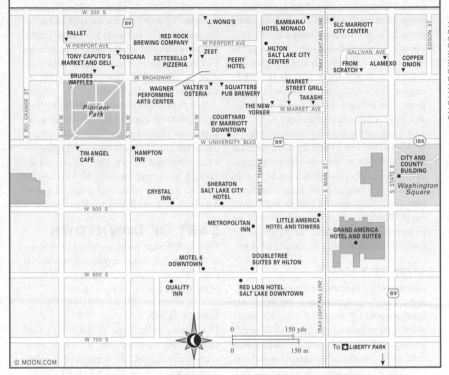

South of Downtown Salt Lake City

W 200 S

89

PALLET ▼

W PIERPORT AVE

RED ROCK BREWING COMPANY ▼

J. WONG'S ▼

W PIERPORT AVE

BAMBARA/ HOTEL MONACO ▼

SLC MARRIOTT CITY CENTER ▼

EDISON ST

TONY CAPUTO'S MARKET AND DELI ▼   TOSCANA ▼   SETTEBELLO PIZZERIA ▼

ZEST ▼

PEERY HOTEL

HILTON SALT LAKE CITY CENTER ●

GALLIVAN AVE

FROM SCRATCH ▼   ALAMEXO ▼

COPPER ONION ▼

BRUGES WAFFLES ▼

W BROADWAY

WAGNER PERFORMING ARTS CENTER

VALTER'S ▼ OSTERIA

SQUATTERS PUB BREWERY ▼

MARKET STREET GRILL ●

TAKASHI ▼

Pioneer Park

S RIO GRANDE ST

S 400 W

S 300 W

S 200 W

THE NEW YORKER ▼

W MARKET AVE

COURTYARD BY MARRIOTT DOWNTOWN

W UNIVERSITY BLVD   89

186

TIN ANGEL CAFÉ ▼

HAMPTON INN ●

CITY AND COUNTY BUILDING

S WEST TEMPLE

S MAIN ST

S STATE E

Washington Square

CRYSTAL INN ●

SHERATON SALT LAKE CITY HOTEL ●

W 500 S

METROPOLITAN INN ●

LITTLE AMERICA HOTEL AND TOWERS ■

GRAND AMERICA HOTEL AND SUITES ■

MOTEL 6 DOWNTOWN ●

DOUBLETREE SUITES BY HILTON ●

W 600 S

QUALITY INN ●

RED LION HOTEL SALT LAKE DOWNTOWN ■

TRAX LIGHT RAIL LINE

89

0   150 yds

0   150 m

W 700 S

To ★ LIBERTY PARK

© MOON.COM

an indoor pool, a recreation area, and a fine-dining restaurant.

SOUTH OF DOWNTOWN

Just south of the religious sites and convention areas downtown is a large complex of hotels and motels, mostly representatives of large chains, with rooms in almost every traveler's price range. These lodgings aren't entirely convenient for travelers on foot, but if you have a car or intend to ride buses or TRAX (unfortunately, the free public transit zone doesn't extend this far south, but the zone is just a short walk from these hotels), these are some of the newest and nicest places to stay in the city.

$50-100

These budget motels won't satisfy finicky travelers, but they're reliable standards. **Motel 6 Downtown** (176 W. 600 S., 801/531-1252, $64-82) is a standard motel, but it does have a pool. Pets are allowed at the **Quality Inn Downtown** (616 S. 200 W., 801/534-0808, www.rodewayinn.com, $99-109). The **Metropolitan Inn** (524 S. West Temple St., 801/531-7100, www.metropolitaninn.com, $79-149) has Tempurpedic mattresses in the guest rooms, all with coffeemakers and access to a heated pool and a hot tub. Pets are accepted.

$100-150

If you're looking for comfortable rooms without breaking the bank, the ★ **Little America Hotel and Towers** (500 S. Main St., 801/363-6781 or 800/304-8970, http://saltlake.littleamerica.com, $119-319) is a great place to stay. This large lodging complex, with nearly 850 guest rooms, offers three types of room: Courtside rooms and garden suites are scattered around the hotel's nicely manicured grounds, with most guest rooms overlooking a pool or fountain. Tower suites are executive-level suites in a 17-story block offering some of SLC's best views. All guests share the hotel's elegant public areas, two pools, and a fitness room. The restaurant is better than average, and there is free airport transfer.

Another of the nicer-for-the-money hotels in this part of Salt Lake City is the **Crystal Inn** (230 W. 500 S., 801/328-4466 or 800/366-4466, www.crystalinnsaltlake.com, $134-174). Guest rooms here are very large and nicely furnished; all come with fridges and microwaves. There's a free hot breakfast buffet for all guests. For recreation, there's an indoor pool, an exercise room, a sauna, and a hot tub.

$150-200

One of the best situated of all the south downtown motels is **Courtyard by Marriott Downtown** (130 W. 400 S., 801/531-6000, www.marriott.com, $195-234). It's centrally located to all the restaurants and happenings in the city's fast-changing warehouse-loft district. There's a pool, a hot tub, a fitness facility, and an airport shuttle.

Hampton Inn (425 S. 300 W., 801/741-1110, http://hamptoninn.hilton.com, $179-209) offers complimentary breakfast, an indoor pool, a hot tub, and a business center.

If you're in Salt Lake for an extended time or are traveling with a family, consider the **DoubleTree Suites by Hilton** (110 W. 600 S., 801/359-7800, http://doubletree3.hilton.com, $160-195). All suites have efficiency kitchens with a coffeemaker, a fridge, and a microwave along with separate living and sleeping areas; there are two two-bedroom units. Facilities include a pool, a sauna, an exercise area, a restaurant, and a lounge.

Over $200

The behemoth ★ **Grand America Hotel and Suites** (555 S. Main St., 801/258-6000

or 800/304-8696, www.grandamerica.com, $309-409) is a full Salt Lake City square block (remember, that's 10 acres), and its 24 stories contain 775 guest rooms, more than half of them suites. Guest rooms have luxury-level amenities; expect all the perks and niceties that modern hotels can offer, delivered in an over-the-top package that borders on the indulgences of Las Vegas hotels.

Sheraton Salt Lake City Hotel (150 W. 500 S., 801/401-2000 or 888/627-8152, www.sheratonsaltlakecityhotel.com, $214-289) is one of the city's best addresses for high-quality comfort and service. The lobby areas are very pleasant, and facilities include a great pool, an exercise room, and a spa. The rooftop restaurant and lounge are also notable.

EAST OF DOWNTOWN

There aren't many lodging choices in this part of the city, but this is a pleasant residential area without the distinct urban jolt of much of the rest of central Salt Lake City.

Under $50

The Avenues (107 F St. at 2nd Ave., 1 mile east of Temple Square, 801/363-3855, www.saltlakehostel.com, $34 dorm, $64 d) offers dorm rooms with use of a kitchen, a TV room, and laundry. Although you're likely to meet travelers from all over the world, the hostel is a bit on the shabby side. Beds are available in the dorm (sheets included) or in private rooms, some of which have private baths. From downtown, head east on South Temple Street to F Street, then turn north and go two blocks.

$150-200

The **Anniversary Inn** (460 S. 1000 E., 801/363-4900 or 800/324-4152, www.anniversaryinn.com, $179-229) caters to couples and newlyweds interested in a romantic getaway. All 32 guest rooms are imaginatively decorated according to a theme: Beds may be in a covered wagon or a vintage rail car, and baths may be in a sea cave. Chances are good that your guest room will have its own private waterfall. You get to pick your suite from choices that include The Lighthouse, The Opera House, South Pacific, and Venice. These guest rooms aren't just filled with kitsch; they are luxury-class accommodations with big-screen TVs, hot tubs, stereos, and private baths. Rates vary widely by room. There's also a second Anniversary Inn (678 E. South Temple St.).

Right in the University of Utah's Research Park, the **Marriott University Park Hotel and Suites** (480 Wakara Way, 801/581-1000, www.marriott.com, $150-200) is one of the city's best-kept secrets for luxurious lodgings in a lovely setting. You can't miss with the views: All guest rooms either overlook the city or look onto the soaring peaks of the Wasatch Range, directly behind the hotel. Guest rooms are very nicely appointed—the suites are some of the best in the city. All guest rooms have minibars, fridges, and coffeemakers.

WEST OF DOWNTOWN

Nearly all of the following hotels offer transfers to the Salt Lake City Airport. Those with the lowest-numbered addresses on West North Temple Street are closest to downtown; these hotels are about one mile from Temple Square and downtown, and they are inexpensive options if you're looking for a centrally located place to stay.

$50-100

Budget rooms are available at the **Motel 6 Airport** (1990 W. North Temple St., 801/364-1053, www.motel6.com, $64-66), where there's a pool.

Practically next door to the airport terminal is the **Ramada Salt Lake City** (5575 W. Amelia Earhart Dr., 801/537-7020, www.ramada.com, $85-129), with a pool and a spa.

$150-200

The **Radisson Hotel Salt Lake City Airport** (2177 W. North Temple St., 801/364-5800, www.radisson.com, $147-202) is a very attractive lodgelike building with nicely furnished guest rooms. Guests receive a complimentary continental breakfast and a newspaper, and

in the evenings there's a manager's reception with free beverages. Facilities include a pool, a spa, and a fitness room. Suites come with a loft bedroom area.

At the **DoubleTree by Hilton SLC Airport** (5151 Wiley Post Way, 801/539-1515, doubletree3.hilton.com, $159-189), guest rooms are very spacious and nicely furnished, and facilities include two pools, a putting green, a sports court, an exercise room, and a spa. The hotel even has its own lake.

CAMPGROUNDS

Of the several commercial campgrounds around the periphery of Salt Lake City, **Camp VIP/Salt Lake City KOA** (1400 W. North Temple, 801/328-0224, www.koa.com, year-round) is the most convenient, located between downtown and the airport. It offers sites for tents ($37) and RVs (from $59) with showers, a swimming pool, a game room, a playground, a store, and laundry. From I-15 northbound, take exit 311 for I-80; go west 1.3 miles (2.1 km) on I-80, exit north for 0.5 mile on Redwood Road (Hwy. 68), then turn right and continue another 0.5 mile on North Temple Street. From I-15 southbound, take exit 313 and go south 1.5 miles (2.4 km) on 900 West, then turn right and drive less than 1 mile (1.6 km) on North Temple Street. From I-80, take either the North Temple exit or the one for Redwood Road (Hwy. 68).

There are two good U.S. Forest Service campgrounds in Big Cottonwood Canyon, about 15 miles (24 km) southeast of downtown Salt Lake City, and another two in Little Cottonwood Canyon, about 19 miles (31 km) southeast of town. All have drinking water, and all prohibit pets because of local watershed regulations; rates range $21-23, and one can be reserved (877/444-6777, www.recreation.gov, $9 online, $10 phone reservation fee).

In Big Cottonwood Canyon, **Spruces Campground** (9.1 miles/14.6 km up the canyon, elev. 7,400 feet) is open early June-mid-October. The season at **Redman**

Campground (elev. 8,300 feet, first-come, first-served) is mid-June-early October. It's between Solitude and Brighton, 14 miles (22.5 km) up Big Cottonwood Canyon.

Little Cottonwood Canyon's **Tanners Flat Campground** (4.3 miles/6.9 km up the canyon, elev. 7,200 feet, first-come, first-served) is open mid-May-mid-October. **Albion Basin Campground** (elev. 9,500 feet, first-come, first-served) is high in the mountains a few miles past Alta Ski Area and is open early July-late September; go 11 miles (17.7 km) up the canyon (the last 2.5 miles/4 km are gravel).

Information and Services

Salt Lake City's visitors centers are well stocked with information and enthusiastic volunteers. Couple that with excellent public transportation, and you'll find the city and surrounding areas easy to negotiate despite the intimidating sprawl.

INFORMATION
Tourism Offices
Volunteers at the **Salt Lake Convention and Visitors Bureau** (downtown in the Salt Palace, 90 S. West Temple St., Salt Lake City, UT 84101, 801/534-4900, www.visitsaltlake. com, 9am-5pm daily) will tell you about the sights, facilities, and goings-on in town. The office also has many helpful magazines and brochures.

The **Utah Travel Council** (300 N. State St., 801/538-1030, www.utah.com, 8am-5pm Mon.-Fri., 10am-5pm Sat.-Sun.) publishes a well-illustrated *Utah Travel Guide,* travel maps, and other helpful publications. The staff at the Travel Council information desk provides advice and literature about Utah's national parks and monuments, national forests, Bureau of Land Management areas, and state parks as well as general travel in the state.

U.S. Forest Service
Although visiting the U.S. Forest Service headquarters or a ranger station is always an option, travelers may find it easier to go to REI (3285 E. 3300 S., 801/486-2100), where the Forest Service maintains the **Public Lands Information Center** (801/466-6411, 10:30am-5:30pm Mon.-Fri., 9am-1pm Sat.). The staff is often more oriented to serving outdoor recreationalists than is staff at ranger stations. A full selection of maps, books, and printed material is available.

The **Uinta-Wasatch-Cache National Forest** supervisor's office (857 W. South Jordan Pkwy., South Jordan, UT, 84109, 801/999-2103, www.fs.usda.gov/uwcnf, 8am-4:30pm Mon.-Fri.) has general information and forest maps for all the national forests in Utah, and some forest and wilderness maps of Nevada, Idaho, and Wyoming.

SERVICES
There is a main **post office** (230 W. 200 S., 801/974-2200) downtown. The University of Utah has a post office in the bookstore.

Salt Lake City is a major regional banking center, and you'll have no trouble with most common financial transactions. ATMs are everywhere and make obtaining money easy. If you are depending on foreign currency, consider changing enough for your trip around Utah while you're in Salt Lake City. Exchanging currency is much more difficult in smaller rural towns.

Minor medical emergencies can be treated by **InstaCare Clinics** (389 S. 900 E., 801/282-2400, 9am-9pm daily), with more than 30 outlets in the greater Wasatch Front area. Hospitals with 24-hour emergency care include **Salt Lake Regional Medical Center** (1050 E. South Temple St., 801/350-4111), **LDS Hospital** (8th Ave. and C St., 801/350-4111), **St. Mark's Hospital** (1200 E. 3900 S.,

801/268-7111), and **University Hospital** (50 N. Medical Dr./1900 East, 801/581-2121).

For a 24-hour pharmacy, try **Rite Aid** (5540 S. 900 E., 801/262-2981). If you're looking for a drugstore, check the phone book for **Smith's Pharmacy;** there are more than 25 in the Salt Lake metro area.

The **American Automobile Association** (AAA) has offices at 560 East 500 South (801/541-9902).

Transportation

AIR

Salt Lake City International Airport (SLC, 776 N. Terminal Dr., 801/575-2400, www.slcairport.com) is conveniently located 7 miles (11.3 km) west of downtown; take North Temple or I-80 to reach it. Most major U.S. carriers fly into Salt Lake City, and it is the western hub for Delta Air Lines, the region's air transportation leader.

Delta Connections (800/325-8224, www.skywest.com) is Delta's commuter partner and flies from SLC to Cedar City and St. George in Utah and to smaller cities in adjacent states.

The airport has three terminals; in each you'll find a ground-transportation information desk, food service, motel-hotel courtesy phones, and a ski-rental shop. Auto rentals (Hertz, Avis, National, Budget, and Dollar) are in the parking structure immediately across from the terminals. Just follow the signs.

Staff at the ground-transportation information desks will know the bus schedules into town and can advise on limousine services direct to Park City, Sundance, Provo, Ogden, Brigham City, Logan, and other communities. By far the easiest way to get from the airport to downtown is via the TRAX rail line, which runs between the SLC airport and the Salt Lake Central Station. The train stop is located at the south end of Terminal 1. Trains run every 15 minutes on weekdays, every 20 minutes on weekends; hours are 6am-11pm Mon.-Sat., 9:45am-10pm Sun. One-way fare is $2.50.

If you're flying in from Phoenix or Los Angeles, consider the Provo airport, which is less than an hour from SLC by car, and served by budget airline Allegiant. However, when flying on Allegiant, as with other budget airlines, travelers should expect to pay extra for "extras" such as carry-on bags and water.

TRAIN

Amtrak (340 S. 600 W., information and reservations 800/872-7245, www.amtrak.com) trains stop at the Salt Lake Central Station (300 S. 600 W.), which also serves as a terminus for local buses, light rail, and commuter trains. The only Amtrak train that currently passes through the city is the *California Zephyr,* which runs west to Reno and Oakland and east to Denver and Chicago once daily in each direction. Call for fares, as Amtrak prices tickets as airlines do, with advance-booking discounts, special seasonal prices, and other special rates available. Amtrak office hours, timed to meet the trains, are irregular, so call first.

LONG-DISTANCE BUS

Salt Lake City is at a crossroads of several major interstate highways and has good **Greyhound** bus service (300 S. 600 W., 801/355-9579, www.greyhound.com). Generally speaking, buses go north and south along I-15 and east and west along I-80. In summer, one bus daily leaves from Salt Lake City for Yellowstone National Park.

LOCAL BUS AND LIGHT RAIL

Utah Transit Authority (UTA, 801/287-4636, www.rideuta.com, 6am-7pm Mon.-Sat.) provides inexpensive bus and light rail train service in town and to the airport, the

University of Utah, and surrounding communities. Buses go as far north as Ogden, as far south as Provo and Springville, and as far west as Tooele. TRAX light rail trains connect the Vivint Smart Home Arena, the University of Utah, downtown Salt Lake City, the airport, and the southern suburbs. No charge is made for travel downtown within the Free-Fare Square area, generally bounded by North Temple Street, 500 South, 200 East, and 400 West; on TRAX, service is fare-free to Salt Lake Central Station at 600 West.

A TRAX line connects Salt Lake City International Airport with Salt Lake Central Station, which you can board a light rail train at the airport and ride public transport downtown—or with a bit of patience, to your Wasatch Front ski area.

During the winter ski season, skiers can hop on the Ski Bus Service to Solitude, Brighton, Snowbird, and Alta ski areas from downtown, the University of Utah, and other locations. A bus route map and individual schedules are available on the website and at the ground transportation information desk at the airport, at the Salt Lake Convention and Visitors Bureau downtown, and at Temple Square visitors centers. Free transfers are provided on request when the fare is paid. On Sunday, only the airport, Ogden, Provo, and a few other destinations are served. UTA shuts down on holidays. Fares are $2.50 for two hours of travel on both TRAX and the buses; a day pass is $6.25.

BIKE SHARING

The nonprofit **GREENbike** (801/333-1110, http://greenbikeslc.org) makes bikes available at some 20 stations in central Salt Lake City. The system is easy to use. Pay a small membership fee online, then download an app to find stations and bike availability. You can take any bike from any station as many times as you wish, within the terms of your membership. When you're done with your trip, return your bike to any station. The bright green bikes all have a basket large enough for a briefcase or knapsack; automatic front and rear LED lights, adjustable seat; and built-in cable lock. Though annual memberships are available, most visitors will opt for a 24-hour pass ($7) or a four-day pass ($15); both allow for unlimited 30-minute trips.

CAR RENTAL

All the major companies and many local outfits are eager to rent you a set of wheels. In winter you can find "skier-ized" vehicles with snow tires and ski racks ready to head for the slopes. Many agencies have an office or delivery service at the airport: **Avis Rent A Car** (Salt Lake City International Airport, 801/575-2847 or 800/331-1212, www.avis.com), **Budget Rent A Car** (641 N. 3800 W., 801/575-2586 or 800/527-0700, www.budget.com), **Dollar Rent-A-Car** (601 N. 3800 W. and Salt Lake City International Airport, 801/575-2580 or 800/421-9849, www.dollar.com), **Enterprise Rent-A-Car** (151 E. 5600 S., 801/266-3777 or 801/534-1888, www.enterprise.com), **Hertz** (Salt Lake City International Airport, 801/575-2683 or 800/654-3131, www.hertz.com), **National Car Rental** (Salt Lake City International Airport, 801/575-2277 or 800/227-7368, www.nationalcar.com), and **Payless Car Rental** (1974 W. North Temple St., 801/596-2596 or 800/327-3631, www.paylesscar.com).

TAXI

City Cab (801/363-8400), **Ute Cab** (801/359-7788), and **Yellow Cab** (801/521-2100) have 24-hour service. Lyft and Uber are also available.

Vicinity of Salt Lake City

Travelers may think that northern Utah is dominated by the sprawling suburbs of the Wasatch Front. However, there is plenty to see and do in the state's chunky panhandle. Great Salt Lake, one of Utah's signature features, is a remnant of a network of ice age lakes that once covered the West. It's not exactly easy to visit the lake itself—and at certain times of the year, not exactly pleasant—but this one-of-a-kind destination does merit a detour to scenic Antelope Island, where bison and bighorn sheep graze alongside the island's namesake pronghorn, or a visit to Great Salt Lake State Park to explore the southern shores by kayak.

The region has a rich railroad history. Ogden was born of the railroads, and the city's historic downtown is dominated by Union Station, now home to multiple museums. The first transcontinental railway joined the Atlantic and Pacific coasts near here in 1869, at Promontory Summit. This windswept pass is preserved as the Golden Spike National Historic Site, with a visitors center and exhibits to beguile the student of history and the rails.

Logan is one of Utah's most pleasant towns, home to Utah State University and a profusion of summer festivals, including the Utah Opera Festival. The town's alpine setting and surrounding dairy farms make the deserts and saline lakes of Utah seem far away.

The mountains of the Wasatch Range east of both Logan and Ogden are filled with great recreational opportunities. Ogden Canyon, just east of town, is the site of good hiking trails and the road to some of the state's best skiing at Snowbasin. Logan Canyon includes trails to lakes and wildflower meadows.

GREAT SALT LAKE STATE PARK

The lake is popular for sailing, kayaking, and pleasure boating, and **Great Salt Lake State Park** (14 miles/22.5 km west of Salt Lake City,

take I-80 exit 104, 801/250-1898, sunrise-sunset, $3 per vehicle), with paved launches, is the primary marina along the southern shores. A small (five-site) campground ($20, www.reserveamerica.com) is right on the lakeside, but is really just a parking lot and best for RVs. In addition, there's a visitors center and gift shop, a picnic area, and restrooms. Adjacent to the marina is a beach, and when the lake waters are high enough, this is a good spot to go swimming, wading, or just floating. Because of the salty residue that the water can leave on your skin, you'll also be glad that the park offers freshwater showers.

Gonzo Boat Rentals and Tours (801/698-6288, www.gonzofun.com) offers kayak, paddleboard, and pedal boat rentals from the marina, mostly on weekends, though call ahead to arrange customized tours and excursions.

OGDEN

Located at the northern edge of the Wasatch Front urban area, Ogden, off I-15 and 35 miles (56 km) north of Salt Lake City, remains very much its own city even as it is engulfed by suburbs. Ogden was one of the West's most important rail hubs at the beginning of the 20th century, and in the downtown area, vestiges of the city's affluence remain in the grand architecture and the impressive Union Pacific Depot.

Ogden is named for Peter Skene Ogden of the Hudson's Bay Company. He explored and trapped in the upper reaches of the Ogden and Weber Valleys in 1828-1829, but he never descended to the site of the city that bears his name. In 1846, Miles Goodyear established an out-of-the-way trading post and stockade here, one of the first permanent settlements in Utah, and named it Fort Buenaventura.

Arrival of the transcontinental railroad in 1869 changed Ogden forever. Although the railroad's Golden Spike had been driven at

Vicinity of Salt Lake City

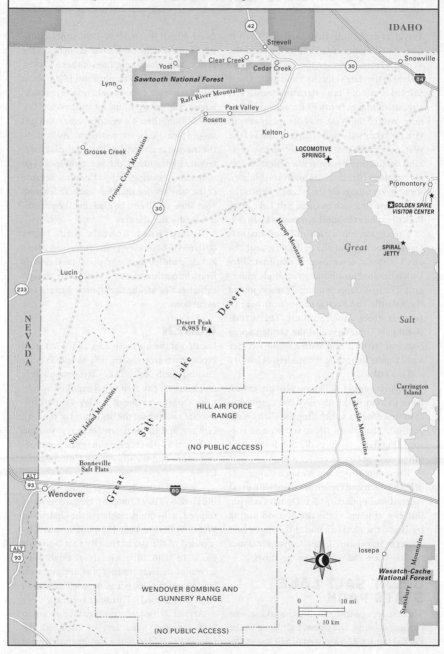

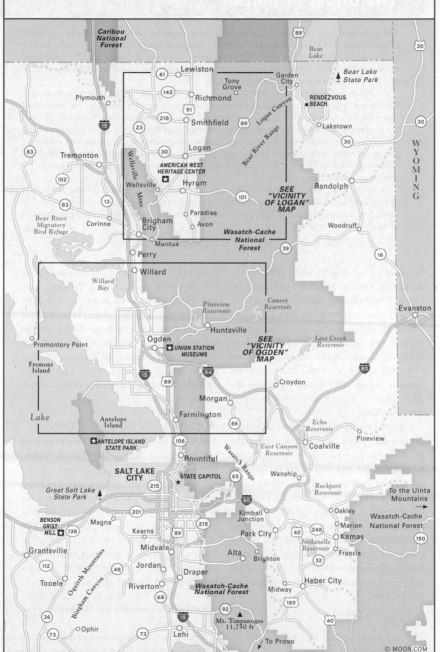

Caribou National Forest

Bear Lake

30

WYOMING

61 Lewiston

142 Richmond

Tony Grove

Garden City

Bear Lake State Park

RENDEZVOUS ■ BEACH

Plymouth

91

218

23

15

Smithfield

89

Logan Canyon

Laketown

30

30

83

Tremonton

30 Logan

American West Heritage Center ★

Bear River Range

Randolph

102

Wellsville Mtns

Wellsville

Hyrum

101

SEE "VICINITY OF LOGAN" MAP

Woodruff

83 13

Bear River Migratory Bird Refuge

Corinne

Paradise

Avon

Brigham City

Mantua

Wasatch-Cache National Forest

39

16

Perry

Willard

Willard Bay

Pineview Reservoir

Causey Reservoir

Evanston

Promontory Point

Ogden

★ Union Station Museums

Huntsville

SEE "VICINITY OF OGDEN" MAP

Lost Creek Reservoir

80

Fremont Island

15

89

84

Croydon

Lake

Antelope Island

Morgan

Farmington

66

Echo Reservoir

Pineview

★ Antelope Island State Park

106

East Canyon Reservoir

Coalville

Bountiful

Wasatch Range

Salt Lake City

★ State Capitol

State Capitol

65

Wanship

Rockport Reservoir

To the Uinta Mountains →

Great Salt Lake State Park

215

Benson Grist Mill 138

Magna

201

Kearns

89

215

80

Kimball Junction

Oakley

Marion

Kamas

Wasatch-Cache National Forest

Grantsville

Midvale

Park City

40

248

150

112

Oquirrh Mountains

48

Jordan

Draper

Alta

Brighton

Jordanelle Reservoir

Francis

32

Tooele

Riverton

68

Wasatch-Cache National Forest

Midway

Heber City

189

36

Bingham Canyon

92

Mt. Timpanogos 11,750 ft

40

73

Ophir

73

Lehi

To Provo

© MOON.COM

The Ghost of Saltair

Bathers have enjoyed hopping into Great Salt Lake ever since the 1847 arrival of Mormon pioneers. Extreme buoyancy in the dense water makes it impossible for a bather to sink—no swimming ability needed! But if you put your head underwater, you'll quickly realize that the salty water causes great irritation to the eyes, throat, and nose. Also note that algae blooms during summer, and the odor of the water can irritate the nose.

Beginning in the 1880s, several resorts popped up along the lake's east and south shores. Besides bathing, guests could enjoy lake cruises, dances, concerts, bowling, arcade games, and roller-coaster rides. Saltair Resort represented the grandest of the old resorts. Completed in 1893, the Moorish structure rose five stories and contained a huge dance floor, where as many as 1,000 couples could enjoy the orchestra's rhythms. A rail line from Salt Lake City ran out on a 4,000-foot pier to the resort, which stood on pilings over the water. After 1930, low water levels, the Great Depression, fires, and fewer visitors gradually brought an end to Saltair. Its buildings burned for the second time in 1970.

In the 1980s, a developer built a smaller replica of the **Saltair Resort** (13 miles/21 km west of Salt Lake City, near I-80 exit 104, www.thesaltair.com) on Great Salt Lake's southern shore. The building is now mostly used as a concert venue. From the Saltair parking, visitors can cross the beach for a swim in the lake.

Promontory Summit, 55 miles (89 km) to the northwest, Ogden earned the title Junction City as lines branched from it through Utah and into surrounding states. New industries and an expanding non-Mormon population transformed the sleepy farm town into a bustling city. Today, Ogden, with a population of 84,000, serves as a major administrative, manufacturing, and livestock center for the intermountain West; it's also home to a large Air Force base.

Ogden is worth exploring for its museums, historic sites, and access to scenic spots in the Wasatch Range, which looms precipitously just behind the city. From here it's quick to get out into the hinterlands of northern Utah. Ogden Canyon, beginning on the east edge of town and leading into the Wasatch, leads up to lakes, campgrounds, hiking trails, and three downhill ski areas. Several 2002 Winter Olympic events took place in the Ogden area, including the downhill and super-G ski races and the men's and women's curling competition.

Sights

The Salomon Center, at 23rd and Keisel Streets, is a sports, recreation, and fitness center complete with Gold's Gym, a wave pool for surfing practice, a climbing wall, and **iFLY Indoor Skydiving** (801/528-5348, www.iflyutah.com, 11am-9pm Mon.-Sat., $55 and up), a vertical wind tunnel that re-creates the experience of free-fall skydiving. (If skydiving lessons are going on, it's fun just to stop in to watch.) Also at the Center are a Megaplex 13 movie theater and a number of restaurants, mostly chains.

★ UNION STATION MUSEUMS

Travelers thronged into the cavernous **Union Station Building** (2501 Wall Ave., http://theunionstation.org) during the grand old days of railroading. Completed in 1924, it saw more than 120 trains daily during the peak World War II years. When passenger trains stopped serving Ogden in 1977, the station was leased to the city of Ogden. Today, the depot is mostly known for its fine museums and the **Forest Service Information Center** (801/625-5306, 8am-4:30pm Mon.-Fri.), which provides recreation information for public lands in the Wasatch Range.

Union Station's museums and art gallery are well worth a visit. A single ticket allows

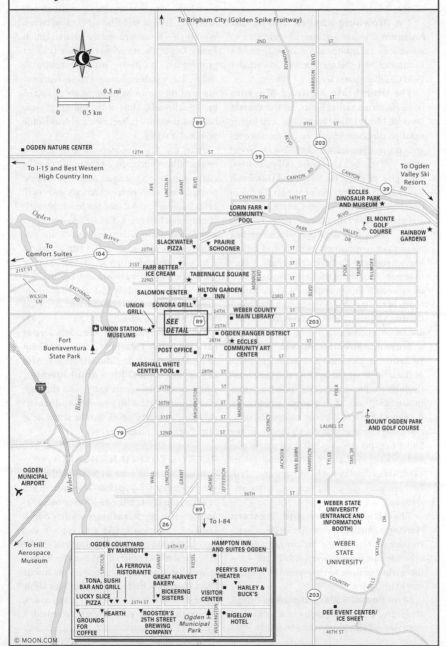

Ogden

To Brigham City (Golden Spike Fruitway)

OGDEN NATURE CENTER

To I-15 and Best Western
High Country Inn

To
Comfort Suites

Ogden River

ECCLES
DINOSAUR PARK
AND MUSEUM

To Ogden
Valley Ski
Resorts

LORIN FARR
COMMUNITY
POOL

EL MONTE
GOLF
COURSE

RAINBOW
GARDENS

SLACKWATER
PIZZA

PRAIRIE
SCHOONER

FARR BETTER
ICE CREAM

TABERNACLE SQUARE

SALOMON CENTER

HILTON GARDEN
INN

UNION
GRILL

SONORA GRILL

SEE
DETAIL

WEBER COUNTY
MAIN LIBRARY

UNION STATION
MUSEUMS

Fort
Buenaventura
State Park

OGDEN RANGER DISTRICT

ECCLES
COMMUNITY ART
CENTER

POST OFFICE

MARSHALL WHITE
CENTER POOL

MOUNT OGDEN PARK
AND GOLF COURSE

OGDEN
MUNICIPAL
AIRPORT

To I-84

WEBER STATE
UNIVERSITY
(ENTRANCE AND
INFORMATION
BOOTH)

To Hill
Aerospace
Museum

WEBER
STATE
UNIVERSITY

OGDEN COURTYARD
BY MARRIOTT

HAMPTON INN
AND SUITES OGDEN

LA FERROVIA
RISTORANTE

GREAT HARVEST
BAKERY

PEERY'S EGYPTIAN
THEATER

TONA, SUSHI
BAR AND GRILL

BICKERING
SISTERS

HARLEY &
BUCK'S

LUCKY SLICE
PIZZA

VISITOR
CENTER

BIGELOW
HOTEL

GROUNDS
FOR
COFFEE

HEARTH

ROOSTER'S
25TH STREET
BREWING
COMPANY

Ogden
Municipal
Park

DEE EVENT CENTER/
ICE SHEET

© MOON.COM

0   0.5 mi
0   0.5 km

admission to all exhibitions (10am-5pm Mon.-Sat., $5 adults, $4 students and over age 61, $3 ages 3-12).

The **Browning-Kimball Classic Car Museum** displays a glittering collection of about a dozen antique autos, ranging from a 1-cylinder 1901 Oldsmobile to a 16-cylinder 1930 Cadillac sports sedan.

The **Utah State Railroad Museum** comprises two rail exhibits. In the **Wattis Dumke Model Railroad** collection, highly detailed dioramas illustrate railroad scenes and construction feats. Eight HO-scale model trains roll through the Ogden rail yard, wind through a model of the Sierra and Humboldt Palisades, cross Great Salt Lake on the Lucin Cutoff, and descend Weber Canyon. Exhibits and photos show railroading history and great trains, such as the Big Boys, which weighed more than one million pounds and pulled heavy freights up the mountain ranges. A documentary film about the first transcontinental railroad is shown on request. Outside, just south of the station, at the **Eccles Railroad Center,** you can visit giant diesel locomotives and some cabooses.

Browning Firearms Museum (upstairs) contains the gun shop and many examples of firearms invented by the Browning family. John M. Browning (1855-1926), a genius in his field, held 75 major gun patents. He developed the world's first successful automatic firearms, which used gases from the bullet to expel the old shell, load a new one, and cock the mechanism. The skillfully done exhibitions display both military and civilian handguns, automatic weapons, rifles, and shotguns.

The **Utah Cowboy and Western Heritage Museum** commemorates Utah's frontier past, honoring the cowboy and the other men and women who settled Utah—and those who continue to champion the Western way of life.

Myra Powell Gallery displays paintings, sculpture, and photography in a former pigeon roost. Exhibitions rotate monthly.

HISTORIC 25TH STREET

When Ogden was the railroad's main transport hub, 25th was the city's main street. Running like a wide boulevard between Washington Boulevard and the palatial Union Pacific Depot, the street boasted the city's first grocery and hardware stores, blacksmith shops, livery stables, hotels, and restaurants, many of them run by immigrants attracted by the railroads. Most of the buildings were built for posterity in redbrick and handsome vernacular styles.

After the city's residents came to rely less on the railway and more on the motor car, the city's orientation changed, and this historic precinct fell into disrepair. Artists and small cafés have since colonized the lovely historic commercial buildings. The street now serves as a combination gallery and restaurant row while still functioning as the city's bowery. It's a pleasant place for a stroll, and many of the shops and cafés are worth a detour. Pick up a brochure detailing histories of many of these buildings from the tourism office on Washington Boulevard.

On summer Saturdays, the **25th Street Farmers and Art Market** (25th St. and Grant Ave.) takes over Ogden Municipal Park. Also in the park is the **Ogden Amphitheater,** which hosts free events early June through mid-August, including movies and classical music concerts; check out the schedule at http://ogdenamphitheater.com.

PEERY'S EGYPTIAN THEATER

You can't miss the unusual facade of the venerable **Peery's Egyptian Theater** (2415 Washington Blvd., 801/689-8700 or 866/472-4627, www.egyptiantheaterogden.com). Looking suspiciously like an Egyptian sun temple, this old-time movie palace and vaudeville theater was built in 1924 in the "atmospheric" style during the fit of Egyptomania that followed the discovery of King Tut's tomb. After falling into disrepair for many years, the old theater was completely refurbished; it

---

1: Ogden's Union Station; 2: Historic 25th Street

1

2

ROOMS

HISTORIC
25th STREET

ROOMS

now serves as Ogden's performing arts center. The interior of the hall is equally astonishing, with a sun that moves across the ceiling, floating clouds, and glittering stars. With columns, hieroglyphs, and mummies everywhere, the theater looks like the set for *Aida*. The Egyptian keeps very busy with a series of top-notch musical performances and regional theater productions.

Adjacent to the Egyptian Theater is the **David Eccles Conference Center** (801/689-8600), a handsome building designed to harmonize architecturally with the theater. Together, the conference center and the theater form the core of Ogden's convention facility.

OGDEN TEMPLE AND TABERNACLE

The **Ogden LDS Temple** (350 22nd St.), once a modern structure much like the Provo Temple, was rebuilt and reopened in 2014, resulting in a much grander and more classical granite-clad building. The **Daughters of Utah Pioneers Museum** is just west of the temple on the corner of Lincoln Street and 21st Avenue. On Tabernacle Square, the white-steepled **Ogden Tabernacle** (2133 Washington Blvd., 9am-5pm Mon.-Sat. in summer), completed in 1956, sits just to the north. Visitors are welcome inside the tabernacle.

FORT BUENAVENTURA STATE PARK

Miles Goodyear built the original **Fort Buenaventura** (office 2450 S. A Ave., 801/399-8009, www.webercountyutah.gov, 9am-dusk daily spring-fall, $2) in 1846 to serve as a trading post and way station for travelers crossing the remote Great Basin region. Now a replica of the tiny fort provides a link with Utah's mountain-man past. The location, dimensions, and materials used for the stockade and three cabins inside closely follow the originals. The 32-acre park has a campground and a pond popular for canoeing in summer (rentals are available). From downtown Ogden, take 24th Street

west across the rail yard and the Weber River, turn left onto A Avenue, and follow the signs.

ECCLES COMMUNITY ART CENTER

A series of monthly changing exhibitions at the **Eccles Community Art Center** (2580 Jefferson Ave., 801/392-6935, www.ogden4arts.org, 9am-5pm Mon.-Fri., 9am-3pm Sat., free), in a historic mansion, displays the best of regional paintings, sculpture, photography, and mixed media. The ornate mansion, once owned by the philanthropic Eccles family, whose name is attached to many arts centers in northern Utah, is an attraction in itself. Turrets, cut glass, and carved woodwork decorate the brick and sandstone structure, built in 1893 in a Richardsonian-Romanesque style. The carriage house in back contains a sales gallery, and the grounds are used as a sculpture garden.

OGDEN NATURE CENTER

The **Ogden Nature Center** (966 W. 12th St., 801/621-7595, www.ogdennaturecenter.org, 9am-5pm Mon.-Fri., 9am-4pm Sat., $5 ages 13-65, $4 age 65 and up, $3 ages 2-12) is a 127-acre wildlife sanctuary on the outskirts of Ogden. It's a popular spot for school field trips and summer camps, and it's also fun just to visit on your own. Hiking trails lead through woods, wetlands, and open fields. Deer, porcupines, muskrat, rabbits, snakes, and about 130 species of birds have been spotted here. The visitors center offers classes, workshops, displays, picnic facilities, and activities year-round. To get here, follow West 12th Street northwest from downtown.

ECCLES DINOSAUR PARK AND MUSEUM

Paths at the leafy **Eccles Dinosaur Park** (1544 E. Park Blvd., 801/393-3466, www.dinosaurpark.org, 10am-7pm Mon.-Sat., 10am-5pm Sun. Labor Day-Memorial Day, 10am-6pm daily Memorial Day-Labor Day, $7 adults, $6 seniors and students, $5 ages 2-12) lead to more than 100 realistic life-size replicas of dinosaurs, complete with robotics, making this a favorite with children. Exhibitions are based on the most up-to-date studies of paleontologists, and the replicas were created by the same folks who build "dino-stars" for Hollywood films. A large museum includes some impressively large dino skeletons and an area to watch technicians work on recently excavated dinosaur bones.

HILL AEROSPACE MUSEUM

Construction of Hill Field began in 1940, just in time to serve the aircraft maintenance and storage needs of the military during the hectic World War II years. The decades since have seen a parade of nearly every type of bomber, fighter, helicopter, trainer, and missile belonging to the U.S. Air Force. At **Hill Aerospace Museum** (7961 Wardleigh Rd., 801/777-6868, www.hill.af.mil, 9am-4:30pm daily, donation), about 90 of these can be seen close-up in outdoor and indoor exhibits. To get here, take I-15 exit 341 for Roy, 5 miles (8 km) south of Ogden, and follow the signs east.

WEBER STATE UNIVERSITY

Weber State University (3848 Harrison Blvd., 801/626-6000, www.weber.edu), pronounced WEE-bur, is southeast of downtown on a bench of prehistoric Lake Bonneville; the Wasatch Range rises steeply behind. Visitors are welcome on campus for the kid-oriented **Museum of Natural Science** (1551 Edvalson St., 801/626-6653, 8am-5pm Mon.-Fri., free), **Shaw Art Gallery** (Kimball Visual Arts building, 801/626-7689, 11am-5pm Mon.-Fri., noon-5pm Sat. during school year), Olympic ice-skating rink, library, student union and bookstore, and cultural and sporting events. **Wilderness Recreation Center** (4022 Taylor Ave., 801/626-6373, www.weber.edu, 8am-6pm Mon.-Sat.), next to the Swenson Gym, rents kayaks, rafts, skis, camping gear, and other sports equipment; although it's geared toward students, the center also rents to visitors and people from the local community.

Events

During the summer, the amphitheater in downtown Ogden's Park (25th St and Washington Ave.) is the site of Thursday evening concerts (www.ogdentwilight.com). Although they're not free, the tickets are inexpensive ($10-15), and acts are fairly big-time (think Chvrches or Flaming Lips). On Saturday mornings during the summer, the entire downtown stretch of 25th Street is taken over by **farmers' market** and craft booths.

Recreation

HIKING

Hikers, trail runners, and winter snowshoers have easy access to trails in and around Ogden. Right in town, the 9.6-mile **Ogden River Parkway** links a number of the city's major parks and attractions along the Ogden River, including Eccles Dinosaur Park and the Utah State University Botanical Gardens. The easternmost end trail is at the mouth of Ogden Canyon, near Rainbow Gardens (1851 Valley Dr.), which is a busy gift shop, and its western terminus is at Fort Buenaventura, just west of 24th Street. Join the trail at 18th Street and Washington Boulevard, at 1700 Monroe Boulevard, or at the east end of Park Boulevard.

Several trails into the Wasatch Range start on the east side of town. Good resources for trail information include the **Forest Service Information Center** in Odgen's Union Station (801/625-5306) and **Weber Pathways** (www.weberpathways.org), a nonprofit trail advocacy group whose excellent printed trail map is widely available around town, including at the visitors center.

The **Bonneville Shoreline Trail** follows the eastern bench of ancient Lake Bonneville along the western edge of the Wasatch Range. This relatively new trail is still being developed, and it may someday run along the entire Wasatch Front. For now, the stretch near Ogden can be accessed from five trailheads (from north to south): Rainbow Gardens, where Valley Drive intersects Highway 39;

22nd Street; 29th Street; 36th Street; and 46th Street. The trail is right on the urban interface, and it is popular with mountain bikers as well as hikers and trail runners. Also right at the eastern edge of town, **Indian Trail,** which follows an old Shoshoni route 4.3 miles (6.9 km) into Ogden Canyon, can be accessed from the 22nd Street trailhead at the western edge of the canyon; follow it to its terminus at the Cold Water Canyon trailhead in Ogden Canyon. There's also a spur trail off Indian Trail leading to a nice viewpoint; about 0.5 mile (0.8 km) up the trail, take a sharp right turn, and head 1.4 miles (2.3 km) uphill to Hidden Valley.

At the eastern edge of the canyon, just across from the Pineview Dam, the easy **Wheeler Creek Trail** is also popular with mountain bikers. Head 1.8 miles (2.9 km) up the canyon to emerge at the Art Nord trailhead; it's also possible to fashion loop hikes from this trail.

Ogden's 9,712-foot **Ben Lomond Peak** was supposedly the inspiration for the Paramount Pictures logo. The 7.6-mile **Ben Lomond Trail** starts from North Fork Park in Liberty. To get here from Ogden, head up Ogden Canyon, go left over the Pineview Reservoir Dam, and keep left. At the four-way stop in Eden, go left on Highway 162 and travel north until you must stop at the three-way stop in Liberty at Liberty Park. Go left (west) at the three-way stop for one block, then go right (north) on 3300 East and follow it 1.5 miles (2.4 km); veer left at the Y intersection and travel one mile to the park and trailhead sign. For an early start, plan to camp at the trailhead.

GOLF

The Ogden area has a number of golf courses, with some of the lowest greens fees you'll find anywhere (all prices are for 18 holes unless noted). Try any of these courses: **Ben Lomond** (1800 N. U.S. 89, 801/782-7754, $28); the municipal courses **El Monte** (1300 Valley Dr., at the mouth of Ogden Canyon, 801/629-0694, nine holes $14) and **Mount Ogden**

(1787 Constitution Way, 801/629-0699, $28); **The Barn Golf Club** (305 W. Pleasant View Dr., North Ogden, 801/782-7320, $28); and **Wolf Creek** (3900 N. Wolf Creek Dr., Eden, 801/745-3365, $39), 15 miles (24 km) east of Ogden.

SKIING

You'll find good **downhill skiing** in the Wasatch Range 15-19 miles (24-31 km) east of Ogden at Snowbasin, Powder Mountain, and Nordic Valley. **Cross-country skiers** can use the easy set tracks at Mount Ogden Golf Course (1787 Constitution Way) or head into the mountains for more challenging terrain. One place that's groomed for classic and skate skiing is the trail system at North Fork Park, at the base of Ben Lomond Peak in Liberty.

SWIMMING

Swim year-round at **Marshall White Center Pool** (222 28th St., 801/629-8346) or at the **Weber State University gym** (3848 Harrison Blvd., 801/626-6466), on the south end of campus. The outdoor **Lorin Farr Community Pool** (1691 Gramercy Ave., 801/629-8291) is open in summer.

Food

Quite a number of good restaurants line 25th Street, the somewhat gentrified Main Street of turn-of-the-20th-century Ogden. In addition to the dining options noted below, there are bakery cafés, a Greek restaurant, sushi joints, taverns with burgers, and home-style Mexican food. If you've got time, just saunter along 25th Street, and you'll be sure to find someplace to suit your fancy.

BREAKFAST AND LIGHT MEALS

If your idea of breakfast is strong coffee, fresh pastries, and the option of an omelet, plan on frequenting ★ **Grounds for Coffee** (111 25th St., 801/392-7370, www.groundsforcoffee.com, 6am-8pm

1: Ogden River Parkway; 2: Lucky Slice; 3: Pineview Reservoir; 4: Shooting Star Saloon

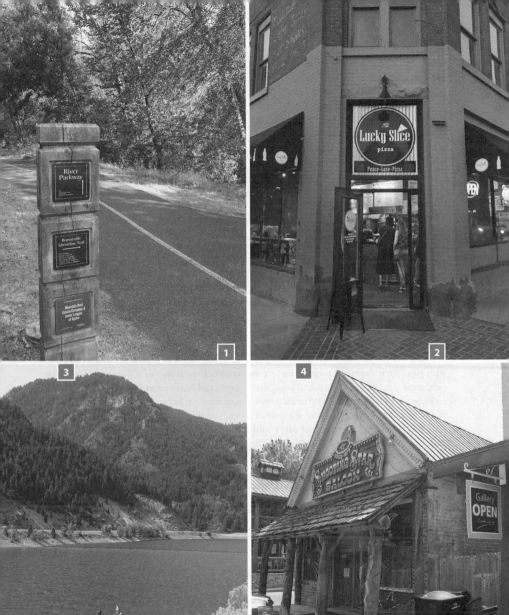

Mon.-Thurs., 6am-10pm Fri.-Sat., 7am-8pm Sun., $5), the city's best coffee shop; there's often entertainment in the evening. The coffee shop is in a beautifully preserved 19th-century storefront along historic 25th Street.

The combined **Zenger's Deli-Great Harvest Bakery** (272 25th St., 801/394-6800, www.ogdenbread.com, 7am-6pm daily, $5-9) serves up hearty baked goods and sandwiches made on tasty whole-grain breads.

An egg sandwich from **Bickering Sisters** (2487 Grant Ave., 801/317-4463, https://thebickeringsisters.com, 7:30-3:30pm daily, $6-9); at lunch stop in for a peppered eggplant and hummus sandwich or a Caesar salad. During the summer, settle in on the patio for your meal.

CASUAL DINING

One of the liveliest places along 25th Street is ★ **Roosters Brewing Company** (253 25th St., 801/627-6171, http://roostersbrewingco.com, 11am-10pm Mon.-Thurs., 11am-11pm Fri.-Sat., 10am-9pm Sun., $10-21), a brewpub with good food (burgers, pizzas, ribs, fresh fish, steaks, and sandwiches) and good microbrews. It's a popular weekend brunch spot, and in summer there's a pleasant shady deck.

If you're looking for unusual pizza and craft beers, head to **Slackwater Pizza** (1895 Washington Blvd., 801/399-0637, http://slackwaterpizzeria.com, 11am-10pm Mon.-Thurs., 11am-11pm Fri.-Sat., 10am-9pm Sun., pizzas $11-15), where you'll find traditional margherita as well as tikka masala and barbecued pork pizzas. Plus, they offer a wide selection of local beers. Slackwater can be very busy and loud; if you just want a slice and a beer, head to 25th where **Lucky Slice** (200 25th St., 801/627-2229, www.theluckyslice.com, 11am-10pm Sun.-Thurs., 11am-2am Fri.-Sat., slices $3.50), serves good slices and whole pies.

Find good upscale non-chain Mexican food, including several varieties of seviche, at **The Sonora Grill** (2310 S. Kiesel Ave., 801/393-1999, www.thesonoragrill.com, 11am-10pm Mon.-Thurs., 11am-11pm Fri.-Sat., 11am-9pm Sun., $11-19), just across from the Salomon Center.

The sushi is fresh and quite lovely at ★ **Tona Sushi Bar and Grill** (210 25th St., 801/622-8662, http://tonarestaurant.com, 11:30am-2:30pm and 5pm-9:30pm Mon.-Thurs., 11:30am-2:30pm and 5pm-10pm Fri.-Sat., rolls $5-15), with a wide range of Japanese dishes besides the sushi and sashimi; stop by for a bento box or rice bowl at lunchtime.

Satisfy a craving for ice cream at **Farr Better Ice Cream** (274 21st St., 801/393-8629, 9am-10pm Mon.-Thurs, 9am-11pm Fri.-Sat.), a long-time Ogden favorite. FYI, ice cream is a favorite Mormon indulgence, and this old-fashioned parlor across from the tabernacle can draw crowds, especially after services.

FINE DINING

Hearth on 25th (195 25th St., 801/399-0088, www.hearth25.com, noon-9pm Mon.-Thurs., noon-10pm Fri.-Sat., $15-37) is a stylish restaurant that takes the concept of "hearth" seriously. Most of the menu features live fire cooking, courtesy of a Tuscan wood-fired oven, and made-from-scratch breads, pastas, and desserts. Expect unusual, inventive dishes such as elk tenderloin or yak meatballs. The restaurant's "pantry" offers a top-notch selection of olive oils and vinegars for purchase.

Harley and Buck's (2432 Washington Blvd., 801/745-2060, http://harleyandbucks.com, 11am-9pm Mon.-Thurs., 11am-10pm Fri.-Sat., $10-29) is an attractive restaurant just around the corner from the 25th Street restaurant row, with dinners ranging from burgers to pastas to steaks and seafood—expect well-prepared upscale versions of American comfort food.

Dine in a covered wagon circled around "camp" at **Prairie Schooner** (445 Park Blvd., 801/392-2712, http://prairieschoonerrestaurant.com, 11am-9pm Mon.-Thurs., 11am-10pm Fri., 3pm-10pm Sat., $12-59). The menu includes everything from burgers to big surf-and-turf combos, with a focus on really good steaks. Kids love this place.

Accommodations

$50-100

Sleep Inn (1155 S. 1700 W., 801/731-6500, www.sleepinn.com, $95), just west of I-15 exit 344, is a good bet if you don't mind staying out by the freeway. It's pet friendly. For a few dollars more, lodging quality increases dramatically.

$100-150

The huge ★ **Bigelow Hotel** (2510 Washington Blvd., 866/627-1900, www.bigelowhotelogden.com, $139-239), a downtown landmark, was built in 1927 in Italian Renaissance Revival style. The lobby is pretty spectacular, and the rooms are all spacious suites, with sitting rooms and separate bedrooms. Pets are allowed in some guest rooms.

At I-15 exit 347, the pet-friendly **Comfort Suites of Ogden** (2250 S. 1200 W., 801/621-2545, www.comfortsuites.com, $109-184) has an indoor pool and a fitness center; all guest rooms have efficiency kitchens and coffeemakers, and rates include continental breakfast. Also at exit 347 is the **Best Western High Country Inn** (1335 W. 12th St., 801/394-9474 or 800/780-7234, www.bestwestern.com, $105-194), with a pool, a spa, and a fitness room. Pets are accommodated, and there's a good restaurant in the motel.

One of Ogden's newest hotels is the ★ **Hilton Garden Inn** (2271 S. Washington Blvd., 801/399-2000, http://hiltongardeninn3.hilton.com, $109-149), a striking-looking hotel right next to the Salomon Center with amenities such as HD TVs, a business center, an indoor pool, and a fitness room. Although breakfast is not included in the basic rates (it's available for about $10 extra per couple), there's a good restaurant in the hotel.

Near the city center and the restaurants on 25th Street is the **Ogden Courtyard by Marriott** (formerly the Summit Hotel, 247 24th St., 801/627-1190, www.marriott.com, $104-119), with an indoor pool, a hot tub, guest laundry, and a business center; there's a lounge and a good restaurant on the premises.

For a unique lodging experience in a pretty setting, consider the ★ **Alaskan Inn** (435 Ogden Canyon, 801/621-8600, www.alaskaninn.com, $130-230), 6 miles (9.7 km) east of Ogden. A 26-unit log lodge and cabin complex, the Alaskan Inn sits along the banks of a mountain stream. Lodging is either in suites in the central lodge building or in individual log cabins. The rustic decor includes hand-hewn pine furniture, brass lamps, and Western art. Breakfast is included in the rates.

$150-200

The ★ **Hampton Inn and Suites Ogden** (2401 Washington Blvd., 866/394-9400, http://hamptoninnogden.com, $154-232) is a grand art deco souvenir of the early 20th century. In addition to comfortable guest rooms and a gracious formal lobby, guests are offered exercise facilities, a business center, and a fine-dining restaurant. The Hampton Inn was completely renovated and refurbished for the Olympics, and it's a charming place to stay, with frequent rate specials on the hotel's website.

CAMPGROUNDS

Camp in town at historic **Fort Buenaventura** (office 2450 S. A Ave., 801/399-8099, www.webercountyutah.gov/parks/fortb, Apr.-Oct., $20); it's a pleasant riverside spot, with canoes available for rent.

Information and Services

The very helpful **Ogden Convention and Visitors Bureau Information Center** (2438 Washington Blvd., 801/778-6250 or 800/255-8824, www.visitogden.com, 9am-5pm Mon.-Fri.) can tell you about the sights, facilities, and goings-on for Ogden and surrounding communities, including Davis, Morgan, and Box Elder Counties.

Visit the **Ogden Ranger District Office** (507 25th St., 801/625-5112, 8am-4:30pm Mon.-Fri.) to find out about local road conditions, camping, hiking, horseback riding, ski touring, snowshoeing, and snowmobiling.

Hospital care and physician referrals are provided by **McKay-Dee Hospital Center**

(4401 Harrison Blvd., 801/387-2800) and **Ogden Regional Medical Center** (5475 S. 500 E., 801/479-2111). There is a **post office** (2641 Washington Blvd., 801/627-4184) downtown.

Getting There

Utah Transit Authority (UTA, 2393 Wall Ave., 877/621-4636, www.rideuta.com, 7am-6pm Mon.-Fri.) buses serve many areas of Ogden and head south to Salt Lake City and Provo; buses operate Monday-Saturday and offer some late-night runs. The UTA's Front Runner commuter train also travels between Salt Lake City and Ogden. **Greyhound** (801/394-5573, www.greyhound.com) provides long-distance service from the bus terminal (2393 Wall Ave.).

Most air travelers use the **Salt Lake City International Airport** (SLC, 776 N. Terminal Dr., 801/575-2400, www.slcairport. com), just 35 miles (56 km) away. Allegiant provides service from Phoenix to **Ogden-Hinckley Airport** (3909 Airport Rd., 801/629-8262, http://flyogden.com).

Yellow Cab (801/394-9411) provides 24-hour taxi service. Lyft and Uber are also available.

WEST OF OGDEN

TOP EXPERIENCE

★ Antelope Island State Park

Just a short distance offshore in the Great Salt Lake, **Antelope Island** (office 4528 W. 1700 S., Syracuse, 801/773-2941, http://stateparks. utah.gov, $10 per car, $3 bicycles and pedestrians) seems a world away, and since it's accessed from its north end, it is closer by road to Ogden than SLC. Its rocky slopes, rolling grasslands, marshes, sand dunes, and lake views instill a sense of remoteness and rugged beauty. An extension of the Oquirrh Mountains, Antelope Island is the largest of the lake's 10 islands. It measures 15 miles (24 km) long and 5 miles (8 km) wide; Frary Peak (elev. 6,596 feet) rises in the center.

The entire island is a state park, accessible via a seven-mile paved causeway. Antelope Island is a great place for mountain biking; park trails are open to hiking, bicycling, and horseback riding, allowing access to much of the island; there's also a marina for sailboats and kayaks and a historic ranch house. The visitors center offers exhibits on the island's natural and human history. Rates for **campsites** (reservations 800/322-3770, http://utahstateparks.reserveamerica.com, $15 for the first night, $12 thereafter) include the park's day-use fee. Showers and restrooms are available in the swimming area in the northwest corner of the island. Take I-15 exit 332, near Layton, and then drive 9 miles (14.5 km) west to the start of the causeway and the entrance booth.

Archaeologists have found prehistoric sites showing that Native Americans came here long ago, perhaps on a land bridge during times of low water levels. In 1843, explorers John Frémont and Kit Carson rode their horses across a sandbar to the island and named it after the antelope (pronghorn) herds that the party hunted for food. The Fielding Garr Ranch, on the southeast side of the island, was established in 1848 and operated until it became part of the park in 1981.

Antelope Island is now home to more than 600 bison as well as deer, bighorn sheep, pronghorn, and other wildlife. The best place to see bison is usually along the road on the east side of the island near the ranch. The yearly bison roundup (late Oct.) is a big event for both cowboys and visitors: The bison are driven to corrals on the north end of the island and given veterinary checkups. Thanks largely to its population of brine flies and shrimp, Great Salt Lake attracts a wide variety of birds and is an important migratory stop. Antelope Island is a good place to look for eared grebes, avocets, black-necked stilts, willets, sanderlings, long-billed curlews, burrowing owls, chukars, and all sorts of raptors. The same insect life that attracts birds can attack visitors, especially during May-June; come prepared to do battle with no-see-ums.

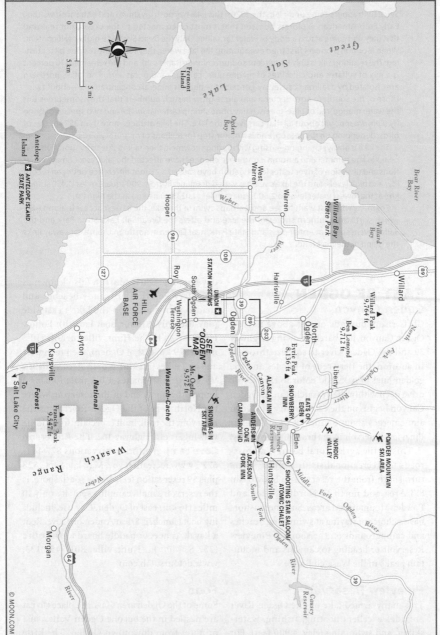

Vicinity of Ogden

Great Salt Lake

Since fur trappers came upon it in the 1820s, this lake has both mystified and entranced visitors. Early Euro-American explorers guessed that it must be connected to the ocean, not realizing that they had come across a body of water far saltier. Only the Dead Sea has a higher salt content. When Mormon pioneers first tried evaporating the lake water, they found the residue bitter tasting: The resulting salt is only 84 percent sodium chloride (table salt), and the remaining 16 percent is a mix of sulfates and chlorides of magnesium, calcium, and potassium. The lake's northern arm, isolated by a railroad causeway, contains the highest mineral concentrations—about twice those of the southern arm. Bacteria and algae grow in such numbers that they sometimes tint the water orange-red or blue-green. A tiny brine shrimp (*Artemia salina*) and two species of brine fly (*Ephydra spp.*) are about all that can live in the lake. The lake attracts more than 257 species of birds, depending on the season, and is a major stop for millions of migratory birds.

The lake is always changing—rising with spring snowmelt, then falling due to evaporation that peaks in late summer and autumn. Long-term changes have affected the lake, too: Climate variations and diversion of river water for irrigation have caused a 21-foot difference between record low and high levels, and the lake's size has varied dramatically from 900 square miles (1,450 square km) at the lowest water level to 2,500 square miles (4,023 square km) at the highest.

For many who just want to see and perhaps swim in the lake, the easiest access is along I-80, which skirts the southern shores of the lake and offers the Great Salt Lake State Park and the Saltair event space; at Antelope Island State Park, near Ogden in northern Utah, a causeway links the island to the mainland.

EAST OF OGDEN

Ogden Canyon

Cliffs rise thousands of feet above narrow Ogden Canyon, just barely allowing Highway 39 and the Ogden River to squeeze through. In autumn, the fiery reds of maples and the golden hues of oaks add color to this scenic drive deep within the Wasatch Range. Ogden Canyon begins on the eastern edge of Ogden and emerges about 6 miles (9.7 km) later at Pineview Reservoir in the broad Ogden Valley.

This fertile agricultural basin is a crossroads for recreationalists. In winter, skiers turn south from the reservoir to Snowbasin Ski Area and north to Nordic Valley and Powder Mountain ski areas. Summer visitors have a choice of staying at swimming beaches and campgrounds on the shore of Pineview Reservoir or heading to canyons and mountain peaks in the Wasatch Range.

Pineview Reservoir

This many-armed lake on the Ogden River provides excellent boating, fishing, water-skiing, and swimming (elev. 4,900 feet). For

day-tripping, **Bluff Marina** (also known as Cemetery Point) offers sandy beaches and shaded picnic areas on the lake's east side (day-use only, $18 for boat launch). Follow Highway 39 to the Huntsville turnoff (10.5 miles/16.9 km east of Ogden), then turn west and go 2 miles (3.2 km). **North Arm Wildlife Viewing Trail** makes a 0.4-mile (0.6-km) loop at the north end of the reservoir, where the North Fork of the Ogden River joins the reservoir; the trail, built especially for wildlife viewing, is off Highway 162. The **Anderson Cove campground** (reservations 877/444-6777, www.recreation.gov, May-late Sept., $28 plus $9 reservation fee), on the south shore, is the reservoir's main camping spot; it's only 10 miles (16 km) east of Ogden. Day use, including boat launch, is $15 at Anderson Cove. Rent a kayak, canoe, or paddle board at **Detours** (237 S. 7400 E., Huntsville, 801/745-3133, www.detoursutah.com).

Food

Some of the Ogden area's favorite places to eat are nestled in the bucolic Ogden Valley, just minutes from downtown Ogden. The little town of Huntsville offers a couple of places to eat and Utah's oldest bar, the ★ **Shooting Star Saloon** (7345 E. 200 S., 801/745-2002, 11-9pm Mon.-Thurs., 11am-10pm Fri.-Sat., 11am-8pm Sun., sandwiches $5-9), which has been in business since 1879. This is a favorite place to come for burgers; the signature model combines a burger and a hot dog. There's interesting graffiti in the restrooms, and the bar boasts the stuffed head of an enormous St. Bernard dog that is rumored to be the subject of Jack London's *Call of the Wild*.

A fun place to eat near Eden is **Eats of Eden** (2529 N. Hwy. 162, 801/745-8618, www.eatsofedenutah.com, 11:30am-9pm Tues.-Sat., $8-11), which serves good sandwiches on homemade bread; the deep-dish pizza hits the spot after a day of skiing.

An old general store houses **Carlos and Harley's Fresh-Mex Cantina** (5510 E. 2200 N., Eden, 801/745-8226, http://carlosandharleys.com, 11am-9pm daily, $9-25); during the summer, you can eat your Tex-Mex food outdoors.

Accommodations

A fun place to stay is the ★ **Atomic Chalet** (5917 E. 100 S., Huntsville, 801/425-2813, www.atomicchalet.com, summer $119, winter $135), a B&B right on Pineview Reservoir 10 miles (16 km) from Snowbasin. It's a lodge-like building with a casual and relaxed vibe, and it's a favorite of skiers in winter, when a two-night minimum stay is required. All four guest rooms have a private bath, fridge, TV, and MP3 player.

At the **Valley House Inn** (7138 E. 200 S. 158, Huntsville, 801/745-8259, http://valleyhouseinn.com, $129-169), a sweet B&B in a historic house, guests can stay upscale-rustic log-walled room and have breakfast delivered to a dining nook. This is a favorite spot for romantic getaways.

On the northern arm of Pineview Reservoir is a charming log B&B, the **Snowberry Inn** (1315 N. Hwy. 158, Eden, 801/745-2634, www.snowberryinn.com, $129-159). The inn

overlooks the reservoir and provides access for water sports and swimming, while Ogden-area ski resorts are only 15 minutes away. All eight guest rooms come with private baths; guests share a hot tub, a billiard table, and a TV room.

A number of condo developments have sprung up in the Ogden Valley to serve the needs of skiers at the local ski areas. For a selection of condo options, check out the listings at http://lakesideresortproperties.com.

CAMPGROUNDS

Camp on the south shore of Pineview Reservoir (and close to the highway) at **Anderson Cove** (801/625-5306, www.recreation.gov, May-late Sept., $28 plus $9 reservation fee).

Several smaller campgrounds (Magpie, Botts, South Fork, Perception Park, Upper and Lower Meadows, and Willows, $20-23) on Highway 39 about 5 to 10 miles (8-16.9 km) east of Huntsville are on the South Fork of the Ogden River.

The **Weber County Memorial Park** (801/399-8230, first-come, first-served, $18) is one mile down the paved road from Causey Reservoir, a narrow crescent-shaped lake in the upper South Fork of the Ogden River. A paved road in the park crosses the river to individual sites; three group sites can be reserved. Water is available late May-mid October. The turnoff for Causey Reservoir is on Highway 39 one mile east of Willows Campground.

Monte Cristo Campground (Highway 39, between mileposts 48 and 49, 30 miles (48 km) east of Huntsville, 21 miles (34 km) west of Woodruff, July-Nov., $23) sits at 8,400 feet elevation in mountain forests of spruce, fir, and aspen.

Getting There

Ogden Canyon begins on the eastern edge of Ogden and extends 6 miles (9.7 km) to Pineview Reservoir in the broad Ogden Valley. Reach the canyon from Ogden by heading east on 12th Street (take I-15 exit 347).

SKI AREAS

Some of the best downhill skiing slopes in Utah are found in the vicinity of Ogden.

Snowbasin

Snowbasin (3925 E. Snowbasin Rd., Huntsville, 801/620-1000 or 888/437-5488, snow report 801/620-1100, www.snowbasin. com) was gussied up substantially for the 2002 Winter Olympics, when it hosted the men's and women's downhill, super-G, and combined competitions. Snowbasin, which is owned by Sun Valley, is now one of Utah's largest ski areas, with an excellent lift system, great panoramic views, and few crowds. Although it gets a bit less snow than the Cottonwood resorts, Snowbasin is well equipped with snow-making machines.

UTA ski buses run to the resort from Ogden and Layton.

TERRAIN AND LIFTS

With more than 3,200 acres of terrain and relatively few other skiers and snowboarders, there's almost always room to roam here. The area is well covered with speedy lifts, meaning that you can spend more time skiing and less time standing in line or sitting on pokey chairlifts. Three triple chairlifts, two high-speed quads, two gondolas, and a short 15-person tram serve 106 runs, of which 20 percent are rated beginner, 50 percent intermediate, and 30 percent expert; snowboarding is allowed. The longest run is 3 miles (4.8 km) and drops 2,400 feet in elevation.

Snowbasin is an expert skier's dream. The north side of the mountain (the John Paul area) has incredible expert terrain—long and *steep*. However, John Paul is sometimes closed for races. There are also extra-black chutes off the top of the Strawberry Express gondola. But intermediate skiers can also have a good, non-terrifying time here. The Strawberry area in particular is full of nicely groomed, long blue cruisers. Beginners will find limited territory but a couple of nice long runs.

The five terrain parks include 65 rails, a large pipe, and many other features.

Ski season at Snowbasin normally runs Thanksgiving-mid-April. Adult lift tickets are $109 full-day, $85 half-day (sold starting at 12:30pm); youth rates are $59 full-day, $45 half-day; ages 65-74 pay $85 full-day, $70 half-day, and people over age 75 pay $39 full-day, $30 half-day.

Near parking area 2, find a 26-kilometer **Nordic area** groomed for classic and skate cross-country skiing (free).

Snowbasin offers a ski school, a ski shop, rentals, and three day lodges.

SUMMER ACTIVITIES

The lifts at Snowbasin remain open in summer for hikers ($14) and bikers ($25), making it easy to reach the high country. Hikers can pull off the ski area access road to hike the **Green Pond Trail,** which heads a relatively gentle 2.5 miles (4 km) up to a picnic area and the pond. Kid-friendly summertime activities include a climbing wall and spider (bungee) jump as well as Sunday-afternoon nature adventures; these are timed to coincide with the more adult-oriented Sunday Brews, Blues and BBQ.

LODGING

Snowbasin doesn't offer slope-side accommodations; however, the ski area is affiliated with **Lakeside Resort** on Pineview Reservoir (6486 E. Hwy 39, Huntsville, 801/745-3194, $199-459 for two-bed condos), a high-end resort a ten-minute's drive away.

Nordic Valley

Nordic Valley (Eden, 801/745-3511, http://nordicvalley.com), is the closest ski area to Ogden, and currently the smallest in the state, though that may be changing with new ownership and plans for a 4.3-mile-long gondola running between North Ogden and Nordic Valley's base area. Of course, such expansion (including nine new lifts) has many hurdles to overcome, but this family-friendly resort may be heading toward the big time.

And Nordic Valley is especially popular with families. It's an unintimidating place to learn to ski. Three chairlifts and a magic carpet serve 19 runs and a terrain park. About 35 percent of the territory is beginner level, 45 percent intermediate, and 20 percent expert. Elevation drop is 1,000 feet. You can ski at night, too—all runs are under lights Monday-Saturday. The season runs daily early December-late March. Adult lift tickets cost $50 full-day, $30-35 half-day, and $35 at night; children's rates are $35 full-day, $27 half-day; night skiing (3pm-8pm) is $30 for adults and $22 for children. The resort has a ski school, a ski shop, and a day lodge.

During the summer, a lift ride is $12, and $15 with a bike. Summer activities include a very long slip 'n' slide and disc golf.

Nordic Valley is 15 miles (24 km) northeast of Ogden; go through Ogden Canyon, turn left at Pineview Dam, and follow the signs.

Powder Mountain

Powder Mountain has long been an under-the-radar sort of destination for die-hard skiers and boarders who are looking for great slopes and conditions, and who aren't bothered about the comparative lack of fancy resort facilities. But PowMow skiers can expect changes; the owners, Summit, are working to make this a socially and environmentally

progressive destination resort that creates "global change" with resort homes and amenities for the global elite. (Think Richard Branson and tech entrepreneurs.) Not surprisingly, the resort village that's being developed is beautifully designed, with some houses that aren't obscenely large and great views over the canyon, which is one of Utah's most scenic.

One triple chairlift and five quads (four fixed and the other detachable) reach two different peaks and serve more than 144 runs (25 percent beginner, 40 percent intermediate, and 35 percent expert). Three surface tows supplement the chairlifts for beginners; for expert skiers, there is a huge skiable area that's not lift-served (snowcats are often used to access more remote areas). High elevations of 6,895-8,900 feet catch plentiful powder snow. In addition, there are two terrain parks for boarders. You can ski at night from the Sundown lift until 9pm. Powder Mountain's season lasts mid-November-mid-April. Adult lift tickets cost $88 day, $30 for night skiing; ages 7-12 are $49 day, $25 night; ages 65-74 pay $66 day, $27 night; military $58; seniors 75 and older are free. Facilities include a ski school, ski shops, rentals, and three day lodges.

Powder Mountain is located above one of Utah's prettiest valleys.

Powder Mountain is 19 miles (31 km) northeast of Ogden; drive through Ogden Canyon, turn left at Pineview Dam, and follow the signs. During the winter, UTA runs a ski bus from Ogden. A shuttle also runs from Eden, and it's well worth taking to avoid the steep, narrow road to the lifts. In summer, mountain bikers are free to use the trails, but there is no lift-assisted hiking or biking.

Food and Accommodations

Powder Mountain is the only one of the Ogden-area ski resorts with slope-side lodging; the **Columbine Inn** (801/745-1414, www.columbineinnutah.com) has simple hotel-style guest rooms ($125-175) as well as condos, suites, and cabins with full kitchens and fireplaces ($350-520). Rates are much lower in summer.

Most skiers and boarders drive up from Salt Lake City or Ogden; the Ogden Valley lodgings are also quite handy, with a number of B&Bs and condos catering to skiers.

Dining options are pretty limited: You can eat at casual or fancy places at Snowbasin such as **Earl's Lodge** (801/621-1000), the mountaintop **Needles Lodge** (801/620-1021, 9am-4pm Sun.-Fri., 9am-8pm Sat. in ski season, $6-20), or at **John Paul Lodge** (801/620-1021, 9am-3pm daily in ski season). Lunch will set you back $10-15 at any of these places.

GOLDEN SPIKE NATIONAL HISTORIC SITE

At 12:47pm on May 10, 1869, rails from the East Coast and the West Coast met for the first time. People across the country closely followed telegraph reports as dignitaries and railroad officials made their speeches and drove the last spikes, then everyone broke out in wild celebration. The joining of rails at this 4,905-foot-high windswept pass in Utah's Promontory Mountains marked a new chapter in the growth of the United States. A transcontinental railroad at last linked both sides of the nation.

HISTORY

The Central Pacific and Union Pacific Railroads, eager for land grants and bonuses, had both been laying track at a furious pace and grading the lines far ahead. So great was the momentum that the grader crews didn't stop when they met but laid parallel grades for 250 miles (405 km) across Utah. Finally, Congress decided to join the rails at Promontory Summit and stop the wasteful duplication of effort. A ragged town of tents, boxcars, and hastily built wooden shacks sprang up along a single muddy street. Outlaws and crooked gambling houses earned Promontory Summit an awful reputation as a real hell-on-wheels town. The party ended six months later when the railroads moved the terminal operations to Ogden. Soon, only a depot, roundhouse, helper engines, and other rail facilities remained. The Lucin Cutoff across Great Salt Lake bypassed the long, twisting grades of Promontory Summit in 1904 and dramatically reduced traffic along the old route. The final blow came in 1942, when the rails were torn up for scrap to feed wartime industries.

★ Golden Spike Visitor Center

The Golden Spike National Historic Site, authorized by Congress in 1965, re-creates this momentous episode of railroad history. The **Golden Spike Visitor Center** (32 miles/52 km west of Brigham City, 435/471-2209, www.nps.gov/gosp, 9am-5pm daily except Thanksgiving, Christmas, and New Year's Day, motor vehicles $10, cyclists $5) offers exhibits and programs that illustrate the difficulties of building the railroad and portrays the officials and workers who made it possible. A short slide show introduces Promontory Summit's history. A 20-minute program, *The Golden Spike*, presents a more detailed account of building the transcontinental railroad. Rangers give talks several times a day in summer. An exhibit room has changing

1: rockets on display outside the Orbital ATK Flight Systems Facility; 2: Spiral Jetty

The Golden Spike Ceremony

In grade school, many of us learned that when the Union Pacific and Central Pacific Railroads met, a solid gold ceremonial stake was driven to mark the spot. One yearns to go to Promontory and pry out that golden spike. But the real story tells us the event was marked with no fewer than two golden spikes, both from California; a silver spike contributed by the state of Nevada; and an iron spike with its body plated in silver and its cap plated in gold, courtesy of the state of Arizona.

A polished myrtle-wood tie was placed at the site to receive the spikes, protecting the precious metals from the damage of driving them into the earth. At the ceremony, Central Pacific president Leland Stanford (founder of Stanford University) took the first swing at the final spike and missed it entirely—but did hit the tie. Union Pacific vice president and general manager Thomas C. Durant next tried his hand and missed not only the spike but the rail and the tie as well. A bystander was finally summoned from the crowd to tap the stake home.

Shortly after the formal ceremony concluded, the valuable spikes and tie were removed and standard fittings were substituted to link the nation by rail.

displays on railroading, and historical markers behind the visitors center indicate the spot where the last spike was driven.

The two locomotives that met here in 1869, Central Pacific's *Jupiter* and Union Pacific's *119*, succumbed to scrap yards around the turn of the 20th century. However, they have been born again in authentic replicas. Every day in summer, the trains steam along a short section of track from the engine house to the historic spot. These runs include arrivals of the *Jupiter* and *119* at 10am and 10:30am, steam demonstrations of both locomotives at 1pm, and departures of the *119* and the *Jupiter* at 4pm and 4:30pm. You can't ride on the engines; they're here mostly for photo ops. During the winter, the locomotives are stored in the engine house; tours are usually available by contacting the visitors center.

Reenactments of the Golden Spike ceremony are held at 11:00am and 1:30pm on Saturdays and holidays between May 1st and Labor Day at trackside in front of the locomotives, the same location where the original ceremony was held more than 145 years ago on May 10, 1869.

The annual **Last Spike Ceremony** (May 10) reenacts the original celebration with great fanfare. The **Railroaders Festival** on the second Saturday of August has special exhibits, a spike-driving contest, reenactments, handcar races, and entertainment. A sales counter offers a good selection of books on railroading, Utah history, and natural history as well as postcards and souvenirs.

From I-15, exit 368 for Brigham City, head west on Highway 13 and Highway 83 and follow the signs for 29 miles/47 km. If you're coming from the north, it's about 29 miles (47 km) from I-84's exit 40; follow signs to Highway 83 and the Golden Spike.

ORBITAL ATK FLIGHT SYSTEMS FACILITY

Many buildings of this giant aerospace corporation lie scattered across the countryside about 6 miles (9.7 km) northeast of the historic site; if you drive this route on the way to or from the Golden Spike site, you can't miss it. You can't tour the facility, but you can visit a display of missiles, rocket engines, and a space shuttle booster casing in front of the administrative offices. Turn north and go 2 miles (3.2 km) on Highway 83 at the junction with the Golden Spike National Historic Site road, 8 miles (12.9 km) east of the visitors center.

SPIRAL JETTY

Although you're more likely to see Spiral Jetty from the air, it is possible to visit this massive earthwork sculpture. Robert Smithson built the giant spiral from mud, salt crystals, and basalt on the northeastern shore of Great Salt

Lake in 1970. The 1,500-foot-long, 15-foot-wide jetty is in a remote area about 16 miles (26 km) southwest of the Golden Spike Visitor Center. Although the gravel roads are generally well graded, it's best to make the drive in a vehicle with decent clearance; don't attempt the trip in wet weather when things can get quite mucky. Find driving directions at www.diaart.org/visit/visit/robert-smithson-spiral-jetty or stop in at the Golden Spike visitor center for a map.

LOGAN

Without question one of the most appealing towns in Utah, Logan (pop. 51,000; surrounding area pop. just over 125,000) is surrounded by the lush dairy and farmlands of the Cache Valley and by the lofty peaks of the Bear River Range. Of all the mountain communities in the American West that advertise their Swiss or Bavarian aspirations, Logan comes closest to actually looking alpine.

The town itself is built on stairlike terraces that mark the ancient shorelines of Lake Bonneville. Logan is also one of the state's festival centers, enlivened by theater, music, and performance series in summer. As everywhere in Utah, the outdoors is never far away: The mountains provide abundant year-round recreation, including scenic drives, boating on nearby Bear Lake, camping, fishing, hiking, and skiing. Logan also makes a good base camp if you are visiting more remote destinations, such as the Golden Spike National Historic Site or Bear Lake.

Sights

Logan has a lovely little downtown, filled with handsome architecture, lined with trees, and flanked by parks. A walk along Main Street is a pleasant diversion, but it's even more fun to walk through the old neighborhoods around downtown. Head west on Center Street for some of the grander historic homes; a good brochure from the **Cache Valley Visitors Bureau** (199 N. Main St., 435/755-1890, www.explorelogan.com, 8am-5pm Mon.-Fri., 9am-1pm Sat. June-Aug., 8am-5pm Mon.-Fri.

Sept.-May) details the history of many of these houses.

MORMON TEMPLE, TABERNACLE, AND HISTORY MUSEUM

The distinctive castellated **Mormon Temple** (175 N. 300 E.) rises from a prominent hill just east of downtown. After Brigham Young chose this location in 1877, church members labored for seven years to complete the temple. Architect Truman O. Angell, designer of the Salt Lake temple, oversaw construction. Timber and blocks of limestone came from nearby Logan Canyon. Only Mormons engaged in sacred work may enter the temple, but visitors are welcome on the grounds to view the exterior.

The tabernacle is also a fine example of early Mormon architecture. Construction of the stone structure began in 1865, but other priorities—building the temple and ward meetinghouses—delayed dedication until 1891. The public may enter the tabernacle, which is downtown at Main and Center Streets.

At the **Daughters of Utah Pioneers Museum** (160 N. Main St., 435/752-5139, 11am-5pm Tues.-Fri., 10am-1pm Sat. June-Aug., 11am-5pm Wed.-Thurs. Sept.-May, free), exhibits show how Logan's early settlers lived. You'll see their tools, household furnishings, clothing, art, and photographs. It is also the chamber of commerce office.

ZOOTAH AT WILLOW PARK

The small **Zootah at Willow Park** (419 W. 700 S., 435/750-9894, http://willowparkzoo.wixsite.com/home, 10am-6pm Mon.-Sat. Memorial Day-Labor Day, 11am-5pm Fri.-Sat. May and Sept., 11am-5pm Fri.-Sat March, April, Oct., and Nov. closed Dec., Jan., Feb., $4 adults, $3 ages 3-11) displays exotic birds such as an Andean condor, a golden pheasant, a mitered conure, and more familiar golden and bald eagles, peacocks, swans, and ducks. In fact, Willow Park has one of the greatest waterfowl collections in the region, showcasing more than 100 species. You'll also see lemurs,

Logan

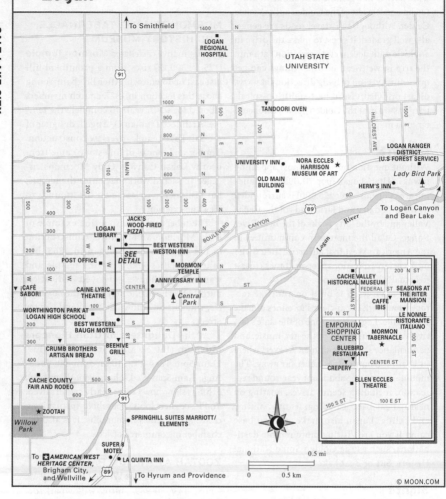

To Smithfield

1400 N

LOGAN REGIONAL HOSPITAL

UTAH STATE UNIVERSITY

91

1000 N
900 N
800 N
700 N
600 N
500 N

500 600
700
m m
100
MAIN

▼ TANDOORI OVEN

HILLCREST AVE

1500 m

UNIVERSITY INN ●

OLD MAIN BUILDING ■

NORA ECCLES HARRISON ★ MUSEUM OF ART

LOGAN RANGER DISTRICT (U.S FOREST SERVICE) ■

Lady Bird Park

HERM'S INN ●

400 300 200
500 400 300
100 200 300 400
N

JACK'S WOOD-FIRED PIZZA ▼

89

RD

CANYON

River

To Logan Canyon and Bear Lake

LOGAN LIBRARY ■

300

200

100

POST OFFICE ■

W
W
W
W

BOULEVARD

BEST WESTERN WESTON INN ■

SEE DETAIL

MORMON TEMPLE ■

ANNIVERSARY INN ●

CENTER

▼ ¡CAFÉ SABOR!

CAINE LYRIC THEATRE ■

WORTHINGTON PARK AT LOGAN HIGH SCHOOL

200

▲ Central Park

ST
S

BEST WESTERN BAUGH MOTEL ●

300

400

CRUMB BROTHERS ARTISAN BREAD ▼

BEEHIVE GRILL ▼

ST
S
m m m m
S
S

CACHE COUNTY FAIR AND RODEO ■

500 S

600

91

★ ZOOTAH

Willow Park

SPRINGHILL SUITES MARRIOTT/ ELEMENTS ●

SUPER 8 MOTEL ●

To ✚ AMERICAN WEST HERITAGE CENTER, Brigham City, and Wellville

89

● LA QUINTA INN

To Hyrum and Providence

Logan

CACHE VALLEY HISTORICAL MUSEUM ■

200 N ST

MAIN ST
FEDERAL ST

SEASONS AT THE RITER MANSION ●

CAFFE IBIS ▼

100 N ST

EMPORIUM SHOPPING CENTER ■

MORMON TABERNACLE ★

LE NONNE RISTORANTE ITALIANO ▼

100 E ST

BLUEBIRD RESTAURANT ▼

CENTER ST

CREPERY ▼

ELLEN ECCLES THEATRE ■

100 S ST

100 E ST

0   0.5 mi

0   0.5 km

© MOON.COM

red foxes, coyotes, elk, a blind yak, a pair of friendly reindeer, and more. The setting offers walkways beside shady willow trees, and children can feed the ducks, geese, and trout. Additionally, Willow Park offers picnic areas and a playground among its large, shady trees.

★ **AMERICAN WEST HERITAGE CENTER**

The **American West Heritage Center** (4025 S. U.S. 89/91, Wellsville, 435/245-6050, www.

awhc.org, 11am-5pm Tues.-Sat. June-Aug., check website for complex fall and winter season openings, $7 adults, $6 ages 3-11, higher prices for some seasonal events), 6 miles (9.7 km) southwest of Logan, is an institution that celebrates the history and culture of the Old West. The center is quite ambitious, and it includes a permanent living-history installation

1: Mormon Temple; 2: the American West Heritage Center

1

2

that highlights the lives and lifestyles of the Native Americans of the Cache Valley, the fur-trapping mountain men who arrived in the 1820s, and the pioneer Mormon farmers who settled here starting in the 1860s. Check the calendar for events such as baby animal days, mountain man camps, Native American encampments, woodworking workshops, art shows, harvest fairs, pioneer cooking contests, and so on.

Adjacent to the center and incorporated into it is the **Ronald V. Jensen Living Historical Farm,** an outdoor museum that re-creates life on a Cache Valley family farm in 1917. Workers dress in period clothing to plow soil, thresh grain, milk cows, shear sheep, and butcher hogs. Buildings here include an 1875 farmhouse, a summer kitchen, a root cellar, a smokehouse, a blacksmith shop, a horse barn, a sheep shed, and a privy or two. Special demonstrations take place all through the year, usually on Saturday. In fall, the cornfield is converted into a maze.

UTAH STATE UNIVERSITY

In 1888, a federal land-grant program opened the way for the territorial legislature to establish the Agricultural College of Utah. The school grew to become Utah State University (USU, www.usu.edu) in 1957 and now has eight colleges, 45 departments, and a graduate school. USU's Aggies number more than 25,000, led by 2,500 faculty and staff. The university has continued its original purpose of agricultural research while diversifying into atmospheric and space sciences, ecology, creative arts, social sciences, and other fields.

Attractions on campus include the **Nora Eccles Harrison Museum of Art** (650 N. 1100 E., 435/797-0163, http://artmuseum.usu.edu, 10am-5pm Tues.-Sat., free), one of the largest permanent collections of art in Utah. In addition to the art housed in the museum, 35 sculptures dot the campus; choose from three different walking tours (1.25 to 3.33 miles/2-5.3 km), depending on how many you want to see.

Old Main Building, with its landmark bell tower, was begun one year after the college was founded and has housed nearly every office and department in the school at one time or another. The oak-shaded campus is northeast of downtown on a bench left by a northern arm of prehistoric Lake Bonneville.

The USU dairy department is justifiably proud of its milk, cheese, and ice cream. Get a double scoop at **Aggie Ice Cream** (750 N. 1200 E., 435/797-2112, https://aggieicecream.usu.edu, 9am-10pm Mon.-Fri., 10am-10pm Sat. May-Sept., 9am-9pm Mon.-Fri., 10am-9pm Sat. Oct.-Apr.).

Entertainment and Events

One of the best reasons to visit Logan is to catch the community's high-quality arts and music festivals. People from all over Utah and the intermountain West come to Logan to take in an opera, a chamber music concert, or an evening of theater in this scenic alpine valley. The **Cache Valley Visitors Bureau** (199 N. Main St., 435/755-1890, www.explorelogan.com) can fill you in on what's happening in the area.

UTAH FESTIVAL OPERA COMPANY

The professional **Utah Festival Opera and Musical Company** (59 S. 100 W., 435/750-0300 or 800/262-0074, www.ufoc.org) takes over the beautifully restored **Ellen Eccles Theatre** (43 S. Main St.) mid-July-early August. The fact that a small Utah agricultural college town has its own prominent opera company is slightly unusual. Two factors account for the opera and musical company's hearty success. Michael Ballam, a Logan-area native and professional opera singer, decided in 1993 to start an opera company in Utah; at the same time, Logan's old movie palace and vaudeville hall, the Capitol Theatre, was remodeled and transformed into a world-class performing arts center. Renamed the Ellen Eccles Theatre, the theater has excellent acoustics and an intimate yet formal atmosphere that perfectly suited Ballam's operatic vision. Utah Festival Opera currently stages five operas and musicals, plus a number of music performances during its month-long festival season.

LYRIC REPERTORY COMPANY
The **Lyric** (28 W. Center St., 435/797-8022, mid-June to mid-Aug.) provides a summer season of musicals, comedies, and dramas in the historic **Caine Lyric Theatre** in downtown Logan. Visiting equity actors lead the shows produced by Utah State University's drama department. Other Logan-area summer stock theaters also present light comedies and musicals.

Recreation
PARKS AND SWIMMING POOLS
Willow Park (450 W. 700 S.) is a good place for a picnic and has the added attractions of a small zoo, a playground, volleyball courts, and a softball field. **Bicentennial Park** (100 S. Main St.) offers picnic spots downtown. The outdoor **Logan Aquatic Center** (451 S. 500 W., 435/716-9280, June-Labor Day) has a 50-meter lap pool, a diving pool, and a kids pool with two waterslides. The **Community Recreation Center** (195 S. 100 W., 435/750-9877) features tennis and handball-racquetball courts, basketball, volleyball, a weight room, an indoor track, table tennis, a sauna, and a whirlpool.

GOLF
The cool and verdant Cache Valley is especially suited to golf, and there are some dandy courses in the Logan area. Play at the 18-hole municipal **Logan River Golf Course** (550 W. 1000 S., 435/750-0123, $30); the 18-hole **Birch Creek Golf Course** (600 E. Center St., Smithfield, 435/563-6825, $30), 7 miles (11.3 km) north; or the small but pretty nine-hole **Sherwood Hills** (Sardine Canyon, U.S. 89/91, 435/245-6055, $15 for nine holes), 13 miles (21 km) southwest of town.

WINTER SPORTS
Ice-skating is popular in winter at **Central Park** (85 S. 300 E.). The **Beaver Creek Lodge** (Hwy. 39, 435/946-4485 or 800/946-4485, http://beavercreeklodge.com), 28 miles (45 km) east of Logan on Highway 39 near the Idaho border, offers snowmobile rentals plus cross-country ski trails in winter. Just next door is the **Beaver Mountain Ski Area** (Garden City, 435/946-3610 or 435/753-0921, www.skithebeav.com, 9am-4pm daily early Dec.-late Mar., $50 adults, $40 over age 69 and under age 12), a family-owned downhill area served by four lifts.

Food
If you're looking for a really good cup of coffee, a pastry, or perhaps a salad for lunch, head to pleasantly alternative **Caffe Ibis** (52 Federal Ave., 435/753-4777, www.caffeibis.com, 6am-7pm Mon.-Sat., 8am-6pm Sun., $2-10). Another great spot for pastries and sandwiches is **Crumb Brothers Artisan Bread** (291 S. 300 W., 435/792-6063, http://crumbbrothers.com, 7am-6pm Mon.-Sat., 9am-3pm Sun., $3-9), in a pretty setting near many of Logan's historic homes. Or go *un peu* French at the **Crêpery** (25 W. Center St., 435/752-5766, www.the-crepery.com, 7am-9pm Mon.-Thurs., 7am-10pm Fri.-Sat., 9am-2pm Sun., $5-7), but be prepared to expand your crêpe horizons to include a s'more version (called Scout Camp) or the Mac Daddy, with chicken, bacon, avocado, and a cheesy sauce.

If you're headed up Logan Canyon, take a little detour onto the old highway to find hip **Herm's Inn** (1420 E. Canyon Rd., 435/792-4321, www.hermsinn.com, 7am-2pm daily, $7-10), housed in a historic brick building; it has a great full breakfast. Lunch features classic sandwiches (tuna melt, club) and salads (cobb).

It pays to venture to the university area to find **Tandoori Oven** (720 E. 1000 N., 435/750-6836, www.tandooriovenlogan.com, 11am-2:30pm and 4pm-9:00pm Mon.-Sat., $10-16), part of a minimart. The Indian food is delicious, and the restaurant gets crowded at dinnertime.

Head to the old train depot at the west end of Center Street, where **¡Cafe Sabor!** (600 W.

Center St., 435/752-8088, www.cafesabor.com, 11am-10pm Mon.-Thurs., 11am-10:30pm Fri.-Sat., $9-17) offers Mexican and Southwest-inspired fare. The tortillas and salsas are all made fresh on the premises, but the highlight may be outdoor dining on the shaded passenger platforms.

For something uniquely Loganesque, try the over-100-year-old **Bluebird Restaurant** (19 N. Main St., 435/752-3155, www.thebluebirdrestaurant.com, 11am-9:30pm Mon.-Thurs., 11am-10pm Fri.-Sat., $8-16), a beautifully maintained soda fountain, chocolatier, and restaurant that appears unchanged since the 1930s. Except for the candy, the food is secondary to the atmosphere.

Another only-in-Utah place is the **Beehive Grill** (255 S. Main St., 435/753-2600, www.thebeehivegrill.com, 11am-9pm Mon.-Thurs., 11am-10pm Fri.-Sat., $7-17), a root beer brewpub. It's owned by the same people that brew beer at Moab Brewery, and it also serves the alcoholic stuff as well as better-than-average pub food, including vegan and gluten-free options.

High-quality northern Italian cooking is served up in a charming atmosphere, with live jazz on weekend nights, at ★ **Le Nonne Ristorante Italiano** (129 N. 100 E., 435/752-9577, www.lenonne.com, 5:30pm-9:30pm Mon.-Sat., $10-23). The chef-owner hails from Tuscany, and the cuisine reflects cooking learned from his *nonne* (grandmothers).

Jack's Wood Fired Oven (256 N. Main St., 435/754-7523, www.jackswoodfiredoven.blogspot.com, 11:30am-9pm Mon.-Thurs, 11:30am-10pm Fri.-Sat., about $15) turns out tasty thin-crust pizza (including gluten-free) with some inventive topping combos (e.g., the pig and peach, which includes both of these plus huckleberries).

One of the most stylish restaurants around these parts is **Elements** (640 S. 35 E., 435/750-5171, http://theelementsrestaurant.com, 11am-9pm Mon.-Thurs., 11am-10pm Fri.-Sat., $13-30), which serves well-prepared updated American cuisine from its location next to the Marriott Springhill Suites. Even the cheapest menu item, a burger with onion marmalade, buttermilk blue cheese, and applewood bacon, is quite good. Higher up the food chain, check out the Frenched pork chop served with molasses mustard glaze with bourbon apple butter. If the weather is nice, ask to be seated outside.

Accommodations

Logan's motels are generally well-maintained and moderately priced. For a basic, inexpensive guest room at a busy road junction south of downtown, try the **Super 8 Motel** (865 S. U.S. 89/91, 435/363-0050, $56-81).

Right downtown, the ★ **Best Western Baugh Motel** (153 S. Main St., 435/752-5220, www.bestwesternbaugh.com, $112-142) offers large, recently remodeled guest rooms, an outdoor swimming pool, and an exercise room.

Head uphill from downtown for a guest room at the ★ **University Inn** (4300 Old Main Hill, 435/797-0017, http://uicc.usu.edu, $129-159), a modern, mirrored-glass building on the USU campus. Although it's a ways from downtown, it's convenient to university-area restaurants and the Aggie Ice Cream Shop—in fact, guest rooms come with vouchers for free ice cream and a chance to work off some of the butterfat at the university's rec center.

The ★ **Best Western Weston Inn** (250 N. Main St., 435/752-5700 or 800/280-0707, www.westoninn.com, $120-185) has a great location in the center of downtown as well as an indoor pool, a hot tub, and complimentary breakfast; it accepts some pets and has an electric car charging station.

The **Springhill Suites Logan** (635 S. Riverwoods Pkwy., 435/750-5180, www.marriott.com, $151-209) is the most upscale hotel in town, with modern decor, a pool and a fitness center, and complimentary breakfast. Although its address is confusing, it's basically on South Main Street, right next to the equally upscale Elements restaurant.

One of the more unusual places to stay in Logan is **Anniversary Inn** (169 E. Center St., 435/752-3443, www.anniversaryinn.

com/logan, $159-259), a complex of heritage homes with more than 30 themed guest rooms, including the "African Safari." The decor is fun, but it can be a bit over-the-top. All guest rooms have big-screen TVs and private baths with jetted tubs; breakfast is delivered to your room and each room has a bottle of non-alcoholic cider and a cheesecake. Children are not permitted, and reservations are required.

Just a block off Main Street in a pretty neighborhood, **Seasons at the Riter Mansion** (168 N. 100 E., 435/752-7727 or 800/478-7459, www.theritermansion.com, $99-169) is a B&B that's a popular spot for weddings (don't plan to stay here on a June weekend). Unlike many B&Bs, families with kids are welcome; of the six guest rooms, one is a family suite, and another is geared toward business travelers.

CAMPGROUNDS

U.S. Forest Service campgrounds, 6 miles (9.7 km) east of town on U.S. 89 in Logan Canyon, are the best bets for tent campers. At Hyrum State Park, the **Lake View Campground** (Hwy. 165, 435/245-6866, reservations 800/322-3770, http://stateparks.utah.gov, $25-30) is on a reservoir about 7 miles (11.3 km) south of town. **Traveland RV Park** (2020 S. U.S. 89/91, 435/787-2020, www.travelandrvpark.net, year-round, $35) is best for large RVs; many occupants are longer-term residents.

Information and Services

The **Cache Valley Visitors Bureau** (199 N. Main St., 435/755-1890, www.explorelogan.com, 8am-5pm Mon.-Fri.) is housed in a beautiful old courthouse downtown and has information for Cache and Rich Counties, including Logan and Bear Lake. To learn more about local history and architecture, ask for *Logan's Historic Main Street,* a brochure outlining a self-guided 45-minute walking tour. For recreation information and maps of the surrounding mountain country, visit the **Logan Ranger District Office** (1500 E. U.S.

89, 435/755-3620, 8am-4:30pm Mon.-Fri. fall-spring, 8am-5pm Mon.-Fri. summer), at the entrance to Logan Canyon.

Logan Regional Hospital (1400 N. 500 E., 435/716-1000) provides 24-hour emergency care. There is a **post office** (151 N. 100 W., 435/752-7246).

Getting There

Salt Lake Express (800/356-9796, www.saltlakeexpress.com) buses stop at several Logan hotels and make 12 trips a day to Salt Lake City and the SLC airport; the fare is $25-37. Free **city buses** (435/752-2877, www.cvtdbus.org) run throughout town. Pick up schedules and a map at the visitors bureau (199 N. Main St.).

VICINITY OF LOGAN
Crystal Hot Springs

Southwest of Logan, and just east of I-15, **Crystal Hot Springs** (8215 N. Hwy. 38, Honeyville, 435/339-0038, www.crystalhotsprings.net, 10am-10pm Mon.-Thurs., 10am-11pm Fri.-Sat., 10am-8pm Sun., Memorial Day-Labor Day, noon-10pm Mon.-Thurs., noon-11pm Fri., 10am-1:30pm Sat., 11am-7:30pm Sun. Labor Day-Memorial Day, $9 adults, $7 seniors and ages 3-12) is fed by natural hot and cold springs. The little resort has a large swimming pool, a hot soaking pool, a waterslide, and campsites (tents $30, hookups $40).

Hardware Ranch and Blacksmith Fork Canyon

The **Utah Division of Wildlife Resources** (435/753-6206, http://wildlife.utah.gov/hardwareranch) operates this ranch in the middle of the northern Wasatch Range to provide winter feed for herds of elk. In winter, concessionaires offer sleigh rides ($5 adults, $3 ages 4-8) for a closer look at the elk, and wagon rides if there's not enough snow. A **visitors center** (noon-5pm Mon. and Fri., 10am-5pm Sat.-Sun. mid-Dec.-Feb.), with displays, is also open in winter. During the spring calving season, you might see newborn

Vicinity of Logan

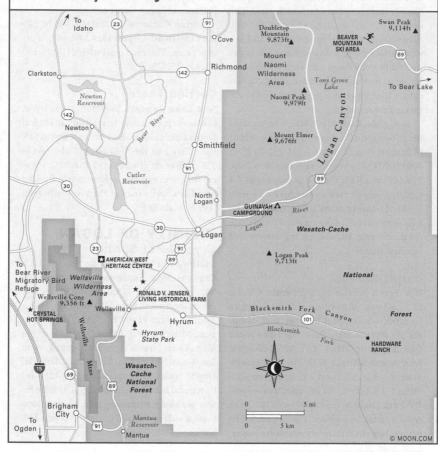

baby elk. You're not likely to see elk here in the summer months, but the drive in is still pretty. Call before heading out; the ranch has some seasonal closures.

Logan Canyon

From its mouth on the east edge of Logan, Logan Canyon, with its steep limestone cliffs, winds more than 20 miles (32 km) into the Bear River Range, a northern extension of the Wasatch Mountains. Paved U.S. 89 follows the canyon and is a designated scenic byway. If you're looking for a day trip out of Logan, just head up the canyon; you'll pass lots of picnic areas, campgrounds, fishing spots, and hiking trails, where you can easily spend a few blissful hours.

Steep slopes on the west rise to rolling plateau country across the top of the range, and moderate slopes descend to Bear Lake on the east. The route climbs to an elevation of 7,800 feet at Bear Lake Summit, which offers a good view of the lofty Uintas of northeastern Utah. In autumn, maples of the lower canyon turn a brilliant crimson while aspens in the higher country are transformed to gold. Roadside geological signs explain features in Logan Canyon. Picnicking is free at picnic areas, but you have to pay to picnic at some campgrounds.

A mile-by-mile guide to the canyon is available from the **Cache Valley Visitors Bureau** (199 N. Main St., 435/755-1890, www.explorelogan.com, 8am-5pm Mon.-Fri.) in Logan.

HIKING

A number of easy to moderate hikes make Logan Canyon a lovely and convenient destination for a little exercise and an eyeful of nature. Four miles (6.4 km) up the canyon, **Riverside Nature Trail** winds along the Logan River between Spring Hollow and Guinavah Campground, a 1.5-mile (2.4 km), one-way, stroll with good bird-watching opportunities. From Guinavah, you can loop back to Spring Hollow via the **Crimson Trail;** this more strenuous trail takes you up the limestone cliffs and down in another 2 miles (3.2 km). It takes its name from the autumn colors visible along the way. Five miles (8 km) up is the **Wind Cave trailhead.** Wind Cave, with eroded caverns and arches, is 1 mile (1.6 km) and a 1,100-foot climb from the trailhead.

Jardine Juniper Trail begins at Wood Camp Campground, 10 miles (16 km) up the canyon. The trail climbs 1,900 vertical feet in 4.4 miles (7 km) to Old Jardine, a venerable Rocky Mountain juniper tree. Still alive after 1,500 years, it measures about 27 feet in circumference and 45 feet high. A mile farther up the canyon is **Logan Cave,** a 2,000-foot-long cavern where a gate protects the endangered Townsend's big-eared bats that nest and hibernate here.

Forest Road 174 takes off to the north about 20 miles (32 km) from Logan and provides access to **Tony Grove Lake,** an exceptionally pretty, high mountain lake (elev. 8,050 feet) with a nature trail, a campground, and trails into the Mount Naomi Wilderness. The 8-mile (12.9-km) round-trip hike to Naomi Peak is known for its wildflower displays.

At **Bear Lake Summit,** 30 miles (48 km) from Logan, the **Limber Pine Nature Trail** originates at the parking area on the right and terminates at a massive limber pine 25 feet in circumference and 44 feet high. At one time this tree was thought to be the world's oldest and largest limber pine, but a forestry professor at USU discovered that it is really five trees grown together and "only" about 560 years old. The easy, self-guided walk takes about an hour; Bear Lake can be seen to the east.

SKIING

Beaver Mountain Ski Area (Garden City, 435/753-0921, www.skithebeav.com, 9am-4pm daily early Dec.-late Mar., $50 adults, $40 over age 65 and under age 11) operates four chairlifts serving 47 runs, the longest of which is 2.25 miles (3.6 km) and drops 1,600 vertical feet. A cafeteria, ski shop, rentals, and lessons are available at the day lodge. Half-day passes are available for about $10 less. Go northeast 28 miles (45 km) on U.S. 89, then north 1.5 miles (2.4 km) on Highway 243.

ACCOMMODATIONS

A handsome timber and stone lodge, **Beaver Creek Lodge** (435/753-1076 or 800/946-4485, www.beavercreeklodge.com, $149-159) not only offers guest rooms, but also has horseback trail rides, snowmobile or four-wheeling rentals, and cross-country ski trails in winter. The layout and modest size of the lodge make it a good place for group get-togethers. The lodge is about 28 miles (45 km) northeast of Logan on U.S. 89, just past the turnoff for Beaver Mountain Ski Area.

CAMPGROUNDS

There are 10 Forest Service campgrounds along U.S. 89 in Logan Canyon, so finding a place to pitch a tent is usually pretty easy. The closest ones to Logan are **Bridger** (no reservations, mid-May-early Sept., $20) and **Spring Hollow** (877/444-6777, www.recreation.gov, mid-May-mid-Oct., $22, $9 reservation fee) Campgrounds, 3 and 4 miles (4.8-6.4 km) from town, respectively. **Guinavah-Malibu Campground** ($22, reservations accepted) is just a few miles farther, and **Wood Camp**

Campground (U.S. 89, 435/755-3620, no reservations, mid-May-mid-Oct., $20) is 10 miles (16 km) up Logan Canyon. **Tony Grove Lake Campground** (877/444-6777, www.recreation.gov, mid-June-Sept., $22, $9 reservation fee) is 19 miles (31 km) east of Logan at an 8,100-foot elevation. Expect cool temps and possibly snow in summer. The 7,000-foot-high **Sunrise Campground** (877/444-6777, www.recreation.gov, late May-Sept., $20, $9 reservation fee), about 30 miles (48 km) from Logan, has good views of Bear Lake.

TOOELE AND VICINITY

To sound like a native, pronounce the town's name too-WILL-uh. The origin of the word is uncertain, but it may honor the Goshute chief Tuilla. The sprawling town (pop. 34,000) lies 34 miles (55 km) west of Salt Lake City between the western foothills of the Oquirrh Mountains and the Great Salt Lake. Mormon pioneers settled here in 1849 to farm and raise livestock, but today the major industries are the nearby Tooele Army Depot, the Dugway Proving Ground, and mining. In recent years, Tooele has become a bedroom community for Salt Lake City workers. Visitors wanting to know more about the region's history will enjoy the area's several museums.

Sights

TOOELE VALLEY RAILROAD MUSEUM

A steam locomotive and a collection of old railroad cars surround Tooele's original train station (1909), now the **Tooele Valley Railroad Museum** (35 N. Broadway, 435/882-2836, 1pm-4pm Wed. and Fri., 1pm-7pm Thurs., 10am-4pm Sat. Memorial Day-Sept., donation). Step inside to see the restored station office and old photos showing railroad workers, steam engines, and trestle construction. Mining photos and artifacts illustrate life and work in the early days at Ophir, Mercur, Bauer, and other once-booming communities

now faded to ghosts. Two railroad cars, once part of an air force mobile ballistic missile train, contain medical equipment and antique furniture. Outside, kids can ride the scale railway on some Saturdays, check out a caboose, or explore a replica of a mine.

TOOELE PIONEER MUSEUM

Meet Tooele's pioneers through hundreds of framed pictures and see their clothing and other possessions at the downtown **Pioneer Museum** (47 E. Vine St., 435/882-3168, www.tooelepioneermuseum.org, 10am-1pm Tues., 10am-4pm Fri.-Sat. May-Sept., free). The small stone building dates from 1867 and once served as a courthouse for Tooele County. The little log cabin next door, built in 1856, was one of the town's first residences.

★ BENSON GRIST MILL

Pioneers constructed the **Benson Grist Mill** (325 Hwy. 138, one block west of Mills Junction, 435/882-7678, http://bensonmill.org, 10am-6pm Thurs.-Sat. May-Oct., free), one of the oldest buildings in western Utah, 8 miles (12.9 km) north of Tooele in 1854. Wooden pegs and rawhide strips hold the timbers together. E. T. Benson, grandfather of past Mormon Church president Ezra Taft Benson, supervised its construction for the church. The mill produced flour until 1938, then ground only animal feed until closing in the 1940s. Local people began to restore the exterior in 1986. Much of the original machinery inside is still intact, and it offers a fascinating glimpse of 19th-century agricultural technology. Antique farm machinery, a granary, a log cabin, a blacksmith shop, and other buildings stand on the grounds to the east. Ruins of the Utah Wool Pullery, which once removed millions of tons of wool from pelts, stand to the west.

BONNEVILLE SEABASE

Scuba divers can enjoy ocean-type diving in the middle of the Bonneville mudflats. A natural 60-foot-deep pool at **Bonneville Seabase** (1600 N. Hwy. 138, 435/884-3874, www.seabase.net, 9am-3pm Thurs.-Fri.,

1: Tony Grove Lake; 2: the well-preserved Benson Grist Mill

8am-3:30pm Sat.-Sun., reservations highly recommended) was found to have salinity so close to that of the ocean that marine creatures could thrive in it. Several dozen species have been introduced, including groupers, stingrays, triggerfish, damsel fish, clown fish, and lobsters. The springs are geothermally heated, so winter cold is no problem. The original pool has been expanded, and dredging created new pools. User fees run $20 per person; you can rent full equipment for scuba diving ($22) or snorkeling ($11). Bonneville Seabase is 5 miles (8 km) northwest of Grantsville, or 15 miles (24 km) northwest of Tooele. If you are coming directly on I-80, take exit 84, turn toward Grantsville, and drive 5 miles (8 km).

Food

Tooele is not known for its food, though there are plenty of fairly nondescript chain restaurants. **Thai House** (297 N. Main St., 435/882-7579, www.thaihouseutah.com, 11am-9:30pm Mon.-Fri., 2pm-9:30pm Sat., $10-17) is a good bet for something a little different. If you're thirsty and looking for some good pub grub, head to **Bonneville Brewery** (1641 N. Main St., 435/248-0646, www.bonnevillebrewery. com, 11am-10pm Mon.-Thurs., 11am-11pm Fri., 10am-11pm Sat., 10am-10pm Sun., $8-25), a handsome brewpub with good burgers, pizzas, salads, and such specialties as pork tenderloin skewers topped with a lemon dill sauce.

Accommodations

There are a number of chain hotels at Tooele. The following are recommended hotels in all price brackets. The **Oquirrh Mountain Inn Motel & RV Resort** (8740 N. Hwy. 36, 801/250-0118, www.oquirrhinn.com, $72) is a comfortable, inexpensive motel north of town, near Great Salt Lake and I-80. If you are passing through and looking for economy lodging, it's a good place to stay (RVers can stay for $25). In town, the **Hotel American** (491 S. Main St., 435/882-6100, www.hotel-american.com, $99-129) offers full breakfasts, kitchenettes and efficiency kitchens, laundry facilities, a pool, and a spa. Since lots of people travel to Tooele on work assignments, this extended-stay hotel is popular. The reliable **Best Western Inn Tooele** (365 N. Main St., 435/882-5010, $126) has a pool and a free breakfast bar.

Information

Visit **Explore Tooele** (866/123-4567, www. exploretooele.com) for more information about the sights and services.

Getting There

Utah Transit Authority (UTA, 435/882-9031, www.rideuta.com) buses connect Tooele with Salt Lake City and other towns of the Wasatch Front Monday-Friday. The main bus stop is at Main Street and 400 South.

Great Salt Lake Desert

Lake Bonneville once covered 20,000 square miles (32,186 square km) of what is now Utah, Idaho, and Nevada; when the lake broke through the Sawtooth Mountains, its level declined precipitously, leaving the 2,500-square-mile (4,023-square-km) Great Salt Lake and huge expanses of salt flats to the south and west. These salt flat remnants of Lake Bonneville in the western exurbs of Salt Lake City are almost completely white and level, and they go on for more than 100 miles (161 km). It is commonly said that one can see the earth's curvature at the horizon, although this apparently takes a very discerning eye.

You're most likely to visit the sites in the Great Salt Lake Desert if you're traveling along I-80 between Salt Lake City and the Nevada border, but it's good to know that towns like Wendover offer lodging and dining options, and that the surrounding deserts offer such curiosities as race tracks and scuba diving.

Out in the Desert

Two military installations, the Utah Training and Test Range and the Dugway Proving Ground, along with the Tooele Army Depot, a chemical and biological weapons storage area, occupy much of the land in the Great Salt Lake Desert. They are all extremely high-security areas.

UTAH TRAINING AND TEST RANGE

The Utah Training and Test Range (UTTR) provides the huge amount of land necessary to train military air crews and test weapons. It is, put simply, a bombing range, with many mock targets erected for fighter pilots and their crews to use for practice. The UTTR was created in 1979 for cruise-missile testing. The large amount of land and airspace required for that purpose has made the UTTR a natural place to test smart munitions, long-range standoff weapons, remote-controlled or unpiloted air vehicles, boost-glide precision-guided munitions, air-to-air missiles, and autonomous loitering antiradiation missiles, as well as to dispose of unwanted explosives.

The UTTR also has the largest overland contiguous block of supersonic authorized restricted air space in the continental United States. The airspace is situated over 2,675 square miles (4,034 km) of Department of Defense land, administered by the U.S. Air Force. The UTTR works closely with the U.S. Army at Dugway Proving Ground.

Although the UTTR quite obviously does not allow visitors, the Hill Aerospace Museum, located at the Hill Air Force Base just south of Ogden in the town of Roy, is open to the public and has many displays of military aircraft.

DUGWAY PROVING GROUND

The primary mission of Dugway Proving Ground is to evaluate, test, and develop chemical defenses; biological defenses; and incendiary, smoke, and obscurant systems and to conduct environmental technology testing. Dugway sells its services to all authorized customers, including the U.S. and foreign governments as well as nongovernmental organizations. In addition, Dugway is a major range and test facility for chemical and biological defense testing.

Dugway Proving Ground encompasses about 800,000 acres. In addition to chemical and biological defensive testing and environment characterization and remediation technology testing, Dugway is the Defense Department's leader in testing battlefield smokes and obscurants. The installation consists of more than 600 buildings.

As if all this weren't enough, Dugway has developed a following among ufologists, who suspect that the base's secret status, underground facilities, and low profile make it the perfect place for the sequestering of alien artifacts and other items of extraterrestrial origin.

TOOELE ARMY DEPOT

In the summer of 1996, the army began burning part of the nation's store of chemical weapons at the Tooele Army Depot, 10 miles (16 km) south of the town of Tooele and 55 miles (89 km) from Salt Lake City. The depot held the nation's single largest cache of chemical weapons, with 44 percent of the arsenal stored in underground bunkers called igloos. Part of the reason for burning the weapons, besides the requirements of treaties with the former USSR, was that there was a far greater risk of leakage and environmental damage in leaving the chemical agents in bunkers than there was in incinerating them. The chemicals destroyed include sarin, mustard gas, nerve gas, and lewisite, a skin-blistering agent. The last of Tooele Army Depot's chemical weapons were destroyed in 2007. The depot now tests and stores weapons for use in wars and for training.

BONNEVILLE SALT FLATS INTERNATIONAL SPEEDWAY

A brilliant white layer of salt left behind by prehistoric Lake Bonneville covers more than 44,000 acres of the Great Salt Lake Desert. For much of the year, a shallow layer of water sits atop the salt flats. The hot sun usually dries out the flats enough for speed runs in summer and autumn.

Cars began running across the salt in 1914 and continue to set faster and faster times. Rocket-powered vehicles have exceeded 600 miles (970 km) per hour. Expansive courses can be laid out; the main speedway is 10 miles (16 km) long and 80 feet wide. A small tent city goes up near the course during the annual **Speed Week** in August; vehicles of an amazing variety of styles and ages take off individually to set new records in their classes. The salt flats, just east of Wendover, are easy to access: Take I-80 exit 4 and follow the paved road 5 miles (8 km) north, then east. Signs and markers indicate if and where you can drive on the salt. Soft spots underlaid by mud can trap vehicles venturing off the safe areas. Take care not to be on the track when racing events are being held.

WENDOVER

Wendover began in 1907 as a watering station serving construction of the Western Pacific Railroad. The highway went through in 1925, marking the community's beginnings as a stop for travelers, and its population swelled during World War II, when the air base was active. Wendover now has the tacky grandiosity of a Nevada border town.

Wendover has a split personality—half of the town lies in Utah and half in Nevada. On both sides you'll find accommodations and restaurants where you can take a break from long drives on I-80. Six casinos on the Nevada side provide a chance to lose your money at the usual games. Most of the town's visitor facilities line Wendover Boulevard, also known as State Highway, which parallels the interstate. Lodgings are cheaper on the Utah side, but prices go up and availability goes down during mid-August Speed Week. The **Motel 6** (561 E. Wendover Blvd., 435/665-2267, $47) is a fine place for a night.

Park City and the Wasatch Range

Immediately east of Salt Lake City, the Wasatch Range soars to over 11,000 feet. Its steep canyons and abundant snowfall make for legendary skiing.

Salt Lake City's nearby ski areas are in three adjacent areas. Big Cottonwood Canyon, home to the Solitude and Brighton ski and snowboard areas, is just southeast of the city; the next canyon south, Little Cottonwood, has Snowbird and Alta, two world-class resorts. When the snow melts, the hiking is every bit as great as the skiing and boarding, and many of the resorts have summer operations with lift-assisted mountain biking being the most popular activity.

About 45 minutes east of Salt Lake via I-80, Park City is home to two ski areas: Deer Valley and the Park City Mountain Resort, which, with 7,300

Highlights

Look for ★ to find recommended sights, activities, dining, and lodging.

★ **Snowbird Ski and Summer Resort:** With both winter skiing and summer activities, the adrenaline never stops at Snowbird. End the day with relaxation at the swank Cliff Lodge and Spa (page 122).

★ **Alta Ski Area:** Here's where old skiers come to ski their tails off! Alta is a haven for skiers—no snowboarding allowed—with homey accommodations. Don't be surprised if a 70-year-old helps you up from a fall (page 126).

★ **Deer Valley Resort:** Show off your new ski outfit at Deer Valley, where you may ride the lift with a big-time CEO but are just as likely to cruise down a perfectly groomed run with the fun-loving members of a blue-collar ski club (page 137).

★ **Utah Olympic Park:** Bobsled, luge, and ski-jump competitions were held here during the 2002 Winter Olympics. Today, come here to watch ski jumping or take a bobsled ride, winter or summer (page 141).

★ **Ski Utah Interconnect:** Learn the local geography by skiing a challenging backcountry tour (page 141).

★ **Wasatch Mountain State Park:** Along with camping, hiking, and great scenic views, Utah's largest state park has one of the best public golf courses anywhere (page 151).

skiable acres, is the largest ski and snowboard resort in the United States. Park City is also the site of the annual Sundance Film Festival.

Although the entire northern Wasatch region is within commuting distance of Salt Lake City, skiers who can afford the somewhat pricey accommodations should try to spend at least a couple of nights at one of the many lodges, which range from Alta's friendly down-home places to Deer Valley's equally friendly but ultrachic digs.

PLANNING YOUR TIME

In the winter, if you have only a few days, it's best to pick an area—Big Cottonwood Canyon, Little Cottonwood Canyon, or Park City—and base yourself there for skiing and boarding. It's not really necessary to have a car, especially in the Cottonwood Canyon areas; if you want to explore another ski area for a day, it's generally cheaper to use a shuttle service than to rent a car. If not everybody in your group is interested in skiing all day long, Park City is the best bet—it's a real town with as much activity off the slopes as on them.

In the summer, it's nice to have a car (or a bike) and the freedom to poke around the mountains. Increasingly, the ski areas have structured summer activities, but there are also plenty of trails, and the summertime quiet of these canyons makes them good places to camp and hike.

Big Cottonwood Canyon

Cliffs tower thousands of feet from the gateway to Big Cottonwood Canyon. Skiers come in season to try the downhill slopes at Solitude and Brighton and to cross-country ski at the Solitude Nordic Center or on snow-covered campground loop roads. Enter the canyon from Wasatch Boulevard and 7000 South, about 15 miles (24 km) southeast of downtown Salt Lake City. The 14-mile road to Brighton Basin passes several summertime picnic areas and reveals splendid vistas at each turn while climbing to an elevation of 8,700 feet. The summertime-only Guardsman Pass Road turns off just before Brighton and winds up to Guardsman Pass (elev. 9,800 feet) at the crest of the Wasatches, then drops down into either Park City or Heber City on the other side; the mostly unpaved road is usually open late June-mid-October.

SOLITUDE MOUNTAIN RESORT

The best thing about **Solitude** (801/534-1400 or 800/748-4754, http://solitudemountain.

com) is reflected in its name—it's rarely crowded. The other thing that makes this ski area distinctive is the European-style village at the base area. The village square is closed to cars; day visitors park in a lot about a five-minute walk away, and underground parking lots stow condo guests' vehicles. The inn and several condos face the pedestrian area. From all the lodgings, it's only a short walk to the lifts.

Ski season at Solitude runs from about Thanksgiving until the third week in April, depending on snow.

History

This area was originally called Solitude by silver miners in the early 1900s. It became a ski area served by two chairlifts in 1957, and in 1989 the Emerald Express became Utah's first high-speed quad lift. Until the Creekside condominiums opened in 1995, Solitude was entirely a day-use area. In 2018, Alterra Mountain Company, the owners of Deer Valley Resort, purchased of Solitude;

Park City and the Wasatch Range

To Salt Lake City

"This Is the Place" State Park

★ UNIVERSITY OF UTAH

152

80

215

Lone Peak 11,253ft

Little Cottonwood Canyon

210

Twin Peaks 11,326ft

Big Cottonwood Canyon

152

Mt. Olympus 9,026 ft

Wasatch-Cache National Forest

Mill Creek Canyon

Parleys Canyon

Emigration Canyon

Gobbler's Knob 10,246 ft

LOG HAVEN RESTAURANT

Parleys Canyon

65

Maybird Lakes

TANNERS FLAT CAMPGROUND

Red Pine Lake

White Pine Lake

SNOWBIRD TRAM

ALTA SKI AREA

SKI UTAH INTERCONNECT

SPRUCES CAMPGROUND

SOLITUDE SKI RESORT

REDMAN CAMPGROUND

Wasatch Range

Lambs Canyon

Desolation Lake

80

SNOWBIRD SKI AND SUMMER RESORT

Hidden Peak 11,000ft

ALBION BASIN CAMPGROUND

Brighton Lakes Trail

BRIGHTON SKI RESORT

Guardsman Pass

SILVER FORK LODGE

Ski Interconnect

UTAH OLYMPIC PARK

CANYONS VILLAGE

224

PARK CITY MOUNTAIN RESORT

Kimball Junction

Coalville

WASATCH MOUNTAIN STATE PARK

224

CLOSED IN WINTER

224

SEE "PARK CITY" MAP

Park City

248

80

40

113

Midway

To Deer Creek State Park

40

Heber City

Hailstone

Jordanelle Reservoir

Jordanelle State Park

Rockport Reservoir

DEER VALLEY RESORT

248

0   2 km

0   2 mi

22

recent infrastructure improvements include installation of a new detachable high-speed quad lift and a new ski run from the top of the existing Apex Express chairlift to the bottom terminal of the realigned Summit Express chairlift.

Terrain and Lifts

Skiers can choose from a wide variety of runs—there are plenty of wide blue cruisers and when conditions are favorable, gates open to expert terrain, including Honeycomb Canyon, containing more than 400 acres of ungroomed powder skiing on the back side of the resort. The Honeycomb lift, a fixed quad, makes this challenging, largely natural area relatively accessible to expert skiers or boarders.

One of the nice things about Honeycomb Canyon is that along with all the 50-degree-slope double-black-diamond tree runs, there's one run that's accessible to strong intermediate skiers and snowboarders. Woodlawn, a blue-black run, starts at the top of the Summit lift and goes right down the center of the canyon. There's one short steep section and a lot of moguls before it reaches the bottom of the Honeycomb lift, but on a clear day with good snow conditions, it's a great challenge for an advancing skier. In less than perfect conditions, it's terrifying and best left to the experts. Another good challenging intermediate run is Dynamite, also starting at the top of the Summit lift.

Day skiers (as opposed to resort guests) generally head out from the Moonbeam base area, where a quad lift shuttles skiers and boarders up to a network of green and blue runs. A large day lodge at the Moonbeam base has lockers, a café and bar, and a comfortable area where you can sit and wait for your die-hard companions to come off the mountain.

In all, there are more than 1,200 skiable acres, rated 10 percent beginner, 40 percent intermediate, and 50 percent advanced, served by eight lifts, including three high-speed quads. The green and blue runs are mostly clumped together, which makes it difficult for an expert and a novice to ski in the same area and meet up for lift rides together. Although Solitude does permit snowboarding and has a terrain park, most Big Cottonwood boarders head to Brighton.

Lift tickets for adults cost $88, half-day tickets are $71, seniors over age 69 pay $62, lift tickets for ages 7-13 are $56; those under age 7 ski free. Buy a Solbright pass ($115) if you want to ski over the summit to access Brighton's lifts.

Lifts run 9am-4pm daily. For more information, check http://skisolitude.com. Solitude has a ski school, rentals, and kids' programs.

Solitude Nordic Center

Plenty of snow and nicely groomed tracks make Solitude's **Nordic Center** (Silver Lake Day Lodge, 801/536-5774 or 800/748-4754, ext. 5774, http://solitudemountain.com, 8:30am-4:30pm daily mid-Nov.-mid-Apr., $20 ages 7-64, $18 senior) one of the best places in Utah for both traditional cross-country skiers and skate skiers. The 12.4 miles (20 km) of groomed trails are relatively easy to ski, with level loops for beginners and rolling terrain for more experienced skiers. An additional 6.2 miles (10 km) of trails are groomed for snowshoers. Don't hesitate to try the gentle, mostly downhill ski from the Nordic Center lodge to the downhill skiing base area at Solitude.

The Nordic Center is in the Silver Lake Day Lodge, about 2 miles (3.2 km) up the road from Solitude's downhill area, almost all the way to Brighton. Shuttles run at 10am, 1pm, and 3:30pm daily from Solitude Village. A shop at the Nordic Center offers rentals (touring, racing, telemark, and snowshoes), sales, instruction, day tours, and advice on backcountry touring and avalanche hazards. Tickets can be purchased here or at Solitude's downhill ski area. The ski area is 12 miles (19.3 km) up Big Cottonwood Canyon and only a 28-mile drive southeast of downtown Salt Lake City.

If you're not so fussy about skiing on groomed trails, explore the loop trails at

Getting to the Slopes

Don't assume that you'll need a rental car for your ski trip to Utah, even if you want to visit more than one resort. The cheapest way to arrange a ski trip is to stay in Salt Lake City and take the UTA bus to the mountains.

UTA buses (801/743-3882, www.rideuta.com, $4.50 one-way in winter) run between Salt Lake City and Solitude and Brighton resorts, with stops at many hotels and park-and-rides. To reach Snowbird and Alta resorts, take the TRAX light rail from downtown south to the 7200 South station. Bus 960 travels up Big Cottonwood Canyon; bus 990 goes up Little Cottonwood. The bus ride from the 7200 South TRAX station to Alta takes a little over an hour. Buses run throughout the day daily in winter.

Even easier is taking a bus—either public or private—to a ski resort, where you'll stay in resort lodgings. From the airport, **Canyon Transportation** (800/255-1841, http://canyontransport.com, $39 one-way, $76 round-trip) runs regular shuttles up Big and Little Cottonwood Canyons, with stops at Alta, Solitude, and Brighton. Runs to Park City are $45 one-way and $78 round-trip. **Alta Shuttle** (801/274-0225 or 866/274-0225, www.altashuttle.com, any trip $38 one-way) runs shuttles to and from the airport and Alta and Snowbird resorts in Little Cottonwood Canyon, and the Park City resorts.

Once you get to your destination, don't feel like you're tied to your chosen ski area. It's easy to take UTA buses between Snowbird and Alta or between Solitude and Brighton. For longer trips, private shuttle buses travel between Big and Little Cottonwood Canyons and the Park City resorts.

Spruces Campground, 9.7 miles (15.6 km) up Big Cottonwood Canyon. These trails are also popular with snowshoers.

Summer Activities

During the summer, the Sunrise lift (a single round-trip lift ride costs $12 pp) and most summer activities operate 10am-6pm, Friday-Sunday.

MOUNTAIN BIKING

Twenty miles (32 km) of single track within the resort area, plus easy access to nearby Wasatch National Forest roads and trails, make Solitude a fun place to bike. Bicycles are permitted on the Sunrise lift (Fri.-Sun. summer, single lift ticket $12, full-day lift pass $20). Full-suspension mountain bikes ($40 for 2 hours, $55 full-day) are available for rent.

DISC GOLF

The 18-hole course is free, although you may want to ride the Sunrise lift ($12 per ride) to

---

1: hiking in Big Cottonwood Canyon; **2:** Solitude Mountain Resort

get to the first hole, which is at 9,000 feet elevation, a pretty good hike up the mountain from the base area.

Food

The Inn at Solitude's restaurant, **St. Bernard's** (801/535-4120, http://solitudemountain.com, 7am-10am daily and 4:30pm-9pm Wed.-Sun. winter, $38), is the place to go for a popular and surprisingly good buffet dinner; dinner reservations are recommended.

For a quick slice of pizza, an espresso, or good ice cream, stop by the **Stone Haus Pizzeria and Creamery** (801/536-5767, 7:30am-9pm Sun.-Thurs., 7:30am-10pm Fri.-Sat. winter, 8am-8pm Mon.-Thurs. 7:30am-9pm Fri.-Sat., 7:30am-8pm Sun. summer, $9-15), right in the village square. During summer, you'll be able to spot the distinctive grass roof; in the winter it's where cross-country skiers gather for a free shuttle to the Nordic area.

Snowshoe (approximately 0.75 mile, snowshoes provided) to the trailside ★ **Yurt** (801/536-5765, 5:30pm Thurs.-Sat., 5pm Sun.

winter) for a five-course dinner ($135). Only 24 people are seated each evening; reservations are required, and it's best to make them well in advance.

Outside the main resort complex, the **Silver Fork Lodge** (11332 E. Big Cottonwood Canyon, 801/533-9977, www.silverforklodge. com, 8am-9pm daily, $12-38) has a friendly Western atmosphere. The restaurant uses a 70-year-old sourdough starter to make its pancakes. For dinner, go high-end with steak or blue-collar with meatloaf; there's also pulled pork and ribs done in the smoker.

Accommodations

Most lodgings at Solitude are in the European-style ski village at the base of the slopes and are owned and managed by Solitude Mountain Resort (801/534-1400 or 800/748-4754, http://solitudemountain.com). Rates at all of the Solitude-owned lodgings drop by at least half during the summer.

The **Inn at Solitude** ($277-462 winter, $149-179 summer) is a few steps from the base area lifts. As ski resort hotels go, it's rather intimate, with 46 guest rooms, a fancy restaurant and bar, a spa, and other amenities.

The **Village at Solitude Condominiums** offers condo units ($459-834 winter, $207-388 summer) in three different developments: Creekside is right next to the base area lifts; Powderhorn is only a few steps farther; and Eagle Springs, although a slightly longer walk to the lifts, has easy access to Club Solitude's indoor pool and exercise room. All have fireplaces, full kitchens, TVs and DVD players, and private decks, and come with 1-3 bedrooms. Just outside the main village area, find the **Crossings,** with three-bedroom town houses ($814 winter, $363 summer).

About one mile from Solitude, and not part of the resort village, is the **Silver Fork Lodge** (11332 E. Big Cottonwood Canyon, 801/649-9551, www.silverforklodge.com, 3-night minimums in winter, $185-240 per night, $110-165 in spring and fall, includes breakfast), which has eight rustic B&B rooms without TVs or telephones. The Silver Fork is largely known for its restaurant.

Getting There

From Salt Lake City, take I-80 east to I-215 south to exit 6 (6200 South); follow 6200 South, which becomes Wasatch Boulevard. Follow the signs to Big Cottonwood Canyon; Solitude is 14 miles (22.5 km) up Big Cottonwood Canyon.

UTA buses and Canyon Transportation shuttles serve all resorts in Big Cottonwood Canyon.

TOP EXPERIENCE

BRIGHTON RESORT

Brighton (801/532-4731 or 855/201-7669, www.brightonresort.com, 9am-4pm daily mid-Nov.-mid-Apr., night skiing 4pm-9pm Mon.-Sat. early Dec.-Mar.) is a longtime favorite with local families for the excellent skiing and friendly, unpretentious atmosphere. There's no Euro-village resort here; it's all about being on the mountain. It's also the least expensive and most snowboard-friendly of the Cottonwood resorts and is the only place near Salt Lake with a real night-skiing program. The resort is in the Uinta-Wasatch-Cache National Forest and does not have a commercial summer season, but there are plenty of places to hike in the area.

History

This is Utah's oldest ski resort, dating from 1936, when ski-club members built a "skier tow" from half-inch wire rope and an old elevator drum. Two years later, a T-bar tow was erected, and in 1946, the area's first actual chairlift traveled up Mount Millicent.

Terrain and Lifts

Brighton skiers and boarders are serious about their mountain time, and the resort has cooperated by making all of its terrain accessible by high-speed quad lifts, which climb as high as 10,500 feet for a 1,875-foot vertical descent to the base. In addition to the 66 runs and trails at Brighton, you can hop on the Sol-Bright run to visit Solitude ski area; a lift there will put you back on a trail to Brighton. Although a lot of the territory is suitable for beginners and intermediates, Brighton does offer some difficult powder-bowl skiing and steep runs.

Absolute beginners can step onto the Magic Carpet and be gently carried up to the Explorer area, which is also served by a slow-moving (and thus easy to mount and dismount) lift. Beginners with a few runs behind them and cautious intermediate skiers and boarders should venture onto the Majestic lift, which serves a good network of wide tree-lined green and blue runs. More advanced skiers will prefer the bowls in the Millicent and Evergreen areas. One of the things that makes Brighton so popular with snowboarders (besides the fact that they're welcome here) is its lack of long run-outs. It also has an open-backcountry policy, although it's unwise to head off into the backcountry unless you're with locals who grew up skiing and boarding here.

Brighton's terrain parks are among the best in the West. Snowboarders looking for a challenge should head up the Crest Express quad and play around the My-O-My and Candyland terrain parks. Just down the slope from these areas are two more terrain parks and a half-pipe.

Brighton has a ski and snowboard school, rentals, ski shops, a couple of cafeterias, and a sit-down restaurant in the lodge. Many Utah residents learned to ski at Brighton, and its snowboard classes are considered to be especially good.

Lift tickets for adults cost $85 for a full day, $68 half-day (morning or afternoon), and $45 at night. Seniors age 65 and up pay $57, youths 11-13 ski for $53, and children under age eight ski free with a paying adult.

Food
Slope-side restaurants include the cafeteria **Alpine Rose** (801/532-4731, ext. 252, 8am-9pm Mon.-Sat., 8am-4pm Sun. mid-Dec.-mid-Mar., 9am-4pm daily mid-Mar.-mid-Dec.,

$6-12), a good lunch spot; the **Millicent Chalet** (801/532-4731, ext. 219, 9am-9pm Mon.-Sat., 9am-4pm Sun. winter, 9am-3pm Mon.-Wed, 9am-8pm Thurs.-Sun. spring-fall, $6-12) at the base of the Millicent quad; and **Molly Green's** (801/532-4731, ext. 206, 11am-11pm Mon.-Sat., 10am-8pm Sun. mid-Dec.-mid-Mar., 11am-8pm daily mid-Mar.-mid-Dec., dinner $9-18, age 21 and over only), a bar and grill with table service.

Accommodations
Adjacent to the slopes is resort-owned **Brighton Lodge** (800/873-5512 or 855/201-7669, $129-209), which offers accommodations with a heated outdoor pool and a spa adjacent to the restaurant. It's much smaller than most ski-resort lodges and very casual. A few hostel rooms (twin beds or bunks and shared baths, $139) are available along with regular guest rooms ($155) and suites ($219). If you want a more upscale setting, stay just down the hill at Solitude.

Getting There
Brighton is at the road's end, 2 miles (3.2 km) past Solitude in Big Cottonwood Canyon. From Salt Lake City, take I-80 east to I-215 south. Take I-215 to exit 6 (6200 South) and follow 6200 South, which becomes Wasatch Boulevard. Follow the signs to Big Cottonwood Canyon; Brighton is 16 miles (26 km) up Big Cottonwood Canyon.

UTA buses and Canyon Transportation shuttles serve all resorts in Big Cottonwood Canyon.

HIKING
Hikers in Big Cottonwood Canyon should leave their dogs at home; because of water purity concerns, dogs are prohibited in this watershed. A good map for hikes in the area is the *Trails Illustrated Wasatch Front North*, map 709.

Mineral Fork Trail
Mineral Fork Trail (5 miles/8 km one-way) follows an old mining road past abandoned

mines, cabins, and rusting equipment to a high glacial cirque. Waterfalls, alpine meadows, wildflowers, and abundant birdlife make the steep climb worthwhile. The signed trailhead is on the south side of the road 6 miles (9.7 km) up the canyon (0.8 mile/1.3 km past Moss Ledge Picnic Area). You'll climb 2,000 vertical feet in 3 miles (4.8 km) to the Wasatch Mine, which has mineralized water that makes up much of the flow of Mineral Fork Creek. Another 2 miles (3.2 km) and 1,400 vertical feet of climbing lead to the Regulator Johnson Mine. A loop trip can be made by climbing the ridge west of Regulator Johnson (no trail) and descending Mill B South Fork Trail to Lake Blanche and the main road, coming out 1.5 miles (2.4 km) west of the Mineral Fork trailhead.

Donut Falls

The easy and popular hike to Donut Falls (0.75 mile/1.2 km one-way) starts just past the Jordan Pines campground and follows a trail that's partly through the woods and partly an old dirt road to the waterfall, which spurts from a "doughnut hole" in a rock. Rockfall and erosion have actually made the effect a bit less doughnut-like in recent years.

Brighton Lakes Trail

Brighton Lakes Trail (3 miles/4.8 km one-way) winds through some of the prettiest lake country in the range. Families enjoy outings on this easy trail, which begins in Brighton behind the Brighton Lodge. Silver Lake has a boardwalk giving full access to fishing docks. The first section follows Big Cottonwood Creek

through stands of aspen and evergreens. The trail continues south across meadows filled with wildflowers, then climbs more steeply to Brighton Overlook, one mile from the start. Dog Lake, surrounded by old mine dumps, lies 200 yards to the south. Continue on the main trail 0.5 mile to Lake Mary, a large, deep lake below Mount Millicent. Lake Martha is another 0.5 mile up the trail. Another mile of climbing takes you to Lake Catherine, bordered by a pretty alpine meadow on the north and the steep talus slopes of Sunset and Pioneer Peaks on the south. Total elevation gain for the three-mile hike to Lake Catherine is 1,200 feet. Hikers can also go another 0.5 mile to Catherine Pass and descend 1.5 miles (2.4 km) to Albion Basin in Little Cottonwood Canyon. Sunset Peak (10,648 feet) can be climbed by following a 0.5-mile trail from the pass.

CAMPGROUNDS

All Uinta-Wasatch-Cache National Forest campgrounds have water during the summer. Reserve at 877/444-6777 or www.recreation.gov ($10 reservation fee). Note that in order to protect the Salt Lake City watershed, dogs are not permitted at these campgrounds, and this is strictly enforced.

At an elevation of 7,500 feet, **Spruces Campground** (9.7 miles/15.6 km up the canyon, late May-mid-Oct., $23) is the largest campground in the area. **Redman Campground** (13 miles/21 km up the canyon, mid-June-early Oct., $23) is located between Solitude and Brighton at an elevation of 8,300 feet.

1: Lake Mary; **2:** the Albion Basin

Little Cottonwood Canyon

The road through this nearly straight glacial valley ascends 5,500 vertical feet in 11 miles (17.7 km). Splendid peaks rise to more than 11,000 feet on both sides of the canyon. In winter and spring, challenging terrain attracts skiers to the Snowbird and Alta ski areas. Enter Little Cottonwood Canyon from the junction of Highway 209 and Highway 210, 4 miles (6.4 km) south of the entrance to Big Cottonwood Canyon.

Granite for the Salt Lake Temple came from quarries one mile up the canyon on the left. Here also are the Granite Mountain Record Vaults, containing genealogical and historical records of the LDS Church stored on millions of rolls of microfilm. Neither site is open to the public.

★ SNOWBIRD SKI AND SUMMER RESORT

When you drive up Little Cottonwood Canyon, **Snowbird** (801/933-2122 or 800/232-9542, road and snow report 801/933-2100, www.snowbird.com) is the first resort you approach. It's about a 40-minute drive from the heart of downtown Salt Lake City. Aside from sheer convenience, Snowbird is known for its great snow—an average of 500 inches a year, and much of that classified as champagne powder. It's a big, fun place to ski or board, with lots of varied terrain.

History

Snowbird's cofounder and developer, Dick Bass, was well known in mountaineering circles as the author of *Seven Summits,* his account of climbing the highest peak on every continent. He reportedly had the vision for this resort, including the deluxe Cliff Lodge, while he was holed up in a tent on Mount Everest. The soaring 11-story windowed atrium at the sturdy concrete Cliff imparts a sense of openness that was so sorely lacking in

that Everest tent. Along with open space and light, Bass also had a vision of a spa.

It was important to Bass to build an environmentally friendly resort, and much effort was taken to preserve trees and improve the quality of the watershed, which had been degraded by mining. Mine tailings were removed and lodges built in their place to avoid harming existing trees and vegetation.

In 2014, Bass sold majority interest in Snowbird to Ian Cumming and his family; Cumming died in 2018 as this book was being updated.

Terrain and Lifts

Snowbird is on the west side of the Wasatch Range, with ski runs mostly on the north face of the mountains. There are three distinct areas to ski at this large and varied resort: Peruvian Gulch, Gad, and Mineral Basin on the back side. And if 2,500 skiable acres aren't enough to keep you busy, you can buy a special lift ticket that allows skiing between Snowbird and neighboring Alta.

Plenty of lifts serve Snowbird, including six high-speed quads and a tram that can ferry up to 125 skiers at a time to the top of Peruvian Gulch. The runs here are also long (Chip's Run, from the top of the tram, is 2.5 miles/4 km), meaning that you don't have to hop a lift every few minutes. Unless it's a powder day, when locals call in sick and head for the mountains, lines are rarely a problem, especially midweek. The one place that does get crowded is the tram; lines can be quite long, especially first thing in the morning and just after lunchtime. But the tram really is the way to get up the mountain quickly and has access to the best territory.

Twenty-seven percent of the runs are classed as beginner, 38 percent intermediate, and 35 percent advanced. There are also plenty of ungroomed areas in the backcountry. Snowbird's ski and snowboard schools

Multi-Resort Passes

In 2018, Utah ski resorts teamed up with other North American ski areas to offer the **IKON Pass** (www.ikonpass.com), which gives access to 23 destinations, including Deer Valley, Alta, and Snowbird. A $599 season pass has blackout dates around holidays and "limited access" to all of the Utah resorts, meaning that the pass is only good for five days at a particular resort. One caveat: Alta and Snowbird are lumped together as one resort in the IKON Pass; five days of access to AltaSnowbird are permitted (not five days at each). For $899, blackout days are eliminated, but the access limits remain. For skiers and boarders who live or travel in the West or Rocky Mountain states, this pass is a good way to explore. The participating resorts include some great places, including Big Sky, Jackson Hole, Steamboat.

Another pass is offered by the **Mountain Collective** (mountaincollective.com), which includes two days of access to each of sixteen resorts, including Alta, Snowbird, and Snowbasin in Utah. An adult pass costs $409; kids 12 and under can get a pass for $1. Other areas included in this pass are Big Sky, Jackson Hole, and Sun Valley. An additional benefit of this pass is that it may give you a discount at some Alta-area lodgings.

and separate bunny hill make it a good place to learn. The longest descent is 3.5 miles (5.6 km) and drops 3,200 feet. Guided ski tours of about two hours (free with lift-ticket purchase) leave from the Snowbird Plaza deck at 9:30am and 10:30am daily and tour mostly blue runs.

Snowboarders can find a terrain park on the Big Emma run, under the Mid-Gad lift. The terrain, with lots of natural chutes, lends itself to snowboarding.

Skiers and snowboarders alike should be sure to check out the Mineral Basin area. Reach it by taking the tram to the top of Hidden Peak (11,000 feet) and then heading over to the back side of the mountain, or by riding the Peruvian Express lift and then riding a "magic carpet" through a 600-foot-long tunnel to Mineral Basin. Two high-speed quads serve a great network of runs on this side of the mountain.

Ski instruction and programs are available for both children and adults. Snowbird also offers a number of adaptive ski programs (801/933-2188, http://wasatchadaptivesports. org). Sit-skis, mono-skis, and outriggers make skiing possible for people with mobility impairments.

Lift tickets for adults cost $119-129 (higher price is during President's Day weekend); add access to Alta's lifts and you'll pay $139. Seniors pay $99-109, youth (ages 7-12) tickets are $88; two children age six and under can ski free with each adult. Half-day and multiday passes are also available. The exceptionally long season at Snowbird runs mid-November-May, although many lifts close by May 1. Even confirmed Alta skiers head to Snowbird for their late-spring skiing.

Wasatch Powderbird Guides (801/742-2800, www.powderbird.com) offers helicopter skiing in the peaks above the regular runs. Rates start at $1,260 for six or seven runs; check the website for the rather complex rate and package information.

Summer Activities

Snowbird offers a full array of family recreation and resort facilities to summer visitors. In fact, the base area can take on an amusement park-like atmosphere with all the kids' activities. All lodging, spa, and recreational facilities remain open, as do many restaurants and retail outlets.

Get away from the hubbub at the base with a tram ride to 11,000-foot Hidden Peak (11am-8pm daily) for a fantastic panorama of the Wasatch Range, the surrounding valleys, and the distant Uinta Mountains. Round-trip one-ride tickets are $20 adults, $17 children 7-16 and seniors, and free for children under age 7. The Peruvian chairlift also runs in the

The Greatest Snow on Earth

What makes Utah's snow so great? In a word, geography. Storms come in from the Pacific, pushed by a cold jet stream across the Great Basin. When these storm clouds encounter the Wasatch peaks, the jet stream forces them upward into even colder air, where they release their moisture. The extremely cold temperatures ensure that this moisture falls as light, dry snow.

Storm fronts often become trapped in the Salt Lake Valley, laden with moisture and too heavy to rise out of the Great Basin. These heavy clouds make it partway out of the basin, dump snow on the nearby mountains, then drop back to the Great Salt Lake, where they pick up more moisture. This cycle continues until the storm weakens and the clouds release enough moisture to float over the tops of the mountains and continue eastward.

summer; jeep trails connect the two lifts, and a pass is good on either one.

Mountain bikers can ride the 7.5-mile Big Mountain Trail downhill from the top of the tram to the base; a special biking tram pass ($25 adult, $19 youths 16 and younger) is required.

The resort's summer commercial emphasis is on vaguely extreme sports, including the mountain coaster (think personal roller coaster, $25 adult, $20 child per ride), although there are also plenty of general fitness and outdoor activities. An all-day pass for activities, including the coaster, jumping alpine slide, climbing wall, and more, goes for $49 or $36 for children under 48 inches tall.

The **Activity Center** (in the Snowbird Center, 801/933-2147) is the hub for summer activities. It also rents mountain bikes and can arrange horseback rides in Mineral Basin. A hiking map available at the center shows local trails and jogging loops. Guided hikes are available, and there's a nature trail adapted for guests with disabilities. If you're looking to relax, there's also the Cliff Spa and Salon, with beauty and massage treatments. Snowbird is also the site of frequent summertime musical and arts events.

Spa

The Cliff Spa (801/933-2225) offers all sorts of massage therapies, facials, manicures, yoga and Pilates classes, a weight room, cardio equipment, and its own rooftop outdoor pool. It's much nicer and more complete than most

hotel spas. A day pass ($20 summer, $30 winter for hotel guests, $25/30 for general public) to the spa permits access to yoga classes and workout facilities; people who aren't staying at the Cliff are welcome. It's best to make an appointment for massages and other treatments at least a day or two in advance.

Food

Serious skiers will no doubt eat lunch either on the mountain at the **Mid-Gad Restaurant** or at the **Forklift,** a sandwich-and-burger joint near the base of the tram. While these places are perfectly acceptable refueling stations, be aware that there are a couple of very good restaurants at Snowbird, plus the new and eye-popping **Summit Restaurant** (801/933-2222, 9am-3pm daily, $12-17), located at the top of the Hidden Peak tram, at 11,000 feet. This soaring all-windows structure houses an upscale cafeteria-style restaurant.

The ★ **Aerie** (801/933-2160 or ext. 5500, 4pm-9pm daily, $15-32) is the Cliff's fancy 10th-floor restaurant, offering excellent steaks and pasta and fine sunset views of the mountains. If you'd like to partake of the Aerie's scenery but aren't up for the splurge, check out the sandwiches and small plates menu in the Aerie's lounge.

Another relatively elegant dinner restaurant is the **Lodge Bistro** (807/933-2145 or ext. 3042, 5:30pm-9pm Thurs.-Mon. winter only, $15-45), located in the Lodge at Snowbird. Dinners have a French influence, and it's easy to make a meal of small plates ($9-21).

The grab-and-go espresso bar in the Cliff's **Atrium** (801/933-2140, 7am-4pm daily winter, 7am-10:30am daily summer, breakfast buffet $5-6) has granola, pastries, and fruit. It's quick and has a splendid view of the mountain. For those who aren't in a hurry to hit the slopes, the Atrium also serves a breakfast buffet ($19 adults, $11 children). For a not-too-extravagant dinner, the **El Chanate** (801/933-2025 or ext. 5100, 11am-9pm daily winter only, $12-24) has reasonably priced (but not wildly exciting) Mexican food and an astounding array of tequilas. It's tucked away in the bottom of Cliff Lodge.

In the Iron Blosam Lodge, the casual **Wildflower Restaurant** (807/933-2230 or ext. 1042, 5pm-10pm daily winter, $13-20) has satisfying Italian dinners and good views.

Down at the bottom of the canyon, about 15 miles (24 km) from Snowbird, the **Market Street Grill** (2985 E. Cottonwood Pkwy., 801/942-8860, https://marketstreetgrill.com, 11:30am-2pm and 5pm-9pm Mon.-Thurs., 11:30am-3pm and 5pm- 9:30pm Fri., 4pm-9:30pm Sat., 9am-3pm and 4pm-9pm Sun., $15-50) is an excellent seafood restaurant and oyster bar with a classy, bustling atmosphere.

Accommodations

All of Snowbird's accommodations are run by the resort; the best way to find out about the many options is simply to call the central reservation line (800/232-9542) or check the website (www.snowbird.com). Rates vary wildly according to season, day of week, and view but are generally quite high during the winter, dropping to about half the winter rate during the summer.

The most upscale place to stay at Snowbird is the ski-in, ski-out ★ **Cliff Lodge,** with more than 500 guest rooms, four restaurants, conference facilities, retail shops, a year-round outdoor pool, and a top-notch spa. One very nice practical detail is the ground-floor locker (complete with boot dryer) assigned to each guest. The Cliff is swanky without being snobbish or stuffy—you don't have to look like the current season's Bogner catalog to fit in

here (though many guests do). Standard winter room rates run about $450 (even the most basic rooms can sleep four), with many package deals available, including better rates on multiday packages that include lift tickets. During the summer, it's common to find rates around $150. The west wing of the Cliff has been remodeled into condo units; studios with kitchens and hot tubs at the **Cliff**.

The **Lodge at Snowbird,** the **Inn at Snowbird,** and the **Iron Blosam Lodge,** which has timeshare units and requires a Saturday-Saturday stay, are the resort's three condominium complexes. Though they aren't quite as grand as the Cliff, they're perfectly nice and quite practical places to stay. The three are pretty similar, with guest laundries, pools, steam and sauna areas, restaurants, and many kitchen units. All of these places are a short walk from the tram loading area. Most are one-bedroom units with rates starting at $275.

More condos are available through **Canyon Services** (888/546-5707, www.canyonservices.com). These upscale accommodations are found between Snowbird and Alta, and they are available in several different complexes and in units with 2-7 bedrooms; winter rates are mostly $500-600 per night (though if you book early you might find a two-bedroom condo for under $300), with a five-night minimum.

If these prices seem prohibitive, remember that Salt Lake City is just down the hill, and city buses run up the canyon several times a day.

Getting There

The resort at Snowbird is 6 miles (9.7 km) up Little Cottonwood Canyon and 25 miles (40 km) southeast of downtown Salt Lake City. Snow tires are required November 1-May 1 with tire chains in the car. During extremely heavy snowstorms, the canyon may be temporarily restricted to vehicles with 4WD or chains.

UTA buses and Canyon Transportation shuttles serve all resorts in Little Cottonwood

Canyon. Snowbird provides free shuttle service between the different areas of the resort during skiing hours.

★ ALTA SKI AREA

Alta (801/359-1078, snow report 801/572-3939, www.alta.com) has a special mystique among skiers. A combination of deep powder, wide-open terrain, charming accommodations, and the polite but firm exclusion of snowboards make it special, as does its clientele. Many Alta skiers have been coming here for years—it's not uncommon to share a lift with a friendly 70-year-old who, upon debarking the lift, heads straight for the steepest black run.

Do not come to Alta expecting to do anything but ski. There is no shopping, no nightlife, no see-and-be-seen scene. Unlike Park City's resorts, there are no housing developments surrounding the runs at Alta or Snowbird, which gives them a feeling of remoteness. The lack of development around Alta is largely thanks to the late Bill Levitt, owner of the Alta Lodge and mayor of Alta for 34 years, who fought developers all the way to the U.S. Supreme Court.

Dogs are not permitted in the town of Alta, unless they receive a special permit. Appeal to the powers-that-be at the town offices, if necessary.

History

The little town of Alta owes its original reputation to rich silver veins and the mining camp's rip-roaring saloon life. Mining started in 1865 with the opening of the Emma Mine and peaked in 1872, when Alta had a population of 5,000 served by 26 saloons and six breweries. Crashing silver prices the following year and a succession of deadly avalanches ended the boom. Little remains from the old days except abandoned mine shafts, a few shacks, and the cemetery.

By the 1930s, only one resident was left, George Watson, who elected himself mayor. In 1938 he deeded 1,800 acres to the U.S. Forest Service. There is some present-day speculation that Watson didn't ever really own the deeded land, but he did take advantage of the tax breaks he got by handing it over to the government.

Ski enthusiasts brought Alta back to life. The Forest Service hired famous skier Alf Engen to determine Alta's potential as a site for a future ski area. In 1939 Alta's Collins

Alta Ski Area

chairlift became the second lift in the United States; detractors complained that the $1.50 per day lift tickets reserved the sport for the rich. Some of the original Collins single chairs are still around; look for them in the Wildcat Base parking lot near the Goldminer's Daughter Lodge.

Terrain and Lifts

The first thing to know about Alta is that it's for skiers; snowboards aren't allowed. And, even though it's right next door to Snowbird, it feels totally different. Whereas Snowbird feels big and brawny, Alta has an almost European quality. To keep the slopes from becoming too crowded, Alta limits the number of skiers allowed, although it's rare that anyone is turned away; this mostly happens during the holidays and on powder-filled weekends.

Alta's season usually runs mid-November-April. Average total snowfall is about 500 inches per year, and snow levels usually peak in March, with depths of about 120 inches. Lifts include three high-speed quads, a high-speed triple, four slower chairlifts, and several tow ropes. Even though Alta has the reputation of being an experts' ski area, there's a fair amount of very nice beginner territory. Of the 116 runs, 25 percent are rated beginner, 40 percent intermediate, and 35 percent advanced. The longest run is 3.5 miles (5.6 km) and drops 2,020 vertical feet. Skiers should keep their eyes open as they ride the lifts porcupines are a common sight in the treetops here.

A good strategy for skiing Alta's 2,200 acres is to begin the day skiing from the Albion Base on the east side of the resort, perhaps even warming up on the mile-long green Crooked Mile run near the Sunnyside lift before heading up the Supreme lift to the top of Albion Basin, with fairly steep blue runs and some of Alta's famously "steep and deep" black runs. Later in the day, move over to the Wildcat side, after the sun has had a chance to soften the snow there.

Holders of the Alta-Snowbird pass can cut over to Snowbird's Mineral Basin area from the top of Alta's Sugarloaf lift. The cut-across is not difficult, and Mineral Basin is a fun place to ski.

Alta's **Alf Engen Ski School** (801/359-1078) offers a wide variety of lessons; rentals and child-care services are also available. Guided snowcat skiing and snowboarding in the Grizzly Gulch backcountry is available for expert skiers and boarders with lots of off-trail experience. A two-hour beginner group class costs $70; call the ski school to reserve a spot.

Lift tickets for adults cost $104 for adults, $54 for skiers under age 12.

Cross-Country Skiing

Cross-country skiers can follow a 1.9-mile loop groomed for both classic and skate skiing (free); it's not the world's most exciting trail—it essentially parallels the tow rope that runs between the Wildcat and Albion lifts—but it's a good place to learn cross-country techniques or get your legs in shape at the beginning of the season.

More ambitious cross-country skiers can head up the unplowed summer road to Albion Basin. Snowcats often pack the snow. The road begins at the upper end of the Albion parking lot, then climbs gently to the top of the Albion lift, where skiers can continue to Albion Basin. Intermediate and advanced skiers can also ski to Catherine Pass and Twin Lakes Pass. Cross-country skiers may ski the beginner (green) Alta trails.

Food

Since virtually all of Alta's lodges include breakfast and dinner for their guests, Alta does not have a highly developed restaurant scene. All of the lodge dining rooms are open to the public; of these, the Rustler and Alta Lodge are particularly good places for dinner.

Stop for lunch on the mountain at **Watson Shelter** (801/799-2296, 10:30am-3:30pm daily, $8-13), midmountain beneath the top of the Wildcat lift. Upstairs, **Collin's Grill**

Dealing with High Altitude

Suppose some skiers leave their sea-level hometown at 5pm on Thursday, fly to Salt Lake City, and get the first tram up from the Snowbird base area at 9am on Friday. By 9:15am, they're at 11,000 feet. No wonder they feel tired before they even start skiing.

It's hard to predict who will be immobilized by the altitude. Men seem to have more problems than women, and athletes often feel worse than more sedentary people. But the altitude (and the dry air that goes along with it) can have a host of effects.

EFFECTS OF HIGH ALTITUDE

• Sleeplessness.

• Increased drug potency, especially with tranquilizers and sedatives.

• Increased UV radiation. People taking tetracycline are especially sensitive to the sun.

• Stuffy nose. The dry air can make your sinus tissues swell and feel stuffy. Antihistamines or decongestants just make the tissues swell more.

• Increased sensitivity to MSG.

• Increased flatulence.

• Slightly decreased fertility (decreased testosterone production in men; delayed ovulation in women).

• Slow-drying, thick nail polish.

TIPS

• Don't expect to go full steam all at once. Day two can be particularly rough; don't feel bad about knocking off early and taking a nap. Rest is good, even when sleep is difficult.

• Don't take it too easy; it's best to get some light exercise.

• Drink lots of water and avoid alcohol for the first two or three days.

• Decrease salt intake to prevent fluid retention.

• Breathe deeply.

• Wear sunglasses or goggles. It is easy to sunburn your eyes and damage your corneas.

• Use a vaporizer at night; most ski resorts have them in the guest rooms.

• Try not to arrive with a cold. (Ha!)

• If you're seriously prone to high altitude's ill effects, consult your doctor before your trip. Diamox, a prescription drug, stimulates the respiratory system and decreases fluid retention, easing the effects of high altitude.

(801/799-2297, 11:30am-2:30pm daily, $16-25) is a sit-down restaurant.

Alta's one real restaurant of note is the **Shallow Shaft** (801/742-2177, www.shallowshaft.com, 5:30pm-8:30pm daily, $24-65), across the road from Alta Lodge. Although the place looks a little dubious from the outside, the interior has great views of the ski mountain. Along with a fairly small menu of good steaks (including a buffalo tenderloin), fish, and pasta, the wine list is as good as you'll find in Utah.

Accommodations

Alta's accommodations are excellent, though pricey: Even bunk beds in a dorm room cost over $100. There's an additional room tax of more than 12 percent, and most lodges tack on a 15 percent service charge in lieu of tipping. Note, however, that room rates at all of the lodges listed here include breakfast and dinner. In summer, room rates drop by nearly half.

The easiest way to find a room is go to the lodging page on Alta's website; from here you can enter your dates of travel and link to local lodges and condos. The local visitor's bureau website (discoveralta.com) has a similar feature.

In Alta, one of the most charming and most central places to stay is the **Alta Lodge** (801/742-3500 or 800/707-2582, www. altalodge.com, dorm bed $141-166 pp, standard room $456-594 includes breakfast, afternoon tea, and dinner), an old-fashioned ski lodge that oozes authenticity. Alta Lodge, built in 1939, is not fancy. In fact, descending the four flights of wood-plank stairs from street level is a bit like entering a mine. Fortunately, at the bottom of this shaft, guests may be greeted by a friendly dog, engaging people, and a supersize bottle of sunscreen at the check-in window. The atmosphere is relaxed, and the Sitzmark Club, the lodge's bar, is lively. There are no TVs in the guest rooms at Alta Lodge (but there is Wi-Fi), but a game room off the lobby has a big-screen TV. The lodge also has a good ski-and-play program for kids.

The most luxurious place to stay in town is ★ **Alta's Rustler Lodge** (801/742-4200, www.rustlerlodge.com, dorm bed $192 pp, standard room $474-754 d, includes breakfast and dinner), with a heated outdoor pool, a fine-dining restaurant, and spacious guest rooms. But even here there's no pretense. Après-ski, it's common to see guests wandering around the lobby swathed in their thick hotel bathrobes. The Rustler spa offers massage, facials, full-body skin care, and altitude therapy; call the lodge to book an appointment.

Alta's oldest, and previously smallest and most rustic place, to stay is the newly luxurious **Snowpine Lodge** (801/742-2000, www. thesnowpine.com, dorm bed $175-200, standard room $604 d, includes breakfast and dinner). It was built as a Works Progress Administration (WPA) project in 1938, and its original design was a smaller version of Timberline Lodge on Oregon's Mount Hood, another WPA ski lodge. In 2018, the Snowpine reopened after closing for an extensive remodel and expansion; it no longer looks like a rustic WPA lodge!

The **Alta Peruvian Lodge** (801/742-3000 or 800/453-8488, www.altaperuvian.com, dorm bed $199, standard room $429 includes breakfast, lunch, and dinner) is another good choice, with its large heated outdoor pool and grand lobby. Like most of the other local lodgings, the Peruvian has a colorful history. In 1947 its owner acquired two hospital barracks from Brigham City, over 100 miles (161 km) to the north, hauled them to Alta, and hooked them together. Although the original structure still stands in a convenient location near the Wildcat Base, the lodge has been considerably updated and modernized.

The **Goldminer's Daughter Lodge** (801/742-2300, www.goldminers daughterlodge.com, dorm bunk usually for men $185 pp, standard room $400-667, includes breakfast and dinner) is close to the base of the Wildcat lift, near the large parking area, with easy ski-in, ski-out access. (All of Alta's lodgings have easy access from the slopes, but most are up-slope from the lifts, meaning that at the end of the day, you've got to be hauled back to your lodge on a tow rope.) While the Goldminer's Daughter doesn't have quite the history or ambience of many of Alta's lodgings, it's plenty comfortable.

In addition to the traditional ski lodges, there are condos available for rent, including a wide range of properties through **Alta**

Chalets (801/424-2426, www. altachalets. com). Be sure to pick up groceries in Salt Lake City; there are no food stores up here.

Getting There and Around

Alta is 8 miles (12.9 km) up Little Cottonwood Canyon. Snow tires are required in the canyon November 1-May 1 with tire chains in the car. During extremely heavy snowstorms, the canyon may be temporarily restricted to vehicles with 4WD or chains; occasionally it shuts down entirely.

Parking can be difficult in Alta. Pay attention to the No Parking signs, as parking regulations are enforced.

UTA buses and Canyon Transportation shuttles serve all resorts in Little Cottonwood Canyon. **Alta Shuttle** (801/274-0225 or 866/274-0225, www.altashuttle.com, $38 one-way) runs between the airport and Alta.

It's easy to get around Alta without a car, thanks to the **Alta Town Shuttle** (8:30am-5:30pm daily winter, free), which swings by most of the local condos and the Wildcat Base on its continuous loop.

HIKING

Make sure not to take a dog on a hike—or a drive—up Little Cottonwood Canyon. Because this heavily used canyon is part of the Salt Lake City watershed, environmental regulations prohibit pets, even in the car.

White Pine, Red Pine, and Maybird Gulch

These trails lead to pretty alpine lakes. Red Pine and Maybird Gulch are in the Lone Peak Wilderness (www.fs.usda.gov/uwcnf). All three trails begin from the same trailhead and then diverge into separate valleys. On any one of them, you'll enjoy wildflowers and superb high-country scenery. This whole area is heavily used by hikers.

Start from White Pine trailhead (elev. 7,700 feet), 5.3 miles (8.5 km) up the canyon and 1 mile (1.6 km) beyond Tanners Flat Campground. The trails divide after 1 mile

(1.6 km) ; turn sharply left for White Pine Lake or continue straight across the stream for Red Pine Lake and Maybird Gulch. Red Pine Trail contours around a ridge, then parallels Red Pine Fork to the lake (elev. 9,680 feet)—a beautiful deep pool ringed by conifers and alpine meadows. Maybird Gulch Trail begins 2 miles (3.2 km) up Red Pine Trail from White Pine Fork and leads to tiny Maybird Lakes. From the trailhead, White Pine Lake is 3.5 miles (5.6 km) with 2,300 feet of elevation gain, Red Pine Lake is 3.5 miles (5.6 km) with 1,920 feet of elevation gain, and Maybird Lakes are 4.5 miles (7.2 km) with 2,060 feet of elevation gain.

Peruvian Gulch-Hidden Peak Trail

These Snowbird area trails give you the advantage of hiking just one way from either the top or bottom by using the Snowbird tram ($20). From the top of Hidden Peak (elev. 11,000 feet), the trail crosses open rocky country on the upper slopes and spruce- and aspen-covered ridges lower down, then follows an old mining road down Peruvian Gulch. Elevation change along the 3.5-mile (5.6-mile) trail is 2,900 feet.

Catherine Pass

It's a lovely 1.5-mile hike to Catherine Pass (with 900 feet of elevation gain) and just under 5 miles (8 km) to Brighton. After the big parking area just past the Snowpine Lodge, the road becomes dirt; follow it another 2 miles (3.2 km) to a trailhead for Catherine Pass.

Cecret Lake Trail

At the end of the road past Snowpine Lodge is the Albion Basin Campground and Cecret Lake Trail, which climbs glacier-scarred granite slopes to a pretty alpine lake (elev. 9,880 feet) below Sugarloaf Mountain. Wildflowers put on colorful summer displays along the way. The trail is just one mile long and makes a good family hike; elevation gain is 360 feet. Continue another mile for fine views south to Mount Timpanogos from Germania Pass.

CAMPGROUNDS

Tanners Flat Campground (with water, mid-May-mid-Oct., $23) is 4.3 miles (6.9 km) up Little Cottonwood Canyon at an elevation of 7,200 feet. **Albion Basin Campground** (with water, late June-mid-Sept., $21) is 11 miles (17.7 km) up the road, near the head of the canyon, at an elevation of 9,500 feet; the last 2.5 miles (4 km) are gravel road. Both campgrounds accept reservations (877/444-6777, www.recreation.gov, $10 reservation fee).

Park City

Although Park City locals began messing around on skis and building ski jumps in the 1930s, a proper ski resort didn't open until 1963. These ski pioneers wouldn't recognize the area any more.

With multiple ski areas and the Utah Olympic Park, Park City (pop. about 8,000) is noted worldwide for its snow sports: The U.S. national ski team trains here, and many of the 2002 Winter Olympic competitions took place in the valley. In summer, guests flock to the resorts to golf and explore the scenic mountain landscapes on horseback, mountain bike, or foot.

However, there's a lot more to Park City than recreation: The well-heeled clientele that frequents the resorts has transformed this old mining town into the most sophisticated shopping, dining, and lodging center in Utah. However, such worldly comforts come at a cost. Condominium developments and trophy homes stretch for miles, encroaching on the beauty that brought people here in the first place.

Even if you're not a skier or hiker, plan to explore Park City's historic downtown. Late-19th-century buildings along Main Street and on the hillsides recall Park City's colorful and energetic past. Here you'll find a historical museum, art galleries, specialty shops, and fine restaurants. A busy year-round schedule of arts and cultural events (including the Sundance Film Festival), concerts, and sports also help keep Park City hopping.

ORIENTATION

Park City is in a mountain valley (elev. 7,000 feet) on the east side of the Wasatch Range, 31 miles (50 km) east of Salt Lake City via I-80 and Highway 224. The principal exit for Park City is called Kimball Junction, and although Park City proper is 7 miles (11.3 km) south, the condominiums and shopping centers begin immediately. Just south of Kimball Junction is the Canyons Village (part of the sprawling Park City Mountain Resort), with its mammoth lodges, and Utah Olympic Park, the ski-jump facility. In Park City proper, the Park City Mountain Resort is just west of downtown; most businesses stretch along historic Main Street. Two miles (3.2 km) southeast of Park City is Deer Valley, the state's most exclusive ski resort and an upscale real estate development.

SIGHTS

No matter what else you do in Park City, spend an hour or two wandering along historic Main Street. Even with the influx of galleries, gift shops, and trendy restaurants, there's still considerable Old West charm here.

Park City Museum

Drop in to the renovated and expanded **Park City Museum** (528 Main St., 435/649-7457, www.parkcityhistory.org, 11am-6pm Mon.-Sat., noon-6pm Sun., $12 adults, $5 ages 7-17) to see historical exhibits on Park City's colorful past. In October 1868, with winter fast approaching, three off-duty soldiers from Fort

Park City

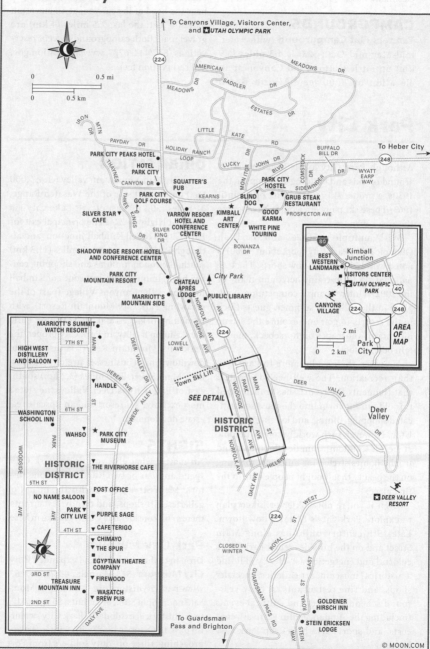

0   0.5 mi

0   0.5 km

To Canyons Village, Visitors Center,
and ✪UTAH OLYMPIC PARK

224

AMERICAN
MEADOWS DR
SADDLER DR
MEADOWS DR

ESTATES DR

IRON MTN DR
PAYDAY DR
HOLIDAY RANCH LOOP
LITTLE KATE
RD
LUCKY DR
JOHN DR
BLVD
BUFFALO BILL DR
To Heber City
248

PARK CITY PEAKS HOTEL
HOTEL PARK CITY
THAYNES
CANYON DR
SQUATTER'S PUB
KEARNS
MONITOR DR
COMSTOCK DR
WYATT EARP WAY
SIDEWINDER
DR

PARK CITY GOLF COURSE
THREE KINGS
PARK CITY HOSTEL
BLIND DOG
GRUB STEAK RESTAURANT

SILVER STAR CAFE
SILVER KINGS DR
YARROW RESORT HOTEL AND CONFERENCE CENTER
KIMBALL ART CENTER
GOOD KARMA
WHITE PINE TOURING
PROSPECTOR AVE

SHADOW RIDGE RESORT HOTEL AND CONFERENCE CENTER
BONANZA DR

PARK CITY MOUNTAIN RESORT
CHATEAU APRÈS LODGE
City Park
PUBLIC LIBRARY

MARRIOTT'S MOUNTAIN SIDE

NORFOLK AVE
EMPIRE AVE
224

LOWELL AVE

80
BEST WESTERN LANDMARK
Kimball Junction
VISITORS CENTER
✪ UTAH OLYMPIC PARK
40
CANYONS VILLAGE
224
248

0   2 mi

0   2 km

AREA OF MAP

Park City

MARRIOTT'S SUMMIT WATCH RESORT
7TH ST
MAIN ST
DEER VALLEY DR
HANDLE
HEBER AVE
SWEDE ALLEY
Town Ski Lift
SEE DETAIL

HIGH WEST DISTILLERY AND SALOON ▼

WASHINGTON SCHOOL INN
6TH ST
PARK AVE
WAHSO
★ PARK CITY MUSEUM

WOODSIDE AVE

HISTORIC DISTRICT
5TH ST

NO NAME SALOON
PARK CITY LIVE
4TH ST

▼ THE RIVERHORSE CAFE

POST OFFICE

▼ PURPLE SAGE
▼ CAFE TERIGO
▼ CHIMAYO
▼ THE SPUR
EGYPTIAN THEATRE COMPANY
▼ FIREWOOD

3RD ST
TREASURE MOUNTAIN INN
2ND ST
WASATCH BREW PUB

DALY AVE

HISTORIC DISTRICT

PARK
WOODSIDE
MAIN ST
NORFOLK AVE
DALY AVE
HILLSIDE

224

DEER VALLEY

DEER VALLEY DR

CLOSED IN WINTER

224

WEST ST

ROYAL ST

GUARDSMAN PASS RD

STEIN ST

ROYAL ST EAST

✪ DEER VALLEY RESORT

GOLDENER HIRSCH INN

STEIN ERICKSEN LODGE

To Guardsman Pass and Brighton

© MOON.COM

Douglas discovered a promising outcrop of ore on a hillside 2 miles (3.2 km) south of the present town site. Their sample assayed at 96 ounces of silver per ton, with lesser values of lead and gold. Two years later, the Flagstaff Mine began operation, and development of one of the West's richest mining districts took off. What had been a peaceful valley with grazing cattle now swarmed with hordes of fortune hunters and rang with the sound of pickaxes. In 1898, a fire raced along Main Street, reduced 200 businesses and houses to ashes, and left much of the population homeless. Determined citizens immediately set to work rebuilding, and they constructed a new downtown within three months. Many of the businesses you see along Main Street date from that time. The museum is in the old City Hall Building, built in 1885 and rebuilt after the 1898 fire. There are great photos of skiers from the 1930s, and a car from an old underground chairlift (remember, this was a mining town). Go downstairs to see the original jail, known as the dungeon.

Kimball Art Center

The large civic **Kimball Art Center** (1401 Kearns Blvd., 435/649-8882, www.kimball-art.org, 10am-5pm Mon.-Fri., noon-5pm Sat.-Sun., donation) exhibits works by noted artists and sponsors classes and workshops. Galleries display monthly changing shows of paintings, prints, sculptures, ceramics, photography, and other media. Look for other art galleries along Main Street.

PARK CITY MOUNTAIN RESORT

Park City Mountain Resort (office 435/658-9454, general inquiry 800/222-7275, www.parkcitymountain.com) is the second largest ski and snowboard resort in the United States (Powder Mountain, near Ogden, is larger). This mega-resort is the creation of Vail Resorts, a ski resort, lodging and real estate consortium with nine mountain resorts and three urban ski areas in seven U.S.

states and three countries (these include Vail, Breckenridge, and Beaver Creek in Colorado; Heavenly in California; Whistler-Blackcomb in British Columbia; and Perisher in Australia).

The Quicksilver Gondola links the Park City and Canyon ski areas (the former has a downtown base, while the Canyons base is near Kimball Junction). The gondola runs both ways, linking the two formerly separate resorts via a midstation atop Pine Cone Ridge; trails have been cut to take advantage of the territory between the two main areas. In total, the combined resort has three distinct base areas, nine hotels, more than two dozen restaurants, and 7,300 skiable acres encompassing a 22-mile network of nearly 350 trails linked by 48 lifts, seven terrain parks, 14 bowls, six natural half-pipes, one superpipe, and one minipipe. Ski season usually runs mid-November-mid-April. Lifts operate 9am-4pm daily; night skiing runs 4pm-9pm daily late December-March.

The other big change has to do with ticketing. Of course, a single ticket now gets skiers onto all the trails that used to be limited to the Park City and Canyons resorts, but ski passes to the merged resort also provide access to other Vail Resorts ski areas. Depending on which Epic Pass option you purchase, your Park City pass can get you unlimited free access to Vail, Keystone, Arapahoe Basin, and other Vail Resorts ski areas.

Park City Mountain Resort has dynamic pricing for **lift tickets,** which means prices change from day to day based on demand. It's a little cheaper to buy tickets online in advance. These are the base rates: $142 adults, $98 seniors, $91 ages 7-12.

Note that if the snow in Park City is iffy, it's often better over in the Cottonwood Canyons.

Park City Base Area

The town of Park City has two access points to the resorts' lifts. The **Park City Town Lift** loads right above Main Street, while the **Park City Base Lift** is about 0.5 mile north at the Resort Center. The main resort parking lot is

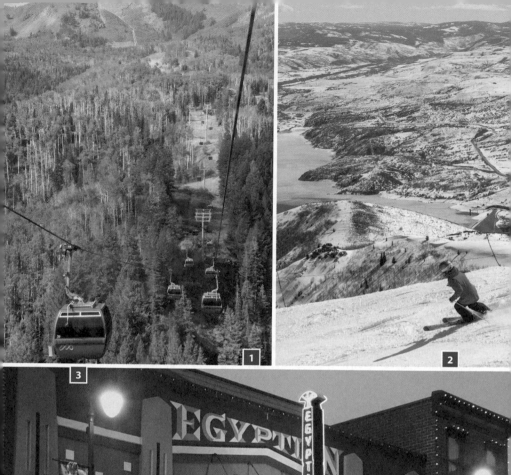

here, as well as the hub for the resort's extensive public transport buses and shuttles.

These lifts provided access to all the snowboarding events and the men's and women's giant alpine slalom in the 2002 Winter Olympics.

TERRAIN AND LIFTS

From these two base areas, four high-speed six-passenger lifts, three high-speed quads, and nine slower chairlifts carry up to 20,200 skiers per hour high onto the eastern slope of the Wasatch Range. If you choose to stay within the bounds of the previous Park City runs, you'll find more than 100 trails (17 percent easier, 52 percent more difficult, and 31 percent most difficult) and three terrain parks and a superpipe. Experienced skiers and boarders can enjoy the powder in five open bowls near the top of the mountain on a total of 650 acres. The total vertical drop is 3,100 feet from the top of Jupiter Bowl to the Resort Center.

Blue runs dominate the lower and middle part of the mountain. Intermediate skiers and boarders will appreciate the hillside full of blue cruisers off the King Con high-speed quad; even beginners can get a nice long run from midmountain (it's easy to get to by riding first the Town Lift, then Bonanza) by following the Home Run trail back to the Town Lift base. The Jupiter and McConkey's lifts ferry expert skiers and boarders to a series of steeper bowls. Actually, the lifts get you to only a couple of areas near the bowls; after getting off the lifts, many people hike along the ridges to find just the right run down.

Mountain hosts are posted around this sprawling resort, helping visitors find their way back to the Town Lift base or over to the challenging Jupiter Bowl area. The Park City base and the adjacent resort village offer a ski school, rentals, ski shops, ice-skating, and restaurants (three are on the slopes).

And of course the Quicksilver Gondola

links these Park City runs to the Canyons Village ski area. Catch this gondola from the base of the Silverlode Express.

Skiing at Park City Mountain Resort is one of several outdoor activities that people with disabilities can learn with the help of the **National Ability Center** (435/649-3991 voice or TDD, www.discovernac.org), located on the edge of town. The center provides special equipment and instruction at affordable rates, offers programs to people of all ages, and is open for summer programs as well.

SUMMER ACTIVITIES

Although the Park City base shuts down most of its lifts for the summer, the resort remains open and maintains 30 miles (48 km) of trails for mountain bikers, hikers, and horseback riders; you can ride up the Crescent or Payday Lift ($24 day pass) with your bike or picnic hamper. A free map of designated mountain biking trails is available from the resort and local bike shops.

Summer or winter, thrill seekers can ride the **Alpine Coaster** (11am-8pm Mon.-Thurs., 11am-9pm Fri.-Sat., 11am-6pm Sun. mid-June-Labor Day, shorter hours mid-May-mid-June and Labor Day-mid-Oct., noon-4pm daily winter, $26 driver, $10 youth passenger) through the aspen glades on an elevated track as it winds over a mile of curves, bends, and loops. Ride a lift to the top of the track, suck in your breath, and plummet downhill on this roller coaster-like ride.

In addition to the Alpine Coaster, which runs on tracks, the ski area has an **Alpine Slide** (11am-8pm Mon.-Thurs., 11am-9pm Fri.-Sat., 11am-6pm Sun. mid-June-Labor Day, shorter hours mid-May-mid-June and Labor Day-mid-Oct., $22 adults per ride, $9 under 48 inches tall and older than age 2), which is like a toboggan on a giant curving sliding board. A chairlift takes you to the start of a 0.5-mile track that twists and winds down the hillside. No special skills are needed to ride the little wheeled sled.

Even more frightening are two **ziplines** (11am-8pm Mon.-Thurs., 11am-9pm Fri.-Sat.,

1: Red Pine gondola at Canyons Village; **2:** Deer Valley Resort; **3:** the Egyptian Theatre

11am-6pm Sun. mid-June-Labor Day, shorter hours mid-May-mid-June and Labor Day-mid-Oct., $30-59 for a combo ticket). The longest, called the ZipRider, makes a 60-second, 500-foot plunge along 2,300 feet. At its highest point, the rider is suspended 110 feet off the ground. Riders must weigh 75-275 pounds. A second zipline, called the Flying Eagle, is a two-person ride with no weight minimum.

Other summer activities include a climbing wall, horseback rides, miniature golf, and hiking.

Canyons Village Base Area

Canyons Village, with lifts reaching nine separate peaks along the Wasatch Mountains, is the second base for the combined Park City Mountain Resort. At the base of the slopes are a number of large lodge hotels with enough restaurants and shops to make this ski base seem like its own town.

Canyons Village is the first ski resort you reach driving 27 miles (43 km) east from Salt Lake City via I-80 and Highway 224. Free shuttle buses run between the Canyons Village and Park City bases.

TERRAIN AND LIFTS

Not counting the Cabriolet gondola from the day-use parking area, another gondola from housing to the base, and a couple of surface tows, the Canyons Village base has 19 lifts, including an eight-passenger gondola, a detachable six-pack, and five high-speed quads. The 182 ski trails are rated 10 percent beginner, 44 percent intermediate, and 46 percent advanced and expert. The longest run is 2.5 miles (4 km) and drops 3,190 vertical feet. For snowboarders, there are six natural half-pipes and one terrain park.

And if you'd prefer to check out the conditions at the Park City base, just take the Quicksilver Gondola and Silverlode Express over to the Park City runs; it's all included in your ticket.

To begin a day at the Canyons, ride the Cabriolet from the parking area to the resort base. From the base, you'll have to wait in line for the Red Pine gondola, which soars over mountains, valleys, and terrain parks to the Red Pine Lodge, the midmountain base. From here, ski down to the Tombstone Express, ride that lift, and from there continue working your way south (left on the trail map) to the top of the Dreamscape lift, which lets out onto a mountainside full of nice blue runs.

Expert skiers and boarders can go from Tombstone to Ninety-Nine 90, a high-speed quad serving expert runs. The views from the top are breathtaking, and the trails there send you meandering through glade steeps, open bowls, and narrow chutes. You could spend a whole day here, especially after a big snowfall. Also, from here you can access backcountry skiing on huge bowls way above the tree line. There is a short hike, but it's well worth it.

At the end of the day, ride up on the Super Condor Express, then head home on Upper Boa to Willow Drain, a long, easy cruise marred only by an uphill walk at the end. If you can't bear to walk, just ride the gondola back down to the base.

The Canyons Village base offers day care, supervised lunches, ski lessons, and rentals for the younger set. Canyons Village includes a ski school, a rental and sales shop, half a dozen restaurants (three midslope), and free shuttles from lodges and hotels in Park City.

SUMMER ACTIVITIES

The **Red Pine gondola** (10am-6pm daily late June-Aug., 10am-6pm Fri.-Sun. Sept., $24 adults, $21 juniors under 12 or under 54 inches, free children age 4 and under) lifts you up to the Red Pine Lodge, where you can eat lunch or embark on a day hike or a mountain bike ride (bikes are permitted on the gondola, but dogs aren't). There's also a disc golf course (free) near the top of the gondola.

A mountain bike park has trails studded with features that demand good bike-handling skills. Two shorter chairlifts offer access to the bike park; a full-day lift ticket includes the gondola and goes for $30.

The resort can also arrange backcountry horseback rides and other summer activities.

Food

Midmountain, at the top of the Red Pine gondola, the **Red Pine Lodge** (435/615-2888, 8:30am-4pm daily, $7-15) is a good place to grab a breakfast burrito or some lunch without having to disrupt a day on the slopes. It serves the typical pizza, burgers, soup, and salad. Better, indeed excellent, food is served at the **Lookout Cabin** (435/615-2892, 11:30am-3pm daily, $19-25, reservations suggested), a sit-down restaurant just down from the top of the Orange Bubble lift. Warm up with a bowl of bison chili or stay light for afternoon skiing with an amazingly good salmon salad. Also on the Canyons side, a genuinely good lunch spot is ★ **Cloud Dine** (435/615-2892, 10am-3:30pm daily, $15-30), at the top of the DreamCatcher and DreamScape lifts, is a newer restaurant with sandwiches, flatbreads, pizza and fresh donuts…all quite good.

In the Grand Summit Hotel, **The Farm** (435/615-8080, 11:30am-10pm Tues.-Sun., $18-40) uses locally sourced ingredients; for dinner you could have steelhead trout with pasta, wild mushrooms, and truffled leek cream.

Accommodations

By far the easiest way to navigate the nearly endless lodging options at Canyons Village, and other Park City Mountain Resort hotels, is to contact **Park City Mountain Central Reservations** (435/602-4099, 800/331-3178, www.parkcitymountain.com) or use the website's search engine.

The Grand Summit Hotel, Sundial Lodge, and Silverado Lodge are at the base of Canyons Village ski slopes. Facilities at the **Grand Summit,** which directly fronts the gondola loading platform, include a full-service health club and a spa, with an indoor-outdoor pool, three on-site restaurants, a bar, and a brewpub. The **Sundial Lodge,** about 100 yards from the gondola, has an outdoor heated pool, a hot tub, and an on-site exercise facility. The **Silverado** is a few steps farther downhill, and it is the least expensive place at the resort.

It has the requisite outdoor heated pool, hot tub, and exercise room. The Hyatt **Escala Lodges** are near the base of the Sunrise lift.

These enormous hotels are built on a scale unlike any other lodgings in Park City and vie with Canadian national park resorts in terms of grandness and scope. All of the lodges have a mix of hotel rooms and condos; expect to pay $350-750 for the most basic (though luxurious) guest rooms during ski season. However, if you book far in advance, it's possible to find rooms in the $250-350 range. Condos can get quite elaborate and expensive, topping out at more than $1,000 per night.

Just a little way downslope, and served by the Waldorf gondola, is the **Waldorf Astoria Park City** (2100 W. Frostwood Blvd., 435/647-5500, www.parkcitywaldorfastoria.com, $900 and up during ski season, $300 and up in summer), the only lodge that's not booked through the ski resort. On top of the room rate, expect to pay an additional mandatory $35 resort fee.

Although the resort lodgings are prohibitively expensive for many travelers, two of Park City's least expensive hotels, the **Best Western Landmark** (6560 N. Landmark Dr., 435/649-7300, www.bwlandmarkinn.com, $225-329) and the **Holiday Inn Express** (1501 West Ute Blvd., 435/658-1600, www.holidayinn.com, $140-165) are near Kimball Junction, about one mile from the Canyons.

TOP EXPERIENCE

★ DEER VALLEY RESORT

Deer Valley Resort (435/649-1000 or 800/424-3337, ski report 435/649-2000, www.deervalley.com) is the crème de la crème of Utah ski areas. You'll find good, uncrowded skiing on immaculately groomed trails with all the extras of upscale accommodations, gourmet dining, attentive service, and polished brass everywhere. Lift operators steady the chairs as you plunk your bottom down, mountain guides lead free tours, and at the top of nearly every lift, a friendly green-parka-clad host points you to a run that's right for you. If you're with kids who don't ski (or can't last a full day), sign them up for childcare (if you're prepared to pay about $150!). Despite its reputation as being a cushy, glitzy area for spoiled rich folks, the skiing here can be great, and the people riding the lifts are by and large friendly and interesting.

Deer Valley is a ski-only resort; it prohibits snowboards. The ski area is 1.5 miles (2.4 km) south of downtown Park City (33 miles/53 km east of Salt Lake City), and free shuttle buses connect the resort and the town.

History

Although a small ski operation called Snow Park was in this area 1947-1965, Deer Valley did not open until 1981. The owners, Edgar and Polly Stern, wanted to provide a resort that was both easy to get to and more luxurious than other ski areas. Like Park City's other ski areas, Deer Valley was built on private land (as opposed to the Cottonwood areas, which are on U.S. Forest Service leases) and is fueled by development. It's rather like the typical golf course development, where expensive homes are built immediately adjacent to the area, meaning that you're frequently skiing past incredibly huge, expensive homes. The 2002 Olympic slalom, mogul, and aerial events were held at Deer Valley. In 2017, Deer Valley was acquired by the Alterra Mountain Company, a newly formed resort company that also picked up Steamboat, Squaw Valley, and about 10 other ski resorts.

Terrain and Lifts

Deer Valley spans six mountains: Bald Eagle Mountain, Bald Mountain, Little Baldy Peak, Empire Canyon, Lady Morgan, and Flagstaff Mountain. The main base area and parking is at Snow Park, but the midmountain Silver Lake area is much more of a hub. In fact, at the end of the day, you can't just ski straight down to the parking area; instead, you must make your way to Silver Lake, take a short ride on the Homestake lift out of the valley, then ski down Bald Eagle Mountain to the base. If you're coming in from other Park City areas, consider avoiding parking challenges by hopping the free bus; it stops at both the Snow Park and Silver Lake day lodges.

The slopes are served by 21 lifts (9am-4:15pm), including 1 high-speed four-passenger gondola and 12 high-speed quads, providing 101 runs, 6 bowls, and a vertical drop of 3,000 feet. The longest run is 2.8 miles (4.5 km). Twenty-seven percent of the skiing is rated easier, 41 percent more difficult, and 32 percent most difficult. Deer Valley has the reputation of coddling skiers (and it's true that the resort provides a green or blue way down from the top of every lift), but there's plenty of challenging territory for advanced skiers, especially in Empire Canyon, which has good access via the Lady Morgan lift.

Deer Valley is famous for its meticulously groomed trails. To find out what has been groomed, check the boards at the top of every mountain. Mountain hosts can also steer you to freshly groomed trails or onto ungroomed powder.

The majestic **Snow Park Lodge** (elev. 7,200 feet) contains the main ticket office, a ski school, rentals, a ski shop, child-care service, a gift shop, and a restaurant. You can drive 3 miles (4.8 km) and 1,000 feet higher to **Silver Lake Lodge** (parking is more limited), a major hub of activity on the mountain, with more restaurants and luxury hotels.

Bald Eagle Mountain, near the Snow Park base, contains the main beginners' area and served as a site for events in the 2002 Olympics. Aspiring slalom skiers can take a run on the Know You Don't slalom course; the Champion mogul course is also open to the public. At 9,400 feet, Bald Mountain is steeper and more exposed; its intermediate and advanced runs have spectacular views but often get skied out in the afternoon. Find steep, ungroomed trails in the Sultan and Mayflower areas.

On the right (west) side of Flagstaff Mountain (elev. 9,100 feet), the snow often holds up well, making its intermediate and beginner ski trails good bets for skiing later in the day. Blue runs off the Northside Express are good for intermediates. The Flagstaff area also has tree skiing and access to Ontario Bowl. Empire Canyon (elev. 9,570 feet) has skiing for all abilities, including a family ski area off the Little Chief lift, challenging but skiable intermediate terrain, and some of the most advanced skiing at Deer Valley, including eight chutes and three bowls. The classic last run of the day is Last Chance, which goes past stunning ski houses and some fairly amazing yard art all the way to the parking area. Tired skiers can also board the Silver Lake Express from the top and ride it back to the Snow Park base.

To prevent overcrowded trails, Deer Valley restricts the number of skiers on the mountain and often needs to restrict ticket sales during Christmas, New Year's, and Presidents Day weeks. If you're planning on skiing here during the holidays, reserve lift tickets at least a few days in advance.

Lift tickets are full-day $135 adults, $84 ages 5-12, $32 ages 1-4, $94 over age 64, afternoon $111 adults, $69 ages 5-12, $27 ages 1-4, $81 over age 64. Holiday rates are bumped up by about $10. Beginner passes limit skiers to just a few lifts, but are only $40.

Summer Activities

Hikers and sightseers can catch the Sterling, Silver Lake, and Ruby Express lifts (10am-5pm daily mid-June-Labor Day, full-day pass all lifts $45, single ride two lifts $20) to explore more than 50 miles (81 km) of trails running from the peak. The same rates apply to bike riders; helmets are required. Mountain biking instruction, rentals, and tours are available; call the resort (888/754-8477) for more information. Summer is also the season for off-road cycling events, Utah Symphony concerts, and music festivals. For horseback rides, call Deer Valley Stables (866/783-5819).

Food

The midmountain lodges here are unique because you can actually drive to them.

SILVER LAKE

Several cafeteria-style restaurants make the Silver Lake Lodge a good spot for a quick lunch. On a sunny day, stretch out in the lawn chairs on McHenry's Beach, the big sunny spot in front of the lodge, with your meal, perhaps warming up with a bowl of pho from **Bald Mountain Pho** (435/649-1100, 11:30am-2pm daily winter, $14) in the Silver Lake Lodge. There are also a couple of small coffee shops on the mountain—they serve Deer Valley's trademark turkey chili ($10-12) and good cookies. At any of Deer Valley's restaurants, look for cheese from **Deer Valley Artisan Cheese,** made using cow and goat milk from the nearby Heber Valley.

For a sit-down lunch, après-ski snacks, or dinner, the **Royal Street Café** (435/645-6724, 11:30am-8pm daily winter, 11:30am-2pm daily summer, $12-28) in the Silver Lake Lodge is a good bet. At dinnertime, the award-winning **Mariposa** (435/649-1000, 5:45pm-9pm Tues.-Sun. in ski season, $18-42) is a wonderful splurge, preparing "classic and current" cuisine; fresh fish, rack of lamb, steaks, chicken, and other meats receive savvy sauces and preparations. Reservations are recommended.

An unexpected treat in Deer Valley is the warm greeting and delicious eastern Mediterranean cooking at **Reefs** (at the Deer Valley Club, 7720 Royal St., 435/658-0323, www.reefsrestaurant.com, 4:30pm-10pm Mon.-Sat., plus Sun. during ski season, $14-36), where you'll enjoy Lebanese- and Turkish-style standards in addition to ringers such as poke and sashimi.

At the **Goldener Hirsch Inn** (435/655-2563, 11:30am-10pm daily, $29-50, reservations recommended) in Silver Lake Village, dishes reflect both an Austrian heritage and New World pizzazz: Wiener schnitzel ($48) is the house specialty, and fondue ($46) is a popular après-ski option.

It's a treat to visit the Stein Eriksen Lodge, and a meal the elegant **Glitretind Restaurant** (435/645-6455, steinlodge.com, 7am-9pm daily, $28-58, reservations recommended) gives you a good reason to do so; it serves contemporary cuisine and has one of the state's largest wine lists.

SNOW PARK

If you take an informal survey of lift riders here, the most popular meal in Deer Valley seems to be the **Seafood Buffet** at the **Snow Park Lodge** (435/645-6632, 6:15pm-9pm Mon.-Sat. in ski season, $70 adults, $37 children). Both quality and quantity are unstinting.

From the base, take a funicular up to the massive St. Regis Resort to find Jean-Georges Vongerichten's ★ **J&G Grill** (2300 Deer Valley Dr. E., 435/940-5760, www.jggrilldeercrest.com, 7am-2pm and 6pm-9pm daily, $31-45), where the meats are grilled simply, but the quality of the ingredients and the elegance of the restaurant make it one of the area's finest. If you want to sample the atmosphere and have a drink and a burger ($20), head to the bar but consider leaving your stinky ski parka in the car.

Accommodations

There are abundant condominium lodgings in Deer Valley, many almost immediately adjacent to the slopes. The best way to book lodgings is to contact **Deer Valley Central Reservations** (435/645-6528 or 800/558-3337, www.deervalley.com) and let them guide you through the process. The website has a good interactive map that will give you an overview of the accommodations and prices. Package deals are often available, but rates are still high—it's hard to find a condo for under $800 or a hotel room for less than $350 per night, and the least expensive rooms tend to book up fast. But remember, you're only a couple of miles from Park City and about an hour from Salt Lake. It's worth skiing Deer Valley even if you can't afford to sleep here.

Accommodations are in two main areas: **Snow Park,** the Deer Valley base area, which is about 1 mile from downtown Park City, and the **Silver Lake** area, located midmountain approximately 3.2 miles (5.1 km) from the

Snow Park base area. A short distance past Silver Lake is the Empire Pass area, with a few condos. Both Snow Park and Silver Lake lodges are just day lodges.

SILVER LAKE

If money is no object, book a room at the luxurious **Stein Eriksen Lodge** (7700 Stein Way, 435/649-3700 or 800/453-1302, www.steinlodge.com, roughly $700-3,600), a midmountain ski in-ski out hotel the Silver Lake area. The lodge is like a Norwegian fantasy castle built of log and stone. Guest rooms are exquisitely appointed, and there's a day spa with a pool and a fitness room. The restaurant here is one of the best rated in the area. You can book a guest room here either through the lodge itself or through Deer Valley Central Reservations.

Another extremely comfortable place is the **Goldener Hirsch Inn** (7570 Royal St. E., 435/645-6528 or 800/558-3373, www.goldenerhirschinn.com, $700-1250) in exclusive Silver Lake Village. It's a small Austrian-style ski-in, ski-out inn with beautifully furnished guest rooms (the gorgeous hand-carved beds were imported from Austria), hot tubs, a sauna, a lounge, meeting facilities, and underground parking. The restaurant is also extremely good.

SNOW PARK

At the Snow Park base, **The Lodges at Deer Valley** (435/645-6528 or 800/558-3337, www.deervalley.com, rooms $445-495, condos $675-1,000+) has hotel rooms, which have minifridges and toasters, along with full-kitchen condos; the complex has a year-round outdoor pool and hot tub. These are joined by many, many other condos; central reservations can help you select a place.

Another premium place to stay near the base of the lifts is **The St. Regis Deer Valley** (2300 Deer Valley Drive East, 435/940-5700, www.stregisdeervalley.com, $750-1,040) with beautifully outfitted rooms that mix rustic and stylishly contemporary decor. The St. Regis sits on a bluff above the Snow Park lifts, and primary access to the lifts at Deer Park Resort is via a funicular. As you might expect, the dining here is superb, with five options, including the resort's destination restaurant, the **J&G Grill** (J&G, as in celebrity chef Jean-Georges Vongerichten).

EMPIRE VALLEY

High above Deer Valley, at an elevation of 8,300 feet, is **Montage Deer Valley** (9100 Marsac Ave., 435/604-1300, www. montagehotels.com/deervalley, $1,245-- 2,075), a premium resort hotel with the monumentality of a grand mountain lodge and the finesse of a refined luxury hotel. In addition to fine dining (five dining options) and a 35,000-square-foot spa, the Montage offers ski-in, ski-out access to Deer Valley Resort out your backdoor via the Empire and Ruby Express lifts.

RECREATION

Most sports stores in Park City (and there are lots of them) rent skis and related equipment in winter and bicycles and camping gear in summer. It's also easy to rent equipment, including mountain bikes in the summer, at the ski resorts.

White Pine Touring (1790 Bonanza Dr., 435/649-8710, www.whitepinetouring.com, 9am-6pm daily) rents cross-country skis, snowshoes, mountain-climbing equipment, camping gear, and mountain bikes.

Jans Mountain Outfitters (1600 Park Ave., 435/649-4949, www.jans.com, 8am-7pm daily winter-summer, 8am-7pm daily fall) has downhill, telemark, and cross-country ski rentals, snowboards, snowshoes, mountain bikes, and fly-fishing gear.

Winter
★ UTAH OLYMPIC PARK
Built for the 2002 Olympics, **Utah Olympic Park** (3000 Bear Hollow Dr., near the Canyons, 435/658-4200, http:// utaholympiclegacy.org/, noon-4pm winter, noon-5pm March-April, noon-6pm daily summer, basic admission is free and includes

two museums devoted to winter sports) was the site of the bobsled, luge, and ski-jump competitions.

The mission of the park now is to train aspiring athletes, and visitors can often watch them. During the summer, freestyle skiers do acrobatic jumps and plunge into a huge swimming pool. On Saturday afternoons in summer, there's a freestyle aerial show.

It's also possible to actually do something here, such as take a vigorous (some would say harrowing) bobsled run (summer $75, must be over age 13, winter rides $175, must be over age 15, reservations strongly advised) with a professional driver; a day pass gives visitors access to a variety of activities, including a zipline, a ropes course and a drop tower (don't ask...just close your eyes and go!).

WHITE PINE TOURING
Park City's cross-country ski center, **White Pine Touring** (Park Ave. and Thaynes Canyon Dr., 435/649-6249, www. whitepinetouring.com, 9am-6pm daily, mid-Nov.-early Apr., $18 adults, $8 ages 6-12, free under age 7 or over 64,), offers rentals, instruction, and guided snowshoe tours. It has a touring center and about 12.4 miles (20 km) of groomed trails right in town. White Pine also has a yurt ($175-200) in the Uinta Mountains that's available year-round. There is a year-round office and shop (1790 Bonanza Dr., 435/649-8710, 9am-7pm daily).

★ SKI UTAH INTERCONNECT
If you look at the map, you'll see that Snowbird, Alta, Solitude, Brighton, Deer Valley, and Park City Mountain Resort are not that far from one another and can be linked by backcountry routes. Experienced skiers who are up for a challenging day can explore the backcountry among these ski areas in Big and Little Cottonwood Canyons and Park City with **Ski Utah Interconnect** (801/534-1907, www.skiutah.com, mid-Dec.-mid-Apr., $395, reservations required), which provides a guide service for extensive touring

of Wasatch Front ski areas. Touring is with downhill equipment and requires legs of steel and the ability to ski ungroomed powder all day long and do a bit of hiking to reach those great bowls and chutes. Tours on Monday, Tuesday, Wednesday, Friday, and Sunday depart from Deer Valley and move on to Park City Mountain Resort, Solitude, Brighton, Alta, and Snowbird. On Thursday and Saturday, tours start at Snowbird and visit Alta, Brighton, Solitude, and a lot of backcountry terrain; these tours are somewhat more rigorous than those starting at Deer Valley. Rate includes guide service, lunch, lift tickets, and transportation back to the point of origin.

SLEIGH RIDES

Riding a horse-drawn sleigh to a Western dinner or an evening of entertainment is quickly becoming a Park City tradition. One of the more elaborate activities is offered by **Snowed Inn Sleigh Company** (435/647-3310, www.snowedinnsleigh.com, $129 adults, $84 children, reservations required), which takes guests on a sleigh ride to a lodge where dinner is served; short rides without dinner are also available ($25). Another sleigh (or heated snow-cat) ride heads to **The Viking Yurt** (435/647-3310, vikingyurt.com, $181) for a six-course dinner.

Summer
BALLOONING

A flight above Park City on a hot-air balloon is an exhilarating experience. Balloons take off in the early morning year-round, weather permitting, and trips typically include a continental breakfast and postflight champagne toast. The cost is $250 for one hour with either **Park City Balloon Adventures** (435/645-8787 or 800/396-8787, www.pcballoonadventures.com) or **Skywalker Balloon Company** (435/824-3934, http://skywalker.at). If you're content to just watch from the ground, visit during September, when the Autumn Aloft festival fills the sky with balloons.

FISHING

Fly-fishing is a favorite pastime in the mountain streams and lakes of the Wasatch Mountains. The Weber and Provo Rivers are well known for their wily native cutthroat, wild brown, and rainbow trout as well as Rocky Mountain whitefish. Get your fishing license, supplies, and a guide at **Trout Bum 2** (4343 N. Hwy. 224, Suite 101, 435/658-1166 or 877/878-2862, www.troutbum2.com, 8am-6pm Mon.-Sat., 8am-5pm Sun. summer, 9am-5pm Mon.-Sat., 9am-4pm Sun. winter).

GOLF

The Park City area has a number of 18-hole courses, including the city-owned **Park City Golf Club** (Park Ave. and Thaynes Canyon Dr., 435/615-5800, www.parkcitygolfclub.org, nonresidents $52). Opened in 2014, the **Canyons Golf Course** (4000 Canyons Resort Dr., 435/615-4728, www.parkcitymountain.com, $70) is a 6,256-yard, par-70 course, designed by Gene and Casey Bates, with a number of holes built right on the ski runs of Park City Mountain Resort. **Wasatch Mountain State Park** (435/654-0532, wasatchgolfcourse.com, $50), a short distance away in Midway, has two outstanding public courses.

HIKING

The ski areas open their trails to hikers in summer; pick up a trail map and just head out. **Deer Valley** (435/649-1000 or 800/424-3337, www.deervalley.com) or **Park City** (435/649-8111, www.parkcitymountain.com) both offer lift-assisted hiking that takes walkers up to the high country without a wind-sucking foot ascent; see individual resorts for information. From downtown Park City, follow trail signs to the slopes; well-marked trails start just on the edge of town and head uphill. Mountain Trails Foundation (http://mountaintrails.org), a trail advocacy organization, has good interactive maps on their website.

When hiking around Park City, stay clear of relics of the mining past that lie scattered about. You're likely to come across miners' cabins in all states of decay, hoist buildings, aerial tramway towers, rusting machinery, and great piles of mine tailings. Unlike other parts of the Wasatch Range, most of the land here belongs to mining companies and other private owners. Visitors need to keep a distance from mine shafts—which can be hundreds of feet deep—and respect No Trespassing signs.

HORSEBACK RIDING
Red Pine Adventures (2050 White Pine Canyon, 435/649-9445 or 800/417-7669, www.redpinetours.com, from $75) offers trail rides of varying lengths; 1.5-hour rides start several times a day.

MOUNTAIN BIKING
This is a favorite summer activity in the Park City area, with more than 350 miles (565 km) of mountain bike trails. Some of the local landowners, including ski resorts and mining companies, have offered access to their land and have even built trail sections at their own expense. Helmets are always required when riding on private land. Both Park City resorts keep at least one lift open for bikers and hikers during the summer. **Deer Valley** (435/649-1000 or 800/424-3337, www.deervalley.com) has 55 stunning miles (89 km) of single- and double-track trails; **Park City** (435/649-8111, www.parkcitymountain.com) has 35 miles (56 km) of trails, including some fine downhills from the top of the Canyons area's Red Pine lift.

Mountain bikers can also access any number of side trails off the rail trail described below. Check out Mountain Trails Foundation's online map (http://mountaintrails.org/map/) to plan a route.

A good place for an easy-going ride is the **Historic Union Pacific Rail Trail State Park** (435/649-6839, http://stateparks.utah.gov, dawn-dusk daily year-round, free), a multiuse nonmotorized trail built to accommodate hikers, bicyclists, horseback riders, and cross-country skiers. The trail parallels I-80 and runs about 30 miles (48 km) from Deer Valley through Park City and the town

of Coalville north to Evanston, Wyoming. In Park City, from Park Avenue, turn onto Kearns Boulevard, then right onto Bonanza Drive. After about 200 yards, turn left onto Prospector Avenue, where you can catch the trail behind the Park City Plaza; the parking area is on the right. Rent a bike from **White Pine Touring** (1790 Bonanza Dr., 435/649-8710, 9am-7pm daily); their shop has easy access to the trail. If you're visiting in 2019, check the website before heading out; work is scheduled that will close parts of the trail.

WATER SPORTS
Hone your stand-up paddling skills with **PCSUP** (1375 Deer Valley Rd. S., 801/558-9878, www.parkcitysup.com); board rentals are available. **Boating, waterskiing,** and **stand-up paddling** are popular activities at the Jordanelle, Rockport, and Echo Reservoirs.

ENTERTAINMENT AND EVENTS
Events
One of the state's biggest—and certainly glitziest—events takes over Park City every January (see callout about the Sundance Film Festival). But that's not the only event that draws visitors to this resort town. Also in January, the FIS Freestyle World Cup brings daredevil skiers to the slopes at Deer Valley, and not surprisingly, Fourth of July weekend is a time to whoop it up at a parade, rodeo, and concert.

Nightlife
As you'd expect in a ski resort, nightlife centers on bars and dance clubs. The principal hangouts are on Main Street, although all the lodges and resorts and most of the larger hotels have bars and clubs of their own. The trendy **Park City Live** (427 Main St., 435/649-9123, http://parkcitylive.net) is the largest music venue in town, with long lines at the door, a large crowded dance floor, and special VIP tables. The more down-home **No Name Saloon** (447 Main St., 435/649-6667, www.nonamesaloon.net, 10am-2am daily)

is a sports bar with food, including what's often called the town's best burger; head up to the rooftop to spy on Main Street action. Duck into **The Spur** (352 Main St., 435/615-1618, www.thespurbarandgrill.com, 10am-1am) for rock, acoustic folk, or bluegrass and a friendly, convivial atmosphere. Right by the Town Lift, **The Cabin** (825 S. Main St., 435/565-2337, www.thecabinparkcity. com, noon-1am daily) has music every night, a good list of beers and cocktails (including the $30 Elkupine).

One of the best bars in town, **High West Distillery and Saloon** (703 Park Ave., 435/649-8300, www.highwest.com, 11am-10pm daily), is conveniently located at the bottom of Park City Mountain Resort's Quittin' Time run. Housed in a collection of historic buildings a block off Main Street, High West is classy in an old-fashioned Western ski town kind of way. Head out of town to Wanship to visit the High West distillery (435/649-8300); it's located at the Blue Sky Lodge (yet to be opened when we visited in 2018) and offers tours Wednesday-Sunday (call for a reservation).

You can drink a microbrew and chat with friends at **Wasatch Brew Pub** (250 Main St., 435/649-0900, www.wasatchbeers.com, 11am-10pm Mon.-Fri., 11am-11pm Sat.-Sun.) or head north of the Main Street neighborhood to **Squatters Pub** (1900 Park Ave., 435/649-9868, www.squatters.com, 8am-10pm Sun.-Thurs., 8am-11pm Fri.-Sat.).

The Arts
CONCERTS
Summer is music-festival time in Park City. The Utah Symphony and other classical performers, including the Utah Opera, take the stage at Deer Valley's outdoor amphitheater (2250 Deer Valley Dr. S., 801/533-5626, www. deervalleymusicfestival.org) from early July to the second week of August for a summer concert series. The Park City Beethoven Festival (435/649-5309, www.pcmusicfestival.com) offers chamber music at various locations around town from spring through fall.

THEATER
The **Egyptian Theatre Company** (www. egyptiantheatrecompany.org) puts on dramas, concerts, comedies, musicals, and children's shows year-round in the historic Egyptian Theatre (328 Main St., 435/649-9371). The Egyptian also hosts concerts (Herman's Hermits, anyone?) and comedy.

Cinema
Of course the big event is the annual **Sundance Film Festival** (www.sundance. org, mid-late Jan.), which spotlights more than 200 films from around the world and involves at least as many parties as films. Festival ticket packages range from $500 for 10 tickets to up to $6,500 for a full season pass and a couple of parties. Buy these online, as the premium packages sell out early. Toward the end of the festival, individual tickets are often available for $20. Also note that a number of festival screenings take place in Salt Lake City.

The **Park City Film Series** (1255 Park Ave., 435/615-8291, www.parkcityfilmseries. com, Sept.-June) offers art, foreign, and classic films.

Arts Festivals
In early August, more than 220 artists exhibit their work on Main Street for the **Kimball Arts Festival** (435/649-8882, www. kimballartcenter.org, $12), a fundraiser for the excellent Kimball Arts Center. Contact the Park City Visitor Information Center (1794 Olympic Parkway, 435/658-9616, www. visitparkcity.com) for the latest news on other happenings around town.

SHOPPING
Park City's primary shopping venue is historic **Main Street,** which is lined with upscale boutiques, gift shops, galleries, craft shops, and sporting goods stores.

Markets
The open-air **Park Silly Sunday Market** (435/714-4036, http://parksillysundaymarket. com, 10am-5pm Sun. early June-late Sept.)

Sundance Film Festival

Robert Redford began this noted festival in 1981 as a venue for independent films that otherwise had a difficult time reaching the screen or a mass audience. Since then, the **Sundance Film Festival** (435/658-3456, www.sundance.org) has become the nation's foremost venue for new and innovative cinema. The festival is held in the second half of January at the height of the ski season, so Park City is absolutely packed and then some during that time. As the festival has grown, some films are now shown in Salt Lake City theaters, as well as in Peery's Egyptian Theater in Ogden. Definitely make plans well in advance if you want to attend any of the screenings or festival activities.

Tickets to the screenings can be hard to come by, especially for films with advance buzz or big stars; if you can't get tickets, put your name on waiting lists or join the lines at the theaters for canceled tickets. However, tickets to less well-known films are usually available at the last minute. If you are coming to Park City expressly to see the films, inquire about package tours that include tickets.

Park City is exciting during the festival, as the glitterati of New York and Hollywood descend on the town. You'll see movie stars, some wild clothing, and lots of deal making.

takes over the lower stretch of Main Street. You'll find lots of arts and crafts, handmade clothing and hats, and at the bottom of the street, food carts and live music. It makes for agreeable shopping and fascinating people watching. The **Park City Farmers Market** (noon-6pm Wed. early June-Oct.) is held at Canyons Village's main parking lot (Canyon Resort Dr., 0.25 mile west of Hwy. 224).

Books and Cards

Dolly's Bookstore (510 Main St., 435/649-8062, http://dollysbookstore.com, 10am-10pm daily) has a good selection of books for all ages and interests. **Atticus** (738 Main St., 435/214-7241, www.atticustea.com, 7am-5pm daily) combines the virtues of a used-book store, tea and sandwich shop, and events center. It's a fun place to hang out and catch Park City's subtle arty alternative vibe.

Clothing

Panache (738 Main St., 435/649-7037, 10am-7pm Mon.-Sat., 10am-6pm Sun.) offers stylish high-end women's clothing and jewelry. **Olive & Tweed** (608 Main St., 435/649-9392, 10am-9pm daily) is an artisans co-op featuring women's clothing, jewelry, and lots of gifts. **Cake Boutique** (511 Main St., 435/649-1256, 10am-7pm Mon.-Sat., 11am-6pm Sun.) is a fashion-forward clothing store that veers toward designer hipster wear with lots of denim.

If you like the upscale Western look common in Park City, pick up some togs at **Park City Clothing Company** (558 Main St., 435/649-0555, 10am-6pm daily), with pearl-snap shirts, hats, boots, and jewelry amid the Coca-Cola memorabilia. If it's mostly boots that you're interested in, check out the walls of Western-style boots at **Burns Cowboy Shop** (363 Main St., 435/649-6300, 9am-6pm Mon.-Sat.).

If your budget doesn't allow for shopping in Park City's high-end boutiques, check the good selection of pre-owned clothing at **Exchange Consignment** (1755 Bonanza Dr., 435/649-3360, 11am-5pm Mon.-Sat.).

Galleries

There are nearly as many art galleries in tiny Park City as in Salt Lake City; it's a major scene, with lots of high-end art. Most galleries are along busy Main Street, so they aren't hidden away. Here are some favorites.

Gallery MAR (436 Main St., 435/649-3001, www.gallerymar.com, 10am-9pm daily) represents a wide selection of mostly representational artists. **Julie Nester Gallery** (1280 Iron Horse Dr., 435/649-7855, www.julienestergallery.com, 10:30am-6pm

Mon.-Fri., 10am-5pm Sat.) represents a number of national contemporary artists, with more sophisticated works than you'd usually expect in a resort town. **Mountain Trails Gallery** (301 Main St., 435/615-8748, www. mountaintrailsgalleries.com, 10am-9pm daily) is Park City's top purveyor of Western and wildlife art, in both painting and sculpture. Check out the work of emerging and mid-career artists from Utah and around the West at **Terzian Galleries** (625 Main St., 435/649-4927, www.terziangalleries. com, 11am-5pm Mon.-Thurs., 11am-6pm Fri.-Sat.). For Native American art, antiques, and collectibles, go to the **Crosby Collection** (419 Main St., 435/658-1813, www.crosbycollection.com, 10am-6pm daily).

Park City's real jewel of a gallery is **Kimball Arts Center** (401 Kearns Blvd., 435/649-8882, www.kimball-art.org, 10am-5pm Mon.-Fri., noon-5pm Sat.-Sun., donation), a nonprofit community arts center where there's always interesting art to experience. It's an arts education hub plus a sales and exhibition gallery, and it's a great place to catch the spirit of the local artistic community.

FOOD

Park City has the greatest concentration of good restaurants in Utah; the listings below are just a smattering of what you'll find in a very small area. The five blocks of historic Main Street alone offer many fine places to eat, and each of the resorts, hotels, and lodges offers more options. Note that many of the restaurants close in May and November—the so-called mud season. During ski-season weekends, dinner reservations are strongly advised for all but the most casual restaurants.

Main Street and Vicinity

At the top of Main Street, **Wasatch Brew Pub** (250 Main St., 435/649-0900, www. wasatchbeers.com, 11am-10pm Mon.-Fri., 10am-10pm Sat.-Sun., $10-23) is a reliable place for budget travelers to find sustenance in downtown Park City. The pub-style food is

fine, and beer is very good; in nice weather, there's a patio for outdoor dining.

Locally sourced meats are grilled on, well, a wood fire, at **Firewood** (306 Main St., 435/252-9900, www.firewoodonmain.com, 5:30pm-9:30pm Sun.-Thurs., 5:30pm-10pm Fri.-Sat., $29-46)...or, skip the meat and go for excellent grilled cauliflower.

Chimayo (368 Main St., 435/649-6222, www.chimayorestaurant.com, 5pm-10pm daily winter and summer, hours vary in other seasons, $32-50) is the area's leading purveyor of contemporary Southwest cuisine such as trout fajitas seared with green pepitas and served with chipotle sour cream, guacamole and pico de gallo. One of the most romantic restaurants in Park City is **Wahso** (577 Main St., 435/615-0300, www.wahso.com, 5pm-9:30pm Sun. and Wed.-Thurs., 5pm-10pm Fri.-Sat., $28-52). Its name is both Chinese and French (from *oiseau*, meaning "bird"), as is the cuisine at this stylish, slightly formal restaurant. French sauces meet Chinese cooking techniques and vice versa.

The inspiration for the food at pleasant **Cafe Terigo** (424 Main St., 435/645-9555, www.cafeterigo.com, 11:30am-2:30pm and 5:30pm-9:30pm daily, $28-40) is Italian, but dishes such as pan-seared scallops with sweet corn risotto and red pepper puree show that ingredients and techniques have been substantially updated. The atmosphere in the restaurant and on the side patio is simultaneously calming and fun.

Another signature (and very classy) Park City restaurant, **Riverhorse on Main** (540 Main St., 435/649-3536, http:// riverhorseparkcity.com, 5pm-10pm daily and 11am-2pm Sat.-Sun., $42-92) in the old Masonic building, serves carefully prepared American standards with a few restrained flourishes; after a day of skiing, splurge on the trio of wild game.

The traditional foods of the American West are celebrated and expanded on at the fun, stylish ★ **Purple Sage** (434 Main St., 435/655-9505, www.purplesageparkcity.com, 5:30pm-10pm nightly in winter, closed Sun. in other seasons, $28-45), where such dishes as meatloaf, cowboy steaks, and sweet corn-battered trout are prepared to exacting standards. Although ★ **High West Distillery and Saloon** (703 Park Ave., 435/649-8300, www.highwest.com, 11am-10pm, daily, $16-34) is a great place to get an après-ski drink, it's also one of Park City's best restaurants. Try the three-bean bourbon chili topped with fried quinoa. Kids are welcome here, and there's a special menu with them in mind. (Hot tip: High West now has a location at the SLC airport; have a pulled pork sandwich before boarding your flight home!)

Just a block off Main Street, **Handle** (136 Heber St., 435/602-1155, http://handleparkcity.com, 5pm-10pm daily, $16-70) focuses on seasonal and local ingredients; go with a selection of small plates such as buffalo-wing-style cauliflower or a squash tostada.

Prospector Square and Vicinity

One of Park City's best restaurants is the ★ **Blind Dog** (1251 Kearns Blvd., 435/655-0800, http://blinddogpc.com, 5pm-9:30pm Tues.-Sat., $22-36). The food here is seriously good, and although crab cakes ($34, or $18

as an appetizer) are favorites, the Dog is also known for its sushi (rolls $10-18). In the same Boneyard complex find a saloon and a wine bar.

A good, reasonably priced, and healthy bet for any meal of the day is **Good Karma** (1782 Prospector Ave., 435/658-0958, http://goodkarmarestaurants.com, 8am-2:30pm and 5pm-9pm daily, $9-14), a sweet but tiny spot in Prospector Square with tasty Indo-Persian food (standard American fare is served at breakfast); sit out back in the courtyard.

For a Western steak house atmosphere, go to **Grub Steak Restaurant** (2093 Sidewinder Ave., 435/649-8060, www.grubsteakrestaurant.com, 11:30am-2pm and 5pm-9pm Mon.-Thurs., 11:30am-2pm and 5pm-9:30pm Fri., 5pm-9:30pm Sat., 5pm-9pm Sun., $21-84) in the Inn at Prospector Square. The steaks, prime rib, grilled chicken, and seafood are excellent, and dinners come with a trip to the salad bar.

On Park Avenue at Kearns Boulevard is **Squatters Roadhouse Grill** (1900 Park Ave., 435/649-9868, www.squatters.com, 8am-10pm Sun.-Thurs., 8am-11pm Fri.-Sat., $10-20), a brewpub with above-average pub grub. Vegetarians should check out the charbroiled tofu tacos.

PARK CITY

PARK CITY AND THE WASATCH RANGE

High West Distillery and Saloon

Luck into an outside table at the tiny ★ **Silver Star Cafe** (1825 Three Kings Dr., 435/655-3456, www.thesilverstarcafe.com, 8am-9pm Sun.-Wed., 8am-10pm Thurs.-Sat. in winter, call for hours in other seasons, $23-38) and you'll have a great view of Park City. It's a favorite spot for brunch ($14-17) or a couple of small plates after hiking or skiing, or a dinnertime singer-songwriter concert, when the music complements the Silver Star's "American roots" food and easygoing atmosphere.

ACCOMMODATIONS

Park City is awash in condos, hotels, and B&Bs; guest capacity far exceeds the town's permanent population. Rates peak at dizzying heights during the ski season, when accommodations may also be hard to find. Most lodgings have four different winter rates, which peak at the Christmas holidays, during the Sundance Film Festival, and in February-March; there are different rates for weekends and weekdays as well. Many lodgings have rooms at a wide range of prices, from hostel rooms to basic hotel rooms to multiroom suites, so remember that the following price categories are for a standard double room in the winter high (but nonholiday) season. Summer rates are usually about half those given below. During ski season, many lodgings ask for minimum stays—sometimes a weekend, sometimes a full week. Park City's hotel tax is 10.35 percent; add this to any rate you're quoted.

The following accommodations are in addition to the lodges and hotels operated by or located at **Deer Valley** (435/645-6528 or 800/558-3337, www.deervalley.com) and by the **Park City Mountain Resort** (lodging 435/602-4099 or 800/331-3178, www.parkcitymountain.com).

Reservation Services

Undoubtedly the easiest way to find a room or condo in Park City is to contact one of the many reservation services; most also offer ski, golf, or other recreational packages. For general Park City lodging, try **Park City Lodging** (855/348-6759, www.parkcitylodging.com) and **Resort Property Management** (435/655-6529 or 800/645-4762, www.resortpropertymanagement.com). **All Seasons Resort Lodging** (888/667-2775, www.allseasonsresortlodging.com) handles a vast number of condo units throughout the valley. The **Park City Area Chamber of Commerce** (www.visitparkcity.com) also has an online lodging locator.

$50-100

A welcome addition to Park City's lodging scene is the **Park City Hostel** (1781 Sidewinder Dr., 435/731-8811, www.parkcityhostel.com, dorm bed $35, private room $75 d). Although you may find yourself sleeping in a bunk bed (though there are a fair number of private rooms), this newer, well-kept hostel in Prospector Square is a real boon for budget travelers in this spendy town.

Park City's classic budget ski lodge, **Chateau Après Lodge** (1299 Norfolk Ave., 435/649-9372, www.chateauapres.com, men's dorm bed $40-50, private room $145 d; open for groups only in summer), is a short walk from the Park City Mountain Resort base. The lodge has a dedicated following among serious skiers, and although even the men's dorm is a barracks and regular guest rooms are far from elegant, this family-run lodge is a great deal. It's also convivial; meet skiers from all over the world at the breakfast buffet.

Although it's not in town, the **Best Western Holiday Hills** (200 S. 500 W., Coalville, 435/336-4444 or 866/922-7278, www.bwstay.com, $95-119), about 20 minutes northeast of Park City, is a reasonable bet for travelers who want a comfortable guest room (with continental breakfast included) that's probably cheaper than your lift ticket. It's located just off I-80 at exit 162.

It's also possible to find high-quality lodgings in this price range in Heber City, about 20 minutes from Park City. And remember, Park City is less than 35 miles (56 km) from Salt Lake City.

$100-200

Out at the Kimball Junction exit on I-80 is the **Best Western Landmark Inn** (6560 N. Landmark Dr., 435/649-7300 or 800/548-8824, www.bwlandmarkinn.com, $225-329), with a pool, a spa, a breakfast buffet, and a free shuttle to ski areas and downtown Park City. If you want a high-quality reasonably priced (for Park City) hotel room and don't mind being a bit removed from the action, this is a good bet. During the summer, guest rooms are about $50 cheaper.

A few other chain hotels are located near the freeway, close to Park City's Canyons Village.

Prospector Accommodations (2200 Sidewinder Dr., 435/649-7100 or 888/575-2775, www.allseasonsresortlodging.com, standard rooms $149-319, two-bedroom condos $160-1000) is one of several hotel-condominium complexes managed by All Season Resorts. Several different room types are scattered through eight different buildings about one mile from Main Street and the main Park City lifts; the city's free shuttle bus stops here. Guests can use the adjacent Silver Mountain Sports Club. Note that many of these units require a five-night minimum stay.

$200-300

Right downtown is the ★ **Treasure Mountain Inn** (255 Main St., 435/649-7334 or 800/344-2460, www.treasuremountaininn. com, $215-450). Treasure Mountain is a large complex of three buildings with several room types, all with kitchens. Refurbished guest rooms are large and beautifully furnished. If you want a quiet room in this extremely central locale, ask for one that faces the back pool and garden.

A little way from downtown is the **Park City Peaks Hotel** (2121 Park Ave., 435/649-5000 or 800/649-5012, www.parkcitypeaks. com, $229-329). It is an upscale hotel that is notable mainly because its summer rates are sometimes well under $100.

Not surprisingly, downtown Park City is peppered with chain lodgings; you can usually find a room for about $250-300 in the winter, a bit less in the summer, and substantially less in the spring and fall.

Over $300

Despite its pedestrian name, the Marriott-owned **Hotel Park City** (2001 Park Ave., 435/200-2000, www.hotelparkcity.com, $685-1,700) is quite sumptuous, even by Park City standards. This all-suite hotel has comfy leather sofas, luxurious baths, a heated outdoor pool, a spa and fitness center, and a good restaurant. It is a little too far to walk from the hotel to Main Street. During the slow spring and fall seasons, rates can drop to about $250.

A landmark Park City boutique hotel just a block off Main Street is the **Washington School House Hotel** (543 Park Ave., 435/649-3800 or 800/824-1672, www. washingtonschoolhouse.com, $875-3,100). The quarried limestone inn was built in 1889 as the town's elementary school and is now one of the most luxurious lodgings in Park City. There are four large standard guest rooms and four suites furnished with well-chosen antiques and art, an outdoor heated pool, hot tub, sauna, and ski lockers. During the summer it's possible to get a room for about $450.

A less vaunted but still quite luxurious and extra-friendly B&B with full breakfast is the **Torchlight Inn** (255 Deer Valley Dr., 435/612-0345, www.torchlightinn.com, $343-484). This newer inn is on the edge of downtown Park City.

Marriott's Summit Watch Resort (780 Main St., 435/647-4100, www.marriott.com, hotel room with kitchenette $349-522) is a cluster of condominium hotels at the base of Main Street near the Town Lift, with options ranging from studios to two-room villas. All guest rooms have kitchen facilities; there's a central pool, and all the dining that downtown Park City offers is within a five-minute stroll.

Right at the main base of the Park City Mountain Resort and just a few dollars more expensive is **Marriott's MountainSide** (1305 Lowell Ave., 800/940-2000, www. marriott.com, hotel room with kitchenette $349-540); if you are looking for top-notch ski-in, ski-out lodging, this is a good choice. Although you can walk to town from here, it's a bit of a schlep in the winter.

Campgrounds
Park City RV Resort (2200 W. Rasmussen Rd., 435/649-2531, www.parkcityrvresort. com, tents $28, hookups $37-42) offers seasonal tent and year-round RV sites with showers and laundry. From I-80, take exit 145 for Park City and travel west one mile on the north frontage road. The campground is about 6 miles (9.7 km) from Park City.

There are good public campgrounds in the Heber City area. **Jordanelle State Park** (435/649-9540 or 435/782-3030, http:// stateparks.utah.gov, campsites $20-30, cabins $70-85) and **Wasatch Mountain State Park** (435/654-1791, http://stateparks.utah. gov, campsites $14-30, cabins $60-80) are both good places to pitch a tent in the summer. Both take reservations (800/322-3770, www.reserveamerica.com).

INFORMATION AND SERVICES
A number of Main Street storefronts advertise "visitors information"; these places are almost invariably real estate offices, although they do have racks of brochures. For the best selection of info and genuinely helpful staff, visit the **Park City Visitor Information Center** (1794 Olympic Pkwy., 435/658-9616, www.visitparkcity.com, 9am-6pm daily)

near Kimball Junction at the turnoff to Utah Olympic Park. There's a branch office in the Park City Museum (528 Main St.).

GETTING THERE AND AROUND
The 32-mile drive from Salt Lake City to Park City takes about 40 minutes (allow more time in the winter). From SLC, take I-15 to I-80 East; follow I-80 for about 24 miles (39 km) to exit 145 (UT 224), which eventually flows into downtown Park City. It's well signed and hard to lose your way.

If you'd rather skip the hassle of driving, **Peak Transportation** (877/474-9019, www. peaktransportation.com, $25-120 one-way depending on number of passengers) and **Canyon Transportation** (800/255-1841, www.canyontransport.com, $45 one-way) both make regular runs between Park City and Salt Lake City International Airport or downtown. Resorts also offer car rentals in Park City.

Park City Transit (recording 435/645-5350) operates a trolley bus up and down Main Street (about every 10 minutes daily) and has several bus routes to other parts of town, including Park City, Canyons Village, and Deer Valley ski areas (every 10-20 minutes daily). All buses are free; pick up a transit guide from the visitors center at Kimball Junction (1794 Olympic Pkwy., 435/658-9616), in the Park City Museum (528 Main St., 435/649-7457), on any of the buses, or on the parkcity.org website. Parking can be extremely difficult in downtown Park City, so it's a good idea to hop a bus. Uber and Lyft also serve Park City.

Heber City and Vicinity

Its setting in a lush agricultural valley surrounded by high mountains has earned Heber City the title of Switzerland of America. Many of its people work at farming, raising livestock, and dairying, as their families have done since pioneer days, although it's also become the site of some fantastically expensive vacation homes. Heber City (pop. 15,000) makes a handy stop for travelers exploring the nearby Wasatch and Uinta Ranges or visiting the large Deer Creek and Strawberry Reservoirs. It also offers reasonably priced accommodations a short drive from Park City. Heber City merges almost seamlessly into the town of Midway, home to several upscale resorts.

SIGHTS

Heber Valley Historic Railroad

Ride a turn-of-the-20th-century train pulled by steam locomotive number 618 past Deer Creek Lake into scenic alpine Provo Canyon. The **Heber Valley Railroad** (450 S. 600 W., 435/654-5601, http://hebervalleyrr.org, year-round, $20-30 adults, $15 ages 3-12) offers three different scenic tours, plus a variety of dinner and adventure options as well, including a train ride to a raft trip down the Provo River ($95 includes train ride, raft trip, and boxed lunch); check the website for details.

Soldier Hollow

Soldier Hollow (435/654-2002, https://utaholympiclegacy.org, trail pass $10), site of the 2002 Olympic and Paralympic cross-country skiing and biathlon events, offers roughly 20 miles (32 km) of trails (including some easy ones added to the Olympic-level course) for cross-country skiing, snowshoeing, biathlon, and mountain biking. There's also a tubing hill ($24 for 2 hours ages 13 and up, $22 ages 6-12 $12 ages 3-5). Rentals are available at the lodge. From Heber City, head west on 100 South to Midway. Take a left on

Center Street (Hwy. 113) in Midway and head south for 3.5 miles (5.6 km) to Soldier Hollow.

Homestead Crater

Just northwest of the town of Midway, on the grounds of the Homestead Resort, is a large volcanic-like cone called the Crater. This geological curiosity is actually composed of travertine deposited by the local hot springs; water once flowed out of the top, but now it's piped to a 65-foot-deep, 95°F pool deep in the Crater's belly. **Homestead Crater** (435/657-3840, 12:30-6:30pm Mon.-Thurs., 10:30am-6:30pm Fri.-Sat., 10:30am-4:30pm Sun., $13-16, reservations required) is accessible for swimming, scuba diving ($22-27), and snorkeling ($18-21).

RECREATION

★ Wasatch Mountain State Park

Wasatch Mountain State Park (435/654-1791, tee times 435/654-0532, http://stateparks.utah.gov, day-use $10, 18 holes of golf $50), Utah's largest state park, encompasses 22,000 acres of valleys and mountains on the east side of the Wasatch Range. Unpaved scenic drives lead north through Pine Creek Canyon to Guardsman Pass Road (turn right for Park City or left over the pass for Brighton), northwest through Snake Creek Canyon to Pole Line Pass and American Fork Canyon, and southwest over Decker Pass to Cascade Springs.

The 1.5-mile **Pine Creek Nature Trail** begins near site 21 in the Oak Hollow Campground. The vast park is also a popular place for off-highway vehicle riding, which is not always a rowdy and reckless pastime; in the fall, join a guided OHV leaf-peeping tour.

The excellent **Lake** and **Mountain Golf Courses** (975 W. Golf Course Dr., 435/654-0532) are in the main part of the park. The newer Gold and Silver courses are at **Soldier**

Hollow Golf Course (1370 W. Soldier Hollow Ln., 435/654-7442), which occupies a corner of the park. A clubhouse includes a pro shop and a café.

Winter brings snow depths of 3-6 feet mid-December-mid-March. Separate **cross-country ski** and **snowmobile** trails begin near Soldier Hollow. **Homestead Adventure Center** (Homestead Resort, 700 N. Homestead Dr., Midway, 435/931-3097) provides equipment for both sports.

To reach the main entrance of Wasatch Mountain State Park, drive west three miles (4.8 km) from Heber City to Midway, then follow signs north 2 miles (3.2 km).

Jordanelle State Park

The large **Jordanelle State Park** reservoir (435/649-9540, http://stateparks.utah.gov), upstream of Heber City on the Provo River, provides recreation for boaters and anglers. It's east of U.S. 40, 6 miles (9.7 km) north of Heber City. There are two recreation areas. **Rock Cliff Recreation Area** (435/782-3030, day-use $10) is at the upper end of the east arm of the reservoir and has restrooms, a nature center, boardwalks with interpretive displays, and pavilions for day use. **Hailstone Recreation Area** (435/649-9540 or 800/322-3770, day-use $10) has a large campground, restrooms and showers, day-use shaded pavilions, a marina with 80 boat slips, a general store, a laundry, and a small restaurant.

Deer Creek State Park

The seven-mile-long Deer Creek Reservoir in **Deer Creek State Park** (Midway, 435/654-0171, http://stateparks.utah.gov, day-use $10) lies in a very pretty setting below Mount Timpanogos and other peaks of the Wasatch Range. A developed area near the lower end of the lake has a campground with showers, a picnic area, a paved boat ramp, a dock, and a fish-cleaning station; elevation is 5,400 feet. **Island Beach Area,** 4.5 miles (7.2 km) to the northeast, has a gravel swimming beach and a marina, is open in summer, with a store, a snack bar, a boat ramp, and rentals of fishing

boats, ski boats, and personal watercraft. Rainbow trout, perch, largemouth bass, and walleye swim in the lake. Good winds for sailing blow most afternoons. You'll often see a lineup of catamarans at the sailboat beach near the campground and crowds of sailboarders at the Island Beach Area. **Deer Creek Island Resort** (Island Beach Area, 435/654-2155, www.deercreekislandresort. com) has boat rentals.

Strawberry Reservoir

The 17,000-acre **Strawberry Reservoir** (435/654-0470) is Utah's top trout fishery and lies on a high rolling plateau 23 miles (37 km) southeast of Heber City. Fishing is good all year (through the ice in winter) for rainbow and cutthroat trout and some brook trout and kokanee salmon. The U.S. Forest Service maintains three marinas around the lake. Several winter parking areas along U.S. 40 provide access for cross-country skiing, snowmobiling, and ice fishing.

ENTERTAINMENT AND EVENTS

Horse shows and rodeos take place throughout the summer in the Heber City area (www.gohebervalley.com). The **Utah High School Rodeo Finals** are held in early June. **Wasatch County Fair Days** features a parade, a rodeo, exhibits, a livestock show, entertainment, and a demolition derby in early August. Labor Day weekend brings **Swiss Days** (https://midwayswissdays.com) to Midway as well as a huge gathering of border collies and their fans to Soldier Hollow for the **Soldier Hollow Classic Sheepdog Championship** (435/654-2002, http://soldierhollowclassic.com).

FOOD
Heber City

American-style cafés line Main Street, along

1: vintage train at the Heber Valley Historic Railroad; **2:** Mountain Golf Course; **3:** Deer Creek State Park; **4:** Snake Creek Grill

with plenty of fast food to serve the skiing crowds. A fun, casual local place with good food is **Spin Cafe** (220 N. Main St., 435/654-0251, http://spincafe.net, 11:30am-8:30pm Mon.-Thurs. 11:30am-9pm Fri.-Sat., 11:30am-8pm Sun., $12-22); the barbecue, burgers, and gelato are the specialties.

The **Snake Creek Grill** (650 W. 100 S., 435/654-2133, www.snakecreekgrill.com, 5:30-9:30pm Wed.-Sat., 5:30-8:30pm Sun., $14-25), housed in a historic Old Western wooden building and tucked behind a miniature Old West complex (which now includes a tattoo parlor), is about as upscale as it gets in Heber City, with surprisingly well-prepared trout, bison burgers, and pasta dishes, and a friendly atmosphere.

Take a drive over to the tiny town of Woodland for a breakfast biscuit sandwich or lunchtime burger at the **Woodland Biscuit Company** (2734 E UT 35, Woodland, 435/783-4202, www.woodlandbiscuitcompany.com, 8am-2pm Fri.-Tues., $9-14).

Midway

In a little strip mall in Midway, find ★ **Tarahumara** (380 E. Main St., 435/654-3465, www.tarahumararestaurant.com, 11am-9pm Mon.-Sat., $10-15), where the Mexican food is shockingly good; the salsa bar is a special treat. The dining room at the **Blue Boar Inn** (1235 Warm Springs Rd., 435/654-1400 or 888/650-1400, www.theblueboarinn.com, 8am-9pm daily, $30-39), which puts out elegant takes on European classic dishes, is also highly regarded.

The casual restaurant at the Homestead Resort is **Fanny's Grill** (700 N. Homestead Dr., 888/327-7220, 7am-2pm daily, $10-15), and it's a good enough place to get a bite to eat after a swim in the Homestead Crater. **Simon's** (5pm-9pm daily, $13-30) is the Homestead's dinner restaurant, with a Western atmosphere and a menu offering American-style comfort food such as fried chicken, beef pot roast, and apple donuts, all made from local ingredients, including

dairy products from the Heber Valley Creamery.

ACCOMMODATIONS

Heber City motels are generally well maintained and reasonably priced. A few miles west, in Midway, are several more expensive and luxurious resorts.

Heber City

The **Swiss Alps Inn** (167 S. Main St., 435/654-0722, www.swissalpsinn.com, $73-90) is a charming budget motel with an outdoor pool, a playground, and two suites with full kitchens.

The **Holiday Inn Express** (1268 S. Main St., 435/654-9990 or 800/315-2621, www.hiexpress.com, $101-114), on the southern edge of town, is a good choice for those who don't appreciate the quirks of small-town budget motels.

Midway

Undoubtedly the truly unique place to stay in the Heber City area is the **Homestead Resort** (700 N. Homestead Dr., 435/654-1102 or 800/327-7220, www.homesteadresort.com, $139-202). This hot spring resort is 3 miles (4.8 km) west of Heber City, near Midway, and features mineral baths, swimming, and accommodations. The natural hot spring water is believed to be good for the skin, and if the water alone doesn't do the trick, the resort's spa services can probably help. The spacious grounds and stately buildings of the Homestead may remind you of grandma's house, and the guest rooms themselves are country-style but comfortable.

Golfers can play at the resort's 18-hole course (18 holes $37-55) but should also note that excellent golf courses are right down the road at Wasatch Mountain State Park. Stables offer horseback riding, hayrides (sleigh rides in winter), and bicycle rentals. Guest rooms should be reserved well in advance, especially for summer weekends. The **Blue Boar Inn** (1235 Warm Springs

Rd., 435/654-1400 or 888/650-1400, www.theblueboarinn.com, $175-295) is near an entrance to Wasatch Mountain State Park and the park's popular golf course. Each of the inn's 12 meticulously decorated guest rooms is devoted to a different poet or author; there's also a very good restaurant and a cozy pub on-site.

The **Zermatt Resort** (784 W. Resort Dr., 435/657-0180 or 866/937-6288, www.zermattresort.com, $189-499) is an imposing Swiss-style lodge with restaurants, swimming pools, a spa, and its own travertine warm-spring plunge.

Sixteen miles (26 km) southeast of Heber City, **Daniels Summit Lodge** (U.S. 40, 435/548-2300 or 800/519-9969, www.danielssummit.com, $129-214) is located near the Strawberry Reservoir. This big country lodge offers plenty of activities, including horseback riding in the summer and snowmobiling in the winter. A restaurant is on-site, so you don't have to drive into town for dinner.

Campgrounds

Wasatch Mountain State Park (435/654-1791, http://stateparks.utah.gov, reservations 800/322-3770 or www.reserveamerica.com, day-use $10, campsites $14-28) has three campgrounds. The large Oak Hollow Campground (tents) and Mahogany Campground (RVs) are just north of the golf course (elev. 5,600 feet). Both have showers and hookups late April or early May-late October. Little Deer Creek Campground (water June-mid-Sept.) is a smaller and more secluded area set in an aspen forest. Groups often reserve all the sites; check with the park office first.

From Heber City, drive west 3 miles (4.8 km) to Midway, then follow signs north for 2 miles (3.2 km) to the main park entrance. Little Deer Creek Campground is reachable by driving a 7-mile (11.3-km) unpaved road to Cascade Springs, then turning north and going 4 miles (6.4 km) on another unpaved road.

Jordanelle State Park (http://stateparks.utah.gov) offers walk-in camping at the **Rock Cliff Recreation Area** (435/782-3030, day-use $10, camping $20-30), at the upper end of the east arm of the reservoir. Facilities include restrooms and hot showers, a nature center, boardwalks with interpretive displays, and pavilions for day use. **Hailstone Recreation Area** (435/649-9540 or 800/322-3770, www.reserveamerica.com, day-use $10, camping $20-30, cabins $70-85) is a large campground on Jordanelle Reservoir with restrooms and showers, day-use shaded pavilions, a marina with 80 boat slips, a general store, a laundry, and a small restaurant. Facilities include wheelchair access with raised tent platforms. Jordanelle State Park is east of U.S. 40, 6 miles (9.7 km) north of Heber City.

River's Edge at Deer Park (7000 N. Old Hwy. 40, 435/654-4049, http://riversedgeatdeerpark.com, year-round, tents $22, RVs $42, yurts $92, cabins $112-399), a private resort about 6 miles (9.7 km) north of Heber City, offers a variety of camping and cabin options just below the Jordanelle Reservoir dam.

Deer Creek State Park (Midway, 435/654-0171 or 800/322-3770, www.reserveamerica.com, day-use $10, camping $20-30) has a campground on the massive Deer Creek Reservoir just off U.S. 189; it is 10 miles (16 km) southwest of Heber City and 17 miles (27 km) northeast of Provo. Deer Creek State Park has many access points around the reservoir, including one with a swimming beach.

The U.S. Forest Service maintains four campgrounds at **Strawberry Reservoir** (435/548-2321, www.recreation.gov, late May-late Oct., $20-31), a popular trout-fishing destination. **Currant Creek Recreation Complex** (435/654-0470, www.recreation.gov, late May-late Oct., $20, plus $10 reservation fee) has a campground. **Currant Creek Nature Trail** begins from Loop D of the campground and climbs 400 vertical feet in a 1.25-mile loop. From Heber City, drive southeast for 42 miles (68 km) on U.S. 40 (past

Strawberry Reservoir), turn northwest onto Forest Road 083, and travel 19.5 miles (31 km) along Currant Creek.

INFORMATION AND SERVICES

The **Heber Valley Chamber of Commerce** (475 N. Main St., 435/654-3666, www. gohebervalley.com, 9am-5pm Mon.-Fri.) dispenses information on businesses in Heber City and Midway. **Heber Ranger District Office** (2460 S. U.S. 40, 435/654-0470, 8am-4:30pm Mon.-Fri.) manages the Uinta National Forest lands east and southeast of Heber City.

The **Heber Valley Hospital** (1485 S. U.S. 40, 435/654-2500) has 24-hour emergency care.

GETTING THERE

To reach Heber City, take I-80 (from about 25 miles/40 km east of Salt Lake City) to exit 146 and head 17 miles (27 km) south on U.S. 40. No public transportation serves this area.

Provo and Central Utah

Just two years after the founding of Salt Lake City, Mormon pioneers pushed south and began settling the Utah Valley area. Today its hub, Provo, is the state's third-largest city and home to bustling Brigham Young University. The university offers a number of excellent museums and a surprisingly diverse collection of paintings and sculpture at its Museum of Art. The attractive and historic city center provides a wide selection of restaurants in vintage storefronts.

The soaring Wasatch peaks offer abundant recreational opportunities, including hiking and fishing, as well as more unusual activities such as Timpanogos Cave National Monument, where guided tours lead deep into limestone chambers hung with dripping stalactites.

Highlights

Look for ★ to find recommended sights, activities, dining, and lodging.

★ **Springville Museum of Art:** Both the building and its collection make this small-town museum, a short drive from Provo, worth visiting. Between late April and early July, the Spring Salon shows off the work of contemporary Utah artists (page 161).

★ **Brigham Young University:** One of the largest church-affiliated schools in the world has several good museums scattered around its beautiful, sprawling campus (page 161).

★ **Timanogos Cave National Monument:** These three limestone caves reward visitors with branching helictites, icicle-like stalactites, rising stalagmites, and graceful flowstone formations in shades of green, yellow, red, and pure white (page 166).

★ **Sundance Resort:** Even if Sundance is out of your price range, it's worth a visit. The restaurants, shops, ski area, artist studios, and most other facilities are open to the public. Everything is tasteful, and to the extent possible, in accordance with nature (page 170).

★ **Topaz Museum and Camp:** Be prepared for exhibits, films, and artifacts that pack an emotional punch at this excellent community museum chronicling the internment of Japanese-Americans during World War II (page 177).

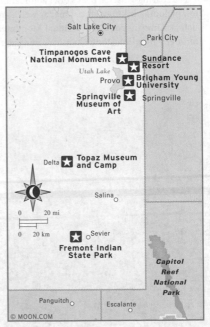

★ **Fremont Indian State Park:** More than 500 rock-art panels provide clues to the lives of the people who lived here some 3,000 years ago (page 181).

Sundance Resort—while much smaller than the Wasatch resorts to the north—the region's top skiing destination, is known for its high-end comforts, deep powder, art events, and celebrity visitors. At the region's southern edge, along I-70, Fremont Indian State Park preserves the remains of a millennium-old Fremont village that was once home to 1,000 residents.

Toward the Nevada border, smaller mountains and hills in west-central Utah form a transition to the basin and range terrain. Out here in the western deserts, remote mountain ranges offer stellar rock-hounding opportunities, and Utah's Wild West remains nearly as wild as ever. Rugged mountain ranges and barren desert valleys have always discouraged all but the most determined individuals. Explorers, pioneers in wagon trains, Pony Express riders, and telegraph linemen crossed this inhospitable

land with only the desire to reach the other side. It took the promise of gold and silver to lure large numbers of people into the jagged hills. Hardy ranchers still brave the isolation to grow hay and run their cattle and sheep.

PLANNING YOUR TIME

Unless you are planning extended stays in Provo or taking a leisurely exploration of the Alpine Scenic Drive and Mount Timpanogos, it's unlikely that you'll be spending much time in central Utah. But it is worth stopping into the small towns along I-15 as you travel between Salt Lake City and southern Utah, and Provo is a good place to spend a night or two. Back-road enthusiasts—many of them motorbikers—enjoy the remote ranch lands along the historic Pony Express trail from Fairfield to the Nevada border, a long day's journey into the desert.

Provo

Provo (pop. 122,000) has a striking setting on the shore of Utah Lake beneath the west face of the Wasatch Range. The city is best known as the home of Brigham Young University (BYU), a large, dynamic school sponsored by the Church of Jesus Christ of Latter-day Saints.

Provo also contains a rich architectural heritage. At the turn of the 20th century, this hard-working young city constructed its civic buildings with style and substance, and its residential areas are filled with Victorian mansions and vernacular workers' homes. The visitors center (utahvalley.com) can provide self-guided tour brochures that describe the city's historic architecture.

Provo boasts one of the most majestic views of any of the Wasatch Front cities along with easy access to the mountains, perhaps

contributing to the city's consistently high marks in many publications' livability ratings. Surprisingly enough, it's even gained a bit of hipster cred in the past few years, with a lively music scene (check out Velour Live Music Gallery, 135 N. University Ave., 801/818-2263, for shows or acoustic open mics).

SIGHTS
Provo Temples

The modern **Provo Utah Temple** (2200 N. Temple Hill Dr.) of white cast stone incorporates floral elements and a central golden spire. It's particularly impressive lit up against the sky at night. The dedication took place in 1972 with 75,000 people in attendance. Church members carry out sacred work within the 283 rooms. Visitors can't go inside but are welcome to visit the landscaped

Provo

To Block
Restaurant

← To Orem

To Salt Lake City

UNIVERSITY PKWY

STATE ST

COLUMBUS LN

89

TIMPVIEW DR

PROVO

2320 N

N TEMPLE DR

2230

2200 N

N

PROVO TEMPLE

189

● BAYMONT INN & SUITES

■ COUGAR STADIUM

TEMPLE VIEW DR

CANYON

● COURTYARD BY MARRIOTT

● SPRINGHALL SUITES PROVO

MARRIOTT CENTER ■

★ MONTE L. BEAN LIFE SCIENCE MUSEUM

CANYON RD

CAMPUS DR

★ BRIGHAM YOUNG UNIVERSITY

HERITAGE BIRCH LN

Wasatch Mtn State Park

★ TIMPANOGOS CAVE NATIONAL MONUMENT

To Salt Lake City

15

Cedar Fort

73

Mt. Timpanogos ▲ 11,750ft

★ SUNDANCE RESORT

40

Fairfield

Orem

○ Provo

★ BRIGHAM YOUNG UNIVERSITY

Utah Lake

○ Springville

Spanish Fork ○

★ SPRINGVILLE MUSEUM OF ART

68

Payson ○

Thistle

1230 N

PROVO RECREATION CENTER ■

To the "Y"

800 N
700 N
600 N

UNIVERSITY

★ MUSEUM OF PEOPLES AND CULTURES

N

North Park

500

400

900 W
800 W
700 W
600 W
500 W
400 W
300 W
200 W
100 W

300 W

▼ BOMBAY HOUSE

100 m
200 m
300 m
400 m
500 E
600 E
700 E
900 E

N
N
N

ST

1100 W
1000 W
100 W

GREYHOUND BUS ■

SEE DETAIL

N

CENTER

← To Utah Lake, Fort Utah, and Provo Municipal Airport

Pioneer Park ▲

100

HINES MANSION B&B ●

200 S

300

400

TEMPLE SITE ★

■ UTAH COUNTY TRAVEL COUNCIL (TOURIST INFO)

POST OFFICE

S

UNIVERSITY

AVE

PROVO MARRIOTT HOTEL

100 ●

■ UINTA NATIONAL FOREST SUPERVISOR

▼ COMMUNAL

BLACK SHEEP CAFE ▼

CENTER ST

100 W

▼ GURU'S

100 m

STATION 22 ▼

500 S

600 S

600 S

189

900 S

920 S

S

15

0   0.25 mi

0   0.25 km

© MOON.COM

EAST BAY GOLF COURSE

↓ To La Quinta and Sleep Inn

S STATE ST

89

To ★ SPRINGVILLE MUSEUM OF ART

grounds. Turn east onto 2230 North from University Avenue, or drive north on 900 East.

A second temple, **Provo City Center Temple** (100 S. University Ave.) stands at the corner of 100 South and University Avenue in downtown Provo, where the city's tabernacle stood until it was destroyed by fire in 2010. The new temple, completed in 2015, is much more traditional looking than the modern building near the university.

Utah Lake State Park

The largest body of freshwater completely within the state, Utah Lake is 24 miles (39 km) long and 11 miles (17.7 km) wide; its average depth is only 9.4 feet. It drains north into the Great Salt Lake. Mountains form the skyline in all directions. Swans, geese, pelicans, ducks, and other migratory birds stop by; the best bird-watching is at the south end of the lake and near the Provo Airport. **Utah Lake State Park** (4400 W. Center St., 801/375-0731, http://stateparks.utah.gov, day-use $10, camping with water and electric hookups $30, open about mid-March-October) provides recreational facilities on the east shore, just a short drive from downtown Provo. Visitors come for waterskiing, sailboarding, paddle boarding, and fishing; four paved boat ramps, docks, and slips are available.

Head west 4 miles (6.4 km) on Center Street from downtown Provo or take the I-15 exit for West Center Street and go west 3 miles (4.8 km).

Bridal Veil Falls

The two-tiered, 607-foot-tall Bridal Veil Falls is at the southern end of Provo Canyon, about 10 miles (16 km) from downtown Provo. Although you can see the falls from the pullout along U.S. 189, it's best to take the exit into the parking area and hike up a short paved path to the pool of water at the base. During the winter, this is a popular spot for ice climbing.

★ Springville Museum of Art

The **Springville Museum of Art** (126 E. 400 S., Springville, 801/489-2727, http://smofa.org, 10am-5pm Tues., 10am-9pm Wed., 10am-5pm Thurs.-Sat., free) started in the early 1900s as the collection of Springville High School, but when it began to receive gifts of major works from artists Cyrus Dallin and John Hafen, townspeople decided that a special building was needed. They built this fine Spanish-style structure during the Depression with federal and Mormon Church assistance. The town has become known as Art City for its patronage. The permanent collection contains 2,000 works, including some of the best by early Utah pioneers and Native Americans as well as the state's modern artists. Twenty-nine galleries display 15 exhibitions each year; there's also a sculpture garden. The annual **Spring Salon** (late Apr.-early July) is a major show of Utah contemporary artists. From Provo, drive 7 miles (11.3 km) south on U.S. 89 (S. State St.) or take I-15 exit 263 and head east.

★ BRIGHAM YOUNG UNIVERSITY

Brigham Young University (north of 800 North, between University Ave. and 900 East, 801/422-9020, www.byu.edu) had a modest beginning in 1875 as the Brigham Young Academy, established under the direction of Mormon Church president Brigham Young. Like the rest of Provo, BYU's population and size have grown dramatically in recent decades. BYU is one of the largest church-affiliated schools in the world. Students aren't required to be Mormons, but about 98 percent of the student body of some 30,000 does belong to the LDS Church. Everyone attending the school must follow a strict dress and grooming code—something you'll notice immediately on a stroll across the pretty campus. Almost all activities shut down for about an hour at 11am Tuesday for a university-wide devotional hour.

You're welcome to visit the more than 600 acres of BYU's vast campus. The expansive **Hinckley Alumni and Visitors Center** (435/422-3257, http://hinckleycenter.byu.edu, 9am-4pm Mon.-Fri.) provides literature and advice about things to see, events, and facilities open to the public.

Museum of Art

BYU is home to one of the largest university art museums in the West, the **BYU Museum of Art** (North Campus Dr., 801/422-8287, http://moa.byu.edu, 10am-6pm Tues., Wed., Sat., 10am-9pm Mon., Thurs., Fri., free except occasional special exhibits), with a collection of more than 17,000 works. On display are famous pieces, including Rembrandt's *Raising of Lazarus,* Gifford's *Lake Scene,* and Andy Warhol's *Marilyn.* The building itself is a work of art, with a polished granite exterior, hardwood floors, and high-ceilinged galleries bathed in natural light.

Monte L. Bean Life Science Museum

Mounted animals and dioramas realistically depict wildlife of Utah and distant lands at the **Life Science Museum** (645 E. 1430 N., 801/422-5051, http://mlbean.byu.edu, 10am-9pm Mon.-Fri., 10am-5pm Sat., free). The exhibits not only identify the many species on display, but also show how they interact within their environments. Special presentations include movies; talks; workshops; and live-reptile, animal-adaptation, and other demonstrations (check the website for a schedule).

Museum of Paleontology

The **Museum of Paleontology** (1683 N. Canyon Rd., 801/422-3680, http://geology.byu.edu/museum, 9am-5pm Mon.-Fri., free), across from Cougar Stadium, features excellent exhibits of dinosaurs and early mammals. BYU has a good program in paleontology, and students excavate bones from Utah and other western states. A viewing window lets you observe researchers cleaning and preparing bones.

Museum of Peoples and Cultures

Originally a place for the Department of Anthropology to stash its collections, the **Museum of Peoples and Cultures** (2201 N. Canyon Rd, 801/422-0020, http://mpc.byu.edu, 9am-5pm Mon. and Wed.- Fri., 9am-7pm Tues. Sept.-Apr., 9am-5pm Mon.-Fri. May-Aug., free) now has a broader collection that communicates knowledge about both modern and ancient peoples of the world. Exhibits reflect research in the Great Basin of Utah, the American Southwest, Mesoamerica, South America, the Near East, and Polynesia; one recent exhibit explored the textiles of the ancient Andes.

RECREATION

Most of Provo's recreation hot spots are northeast of town in the mountains. In town, join BYU students on a hike to the big Y on the side of (naturally) Y Mountain. The steep but not-too-difficult 2.4-mile trip will reward hikers with good views of the valley and town. The trailhead is east of the BYU campus. Take 900 East north and turn right onto 820 North, which becomes Oakmont Lane; turn right onto Oakcliff Drive, right again onto Terrace Drive, which will take you to Y Mountain Trailhead Road.

Two-hour **rafting** trips down the Provo River Canyon ($50 adults, $32 under age 13) and four-hour trips down the Weber River ($95 adults, $73 under age 13) are offered by **High Country Adventure** (801/224-2500, www.highcountryadventure.com, late Apr.-Oct.).

FOOD

Downtown Provo has a pretty good restaurant row along Center Street, on both sides of University Avenue. This is an attractive part of town, with turn-of-the-20th-century storefronts and a shady median that makes the area parklike. It's easy and pleasant just to wander down the street and select a place. There are quite a number of international-cuisine choices, thanks to the university

1: the entrance to Timpanogos Cave; 2: water in the Timpanogos Cave; 3: Provo Utah Temple

crowd; within a few blocks you'll find Italian, Chinese, Peruvian, Salvadoran, and Korean restaurants.

Near the busy intersection of Center Street and University Avenue, find the casual and almost-hip (in a yoga sort of way) **Guru's** (45 E. Center St., 801/377-6980, http://guruscafe. com, 8am-9pm Mon.-Tues., 8am-10pm Wed.-Sat., $8-13), which serves good pasta, rice bowls, wraps, pizzas, and salads. It's also a reliable place for breakfast.

★ **Black Sheep Cafe** (19 N. University Ave., 801/607-2485, www.blacksheepcafe.com, 11:30am-2:30pm and 5pm-9pm Mon.-Fri., 11:30am-2:30pm and 5pm-10pm Fri., noon-3pm and 5pm-10pm Sat., 11am-3pm Sun. in summer, $18-22) serves creative takes on Native American dishes such as Navajo tacos and Southwestern specialties such as posole in a tidy modern dining room, where you can also chat with a jeweler selling his beautiful silver-and-turquoise jewelry.

On the west side of Center Street, **Station 22** (22 W. Center St., 801/607-1803, http://station22cafe.com, 11am-10pm Mon.-Sat., $10-15) is an American roots restaurant, serving hearty comfort food from across the country. Choices range from burgers (including one named for Jack Kerouac) to shrimp and grits, and on to chicken and waffles and poutine. No alcohol, but a large "craft soda" menu features good homemade root beer as well as birch beer, sasparilla, and cream sodas.

North of Center Street on University Avenue is **Bombay House** (463 N. University Ave., 801/373-6677, www.bombayhouse.com, 4pm-10pm Mon.-Sat., $10-18), the city's top choice for Indian food, with excellent tandoori specialties.

A particularly stylish and delicious downtown restaurant is ★ **Communal** (100 N. University Ave., 801/373-8000, www. communalrestaurant.com, 5pm-10pm Mon., 11:30am-2pm and 5pm-10pm Tues.-Fri., 9am-2pm and 5pm-10pm Sat., $33-36), where food is locally sourced (farmers share the spotlight with the chefs) and diners have the option of sharing the large central table (there are also

a few smaller tables). Settle in, get to know your neighbors, and enjoy an order of house-smoked pork shoulder with coleslaw and watermelon. Sides ($8-13) are extra; it's possible to make a meal with an appetizer (perhaps a fennel tart with tomato jam) and a couple of sides.

For more farm-to-table food, head north to Orem, where **Pizzeria Seven Twelve** (320 S. State St., Orem, 801/623-6712, 11:30am-2:30pm and 5pm-10pm Mon.-Fri., 5pm-10pm Sat., $10-16) pulls delicious, seasonally inspired pizzas from a wood-fired oven purportedly heated to 712°F.

Although Sunday brunch can be hard to come by in Provo, **Block Restaurant** (3330 N. University Ave., Provo, 801-885-7558, block-restaurantgroup.com, 11:30am-2pm and 5pm-10pm Mon.-Fri., 10:30am-2pm and 5pm-10pm Sat., 10:30am-2pm Sun., brunch $9-15, dinner $15-36) has it covered with a tasty (and quite rich) avocado Benedict. Dinners, such as trout with celeriac-leek puree, are similarly well prepared with lots of local ingredients. You can even get an alcoholic beverage with your brunch (or dinner) here.

ACCOMMODATIONS

Most of Provo's accommodations are chain motels along South University Avenue, the long commercial strip that runs from I-15 exit 266 to downtown. The downtown area offers older but well-maintained properties. If you're concerned more with price than amenities, look for a string of budget motels at the south end of town.

Tucked just off University Avenue, the **Sleep Inn** (1505 S. 40 E., 801/377-6597, www.sleepinnprovo.com, $97-115) is a good bet and fairly convenient to downtown. Pets are permitted, there's a small pool and an exercise room, and guest rooms have fridges and microwaves.

Just a few miles north of Provo, a **La Quinta** (1100 W. 780 N., Orem, 801/235-9555, $119-129) is right off I-15 and makes a good jumping-off point for trips up Provo Canyon. The **Provo Marriott Hotel** (101 W. 100

N., 801/377-4700, $166-219), in the heart of downtown, is an upscale business and conference hotel. Guest rooms are nicely appointed, and they come with fridges and coffeemakers; facilities include a pool, a spa, and a weight room. Another good choice, north of downtown and close to the university (Freedom Blvd. is the same as 200 West), is the **Courtyard Marriott** (1600 N. Freedom Blvd., 801/373-2222, $136). **SpringHill Suites Provo** (1580 N. Freedom Blvd., 801/373-0073, $166), another Marriott property near the university, has large, nicely furnished guest rooms, an indoor pool, and an on-site restaurant.

The **Baymont Inn & Suites Provo River** (2230 N. University Pkwy., 801/921-5071, www.baymontinns.com, $107-149) has a great setting near the Provo River, with access to biking and walking paths; it has an indoor pool and large guest rooms.

Although Provo's hotels are fine places to stay, if you want to get away from the chains, consider booking a room at the **Hines Mansion B&B** (383 W. 100 S., 801/374-8400, www.hinesmansion.com, $165-225). The decor of the nine guest rooms ranges from a sweet Victorian theme to a Western lodge style; the "Library" room even has a secret passage. Although the B&B is within walking distance of downtown restaurants, it's not in a particularly charming neighborhood.

Campgrounds

The **Lakeshore Campground** (800/322-3770, www.reserveamerica.com, mid-Mar.-Oct., $30 plus $9 reservation fee) at **Utah Lake State Park** has water and showers.

Lakeside RV Campground (4000 W. Center St., 801/373-5267, www.lakesidervcampground.com, year-round, tents $27, RVs $39-42), just before Utah Lake State Park, has showers, a pool, laundry, and a store; tent campers can't have dogs.

INFORMATION AND SERVICES

Utah Valley Convention and Visitors Bureau (220 W. Center St., 801/851-2100 or 800/222-8824, www.utahvalley.org) offers advice on sights and services in Provo and the Utah Valley.

There is a **post office** (95 W. 100 S., 801/275-8777), and medical treatment is available at **Utah Valley Regional Medical Center** (1034 N. 500 W., 801/373-7850).

GETTING THERE

Allegiant Airlines (702/505-8888, www.allegiantair.com) offers flights between the Provo airport (PVU, 5 miles/8 km west of downtown) and Los Angeles and Phoenix. **Enterprise** (801/331-7700) and **Hertz** (801/438-4528) rent cars at the airport.

Utah Transit Authority (UTA) (801/375-4636, www.rideuta.com) provides local bus service in Provo and connects with Springville, Salt Lake City, Ogden, and other towns; buses don't run on Sunday in Provo. **Greyhound** (70 W. 750 S., 801/231-2222, www.greyhound.com) has two northbound and two southbound bus departures daily. **Amtrak** (300 W. 600 S., 800/872-7245, www.amtrak.com) runs the Chicago-Oakland *California Zephyr* train via Provo once daily in each direction.

North of Provo

Along the I-15 corridor between Provo and Salt Lake City are a few sights ranging from the individual and quirky Hutchings Museum to the huge Thanksgiving Point enterprise. The natural areas north of Provo could easily fill a couple days' worth of exploration, but they're also pretty easy to reach from town.

★ TIMPANOGOS CAVE NATIONAL MONUMENT

Beautiful cave formations reward visitors who hike the trail to the entrance of **Timpanogos Cave** (801/75-5239, www.nps.gov/tica, 7am-3pm daily mid-May-Labor Day, cave tours $8 adults, $6 ages 6-15, $4 ages 3-5) on the north side of Mount Timpanogos. Tunnels connect three separate limestone caves, each of which has a different character. The first cave was discovered by Martin Hansen in 1887 while he was tracking a mountain lion. Middle and Timpanogos Caves weren't publicly reported until 1921-1922. Timpanogos Cave so impressed early explorers that a trail, lighting, and national monument protection came soon afterward.

Exhibits and a short slide show presented in the visitors center introduce the formation, history, and ecology of the caves. Be sure to obtain tickets here for the cave tour before starting up the trail.

Allow about 3-4 hours for the complete trip, including 45-60 minutes for the cave tour. The three-mile round-trip hike from the visitors center to the caves is moderately difficult, even though the path is paved; you'll climb 1,065 vertical feet to an elevation of 6,730 feet. Points along the way have fine views up and down American Fork Canyon and out onto the Utah Valley. People with breathing, heart, or walking difficulties shouldn't attempt the trail; wheeled vehicles (including strollers) and pets aren't allowed.

Ranger-led tours start at the end of the hiking trail and wind about 0.3 mile through the caves. The underground temperature is about 45°F all year, so bring a sweater or jacket. The season lasts mid-May-Labor Day; the caves close fall through spring because snow and ice make the trail too hazardous. Tours are very popular; it's a good idea to purchase tickets in advance (877/444-6777, www. recreation.gov, up to 30 days in advance).

If you want to learn more about caving, sign up for an **Introduction to Caving tour** (877/444-6777, www.recreation.gov, 9:30am daily, $16 over age 14, reservations required). These tours are limited to five spelunkers, who can expect to do some scrambling and crawling. In addition to regular hiking clothing, bring clean leather gloves and close-toed hiking boots. Although the tour itself lasts 1.5 hours, plan to spend about 4 hours to complete both the tour and the hike required to get to the starting point.

A snack bar at the visitors center is open in summer. Picnickers can use tables across the road from the visitors center and at a site 0.25 mile west. The visitors center is 2 miles (3.2 km) up American Fork Canyon on the Alpine Scenic Loop (Hwy. 92); to continue along this route and into Forest Service land up American Fork Canyon requires a $6 (for 3 days) pass, but if you're only going to Timpanogos Cave, you do not need to buy a pass.

You can take I-15 exit 279 for American Fork if you're coming north from Provo or I-15 exit 287 for Alpine if you're coming south from Salt Lake City.

ALPINE SCENIC LOOP

This very narrow paved highway twists and winds through some of the most beautiful alpine terrain in Utah. Mount Timpanogos rises to 11,750 feet in the center of the loop and presents sheer cliff faces and jagged ridges in every direction. More than a dozen

North of Provo

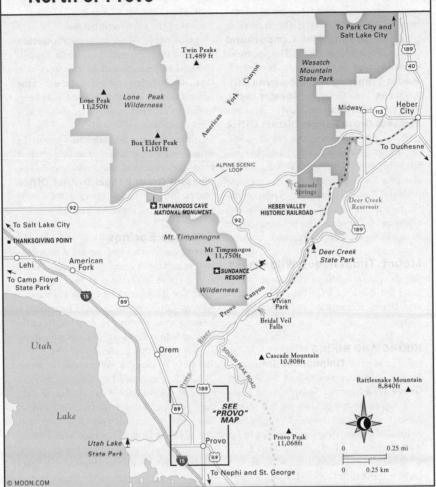

campgrounds and several picnic areas line the way. In order to stop and hike, fish, picnic, or camp, visitors must purchase a recreation pass for the area ($6 per vehicle for 3 days; buy pass at entrance to American Fork Canyon or at self-service locations along the route).

Anglers can try for trout in swift, clear streams. Autumn brings brilliant gold to the aspens and scarlet to the maples. Winter snows close the loop at its higher elevations and attract skiers to Sundance Resort. The most scenic sections of the loop are along American Fork Canyon and its South Fork, Provo Canyon and its North Fork, and on the high pass between these drainages. A drive on U.S. 89 or I-15 completes the approximately 40-mile loop. With a few stops, a full day can easily be spent on the drive. If you'd like to see Timpanogos Cave on the way, begin the loop from the north to avoid waiting in ticket lines, especially on weekend afternoons.

Most of the picnic areas and campgrounds

(801/785-3563 or 877/444-6777, www. recreation.gov, all have water, $24) are along American Fork Canyon at elevations of 5,400-6,200 feet. Higher recreation areas are **Granite Flat Campground** (elev. 6,800 feet, June-Sept.), **Timpooneke Campground** (elev. 7,400 feet, June-Oct.), **Mount Timpanogos Campground** (elev. 6,800 feet, June-Oct.), and **Theater in the Pines Picnic Area** (elev. 6,800 feet). The **Pleasant Grove Ranger District Office** (390 N. 100 E., Pleasant Grove, 801/785-3563) of the Uinta-Wasatch-Cache National Forest has information and maps for recreation areas along the Alpine Scenic Loop and for the Lone Peak and Mount Timpanogos Wildernesses. (You'll pass the office if you take U.S. 89 and Highway 146 between Provo or Orem and the mouth of American Fork Canyon.)

Mount Timpanogos Wilderness

The sheer cliffs of Mount Timpanogos tower 7,000 feet above the Utah Valley and present one of the most dramatic sights of the Wasatch Range.

HIKING AND BIKING

Hike either the **Timpooneke Trail** from Timpooneke Campground or the **Aspen Grove Trail** from the Theater in the Pines Picnic Area; both trailheads are just off the Alpine Scenic Loop. One-way distances to the summit of Mount Timpanogos are 9.1 miles (14.6 km) on the Timpooneke Trail (with 4,350 feet of elevation gain) and 8.3 miles (13.3 km) on the Aspen Grove Trail (with 4,900 feet of elevation gain). A hike on both trails (highly recommended for ambitious hikers) can be done with a car shuttle.

If a trip to the summit sounds too ambitious, hike the mile-long paved trail from on the Aspen Grove Trail to a waterfall. It's a little less than 5 miles (8 km) along the same trail to some mountain lakes, including **Emerald Lake**. The **Summit Trail** branches off west

of Emerald Lake, climbs a steep slope to the jagged summit ridge, then follows the ridge southeast to the top. The deep blue waters of Emerald Lake are directly below.

At the Aspen Grove trailhead, **mountain bikers** can grunt uphill on trails, though some bikers prefer to stick to the road, which is often quite lightly traveled. Just north of the turnoff for Cascade Springs, the Alpine Loop Summit Trailhead provides access to a network of mountain bike trails.

Hiking season is mid-July-mid-October. In winter and spring, hikers must be equipped for and experienced with snow travel. The **Pleasant Grove Ranger District Office** (390 N. 100 E., Pleasant Grove, 801/785-3563) can provide advice on hiking conditions.

Cascade Springs

Crystal-clear water emerges amid lush vegetation and flows down a long series of travertine-specked terraces at this beautiful spot. The springs produce more than seven million gallons of water daily. Boardwalks (some accessible for people with disabilities) and short trails with interpretive signs allow a close look at the stream and pools. Trout can be seen darting through the water (fishing is prohibited). Flora includes maples, oaks, aspens, willows, water birches, box elders, cattails, watercress, and wildflowers. The drive to Cascade Springs is also very pretty, either from the Alpine Scenic Loop or from Heber Valley. A paved road (Forest Rd. 114) branches off the Alpine Scenic Loop near its summit (between mileposts 18 and 19) and winds northeast 7 miles (11.3 km) to the springs. An unpaved road, passable by car if the road is dry, begins on the west edge of Heber Valley and climbs high above the valley, offering good views, and then drops down to the springs; turn west and go 7 miles (11.3 km) on Highway 220 from Highway 113 (between Midway and Charleston) and follow the signs.

1: Alpine Scenic Loop; **2:** Mount Timpanogos; **3:** Cascade Springs; **4:** Sundance Resort

★ **Sundance Resort**

Since actor/director Robert Redford purchased this land in 1969, he has worked toward obtaining an ideal blend of recreation, the arts, and natural beauty. **Sundance** (8841 N. Alpine Loop Rd., 866/259-7468, lodging reservations 800/892-1600, www.sundanceresort.com) sponsors a wide selection of summer arts and music events; workshops, exhibits, and artist residencies provide an intense artistic focus to this remote mountain Eden. Redford also founded the **Sundance Institute** in 1980 as a laboratory for independent filmmakers; the actual Sundance Film Festival is centered in Park City.

DOWNHILL SKIING

Downhill skiing (801/223-4849, mid-Dec.-Apr.) is pretty relaxed at Sundance. The resort's four lifts take skiers high on the southeast slopes of Mount Timpanogos. The 45 runs on 5,000 acres provide challenges for people of all abilities; total vertical drop is 2,150 feet. Ski instruction, rentals, accommodations, restaurants, and packages are available at the resort. On weekends, adult **lift tickets** cost $80 for a full day, $70 half-day; children under age 13 ski for $53 full-day, $49 half-day; seniors pay $30. Prices jump $10 during winter holidays. Night skiing runs 4:30pm-9pm Monday, Wednesday, and Friday-Saturday; night-only lift tickets are $40 adults, $31 children, and $20 seniors.

Sundance Nordic Center (801/223-4170, $18 adults, $9 ages 11-17, free seniors 65 and up) offers more than 10 miles (16km) of Nordic track, lessons, and rentals. About once a month, guides lead a "night-owling" snowshoe hike (reservations required, $45), which begins at 6:30pm and offers a chance to call owls. Full moon tours are also available.

SUMMER ACTIVITIES

Sundance is at least as busy in the summer as in the winter, with activities ranging from the mellow (scenic lift rides $20 adults, $18 children, $17 seniors) to the vigorous (mountain biking $28 with lift access). The Provo River is a great fly-fishing destination, and the resort can set you up with a guide. Horseback rides, river rafting, and hiking are also easy to arrange.

But Sundance's art programs are what make the resort really stand out. The **Art Studio** is the site of daily workshops in drawing and painting, pottery, jewelry making, printmaking, and photography ($95 per class, $65 for kids' classes). A glassblower's studio offers visitors a chance to watch (and buy) but not do.

SUNDANCE ZIPTOUR

The **Sundance ZipTour** is the third longest in the United States, with nearly 2 miles (3.2 km) of linked ziplines. With over 2,100 feet of vertical drop, it's also the steepest of any zipline tour in the United States. With two parallel lines, you'll be able to ride side-by-side with an equally terrified friend at speeds up to 65 miles (105 km) per hour. The basic tours cost $69-99, though check the website for full moon, sunrise, and other specialty tours.

FOOD AND ACCOMMODATIONS

Guest rooms are beautifully decorated; if you've ever received the Sundance catalog, you'll know the sort of high-Western romantic furnishings to expect. Standard guest rooms run $278-358; also available are studios, suites, and multi-bedroom houses. The resort's on-site spa books appointments 9am-9pm Mon.-Sat., 9am-7pm Sun.

Sundance has three dining facilities in the main compound, including the **Foundry Grill** (866/932-2295, 7am-11am, 11:30am-4pm, and 5pm-9pm Mon.-Thurs., 7am-11am, 11:30am-4pm, and 5pm-10pm Fri.-Sat., 9am-2pm and 5pm-9:30pm Sun., dinner entrées $24-44), the elegant and highly recommended ★ **Tree Room** (866/627-8313, 5pm-9pm Tues.-Thurs., 5pm-10pm Fri.-Sat., $32-56), and a deli. The actual bar at the **Owl Bar**

(801/223-4222, 4pm-11pm Mon.-Thurs., 4pm-1am Fri., noon-1am Sat., noon-11pm Sun.) was moved from Thermopolis, Wyoming; it's from the Rosewood Bar, once frequented by the Hole-in-the-Wall Gang.

GETTING THERE
Sundance Resort can easily be reached by taking U.S. 189 from Provo, Orem, or Heber City. Turn northwest and go 2.5 miles (4 km) on Highway 92 (Alpine Scenic Loop).

West Along the Pony Express Route

Follow roads west from Lehi to encounter the deserts of central Utah. Admittedly, there's not much out here in this remote, barren landscape, but for a brief number of years these marginal ranch lands thundered to the hooves of the Pony Express. Fans of end-of-the-road experiences will treasure the opportunity to see the outback in all its dusty glory.

LEHI
While the old ranch community of Lehi is now mostly swallowed by Wasatch Front suburbs, it's distinguished by an outstanding natural history museum and the all-things-to-all-people entertainment center at Thanksgiving Point. It's also the gateway to frontier lore to the west, where Pony Express history is told in historic inns and way stations. From here, you can travel desert back roads along the route of the old Pony Express riders between Fairfield and the Utah border at Ibapah.

John Hutchings Museum of Natural History
The diverse collection at the **John Hutchings Museum of Natural History** (55 N. Center St., 801/768-7631, https://hutchingsmuseum. education, 11am-5pm Tues.-Sat., $4 adults, $3 seniors and ages 3-12) in the town of Lehi, 16 miles (26 km) northwest of Provo on I-15, began as a family museum. Highlights include pioneer rifles, Native American crafts, glittering minerals, ancient fossils, mounted birds of Utah, and colorful tropical shells. It's a popular place for school field trips, and has plenty of hands-on activities for kids.

Thanksgiving Point
A vast park and education-entertainment center, **Thanksgiving Point** (801/768-2300 or 888/672-6040, www.thanksgivingpoint. com, 10am-8pm Mon.-Sat. for most exhibits, fees vary but a $35 adult, $25 child pass gets you into the four main attractions), between Utah Lake and I-15, contains everything from incredible gardens, a business park, a golf course, a formal garden, and a paleontology museum to a petting zoo, plus loads of dining and shopping. Highlights of the park, which is the brainchild of the creators of WordPerfect software, include **Museum of Natural Curiosity** ($20 adults, $15 seniors and ages 3-12), a science museum filled with interactive exhibits (where else can you explore the inside of a giant monkey head?); **Farm Country** ($10 above age 2), a farm and petting zoo, complete with wagon rides and lots of tame animals doing what comes naturally; **Ashton Gardens** ($20 adults, $15 seniors and ages 3-12), containing 55 acres of formal gardens, plus a "waterfall amphitheater"; and the **Museum of Ancient Life** ($20 adults, $15 seniors and ages 3-12), which claims to be the largest dinosaur museum in the world.

There's also a 200-acre, 7,714-yard **18-hole golf course** and a **megaplex theatre**. The **Village at Thanksgiving Point** offers six restaurants and dining halls and almost a dozen shops and stores. More than one million people visit each year, including tens of thousands of kids on school field trips.

Thanksgiving Point will either really appeal to you as a one-stop vacation wonderland or send you screaming in search

History of the Pony Express

In 1860, Pony Express officials put together a chain of stations between St. Joseph, Missouri, and Sacramento, California. Relays of frontier-toughened riders covered the 1,838-mile distance in 10 days. Riders stopped at stations spaced about 12 miles (19.3 km) apart to change horses. Only after changing horses about six times did the rider complete a day's work. Despite the hazards of frontier travel, only one mail pouch was ever lost, and Native American conflicts held up service for only a single month. Historians credit the daring enterprise with providing communications vital to keeping California aligned with the Union during the Civil War and proving that the West could be crossed in all kinds of weather—thus convincing skeptical politicians that a transcontinental railroad could be built. The Pony Express operated for only 18 months; completion of the transcontinental telegraph in October 1861 put the riders out of work. The Pony Express company, which received no government assistance, failed to make a profit for its owners.

of noncommercial, unpackaged pastimes. However, one very good reason to make the stop is to visit the **Museum of Ancient Life**. With more than 122,000 square feet of exhibition space, this museum contains 60 complete dinosaur skeletons, dozens of hands-on displays, research facilities, and a six-story IMAX theater. Most of the featured dinosaurs represent species that once strode across the alluvial sands of ancient Utah, including the first-ever displayed skeleton of a *Supersaurus,* supersize at 110 feet long.

The Thanksgiving Point compound is just west of I-15 exit 287. Admission rates are a complex system of individual and combo tickets; check out the options on the website.

FAIRFIELD
Camp Floyd Stagecoach Inn State Park

A restored inn, an old U.S. Army building, and a military cemetery preserve a bit of pioneer history at **Camp Floyd** (18035 W. 1540 N., Fairfield, 801/768-8932, http://stateparks. utah.gov, 9am-5pm Mon.-Sat., $3 pp, $9 family) in Fairfield, a sleepy village on the other side of Utah Lake from Provo. John Carson, who had been one of the first settlers of the site in 1855, built a family residence and hotel three years later. About the same time, troops of the U.S. Army under Colonel Albert Johnston marched in and established Camp

Floyd nearby. The soldiers had been sent by President Buchanan to put down a rumored Mormon rebellion. Finding that no "Mormon War" existed, the colonel led his men to this site so as not to intimidate the major Mormon settlements. Fairfield jumped in size almost overnight to become Utah's third-largest city, with a population of about 7,000 (including the 3,000 soldiers). Even for the times, it was rowdy—17 saloons served the army men. The camp, later named Fort Crittenden, served no real purpose, however, and it was abandoned in 1861 so that troops could return east to fight in the Civil War.

Carson's hotel, later known as the Stagecoach Inn, continued to serve travelers on the dusty main road across Utah. Pony Express riders, stagecoach passengers, miners, sheepherders, and every other kind of traveler stopped here for the night until the doors closed in 1947. Now the inn is a state park, furnished as in the old days and full of exhibits on frontier life. A shaded picnic area is beside it. The only surviving building of Camp Floyd has been moved across the street to serve as the visitors center; it contains a diorama of the fort and some excavated artifacts. Camp Floyd's well-kept cemetery is a 0.75-mile drive west and south of Fairfield. From Provo or Salt Lake City, take I-15 to Lehi, turn west, and go 21 miles (34 km) on Highway 73.

PONY EXPRESS AND STAGE ROUTE

Relive some of the Old West by driving the Pony Express **National Historic Trail** (801/741-1012, www.nps.gov/poex, no fee) across western Utah. The scenic route goes from spring to spring as it winds through several small mountain ranges and across open plains, skirting the worst of the Great Salt Lake Desert. Interpretive signs and monuments along the way describe how the Pony Express riders swiftly brought the country closer together. The 140 miles (225 km) between Fairfield in the east and Ibapah near the Nevada border provide a sense of history and appreciation for the land lost to motorists speeding along I-80.

Allow at least a full day for the 241-mile drive and bring food, water, and a full tank of gas. The Bureau of Land Management (BLM) has campgrounds at Simpson Springs and south of Callao. No motels or restaurants line the road, and the best bets for gas are Tooele, near the eastern edge of the route, and Wendover, about 50 miles (81 km) north of Ibapah. You can travel the well-graded gravel and dirt roads on this route by car, although a 4WD vehicle with decent clearance will make the trip much more enjoyable; watch for the

usual backcountry hazards of wildlife, rocks, ruts, and washouts. Cell phone coverage is spotty along the route.

You can begin your trip on the historic route from the Stagecoach Inn at Fairfield; this is where the pavement stops! You can also begin at Faust Junction, 30 miles (48 km) south of Tooele on Highway 36, or Ibapah, 51 miles (82 km) south of Wendover off U.S. 93A. The BLM has an information kiosk and small picnic area 1.8 miles (2.9 km) west of Faust Junction. For the latest road conditions and travel information, contact the **BLM Salt Lake District Office** (2370 S. 2300 W., Salt Lake City, 801/977-4300). The following are points of interest along the route.

Simpson Springs

Native Americans had long used these excellent springs before the first nonnatives came through. The name honors Captain J. H. Simpson, who stopped here in 1859 while leading an army survey across western Utah and Nevada. At about the same time, George Chorpenning built a mail station here, which was later used by the Pony Express and Overland Express companies. A reconstructed stone cabin on the old site shows what the station looked like. Ruins of a nearby cabin built

Boyd Pony Express Station

Crossing the Great Basin Desert

Imposing terrain and a scarcity of water discouraged early explorers from crossing the Great Basin region. In 1776, the Spanish became the first nonnatives to visit west-central Utah, when members of the Dominguez-Escalante Expedition left the Utah Lake area and headed southwest, passing near the present-day towns of Delta and Milford.

Most American mountain men of the 1820s also kept to the Great Basin's edge—but not Jedediah Smith. With a party of 17 men, Smith set out in 1826 from northern Utah for Spanish California, searching for new fur-trapping areas. When Smith returned to Utah with two companions, the little group nearly perished in deep snows in the Sierra Nevada and from thirst in the desert.

Government explorer John C. Frémont named and made the first scientific studies of the Great Basin in 1845, putting to rest myths about the Great Salt Lake's monsters, whirlpools, and subterranean outlets to the Pacific.

In the following year, travelers began crossing the Great Basin as a shortcut to California. Horses and mules made the crossing safely, but the Donner-Reed wagon train met with disaster. Mud in the Great Salt Lake Desert slowed the group so much that they ran out of water and lost some of their wagons and oxen. The exhausted and demoralized group reached the Sierra Nevada late in the season, when snowstorms trapped and killed 40 of the 87 emigrants.

In 1859, Captain J. S. Simpson surveyed a military road to the south of the treacherous desert to connect Camp Floyd in central Utah with Carson Valley in western Nevada. Swift riders of the Pony Express used the road, known as the South-Central Overland Route, in 1860-1861, before the telegraph ended this brief chapter of American history. The Lincoln Highway, the country's first designated transcontinental motoring route, included part of this road from 1910 to 1927.

in 1893 contain stones from the first station. The **BLM campground** (nonpotable water, $5) higher up on the hillside has good views across the desert. Simpson Springs is 25 miles (40 km) west of Faust Junction and 67 miles (108 km) east of Callao.

Fish Springs National Wildlife Refuge

The Pony Express station once located here no longer exists, but you can visit the 10,000 acres of marsh and lake of **Fish Springs National Wildlife Refuge** (435/831-5353, www.fws.gov/fishspringsfree), which attracts abundant birdlife and wildlife. Waterfowl and marsh birds stop here in greatest numbers during their early spring and late autumn migrations. Many smaller birds nest here in late spring and early summer. A self-guided auto tour makes an 11.5-mile loop through the heart of the refuge. The refuge is 42 miles (68 km) west of Simpson Springs and 25 miles (40 km) east of Callao.

Boyd Pony Express Station

Portions of the Pony Express station's original rock wall remain, and signs give the history of the station and the Pony Express. Find the station 13 miles (21 km) west of Fish Springs and 12 miles (19.3 km) east of Callao.

Callao

This cluster of ranches dates from 1859, when several families decided to take advantage of the desert grasslands and good springs here. Local people believe that the Willow Springs Pony Express Station site was located off the main road at Bagley Ranch, but a BLM archaeologist contends that the foundation is on the east side of town. Callao is 67 miles (108 km) west of Simpson Springs and 28 miles (45 km) east of Ibapah (via the Pony Express and Stage Routes). A **BLM campground** (no water, free) at the site of a former CCC camp is 4 miles (6.4 km) south of town, beside Toms Creek.

Canyon Station

The original station used by Pony Express riders was in Overland Canyon northwest of Canyon Station. Native Americans attacked in July 1863, burned the first station, and killed the Overland agent and four soldiers. The new station was built on a more defensible site. You can see its foundation and the remnants of a fortification. A signed fork at Clifton Flat points the way to Gold Hill, a photogenic ghost town 6 miles (9.7 km) distant. Canyon Station is north of the Deep Creek Range, 13 miles (21 km) northwest of Callao and 15 miles (24 km) northeast of Ibapah. To reach Canyon Station, follow the signs for Sixmile Ranch, Overland Canyon, and Clifton Flat between Callao and Ibapah.

Ibapah

The tiny settlement of Ibapah ("EYE-buh-paw") is a few miles east of the Nevada state line and north of the Goshute Reservation. From Ibapah you can go north to Gold Hill ghost town (14 miles/22.5 km) and Wendover (58 miles/93 km) or south to U.S. 50/6 near Great Basin National Park via Callao, Trout Creek, and Gandy (90 miles/145 km). The Deep Creek Pony Express Station was 1.5 miles (2.4 km) south of Ibapah on a well-signed gravel road.

Pronounce *Ibapah* to avoid sounding like an outsider. Ibapah is about the same size as Callao and little more than a group of some 20 houses.

South of Provo

Although the I-15 corridor is not particularly exciting, this part of central Utah offers a few historic curiosities from the days of Mormon settlement. Out in the western deserts near Delta there's also excellent rockhounding. The small towns just off the freeway also provide basic lodging and restaurants and can be welcome oases amid this long stretch of forlorn ranch land.

Cove Fort is at the intersection of I-15 and I-70. Here, I-70 cuts east toward Green River and on to Denver, passing Fremont Indian State Park and the beautiful San Rafael Swell along the way. Following this route out of Provo is also a convenient way to reach Arches and Canyonlands National Parks.

SOUTH ALONG I-15

Nephi

The small town of Nephi (pop. 5,600) serves as the commercial center for this region and is the seat of Juab County. The first settlers arrived in 1851 and named the place for a patriarch in the Book of Mormon. Pleasant scents fill the air at the **Nephi Rose Garden**, one block east of Main Street on 100 North. North of Nephi, in Mona, you'll notice fields of lavender. These are part of **Young Living Family Farm** (www.youngliving.com), which grows and distills herbs for essential oils (that's the distillery mentioned on the roadside sign). Young Living, a multi-level marketing company, has lavender farms in the United States, France, and Ecuador and is the world's largest distiller of essential oils.

FOOD

Don't expect high-end food in Nephi; the best local restaurants specialize in country cooking. The longtime local standby is **J. C. Mickelson's Restaurant** (2100 S. Main St., 435/623-0152, www.jcmick.com, 7am-9pm daily, $10-20) at I-15 exit 222, serving pretty basic American-style home cooking with decor accented by a big model train set. Another good spot for burgers, chicken-fried steak, or omelets is **Lisa's Country Kitchen** (735 S. Main St., 435/623-7000, 7am-9pm Mon.-Sat., $7-18), a down-home diner with a friendly atmosphere and a big stone fireplace in the dining area.

South of Provo

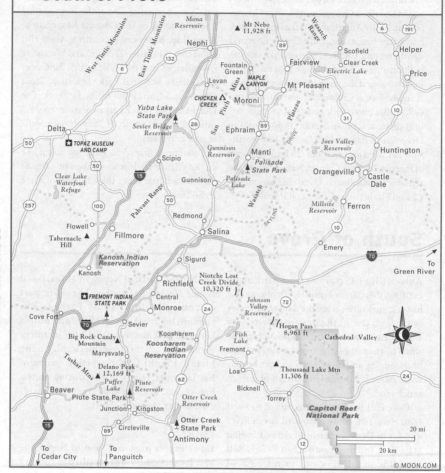

© MOON.COM

ACCOMMODATIONS

Right in town, the **Safari Motel** (413 S. Main St., 435/623-1071, www.nephimotel.com, $53-90) has clean, inexpensive guest rooms plus a pool. It's a good alternative to the chain motels (Super 8, Motel 6) at the freeway exits if you're on a budget.

The **Best Western Paradise Inn** (1025 S. Main St., 435/623-0624 or 800/780-7234, www.bestwesternnephi.com, $110) is the nicest place you'll find to stay in town, with an enclosed pool and complimentary breakfast.

Detour to Delta

The barren Pahvant Valley along the lower Sevier River was considered a wasteland until 1905, when some Fillmore businessmen purchased water rights from Sevier River Reservoir and 10,000 acres of land. The farm and town lots they sold became Delta, the center of one of Utah's most productive agricultural areas. The giant coal-burning Intermountain Power Project, which mostly supplies Los Angeles, and the Brush Wellman beryllium mill have helped boost Delta's population to about 3,500. Miners have been digging into the Drum Mountains northwest of Delta since the 1870s for gold, silver, copper, manganese, and other minerals; some work still goes on there.

Delta, which is 50 miles (81 km) southwest of Nephi on Highway 132, and 35 miles (56 km) northwest of Fillmore via Highway 100 and U.S. 50, makes a handy base for rockhounding and exploring nearby historic sites. In downtown Delta, the **Great Basin Museum** (45 W. Main St., 435/864-5013, http://greatbasinmuseum.com, 10am-5pm Mon.-Sat. Apr.-Oct., 1pm-5pm Thurs. and 10am-5pm Fri.-Sat. Nov.-Mar., free) presents a varied collection of pioneer photos and artifacts, arrowheads, a Topaz Camp exhibit, fossils, and minerals; antique farm machinery stands outside.

ROCKHOUNDING
Beautiful rock, mineral, and fossil specimens await discovery in the deserts surrounding Delta. Sought-after rocks and minerals include topaz, bixbyite, sunstone, geode, obsidian, muscovite, garnet, pyrite, and agate. Some fossils to look for are trilobites, brachiopods, horn corals, and crinoids; the Antelope Springs area west of town is a good place to find trilobites. The **Delta Chamber of Commerce** (80 N. 200 W., 435/864-4316, www.millardcountytravel.com, 10am-5pm Mon.-Fri.) is a good source of local information; it publishes the free *Adventures in Millard County* brochure, which has great information on specific rocks, such as obsidian, sunstone, and topaz, and where to find them.

You can see gemstones from the area at **West Desert Collectors Rock Shop** (278 W. Main St., 435/864-2175, 9am-6pm Mon.-Sat.).

For more of an expedition, head to **Topaz Mountain.** From U.S. 50/6, about 11 miles (17.7 km) northeast of Delta, turn west onto the paved Brush Wellman Road and follow it for 37.3 miles (60 km) to a point where you can clearly see Topaz Mountain. Follow the sign for Topaz Mountain and head up the dirt road north along the east side of the mountain.

Several spur trails lead to rockhounding sites. Primitive camping is permitted, but there is no water.

A commercial enterprise makes it easy, though not cheap, to dig for trilobites and other marine fossils. **U-Dig Fossils** (435/864-3638, www.u-digfossils.com, 9am-6pm Mon.-Sat. Apr.-Oct.) is a private quarry located in Antelope Springs, 52 miles (84 km) west of Delta. It's best to come prepared with work gloves, sturdy shoes, and protective eyewear; U-Dig provides hammers, buckets, and advice. Two hours of digging costs $28 over age 16; it's $16 ages 8-16 and free under age 8. Call ahead, because if business is slow, the quarry closes early. From Delta, head west on U.S. 50/6, turn north at the U-Dig sign between mileposts 56 and 57, and continue another 20 miles (32 km) north to the site.

★ TOPAZ MUSEUM AND CAMP
Topaz is easily Utah's most dispiriting ghost town site. About 9,000 Japanese—most of whom were American citizens—were brought from the West Coast to this desolate desert plain in 1942 for relocation in a Japanese internment camp. Topaz sprang up in just a few months and included barracks, communal dining halls, a post office, hospital, schools, churches, and recreational facilities. Most internees cooperated with authorities; the few who did not were shipped off to a more secure camp. Barbed wire and watchtowers with armed guards surrounded the small city, which was actually Utah's fifth-largest community for a time. All internees were released at war's end in 1945, and the camp came down almost as quickly as it had gone up. Salvagers bought and removed equipment, buildings, barbed wire, telephone poles, and even street paving and sewer pipes.

Even if you don't drive out to the camp, be certain to visit the excellent **Topaz Museum** (55 W. Main St., 435/864-2514, http://www.topazmuseum.org/, 10am-5pm Mon.-Sat., free), which opened in downtown Delta in 2017. A couple of short films (including one taken by an interned man with camera

smuggled into him by a camp official) are excellent and set the stage for a tour of the artifacts and photos from the camp, reconstructed living quarters, and video displays. All of the displays combine to give a moving portrait of life in the camp, and a final exhibit stresses the importance of guarding against infringement of civil liberties.

An uneasy silence pervades the actual internment site today. Little more than the streets, foundations, and piles of rubble remain. You can still walk or drive along the streets of the vast camp, which had 42 neatly laid-out blocks. A concrete memorial stands at the northwest corner of the site.

One way to get here is to go 6 miles (9.7 km) west from Delta on U.S. 50/6 to the small town of Hinckley, turn right (north) and go 4.5 miles (7.2 km) on a paved road (some parts are gravel) to its end, turn left (west) and go 2.5 miles (4 km) on a paved road to its end in Abraham, turn right (north) and go 1.5 miles (2.4 km) on a gravel road to a stop sign, then turn left and go 3 miles (4.8 km) on a gravel road; Topaz is on the left.

FOOD

After a hot afternoon of rockhounding, a burger and big iced tea at the **Ashton's Burger Barn** (304 N. Hwy. 6, 435/864-2288, 10am-9pm Mon.-Sat., $4-6) may be just what you need. There's Mexican food at **El Jalisciense Taco Shop** (396 W. Main St., 435/864-3141, 5:30am-10pm daily, $4-9).

ACCOMMODATIONS AND CAMPING

Delta has several motels on or close to Main Street. The **Budget Motel** (75 S. 350 E., 435/864-4533, $65) is a good bet for those who don't need many amenities. For a step up in style and amenities, the **Days Inn Motel** (527 E. Topaz Blvd., 435/864-3882, $85) has a heated outdoor pool and allows pets.

Antelope Valley RV Park (776 W. Main St., 435/864-1813, http://antelopevalleyrvpark.

1: excavating fossils at U-Dig Fossils in Delta; 2: the Topaz Museum and Camp

com Apr.-Nov., $36-40) is on the west edge of downtown.

INFORMATION AND SERVICES

Delta Chamber of Commerce (75 W. Main St., 435/864-4316, www.millardcountytravel.com, 10am-5pm Mon.-Fri.) can tell you about services in town and sights in the surrounding area.

Fillmore

In 1851, Brigham Young and the Utah Territorial Legislature designated Fillmore as the territorial capital, even before the town was established. They chose this site in the Pahvant Valley because it was in the approximate geographic center of the territory. Their plans didn't work out, but Fillmore (pop. 2,500) has become the center of a large agricultural region and the Millard County seat. A state historical museum in the Territorial Statehouse contains a wealth of pioneer history.

TERRITORIAL STATEHOUSE STATE PARK

Completed in 1855, the **Territorial Statehouse** (50 W. Capitol Ave., 435/743-5316, http://stateparks.utah.gov, 9am-5pm Mon.-Sat., $2 pp) is Utah's oldest government building. Architect Truman O. Angell designed the three-story sandstone structure, originally planned to have four wings capped by a large Moorish dome. Only the south wing was completed, though, because antagonism between the U.S. government and the Mormons blocked the appropriation of expected federal funds. Several legislatures met here, but only the fifth session, in 1855, stayed for its full term; the sixth and eighth sessions opened here, then quickly adjourned to Salt Lake City's better-suited facilities.

Historic photos and paintings show pioneer families and leaders of the church and government in early Utah. You can visit a pair of 1880s log cabins on the grounds; one has pioneer furnishings, the other a wagon. Peek in the windows of the restored 1867 Little Rock

School House nearby. Rose gardens flank the statehouse, which is downtown behind the Millard County courthouse. Also part of this complex are the municipal swimming pool and some lovely shaded picnic spots.

FOOD, ACCOMMODATIONS, AND CAMPING

A good bet in Fillmore is the **Comfort Inn and Suites** (940 S. Hwy. 99, 435/743-4334, $99-134), a surprisingly nice place for this small town. It has a small indoor pool and complimentary breakfast. The **Best Western Paradise Inn** (905 N. Main St., 435/743-6895, $98) is at I-15 exit 167 and has a heated pool and a restaurant. The best place in town for a bite to eat and some local atmosphere is ★ **Cluff's Carhop Cafe** (260 N. Main St., 435/743-5510, 11am-8:30pm Mon.-Fri., 11am-4:30pm Sat., about $8), a cute retro-style burger joint with tables under shade trees.

Open year-round, **Wagons West RV Campground** (545 N. Main St., 435/743-6188, $20-40) has showers, laundry, and a store; both tents and RVs are welcome. **Fillmore KOA** (900 S. 410 W., 435/743-4420, www.koa.com, Mar.-early Dec., tents $35, RVs $40-46, cabins $55-75), 0.5 mile off the south end of the business loop near I-15 exit 163, has showers, laundry, and a store.

Beaver

Beaver (pop. 3,000) is a handy stop just east of I-15. Main Street (the I-15 Business Loop) has a good selection of motels and restaurants.

SIGHTS

More than 200 historic houses of architectural interest lie scattered around town. You'll see many of them by driving along the side streets. A large stone building remaining from Fort Cameron, constructed during a mining boom in 1872, still stands on the east edge of town, across the highway from the golf course. The old **Beaver County Courthouse** (190 E. Center St., 11am-5pm Tues.-Sat., free), with an ornate clock tower,

represents the architectural splendor of its period. Building started in 1877, and the courthouse served Beaver County from 1882 until 1975. It now houses a historical museum. The adjacent Historical Park, on Center Street, one block east of Main Street, has a statue of Philo T. Farnsworth (1906-1971), the Father of Television, who was born in a log cabin near Beaver.

FOOD

You'll find old-fashioned American food at **Arshel's Cafe** (711 N. Main St., 435/438-2977, 7am-9pm daily, $7-20). A fixture in Beaver since the 1930s, this is the kind of diner where you ought to save room for homemade pie after your meal.

ACCOMMODATIONS AND CAMPING

Several chain motels are along the business route through town between I-15 exits 109 and 112. Two places stand out as being especially comfortable. The **Best Western Butch Cassidy Inn** (161 S. Main St., 435/438-2438, www.bestwestern.com, $90-155) and the **Comfort Inn** (1540 S. Main St., 435/438-6283, $108-144) are both pleasant and have pools.

At the north edge of town, **Beaver KOA** (Manderfield Rd., 435/438-2924 or 800/562-2912, Mar.-Oct., tents $29, RVs $43-46) has showers, Wi-Fi, a store, laundry, and a pool; take I-15 exit 112, go south 0.6 mile on the business loop, then turn left onto Manderfield Road.

EAST ON I-70

Though the first 50 miles (81 km) of this route are fairly nondescript (save for the excellent museum at Fremont Indian State Park), after Fremont Junction the scenery becomes very dramatic as the freeway begins dropping through the formations of the San Rafael Swell. Though there are no gas stations, restaurants, or other motorist services between Salina and Green River, a distance of 110 miles (177 km), there's plenty to look at. Take advantage of the frequent wayside exits to take photos.

Cove Fort

In 1867, during the Black Hawk War, LDS Church president Brigham Young ordered construction of **Cove Fort** (Hwy. 161, near the junction of I-15 and I-70, 435/438-5547, www.covefort.com, 9am-dusk daily, free) to protect travelers on the overnight journey between Fillmore and Beaver. Walls of volcanic basalt 13 feet high contained 12 rooms and a cistern and enclosed an area of 10,000 square feet. Gun ports at the two entrances and along the upper walls discouraged Native Americans from ever attacking the fort. Church volunteers lead informal tours and relate the fort's history. Cove Fort is at the junction of I-15 and I-70. Take I-70 exit 1 and go northwest one mile, or take I-15 exit 135 and go southeast 2 miles (3.2 km).

★ Fremont Indian State Park

The prehistoric Fremont people lived over much of what is now Utah, but archaeologists weren't aware of this group's identity until 1931. During construction of I-70 in 1983, a large site was discovered and excavated in Clear Creek Canyon. The Five Finger Ridge Village site probably had more than 150 occupants at its peak, around AD 1100; more people lived nearby in the canyon. The Fremont farmed in the canyon bottom and sought game and wild plants for food. They lived in pit houses and stored surplus food in carefully constructed granaries. More than 500 rock-art panels in the canyon depict the religious and hunting aspects of Fremont life in a cryptic form. Nothing remains at the village site, located across the canyon; workers constructing I-70 cut most of the ridge away to use as fill after the scientific excavations had been completed.

The park's **visitors center** (3820 W. Clear Creek Canyon Rd., 435/527-4631, http://stateparks.utah.gov, 9am-6pm daily in summer, 9am-5pm daily fall-spring, $4 pp or $8 per vehicle) has excellent displays of artifacts found during excavations. Many aspects of Fremont life remain a mystery, but exhibits present ideas of how they may have lived here. A short video introduces the Fremont, their foods, events that may have caused their departure, and the excavation of Five Finger Ridge Village. Models illustrate pit-house construction and how Five Finger Ridge Village might have looked. A full-size replica of a pit house includes audio explanations of the functions of the dwelling.

Three short trails begin outside the visitors center and lead up Coyote Canyon. Park staff can tell you about many other trails and rock-art sites in the area.

The park is near I-70 exit 17 in Clear Creek Canyon, 16 miles (26 km) east of I-15. A short scenic drive with many pullouts to view rock art or granaries follows the old highway 9 miles (14.5 km) through Clear Creek Canyon between the visitors center and I-70 exit 8 for Ranch.

Richfield

The seat of Sevier County and the center of a large agricultural region, Richfield (pop. 7,700) has a few motels and restaurants; most are along the I-70 business route. This is the best-equipped town for travelers for miles around.

FOOD

Stop for a surprisingly good lunch at **Big Daddy's Deli** (60 W. 100 N., 435/896-5239, 10am-6pm Mon.-Fri., $5-14); your sub will get you through to dinner and then some.

ACCOMMODATIONS AND CAMPING

There's an abundance of chain motels at the freeway exit, and also a few more modest budget choices close to the old downtown. **Appletree Inn** (145 S. Main St., 435/896-5481, http://appletreeinn.net, $50-100) is a pretty basic budget motel but inexpensive and close to the freeway. The **Comfort Inn** (1070 W. 1250 S., 435/893-0119, $89-109) is a little more expensive but a step up; it's pet-friendly and has an indoor pool.

The **Hampton Inn** (1100 W. 1350 S., 435/896-6666, $119) has an indoor pool and a fitness room. **Holiday Inn Express** (20

W. 1400 N., 435/896-8552, $116) is one of the newest hotels in Richfield, with an outdoor pool, a complimentary breakfast buffet, and large, comfortable guest rooms. **Richfield KOA** (600 W. 600 S., 435/896-6674 or 888/562-4703, www.koa.com, year-round, tents $31, RVs $42-45, camping cabins $65-125) has a pool, a store, showers, and laundry.

Salina

Salina (suh-LINE-uh) is a Spanish word for "salt mine," one of which is found nearby. The first pioneers arrived in 1863, but conflicts with Native Americans forced them to evacuate the site from 1866 to 1872. Today, Salina is a handy stop for travelers, strategically located at the junction of U.S. 89 and I-70.

You'll find several motels and places to eat downtown and near the I-70 interchange. The most appealing is the **Scenic Hills Super 8** (375 E. 1620 S., 435/529-7483, $88-118), out by the freeway exit, with an adjacent 24-hour Denny's restaurant (and a fridge and microwave for those leftovers). **Butch Cassidy Campground** (1100 S. State St., 435/529-7400, tents $12 pp, RVs $32-42), between I-70 exit 54 and downtown, offers sites for tents and RVs with showers, a store, and laundry.

There are a number of chain restaurants at the freeway exit, but for a more unique experience, drive downtown to the **Mom's Café** (10 E. Main St., 435/529-3921, 7am-9pm daily, $5-19), where you can sample Utah scones and much-lauded liver and onions, in a vintage storefront.

East Across the San Rafael Swell

Once you leave Salina on I-70, it's 106 miles (171 km) to Green River—and the next gas station, restaurant, or lodging. It's apparently the longest stretch of interstate in the entire federal system with no services. However, it's also one of the most scenic. I-70 crosses the huge fold and uplift of the San Rafael Swell, passing through a dramatic landscape of stone castles, canyons, ghost rocks, fins, and turrets of deep red sandstone. There are frequent viewpoints, and at these you'll frequently find Native Americans selling art and jewelry.

The highlight of the route is the San Rafael Reef, where I-70 corkscrews down (or up, if you're heading westward) a 2,100-foot escarpment of Navajo and Wingate sandstone, the same formations that make up Arches National Park and the cliffs above Moab. Drive carefully down this steep, curving road, and be especially attentive to trucks. San Rafael Reef is about 15 miles (24 km) west of Green River.

Dinosaur Country

Northeastern Utah's diverse landscape com-
prises barren desert, deep canyons, high plateaus, and the lofty forested Uinta Mountains. Well-preserved bones unearthed in the region tell of a time about 140 million years ago when dinosaurs roamed in a relatively moist subtropical climate amid tree ferns, evergreens, and ginkgo trees. Dinosaur National Monument preserves a fossil quarry; more bones reside in museums in Vernal, Price, and Castle Dale; and excavations are still underway at the Cleveland-Lloyd Dinosaur Quarry.

This subtropical prehistory also laid down vast formations rich in coal and oil, and resource extraction has become a big business here; cities like Vernal are surprisingly bustling and prosperous.

Many visitors come to northeastern Utah for recreation. The high

Highlights

Look for ★ to find recommended sights, activities, dining, and lodging.

★ **Mirror Lake Highway:** Utah's most spectacular alpine drive climbs to the crest of the western Uinta Mountains, offering access to great campgrounds and hiking trails along the way (page 188).

★ **Utah Field House of Natural History State Park Museum:** This great collection of dinosaur bones gets even adults excited about paleontology (page 191).

★ **Red Canyon Visitor Center:** The view of **Flaming Gorge** through the visitor center's picture window offers inspiration to hike the nearby trails at the gorge's rim (page 204).

★ **Nine Mile Canyon Backcountry Byway:** This 40-mile (64-km) byway tours some outstanding Fremont Indian sites, including granaries, pictographs, and petroglyphs (page 211).

★ **Wedge Overlook:** Follow good dirt roads east from the town of Castle Dale into the San Rafael Swell, where you'll have a good look at Utah's Little Grand Canyon, with the San Rafael River far below (page 215).

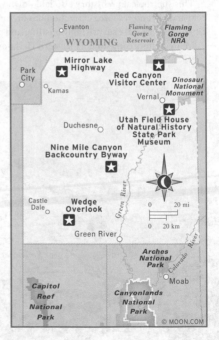

country of the Uinta Mountains offers alpine scenery and good hiking, and the Flaming Gorge National Recreation Area has excellent fishing and boating in a highly colored desert canyon. This region is trenched by the Green River and its tributaries, which offer lively white-water rafting. The San Rafael Swell represents the northern edge of the Colorado Plateau and offers backcountry travelers an untrammeled landscape rich with relics of the ancient Fremont people who made their homes in this rugged country.

PLANNING YOUR TIME

Vernal makes a good base for exploring the Flaming Gorge and Dinosaur National Monument, although campers will find plenty of good sites in both areas. It's worth spending at least two days here: one at the national monument and another at Flaming Gorge. If you have an extra day, plan to take a rafting trip on the Green River.

Another good hub is the town of Price, with a number of lodgings and good access to the San Rafael Swell and Cleveland-Lloyd Dinosaur Quarry.

Finally, if mountain hiking or backpacking is your objective, the Uintas are the best place to spend your time . . . from a day trip out to the Mirror Lake Highway to a week-long backpacking trip. But don't plan such a trip too early in the summer; in heavy snow years it can take until late June for the road to open and the trails to clear of snow.

In summer, come prepared for hot days and chilly nights; the valleys have average highs of about 90°F, but temperatures drop to the low 50s at night. The Wasatch Plateau and Uinta Mountains experience cool weather year-round. Above 10,000 feet, summer highs rarely exceed 70°F during the day and drop to the 30s and 40s at night; freezing weather may occur at any time of year.

Uinta Mountains

The Uintas (yoo-IN-tuhs) contain lofty peaks, lush grassy meadows, fragrant coniferous forests, crystal clear streams, and a multitude of tiny alpine lakes. Kings Peak tops the range at 13,528 feet—the highest point in the state. Unlike most other major ranges of the United States, the Uintas run east-west. Underground forces pushed rock layers up into a massive dome 150 miles (242 km) long and 35 miles (56 km) wide. Ancient Precambrian rocks exposed in the center of the range consist largely of quartzite (metamorphosed sandstone). Outcrops of progressively younger rocks are found away from the center. Glaciers have carved steep ridges and broad basins and left great moraines. Barren rock lies exposed across much of the land, including the peaks and high ridges.

Despite their great heights, the Uintas have a gentler terrain than the precipitous Wasatch Range. High plateaus and broad valleys among the peaks hold the abundant rain and snowfall in marshes and ponds, supporting large populations of wildlife and fish.

The Uintas' many lakes are stocked regularly, and fishing is popular. One feisty and locally popular fish is the tiger trout, a cross between brown and brook trout.

Visiting the Uintas

Winding over the western end of the range from the town of Kamas to the Wyoming border, Highway 150 offers splendid panoramas and access to fishing lakes and hiking trails. On the east, U.S. 191 and Highway 44 provide access to the Uintas and Flaming Gorge

Dinosaur Country

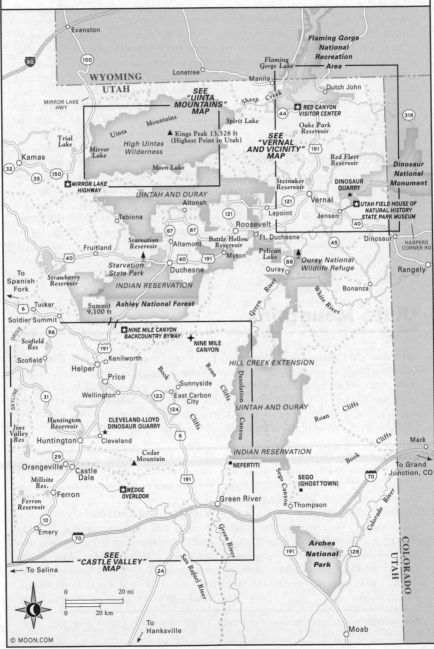

Evanston

Flaming Gorge National Recreation Area

WYOMING
UTAH

Lonetree

Flaming Gorge Lake

Manila

Dutch John

MIRROR LAKE HWY

SEE "UINTA MOUNTAINS" MAP

Sheep Creek

RED CANYON VISITOR CENTER

Spirit Lake

Oaks Park Reservoir

Uinta Mountains

Kings Peak 13,528 ft
(Highest Point in Utah)

SEE "VERNAL AND VICINITY" MAP

Trial Lake

High Uintas Wilderness

Mirror Lake

Red Fleet Reservoir

Dinosaur National Monument

Kamas

Moon Lake

Steinaker Reservoir

DINOSAUR QUARRY

MIRROR LAKE HIGHWAY

UINTAH AND OURAY

Altonah

Vernal

UTAH FIELD HOUSE OF NATURAL HISTORY STATE PARK MUSEUM

Tabiona

Lapoint

Jensen

Roosevelt

Ft. Duchesne

Dinosaur

Starvation Reservoir

Altamont

Bottle Hollow Reservoir

HARPERS CORNER RD

Fruitland

Myton

Pelican Lake

Ouray National Wildlife Refuge

Rangely

Starvation State Park

Duchesne

Ouray

To Spanish Fork

Strawberry Reservoir

INDIAN RESERVATION

Bonanza

White River

Green River

Tucker

Summit 9,100 ft

Ashley National Forest

Soldier Summit

NINE MILE CANYON BACKCOUNTRY BYWAY

NINE MILE CANYON

Scofield Res

HILL CREEK EXTENSION

Scofield

Kenilworth

Helper

Book Cliffs

Roan Cliffs

Desolation Canyon

Price

Sunnyside

East Carbon City

UINTAH AND OURAY

Wellington

Roan Cliffs

Cliffs

Huntington Reservoir

CLEVELAND-LLOYD DINOSAUR QUARRY

Book Cliffs

Mack

Joes Valley Res

Huntington

Cleveland

Cedar Mountain

INDIAN RESERVATION

To Grand Junction, CO

Orangeville

NEFERTITI

Millsite Res.

Castle Dale

Sego Canyon

SEGO (GHOST TOWN)

Ferron

WEDGE OVERLOOK

Colorado River

Ferron Reservoir

Thompson

Emery

Green River

COLORADO
UTAH

SEE "CASTLE VALLEY" MAP

Arches National Park

To Salina

San Rafael River

To Hanksville

Moab

© MOON.COM

0   20 mi

0   20 km

Uinta Mountains

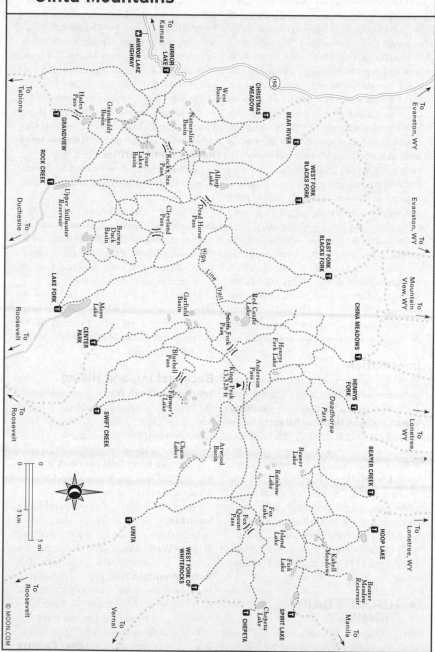

© MOON.COM

Reservoir from Vernal. Unpaved roads also lead to trailheads on all sides of the range. Developed and primitive campgrounds can be found along these highways and at other locations, including many of the trailheads.

Most people prefer to visit the Uintas mid-June-mid-September. Campers should be prepared for cold nights and freezing rain even in the warmest months. Afternoon showers are common in summer. Arm yourself with insect repellent to ward off the mosquitoes, especially in July. Snow stays on the ground until well into June, and the meltwater can make trails muddy until early July. The lakes and campgrounds along Highway 150 become crowded on summer weekends and holidays, although you can usually get off by yourself with a short hike into the backcountry.

An extensive trail system with about 20 trailheads goes deep into the wilderness and connects with many lakes. A great number of trips are possible, from easy day hikes to rigorous long-distance treks. Winter snows close Highway 150 and the back roads, at which time snowmobilers and cross-country skiers come out to enjoy the snowy landscapes.

Information

The U.S. Forest Service manages the Uintas and surrounding forest lands. Northern and western parts are administered by the **Uinta-Wasatch-Cache National Forest** (info desk inside REI, 3285 E. 3300 S., Salt Lake City, 435/446-6411, www.fs.usda.gov/uwcnf). Most of the southern and eastern areas are part of the **Ashley National Forest** (355 N. Vernal Ave., Vernal, 435/789-1181, www.fs.usda.gov/ashley). For specific information, it's best to contact the district office closest to the trailhead. Pick up a copy of the Trails Illustrated High Uintas Wilderness topo map (1:75,000 scale) at the Salt Lake City REI or at a ranger station.

★ MIRROR LAKE HIGHWAY

Kamas is the start of what is probably Utah's most spectacular alpine drive. The Mirror Lake Highway (Hwy. 150) begins here at an elevation of 6,500 feet and climbs to the crest of the western Uinta Mountains at Bald Mountain Pass (elev. 10,678 feet) before descending on the other side and continuing to Evanston, Wyoming. Busy Evanston is about 75 miles (121 km) from Kamas and has several motels, fast-food restaurants, a couple of places to buy groceries, and access to I-80.

The nearest motels to Kamas are in Heber City (17 miles/27 km southwest) and Park City (19 miles/31 km west). The **Heber-Kamas Ranger District Office** (50 E. Center St., 435/783-4338) can advise on road conditions, campgrounds, hiking, cross-country skiing, and snowmobiling.

You can drive scenic Mirror Lake Highway mid-June-mid-October; dates may vary depending on snow levels. A $6 three-day recreation pass, available at the start of the highway and at several points along the way, is required if you're going to park and hike.

The first 25 miles (40 km) of the highway are pretty, but relatively flat. Shortly after passing Provo River Falls, the road climbs sharply, and the views open up to include rugged mountain peaks.

Backpacking and Hiking

Yellowpine Creek Trail begins just north of the Yellow Pine Campground (mile 6.7) and goes up the creek to Lower Yellowpine Lake (elev. 9,600 feet, 4 miles/6.4 km one-way) and beyond; this is a good hike early in the season.

The **Provo River Falls overlook** (mile 24) isn't a formal trail, but it's a great place to get out of the car and explore.

Several trails start at the **Crystal Lake trailhead,** near the Trial Lake Campground (mile 25.4). It's just 1 mile from the trailhead to pretty **Wall Lake,** a good destination for families or easy-going backpackers. The **Notch Mountain Trail** goes north past Wall and Twin Lakes, through the Notch to Ibantik and Meadow Lakes, to the Weber River (elev. 9,000 feet, 6.5 miles/10.5 km one-way), and to Bald Mountain Pass (elev. 10,678 feet, 10 miles/16 km one-way). The **Lakes Country**

Trail starts at the Crystal Lake trailhead and goes west past Island, Long, and other lakes before joining the Smith-Morehouse Trail after 3 miles (4.8 km).

At **Bald Mountain Pass** (mile 29.1, elev. 10,678 feet), the **Bald Mountain National Recreation Trail** climbs to the summit of Bald Mountain (elev. 11,947 feet) with great views all the way. The 2-mile (3.2 km) each way trail climbs 1,269 vertical feet, putting you in the middle of the Uinta Range's alpine grandeur. Expect a strenuous trip because of the high elevation and steep grades; carry rain gear to fend off the cold wind, even in summer, and possible storms. From the top, weather permitting, you'll enjoy panoramas of the High Uintas Wilderness, the Lakes Roadless Area, and the Wasatch Range. **Notch Mountain Trail** also begins near the picnic area and connects with Trial Lake.

At **Hayden Pass** (mile 34.2, elev. 10,200 feet) find the **Highline trailhead;** this is the closest point on the highway to the **High Uintas Wilderness.** The Highline Trail tends to be muddy, rocky, and heavily used. It winds east from here across the Uintas nearly 100 miles (161 km) to East Park Reservoir, north of Vernal, and is the main east-west trail in the Uintas. The highway makes a gradual descent from the pass along Hayden Fork of the Bear River. A gentler alternative starting less than a mile (1.6 km) from the pass goes to **Ruth Lake trailhead** (mile 35); it's an easy 0.75 mile (1.2 km) to the lake.

Campgrounds

Mirror Lake Highway is well supplied with campgrounds; you'll find one every few miles. Campgrounds tend to fill on summer weekends, but some campsites can be reserved (877/444-6777, www.recreation.gov); dispersed camping is permitted in most areas, and you'll see many people camping (mostly in RVs or pickup campers) in roadside pullouts. Of the many campgrounds, here are just a few that have access to hiking trails or lakes.

Early in the season, **Yellow Pine Campground** (mile 6.7, elev. 7,200 feet, no water, late May-late Oct., $18) is a good bet, as is the trail that starts here. **Soapstone Campground** (mile 15.5, water early June-mid-Sept., $23, reservations available) has sites along the Provo River amid lodgepole pines at 8,200 feet.

Trial Lake Campground (mile 25.4, water late June-early Sept., $23) is 0.25 mile (0.4 km) to the left of the highway on Spring Canyon Road. Sites are on the southeast shore of the lake in a pine and spruce forest at 9,500 feet. There's a parking area near the dam for anglers. Spring Canyon Road continues past the dam to Washington and Crystal Lakes and Crystal Lake trailhead.

Mirror Lake Campground (mile 31.2, water early July-early Sept., $23, reservations available) is the largest campground (91 sites) on the Mirror Lake Highway. Sites are near the lake in a forest of spruce, fir, and lodgepole pine at 10,200 feet. Anglers can park at the south end of the lake and at the Mirror Lake trailhead. Boats can be hand-launched; no motors are permitted on the lake. Trails lead into the High Uintas Wilderness.

Cross-Country Skiing

Snowplows keep the highway cleared in winter to Soapstone, 15.5 miles (25 km) from Kamas, to provide access for cross-country skiing and snowmobiling. Five trails used by both skiers and snowmobilers begin along the highway and at Soapstone. Skiers using snowmobile trails will find the most solitude on weekdays.

Beaver Creek Cross-Country Trail begins at the Yellowpine trailhead (6 miles/9.7 km east of Kamas, $3) and parallels the highway to Pine Valley Campground, a distance of 6.5 miles (10.5 km) one-way with an elevation gain of 440 feet. This trail is easy; branching off from it are other ski trails rated intermediate and advanced. Dogs are allowed only on odd-numbered days. You can obtain information and brochures for these and other skiing areas from the Heber-Kamas Ranger District Office.

Vernal

One of the oldest and largest communities in northeastern Utah, Vernal makes a handy base for travels to the many sights of the region. The perennial waters of Ashley Creek—named for mountain man William H. Ashley, who passed by in 1825—attracted the first settlers to the valley during the early 1870s.

Natural resource extraction is a major contributor to Vernal's economy. Growth of the oil industry in recent decades has been a mixed blessing because of its boom-and-bust cycles.

SIGHTS
★ Utah Field House of Natural History State Park Museum

The **Utah Field House Museum** (496 E. Main St., 435/789-3799, http://stateparks. utah.gov, 9am-7pm daily Memorial Day-Labor Day, 9am-5pm daily Mar.-Memorial Day, Labor Day-Oct., 9am-5pm Mon.-Sat. Nov.-Feb., $7 adults, $3.50 children, under age 6 free) is a good place for both adults and children to learn about the dinosaurs that once roamed the Uinta Basin. Full-size models stalk or fly in the Dinosaur Gardens outside, and a 90-foot-long *Diplodocus* skeleton greets visitors in the museum's rotunda. The Jurassic Hall houses dinosaur fossils, including the most complete skeleton that exists of the sauropod *Haplocanthosaurus,* and the Eocene Gallery has displays of 45-million-year-old skulls of ancient mammals, crocodiles, and alligators that once roamed across what is now Utah. A replica of a dig site allows visitors to excavate fossils and experience a paleontology lab. A colorful geologic mural shows the structure of rock layers in northeastern

Utah. Don't skip the short video at the museum's entrance; it's interesting and kind of fun and will help you appreciate the museum's contents. An expansion to the museum houses a paleontology lab.

Uintah County Heritage Museum

The **Uintah County Heritage Museum** (328 E. 200 S., 435/789-7399, www. uintahmuseum.org, 9am-7:30pm Mon.-Thurs., 9am-6pm Fri., 10am-4pm Sat. Memorial Day-Labor Day, 9am-6pm Mon.-Fri., 10am-4pm Sat. Labor Day-Memorial Day, free) is at the Western Park Complex, Vernal's convention center, amphitheater, equestrian center, and racetrack. This pioneer museum and art gallery places special emphasis on Utah's outlaw heritage (real or imaginary). Also housed here is the **Ladies of the White House Doll Collection,** created by a local doll maker and artist. Each doll wears a hand-sewn reproduction of a dress worn at an Inaugural Ball.

Dry Fork Petroglyphs

Several panels of striking petroglyphs are located along a sharp sandstone bluff about 8 miles (12.9 km) northwest of Vernal. Considered to be some of the best rock art in the United States, what makes these carvings so notable is the fact that they contain dozens of nearly life-size human figures, many with elaborate headdresses and ornamentation, and others with gory injuries. The significance of these murals is unknown, although they were probably carved by the Fremont and are reckoned to be between 1,200 and 1,600 years old.

To reach the Dry Fork Petroglyphs (also called the McConkie Ranch Petroglyphs), drive west from Vernal on Main Street and turn north onto 500 West. Follow the main road when it turns to the left onto Highway

1: Bald Mountain and the Mirror Lake Highway in the Uinta Mountains; **2:** life-sized dino replicas at the Utah Field House Museum

Vernal and Vicinity

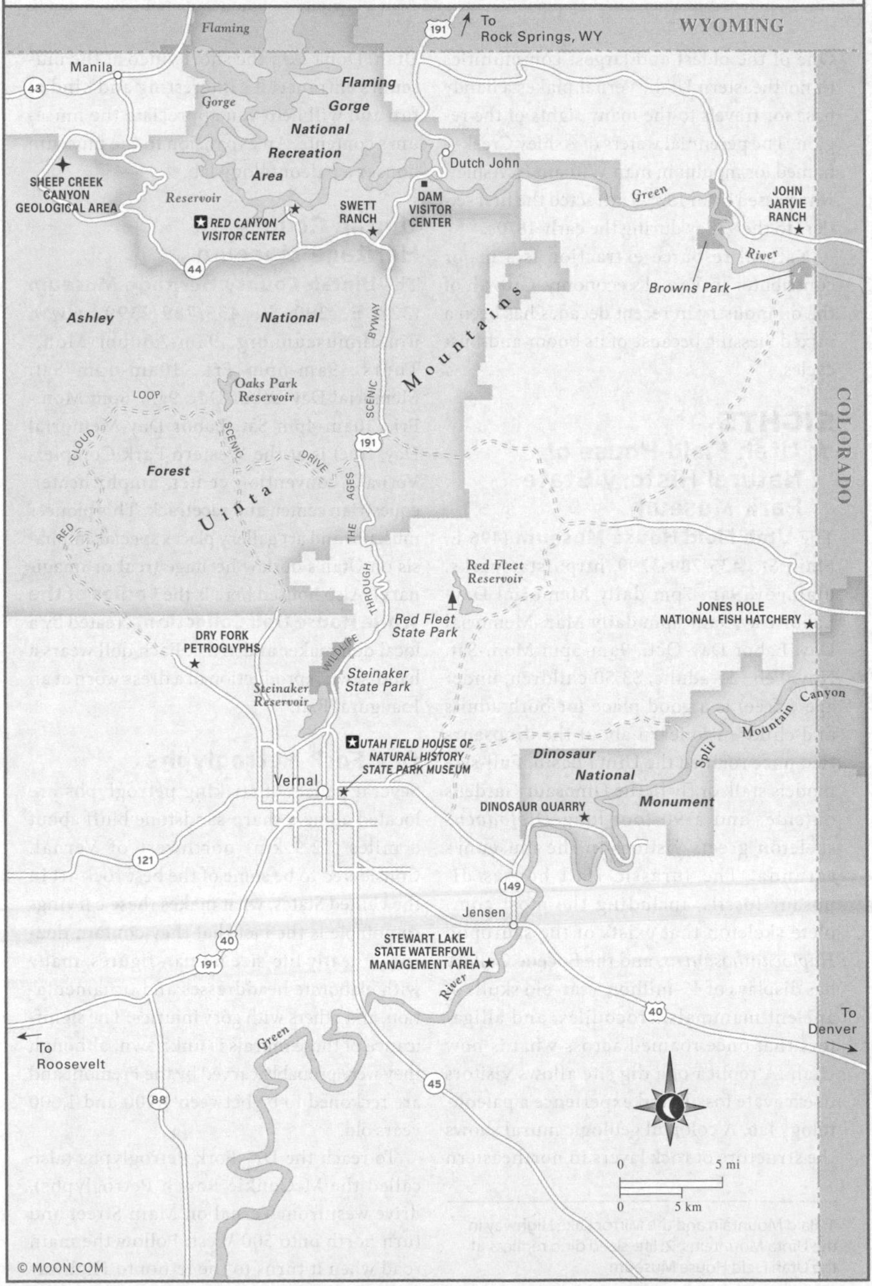

WYOMING

To
Rock Springs, WY

191

Flaming

Manila

43

Flaming
Gorge

Gorge

National

Recreation

Area

Dutch John

Reservoir

DAM
VISITOR
CENTER

SWETT
RANCH

Green

RED CANYON
VISITOR CENTER

44

Browns Park

River

JOHN
JARVIE
RANCH

SHEEP CREEK
CANYON
GEOLOGICAL AREA

Ashley

National

M
o
u
n
t
a
i
n
s

Oaks Park
Reservoir

LOOP

Forest

CLOUD

RED

Uinta

SCENIC BYWAY

191

Red Fleet
Reservoir

JONES HOLE
NATIONAL FISH HATCHERY

SCENIC

DRIVE

THROUGH THE AGES

Red Fleet
State Park

DRY FORK
PETROGLYPHS

WILDLIFE

Split

Mountain

Canyon

Steinaker
Reservoir

Steinaker
State Park

Dinosaur

UTAH FIELD HOUSE OF
NATURAL HISTORY
STATE PARK MUSEUM

National

Vernal

Monument

DINOSAUR QUARRY

121

149

Jensen

40

STEWART LAKE
STATE WATERFOWL
MANAGEMENT AREA

191

River

To
Denver

40

To
Roosevelt

Green

45

88

COLORADO

0   5 mi

0   5 km

© MOON.COM

121 and continue until the junction with 3500 West. Turn right (north) and follow this road for 6.8 miles (10.9 km); it will head west and become Dry Fork Settlement Road. Watch for signs and follow a private ranch access road to the marked parking area.

The petroglyphs are on private property, and donations are gladly accepted; there are no facilities. Be sure to stay on the trails, and don't get discouraged—the best of the carvings are about 15 minutes into the cliff-side hike. This area is very rich in petroglyphs, and you could easily spend hours wandering along the cliffs.

ENTERTAINMENT AND EVENTS

The **Outlaw Trail Theater** (Outlaw Trail Amphitheater, Western Park, 302 E. 200 S., 888/240-2080, http://outlawtrailtheater.com, 8pm most nights mid-June-early July, $9-14) is a community theater presenting Broadway shows every year.

The **PRCA Dinosaur Roundup Rodeo** (800/421-9635, www.vernalrodeo.com) in mid-July is Vernal's biggest event of the year and includes a parade and country music showdown. A parade celebrates **Pioneer Day** on July 24. The **Uintah County Fair**

(435/789-7396, www.uintahcountyfair.com) comes to town the first week of June.

RECREATION
Mountain Biking

Forget Moab—Vernal has great mountain biking and far less hype. McCoy Flats, 10 miles (16 km) west of Vernal, has about 35 miles (56 km) of trails, all starting from a trailhead on McCoy Flats Road. Another good trail system is in the Red Mountain area north of town. Check in at **Altitude Cycle** (580 E. Main St., 435/781-2595, 10am-6pm Tues.-Fri., 9am-5pm Sat.) for info on trails. The Utah Mountain Biking website (www.utahmountainbiking.com) has good descriptions of local trails, as does the Dinosaurland site (www.dinoland.com).

River Rafting

River trips down the Green River's Split Mountain Gorge through Dinosaur National Monument provide the excitement of big rapids and the beauty of remote canyons. The Yampa River, a tributary of the Colorado, joins the Green River in Dinosaur National Monument. Both are good rafting destinations. Experienced rafters will enjoy the challenge of the Class III-IV run down

petroglyphs in Dry Fork Canyon

the Cross Mountain Gorge in the Yampa River. One-day trips on the Green River through Split Mountain Canyon or below Flaming Gorge Dam and longer trips on the Green and Yampa are offered by **Don Hatch River Expeditions** (435/789-4316 or 800/342-8243, www.donhatchrivertrips. com). **Adrift Adventures** (9500 E. 6000 S., Jensen, 800/824-0150, https://adrift. com) has day trips through Split Mountain Canyon, and **Dinosaur River Expeditions** (550 E. Main St., 435/499-9181, www. dinosaurriverexpeditions.com) runs day trips in Flaming Gorge. Expect to pay about $115 adults, $95 children for day trips and about $250-3500 per day for longer excursions.

FOOD

A favorite and extremely casual spot for a burger, sweet potato fries, and Utah microbrew is the **Dinosaur Brew Haus** (550 E. Main St., 435/781-0717, 11am-9pm daily, $9-16). The **Vernal Brewing Company** (55 S. 500 E., 435/781-2337, www.vernalbrewingco. com, 11:30am-9pm Sun.-Thurs., 11:30am-10pm Fri.-Sat., $13-33) is a newer, more upscale pub across from the dinosaur museum, with beers ranging from a lager to a milk stout, decent pizza and creative specials, including bacon confit game hen served with quinoa. The **Quarry Steakhouse** (25 S. Vernal Ave., 435/789-8578, 11am-9pm Mon.-Thurs., 11am-10pm Fri.-Sat., $14-36) is a casual family-run restaurant with burgers, grilled chicken, steaks, and a couple of beers on tap; in the summer, you can dine on a flower basket-lined patio.

Hungry for pizza? **Antica Forma** (251 E. Main St., 435/374-4138, 11am-9pm Mon.-Thurs., 11am-10pm Fri.-Sat., $12-23) is far the best bet in Vernal; it's also a good place to pick up a panini or sandwich to pack along for lunch or settle in for a lasagna dinner.

ACCOMMODATIONS

Vernal is the lodging hub for many people who work in the area's oil fields, so motels can be booked pretty full. Weekend prices tend to be a little lower and rooms easier to book.

The **Econo Lodge Downtown** (311 E. Main St., 435/789-2000, www.econolodge. com, $50-60), near the Field House museum, offers clean and basic guest rooms with microwaves and fridges. Another good in-town motel with reasonable rates is **Antlers Inn** (423 W. Main St., 435/789-1202, $75); make sure ask at the desk for a breakfast voucher for the restaurant next door.

Well south of town along U.S. 191 is the **Quality Inn** (1684 W. U.S. 40, 435/789-9550, $73-149), with an indoor pool, a hot tub, and a well-regarded restaurant. The **Best Western Dinosaur Inn** (251 E. Main St., 435/315-0123, $90-100) has a pool, a hot tub, and an exercise room. The **Springhill Suites** (1250 W. U.S. 40, 435/781-9000, $124-134) is pretty stylish for Vernal, with modern decor, an indoor pool, a fitness center, and a breakfast buffet. One of Vernal's newest hotels is the **Ledgestone Hotel** (679 W. Main St., 435/789-4200, $89-99), where all rooms have kitchenettes.

A few miles east of Vernal in Jensen, the **Jensen Inn** (5056 S. 9500 E., 435/789-5905, www.thejenseninn.com, $100-125) has B&B rooms in a large house in a rural setting. This makes a convenient base for exploring Dinosaur National Monument.

Campgrounds

Unless you really need to be in Vernal, or can't drive a mile (1.6 km) farther, it's best to camp north of town toward Flaming Gorge or east in Dinosaur National Monument. But if you must stay in Vernal, or you want full hookups, **Dinosaurland KOA** (930 N. Vernal Ave., 435/789-2148 or 800/562-7574, www.dinokoa.com, Apr.-Oct., tents $28, hookups $48-73) is on the north side of town. It has showers, a pool, laundry, and miniature golf. **Fossil Valley RV Park** (999 W. U.S. 40, 435/789-6450, www.fossilvalleyrvpark.com, Apr.-Nov., hookups $35-41) has showers and laundry.

INFORMATION AND SERVICES

The **Utah Welcome Center** (435/789-6932, 9am-dusk daily), off U.S. 40 in Jensen, a few miles east of Vernal, has lots of information on northeastern Utah and the rest of the state. Contact the **Dinosaurland Travel Board** (800/477-8558, www.dinoland.com) for visitor info and events.

Contact the **Vernal Ranger District Office** (355 N. Vernal Ave., 435/789-1181, www.fs.usda.gov/ashley, 8am-5pm Mon.-Fri.)

of the Ashley National Forest for information about scenic drives, camping, hiking, cross-country skiing, and snowmobiling in the eastern Uinta Mountains. The **Bureau of Land Management Vernal District Office** (170 S. 500 E., 435/781-4400, www.blm.gov/ut, 7:45am-4:30pm Mon.-Fri.) offers information on the John Jarvie Historic Ranch in the northeast corner of the state and areas south of Vernal.

Ashley Regional Medical Center (151 W. 100 N., 435/789-3342) provides hospital care.

Vicinity of Vernal

From Vernal, U.S. 191 heads north, up and over the Uinta Mountains, to Flaming Gorge, where a dam backs up the Green River. The drive is picturesque but not entirely pristine—views include vast phosphate mining operations and scars from off-road vehicles. For the best photos, head up here in the evening, when the light is beautiful.

Few paved roads cross the vast area south of Vernal between U.S. 40 and I-70. The Green River flows south from here through the spectacular Desolation and Gray Canyons; most river-runners put in for this stretch at Sand Wash, accessible by dirt roads from Price or the crossroads hamlet of Myton (on U.S. 40 between Roosevelt and Duchesne) or by airplane from the town of Green River (there's an airstrip at Sand Wash).

Most travelers don't linger along the U.S. 40 corridor west of Vernal; however, there are several jumping-off spots to the Uinta Mountains, north of the highway, along this route. If you just need a place to take a break from driving on U.S. 40, Starvation Reservoir is a good bet.

NORTH OF VERNAL
Wildlife Through the Ages Scenic Byway

This scenic interpretive route follows U.S. 191 and Highway 44 north from Vernal to

Flaming Gorge Reservoir. As the road climbs, you cross 19 geologic formations—an exceptionally thick geologic layer cake—revealing rock layers from the period of the creation of the Uinta Mountains and on through the periods of erosion that followed. The 30-mile (48-km) drive begins 4 miles (6.4 km) north of town on U.S. 191; a tour map at a pullout shows the formations to be seen ahead. Signs on the drive identify and briefly describe each formation from the Mancos (80 million years old) to the Uinta Mountain Group (one billion years old).

Steinaker State Park

Water sports, fishing, camping, and picnicking at 750-acre Steinaker Reservoir at **Steinaker State Park** (4335 N. U.S. 191, 435/789-4432, http://stateparks.utah.gov, year-round, day-use $8) make this a popular place to escape the desert heat in summer. The **campground** (800/322-3770, http://utahstateparks.reserveamerica.com, $9 reservation fee, tents $15, RVs $23-28) is at an elevation of 5,500 feet; it's open year-round but the water is turned off in the winter. From Vernal, go north 6 miles (9.7 km) on U.S. 191, then turn left and continue 2 miles (3.2 km).

Red Fleet State Park

Colorful cliffs and rock formations, including

three large outcrops of red sandstone, inspired the name of Red Fleet Reservoir in **Red Fleet State Park** (8750 N. U.S. 191, 435/789-4432, http://stateparks.utah.gov, year-round, day-use $8). Like the larger Steinaker Reservoir, Red Fleet stores water for irrigation and municipal use and has a **campground** (800/322-3770, http://utahstateparks.reserveamerica.com, $9 reservation fee, tents $15, RVs $25 with hookups); the park also rents canoes, kayaks, and stand-up paddleboards. From Vernal, go north 10 miles (16 km) on U.S. 191 to milepost 211, then turn right and continue 2 miles (3.2 km) on a paved road to its end.

A moderately rigorous 2.5-mile (4-km) round-trip hike from the northern section of the park leads through desert landscape to a **dinosaur trackway** on the north shore of Red Fleet Reservoir. Three-toed upright dinos laid down these tracks in a soft mud playa (now Navajo sandstone) about 200 million years ago. It's easiest to see these sometimes elusive tracks on a cloudy day or when the sun is low in the sky. Find the turnoff from U.S. 191 across from the big Simplot sign; follow this road 2.3 miles (3.7 km) east to the trailhead.

Red Cloud Loop Scenic Drive

This 45-mile (72 km) loop winds through scenic canyons and mountains northwest of Vernal. Allow about three hours just for the drive. Side roads go to East Park and Oaks Park Reservoirs, campgrounds, fishing streams, and hiking areas. Aspen trees put on a brilliant display in autumn. About half the drive follows unpaved forest roads, so it's a good idea to check road conditions first with the **U.S. Forest Service Office** (353 N. Vernal Ave., Vernal, 435/789-1181). Cars with good clearance can usually make the trip if the roads are dry. Drive 20 miles north from Vernal on U.S. 191 (or 15 miles/24 km south from the junction of U.S. 191 and Highway 44 in Flaming Gorge National Recreation Area) and turn west onto the paved East Park Reservoir Road at the Red Cloud Loop sign. Signs then show the rest of the way. The

Jensen Welcome Center's brochure *Red Cloud Loop* describes points of interest.

It's easy to find a campsite along Red Cloud Loop. **East Park Campground** (mid-June-mid-Sept., $12) at East Park Reservoir (elev. 9,000 feet) has water; go 20 miles (32 km) north of Vernal on U.S. 191, then 10 miles (16 km) northwest on forest roads. All but the last mile are paved. Other campgrounds include **Oaks Park** (June-mid-Sept., free), **Paradise Park** (elev. 10,000 feet, June-mid-Sept., $5), **Kaler Hollow** (elev. 8,900 feet, June-Oct., free), and **Whiterocks** (mid-May-mid-Sept., $8). Of these, only Whiterocks, in a popular OHV area, has drinking water.

ROOSEVELT AND VICINITY

Roosevelt (pop. 6,900) is the largest town in Duchesne County and a supply center for surrounding agricultural and oil businesses and for the Utes. Roosevelt offers a few places to stay and eat along the main highway (200 East and 200 North downtown). The community is 30 miles (48 km) west of Vernal and 146 miles (235 km) east of Salt Lake City. Travelers can head north to Moon Lake and the High Uintas Wilderness. A scenic backcountry drive goes south to the many rock-art sites in Nine Mile Canyon.

Fishing Resorts

Anglers will love **LC Ranch** (14535 W. 4000 N., Altamont, 435/454-3750, www.lcranch.com, $100-150 for two people), just north of Altamont. The ranch was established in 1901 by an enterprising homesteader who decided to develop his holdings into a series of streams and ponds. Now a private reserve, the ranch contains 28 lakes and ponds filled with brookies, rainbow, and brown trout (extra fees charged for fishing and guides). Accommodations are in upscale cabins or larger lodges (a large lodge can sleep eight, $500), including one decorated with more than 30 trophy mounts.

An exclusive resort in the area is ★ **Falcon's Ledge** (P.O. Box 67, Altamont,

435/454-3737, www.falconsledge.com, $195, includes breakfast), an Orvis-endorsed lodge built to cater to fly fishers and upland game bird hunters, although the luxury guest rooms and fine restaurant attract an increasing number of people who simply want to enjoy solitude and soft recreation. Guest rooms are located in a central lodge and are extremely comfortable. Breakfast is included, but other meals are by reservation only and are served family-style. Two days of guided fishing and three nights of lodging (meals included) runs upward of $650 per person.

Ashley National Forest

Moon Lake is in the Uintas, about 45 miles (72 km) due north of Duchesne and 50 miles (81 km) northwest of Roosevelt. Access roads are paved, except for a 7-mile (11.3-km) section crossing tribal lands. **Moon Lake Resort** (summer 435/454-3142, winter 970/731-9906, www.moonlakeresort.com, $85-185) offers cabins of varying degrees of rusticity (most have a bathroom) and boat rentals mid-May-mid-October.

Major access points to the High Uintas Wilderness near Roosevelt are (from west to east): Lake Fork at Moon Lake (three trails), Center Park at the head of Hells Canyon, Swift Creek on the Yellowstone River (two trails), Uinta Canyon on the Uinta River, and West Fork of Whiterocks River. Five campgrounds are located along the Yellowstone River on Forest Roads 119 and 124 northwest of Roosevelt. Elevations are around 8,000 feet. **Swift Creek Campground** ($8) is highest at 8,100 feet; all have water and charge a fee from late May until the week after Labor Day. **Uinta Canyon** ($5) has no water and but is along the Uinta River at an elevation of about 7,600 feet; take Highway 121 and Forest Road 118 north of Roosevelt.

DUCHESNE AND VICINITY

The small community of Duchesne (doo-SHAYN, pop. 1,700), at the confluence of the Duchesne and Strawberry Rivers, is the seat of thinly settled Duchesne County, where ranching, farming, and the oil industry provide most of the employment. Main attractions for visitors are the High Uintas Wilderness and other sections of the Ashley National Forest, Starvation Lake, and fishing on the Duchesne and Strawberry Rivers. Although there are motels and a café in town, there are more accommodations down the road in Roosevelt.

Highway 35 heads northwest out of Duchesne and provides access to the Uinta Mountains. It's a long haul to get to these pretty spots; the **Duchesne Ranger District Office** (85 W. Main St., 435/738-2482, www.fs.usda.gov/ashley) of the Ashley National Forest has information on campgrounds, trailheads, and road conditions for this part of the Uintas.

From Duchesne, U.S. 191 goes southwest 56 scenic miles (90 km) over the West Tavaputs Plateau to Price. The route follows the Left Fork of Indian Canyon to a pass at an elevation of 9,100 feet and then descends through Willow Creek Canyon to the Price River. Snow may close the road in winter.

Starvation State Park

The large Starvation Reservoir in **Starvation State Park** (435/738-2326, http://stateparks.utah.gov, year-round, day-use $10, camping $25-28) is among rolling hills of high-desert country 4 miles (6.4 km) west of Duchesne. Waterskiing is the biggest summer activity, followed by fishing, sailboarding, and sailing. Anglers catch walleye (a state record was taken here), smallmouth bass, and some largemouth bass and German brown trout. A marina is open mid-April through Labor Day with boat rentals (fishing, ski boats, and other watercraft) and a store. Other facilities include a paved boat ramp, a fish-cleaning station, and a dump station. The park's summer season (Memorial Day-Labor Day) is sometimes extended up to a month earlier and later. A paved 4-mile (6.4-km) road to the park turns off U.S. 40 just west of Duchesne.

Dinosaur National Monument

Dinosaur National Monument (4545 E. U.S. 40, Dinosaur, CO, 435/781-7700, www.nps.gov/dino, $25 per vehicle, $20 per motorcycle, $15 pedestrians and bicyclists) owes its name and fame to one of the world's most productive sites for dinosaur bones.

The monument straddles the Utah-Colorado border, but only the area around the quarry, in the western end of the monument, has dinosaur bones. The spectacular canyons of the Green and Yampa Rivers form another aspect of the monument. Harpers Corner Scenic Drive winds onto high ridges and canyon viewpoints in the heart of Dinosaur National Monument. River running allows a close look at the geology and wildlife within the depths and provides the bonus of thrilling rapids.

Elevations range from 4,750 feet at the Green River near the quarry to 9,006 feet atop Zenobia Peak of Douglas Mountain. The high country is part of the east flank of the Uinta Mountains, which has geology that is graphically revealed in the deep canyons of the Green and Yampa Rivers.

DINOSAUR QUARRY AREA

Visitors Center

The **Quarry Visitor Center** (Hwy. 149, 435/781-7700, 8am-6pm daily mid-May-mid Sept., 9am-5pm daily mid-Sept.-mid-May), located 7 miles (11.3 km) north of Jensen, is the jumping-off place for a visit to the Quarry Exhibit Hall.

Quarry Exhibit Hall

Approximately 1,500 bones of 11 different dinosaur species cover a rock face at the Quarry Exhibit Hall, located in a striking new building a short drive from the visitors center. The ranger talks at the quarry are worth catching, and this is one of the few museums where visitors are actually allowed to touch the dinosaur bones. As well as the bones themselves, the exhibit hall houses reconstructions of dinosaurs whose bones were found scattered in the quarry.

The quarry was discovered in the early 1900s and excavated from about 1909 to 1924. Bones were carefully exposed, and even though some were shipped off to museums around the world, most were left in the soil as they were found. The quarry has produced more complete skeletons, skulls, and juvenile specimens than any other site in the world. But the quarry wall is not the only place in the monument where dinosaur bones are sequestered. In 2010, paleontologists discovered the complete skull of a new, large plant-eating dinosaur, *Abydosaurus mcintoshi,* from the monument's Cedar Mountain Formation.

During the summer season, visitors must first stop by the Quarry Visitor Center and board a shuttle bus to the quarry site. Buses leave every 15 minutes 8am-5pm daily. In the early fall and late spring, pick up a pass at the visitors center; this will allow you to drive the steep 0.25 mile (0.4 km) to the quarry. During the winter, early spring, and late fall, rangers guide car caravans from the visitors center to the Quarry Exhibit Hall at 9:30am, 10:30am, 11:30am, 1pm, 2pm, 3pm, and 4pm daily.

Cub Creek Scenic Drive

Stop at the Quarry Visitor Center or a roadside pullout for the booklet *Tour of the Tilted Rocks,* which describes numbered points of interest for an auto tour on Cub Creek Road. The drive begins at the Quarry Visitor Center and goes 10 miles (16 km) past the quarry turnoff to a historic ranch, passing sites of Fremont rock art and the Split Mountain and Green River Campgrounds on the way. A small overhang known as the **Swelter Shelter** contains some petroglyphs. The pullout is 1 mile (1.6 km) beyond the quarry turnoff; a trail

Dinosaur National Monument

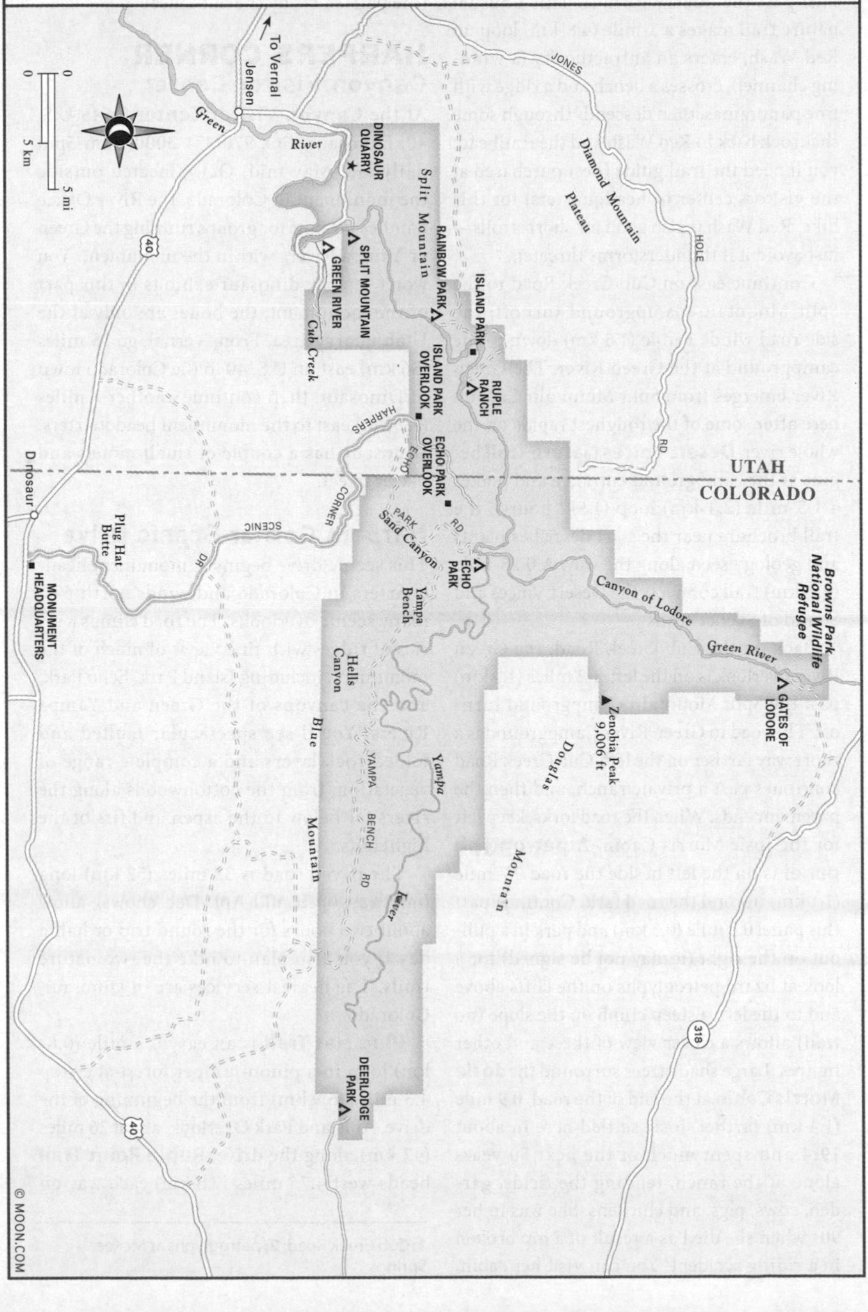

To Vernal

Jensen

Green River

JONES

Diamond Mountain Plateau

DINOSAUR QUARRY

Split Mountain

RAINBOW PARK

SPLIT MOUNTAIN

GREEN RIVER

Cub Creek

ISLAND PARK

ISLAND PARK OVERLOOK

RUPLE RANCH

ECHO PARK OVERLOOK

HARPERS

ECHO

CORNER

Sand Canyon

PARK

RD

ECHO PARK

Yampa Bench

HOLE

RD

UTAH
COLORADO

Browns Park National Wildlife Refugee

Canyon of Lodore

Green River

GATES OF LODORE

Plug Hat Butte

SCENIC

DR

Dinosaur

MONUMENT HEADQUARTERS

Hells Canyon

Blue Mountain

Yampa

YAMPA BENCH RD

Douglas Mountain

Zenobia Peak 9,006 ft

River

DEERLODGE PARK

318

40

40

© MOON.COM

leads 200 feet to the cave. **Sound of Silence Hiking Trail** begins on the left 1.9 miles (3 km) past the quarry turnoff. This unusual nature trail makes a 3-mile (4.8-km) loop up Red Wash, enters an anfractuosity (a winding channel), crosses a bench and a ridge with fine panoramas, then descends through some slickrock back to Red Wash and the trailhead; you'll need the trail guide (best purchased at the visitors center or headquarters) for this hike. Red Wash is also good for short strolls—just avoid it if thunderstorms threaten.

Continue east on Cub Creek Road to the Split Mountain Campground turnoff; the side road winds 1 mile (1.6 km) down to the campground at the Green River. The Green River emerges from Split Mountain Canyon here after some of the roughest rapids on the whole river. **Desert Voices Nature Trail** begins at the campground entrance and makes a 1.5-mile (2.4-km) loop (1.5-2 hours); the trail brochure near the start describes plants and geology seen along the way. A 0.25-mile (0.4-km) trail connects the Desert Voices and Sound of Silence trails.

Back on the Cub Creek Road, the Green River overlook is on the left, 1.2 miles (1.9 km) past the Split Mountain Campground turnoff. The road to Green River Campground is a short way farther on the left. Cub Creek Road continues past a private ranch, and then the pavement ends. When the road forks, keep left for the Josie Morris Cabin. A **petroglyph panel** is on the left beside the road 0.7 mile (1.1 km) beyond the road fork. Continue past this panel 0.2 mile (0.3 km) and park in a pullout on the right (it may not be signed) for a look at lizard petroglyphs on the cliffs above and to the left; a steep climb up the slope (no trail) allows a closer view of these and other figures. Large shade trees surround the **Josie Morris Cabin** at the end of the road, 0.9 mile (1.4 km) farther. Josie settled here in about 1914 and spent much of the next 50 years alone at the ranch, tending the fields, garden, cows, pigs, and chickens. She was in her 90s when she died as a result of a hip broken in a riding accident. You can visit her cabin,

outbuildings, and orchards; be sure to walk 0.25 mile (0.4 km) or so up a lovely box canyon (the path starts by the outhouse).

HARPERS CORNER
Canyon Visitor Center

At the **Canyon Visitor Center** (4545 U.S. 40, Dinosaur, CO, 970/374-3000, 9am-5pm daily late May-mid. Oct.), located outside the monument in Colorado, the River Office handles permits for groups running the Green or Yampa Rivers within the monument. You won't see any dinosaur exhibits in this part of the monument; the bones are only at the Utah quarry area. From Vernal, go 35 miles (56 km) east on U.S. 40 to the Colorado town of Dinosaur, then continue another 2 miles (3.2 km) east to the monument headquarters. Dinosaur has a couple of small motels and places to eat.

Harpers Corner Scenic Drive

This scenic drive begins at monument headquarters in Colorado and winds north past many scenic overlooks. The road climbs a series of ridges with fine views of much of the monument, including Island Park, Echo Park, and the canyons of the Green and Yampa Rivers. You'll see spectacular faulted and folded rock layers and a complete range of vegetation, from the cottonwoods along the rivers far below to the aspen and firs of the highlands.

The paved road is 32 miles (52 km) long (one-way, open mid-Apr.-Dec. snows); allow about two hours for the round trip or half a day if you also plan to hike the two nature trails. The nearest services are in Dinosaur, Colorado.

Plug Hat Trail is an easy 0.5-mile (0.8-km) loop in a piñon-juniper forest at a stop 4.3 miles (6.9 km) from the beginning of the drive. At Island Park Overlook, about 26 miles (42 km) along the drive, **Ruple Point Trail** heads west 4.75 miles (7.6 km) each way on

1: Cub Creek Road; **2:** petroglyphs at McKee Springs

an old jeep road to an overlook of the Green River in Split Mountain Canyon; carry water. The drive ends at Harpers Corner, a long and narrow peninsula. You can continue 1.5 miles (2.4 km) on foot to the very tip by taking the **Harpers Corner Trail.** Cliffs on each side drop to a bend of the Green River at the beginning of Whirlpool Canyon, about 2,500 feet below. Echo Park, Steamboat Rock, and the sinuous curves of the Yampa River Canyon are also visible. Allow 1.5-2 hours for the easy to moderate walk.

Echo Park

A rough dirt road branches off Harpers Corner Road 25 miles (40 km) from monument headquarters and winds down more than 2,000 vertical feet in 14 miles (22.5 km) to Echo Park. The setting of Echo Park, near the confluence of the Green and Yampa Rivers, is one of the prettiest in the monument. The massive sandstone fin of Steamboat Rock looms into the sky across the Green River. Echo Park offers a campground, river access for boaters (permit required), and a ranger station (summer only). Cars with good clearance can often make this side trip, although it's better to have a truck; RVs and trailers shouldn't attempt it. As with all dirt roads in Dinosaur National Monument, it shouldn't be driven in any vehicle when it's wet. The clay surface becomes extremely slick after rains but usually dries out in 2-3 hours.

RAINBOW PARK AND ISLAND PARK

Rainbow Park and Ruple Ranch are on the west shore of the Green River at opposite ends of Island Park. Both offer places to launch or take out river boats. **Petroglyphs** are a short walk from the pullout at McKee Springs. The **Ruple Ranch** is a former sheep and cattle ranch; the original corrals and loafing shed are still on-site. The easiest access is from the quarry area; distances are 30 miles (48 km) to Rainbow Park and about another 5 miles (8 km) to Ruple Ranch via the rough and unpaved Island Park Road. Vehicles with good clearance may be able to drive in, but the road is impassable during wet weather.

GATES OF LODORE

Remote Gates of Lodore, on the Green River, has a campground, a boat launching area for river runners, and a ranger station—all open year-round. The **Gates of Lodore Nature Trail** follows the Green River downstream to the dramatic entrance of Lodore Canyon, an easy 1.5-mile (2.4-km) round-trip; pick up a trail brochure at the ranger station or the trailhead. The Gates of Lodore is 108 miles from monument headquarters via U.S. 40, Highway 318, and a long 10 miles (16 km) of gravel road.

RIVER RUNNING

Trips down the Green or Yampa Rivers feature outstanding scenery and exciting rapids. All boaters in the monument must have permits or be with a licensed river-running company, even for day trips. Applications for a permit lottery are accepted December 1-January 31 and are available online (www.recreation.gov, permit application $15, permit fee $20 for one day). If you miss the lottery, visit www.recreation.gov or call the monument's River Office (970/374-2468, 8am-noon Mon.-Fri.) to check on available launch dates. One-day permits are the easiest to get. The *Dinosaur River Guide,* by Laura Evans and Buzz Belknap, has maps and descriptions of both rivers in the monument; be aware that neither river is for novice rafters; rapids are as high as Class 4.

Guided trips are often best for first-time visitors. The following raft companies are among those authorized to guide one-day and multiple-day trips in the monument: **Adrift Adventures** (9500 E. 6000 S., Jensen, 435/789-3600 or 800/824-0150, www.adrift.com), **Don Hatch River Expeditions** (435/789-4316 or 800/342-8243, www.donhatchrivertrips.com), and **Dinosaur Expeditions** (800/345-7238, www.dinosaurriverexpeditions.com). The most popular one-day run on the Green

River begins at Rainbow Park or Ruple Ranch. Rafters bounce through the Class I-III rapids of Split Mountain Canyon for 9 miles (14.5 km) to takeouts at Split Mountain Campground. Commercial day trips run about $100-120 for adults, $75-100 children.

Longer trips usually begin on the Green River at Gates of Lodore in the north end of the monument. Echo Park marks the end of Lodore Canyon. The Yampa River, the last major undammed tributary of the Colorado River system, joins the Green here and noticeably increases its size and power. Trips usually end with a series of rapids through Split Mountain Canyon. A three-day commercial trip costs about $800.

CAMPGROUNDS

Dinosaur National Monument has two pleasant riverside campgrounds—Green River and Split Mountain—within about a mile (1.6 km) of each other. **Green River Campground** (year-round, has water, $18) is 5 miles (8 km) east of the Quarry Visitor Center in Jensen. **Split Mountain Campground** (has water) is a group campground ($40) during the high season. It serves as a general purpose campground from the first week of October to mid-April; during this time, there is a $6 fee. It's 4 miles (6.4 km) east of Dinosaur Quarry, then 1 mile (1.6 km) north on Split Mountain Road.

There are several other campsites in the monument. One of the nicest is **Echo Park Campground** (year-round, has water, $6-10), 38 miles north of monument headquarters, with several walk-in tent sites. The last 13 miles (21 km) of the road to Echo Park are unpaved and impassable when wet. RVs and trailers are not recommended. A small campground at **Gates of Lodore** (year-round, has water, $6-10) has a boat launch. **Deerlodge Park Campground** (year-round, has water, $6-10), at the east end of the monument, sits just upstream from the Yampa River Canyon. River trips on the Yampa usually begin here. Deerlodge is 53 miles (85 km) from monument headquarters by paved roads. A small primitive campground at **Rainbow Park** (year-round, no water, $6) is 26 miles (42 km) from Dinosaur Quarry on an unpaved road.

All campsites in the monument are available on a first-come, first-served basis.

Flaming Gorge National Recreation Area

The Flaming Gorge Dam impounds the Green River just south of the Wyoming border, backing up a reservoir through 91 miles (148 km) of gentle valleys and fiery red canyons. The rugged land displays spectacular scenery where the Green River cuts into the Uinta Mountains—cliffs rising as high as 1,500 feet, twisted rock formations, and sweeping panoramas. Although much of the lake is in Wyoming, most of the campgrounds and other visitor facilities, as well as the best scenery, are in Utah.

A $5 recreation pass is required if you do anything but drive through the area. Purchase a pass at the U.S. Forest Service offices in Manila or Vernal, at the Flaming Gorge Dam, the Red Canyon Visitor Center, or at one of several self-service pay stations.

FLAMING GORGE DAM AND VISITOR CENTER

Nearly one million cubic yards of concrete went into this massive dam, which was completed in 1964. The **visitors center** (435/885-3135, www.fs.usda.gov/ashley, tours 9am-5pm daily Apr. 15-Sept. 15) has a large 3-D map of the area, exhibits, and video programs. The dam and visitors center are 6.5 miles (10.5 km) northeast from the junction with Highway 44 on U.S. 191, and 2.8 miles (4.5 km) southwest of Dutch John.

★ RED CANYON VISITOR CENTER

The **Red Canyon Visitor Center** (435/889-3713, 10am-5pm Mon.-Fri., 9am-6pm Sat.-Sun. Memorial Day-Labor Day, $5 recreation pass required) has what may be Utah's best picture window onto sheer cliffs dropping 1,360 feet to the lake below. Nearby viewpoints, connected by a trail along the canyon rim, offer splendid panoramas up and down the canyon and to the lofty Uinta Mountains in the distance. The visitors center is 3.5 miles (5.6 km) west on Highway 44 from the junction with U.S. 191, then 3 miles (4.8 km) in on a paved road.

SHEEP CREEK CANYON GEOLOGICAL AREA

Canyon walls on this scenic loop drive reveal rock layers deformed and turned on end by immense geological forces. The earth's crust broke along the Uinta North Fault, and the south side rose 15,000 feet relative to the north. Fossils of trilobites, corals, sea urchins, gastropods, and other marine animals show that the ocean once covered this spot before the uplifting and faulting. Rock layers of yet another time preserve fossilized wood and tracks of crocodile-like reptiles.

The road through Sheep Creek Canyon is paved but has some narrow and rough places; it's closed in winter. The 13-mile (21-km) loop branches off Highway 44 south of Manila between mileposts 14 and 15 and rejoins Highway 44 at milepost 22; the loop can be done in either direction, and a short nature trail at the northern end of the loop drive is a good place to look for the local bighorn sheep. The *Wheels of Time* geology brochure, available at visitors centers, describes geologic formations at marked stops. Two primitive campgrounds (outhouses but no water or established sites)

are just off Highway 44, along lower Sheep Creek, a short way from the entrance to the scenic loop.

SWETT RANCH

Oscar Swett homesteaded near Flaming Gorge in 1909, when he was just 16 years old, then built up a large cattle ranch in this isolated region. With the nearest store days away, Oscar ran his own blacksmith shop and sawmill and did much of the ranch work; his wife, Emma, tended the garden, made the family's clothing, raised nine children, and helped with the ranch chores. You can experience some of the early homestead life on a visit to **Swett Ranch** (435/789-1181, 9am-4pm Thurs.-Mon. Memorial Day-Labor Day). Drive north 0.3 mile (0.5 km) on U.S. 191 from the Highway 44 junction (or south 1.6 miles/2.6 km from Flaming Gorge Lodge), then turn west and follow the signs 1.3 miles (2.1 km) on a dirt road.

DUTCH JOHN

Dutch John sprang up in 1957-1958 to house workers during the construction of Flaming Gorge Dam and had a peak population of about 3,000. About 150 current residents work for various state and federal agencies. **Dutch John Resort** (1050 South Blvd., Dutch John, 435/885-3000, www.dutchjohnresort.com), at the turnoff for Dutch John on U.S. 191, has an RV park ($15-35), cabins ($49-249), a snack bar, raft rentals and shuttle services, and hot showers.

MANILA

The tiny town of Manila is a handy, though rather bare bones, base for travel in the Flaming Gorge area. The town is 63 miles (101 km) northwest of Vernal and 46 miles (74 km) south of Green River, Wyoming, and is home to the **Flaming Gorge Ranger District Manila Headquarters Office** (25 W. Hwy. 43, Manila, 435/784-3445, www.fs.usda.gov/

1: view of the Flaming Gorge; **2:** Sheep Creek Canyon Geological Area

ashley, 8am-4:30pm Mon.-Fri.), at the junction of Highway 44 and Highway 43. Gas up in Manila if you're running low.

RECREATION

Some of northeastern Utah's best mountain biking can be found around the Flaming Gorge area. Boating on the clear blue waters of the lake or the river below is one of the best ways to enjoy the sights. Waterskiers have plenty of room on the lake's 66 square miles (106 square km). Swimming is also popular, as is scuba diving; **Atlantis Divers** (206 W. Main St., Vernal, 435/789-3616, www.atlantisdivers.com) is the best resource for diving in the reservoir. Anglers regularly pull trophy trout and smallmouth bass from the lake and trout from the river. Rafting the lively Green River below the dam offers a thrilling ride that anyone with care and proper safety equipment can take. The U.S. Forest Service and private concessions offer boating facilities and about two dozen campgrounds in the recreation area.

Peace, quiet, and snow prevail in winter. Dedicated anglers still cast their lines into the Green River or fish through the lake ice. Cross-country skiers and snowmobilers make their trails through the woods. Campgrounds are closed, although snow campers and hardy RVers can stop for the night in parking areas.

Flaming Gorge Reservoir

Marinas along the lake's length offer rentals, fuel docks, guides, and supplies. Free paved boat ramps at these and several other locations are maintained by the Forest Service. **Cedar Springs Marina** (Dutch John, 435/889-3795, www.cedarspringsmarina.com, May-Sept.) is 2 miles (3.2 km) south of the dam at the lower end of the lake, and **Lucerne Valley Marina** (Manila, 435/784-3483, www.flaminggorge. com, Mar.-mid-Nov.), 8 miles (12.9 km) east of Manila, provides services, including watercraft rentals ranging from paddleboards to houseboats, on the broad central section of the lake.

The Green River Below Flaming Gorge Dam

The Green bounces back to life in the Little Hole Canyon below the Flaming Gorge Dam and provides enjoyment for boaters, anglers, and hikers.

RAFTING TRIPS

Visitors with canoes, kayaks, and dories can float all sections of the Green River between the dam and Gates of Lodore, although river experience is needed. Raft rentals and shuttle services are provided by **Flaming Gorge Resort** (435/889-3773, www. flaminggorgeresort.com) and **Dutch John Resort** (435/885-3000, www.dutchjohnresort. com). Rentals typically cost $50-100 per day, depending on the size of the raft; vehicle shuttles cost about $45 to Little Hole, a 2.5-hour river trip. The 10 Class II rapids between the dam and Little Hole lend some excitement to the trip but aren't usually dangerous, although the water is quite cold. No motors are allowed between the dam and Indian Crossing. Water flow varies according to power needs; allow more time if the flow is small. Call the Bureau of Reclamation (435/885-3121) for present conditions.

The put-in is at the end of a 1.4-mile (2.3-km) paved road that turns off U.S. 191 (it may not be signed) 0.3 mile (0.5 km) east of the dam. The parking area at the river is small and is for unloading boats and passengers only. The main parking areas are 0.7 mile (1.1 km) back up the road. Drivers can take either of two foot trails that descend from the parking lots to the river. The shuttle to Little Hole is only 8 paved miles (12.9 km) via Dutch John.

FISHING

Anglers can follow the **Little Hole National Recreation Trail** along the north bank of the Green River through Red Canyon for 7 miles (11.3 km) between the main parking area below the dam and Little Hole. Many good fishing spots dot the way. No camping, horses, ground fires, or motorized vehicles are allowed. The Green River downstream from the dam has a reputation for some of the West's best river fishing. Modifications to the dam allow the ideal temperature mix of warmer water near the lake's surface and cold water from the depths. Special regulations apply here to maintain the high-quality fishing (check for current regulations). Anglers using waders should wear life jackets in case the river level rises unexpectedly; neoprene closed-cell foam waders are recommended for extra flotation and protection against hypothermia.

Hiking and Biking

The **Canyon Rim Trail** is a popular 4.2-mile (6.8 km) each way hike or mountain bike ride with trailheads at Red Canyon Visitor Center and the Greendale Overlook, a short distance from the junction of U.S. 191 and Highway 44. **Browne Lake** is a popular starting point for hikes outside the recreation area: Trail 005 goes to the **Ute Mountain Fire Lookout Tower,** a national historic site (2 miles/3.2 km one-way); Trail 016 goes to **Hacking Lake** (7 miles/11.3 km one-way); Trail 012 goes to **Tepee Lakes** (5 miles/8 km one-way) and **Leidy Peak** (elev. 12,028 feet, 8 miles/12.9 km one-way); and Trail 017 goes to **Spirit Lake** (15 miles/24 km one-way). Browne Lake is 4.5

miles (7.2 km) west of the Sheep Creek loop drive on unpaved Forest Road 221, then 1.5 miles (2.4 km) southeast on the Browne Lake road; see the Ashley National Forest map.

Stop by **Altitude Cycle** (580 E. Main St., Vernal, 435/781-2595) for a guide to mountain bike trails in northeastern Utah. Rentals are available at the Red Canyon Lodge. Visitors centers and U.S. Forest Service offices have maps of hiking and mountain bike trails and can suggest dirt roads suitable for either activity.

FOOD AND ACCOMMODATIONS

The nicest place to stay in the Flaming Gorge area is **Red Canyon Lodge** (2450 Red Canyon Rd., 435/889-3759, www. redcanyonlodge.com, early Apr.-late Oct. and Sat.-Sun. winter, $129-159), which sits beside Greens Lake, a short distance from the Red Canyon Visitor Center. The lodge has an assortment of cabins that sleep up to six, some with kitchenettes, some with microwaves and fridges. A restaurant opens daily for breakfast, lunch, and dinner; a store offers fishing supplies, a few groceries, bike rentals, horseback riding, and boat rentals on Greens Lake.

Flaming Gorge Resort (1100 E.

view of the Green River from the Canyon Rim Trail

Flaming Gorge Resort, 435/889-3773, www. flaminggorgeresort.com, $125-165), 7 miles (11.3 km) southwest of Dutch John, offers motel rooms and condos year-round and a popular restaurant serving breakfast, lunch, and dinner daily year-round. The lodge also has an RV park, a store, raft rentals, shuttles, and guided river fishing trips.

Campgrounds

Three campgrounds (435/784-3445 or 877/444-6777, www.recreation.gov, mid-May-mid-Sept., $20) are near the Red Canyon Visitor Center: **Red Canyon, Canyon Rim,** and **Greens Lake.** At 7,400 feet, expect cool evenings and mornings. **Lucerne Campground** (877/444-6777,

www.recreation.gov, May-Sept., $20), 8 miles (12.9 km) east of Manila, is on the shores of the Flaming Gorge Reservoir. Several primitive campgrounds on the lake can be reached only by boat or trail. In Manila, the **Flaming Gorge KOA** (320 W. Hwy. 43, 435/784-3184, mid Apr.-Nov., tents $30, hookups $41, cabins $56) has showers, laundry, a pool, a playground, and cabins (bring sleeping bags).

GETTING THERE

Flaming Gorge NRA can easily be reached by heading north 35 miles (56 km) on U.S. 191 from Vernal. In Wyoming, head south on Highway 530 from the town of Green River or on U.S. 191 from near Rock Springs.

Price

In the beginning, Price was a typical Mormon community. Ranchers and farmers had settled on the fertile land surrounding the Price River in 1879. Four years later, everything changed when the railroad came through. A flood of immigrants from all over the world arrived to work in the coal mines and other rapidly growing enterprises (an informal census taken in a pool hall at nearby Helper in the 1930s found 32 different nationalities in the room). Coal mining has had its ups and downs over the last 100 years but continues to be the largest industry in the area. Price (approximate pop. 8,000) is a good base for exploring the surrounding mountains and desert.

SIGHTS

USU Eastern Prehistoric Museum

The **Utah State University Eastern Prehistoric Museum** (155 E. Main St., 435/613-5060, http://usueastern.edu/museum, 9am-5pm Mon.-Sat., $6 adults, $5 seniors, $3 ages 2-12), a museum of natural and human history, has simple, old-school, nonflashy displays and is a must-stop for anyone interested

in the prehistoric creatures and the people who lived in Utah thousands of years ago. Dinosaur displays include the skeletons of a fierce flesh-eating allosaurus, a plant-eating *Camptosaurus* (not to be fooled with either), a *Camarasaurus*, a *Chasmosaurus*, a *Prosaurolophus*, and a stegosaurus. See bones of the huge Huntington Canyon mammoth discovered nearby, the colorful gemstones of the mineralogy exhibits, and artifacts of the prehistoric Fremont and the modern Utes in the outstanding Native American collection. The power and mystery of prehistoric rock art is conveyed in a replica of the Barrier Canyon Mural. Contemporary art is on display in rotating exhibits; another display monitors earthquake activity around the world in real time. Kids can explore the hands-on displays in the Children's Room.

FOOD

A number of cafés and diners along Main Street serve standard American fare, but two of the best local restaurants are just out of town. Venture a short distance north toward Helper to find the comfortable

Grogg's Pinnacle Brewing Co. (1653 N. Carbonville Rd., 435/637-2924, www. groggspinnaclebrewing.com, 11am-9pm Mon.-Thurs., 11am-10pm Fri.-Sat., 11am-8pm Sun., $10-24), the local brewpub, with burgers, sandwiches, and full dinners to accompany the handcrafted beers. Just southeast of Price, in Wellington, is the local favorite **Cowboy Club** (31 E. Main St., 435/637-4223, www. cowboyclubut.com, 7am-10pm Sun.-Thurs., 7am-11pm Fri.-Sat., $10-35); although the exterior of the building is a little forbidding, it's worth going in for a steak or sausage made from homegrown lamb.

In downtown Price, **Farlaino's Cafe** (87 W. Main St., 435/637-9217, 7am-7pm Mon.-Sat., $7-12) is an old-fashioned diner that's a good spot for a full breakfast (sit on a spinning stool at the counter and get to know the regulars); at lunch, both Italian and American food is served.

ACCOMMODATIONS

Price has the Castle Valley's best selection of lodgings and reasonable prices, which make it a good, if relatively unexciting, base for exploration of this part of Utah.

At the west end of Main Street is a shopping center complex that includes the **National 9 Price River Inn** (641 W. Price River Dr., 435/637-7000, www.national9price.com, $60). Just to the north is the friendly family-run ★ **Legacy Inn** (145 N. Carbonville Rd., 435/637-2424, www.legacyinnutah.com, $60-70), with an adjoining RV park ($25-40).

One of Price's nicest motels are on the east end of town near a clutch of fast-food restaurants and the local supermarket mall. The **Greenwell Inn** (655 E. Main St., 435/637-3520 or 800/666-3520, www.greenwellinn. com, $53-110) has a pool, an exercise room, a bar, and a decent restaurant.

INFORMATION AND SERVICES

Castle Country Travel Office (751 E. 100 N., 435/636-3701, www.castlecountry.com) offers literature and ideas for travel in Price

and elsewhere in Carbon and Emery Counties from a booth in the Eastern Prehistoric Museum (155 E. Main St., 435/613-5060). The **Manti-La Sal National Forest Offices** (599 W. Price River Dr., 435/637-2817, www. fs.usda.gov/mantilasal, 8am-4:30pm Mon.-Fri.), across from the Creekview Shopping Center on the west edge of town, has information about recreation in the beautiful alpine country of the Wasatch Plateau to the west.

Staff at the **Bureau of Land Management** (125 S. 600 W., 435/636-3600, www.blm.gov/ut) can tell you about exploring the San Rafael Swell, Cleveland-Lloyd Dinosaur Quarry, and Nine Mile Canyon as well as about boating the Green River through Desolation, Gray, and Labyrinth Canyons.

Castleview Hospital (300 N. Hospital Dr., 435/637-4800) is on the west edge of town.

GETTING THERE

Amtrak (800/872-7245, www.amtrak.com) runs its *California Zephyr* trains via nearby Helper, once daily in each direction, on their way between Denver and Salt Lake City.

VICINITY OF PRICE
Helper

North of Price, just as the highway enters a narrow canyon, is the town of Helper, a colorful mix of decrepitude, history, and art. In 1883, the Denver and Rio Grande Western Railroad began building a depot, roundhouse, and other facilities here for its new line. Trains headed up the long grade to Soldier Summit needed extra locomotives, or "helpers," based at the little railroad community, so the place became known as Helper. Miners later joined the railroad workers, and the two groups still make up most of the current population of 2,500. The fine examples of early 20th-century commercial and residential buildings in downtown Helper have earned designation as national historic sites. The local economy has suffered downturns from layoffs in the railroad and coal industries, and this is reflected in the many vacant structures awaiting new owners.

However, the vacated structures have begun to attract artists who need inexpensive studio space, and an arts community is taking hold. The excellent **Helper Arts & Music Festival,** held in mid-August, showcases the local arts scene.

WESTERN MINING AND RAILROAD MUSEUM

A venerable red caboose and examples of coal-mining machinery sit outside in downtown Helper next to the **Western Mining and Railroad Museum** (296 S. Main St., 435/472-3009, 10am-5pm Mon.-Sat. May 15-Sept. 14, 11am-4pm Tues.-Sat. Sept 15.-May 14, $5 donation suggested). Inside, you'll see two elaborate model railroad sets and photos of old steam locomotives in action. A mine room has models of coal mines (all are underground in this area) and equipment worn by the miners. Other exhibits illustrate Utah's two great mine disasters—the 1900 Scofield tragedy, in which 200 men and boys died, and the 1924 Castle Gate explosion, which killed 173. Other bits of history include ghost town memorabilia, a Butch Cassidy exhibit, and a dentist's office. The map room displays original maps showing hundreds of miles of tunnels. The brick building housing the museum dates from about 1914, when it was the Hotel Helper; from 1942 to 1982 it served as a YMCA for railroad workers.

PRICE CANYON RECREATION AREA

A pleasant spot in the woods, the **Price Canyon Recreation Area** (435/636-3600, camping $8) makes a good stopping place for a picnic or camping. From the turnoff 8.2 miles (13.1 km) north of Helper, follow a narrow paved road 3 miles (4.8 km) to the picnic area, a canyon overlook, and the campground (elev. 8,000 feet). **Bristlecone Ridge Trail** begins at the far end of the campground loop and winds through forest to a ridgetop. Grand views from the top take in surrounding mountains along with Price and Crandall

Canyons below. The moderately difficult hike is about 2 miles (3.2 km) round-trip, with an elevation gain of 700 feet. Bristlecone pines live on the ridge. Take U.S. 6 north from Helper and turn left at the sign for the recreation area.

SCOFIELD STATE PARK

The large reservoir at **Scofield State Park** (435/448-9449, http://stateparks.utah.gov, day-use $7), popular with anglers (including wintertime ice-fishers), boaters, and water-skiers, is in a broad mountain valley at an elevation of 7,600 feet. The Mountain View area on the northwest side of the lake has boat rentals, a boat ramp, and a dock. The **Mountain View Campground** (800/322-3770, http://utahstateparks.reserveamerica.com, $20) here has showers. **Madsen Bay Campground** ($25), at the far north end of the reservoir, has RV hookups. From Price, drive 23 miles (37 km) north on U.S. 6, then turn left and follow Highway 96 for 13 miles (21 km). Other approaches are from Provo (66 miles/106 km) via Soldier Summit or from Highway 31, where it crosses the Wasatch Plateau to the south.

Use the park as a base camp for hiking trips in the Manti-La Sal Mountains. Find the trailhead for the 10-mile **Fish Creek National Recreation Trail** west of the reservoir (at the small **Fish Creek Campground**, $7). The easy trail follows the creek through meadows and forests of aspens and evergreens. This is a good area to look for wildlife, including moose, elks, mule deer, black bears, mountain lions, bobcats, and beavers. Anglers will find many places to cast a line; special fishing regulations (posted) apply in upper Fish Creek. The trail is good for both day and overnight hikes; after 10 miles, the trail ends on North Skyline Drive. From Scofield, go northwest 3.7 miles (6 km) on a partly paved road, then turn left and go 1.5 miles (2.4 km) at a fork up Fish Creek Valley. This last section of road is slippery when wet and may be too rough for cars at any time.

★ Nine Mile Canyon Backcountry Byway

A drive through this scenic canyon takes you back in time to when the Fremont Indians lived and farmed here, about 900 years ago. Although their pit-house dwellings can be difficult for a nonarchaeologist to spot, the granaries and striking rock art stand out clearly. The canyon is especially noted for its abundant **petroglyphs** and smaller numbers of **pictographs.** You'll also see several ranches and the never large, now abandoned **ghost town** of Harper. In the late 1800s and early 1900s, these roads through Nine Mile Canyon formed the main highway between Vernal and the rest of Utah.

Although the distances may discourage the more casual traveler, the road from the south (Wellington area) is now completely paved; the approach from the north (Myton) is partly unpaved and carries heavy truck traffic due to oil drilling and natural gas exploration in the area.

A brochure and road log describes the various rock-art sites, ancient villages, and historic relics for Nine Mile Canyon. Obtain a copy at the website (www.castlecountry. com) or at the Castle Country Travel Office (751 E. 100 N., Price, 435/636-3701, www. castlecountry.com), the Eastern Prehistoric Museum (155 E. Main St., Price, 435/613-5060), or the BLM office (600 Price River Dr., Price, 435/637-4591, www.blm.gov/ut).

The eastern end of the canyon, with large rock-art panels at Daddy Canyon (mile 43.8) and up the Cottonwood Canyon (miles 45-46), has an especially large concentration of rock-art and Fremont sites.

No camping is allowed on the public land in the canyon, but the **Nine Mile Ranch Bunk and Breakfast** (435/637-2572, http://9mileranch.com) offers B&B lodging in the ranch house ($80-95), camping ($15), as well as simple lodging in four cabins ($60-95). The proprietors can also take you on a guided trip through the canyon.

GETTING THERE

Nine Mile Canyon is actually more than 40 miles (64 km) long; the origin of its misleading name is unclear. The drive is about 120 miles (193 km) round-trip from Price and takes most of a day, but it's a day well spent. From Price, drive 10 miles (16 km) southeast (3 miles/4.8 km past Wellington) on U.S. 6/191 and turn north onto 2200 East (Soldier Creek Rd.) at a sign for Nine Mile Canyon. The road passes Soldier Creek Coal Mine after 13 miles (21 km), continues climbing to an aspen-forested pass, and then drops into the canyon.

Nine Mile Canyon can also be reached from the north, from near Myton (on U.S. 40/191) in the Uinta Basin, via Wells Draw and Gate Canyon. Gate Canyon is the roughest section and may be impassable after storms. The turnoff for the northern approach from U.S. 191 is 1.5 miles (2.4 km) west of Myton; the turn is marked, and BLM signs guide you south. In about 2 miles (3.2 km), bear right and continue south. It's 26 miles (42 km) from U.S. 191 to the bottom of Nine Mile Canyon.

Range Creek Archaeological Remains

In 2001, rancher Waldo Wilcox sold his ranch in the Book Cliffs canyons, some 30 miles (48 km) east of Price, to the nonprofit Trust for Public Land. The ranch, which stood in the rugged Range Creek Canyon, was transferred to the State of Utah to be preserved for its incredible wealth of Fremont archaeological sites, including pit houses, petroglyphs, and stone granaries.

The site contains more than 400 individual Fremont sites that went untouched for some 700 years. The Fremont, who lived in south-central Utah from around AD 200 to 1300, evolved from a hunter-gatherer culture to farming, then, like the Ancestral Puebloans to the south, abruptly disappeared from their highly developed longtime settlements. Though Fremont archaeological sites are relatively common in Utah and western Colorado, few are as large and intact as those at Range Creek.

The Range Creek Ranch is now open to a very limited number of visitors. Under a program operated by the **Utah Museum of Natural History** (801/581-6927, http://umnh.utah.edu), 28 visitors per day are allowed to visit the ranch and archaeological sites May 15-November 30. Visitors can apply for an individual permit, which costs $1 and allows five days' admission to the site but provides no guides or tours—you're on your own when you get there (there's a rough campground near the trailhead). Visitors may enter the ranch only on foot or horseback. For most, it's far more comfortable to schedule a guided tour of the archaeological site through one of the four accredited tour operators.

To reach the ranch trailhead, which involves two hours of rugged backcountry driving from Price, schedule a tour with one of the following outfitters. **Tavaputs Plateau Guest Ranch** (435/637-1236, www.tavaputsranch.com, $150 pp) runs trips to Range Creek several days per month late June-September. You can also arrange to spend the

night at the guest ranch ($200 pp). Overnight tours are run by **Canyonlands Field Institute** (1320 S. U.S. 191, Moab, 435/259-7750 or 800/860-5262, http://cfimoab.org); three-day camping trips are offered a couple of times a year ($680 pp). Meals, tents, and transportation to and from the town of Green River are provided. Only eight people are allowed on each trip, so be sure to reserve in advance. **Carbon County Outdoor Recreation** (30 E. 200 S., Price, 435/636-3702, www.carbon.utah.gov/Recreation, $85) also offers several trips a year.

Range Creek is very remote, and access roads are rough; a 4WD vehicle is recommended. From Price, head southeast through Wellington and turn east (left) onto Highway 123 to East Carbon. Turn south onto Highway 124 and follow it for 10 miles (16 km), past Horse Canyon Mine. About 1 mile (1.6 km) past the mine, turn left and drive 9 miles (14.5 km) to the North Gate entrance to Range Creek. Camping is permitted here, and a trail heads into the archaeological area. Be sure to bring plenty of water.

Castle Valley and North San Rafael Swell

High cliffs of the Wasatch Plateau rise fortresslike to the west above Castle Valley, which is traversed by Highway 10 between Price to the north and I-70 to the south. The wide band of the 10,000-foot-high uplands wrings all the moisture out of east-flowing storm systems, creating rain shadows. However, perennial streams flow down the rugged canyons, enabling farmers to transform the desert into verdant orchards and fields of crops. To the east is the isolated and relatively unexplored canyon country of the San Rafael Swell.

The barren mesas and badland formations, especially along the southern section of Highway 10, make for fine scenery.

However, the real attraction of this area is the backcountry routes that lead to wild and undeveloped destinations. Unpaved roads lead west into the Wasatch Plateau, and up steep canyons to lakes and pretty alpine country to link up with Skyline Drive or to cross the range to the Sanpete Valley and U.S. 89. Backcountry explorers can follow unpaved roads east to the San Rafael Swell, an area of great dramatic beauty and unparalleled recreational opportunity that has somehow avoided the fame and throngs of the state's other canyon country. Destinations included in this near-wilderness are dinosaur fossil quarries and remote vista points and trailheads.

Castle Valley

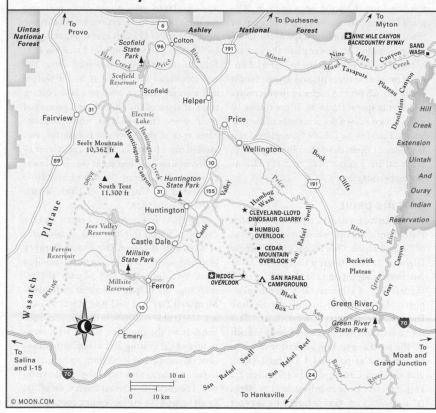

HUNTINGTON

This small town at the mouth of Huntington Canyon dates from 1878 and has a population of a little over 2,000. The town gained attention in 2007 when a mine collapsed, trapping six miners; a few days later, three rescue workers were killed in another collapse. Travelers can head west on paved Highway 31 and soon be in the cool forests and meadows of the Wasatch Plateau, or head east to the Cleveland-Lloyd Dinosaur Quarry and the San Rafael Swell.

Huntington State Park

The 250-acre Huntington Reservoir at

Huntington State Park (435/687-2491, http://stateparks.utah.gov, day-use $7), located 1 mile (1.6 km) north of Huntington on Highway 10, is a popular destination for picnicking, camping, swimming, fishing, boating, and waterskiing. Lots of grass and shade trees and a swimming beach make the park especially enjoyable in summer. Anglers catch mostly largemouth bass and bluegill and some trout; crayfishing is good, if that excites you. The **campground** (800/322-3770, http://utahstateparks.reserveamerica.com, Mar.-Oct., $25-28) has showers; reservations are a good idea for summer weekends. In winter, the park is open for ice-skating and ice fishing.

Huntington Canyon

Highway 31 turns west up Huntington Canyon from the north edge of town. The giant Huntington power plant looks out of place in the agrarian landscape of the lower canyon; beyond the power plant the canyon narrows as the road climbs higher and enters groves of spruce, fir, and aspen. Forest roads branch off the highway to reservoirs and scenic spots. Highway 31 continues 10 miles (16 km) down the other side of the plateau to Fairview on U.S. 89. Snowplows keep Highway 31 open in winter, although drivers must have snow tires or carry chains November-March.

SKYLINE DRIVE

Skyline Drive is near the top of the Wasatch Plateau amid expansive meadows and groves of fir and aspen. One access point is from Highway 31 (Huntington Canyon Rd.); the junction for southbound Skyline Drive is on the left side of Highway 31 between mileposts 14 and 13; the turnoff for Skyline Drive to the north is 5 miles (8 km) farther west along the highway. Roads branch off the northern section of Skyline Drive to Gooseberry Campground (1.5 miles/2.4 km), Flat Canyon Campground (4.5 miles/7.2 km), Electric Lake (6 miles), and Scofield (17 miles/27 km). **Gooseberry Reservoir Campground** (435/283-4151 or 877/444-6777, www.recreation.gov, June-Sept., no water, $10) is near Lower Gooseberry Reservoir at an elevation of 8,400 feet; take the north Skyline Drive turnoff and follow signs 1.5 miles (2.4 km) to this scrubby open spot. **Flat Canyon Campground** (435/283-4151 or 877/444-6777, www.recreation.gov, June-Sept., $10) also provides a good base for fishing lakes of the high country, although there's little shade. Campsites are available via a 5.5-mile (8.9-km) paved road from the north Skyline Drive turnoff; the elevation is 8,800 feet. Boulger Reservoir is 0.25 mile from this campground, Electric Lake is 1 mile (1.6 km), and Beaver Dam Reservoir is also 2 miles (3.2 km).

CLEVELAND-LLOYD DINOSAUR QUARRY

You can learn more about dinosaurs and see their bones in an excavation site in the desert 22 miles (35 km) east of Huntington (or 30 miles/48 km south of Price via U.S. 10). Dinosaurs stalked this land about 147 million years ago, when it had a wetter and warmer climate. Mud in a lake bottom trapped some of the animals and preserved their bones. The mud layer, which later became rock of the Morrison Formation, has yielded more than 12,000 bones of at least 14 different dinosaur species at this site. Local ranchers discovered the bones and then interested the University of Utah, which started digs in 1928.

The BLM has a visitors center, quarry exhibits, a nature trail, and picnic sites at **Cleveland-Lloyd Dinosaur Quarry** (435/636-3600, www.blm.gov/ut, 10am-5pm Mon.-Sat., noon-5pm Sun. Memorial Day-mid-Aug, 10am-5pm Thurs.-Sat., late Mar.-Memorial Day and mid-Aug.-Oct., $5 over age 15). Inside the visitors center, you'll see exhibits on the dinosaur family tree, techniques of excavating and assembling dinosaur skeletons, and local flora and fauna. A fierce allosaurus skeleton cast gazes down on you. The enclosed dinosaur quarry, about 100 yards behind the visitors center, contains excavation tools and exposed allosaurus, stegosaurus, *Camptosaurus*, and *Camarasaurus* bones. The 1.4-mile (2.3 km) **Rock Walk Nature Trail** begins outside; a brochure outlines geology, dinosaurs, uranium mining, and ecology.

The long, slow drive in is on graded dirt roads, although rains occasionally close them. From Price, drive south 13 miles (21 km) on Highway 10, turn left and go 17 miles (27 km) on Highway 155, and follow the unpaved roads. From Huntington, go northeast 2 miles (3.2 km) on Highway 10 and turn right at 20 miles (32 km) onto Highway 155 and unpaved roads. Signs at the turnoffs from Highway 10 indicate the days and hours the quarry is open. If it's closed, there's nothing to see. Visitors are not allowed to collect dinosaur bones at the quarry or on other public lands; bones are of greater scientific value when researchers can examine them in place.

CASTLE DALE

Castle Dale has a good museum: the **Museum of the San Rafael** (70 N. 100 E., 435/381-3560, www.emerycounty.com/sanrafaelmuseum, 10am-4pm Mon.-Fri., 10am-2pm Sat., donation), housed in a pretty building diagonally across the street from the courthouse. It includes a paleontology room with life-size skeletons of dinosaurs, such as a 22-foot *Albertosaurus*. The dinosaurs displayed include only those species that have been found in Emery County. There are also exhibits of the prehistoric Fremont and Ancestral Puebloan peoples, including a rabbit-fur robe, pottery, baskets, tools, jewelry, and the famous Sitterud Bundle (a bow maker's kit).

THE SAN RAFAEL SWELL

About 65 million years ago, immense underground forces pushed rock layers into a dome about 80 miles long (north-south) and 30 miles wide. Erosion has exposed the colorful layers and cut deep canyons into this formation. I-70 divides the swell into roughly equal north and south halves. In the north, a 29-mile (47-km) scenic drive, passable by cars in dry weather, branches off the road to Cedar Mountain and goes south past the Wedge Overlook, descends through Buckhorn Wash, crosses the San Rafael River, then winds across the desert to I-70. For good maps and photos, visit http://theswellutahcom.

★ Wedge Overlook

An impressive panorama takes in surrounding mountains and canyons and the 1,000-foot sheer drop into the Little Grand Canyon. Rain and snowmelt on the Wasatch Plateau feed tributaries of the San Rafael River, which has cut this deep canyon through the San Rafael Swell. Downstream from the Little Grand Canyon, the river plunges through narrow canyons of the Black Boxes and flows across the San Rafael Desert to join the Green River.

From Highway 10 just north of Castle Dale (between mileposts 39 and 40), follow signs east on the well-maintained dirt Green River Cutoff Road for 13.7 miles (22 km) to a four-way intersection. Turn south and stay on the main road for 6.1 miles (9.8 km) to the Wedge Overlook. Campsites are scattered around the Wedge area.

The Wedge Overlook is also the site of good mountain biking, including easy dirt-road riding that's suitable for families or novice riders.

Floating the Little Grand Canyon

The 15-mile (24-km) trip on the San Rafael River through this canyon provides one of the best ways to enjoy the scenery. The swift waters have a few riffles and small sand waves but no rapids. Inflatable kayaks, and rafts can do the excursion in 5-6 hours with higher spring flows. An overnight trip will allow more time to explore side canyons. The best boating conditions occur during the spring runoff in May-June. Some people float through with inner tubes later in the summer. Life jackets should always be worn. No permits are needed for boating or floating, but check with the **BLM office** (600 Price River Dr., Price, 435/637-4591, www.blm.gov/ut) for advice on hazards, river flow, and road conditions. Put-in is at Fuller's Bottom; the turnoff is near the one for the Wedge Overlook, and then it's 5.4 miles (8.7 km) to the river. Takeout is at the San Rafael Bridge Campground. Extremely dangerous rapids and waterfalls lie downstream from the campground in the Black Boxes; don't attempt these sections unless you really know what you're doing.

Campground

The small primitive **San Rafael Bridge Campground** (435/636-3600, no water, $6)

at the San Rafael River makes a handy but bare-bones base for a back-roads exploration of the San Rafael Swell. The road descends into the main canyon via pretty Buckhorn Wash (look for the pictographs here) to the camping area. The swinging bridge, built by the Civilian Conservation Corps in 1937, isn't open to motor vehicles, but it's safe to walk across; a newer bridge is open to cars and trucks. Hikers can explore the canyons above and below the campground on day and overnight trips. Autumn has the best temperatures and lowest water levels; wear shoes suitable for wading.

From Highway 10 north of Castle Dale, head east on the well-maintained dirt Green River Cutoff Road for 13.7 miles (22 km) to a four-way intersection. Continue 12 miles (19.3 km) past the Wedge Overlook turnoff to the bridge and campground. From the campground, the road continues south 20 miles (32 km) to I-70 at exit 129 for Ranch.

Green River and Vicinity

The town of Green River rests midway between two popular river-rafting areas. The Green River's Desolation and Gray Canyons are upstream, while Labyrinth and Stillwater Canyons are downstream. Several river companies organize day and multiday trips through these areas.

GREEN RIVER

Green River (population about 950) is, except for a handful of motels and a lively tavern, pretty rundown, but it's the only real settlement on the stretch of I-70 between Salina and the Colorado border. Travelers can stop for a night or a meal, set off on a trip down the Green River, or use the town as a base for exploring the scenic San Rafael Swell country nearby.

Green River is known for its melons. In summer, stop at roadside stands and partake of wondrous cantaloupes and watermelons. The blazing summer heat and ample irrigation water make such delicacies possible. **Melon Days** (3rd weekend in Sept.) celebrates the harvest with a parade, a city fair, music, a canoe race, games, and lots of melons.

John Wesley Powell River History Museum

Stop by the fine **John Wesley Powell River History Museum** (1765 E. Main St., 435/564-3427, http://johnwesleypowell.com, 9am-7pm Mon.-Sat., noon-5pm Sun. Apr.-Oct., 9am-5pm Tues.-Sat. Nov.-Mar., $6 adults, $2 ages 3-12) to learn about Powell's daring expeditions down the Green and Colorado Rivers in 1869 and 1871-1872. An excellent multimedia presentation about both rivers uses narratives from Powell's trips. Historic riverboats on display include a replica of Powell's *Emma Dean*.

Desolation and Gray Canyons

The Green River leaves the Uinta Basin and slices deeply through the Tavaputs Plateau, emerging 95 miles downstream near the town of Green River. River-runners enjoy the canyon scenery, hiking up side canyons, a chance to see wildlife, and visits to Fremont rock-art sites. John Wesley Powell named the canyons in 1869, designating the lower 36 miles Gray Canyon. Boaters usually start at Sand Wash, the site of a ferry that operated here from the early 1920s to 1952; a 42-mile (68-km) road (36 miles/58 km unpaved) south from Myton is the best way in. Another road turns east from Gate Canyon near Nine Mile Canyon. Some people save the 200-mile (320-km) car shuttle by flying from the town of Green River to an airstrip on a mesa above Sand Wash.

1: the Wedge Overlook in the San Rafael Swell; 2: paddling into the Labyrinth Canyon on the Green River

RAFTING

The river has a few Class III rapids interspersed with flat water, making for a good family adventure. Outfitters normally fly rafting parties in to a remote airstrip at Sand Wash, south of Myton, and take 5-7 days to complete the 85-mile (137-km) trip (prices vary). Outfitters also offer day-long canoe trips through the lower sections of the Gray Canyon, usually for around $75.

For guided one-day or multiday Desolation and Gray Canyon float trips, contact one of the following local companies: **Holiday River Expeditions** (435/564-3273 or 800/624-6323, www.bikeraft.com, 5 days $1,150, 6 days $1,225) or **Adrift Adventures** (435/259-8594 or 800/874-4483, www.adrift.net, 5 days $988, you row).

Experienced kayakers or rafters can make the trip on their own. Drive in from Price or Myton or arrange a flight to the put-in at Sand Wash with Moab-based **Redtail Aviation** (800/842-9251, www.flyredtail.com, $183 pp). You need both a permit and river-running experience to float the canyons on your own. Contact the **BLM Price Field Office** (600 Price River Dr., Price 435/636-0975, www.blm.gov/ut or www.recreation.gov) for permitting information; the BLM also has a complete list of licensed outfitters.

Labyrinth and Stillwater Canyons

The Green River's Labyrinth and Stillwater Canyons are downstream, between the town of Green River and the river's confluence with the Colorado River in Canyonlands National Park. Primarily a canoeing or kayaking river, the Green River at this point is calm and wide as it passes into increasingly deep, rust-colored canyons. This isn't a wilderness river; regular powerboats can also follow the river below town to the confluence with the Colorado River and head up the Colorado to Moab, two or three days and 186 river miles (299 km) away.

The most common trip on this portion of the Green River begins just south of town and runs south through the Labyrinth Canyon, ending at Mineral Bottom, a distance of 68 river miles (109 km). **Moab Rafting and Canoe Company** (420 Kane Creek Blvd., Moab, 435/259-7722, http://moab-rafting.com, 3-day guided trip from $749 pp, depending on group size) offers this trip in canoes and offers unguided raft rentals, too. **Tex's Riverways** (435/259-5101, www.texsriverways.com) offers canoe and touring kayak rentals and all the other equipment you need to outfit a self-guided multiday trip, plus shuttle services to and from the river. Permits are required to paddle in Labyrinth Canyon; they're free and available to download from the BLM website (www.blm.gov) or can be picked up in town at the John Wesley Powell Museum (1765 E. Main St.) or Green River State Park (150 S. Green River Blvd.).

Crystal Geyser

With some luck, you'll catch the spectacle of this cold-water geyser on the bank of the Green River. The gusher shoots as high as 60 feet, but only 3-4 times daily, so you may have to spend half a day here in order to see it. The eruption, typically lasting seven minutes, is powered by carbon dioxide and other gases. A 2,267-foot-deep petroleum test well drilled in 1935-1936 concentrated the geyser flow, but thick layers of old travertine deposits attest that mineral-laden springs have long been active at this site. Colorful newer travertine forms delicate terraces around the opening and down to the river. The orange and dark red of the minerals and algae make this a pretty spot, even if the geyser is only quietly gurgling.

Crystal Geyser is 10 miles (16 km) south of Green River by road; boaters should look for the geyser deposits on the left, about 4.5 river miles downstream from Green River. From downtown, drive east 1 mile on Main Street, turn left, and go 3 miles on signed Frontage Road (near milepost 4), then turn right and go 6 miles (9.7 km) on a narrow paved road just after going under a railroad overpass. The road goes under I-70; keep right at a fork near some power lines. Some washes have to be crossed, so the drive isn't recommended after rains. When the weather is fair, cars shouldn't have a problem.

Food

Other than motel restaurants and fast food, the one really notable place to eat in Green River is ★ **Ray's Tavern** (25 S. Broadway, 435/564-3511, 11am-9pm daily, $8-27). Ray's doesn't look like much from the outside, but inside you'll find a friendly welcome, tables made from tree trunks, and some of the best steaks, chops, and burgers in this part of the state. Don't expect haute cuisine, but the food is good, and the atmosphere is truly Western; beer drinkers will be glad for the selection of regional microbrews after a long day navigating the river or driving desert roads.

Grab a taco from **La Pasadita** (215 E. Main St., 435/564-8159, 8am-10pm daily, $6-10), a taco truck in the parking lot of an old gas station. The food is good, and the scene is convivial at the picnic tables set up for diners.

Directly adjacent to the River Terrace hotel is a decent American-style restaurant, **The Tamarisk** (880 E. Main St., 435/564-8109, 7am-10pm daily, $12-19), with riverfront views.

Accommodations

Green River has a few rather shabby older motels as well as newer chain motels from which to choose. Unless noted, each of the following has a swimming pool—a major consideration in this often-sweltering desert valley.

If you're on a budget, the **Robber's Roost Motel** (325 W. Main St., 435/564-3452, www.rrmotel.com, $48-57) is cheap and basic and right in the center of town; it does not have a pool. Green River's newer motels are on the east end of town. The **Super 8** (1248 E. Main St., 435/564-8888 or 800/888-8888, $99-111), out by I-70 exit 162, is a good value, with spacious, comfortable guest rooms.

The nicest place to stay in town is the ★ **River Terrace** (1740 E. Main St., 435/564-3401 or 877/564-3401, www.river-terrace.com, $139-150), with somewhat older but large guest rooms, some of which overlook the Green River and some with balconies. Breakfast is included, with a restaurant adjacent to the hotel. The very pleasant outdoor pool area is flanked by patios, gardens, and shaded tables.

CAMPGROUNDS

Several campgrounds, all with showers, offer sites for tents and RVs year-round.

Crystal Geyser burbles, and occasionally spouts, alongside the Green River.

Green River State Park (150 S. Green River Blvd., 435/564-3633 or 800/322-3770, www.reserveamerica.com, year-round, $5 day-use, $25 regular sites, $35 with hookups, $75 cabins) has a great setting near the river; it's shaded by large cottonwoods and has a boat ramp. **Shady Acres RV Park** (350 E. Main St., 435/564-8290 or 800/537-8674, www.shadyacresrv.com, year-round, $20-29 tents, $40-43 with hookups, $50 cabins) is not all that shady and may be a bit too close to the noisy road for tent campers; it has a store, showers, and a laundry. **Green River KOA** (235 S. 1780 E., 435/564-3651, $30-35 tents, $46-50 with hookups, $63-85 cabins) has campsites and cabins (bring sleeping bags) across from the John Wesley Powell Museum and next to the Tamarisk Restaurant.

SEGO CANYON

Prehistoric rock art and the ruins of a coal-mining town are within scenic canyons of the Book Cliffs, just a short drive north from Thompson Springs and I-70.

Sego Canyon is a showcase of **prehistoric rock art,** preserving rock drawings and images that are thousands of years old. The Barrier Canyon-style drawings may be 8,000 years old; the more recent Fremont-style images were created in the last 1,000 years. Compared to these ancient pictures, the Ute etchings are relatively recent; experts speculate that they may have been drawn in the 1800s, when Ute villages still lined Sego Canyon. Interestingly, the newer petroglyphs and pictographs are less representational than the older ones. The ancient Barrier Canyon figures are typically horned, ghostlike beings that look like aliens from early Hollywood sci-fi thrillers. The Fremont-style images depict stylized human figures made from geometric shapes; the crudest figures are the most recent. The Ute images are of buffaloes and hunters on horseback.

To reach Sego Canyon, take I-70 exit 185 for Thompson, which is 25 miles (40 km) east of Green River or 5 miles (8 km) east of the U.S. 191 turnoff to Moab, and drive 1 mile (1.6 km) north to Thompson. The small railroad community has a café and a convenience store near I-70. Continue north across the tracks on a paved road, which becomes dirt after 0.5 mile, into Thompson Canyon. At the first creek ford, 3.5 miles (5.6 km) from town, look for petroglyphs and pictographs on cliffs to the left.

A ghost town is 1 mile (1.6 km) up Sego Canyon. Both the Sego and Thompson Canyon Roads lead deeper into the rugged Book Cliffs. Drivers with 4WD vehicles and hikers can explore more of this land, seldom visited except in deer season.

Zion and Bryce

In southwestern Utah, the Mojave Desert, the Great Basin, and the Colorado Plateau meet to create a unique combination of climates and ecosystems. The lofty cliffs of the Colorado Plateau rise east of the desert country with some of the most spectacular scenery on Earth. Great faults break the plateau into a staircase of lesser plateaus across southern Utah and into northern Arizona, where cliffs and canyons dominate the landscape.

Here you'll find two of the nation's most popular national parks, Zion and Bryce Canyon. On the same spring day, you could hike through serpentine canyons or flower-filled meadows, hit the slopes at the Brian Head Ski Area, explore the desert, or play a round of golf.

You can nearly always find pleasant temperatures in some part

Highlights

Look for ★ to find recommended sights, activities, dining, and lodging.

★ **Emerald Pools Trails:** Choose from three trails, each leading to a different magical pool. The highest pool is, of course, the most beautiful, with towering cliffs rising above a white-sand beach (page 234).

★ **The Narrows:** Hike *inside* the Virgin River, between high, fluted walls—only 20 feet apart in some places—where little sunlight penetrates and mysterious side canyons beckon (page 237).

★ **Sunrise and Sunset Points:** Linked by a stretch of the Rim Trail, these two viewpoints in Bryce Canyon National Park offer particularly stunning views at the times of day that give them their names (page 251).

★ **Queen's Garden Trail:** This trail drops from Sunrise Point through the middle of Bryce Amphitheater to a hoodoo resembling a portly Queen Victoria. While it's the easiest hike below the rim, it can still leave flatlanders huffing and puffing (page 254).

★ **St. George Dinosaur Discovery Site:** The local eye doctor peeled back the layers of rock and uncovered some of the best dinosaur tracks ever seen. They're preserved in this museum; just outside, excavation is ongoing (page 273).

★ **Snow Canyon State Park:** Hike trails through red-rock canyons and across lava flows (page 278).

★ **Utah Shakespeare Festival:** Cedar City comes alive with this summer festival, which brings Shakespearean plays to town. The open-air theater-in-the-round is modeled on the original Globe Theatre (page 283).

of this region. Ever since Brigham Young built a winter house at St. George to escape the cold and snow, people have been coming to take advantage of the mild climate. Midwinter temperatures at St. George (elev. 2,880 feet) may drop below freezing at night, but days are typically above 50°F with bright sunshine. Spring and autumn bring ideal weather. Summer, when the highs often top 100°F at the lower elevations, is the time to head for the high country at Cedar Breaks National Monument or Bryce Canyon National Park.

PLANNING YOUR TIME

If you have a week to spend in this corner of Utah, it makes sense to spend a couple of days exploring Zion National Park and another day or two at Bryce Canyon National Park. An ideal week in this part of Utah would begin near St. George, either camping

at Snow Canyon State Park or finding the perfect balance of exertion and relaxation at one of the local spa resorts, then heading to Zion National Park for a couple of days of hiking. From Zion, head east and north to Bryce Canyon National Park for another two days of exploring. Don't forget to venture outside the borders of the national park here to check out the great scenery and trails at nearby Kodachrome Basin State Park and Red Canyon. From the Bryce area, head west across the Markagunt Plateau (spend a summer night at the Cedar Breaks or ski at Brian Head in winter) to Cedar City, where the summertime Shakespeare Festival makes a good end to the trip.

Guided bus and van tours of many of southwestern Utah's grandest sights are available from **Southern Utah Scenic Tours** (435/867-8690 or 888/404-8687, www.utahscenictours.com).

Zion National Park

Zion National Park (435/772-3256, www.nps.gov/zion, $30 per vehicle, $25 per motorcycle, $15 pedestrians and bicyclists) is a magnificent park with stunning, soaring scenery. When you visit Zion, the first thing to catch your attention will be the sheer cliffs and great monoliths of Zion Canyon reaching high into the heavens. Energetic streams and other forces of erosion created this land of finely sculptured rock. Little trickles of water percolating through massive chunks of sandstone have created both dramatic canyons and markedly undesertlike habitats, enabling an incredible variety of plants to find niches here. The large park spreads across 147,000 acres and contains eight geologic formations and four major vegetation zones. Elevations range from 3,666 feet in lower Coalpits Wash to 8,726 feet atop Horse Ranch Mountain.

The canyon's naming is credited to Isaac Behunin, a Mormon pioneer who believed this spot to be a refuge from religious persecution. When Brigham Young later visited the canyon, however, he found tobacco and wine in use and declared the place "not Zion"— which some dutiful followers then began calling it. A scientific expedition led by John Wesley Powell in 1872 helped make the area's wonders known to the outside world. Efforts by Stephen T. Mather, first director of the National Park Service, and others led to designation of Mukuntuweap (Straight Canyon) National Monument in 1909 and the establishment of Zion National Park in 1919.

Zion's grandeur extends all through the year. Even rainy days can be memorable as countless waterfalls plunge from every crevice in the cliffs above. Spring and autumn

Previous: Zion Canyon; beautiful view from Sunset Point; The Narrows.

Zion and Bryce

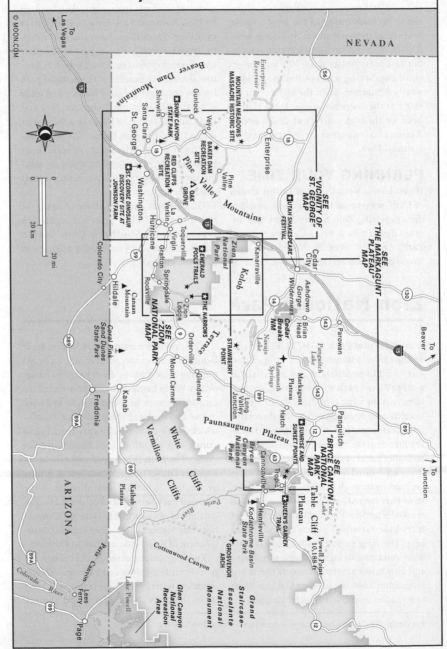

© MOON.COM

NEVADA

To Las Vegas

"THE MARKAGUNT PLATEAU" MAP

"VICINITY OF ST. GEORGE" MAP

SEE "ZION NATIONAL PARK" MAP

SEE "BRYCE CANYON NATIONAL PARK" MAP

Enterprise Reservoir

Beaver Dam Mountains

MOUNTAIN MEADOWS MASSACRE HISTORIC SITE

Gunlock

SNOW CANYON STATE PARK

Shivwits

Santa Clara

St. George

BAKER DAM RECREATION SITE

RED CLIFFS RECREATION SITE

Washington

ST. GEORGE DINOSAUR DISCOVERY SITE AT JOHNSON FARM

Veyo

Pine Valley

Pine Valley Mountains

OAK GROVE

Enterprise

UTAH SHAKESPEARE FESTIVAL

La Verkin

Virgin

Hurricane

Toquerville

Grafton

Springdale

Rockville

EMERALD POOLS TRAILS

Zion National Park

Kolob

Kanarraville

Cedar City

Ashdown Gorge Wilderness

Cedar Breaks NM

Brian Head

Parowan

Zion Lodge

THE NARROWS

Zion

Terrace

STRAWBERRY POINT

Navajo Lake

Panguitch Lake

Mammoth Springs

Markagunt Plateau

Panguitch

To Beaver

Colorado City

Hildale

Canaan Mountain

Coral Pink Sand Dunes State Park

Rockville

Orderville

Mount Carmel

Glendale

Long Valley Junction

Hatch

SUNRISE AND SUNSET POINTS

Bryce Canyon National Park

Cannonville

Tropic

QUEEN'S GARDEN TRAIL

Table Cliff Plateau

Powell Point 10,188 ft

To Junction

Fredonia

Kanab

Mount Carmel

Paunsaugunt Plateau

White Cliffs

Vermilion Cliffs

Kaibab Plateau

Paria River

Cottonwood Canyon

Henrieville

Kodachrome Basin State Park

GROSVENOR ARCH

Grand Staircase-Escalante National Monument

ARIZONA

Colorado River

Lees Ferry

Paria Canyon

Lake Powell

Glen Canyon National Recreation Area

Page

0   20 km

0   20 mi

Avoiding the Crowds

Many areas outside Utah's national parks are often less crowded but equally compelling.

- **Cedar Breaks National Monument** (page 291) preserves an area with formations similar to Bryce Canyon, but without the crowds.

- **Red Canyon** (page 260) is immediately west of Bryce Canyon and shares its geology, but because it's not a national park, you can mountain bike amid the red-rock formations. Dogs are allowed on the trails here, too.

- **Kodachrome Basin State Park** (page 302) between Bryce Canyon and Grand Staircase-Escalante, is ringed by remarkable pink cliffs plus odd rock pillars called sand pipes.

- **Hovenweep National Monument** (page 425) contains the ruins of ancient Ancestral Puebloan stone villages.

- **Natural Bridges National Monument** (page 430) contains rock formations that rival Arches National Park.

- **Dead Horse Point State Park** (page 363), on the road into Canyonlands, provides an eagle's-eye view over the Colorado River Canyon.

- **Goblin Valley State Park** (page 348) has trails among goblin-shaped hoodoos.

---

are the choice seasons for the most pleasant temperatures and the best chances of seeing wildlife and wildflowers. About mid-October-early November, cottonwoods and other trees and plants blaze with color. Summer temperatures in the canyons can be uncomfortably hot, with highs hovering above 100°F. It's also the busiest season. In winter, nighttime temperatures drop to near freezing, and weather tends to be unpredictable, with bright sunshine one day and freezing rain the next. Snow-covered slopes contrast with colorful rocks. Snow may block some of the high-country trails and the road to Lava Point, but the rest of the park is open and accessible year-round.

EXPLORING THE PARK

The highlight for most visitors is Zion Canyon, which is approximately 2,400 feet deep. Zion Canyon Scenic Drive winds along the canyon floor along the North Fork of the Virgin River past some of the most spectacular scenery in the park. (During the spring, summer, and early fall, a **shuttle bus** ferries visitors along this route.) Hiking trails branch off to lofty viewpoints and narrow side canyons. Adventurous souls can continue on foot past the road's end into the eerie depths of the Virgin River Narrows in upper Zion Canyon.

The spectacular Zion-Mount Carmel Highway, with its switchbacks and tunnels, provides access to the canyons and high plateaus east of Zion Canyon. Two other roads enter the rugged Kolob section northwest of Zion Canyon. The Kolob, named after a Mormon term meaning "the brightest star next to the seat of God," is the place to escape the crowds that can fill the trails in Zion Canyon. Kolob Canyons Road, in the extreme northwestern section of the park, begins just off I-15 exit 40 at the Kolob Canyons Visitor Center and climbs to an overlook for great views of the Finger Canyons of the Kolob; the drive is 10 miles (16 km) round-trip. Motorists with more time may also want to drive the Kolob Terrace Road to Lava Point for another perspective on the park; this drive is about 44 miles (71 km) round-trip from Virgin (on Hwy. 9) and has some unpaved sections.

Visitors short on time usually drop in at the visitors center, travel the Zion Canyon Scenic Drive, and take short walks on Weeping Rock

Zion National Park

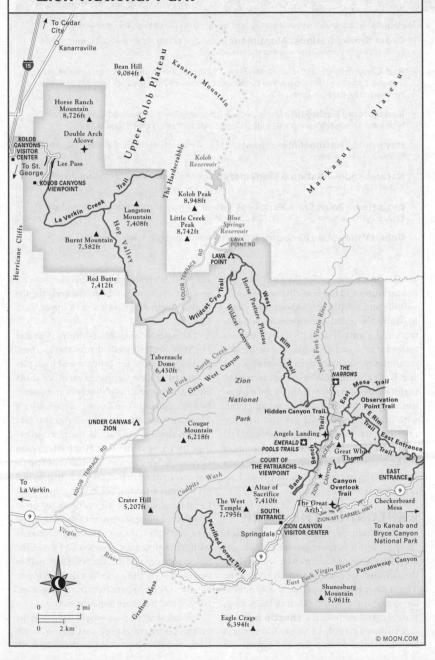

To Cedar City

Kanarraville

15

Bean Hill
9,084ft

Kanarra Mountain

Horse Ranch
Mountain
8,726ft

Upper Kolob Plateau

Double Arch
Alcove

Markagut Plateau

KOLOB
CANYONS
VISITOR
CENTER
To St.
George

Lee Pass

KOLOB CANYONS
VIEWPOINT

The Hardscrabble

Kolob Reservoir

La Verkin Creek

Kolob Peak
8,948ft

Hop Valley

Langston
Mountain
7,408ft

Little Creek
Peak
8,742ft

Blue Springs Reservoir

LAVA
POINT RD

Hurricane Cliffs

Burnt Mountain
7,582ft

Wildcat Cyn Trail

KOLOB TERRACE RD

LAVA
POINT

Red Butte
7,412ft

Wildcat Canyon

Horse Pasture Plateau

West Rim Trail

North Fork Virgin River

Tabernacle
Dome
6,430ft

North Creek

Left Fork

Great West Canyon

Zion

THE
NARROWS

East Mesa Trail

Observation
Point Trail

National

Hidden Canyon Trail

E Rim Trail

UNDER CANVAS
ZION

Cougar
Mountain
6,218ft

Park

Angels Landing

EMERALD
POOLS TRAILS

East Rim Trail

East Entrance

Great White
Throne

Bench Trail

ZION CANYON SCENIC DR

COURT OF
THE PATRIARCHS
VIEWPOINT

EAST
ENTRANCE

To
La Verkin

KOLOB TERRACE RD

9

Crater Hill
5,207ft

Coalpits Wash

Altar of
Sacrifice
7,410ft

Sand Canyon Trail

Canyon
Overlook
Trail

Checkerboard
Mesa

The West
Temple
7,795ft

Petrified Forest Trail

SOUTH
ENTRANCE

The Great
Arch

ZION-MT CARMEL HWY

To Kanab and
Bryce Canyon
National Park

Springdale

ZION CANYON
VISITOR CENTER

9

Virgin River

Grafton Mesa

East Fork Virgin River

Parunuweap Canyon

Shunesburg
Mountain
5,961ft

0   2 mi

0   2 km

Eagle Crags
6,394ft

© MOON.COM

Zion in One Day

Park your car at Zion Canyon Visitor Center. Enjoy the exhibits, then jump on the free park shuttle for a stroll on the Riverside Walk or Weeping Rock Trail, which is only 0.5-mile (0.8-km) round-trip. Jump off the shuttle at Zion Lodge for lunch at the Red Rock Grill. Then take a longer hike: Hidden Canyon is lots of fun and won't utterly deplete experienced hikers. If you don't hike much, the trails to the Emerald Pools are easier. Springdale is just a short walk or shuttle bus ride from the park entrance, and it has several very good restaurants, shops, and galleries.

or Riverside Walk Trails. A stay of two days or longer lets you take in more of the grand scenery and hike other inviting trails.

Tours

The Zion Canyon Field Institute (435/772-3264, https://zionpark) is authorized to run educational programs in the park. These programs range from animal tracking to photography to archaeology. With the exception of ranger-led hikes, Zion Canyon Field Institute classes, the horseback rides from Zion Lodge, and the running commentary from the more loquacious shuttle bus drivers, Zion is a do-it-yourself park. Outfitters are not permitted to lead trips within the park. If you'd like a guided tour outside park boundaries, several outfitters in Springdale lead biking, canyoneering, and climbing trips.

ZION CANYON

During the busy spring, summer, and fall seasons, you'll be traveling up and down Zion Canyon in a shuttle bus. Most visitors find this to be an easy and enjoyable way to visit the following sites. Buses are scheduled to run every 7 to 10 minutes.

Zion Canyon Visitor Center

The park's sprawling visitors center (435/772-3256, 8am-6pm daily mid-Apr.-late May and Sept.-early Oct., 8am-7pm daily late May-Aug., 8am-5pm daily early Oct.-mid-Apr.), between Watchman and South Campgrounds, is a hub of activity.

The plaza outside the building features good interpretive plaques with enough info

to get you going on a hike. Inside, a large area is devoted to backcountry information; staff members can answer your questions about various trails, give you updates on the weather forecast, and help you arrange a shuttle to remote trailheads. The wilderness desk (435/772-0170) opens at 7am daily late April-late November, an hour earlier than the rest of the visitors center. A Backcountry Shuttle Board allows hikers to coordinate transportation between trailheads.

The busiest part of the visitors center is the bookstore, stocked with an excellent selection of books covering natural history, human history, and regional travel. Topographic and geologic maps, posters, and postcards are also sold here.

The best way by far to get a feel for Zion's impressive geology and variety of habitats is to take a hike with a park ranger. Many nature programs and hikes are offered late March-November; check the schedule posted at the visitors center.

Zion Nature Center

At the northern end of South Campground, the Zion Nature Center (2pm-6pm daily Memorial Day-Labor Day) houses programs for kids, including Junior Ranger activities for ages 6-12. Although there's no shuttle stop for the nature center, it's an easy walk along the Pa'rus Trail from the Zion Canyon Visitor Center or the Human History Museum. Check the park newsletter for kids' programs and family hikes. Programs focus on natural history topics such as insects and bats in the park. Many Junior Ranger activities can be

The Rocks of Zion

The rock layers at Zion began as sediments of oceans, rivers, lakes, or sand dunes deposited 65-240 million years ago. The soaring Navajo sandstone cliffs that form such distinctive features as the Great White Throne and the Three Patriarchs were originally immense sand dunes. Look for the slanting lines in these rock walls, which result from shifting winds as the sand dunes formed. Calcium carbonate in the sand piles acted as a glue to turn the dunes into rock, and it's also responsible for the white color of many of the rocks. The reddish rocks are also Navajo sandstone, but they've been stained by iron oxides—essentially rust.

Kayenta shale is the other main rock you'll see in Zion. For an up-close look, check out the streambed at Middle Emerald Pool. The rippled gray rock is Kayenta shale. This shale, which lies beneath Navajo sandstone, is much less permeable than the sandstone. Water can easily trickle through the relatively porous sandstone, but when it hits the impermeable Kayenta shale, it runs along the top surface of the rock and seeps out on the side of the nearest rock face. Weeping Rock, with its lush cliffside springs, is a good place to see the junction between Navajo sandstone and Kayenta shale.

A gradual uplift of the Colorado Plateau, which continues today, has caused the formerly lazy rivers on its surface to pick up speed and knife through the rock layers. You can really appreciate these erosive powers during flash floods, when the North Fork of the Virgin River or other streams roar through their canyons. Erosion of some of the Virgin River's tributaries couldn't keep up with the main channel, and they were left as "hanging valleys" on the canyon walls. A good example is Hidden Canyon, which is reached by trail in Zion Canyon.

Faulting has broken the Colorado Plateau into a series of smaller plateaus. At Zion you are on the Kolob Terrace of the Markagunt Plateau, whose rock layers are younger than those of the Kaibab Plateau at Grand Canyon National Park and older than those exposed on the Paunsaugunt Plateau at Bryce Canyon National Park.

Although some erosive forces, like flash floods, are dramatic, the subtle freezing and thawing of water and the slow action of tree roots are responsible for most of the changes. Water seeps into the Navajo sandstone, accumulating especially in the long vertical cracks in the cliffs. The dramatic temperature changes, especially in the spring and fall, cause regular freezing and thawing, slowly enlarging the cracks and setting the stage for more dramatic rockfalls. Erosion and rockfall continue to shape Zion Canyon. In 1995, a huge rockslide blocked Zion Canyon Scenic Drive and left hundreds of people trapped at the lodge for several days until crews were able to clear a path.

done on your own—pick up a booklet ($1) at the visitors center bookstore.

Zion Human History Museum

The **Zion Human History Museum** (9am-6pm daily mid-Apr.-late May, 9am-7pm daily late May-early Sept., 9am-6pm daily early Sept.-early Oct., 10am-5pm Sat.-Sun. early Oct.-mid.-Apr., entry included in park admission fee) focuses on southern Utah's cultural history, with a film introducing the park and exhibits focusing on Native American and Mormon history. It's at the first shuttle stop after the visitors center. This is a good place to visit when you're too tired to hike any farther or if the weather

forces you to seek shelter. The museum's back patio is a good place to watch the sun rise over the tall peaks of the West Temple and Altar of Sacrifice (so named because of the red streaks of iron on its face).

Court of the Patriarchs Viewpoint

A short trail from the parking area leads to the viewpoint. The Three Patriarchs, a trio of peaks to the west, overlook Birch Creek; they are (from left to right) Abraham, Isaac, and Jacob. Mount Moroni, the reddish peak on the far right, partly blocks the view of Jacob. Although the official viewpoint is a beautiful place to relax and enjoy the view, you'll get an

229

ZION AND BRYCE
ZION NATIONAL PARK

Navajo Sandstone

Take a look anywhere along Zion Canyon and you'll see 1,600-2,200-foot cliffs of Navajo sandstone. The big walls of Zion were formed from sand dunes deposited during a hot dry period about 200 million years ago. Shifting winds blew the sand from one direction, then another—a careful inspection of the sandstone layer reveals the diagonal lines resulting from this "cross-bedding." Researchers have concluded that the vast dunes of southern Utah were formed when the landmass on which they sit was about 15 degrees north of the equator, about the same location as today's Honduras. The shift patterns apparent in the sandstone—the slanting striations easily seen in cliff faces—were caused in part by intense monsoon rains, which served to compact and move the dunes each rainy season.

Eventually, a shallow sea washed over the dunes. Lapping waves left shells behind, and, as the shells dissolved, their lime seeped down into the sand and cemented it into sandstone. After the Colorado Plateau lifted, rivers cut deeply through the sandstone layer. The formation's lower layers are stained red from iron oxides.

even better view if you cross the road and head about 0.5 mile (0.8 km) up Sand Bench Trail.

Zion Lodge

Rustic **Zion Lodge** (435/772-7700, www.zionlodge.com), with its big front lawn, spacious lobby, snack bar, restaurant, and restrooms, is a natural stop for most park visitors. You don't need to be a guest at the lodge to enjoy the ambience of its public areas, and the snack bar is not a bad place to grab lunch.

Cross the road from the lodge to catch the Emerald Pools Trail, or walk 0.5 mile (0.8 km) north from the Zion Lodge shuttle stop to reach the Grotto.

The Grotto

The Grotto is a popular place for a picnic. From here, a trail leads back to the lodge and, across the road, the Kayenta Trail links up with the Emerald Pools trails.

Visible from several points along Zion Canyon Drive is the **Great White Throne.** Topping out at 6,744 feet, this bulky chunk of Navajo sandstone has become, along with the Three Patriarchs, emblematic of the park. Ride the shuttle in the evening to watch the rock change color as the setting sun lights it up.

Weeping Rock

Several trails, including the short and easy

Weeping Rock Trail, start here. Weeping Rock is home to hanging gardens and many moisture-loving plants, including the striking Zion shooting star. The rock "weeps" because this is a junction between porous Navajo sandstone and denser Kayenta shale. Water trickles down through the sandstone, and, when it can't penetrate the shale, moves laterally to the face of the cliff.

While you're at Weeping Rock, scan the cliffs for remains of cables and rigging that were used to lower timber from the top of the rim down to the canyon floor. During the early 1900s, this wood was used to build pioneer settlements in the area.

Big Bend

Look up: This is where you're likely to see rock climbers on the towering walls. Because outfitters aren't allowed to bring groups into the park, these climbers presumably are quite experienced and know what they're doing up there.

Temple of Sinawava

The last shuttle stop is at this canyon, where 2,000-foot-tall rock walls reach up from the sides of the Virgin River. There's not really enough room for the road to continue farther up the canyon, but it's plenty spacious for a fine paved wheelchair-accessible path. The Riverside Walk heads 1 mile (1.6 km)

upstream to the Virgin Narrows, a place where the canyon becomes too narrow for even a sidewalk to squeeze through. You may see people hiking up the Narrows (in the river) from the end of the Riverside Walk. Don't join them unless you're properly outfitted.

EAST OF ZION CANYON

The east section of the park is a land of sandstone slickrock, hoodoos, and narrow canyons. You can see much of the dramatic scenery along the Zion-Mount Carmel Highway (Hwy. 9) between the East Entrance Station and Zion Canyon. If you want to pull off the road and explore, try hiking a canyon or heading up a slickrock slope (the pass between Crazy Quilt and Checkerboard Mesas is one possibility). Highlights on the plateau include views of the White Cliffs and Checkerboard Mesa (both near the East Entrance Station) and a hike on the Canyon Overlook Trail (it begins just east of the long tunnel). Checkerboard Mesa's distinctive pattern is caused by a combination of vertical fractures and horizontal bedding planes, both accentuated by weathering. The highway's spectacular descent into Zion Canyon goes first through a 530-foot tunnel, then a 1.1-mile (1.8-km) tunnel, followed by a series of six switchbacks to the canyon floor.

KOLOB TERRACE

The Kolob Terrace section of the park is a high plateau roughly parallel to and west of Zion Canyon. From the town of Virgin, the steep road runs north through ranch land and up a narrow tongue of land, with drop-offs on either side, then onto a high plateau, where the land widens out. The Hurricane Cliffs rise from the gorge to the west, and the back side of Zion Canyon's big walls are to the east. The road passes in and out of the park and terminates at Kolob Reservoir, which is not in the park, but is a popular boating and fishing destination. This section of the park is much higher than Zion Canyon, so it's a good

place to explore when the canyon swelters in the summertime. It's also much less crowded than the busy canyon. Snow usually blocks the way in winter.

Lava Point

The panorama from Lava Point (elev. 7,890 feet) takes in the Cedar Breaks area to the north, the Pink Cliffs to the northeast, Zion Canyon Narrows and tributaries to the east, the monoliths of Zion Canyon to the southeast, and Mount Trumbull on the Arizona Strip to the south. Signs help identify features. Lava Point, which sits atop a lava flow, is a good place to cool off in summer—temperatures are about 20°F cooler than in Zion Canyon. Aspen, ponderosa pine, Gambel oak, and white fir grow here. A small primitive **campground** (no water, free) near the point offers sites during warmer months. From Virgin, take the Kolob Terrace Road about 21 miles (34 km) north to the Lava Point turnoff; the viewpoint is 1.8 miles (2.9 km) farther on a well-marked but unpaved spur road. (Vehicles longer than 19 feet are prohibited on the Lava Point road.) Expect the trip from Virgin to Lava Point to take about an hour.

Kolob Reservoir

This high-country lake north of Lava Point has good fishing for rainbow trout. An unpaved boat ramp is at the south end near the dam. To reach the reservoir, continue north 3.5 miles (5.6 km) on Kolob Terrace Road from the Lava Point turnoff. The fair-weather road can also be followed past the reservoir to the Cedar City area. Blue Springs Reservoir, near the turnoff for Lava Point, is closed to the public.

KOLOB CANYONS

North and west of Zion Canyon is the remote backcountry of the Kolob. This area became a second Zion National Monument in 1937, and then was added to Zion National Park in 1956. The paved 5-mile (8-km) Kolob Canyons Road begins at the Kolob Canyons Visitor Center just off I-15 and ends at the

1: a relief map of Zion; 2: the Zion Lodge

Flora and Fauna of Zion

Many different plant and animal communities live in the rugged terrain of deep canyons and high plateaus. Because the park is near the meeting place of the Colorado Plateau, the Great Basin, and the Mojave Desert, species representative of all three regions can be found here.

Only desert plants can endure the long dry spells and high temperatures found at Zion's lower elevations; these include cacti (prickly pear, cholla, and hedgehog), blackbrush, creosote bush, honey mesquite, and purple sage. Cacti and yuccas are common throughout the park. Pygmy forests of piñon pine, Utah juniper, live oak, mountain mahogany, and cliffrose grow between about 3,900 and 5,600 feet.

Once you get above the canyon floor, trees such as ponderosa pine and Douglas fir can thrive thanks to the moisture they draw from the Navajo sandstone. White firs and aspens are also common on high cool plateaus. Permanent springs and streams support a profusion of greenery such as cottonwoods, box elders, willows, red birches, horsetails, and ferns. Watch out for poison ivy in moist shady areas.

Colorful wildflowers pop out of the ground—indeed, even out of the rocks—at all elevations from spring through autumn. In early spring, look for the Zion shooting star, a plant in the primrose family found only in Zion. Its nodding pink flowers are easily spotted along the Emerald Pools trails and at Weeping Rock. You're also likely to see desert phlox, a low plant covered with pink flowers, and by mid-May, golden columbine.

Mule deer are common throughout the park. Also common is a type of beaver called a bank beaver, which lives along the banks of the Virgin River rather than in log lodges, which would be too frequently swept away by flash floods. Even though these beavers don't build log lodges, they still gnaw like crazy on trees—look near the base of riverside trees near Zion Lodge for their work. Other wildlife include elk, mountain lions, bobcats, black bears, reintroduced bighorn sheep, coyotes, gray foxes, porcupines, ringtail cats, black-tailed jackrabbits, rock squirrels, cliff chipmunks, beavers, and many species of mice and bats.

Birders have spotted more than 270 species in and near the park, but most common are red-tailed hawks, turkey vultures, quails, mallards, great horned owls, hairy woodpeckers, ravens, scrub jays, black-headed grosbeaks, blue-gray gnatcatchers, canyon wrens, Virginia's warblers, white-throated swifts, and broad-tailed hummingbirds. Zion's high cliffs are good places to look for peregrine falcons; try spotting them from the cliffs at the Angel's Rest trail.

Hikers and campers will undoubtedly see northern sagebrush lizards, and hikers need to watch for western rattlesnakes, although these relatively rare reptiles are unlikely to attack unless provoked.

Timber Creek Overlook and picnic area; it's open year-round.

Kolob Canyons Visitor Center

Although it is small and has just a handful of exhibits, this **visitors center** (435/772-3256, 8am-5pm daily mid-Mar.-mid-Oct., 8am-4:30pm daily mid-Oct.-mid-Mar.) is a good place to stop for information on exploring the Kolob region. Hikers can learn current trail conditions and obtain the permits required for overnight trips and Zion Narrows day trips. The visitors center and the start of Kolob Canyons Road are just off I-15 exit 40.

Kolob Canyons Road

This 5-mile (8-km) scenic drive winds past the dramatic Finger Canyons of the Kolob to Kolob Canyons Viewpoint and a picnic area at the end of the road. The road is paved and has many pullouts where you can stop to admire the scenery. The first part of the drive follows the 200-mile-long (320-km-long) Hurricane Fault that forms the west edge of the Markagunt Plateau. Look for the tilted rock layers deformed by friction as the plateau rose nearly 1 mile. **Taylor Creek Trail,** which begins 2 miles (3.2 km) past the visitors center, provides a close look at the canyons.

Lee Pass, 4 miles (6.4 km) beyond the visitors center, was named after John D. Lee of the infamous Mountain Meadows Massacre; he's believed to have lived nearby for a short time after the massacre. **La Verkin Creek Trail** begins at the Lee Pass trailhead for trips to Kolob Arch and beyond. Signs at the end of the road identify the points, buttes, mesa, and mountains. The salmon-colored Navajo sandstone cliffs glow a deep red at sunset. **Timber Creek Overlook Trail** begins from the picnic area at road's end and climbs 0.5 mile (0.8 km) to the overlook (elev. 6,369 feet); views encompass the Pine Valley Mountains, Zion Canyons, and distant Mount Trumbull.

HIKING
Zion Canyon

The trails in Zion Canyon provide perspectives of the park that are not available from the roads. Many of the hiking trails require long ascents but aren't too difficult at a leisurely pace. Carry water on all but the shortest walks. Descriptions of the following trails are given in order from the mouth of Zion Canyon to the Virgin River Narrows.

Experienced hikers can do countless off-trail routes in the canyons and plateaus surrounding Zion Canyon; rangers can suggest areas. Rappelling and other climbing skills may be needed to negotiate drops in some of the more remote canyons. Groups cannot exceed 12 hikers per trail or drainage. Overnight hikers must obtain backcountry permits from the Zion Canyon or Kolob Canyons Visitor Centers or from https://zionpermits.nps.gov ($5 nonrefundable reservation fee for online reservations). The permit fees are based on group size: $15 for 1-2 people, $20 for 3-7, and $25 for 8-12, plus an additional $5 for online purchases. Some areas of the park—mainly those near roads and major trails—are closed to overnight use. Ask about shuttles to backcountry trailheads outside Zion Canyon at the visitors center's **backcountry desk** (435/772-0170). Shuttles are also available from **Zion Rock and Mountain Guides** (435/772-3303, www.zionrockguides.com) and the **Zion**

Adventure Company (435/772-1001, www.zionadventures.com) in Springdale.

WATCHMAN TRAIL
Shuttle Stop: Zion Canyon Visitor Center

From a trailhead north of Watchman Campground, the trail climbs 370 vertical feet to a bench below Watchman Peak, the prominent mountain southeast of the visitors center. Views encompass lower Zion Canyon and the town of Springdale. The well-graded trail follows a side canyon past some springs, and then ascends to the overlook; the distance is 2.4 miles (3.9 km) round-trip and takes about two hours. In summer, it's best to get an early start. Rangers lead nature walks during the main season.

PA'RUS TRAIL
Shuttle Stops: Zion Canyon Visitor Center and Canyon Junction

This 2-mile (3.2-km) paved trail runs from the South Campground to the Canyon Junction shuttle bus stop. For most of its distance, it skirts the Virgin River and makes for a nice early morning or evening stroll. Listen for the trilling song of the canyon wren, and then try to spot the small bird in the bushes. The wheelchair-accessible Pa'rus Trail is the only trail in the park that's open to bicycles and pets.

SAND BENCH TRAIL
Shuttle Stops: Court of the Patriarchs and Zion Lodge

This easy loop has good views of the Three Patriarchs, the Streaked Wall, and other monuments of lower Zion Canyon. The trail is 1.7 miles (2.7 km) long with a 500-foot elevation gain; allow about an hour or two. During the main season, Zion Lodge organizes three-hour horseback rides on the trail (the horses churn up dust and leave an uneven surface, so most hikers prefer to go elsewhere when the horses are out). The trail soon leaves the riparian forest along Birch Creek and climbs onto the dry benchland. Piñon pine, juniper, sand sage, yucca, prickly pear cactus, and other high-desert plants and animals live here. Hikers can get off the shuttle at the Court of the Patriarchs Viewpoint, walk across the scenic drive, and then follow a service road to the footbridge and trailhead. A 1.2-mile (1.9-km) trail along the river connects the trailhead with Zion Lodge. In warmer months, try to hike in early morning or late afternoon.

★ EMERALD POOLS TRAILS
Shuttle Stop: Zion Lodge

Three spring-fed pools, small waterfalls, and views of Zion Canyon make this climb worthwhile. You have a choice of three trails. The easiest is the paved trail to the Lower Pool; cross the footbridge near Zion Lodge, turn right, and go 0.6 mile (1 km). The Middle Pool can be reached by continuing 0.2 mile (0.3 km) on this trail or by taking a totally different trail from the footbridge at Zion Lodge (after crossing the bridge, turn left, then go right up the trail). Together these trails make a 1.8-mile (2.9-km) round-trip loop. A third trail begins at the Grotto Picnic Area, crosses a footbridge, and turns left to continue 0.7 mile (1.1 km); the trail forks left to the Lower Pool and right to the Middle Pool. A steep 0.4-mile (0.6-km) trail leads from the Middle Pool to Upper Emerald Pool. This magical spot has a white-sand beach and towering cliffs rising above. Allow 1-3 hours to visit the pools and don't expect to find solitude; these relatively easy trails are quite popular.

WEST RIM TRAIL
Shuttle Stop: The Grotto

This strenuous trail leads to some of the best views of Zion Canyon. Backpackers can continue on the West Rim Trail to Lava Point and other destinations in the Kolob region. Start from Grotto Picnic Area (elev. 4,300 feet) and cross the footbridge, then turn right along the river. The trail climbs the slopes and enters the cool and shady depths of Refrigerator Canyon. Walter's Wiggles, a series of 21 closely spaced switchbacks, wind up to Scout Lookout and a trail junction—4 miles (6.4 km) round-trip and a 1,050-foot elevation gain. Scout Lookout

has fine views of Zion Canyon. The trail is paved and well graded to this point. Turn right and go 0.5 mile (0.8 km) at the junction to reach the summit of Angels Landing.

Angels Landing rises as a sheer-walled monolith 1,500 feet above the North Fork of the Virgin River. Although the trail to the summit is rough, chains provide security in the more exposed places. The climb is safe with care and good weather but don't go if the trail is covered with snow or ice or if thunderstorms threaten. Children must be closely supervised, and people who are afraid of heights should skip this trail. Once on top, you'll see why Angels Landing got its name—the panorama makes all the effort worthwhile. Average hiking time for the round-trip between Grotto Picnic Area and Angels Landing is four hours, best hiked during the cooler morning hours.

Energetic hikers can continue 4.8 miles (7.7 km) on the main trail from Scout Lookout to West Rim Viewpoint, which overlooks the Right Fork of North Creek. This strenuous 12.8-mile (21-km) round-trip from Grotto Picnic Area has a 3,070-foot elevation gain. West Rim Trail continues through Zion's backcountry to Lava Point (elev. 7,890 feet), where there's a primitive campground. A car shuttle and one or more days are needed to hike the 13.3 miles (21.4 km) each way from Grotto Picnic Area. You'll have an easier hike by starting at Lava Point and hiking down to the picnic area; even so, be prepared for a long day hike. The trail has little or no water in some seasons.

WEEPING ROCK TRAIL
Shuttle Stop: Weeping Rock

A favorite with visitors, this easy trail winds past lush vegetation and wildflowers to a series of cliffside springs above an overhang. Thousands of water droplets glisten in the afternoon sun. The springs emerge where water seeping through more than 2,000 feet of Navajo sandstone meets a layer of impervious shale. The paved trail is 0.5 mile (0.8 km) round-trip with a 100-foot elevation gain.

Signs along the way identify some of the trees and plants.

OBSERVATION POINT TRAIL

Shuttle Stop: Weeping Rock

This strenuous trail climbs 2,150 feet in 3.6 highly scenic miles (5.8 km) to Observation Point (elev. 6,507 feet) on the edge of Zion Canyon. Allow about five or six hours for the round-trip. Trails branch off along the way to Hidden Canyon, upper Echo Canyon, East Entrance, East Mesa, and other destinations. The first of many switchbacks begins a short way up from the trailhead at the Weeping Rock parking area. The junction for Hidden Canyon Trail appears after 0.8 mile (1.3 km). Several switchbacks later, the trail enters sinuous Echo Canyon. This incredibly narrow chasm can be explored for short distances upstream and downstream to deep pools and pour-offs. **Echo Canyon Trail** branches to the right at about the halfway point; this rough trail continues farther up the canyon and connects with trails to Cable Mountain, Deertrap Mountain, and the East Entrance Station (on Zion-Mt. Carmel Hwy.). The East Rim Trail then climbs slickrock slopes above Echo Canyon with many fine views. Parts of the trail are cut right into the cliffs (work was done in the 1930s by the Civilian Conservation Corps). You'll reach the rim at last after 3 miles (4.8 km) of steady climbing. Then it's an easy 0.6 mile (1 km) through a forest of piñon pine, juniper, Gambel oak, manzanita, sage, and some ponderosa pine to Observation Point. Impressive views take in Zion Canyon below and mountains and mesas all around. The **East Mesa Trail** turns right about 0.3 mile (0.5 km) before Observation Point and follows the plateau northeast to a dirt road outside the park.

HIDDEN CANYON

Shuttle Stop: Weeping Rock

See if you can spot the entrance to Hidden Canyon from below. Inside the narrow canyon await small sandstone caves, a little natural arch, and diverse plant life. The high walls, rarely more than 65 feet apart, block sunlight except for a short time at midday. Hiking distance on the moderately difficult trail is about 3 miles (4.8 km) round-trip between the Weeping Rock parking area and the lower canyon; follow the East Rim Trail 0.8 mile (1.3 km), then turn right and go 0.7 mile (1.1 km) on Hidden Canyon Trail to the canyon entrance. Footing can be a bit difficult in places because of loose sand, but chains provide handholds on the more exposed sections. Steps chopped into the rock just inside Hidden Canyon help bypass some deep pools. Allow 3-4 hours for the round-trip; the elevation change is about 1,000 feet. After heavy rains and spring runoff, the creek forms a small waterfall at the canyon entrance. The canyon is about 1 mile (1.6 km) long and mostly easy walking, although the trail fades away. Look for the arch on the right about 0.5 mile (0.8 km) up the canyon.

RIVERSIDE WALK

Shuttle Stop: Temple of Sinawava

This is one of the most popular hikes in the park, and except for the Pa'rus, it's the easiest. The nearly level paved trail begins at the end of Zion Canyon Scenic Drive and winds 1 mile (1.6 km) upstream along the river to the Virgin River Narrows. Allow about two hours to take in the scenery—it's a good place to see Zion's lovely hanging gardens. Countless springs and seeps on the canyon walls support luxuriant plant growth and swamps. Most of the springs occur at the contact between the porous Navajo sandstone and the less permeable Kayenta Formation below. The water and vegetation attract abundant wildlife; keep an eye out for birds and animals and their tracks. At trail's end, the canyon is wide enough for only the river. Hikers continuing upstream must wade and sometimes even swim. Late morning is the best time for photography. In autumn, cottonwoods and maples display bright splashes of color.

★ **THE NARROWS**

Shuttle Stop: Temple of Sinawava

Upper Zion Canyon is probably the most famous backcountry area in the park, yet it's also one of the most strenuous. There's no trail, and you'll be wading much of the time in the river, which is usually knee- to chest-deep. In places the high fluted walls of the upper North Fork of the Virgin River are only 20 feet apart, and very little sunlight penetrates the depths. Mysterious side canyons beckon.

Hikers should be well prepared and in good condition—river hiking is more tiring than hiking on dry land. The major hazards are flash floods and hypothermia; even in the summer, expect water temperatures of about 68°F (winter temps run around 38°F). Finding the right time to go through can be tricky: Spring runoff is too high, summer thunderstorms bring hazardous flash floods, and winter is too cold. That leaves just part of early summer (mid-June-mid-July) and early autumn (mid-Sept.-mid-Oct.) as the best bets. You can get through the entire 16-mile/26-km (one-way) Narrows in about 12 hours, although two days are best to enjoy the beauty of the place. Children under 12 shouldn't attempt hiking the entire canyon.

Don't be tempted to wear river sandals or sneakers up the Narrows; it's easy to twist an ankle on the slippery rocks. If you have a pair of hiking boots that you don't mind drenching, they'll work, but an even better solution is available from the **Zion Adventure Company** (36 Lion Blvd., Springdale, 435/772-1001, www.zionadventures.com) and other Springdale outfitters. They rent specially designed river-hiking boots, along with neoprene socks, walking sticks, and, in cool weather, dry suits. Boots, socks, and sticks rent for $25 for the first day, $12.50 for each additional day; with a dry suit the package costs $55 for the first day, $27.50 for each

additional day. They also provide valuable information about hiking the Narrows and lead tours of the section below Orderville Canyon (about $160 pp, depending on group size and the season). **Zion Outfitter** (7 Zion Park Blvd., Springdale, 435/772-5090, www.zionoutfitter.com), located just outside the park entrance, and **Zion Guru** (795 Zion Park Blvd., Springdale, 435/632-0432, www.zionguru.com) provide similar services at comparable prices. Talk with rangers at the Zion Canyon Visitor Center before starting a trip; they also have a handout with useful information on planning a Narrows hike. No permit is needed if you're just going partway in and back in one day, although you must first check conditions and the weather forecast with rangers. Permits are required for overnight hikes, which must be "top down," starting at Chamberlain's Ranch and hiking downstream to the Riverside Walk; get permits from the backcountry desk at the visitors center the day before you plan to hike or the morning of your hike (7am-noon), or by applying at https://zionpermits.nps.gov. You will also be issued a plastic bag specially designed to collect human waste. Only one-night stays are allowed. No camping is permitted below Big Springs. Group size for hiking and camping is limited to 12 along the entire route.

A downstream hike saves not only climbing but also the work of fighting the river currents. If you're planning to hike the full length of the Narrows, it is strongly recommended that you take the downstream route. The main hitch is that this requires a shuttle to the upper trailhead near Chamberlain's Ranch, reached by an 18-mile (29-km) dirt road that turns north from Highway 9 east of the park. The lower trailhead is at the end of the Zion Canyon Scenic Drive. The elevation change is 1,280 feet. During the summer, **Zion Adventure Company** (36 Lion Blvd., Springdale, 435/772-1001, www.zionadventures.com, 6:15am and 9:30am, $37 pp, reservations required) offers a daily shuttle to Chamberlain's Ranch. There is a small discount in the fare if you also rent gear from

1: the Angels Landing hike; 2: The Narrows; 3: Hidden Canyon Trail

them. **Zion Rock and Mountain Guides** (1458 Zion Park Blvd., Springdale, 435/772-3303, www.zionrockguides.com) has a similar service.

A good half-day trip begins at the end of the Riverside Walk and follows the Narrows 1.5 miles (2.4 km), or about 2 hours, upstream to Orderville Canyon, then back the same way. Orderville Canyon makes a good destination in itself; you can hike quite a ways up from Zion Canyon.

East of Zion Canyon

You can't take the park shuttle bus to trailheads east of Zion Canyon, although the long-distance East Rim Trail, which starts just inside the park's eastern boundary, joins trails that lead down into Zion Canyon's Weeping Rock trailhead.

The fun **Canyon Overlook Trail** starts on the road east of Zion Canyon and features great views from the heights without the stiff climbs found on most other Zion trails. Allow about one hour for the 1-mile (1.6-km) round-trip; the elevation gain is 163 feet. A booklet available at the start or at the Zion Canyon Visitor Center describes the geology, the plant life, and clues to the presence of wildlife. The trail winds in and out along the ledges of Pine Creek Canyon, which opens into a great valley. Panoramas at trail's end take in lower Zion Canyon in the distance. A sign at the viewpoint identifies Bridge Mountain, Streaked Wall, East Temple, and other features. The Great Arch of Zion—termed a blind arch because it's open on only one side—lies below; the arch is 580 feet high, 720 feet long, and 90 feet deep. The Canyon Overlook Trail begins across from the parking area just east of the longer (west) tunnel on the Zion-Mount Carmel Highway.

Highway 9

Trails in this area head north from Highway 9 west of the town of Springdale and are accessible without paying the park entrance fee.

From the parking area on Highway 9 just west of Rockville, a trail heads 2.5 miles (4

km) up **Huber Wash,** through painted desert and canyons. One of the highlights of hiking in this area, besides the desert scenery, is the abundance of petrified wood. There's even a logjam of petrified wood at the 2.5-mile (4-km) mark, where the trail ends in a box canyon decked with a hanging garden. If you're up to a tricky climb over the petrified logjam, you can climb up and catch the Chinle Trail, then hike 5 miles (8 km) back to the road on that trail. The Chinle Trail emerges onto Highway 9 about 2.5 miles (4 km) east of the Huber Wash trailhead.

During the summer, this area of the park can be extremely hot, and in the early spring it's often too muddy to hike. Thus, this is the ideal autumn hike. Even then it'll be quite warm. Remember to bring plenty of water.

The Huber Wash trailhead is about 6 miles (9.7 km) west of the park entrance on Highway 9, near a power substation. Because the trail starts outside the park, it's not necessary to pay the park entrance fee if all you want to do is hike in this area.

Kolob Terrace

Two trails—West Rim and Wildcat Canyon—begin from Lava Point trailhead in the remote West Rim area of the park. You can reach the trailhead via the Kolob Terrace Road or by hiking the 1-mile (1.6-km) **Barney's Trail** from site 2 in the Lava Point Campground.

The **West Rim Trail** goes southeast to Zion Canyon, 13.3 miles (21.4 km) one-way, with an elevation drop of 3,600 feet (3,000 feet in the last 6 miles/9.7 km). Water can often be found along the way at Sawmill, Potato Hollow, and Cabin Springs.

The **Wildcat Canyon Trail** heads southwest 5 miles (8 km) to a trailhead on Kolob Terrace Road (16 miles/25.7 km north of Virgin); the elevation drop is 450 feet. This trail lacks a reliable water source. You can continue north and west toward Kolob Arch by taking the 4-mile (6.4-km) **Connector Trail** to **Hop Valley Trail.**

Snow blocks the road to Lava Point for much of the year; the usual season is May or

June until early November. Check road conditions with the Zion Canyon or Kolob Canyons Visitor Centers. From the South Entrance Station in Zion Canyon, drive west 15 miles (24.1 km) on Highway 9 to Virgin, turn north and go 21 miles (33.8 km) on Kolob Terrace Road (signed Kolob Reservoir), then turn right and go 1.8 miles (2.9 km) to Lava Point.

A special hike for strong swimmers is the **Left Fork of North Creek,** aka the Subway. This challenging 9-mile (14.4-km) day hike involves, at the very least, lots of route-finding and many stream crossings.

Like the Narrows, the Left Fork can be hiked either partway up, then back down (starting and ending at the Left Fork trailhead), or with a shuttle, from an upper trailhead at the Wildcat Canyon trailhead downstream to the Left Fork trailhead. The top-to-bottom route requires rappelling skills and at least 60 feet of climbing rope or webbing. It also involves swimming through several deep sections of very cold water.

Even though the hike is in a day-use-only zone, the National Park Service requires a special permit, which, unlike other Zion backcountry permits, is available ahead of time through a somewhat convoluted lottery process. Prospective hikers should visit the park's permitting website (https://zionpermits.nps. gov) to be introduced to the complicated lottery system of applying for a permit to hike the Subway. Lotteries are run monthly for hiking dates three months in the future. Each lottery entry costs $5, and each individual hiker can apply only once per month. There's also a last-minute lottery, held two days in advance of the hike. Finally, if there are any remaining permits available, they are dispensed the day before the hike at the visitors center.

The Left Fork trailhead is on Kolob Terrace Road, 8.1 miles (13 km) north of Virgin.

Kolob Canyons

Access these hikes from the Kolob Canyons Road, which begins at I-15 south of Cedar City. You're likely to have the trail to yourself in this section of the park.

TAYLOR CREEK TRAIL

This is an excellent day hike from Kolob Canyons Road. The easy-moderate trail begins on the left 2 miles (3.2 km) from the Kolob Canyons Visitor Center and heads upstream into the canyon of the Middle Fork of Taylor Creek. Double Arch Alcove is 2.7 miles (4.3 km) from the trailhead; a dry fall 0.2 mile (0.3 km) farther blocks the way (water flows over it during spring runoff and after rains). A giant rockfall occurred here in June 1990. From this trail you can also explore the North Fork of Taylor Creek. A separate trail along the **South Fork of Taylor Creek** leaves the drive at a bend 3.1 miles (5 km) from the visitors center, then goes 1.2 miles (1.9 km) upstream beneath steep canyon walls.

KOLOB ARCH

Kolob Arch's 287-foot span makes it one of the world's largest arches. (Landscape Arch in Arches National Park is 3 feet longer, and a 400-foot-long arch in China tops them both.) Kolob's height is over 300 feet, and its vertical thickness is 75 feet. The arch makes a fine destination for a backpacking trip. Spring and autumn are the best seasons to go; summer temperatures rise above 90°F, and winter snows make the trails hard to follow.

You have a choice of two moderately difficult trails. **La Verkin Creek Trail** begins at Lee Pass (elev. 6,080 feet) on Kolob Canyons Road, 4 miles (6.4 km) beyond the visitors center. The trail drops into Timber Creek (intermittent flow), crosses over hills to La Verkin Creek (flows year-round), then turns up side canyons to the arch. The 14-mile (23-km) round-trip can be done as a long day trip, but you'll enjoy the best lighting for photos at the arch if you camp in the area and see it the following morning. Carry plenty of water for the return trip; the climb back to the trailhead can be hot and tiring.

You can also hike to Kolob Arch on the **Hop Valley Trail,** reached from Kolob Terrace Road. The Hop Valley Trail is 7 miles (11.3 km) one-way to Kolob Arch with an elevation drop of 1,050 feet; water is available in Hop Valley and La Verkin Creek. You may have to do some wading in the creek, and the trail crosses private land (don't camp there).

BIKING

One of the fringe benefits of the Zion Canyon shuttle bus is the great bicycling that's resulted from the lack of automobile traffic. It used to be way too scary to bike along the narrow, traffic-choked Zion Canyon Scenic Drive, but now it's a joy.

On the stretch of road where cars are permitted—between the visitors center and Canyon Junction, where the Zion-Mount Carmel Highway meets Zion Canyon Scenic Drive—the 2-mile (3.2-km) paved Pa'rus Trail is open to cyclists as well as pedestrians and makes for easy stress-free pedaling.

If you decide you've had enough cycling, every shuttle bus has a rack that can hold two bicycles. Bike parking is plentiful at the visitors center, Zion Lodge, and most trailheads.

Outside the Zion Canyon area, Kolob Terrace Road is a good place to stretch your legs; it's 22 miles (35.4 km) to Kolob Reservoir. There's really no place to mountain bike within the park, but there are good mountain biking spots, including places to practice slickrock riding, just outside the park

boundaries. It's best to stop by one of the local bike shops for advice and a map of your chosen destination.

Bike rentals and maps are available in Springdale at **Zion Outfitter** (95 Zion Park Blvd., 435/772-5090, http://zionoutfitter.com).

ROCK CLIMBING

Rock climbers come to scale the high Navajo sandstone cliffs; after Yosemite, Zion is the nation's most popular big-wall climbing area. However, Zion's sandstone is far more fragile than Yosemite's granite, and it has a tendency to crumble and flake, especially when wet. Beginners should avoid these walls—experience with crack climbing is a must.

For route descriptions, pick up a copy of *Desert Rock,* by Eric Bjørnstad, or *Rock Climbing Utah,* by Stewart M. Green. Both books are sold at the Zion Canyon Visitor Center bookstore. The backcountry desk in the visitors center also has a notebook full of route descriptions supplied by past climbers. Check here to make sure your climbing area is open—some are closed to protect nesting peregrine falcons—and remember to bring a pair of binoculars to scout climbing routes from the canyon floor.

If you aren't prepared to tackle the

Kolob Arch in Zion's backcountry

2,000-foot-high canyon walls, you may want to check out a couple of bouldering sites, both quite close to the south entrance of the park. One huge boulder is 40 yards west of the park entrance; the other is a large slab with a crack located 0.5 mile (0.8 km) north of the entrance.

During the summer, it can be intensely hot on unshaded walls. The best months for climbing are March-May and September-early November.

If watching the climbers at Zion gives you a hankering to scale a wall, the **Zion Adventure Company** (36 Lion Blvd., Springdale, 435/772-1001, www. zionadventures.com) runs half-day and day-long climbing clinics for beginning and experienced climbers. Similar offerings are provided by **Zion Rock and Mountain Guides** (1458 Zion Park Blvd., Springdale, 435/772-3303, www.zionrockguides.com), **Red Desert Adventure** (435/668-2888, www.reddesertadventure.com), and **Zion Mountain School** (868 Zion Park Blvd., Springdale, 435/663-1783, www.guidesinzion. com), which specializes in private tours. All of these outfitters also guide clients on canyoneering expeditions. Outfitters are not permitted to lead climbs inside the park, so these activities are held outside of the park's boundaries.

HORSEBACK RIDING

Trail rides on horses and mules leave from the corral near **Zion Lodge** (435/679-8665, www. canyonrides.com, mid-Mar.-Oct.) and head down the Virgin River. A one-hour trip ($45) goes to the Court of the Patriarchs, and a half-day ride ($90) follows the Sand Bench Trail. Riders must be at least 7 years old for the short ride and 10 for the half-day ride, and they can weigh no more than 220 pounds.

FOOD AND ACCOMMODATIONS

Within the park, lodging is limited to Zion Lodge and the three park campgrounds (two in Zion Canyon and one up the Kolob Terrace

Road). Look to Springdale or the east entrance of the park for more options.

Zion Lodge

Rustic **Zion Lodge** (435/772-7700, www. zionlodge.com) is in the heart of Zion Canyon, 3 miles (4.8 km) up Zion Canyon Scenic Drive. Zion Lodge provides the only accommodations and food options within the park. It's open year-round; reservations for guest rooms can be made up to 13 months in advance. During high season, all guest rooms are booked months in advance. Accommodations in motel rooms near the main lodge or cute cabins (gas fireplaces but no TV) run around $217; lodge rooms are $227-270.

The **Red Rock Grill** (435/772-7760, 6:30am-10:30am, 11:30am-3pm, and 5pm-10pm daily, dinner reservations required, most dinner entrées $15-30), the lodge restaurant, offers a Southwestern and Mexican-influenced menu daily for breakfast, lunch, and dinner. A snack bar, the **Castle Dome Café** (three meals daily in high season) serves decent fast food, including salads and coffee.

The lodge also has public restrooms, evening programs, a gift shop, and Wi-Fi in the lobby.

Campgrounds
ZION CANYON CAMPGROUNDS
Campgrounds in the park often fill up on Easter and other major holidays. During the summer, they're often full by early afternoon so it's best to arrive early in the day. The South and Watchman Campgrounds, both just inside the south entrance, have sites with water but no showers. **Watchman Campground** (877/444-6777, information 435/772-3256, www.recreation.gov, $20) has 164 sites, some sites with electrical hookups ($30). Prime riverside spots are available. Reservations can be made in advance for some sites at Watchman, which stays open in winter. **South Campground** (information 435/772-3256, $20) has 126 sites, including a few choice walk-in sites and easy access to the Pa'rus Trail. During April and May of some years,

the park campgrounds may have an influx of western tent caterpillars, which defoliate trees; populations vary greatly from year to year. It should be noted that camping in Zion's two big campgrounds can be pretty laid-back; indeed, it can be luxurious. Campers have easy access, via the park's free shuttles, to good restaurants in Springdale. It's also simple enough to find showers in Springdale; just outside the park, Zion Outfitter charges $4; they also have a laundromat.

Private campgrounds are just outside the park in Springdale and just east of the park's east entrance. Camping supplies, sack lunches, and groceries are available just outside the park entrance at **Happy Camper Market** (Springdale shuttle stop, 95 Zion Park Blvd., 435/772-7805, 7am-11pm daily).

KOLOB CAMPGROUNDS

Up the Kolob Terrace Road, there are six first-come, first-served sites at **Lava Point Campground** (no water, free), a small primitive campground that offers sites during warmer months. The **Red Ledge Campground** (435/586-9150, Apr.-Nov., $30) in Kanarraville is the closest commercial campground to the Kolob Canyons area (there's no campground in this part of the park); go 2 miles (3.2 km) north on I-15, take exit 42, and continue 4.5 miles (7.2 km) into downtown Kanarraville. The campground has tent and RV sites, cabins, a store, showers, and a laundry room. The tiny agricultural community here was named after a local Paiute chief. A low ridge south of town marks the southern limit of prehistoric Lake Bonneville. Hikers can explore trails in Spring and Kanarra Canyons within the Spring Canyon Wilderness Study Area just east of town.

GETTING THERE AND AROUND

Zion National Park is 43 miles (69 km) northeast of St. George, 60 miles (97 km) south of Cedar City, 41 miles (66 km) northwest of Kanab, and 86 miles (138 km) southwest of Bryce Canyon National Park. There are two entrances to the main section of the park: From Springdale, you enter the south end of Zion Canyon near the visitors center and the Zion Canyon shuttle buses; from the east, you come in on the Zion-Mount Carmel Highway, pass through a long tunnel, then pop into Zion Canyon a few miles north of the visitors center. Large RVs and bicycles must heed special regulations for the long tunnel on the Zion-Mount Carmel Highway.

There's a separate entrance for the Kolob Canyons area in the park's northwest corner. Reach this area via Kolob Canyons Road, which begins just off I-15's exit 40 at the Kolob Canyons Visitor Center and climbs to an overlook for great views of the Finger Canyons of the Kolob; the drive is 10 miles (16.1 km) round-trip.

A fourth entrance leads to the less-traveled part of the park and is accessed by the Kolob Terrace Road, which heads north from Highway 9 at the tiny town of Virgin and goes to backcountry sites. (There's no entrance station or visitors center on Kolob Terrace Road.)

Zion Shuttles

The road through Zion Canyon is narrow with few pullouts, so to keep the road from becoming a parking lot for enormous RVs, a March-October **shuttle bus** (7am-6pm final two weekends in Feb. and first weekend of March, 7am-7:30pm daily early Mar.-mid May, 6am-8:30pm daily mid May-Sept., 7am-6:30pm daily Oct.) provides regular free service through the canyon.

There are actually two separate bus lines: One line travels between Springdale and the park entrance (8am-9pm daily Mar.-late May, 7am-9:30pm daily late May-late Sept., 8am-7:30pm daily late Sept.-Oct., runs as often as every 6 minutes, less frequently in early morning and late evening, no pets allowed, free), stopping within a short walk of every Springdale motel and near several large visitor parking lots at the edge of town; the other bus line starts just inside the park entrance at the visitors center and runs the length of Zion Canyon Road, stopping at scenic overlooks, trailheads, and Zion Lodge. Lodge guests may obtain a pass authorizing them to drive to the lodge, but in general, private vehicles are not allowed to drive up Zion Canyon.

This is less of a pain than it might seem. It's fine to drive to the campgrounds; in fact, the road between the park entrance and the Zion-Mount Carmel Highway junction is open to all vehicles. Buses run frequently, so there's rarely much of a wait, and most of the bus drivers are friendly and well-informed, offering an engaging commentary on the sights that they pass (even pointing out rock climbers on the canyon walls).

If you get to Zion before 10am or after 3pm, there may be parking spaces available in the visitors center lot. Midday visitors should just park in Springdale (at your motel or in a public lot) and catch a shuttle bus to the park entrance.

Riding the bus is free; its operating costs are included in the park admission fee. No pets are allowed on the buses. In the off-season, November-February, private vehicles are allowed on all roads, and the buses are out of service.

The Zion-Mount Carmel Tunnel

If your vehicle is 7 feet, 10 inches wide, 11 feet, 4 inches tall, or larger, you will need a traffic-control escort through the narrow mile-long Zion-Mount Carmel Tunnel. Vehicles of this size are too large to stay in one lane while traveling through the tunnel, which was built in the 1920s, when autos were not only small but few and far between. Most RVs, buses, trailers, and fifth-wheels, and some camper shells, will require an escort.

If your vehicle requires an escort, expect to pay a $15 fee per vehicle in addition to the park entrance fee (payable at the park entrance station before entering the tunnel). The fee is good for two trips through the tunnel for the same vehicle over a seven-day period.

Although the park service persists in using the term *escort,* you're really on your own through the tunnel. Park staff will stop oncoming traffic, allowing you enough time to drive down the middle of the tunnel, but you do not follow an escort vehicle.

Hours for large vehicles are limited (8am-6pm daily early to mid-March and late Sept.-Nov., 8am-7pm daily mid-Mar.-late April and early Sept.-late Sept., 8am 8pm daily late April-early Sept. and mid-Sept.-late Sept., 8am-4:30pm daily Nov.-early March.) Bicycles must be carried through the long tunnel on a car or truck; it's too dangerous to ride (hitchhiking is permitted).

Vicinity of Zion

Just past the mouth of Zion Canyon near the park's south entrance are several small towns with good—even appealing—services for travelers. Springdale has the widest range of services, including excellent lodgings and restaurants; Rockville has a few B&Bs; and Hurricane is a hub for less expensive chain motels.

SPRINGDALE AND VICINITY

Mormons settled this tiny town (pop. 570) in 1862, but with its location just outside the park's south entrance, Springdale is geared more toward serving park visitors than a typical Mormon settlement. Its many high-quality motels and B&Bs, as well as frequent free shuttle bus service into the park, make Springdale an excellent base for a visit to Zion. Farther down the road toward Hurricane are the little towns of Rockville and Virgin, both of which are quickly becoming suburbs of Springdale.

O. C. Tanner Amphitheater

The highlight at the open-air **O. C. Tanner Amphitheater** (435/652-7994, http://www.

octannershows.com, admission varies) is a series of musical concerts held on Saturday evenings during summer. The amphitheater is just outside the park entrance.

Outfitters

Several good outfitters have shops in Springdale. Here you can buy all manner of gear and outdoor clothing. You can also pick up canyoneering skills, take a guided mountain bike ride (outside the park, of course), or learn to climb big sandstone walls.

Campers who left that crucial piece of equipment at home should visit **Zion Outdoor** (868 Zion Park Blvd., 435/772-0630, www.zionoutdoor.com, 9am-9pm daily), as should anybody who needs to spruce up their wardrobe with some stylish outdoor clothing.

Rent a bike or equipment to hike the Narrows at **Zion Outfitter** (95 Zion Park Blvd., 435/772-5090, http://zionoutfitter.com, 8am-9pm daily).

Canyoneering supplies, including gear to hike the Narrows or the Subway, are available from **Zion Adventure Company** (36 Lion Blvd., Springdale, 435/772-1001, www.zionadventures.com, 8am-8pm daily Mar.-Oct., 8am-7pm daily Nov., 9am-7pm daily Dec.-Feb.), **Zion Guru** (795 Zion Park Blvd., Springdale, 435/632-0432, www.zionguru.com), and **Zion Rock and Mountain Guides** (1458 Zion Park Blvd., Springdale, 435/772-3303, www.zionrockguides.com).

Food

A short walk from the park entrance, **Cafe Soleil** (205 Zion Park Blvd., Springdale, 435/772-0505, www.cafesoleilzionpark.com, 7am-8pm daily) is a bright, friendly place for breakfast or a lunchtime sandwich ($8-10). The town's only supermarket, **Sol Foods** (995 Zion Park Blvd., Springdale, 435/772-3100, www.solfoods.com, 7am-11pm daily) stocks groceries, deli items, hardware, and camping supplies.

★ **Deep Creek Coffee** (932 Zion Park Blvd., Springdale, 435/767-0272, deepcreek-coffee.com, 6:30am-2pm daily) is the hip place

to hang in the morning. Besides excellent coffee drinks and made-from-scratch chai, they serve tasty smoothies, quinoa bowls, and sandwiches ($8-10). For a truly substantial meal, head across the way to **Oscar's Café** (948 Zion Park Blvd., Springdale, 435/772-3232, www.cafeoscars.com, 7am-9pm daily, $10-18), where you can get a good burger or a Mexican-influenced breakfast or lunch. The patio here is set back off the main road and is especially pleasant.

An old gas station has become the ★ **Whiptail Grill** (445 Zion Park Blvd., Springdale, 435/772-0283, www.whiptailgrillzion.com, 11:30-9:30pm daily mid-Feb.-Nov., $11-17), a casual spot serving innovative homemade Mexican-style food, such as incredibly good spaghetti squash enchiladas or fish tacos jazzed up with grape salsa. There's very little seating inside, so plan to eat at the outdoor tables (warmed and lit by gas torches during the evening) or take your meal to go.

A good, reasonably priced place to bring a family with picky eaters is **Zion Pizza and Noodle** (868 Zion Park Blvd., Springdale, 435/772-3815, www.zionpizzanoodle.com, 4pm-10pm daily, $13-16), housed in an old church and serving a good selection of microbrews.

The ★ **Spotted Dog Café** (Flanigan's Inn, 428 Zion Park Blvd., Springdale, 435/772-3244, www.flanigans.com, breakfast buffet 7am-11am daily spring-fall, dinner 5pm-9:30pm daily spring-fall, 5pm-9:30pm Tues.-Sun. winter, dinner $15-19) is one of Springdale's top restaurants; it has a good wine list and a full bar and uses high-quality ingredients in its "American bistro" cuisine, including pepita-crusted grilled trout and game meatloaf (made with bacon, elk, buffalo, and beef). Be sure to order a salad with (or for) your dinner—the house salad is superb. If you want to eat outside, try to get a table on the back patio, which is quieter and more intimate than the dining area out front.

Another very popular place for dinner in Springdale is the **Bit & Spur Restaurant**

(1212 Zion Park Blvd., Springdale, 435/772-3498, www.bitandspur.com, 5pm-close daily spring-fall, weekends only winter, $14-30), a lively Mexican-influenced place with a menu that goes far beyond the usual south-of-the-border concoctions. The sweet-potato tamales keep us coming back year after year.

Springdale's sole brewpub is the **Zion Canyon Brew Pub** (95 Zion Park Blvd., 435/772-0036, www.zionbrewery.com, 11:30am-10pm daily, $9-24), right at the pedestrian gate to the park. The pub offers six flagship brews and many seasonal options, and its upscale pub grub is made from scratch and tasty. Pair a buffalo meatloaf burger with a chocolaty Conviction Stout.

Accommodations

$50-100

The hosts at the **Bunkhouse at Zion B&B** (149 E. Main St., Rockville, 435/772-3393, www.bunkhouseatzion.com, $60-90) are dedicated to living sustainably, and they bring this ethic into their simple two-room B&B. The views are remarkable from this quiet spot in Rockville. They require a two-night minimum stay.

The least expensive lodgings in Springdale are the motel rooms at **Zion Park Motel** (865 Zion Park Blvd., Springdale, 435/772-3251, www.zionparkmotel.com, $79-189), an older well-kept motel with a small pool, located about 1 mile (1.6 km) from the park entrance.

$100-150

Under the Eaves B&B (980 Zion Park Blvd., Springdale, 435/772-3457, www.undertheeaves.com, $109-239) features six homey guest rooms plus a spacious suite, all in a vintage home and a garden cottage. Children over age eight are welcome, and all guests get free breakfast at nearby Oscar's Café.

The **Harvest House B&B** (29 Canyon View Dr., 435/772-3880, www.harvesthouse.net, $140-180) has four guest rooms at the center of Springdale, within easy walking distance of the park entrance. Expect a very friendly welcome; all rooms have private

bathrooms and you'll enjoy the garden setting with year-round outdoor hot tub.

OVER $150

★ **Flanigan's Inn** (428 Zion Park Blvd., Springdale, 435/772-3244 or 800/765-7787, www.flanigans.com, $196-239 guest rooms) is a quiet and convenient place to stay. Guest rooms (and a handful of specialty suites) are set back off the main drag and face onto a pretty courtyard. Up on the hill behind the inn, a labyrinth provides an opportunity to take a meditative walk in a stunning setting. An excellent restaurant (the Spotted Dog Café), a pool, and spa services make this an inviting place to spend several days. Two villas, essentially full-size houses, are also available.

Probably the most elegant place to stay is the ★ **Desert Pearl Inn** (707 Zion Park Blvd., Springdale, 435/772-8888 or 888/828-0898, www.desertpearl.com, $239-284), a very handsome lodgelike hotel perched above the Virgin River. Some guest rooms have views of the river; others face the pool. Much of the wood used for the beams and the finish moldings was salvaged from a railroad trestle made of century-old Oregon fir and redwood that once spanned the north end of the Great Salt Lake. The guest rooms are all large and beautifully furnished, with a modern look.

The closest lodging to the park is at **Cable Mountain Lodge** (147 Zion Park Blvd., Springdale, 435/772-3366 or 877/712-3366, www.cablemountainlodge.com, $199-329). Along with being extremely convenient, it's very nicely fitted out, with a pool, guest rooms with microwaves and fridges or small kitchens, and appealing architecture and decor to go along with the spectacular views. Regular hotel rooms are referred to as studios; a number of suite options are also available.

Just outside the south gates to Zion, the ★ **Cliffrose Lodge** (281 Zion Park Blvd., Springdale, 435/772-3234 or 800/243-8824, www.cliffroselodge.com, $301-316 regular rooms sits on five acres of lovely well-landscaped gardens with riverfront access. The guest rooms are equally nice, especially the riverside rooms, and there's a pool and a laundry room. The Cliffrose is favored by many longtime Zion fans. The entire lodge underwent a property "evolvement" in 2018, with an upgrade of all guest rooms.

For a place with a bit of personality, or perhaps more accurately, with multiple personalities, try the **Novel House Inn at Zion** (73 Paradise Rd., Springdale, 435/772-3650 or 800/711-8400, www.novelhouse.com, $199-219), a small family-run B&B with 10 guest rooms, each decorated with a literary theme and named after an author, including Mark Twain, Rudyard Kipling, and Louis L'Amour. All guest rooms have private baths, TVs and great views, and the B&B is tucked off the main drag. All rooms come with a voucher for complimentary breakfast at Oscar's Café.

Red Rock Inn (998 Zion Park Blvd., Springdale, 435/772-3139, www.redrockinn. com, $209-309) offers accommodations in individual cabins and a cottage suite amid gardens and patios, all with canyon views. Full-breakfast baskets are delivered to your door.

The **Driftwood Lodge** (1515 Zion Park Blvd., Springdale, 435/772-3262, www. driftwoodlodge.net, $179-239) is a six-building complex with a good restaurant, a pool, and a spa on its spacious grounds, and pet-friendly guest rooms with refrigerators and microwaves.

Even though it's a chain motel, the **Holiday Inn Express** (1215 Zion Park Blvd., Springdale, 435/772-3200, www.hiexpress. com, $265-290) is an attractive option; it's part of a complex with a restaurant, a swimming pool, a gift shop, and some of the nicest guest rooms in Springdale. In addition to regular guest rooms, there are also various suites and kitchen units available.

CAMPGROUNDS

If you aren't able to camp in the park, the **Zion Canyon Campground** (479 Zion Park Blvd., Springdale, 435/772-3237, www.zioncamp. com) is a short walk from the park entrance. Along with tent sites (no dogs allowed, $45)

and RV sites ($56), there are motel rooms ($190-250). Although the sites are crammed pretty close together, a few are situated right on the bank of the Virgin River. Facilities include a store, a pizza parlor, a game room, a laundry room, and showers.

The "glamping" phenomenon has come to the Zion area. **Under Canvas Zion** (3955 Kolob Terrace Rd., 435/359-2911, www. undercanvas.com/camps/zion, open early March-mid-Nov.) offers luxury safari tent experiences on 196 acres bordering the west side of the park. Lodging is in a variety of large wall tents or tipis, some with private en-suite bathrooms, and all fitted with fine bedding and furniture. In other words, this isn't exactly roughing it. Tent accommodations that sleep four start at $209 per night, with modern plumbing and bathroom facilities in group shower houses. Top of the line tents with private bathrooms are $474. Adventure packages are also available that customize outdoor activities to your preferences, and also include three camp-cooked meals a day. Under Canvas Zion is 6 miles (9.7 km) north of Virgin on the Kilob Terrace Rd.

The **Hi-Road Zion RV Campground** (877/290-5756, http://zionrv.com, $49 tents, $69-79 tents), is a convenient spot for tenters and RVers immediately east of the park's entrance. In addition to high-elevation access to the park's eastern wonders, this campground offers laundry facilities, indoor showers and restrooms, and full RV hookups. A full service restaurant and gas station are just across the road.

Information and Services

People traveling with their dogs have a bit of a dilemma when it comes to visiting Zion. No pets are allowed on the trails (except the Pa'rus Trail) or in the shuttle buses, and it's absolutely unconscionable to leave a dog inside a car here in the warmer months. Fortunately, the **Doggy Dude Ranch** (800 E. Main, Rockville, 435/772-3105, www. doggyduderanch.com) provides reliable daytime and overnight pet care.

The **Zion Canyon Medical Clinic** (120 Lion Blvd., Springdale, 435/772-3226) provides urgent-care services. You may also want to check out the art galleries along Zion Park Boulevard; some of them have high-quality merchandise.

Getting There

Springdale is located at the mouth of Zion Canyon, just outside the park's main (south) entrance. From I-15 just north of St. George, take exit 16 and head east on Highway 9; it's about 40 miles (64 km). If you're coming from the north, take I-15 exit 22, head southeast through Toquerville, and meet Highway 9 at the town of La Verkin.

GRAFTON

Grafton is one of the best-preserved and most picturesque ghost towns in Utah. Mormon families founded Grafton in 1859 near the Virgin River at a spot 1 mile downstream from the present site, but a big flood two years later convinced them to move here. Hostilities with the Paiutes during the Black Hawk War forced residents to depart again for safer areas from 1866 to 1868. Floods and irrigation difficulties made life hard even in the best of times, and the population declined in the early 1900s until only ghosts remained.

Moviemakers discovered Grafton and used it for *Butch Cassidy and the Sundance Kid,* among other films. A schoolhouse, a store, houses, cabins, and outbuildings still stand. Grafton's cemetery is worth a visit; it's on the left at a turn 0.3 mile (0.5 km) before the town site. From Springdale, follow Highway 9 southwest 2 miles (3.2 km) to Rockville; turn south and go 3.5 miles (5.6 km) on Bridge Road (200 East). The last 2.6 miles (4.2 km) are unpaved but should be passable by cars in dry weather; keep right at a road junction 1.6 miles (2.6 km) past Rockville.

Bryce Canyon National Park

In **Bryce Canyon National Park** (435/834-5322, www.nps.gov/brca, $30 per vehicle, $25 per motorcycle, $15 pedestrians and bicyclists, entry good for seven days and unlimited shuttle use), a geologic fairyland of rock spires rises beneath the high cliffs of the Paunsaugunt Plateau. This intricate maze, eroded from a soft limestone, now glows with warm shades of reds, oranges, pinks, yellows, and creams. The rocks provide a continuous show of changing color throughout the day as the sun's rays and cloud shadows move across the landscape.

Looking at these rock formations is like looking at puffy clouds in the sky; it's easy to find images in the shapes of the rocks. Some see the natural rock sculptures as Gothic castles, others as Egyptian temples, subterranean worlds inhabited by dragons, or vast armies of a lost empire. The Paiute people have a tale of the Legend People that relates how various animals and birds once lived in a beautiful city built for them by Coyote; when the Legend People began behaving badly toward Coyote, he transformed them all into stone.

Bryce Canyon isn't a canyon at all, but the largest of a series of massive amphitheaters cut into the Pink Cliffs. In Bryce Canyon National Park, you can gaze into the depths from viewpoints and trails on the plateau rim or hike down moderately steep trails and wind your way among the spires. A 17-mile (27-km) scenic drive traces the length of the park and passes many overlooks and trailheads. Off-road, the nearly 36,000 acres of Bryce Canyon National Park offer many opportunities to explore spectacular rock features, dense forests, and expansive meadows.

The park's elevation ranges 6,600-9,100 feet, so it's usually much cooler here than at Utah's other national parks. Expect pleasantly warm days in summer, frosty nights in spring

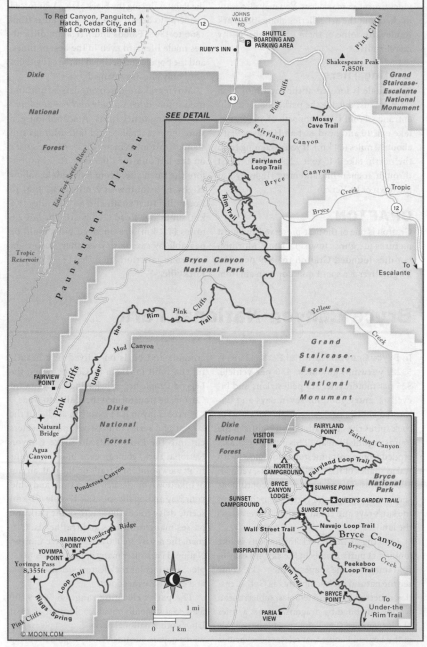

Bryce Canyon National Park

To Red Canyon, Panguitch, Hatch, Cedar City, and Red Canyon Bike Trails

JOHNS VALLEY RD.

12

SHUTTLE BOARDING AND PARKING AREA

RUBY'S INN

P

Shakespeare Peak 7,850ft

Pink Cliffs

Grand Staircase-Escalante National Monument

Dixie

National

Forest

East Fork Sevier River

Paunsaugunt Plateau

63

SEE DETAIL

Fairland Canyon

Fairyland Loop Trail

Bryce

Canyon

Pink Cliffs

Mossy Cave Trail

Rim Trail

Bryce

Creek

Tropic

12

Bryce Canyon National Park

To Escalante

Tropic Reservoir

Rim

the-

Under-

Mud Canyon

Pink Cliffs

Trail

Yellow

Creek

FAIRVIEW POINT

Pink Cliffs

Grand Staircase-Escalante National Monument

Natural Bridge

Dixie

National

Agua Canyon

Forest

Ponderosa Canyon

RAINBOW POINT

Ponderosa Ridge

YOVIMPA POINT

Yovimpa Pass 8,355ft

Loop Trail

Riggs Spring

Pink Cliffs

© MOON.COM

Dixie

National

Forest

VISITOR CENTER

FAIRYLAND POINT

Fairyland Canyon

NORTH CAMPGROUND

Fairyland Loop Trail

Bryce National Park

BRYCE CANYON LODGE

SUNRISE POINT

QUEEN'S GARDEN TRAIL

SUNSET CAMPGROUND

SUNSET POINT

Navajo Loop Trail

Wall Street Trail

Bryce Canyon

INSPIRATION POINT

Bryce

Creek

Rim Trail

Peekaboo Loop Trail

BRYCE POINT

To Under-the -Rim Trail

PARIA VIEW

0   1 mi

0   1 km

Bryce in One Day

Catch the **free park shuttle** near Ruby's Inn, just outside the park entrance. It's worth getting up early so you don't miss the scene at **Sunrise Point.** If you don't want to hike down (and climb back up), take a walk along the **Rim Trail.** Plan to picnic at **Rainbow Point,** at the end of the parkway, with views over much of southern Utah. After lunch, descend from the rim on the **Navajo Loop Trail.** At the bottom of the loop, turn onto the **Queen's Garden Trail** and follow that back up to the rim. The Rim Trail connects the two trailheads. For dinner, the **Lodge at Bryce Canyon** has the best food in the area.

and autumn, and snow at almost any time of year. The visitors center, scenic drive, and a campground stay open year-round.

THE HOODOOS

The park's landscape originated about 60 million years ago as sediments in a large body of water, named Lake Flagstaff by geologists. Silt, calcium carbonate, and other minerals settled on the lake bottom. These sediments consolidated and became the Claron Formation, a soft, silty limestone with some shale and sandstone. Lake Flagstaff had long since disappeared when the land began to rise as part of the Colorado Plateau uplift about 16 million years ago. Uneven pressures beneath the plateau caused it to break along fault lines into a series of smaller plateaus at different levels known as the Grand Staircase. Bryce Canyon National Park occupies part of one of these plateaus—the Paunsaugunt.

The spectacular Pink Cliffs on the east edge contain the famous erosional features known as hoodoos, carved in the Claron Formation. Variations in hardness of the rock layers result in these strange features, which seem almost alive. Water flows through cracks, wearing away softer rock around hard

erosion-resistant caps. Finally, a cap becomes so undercut that the overhang allows water to drip down, leaving a "neck" of rock below the harder cap. Traces of iron and manganese provide the distinctive coloring.

The hoodoos continue to change—new ones form and old ones fade away. Despite appearances, wind plays little role in creating the landscape; it's the freezing and thawing, snowmelt, and rainwater that dissolve weak layers, pry open cracks, and carve out the forms. The plateau cliffs, meanwhile, recede at a rate of about one foot every 50-65 years; look for trees on the rim that now overhang the abyss. Listen, and you might hear the sounds of pebbles falling away and rolling down the steep slopes.

EXPLORING THE PARK

Allow a full day to see the visitors center exhibits, enjoy the viewpoints along the scenic drive, and take a few short walks. Photographers usually obtain best results early and late in the day, when shadows set off the brightly colored rocks. Memorable sunsets and sunrises reward visitors who stay overnight. Moonlit nights reveal yet another spectacle.

Visitors Center

At the **visitors center** (435/834-4747, 8am-8pm daily May-Sept., 8am-6pm daily Apr. and Oct., 8am-4:30pm daily Nov.-Mar.), geologic exhibits illustrate how the land was formed and how it has changed. Historical displays interpret the Paiute people, early explorers, and the first settlers. Trees, flowers, and wildlife are identified. Rangers present a variety of naturalist programs, including short hikes, mid-May-early September; see the posted schedule. From the turnoff on Highway 12, follow signs past Ruby's Inn to the park entrance; the visitors center is a short distance farther on the right.

Tours

The most basic tour of the park, which comes with the price of admission, is a ride on the park shuttle bus. Shuttle buses run every 12 minutes or so during the peak part of the day, and the trip from Ruby's Inn to Bryce Point takes 50 minutes. Of course, the beauty of the shuttle is that you can get off at any stop, hike for a while, and then catch another bus. However, if you're not really planning to hike, consider joining one of the free, twice-daily **shuttle bus tours** (435/834-5290, 9am and 1:30pm, reservations required and available at Ruby's Inn, Ruby's Campground, or the shuttle parking area) of the park. These tours go all the way to Rainbow Point. Shuttle season is early May-mid-October and, unlike at Zion, shuttle use is voluntary.

Ruby's Inn (26 S. Main St., 866/866-6616, www.rubysinn.com), a hotel, restaurant, and recreation complex at the park entrance, is a good place to take measure of the opportunities for organized recreation and sightseeing excursions around Bryce Canyon. The lobby is filled with outfitters who are anxious to take you out on the trail; you'll find lots of recreational outfitters, along with vendors who organize hayrides, barn dances, and chuckwagon dinners. During the summer, Ruby's also sponsors a rodeo (7pm Wed.-Sat., $13 adults, $9 ages 3-12) across from the inn.

Park goers have long explored Bryce Canyon's hoodoos on horseback, and it's still an option offered at Ruby's and at the park lodge. You can also explore the area around Bryce Canyon on a noisier steed. Guided all-terrain vehicle (ATV) tours of Red Canyon are offered by **Ruby's ATV Tours** (435/834-5231, 1-hour trip $70-140 depending on vehicle choice).

If you'd like to get a look at Bryce and the surrounding area from the air, take a scenic flightseeing tour with **Bryce Canyon Airlines** (Ruby's Inn, 435/834-8060), which offers both plane and helicopter tours. There's quite a range of options, but a 35-minute airplane tour ($175 pp, 2-person minimum) provides a good look at the surroundings.

"A Hell of a Place to Lose a Cow"

Mormon pioneer Ebenezer Bryce homesteaded near the town site of Tropic in 1875, but the work of scratching a living from the rugged land became too hard. He left five years later for more promising areas in Arizona. The name of the park commemorates his efforts. He is remembered as saying of the area, "Well, it's a hell of a place to lose a cow."

A later settler, Ruben "Ruby" Syrett, recognized the tourism potential of the area and opened the first small lodge near Sunset Point in 1919, then Ruby's Inn in 1924. Enthusiasm for the scenic beauty led to the creation of Bryce Canyon National Monument in 1923. The name changed to Utah National Park in the following year, and then it took its current name in 1928. Tours organized by the Union Pacific Railroad, beginning in the late 1920s, made Bryce well known and easily visited.

SCENIC DRIVE

From elevations of about 8,000 feet near the visitors center, the park's scenic drive gradually winds 1,100 vertical feet higher to Rainbow Point. About midway you'll notice a change in the trees, from largely ponderosa pines to spruces, firs, and aspens. On a clear day you can enjoy vistas of more than 100 miles from many of the viewpoints. Because of parking shortages on the drive, trailers must be left at the visitors center or your campsite. Visitors who want to see all of the viewpoints should take a walk on the Rim Trail.

Although we present the viewpoints in north-south order, when the park is bustling, it's better to drive all the way to the southern end of the road and visit the viewpoints from south to north, thus avoiding left turns against traffic. Of course, if you're just heading to one viewpoint or trailhead, it's fine to drive directly to it.

Bryce Canyon in Winter

Although Bryce is most popular during the summer months, it is especially beautiful and other-worldly during the winter, when the rock formations are topped with snow. Because Bryce is so high (elevation ranges 8,000-9,000 feet), winter lasts a long time, often into April.

The main park roads and most viewpoints are plowed, and the Rim Trail is an excellent, easy snowshoe or cross-country ski route. The roads to Paria View and Fairyland Point remain un-plowed and are marked as **Paria Ski Trail** (a 5-mile/8-km loop) and **Fairyland Ski Trail** (a 2.5-mile/4-km loop) for snowshoers and cross-country skiers. Rent cross-country ski equipment just outside the park at Ruby's Inn (435/834-5341 or 866/866-6616, www.rubysinn.com). Miles of snowmobile trails are groomed outside the park.

The **Bryce Canyon Snowshoe Program** (435/834-4747, 1pm daily as possible, free) offers free snowshoes, poles, and guided hikes with snowshoe rangers. These 1-mile (1.6-km) outings are designed for beginners and depend on snow depth and ranger availability. On full moon nights November-March, rangers add a moonlit snowshoe hike. During the winter, most of the businesses around the park entrance shut down. The notable exception is Ruby's Inn, which is a wintertime hub of activity. During the winter months, rates drop precipitously—January-March, most guest rooms go for about $70.

Ruby's Inn hosts the **Bryce Canyon Winter Festival** during Presidents Day weekend in February. The three-day festival includes free cross-country skiing and snowshoeing clin-ics, demos, and tours. This is also the time and place to pick up tips on ski archery and winter photography.

Fairyland Point

To reach the turnoff, just inside the park boundary, go north 0.8 mile (1.3 km) from the visitors center, then east 1 mile (1.6 km). Whimsical forms line Fairyland Canyon a short distance below. You can descend into the "fairyland" on the **Fairyland Loop Trail** or follow the **Rim Trail** for other panoramas.

★ Sunrise and Sunset Points

These overlooks are off to the left, about 1 mile (1.6 km) past the visitors center; they're connected by a 0.5-mile (0.8-km) paved section of the **Rim Trail.** Panoramas from each point take in large areas of Bryce Amphitheater and beyond. The lofty Aquarius and Table Cliff Plateaus rise along the skyline to the northeast; you can see the same color-ful Claron Formation in cliffs that faulting has raised about 2,000 feet higher. A short walk down either the **Queen's Garden Trail** or the **Navajo Loop Trail** from Sunset Point will bring you close to Bryce's hoodoos and provide a totally different experience from what you get atop the rim.

Inspiration Point

It's well worth the 0.75-mile (1.2-km) walk south along the **Rim Trail** from Sunset Point to see a fantastic maze of hoodoos in the Silent City. It's also accessible by car from a spur road near the Bryce Point turnoff. Weathering along vertical joints has cut many rows of nar-row gullies, some more than 200 feet deep. It's a short but steep 0.2-mile (0.3-km) walk up to Upper Inspiration Point.

Bryce Point

This overlook at the south end of Bryce Amphitheater has expansive views to the north and east. It's also the start for the **Rim, Peekaboo Loop,** and **Under-the-Rim Trails.** From the turnoff 2 miles (3.2 km) south of the visitors center, follow signs 2.1 (3.4 km) miles in.

Paria View

Cliffs drop precipitously into the head-waters of Yellow Creek, a tributary of the

BRYCE POINT
ELEVATION 8300

SPEED
LIMIT
45

Paria River. You can see a section of the Under-the-Rim Trail winding up a hillside near the mouth of the amphitheater below. Distant views take in the Paria River Canyon, White Cliffs (of Navajo sandstone), and Navajo Mountain. The plateau rim in the park forms a drainage divide. Precipitation falling west of the rim flows gently into the East Fork of the Sevier River and the Great Basin; precipitation landing east of the rim rushes through deep canyons in the Pink Cliffs to the Paria River and on to the Colorado River and the Grand Canyon. Take the turnoff for Bryce Point, and then keep right at the fork.

Farview Point

This sweeping panorama takes in a lot of geology. You'll see levels of the Grand Staircase that include the Aquarius and Table Cliff Plateaus to the northeast, Kaiparowits Plateau to the east, and White Cliffs to the southeast. Look beyond the White Cliffs to see a section of the Kaibab Plateau that forms the north rim of the Grand Canyon in Arizona. The overlook is on the left, 9 miles (14.5 km) south of the visitors center.

Natural Bridge

This large feature is just off the road to the east, 1.7 miles (2.7 km) past Farview Point. The span is 54 feet wide and 95 feet high. Despite its name, this is an arch formed by weathering from rain and freezing, not by stream erosion like a true natural bridge. Once the opening reached ground level, runoff began to enlarge the hole and to dig a gully through it.

Agua and Ponderosa Canyons

You can admire sheer cliffs and hoodoos from the Agua Canyon overlook to the east, 1.4 miles (2.3 km) past Natural Bridge. With a little imagination, you may be able to pick out the Hunter and the Rabbit below. The Ponderosa Canyon overlook, to the east 1.8

1: Bryce Point; 2: Natural Bridge

miles (2.9 km) farther, offers a panorama similar to that at Farview Point.

Yovimpa and Rainbow Points

The land drops away in rugged canyons and fine views are at the end of the scenic drive 17 miles (27 km) south of the visitors center. At an elevation of 9,115 feet, this is the highest area of the park. Yovimpa and Rainbow Points are only a short walk apart yet offer different vistas. The **Bristlecone Loop Trail** is an easy 1-mile (1.6-km) loop from Rainbow Point to ancient bristlecone pines along the rim. The **Riggs Spring Loop Trail** makes a good day hike; you can begin from either Yovimpa Point or Rainbow Point and descend into canyons in the southern area of the park. The **Under-the-Rim Trail** starts from Rainbow Point and winds 23 miles (37 km) to Bryce Point; day hikers can make a 7.5-mile (12-km) trip by using the Agua Canyon Connecting Trail and a car shuttle.

HIKING

Hikers enjoy close-up views of the wonderfully eroded features and gain a direct appreciation of Bryce's geology. Because almost all of the trails head down off the canyon's rim, they're moderately difficult, with many ups and downs, but the paths are well graded and signed. Hikers not accustomed to the 7,000-9,000-foot elevations will find the going relatively strenuous and should allow extra time. Be sure to carry water and drink frequently—staying well hydrated will give you more energy. Rangers stress the fact that most injuries happen because of improper footwear; hike in boots or sturdy trail runners!

Wear a hat and sunscreen to protect against sunburn, which can be a problem at these elevations. Don't forget rain gear; storms can come up suddenly. Always carry water for day trips, as only a few natural sources exist. Ask at the visitors center for current trail conditions and water sources; you can also pick up a free hiking map at the visitors center. Snow may block some trail sections in winter and early spring. Horses are permitted only on

Peekaboo Loop. Pets must stay above the rim; they're allowed on the Rim Trail only between Sunset and Sunrise Points.

Special hazards you should be aware of include crumbly ledges and lightning strikes. People who have wandered off trails or gotten too close to the drop-offs have had to be pulled out by rope. Avoid cliffs and other exposed areas during electrical storms, which are most common in late summer.

Overnight hikers can obtain the required backcountry permit ($5-15 depending on size of group) at the visitors center. Camping is allowed only on the Under-the-Rim and Riggs Spring Loop Trails. Backpack stoves must be used for cooking; wood fires are prohibited. Although there are several isolated springs in Bryce's backcountry, it's prudent to carry at least one gallon of water per person per day. Ask about the location and flow of springs when you register for the backcountry permit.

Don't expect much solitude during the summer on the popular Rim, Queen's Garden, Navajo Loop, and Peekaboo Loop Trails. Fairyland Loop Trail is less used, and the backcountry trails are almost never crowded. September-October are the choice hiking months—the weather is best and the crowds smallest, although nighttime temperatures in late October can dip well below freezing.

Rim Trail

This easy trail follows the edge of Bryce Amphitheater for 5.5 miles (8.9 km) between Fairyland and Bryce Points; the elevation change is 540 feet. Most people just walk sections of it on leisurely strolls or use the trail to connect with five others. The 0.5-mile (0.8-km) section near the lodge between Sunrise and Sunset Points is paved and nearly level; other parts are gently rolling.

Fairyland Loop Trail

This trail winds in and out of colorful rock spires in the northern part of Bryce Amphitheater, a somewhat less-visited area 1 mile (1.6 km) off the main park road. Although the trail is well graded, remember

the 900 vertical feet you'll climb when you make your exit. You can take a loop hike of 8 miles (12.9 km) from either Fairyland Point or Sunrise Point by using a section of the **Rim Trail;** a car shuttle saves 3 hiking miles (4.8 km). The whole loop is too long for many visitors, who enjoy short trips down and back to see this "fairyland."

★ Queen's Garden Trail

A favorite of many people, this trail drops from Sunrise Point through impressive features in the middle of Bryce Amphitheater to a hoodoo resembling a portly Queen Victoria. The hike is 1.5 miles (2.4 km) round-trip and has an elevation change of 320 feet, which you'll have to climb on the way back. This is the easiest excursion below the rim and takes about 1.5 hours. Queen's Garden Trail also makes a good loop hike with the **Navajo Loop** and **Rim Trails;** most people who do the loop prefer to descend the steeper Navajo and climb out on Queen's Garden Trail for a 3.5-mile (5.6-km) hike. Trails also connect with the **Peekaboo Loop Trail** and go to the town of Tropic.

Navajo Loop Trail

From Sunset Point, you'll drop 520 vertical feet in 0.75 mile (1.2 km) through a narrow canyon. At the bottom, the loop leads into deep, dark **Wall Street**—an even narrower canyon, 0.5 mile (0.8 km) long—then returns to the rim; the total distance is about 1.5 miles (2.4 km). Other destinations from the bottom of Navajo Loop Trail are **Twin Bridges, Queen's Garden Trail, Peekaboo Loop Trail,** and the town of Tropic. The 1.5-mile (2.4-km) trail to Tropic isn't as scenic as the other trails, but it does provide another way to enter or leave the park; ask at the visitors center or in Tropic for directions to the trailhead.

Peekaboo Loop Trail

This enchanting walk is full of surprises at every turn—and there are lots of turns.

1: Navajo Loop Trail; 2: the Peekaboo Trail

NAVAJO LOOP
1.3 MI. ROUND TRIP

The trail is in the southern part of Bryce Amphitheater, which has some of the most striking rock features. You can start from Bryce Point (6.5 miles/10.5 km round-trip), from Sunset Point (5.5 miles/8.9km round-trip via Navajo Loop Trail), or from Sunrise Point (7 miles/11.3 km round-trip via Queen's Garden Trail). The loop itself is 3.5 miles (5.6 km) long with many ups and downs and a few tunnels. The elevation change is 500-800 feet, depending on the trailhead you choose. This is the only trail in the park where horses are permitted; remember to give horseback travelers the right-of-way and, if possible, to step to higher ground when you allow them to pass.

Under-the-Rim Trail

The longest trail in the park winds 23 miles (37 km) below the Pink Cliffs between Bryce Point in the north and Rainbow Point in the south. Allow at least two days to hike the entire trail; the elevation change is about 1,500 feet with many ups and downs. Four connecting trails from the scenic drive also allow you to travel the Under-the-Rim Trail as a series of day hikes. Another option is to combine the Under-the-Rim and **Riggs Spring Loop** Trails for a total of 31.5 miles (51 km).

The **Hat Shop,** an area of delicate spires capped by erosion-resistant rock, makes a good day-hike destination; begin at Bryce Point and follow the Under-the-Rim Trail for about 2 miles (3.2 km). Most of this section is downhill, with an elevation change of 900 feet, so you'll have to climb on the way out.

Bristlecone Loop Trail

The easy 1-mile (1.6-km) loop begins from either Rainbow or Yovimpa Point and goes to viewpoints and ancient bristlecone pines along the rim. These hardy trees survive fierce storms and extremes of hot and cold that no other tree can. Some of the bristlecone pines here are 1,700 years old.

Riggs Spring Loop

One of the park's more challenging day hikes or a leisurely overnighter, this trail begins at Rainbow Point and descends into canyons in the southern area of the park. The loop is about 9 miles (14.5 km) long, with an elevation change of 1,625 feet. Of the three backcountry campgrounds along the trail, the Riggs Spring site is most conveniently located, about halfway around the loop. Great views of the hoodoos, lots of aspen trees, a couple of pretty meadows, and great views off to the east are some of the highlights of this hike. Day hikers may want to take a shortcut bypassing Riggs Spring, saving 0.75 mile (1.2 km).

Mossy Cave Trail

This easy trail is not on the main park road; it's just off Highway 12, northwest of Tropic, near the east edge of the park. Hike up Water Canyon to a cool alcove of dripping water and moss. Sheets of ice and icicles add beauty to the scene in winter. The hike is only 1 mile (1.6 km) round-trip, with a small elevation gain. A side trail, just before the cave, branches right a short distance to a little waterfall; look for several small arches in the colorful canyon walls above. Although the park lacks perennial natural streams, the stream in Water Canyon flows even during dry spells. Mormon pioneers labored for three years to channel water from the East Fork of the Sevier River through a canal and down this wash to the town of Tropic. Without this irrigation, the town might not even exist. From the visitors center, return to Highway 12, turn east, and go 3.7 miles (6 km) toward Escalante; the parking area is on the right just after a bridge (between mileposts 17 and 18). Rangers schedule guided walks to the cave and the waterfall during the main season.

MOUNTAIN BIKING

Although mountain biking is prohibited on trails inside the national park, Red Canyon's bike trails, just a few miles west of the park entrance, are spectacularly scenic and exhilarating to ride. Ruby's Inn provides a shuttle service for Red Canyon mountain bikers.

HORSEBACK RIDING

If you'd like to get down among the hoodoos but aren't sure you'll have the energy to hike back up to the rim, consider letting a horse help you along. **Canyon Trail Rides** (Lodge at Bryce Canyon, 435/679-8665, www.canyonrides.com, Apr.-Oct.), a park concessionaire, offers guided rides near Sunrise Point, and both two-hour ($65) and half-day ($90) trips are offered. Both rides descend to the floor of the canyon; the longer ride follows the Peekaboo Loop Trail. Riders must be at least seven years old and weigh no more than 220 pounds; the horses and wranglers are accustomed to novices. **Ruby's Horseback Adventures** (435/834-5341 or 866/782-0002, www.horserides.net, Apr.-Oct.) offers horseback riding in and near Bryce Canyon. There's a choice of half-day ($90) and full-day ($135, including lunch) trips, as well as a 1.5-hour trip ($65). During the summer, Ruby's also sponsors a rodeo (7pm Wed.-Sat., $13 adults, $9 ages 3-12) across from the inn.

FOOD

The dining room at the ★ **Lodge at Bryce Canyon** (435/834-8700, http://brycecanyonforever.com, 7am-10:30am, 11:30am-3pm, and 5:30pm-10pm daily Apr.-Oct., $13-34) is classy and atmospheric, with a large stone fireplace and white tablecloths, and offers food that's better than anything else you're going to find in the area. For lunch, the snack bar is a good bet in nice weather; the only seating is outside on the patio or in the hotel lobby.

A short walk from the main lodge is **Valhalla Pizzeria and Coffee Shop** (435/834-8700, http://brycecanyonforever.com, 6am-10pm daily mid-May-mid-Oct., $10-14). Although the pizza is described as artisanal, don't set your hopes too high. From 11:30am-3pm you can stop by for a slice of pizza (less than $5).

If you're up for a high-volume dining experience, Ruby's Inn **Cowboy Buffet and Steak Room** (26 S. Main St., 435/834-5341, www.rubysinn.com, 6:30am-9:30pm daily

summer, until 9pm winter, $13-28, dinner buffet $23) is an incredibly busy place. It's also one of Bryce Canyon's better restaurants, with sandwiches, steaks, and a buffet with a salad bar. Casual lunch and dinner fare, including pizza, is served in the inn's snack bar, the **Canyon Diner** (6:30am-9:30pm daily May-Oct., $4-12). Note that the vegetarian sandwich here consisted of a slice of American cheese, some lettuce, and a few cucumber slices on a hot dog bun. A third Ruby's restaurant, **Ebenezer's Barn & Grill** (7pm dinner, 8:30pm show daily late Apr.-mid-Oct., $32-38) features cowboy-style food and entertainment that's very expensive for its quality.

Bryce Canyon Resort (13500 E. Hwy. 12, 435/834-5351 or 800/834-0043, www.brycecanyonresort.com, 7am-10pm daily, $8-22), near the turnoff for the park, has an on-site restaurant that features burgers and Mexican food; they also serve Utah beers.

Two long-established restaurants west of the park entrance have a low-key, noncorporate atmosphere and pretty good food. The small family-run restaurant attached to **Bryce Canyon Pines** (Hwy. 12, milepost 10, 435/834-5441 or 800/892-7923, 7am-10pm daily, $15-27) is a homey place to stop for burgers, soup, or sandwiches. The restaurant touts its fruit pies. Two miles west of the park turnoff is **Bryce Point Lodge** (Hwy. 12, 435/834-5227, 7am-10pm daily, $13-28), a popular steak house with an Old West atmosphere.

ACCOMMODATIONS

Travelers may have a hard time finding accommodations and campsites April-October in both the park and nearby areas. Advance reservations at lodges, motels, and the park campground are a good idea; otherwise, plan to arrive by late morning. The Lodge at Bryce Canyon is the only lodge in the park itself, and you'll generally need to make reservations months in advance to get a room in this historic landmark (but it doesn't hurt to ask about vacancies). Other motels are clustered near the park entrance road, but many do not offer much for the money. The quality of lodgings is somewhat better in Tropic, 11 miles east on Highway 12, and in Panguitch, 25 miles to the northwest.

Both of the park's two large campgrounds have some sites available for reservation (877/444-6777, www.recreation.gov, $20 tents, $30 RVs). The rest of the sites are first-come, first-served; arrive by noon in the main season for a better chance of finding a spot.

$100-150

During the winter, it's easy to find inexpensive accommodations in this area; even guest rooms at Ruby's Inn start at about $70. The rest of the year, expect to pay handsomely for the staying close to the park. Several motels are clustered on Highway 12, right outside the park boundary. Many of these have seen a lot of use over the years, usually without a lot of attendant upkeep. If you want something more sumptuous and relaxing, consider staying at a B&B in nearby Tropic.

A reasonably good value for the area can be found at the **Bryce View Lodge** (105 E. Center St., 435/834-5180 or 888/279-2304, www.bryceviewlodge.com, $105-119), which has fairly basic guest rooms set back from the road near the park entrance, across the road from Ruby's Inn (it's owned by Ruby's). The lodge offers an indoor pool and hot tub.

Although "resort" may be stretching it, **Bryce Canyon Resort** (13500 E. Hwy. 12, 435/834-5351 or 866/834-0043, from $132-179) is an older hotel complex with a small pool, a restaurant, a store, and lodging options that include standard motel rooms, suites, and rustic cabins that sleep up to six.

Bryce Point Lodge (1150 Hwy. 12, 435/834-5227, www.fostersmotel.com, $144) has pine-paneled motel rooms in what appear to be older prefab modular structures; these are best suited for budget travelers who don't want to camp and don't plan to spend a lot of time in their rooms. It's 4 miles (6.4 km) west of the park entrance in a small complex with a restaurant and a supermarket.

The sprawling **Best Western Ruby's Inn** (26 S. Main St., 435/834-5341 or 866/866-6616, www.rubysinn.com, $150-160) offers many year-round services on Highway 63 just north of the park boundary; winter rates are considerably lower. The hotel features many separate buildings with guest rooms, as well as an indoor pool and a hot tub and all the bustling activity you could ever want. Kitchenettes and family rooms are also available; pets are allowed. Ruby's Inn is more than just a place to stay, however: This is one of the area's major centers for all manner of recreational outfitters, dining, entertainment, and shopping. Many tour bus groups bed down here. Although it is kind of a zoo, the quality of the guest rooms at Ruby's is generally higher than at other lodgings in the immediate area.

Six miles (9.7 km) west of the park turn-off, **Bryce Canyon Pines Motel** (Hwy. 12, milepost 10, 435/834-5441 or 800/892-7923, www.brycecanyonmotel.com, $140-150 standard rooms) is an older motel with both motel rooms, cottages, two-bedroom family suites with full kitchens, a seasonal covered pool, horseback rides, an RV park, and a restaurant (breakfast, lunch, and dinner daily early Apr.-late Oct.).

Over $150

The newest and best-appointed hotel in the area is the **Best Western Bryce Canyon Grand Hotel** (30 N. 100 E., 435/834-5700 or 866/866-6634, www.brycecanyongrand.com, $219-289). It's across the road from Ruby's, but it's actually a bit of a walk. Rooms have microwaves and refrigerators (unlike many in the area) and the sort of higher-end comforts that are expected in hotels in this price range, including a good breakfast buffet. An outdoor pool is open in the summer; during the winter guests can go across the highway to use the indoor pool at Ruby's.

Set among ponderosa pines a short walk from the rim, the ★ **Lodge at Bryce Canyon** (435/834-8700 or 877/386-4383, www.brycecanyonforever.com, Apr.-Oct., rooms $203-271, cabins $221) was built in 1923 by a division of the Union Pacific Railroad; a spur line once terminated at the front entrance. The lodge is the only lodging in the park itself and has lots of charm; it's listed on the National Register of Historic Places. It also has by far the best location of any Bryce-area accommodations. Accommodations options include suites in the lodge, motel-style guest rooms, and lodgepole pine cabins; all are clean and pleasant but fairly basic in terms of amenities. The location, however, could not be better. Reserving up to a year in advance is a good idea for the busy spring, summer and early fall season; these are popular lodgings.

Activities at the lodge include horseback rides, park tours, evening entertainment, and ranger talks; a gift shop sells souvenirs, while food can be found at both a restaurant and a snack bar.

Campgrounds

The park's two campgrounds both have water and some pull-through spaces. Reservations (877/444-6777, www.recreation.gov, $20 tents, $30 RVs) are accepted for May-September. Otherwise, try to arrive early for a space during the busy summer season; both campgrounds usually fill by 1pm or 2pm. The **North Campground** is on the left just past the visitors center. The best sites here are just a few yards downhill from the Rim Trail, with easy hiking access to other park trails. The **Sunset Campground** is about 2.5 miles (4 km) farther on the right, across the road from Sunset Point. Sunset has campsites accessible to people with disabilities.

Basic groceries, camping supplies, coin-operated showers, and a laundry room are available mid-April-late September at the General Store, between North Campground and Sunrise Point. The rest of the year, you can go outside the park to Ruby's Inn for these services.

The Dixie National Forest has three Forest Service campgrounds located in scenic settings among ponderosa pines, with water available. They'll often have room when campgrounds in the park are full. Sites can be reserved at Pine Lake, King Creek, and Red Canyon Campgrounds (877/444-6777, www.recreation.gov). The **Pine Lake Campground** (mid-May-mid-Sept., $15) is at 7,700 feet, just east of its namesake lake, in a forest of ponderosa pine, spruce, and juniper. From the highway junction north of the park, head northeast 11 miles (17.7 km) on gravel Highway 63, then turn southeast and go 6 miles (9.7 km). Contact the Escalante Ranger District Office (Escalante, 435/826-5400) for information on Pine Lake.

King Creek Campground (usually May-late Sept., $15) is on the west shore of Tropic Reservoir, which has a boat ramp and fair trout fishing. Sites are at 8,000 feet. From Highway 12, west of the park turnoff 2.8 miles (4.5 km), head 7 miles (11.3 km) south on the gravel East Fork Sevier River Road. **Red Canyon Campground** (late May-late Sept., $18) is just off Highway 12, 4 miles (6.4 km) east of U.S. 89. It's at 7,400 feet, below brilliantly colored cliffs. Contact the Powell Ranger District Office (Panguitch, 435/676-9300) for more information on King Creek and Red Canyon Campgrounds.

Camping is available a little farther away at beautiful **Kodachrome Basin State Park** (801/322-3770 or 800/322-3770, www.reserveamerica.com, $20 tents, $45-51 RVs). From Bryce, take Highway 12 east to Cannonville, and then head 9 miles (14.5 km) south to the park.

Private campgrounds in the area tend to cost upward of $35; the base price for camping at Ruby's increases when there are more than two campers. The convenient **Ruby's Inn Campground** (26 S. Main St., 435/834-5301 or 866/878-9373, www.rubysinn.com, Apr.-Oct.) has spaces for tents ($32) and RVs ($45-51); full hookups are available, and showers and a laundry room are open year-round. They've also got a few tepees (from $41) and bunkhouse-style cabins (bedding not provided, $59). All of the considerable facilities at Ruby's are available to campers, and the park shuttle stops here. **Bryce Canyon Pines Campground** (Hwy. 12, milepost

10, 435/834-5441 or 800/892-7923, www. brycecanyonmotel.com, Apr.-Oct., $38 tents, $50 RVs), 4 miles (6.4 km) west of the park entrance, has an indoor pool, a game room, groceries, and shaded sites.

INFORMATION AND SERVICES

The **general store** at Ruby's (26 S. Main St., 866/866-6616) has a large stock of groceries, camping and fishing supplies, film and processing, Native American crafts, books, and other souvenirs. The Bryce **Post Office** is at the store as well. Horseback rides, helicopter tours, and airplane rides are arranged in the lobby. In winter, cross-country skiers can rent gear and use trails located near the inn as well as in the park. Snowmobile trails are available (snowmobiles may not be used within the park). Western-fronted shops across from Ruby's Inn offer trail rides, chuck wagon dinners, mountain bike rentals, souvenirs, and a petting farm.

GETTING THERE AND AROUND

From Bryce Junction (U.S. 89, 7 miles/11.3 km south of Panguitch), turn east and go 14 miles (22.5 km) on Highway 12, then go south 3 miles (4.8 km) on Highway 63. From Torrey, near Capitol Reef National Park, head west 103 miles (166 km) on Highway 12, then turn south and go 3 miles (4.8 km); winter snows occasionally close this section. Both approaches have spectacular scenery.

Park Shuttle Bus

During the peak summer season (8am-8pm daily mid-April-early Oct.), tour buses depart from the front of Ruby's Inn, just outside the park entrance, every 15-20 minutes and stop at all the major viewpoints along the main amphitheater, as well as at the campgrounds, the visitors center, and the Lodge at Bryce Canyon. Passengers can take as long as they like at any viewpoint and catch a later bus—a straight-through ride takes about an hour. The shuttle bus service also makes it easier for hikers, who don't need to worry about car shuttles between trailheads.

Use of the shuttle bus system is included in the cost of admission to the park, but it is not mandatory; you can still bring in your own vehicle. However, park officials note that there is generally one parking space for every four cars entering the park.

Vicinity of Bryce Canyon

Sometimes the tour-bus bustle at Bryce's rim and at the large commercial developments right at the entrance to the park can be a little off-putting. It's easy to escape the crowds by heading just a few miles west on scenic Highway 12.

RED CANYON

The drive on Highway 12 between U.S. 89 and the turnoff for Bryce Canyon National Park passes through this well-named canyon. Because Red Canyon is not part of Bryce Canyon National Park—it's part of Dixie National Forest—many of the trails are open to mountain biking and ATV riding. In fact, this canyon has become very popular as other Utah mountain biking destinations become crowded.

Staff members at the **Red Canyon Visitor Center** (Hwy. 12, between mileposts 3 and 4, 435/676-2676, www.fs.usda.gov/recarea/dixie, dawn-dusk Apr.-Oct.) can tell you about the trails and scenic backcountry roads that wind through the area. Books and maps are available.

Hiking

The U.S. Forest Service maintains many scenic hiking trails that wind back from the highway to give you a closer look at the geology.

The following are open to hikers only; dogs are permitted. **Pink Ledges Trail,** the easiest and most popular, loops 1 mile (1.6 km) past intriguing erosional features from the Red Canyon Visitor Center. Signs identify some of the trees and plants; the elevation gain is 100 feet. The **Birdseye Trail** winds through formations and connects the visitors center with a parking area on Highway 12 just inside the forest boundary, 0.8 mile (1.3 km) away. **Buckhorn Trail** begins from site number 23 in Red Canyon Campground and climbs 1 mile (1.6 km) for views of erosional forms and Red Canyon; the campground is on the south side of Highway 12 between mileposts 3 and 4. The **Tunnel Trail** ascends 300 feet in 0.7 mile (1.1 km) for fine views of the canyon. The trail begins from a pullout on the south side of Highway 12 just west of a pair of tunnels, crosses the streambed, then climbs a ridge to viewpoints on the top. Ask at the visitors center for other good area trails worth exploring.

Mountain Biking

A rather wonderful paved bike trail parallels Highway 12 for 5 miles (8 km) through Red Canyon. Parking lots are located at either end of the trail, at the Thunder Mountain trailhead, and at Coyote Hollow Road.

True mountain bikers will eschew the pavement and head to **Casto Canyon Trail,** a trail that winds 5.5-mile (8.9-km) each way through a variety of red-rock formations and forest. This ride starts west of the visitors center, about 2 miles (3.2 km) east of U.S. 89. Turn north from Highway 12 onto Forest Road 118 and continue about 3 miles (4.8 km) to the Casto Canyon parking lot. For part of the way, the trail is shared with ATVs, but then the bike trail splits off to the right. The usual turnaround point is at Sanford Road.

This ride can be linked with other trails to form a 17-mile (27-km), each way, test of biking skills and endurance, with the route starting and ending along Highway 12. If you don't have a shuttle vehicle at each of the trailheads, you'll need to pedal back another 8 miles (12.9 km) along the paved roadside trail to retrieve your vehicle. Start at Tom Best Road, just east of Red Canyon. You'll climb through forest, turning onto Berry Spring Creek Road and then Cabin Hollow Road. Once the trail heads into Casto Canyon, you'll have 5 downhill miles (8 km) of wonderful red-rock scenery. When you reach the Casto Canyon trailhead, you can choose to return to Highway 12, or you can pedal out to U.S. 89 and Panguitch. Much of the trail is strenuous, and you'll need to take water along because there's no source along the way. There are several side trails to make this into a shorter ride; stop by the visitors center for more information.

BRYCE MUSEUM AND WILDLIFE ADVENTURE

A museum and natural history complex, the **Bryce Museum and Wildlife Adventure** (1945 W. Hwy. 12, 435/834-5555, www.brycewildlifeadventure.com, 9am-7pm daily Apr. 1-Nov. 15, $8) is a wildlife showcase housed in a large building just west of the turnoff to Bryce Canyon. This taxidermy collection depicts more than 800 animals from around the world displayed in dioramas resembling their natural habitats. It's actually quite well done, and kids seem to love it. There's a good collection of Native American artifacts as well, and a beautiful butterfly display. You can also rent ATVs and mountain bikes here.

TROPIC

Mormon pioneer Ebenezer Bryce homesteaded near the town site of Tropic in 1875, but the work of scratching a living from the rugged land became too hard. He left five years later for more promising areas in Arizona. The name of the park commemorates his efforts. He is remembered as saying of the area, "Well, it's a hell of a place to lose a cow." Other pioneers settled six villages near the upper Paria River between 1876 and 1891. The towns of Tropic, Cannonville, and Henrieville still survive. Travelers think of Tropic primarily for its cache of motels lining Main Street (Hwy. 12), but several pleasant

B&Bs also grace the town. Ask to see the small collection of pioneer and Indian artifacts at **Ebenezer Bryce's log cabin** (next to Bryce Pioneer Village at 80 S. Main St.). A **visitor information booth** in the center of town is open 11am-7pm daily early May-late October.

Food

There are a few dining options in town. The best place to start your search for a meal is the **Rustler's Restaurant** (141 N. Main St., 435/679-8633, 7am-10pm daily, $7-22), which is part of Clark's Grocery, an all-around institution that, in addition to selling groceries, serves Mexican food, pasta, pizza, ice cream, and steaks from a variety of venues within a complex that's essentially the town center.

At the Stone Canyon Inn, the **Stone Hearth Grille** (1380 W. Stone Canyon Ln., 435/679-8923, www.stonehearthgrille.com, 5pm-10pm daily mid-Mar.-Oct., $22-38) has an upscale atmosphere and menu. The food is the best for miles around; in good weather, enjoy your meal on the terrace.

Accommodations

$50-100

At the **Bryce Canyon Inn** (21 N. Main St., 435/679-8502 or 800/592-1468, www.brycecanyoninn.com, Mar.-Oct., $79 motel rooms, $164 cabins), the tidy cabins are nicely furnished and are one of the more appealing options in the Bryce neighborhood. The economy motel rooms are small but clean and a good deal.

Up on a bluff on the outskirts of town, the **Buffalo Sage B&B** (980 N. Hwy. 12, 435/679-8443 or 866/232-5711, www.buffalosage.com, $80) has great views and guest rooms decorated in Southwestern style.

Red Ledges Inn (199 N. Hwy. 12, 435/679-8811 or 800/442-1890, www.brycevalleyinn.com, $119-169) has conventional motel rooms in an attractive wood-fronted, Western-style motel. Pets are permitted, but an extra fee is charged.

$100-150

One of the most pleasant places to stay in Tropic is in the **Bryce Country Cabins** (320 N. Hwy. 12, 435/679-8643 or 888/679-8643, www.brycecountrycabins.com, $110-125). The cabins overlook a meadow, and each has a private bath.

At **Bryce Canyon Livery B&B** (660 W. 50 S., 435/679-8780, www.brycecanyonbedandbreakfast.com, $149), every guest room has a private bath; several have balconies with views of Bryce Canyon. They also offer a 3-bedroom cottage with full kitchen (breakfast not included).

OVER $150

The ★ **Stone Canyon Inn** (1380 W. Stone Canyon Lane, 435/679-8611 or 866/489-4680, www.stonecanyoninn.com, $235-360), a couple of miles west of downtown Tropic with views of Bryce, is a strikingly handsome, modern structure with several comfortable two-bedroom guest cabins with kitchens and newly built bungalows configured as suites that can sleep up to four; there are even "treehouses" that allow you to sleep above the trees. A sauna is shared by guests; it's tucked in between the inn and the cottages. Along with these accommodations, which are the region's most luxurious, the Stone Canyon has a notably good restaurant.

At the east end of town, the **Bullberry Inn B&B** (412 S. Hwy 12, 435/679-8820, http://bullberryinn.com, late March.-Oct., $155-145, 2-night minimum) has wraparound porches, and the guest rooms have private baths and rustic-style pine furniture.

CAMPGROUNDS

Head east to Cannonville for **Cannonville/Bryce Valley KOA** (175 N. Red Rock Dr., 435/679-8988 or 888/562-4710, www.koa.com, $36 tents, $41-49 RVs, $86-116 camping cabins), or continue south from Cannonville to **Kodachrome Basin State Park** (801/322-3770 or 800/322-3770, www.reserveamerica.com, $20 tents, $30 RVs).

1: Red Canyon; 2: Tropic cabin accommodations

Getting There

Tropic is just 11 miles east of Bryce Canyon National Park on Highway 12 and is visible from many of the park's viewpoints.

PANGUITCH

Pioneers arrived here in 1864, but conflicts with the Ute people forced their evacuation just two years later. A second attempt by settlers in 1871 succeeded, and Panguitch (the Paiute word for "big fish") is now the largest town in the area.

Panguitch is one of the more pleasant towns in this part of Utah, and there's an abundance of reasonably priced motels, plus a couple of good places to eat. The town is a good stopover on the road between Zion and Bryce National Parks. The early 20th-century commercial buildings downtown have some of their original facades. On side streets you can see sturdy brick houses built by the early settlers.

Travelers in the area during the second weekend in June should try to swing by for the annual **Quilt Walk** (www.quiltwalk.org), an all-out festival with historic home tours, quilting classes, and lots of food. The Quilt Walk commemorates a group of seven pioneers who trudged through snow to bring food back to starving townspeople. They spread quilts on the deep, soft snow and walked on them so as not to sink.

Food

Drop in at **Cowboy's Smokehouse Bar-B-Q** (95 N. Main St., 435/676-8030, 7am-9pm Mon.-Sat. mid-Mar.-mid-Oct., $10-25) for mesquite-grilled meat; live country music, and Western atmosphere are regular features. The **Flying M Restaurant** (580 N. Main St., 435/676-8008, 7am-9pm daily, $8-19) serves hearty breakfasts and standard American comfort food dinners, including homemade turkey potpies.

Depart from the standard American fare at **Tandoori Taqueria** (5 N. Main St., 435/962-9395, www.thetandooritaqueria.com, 4-9pm Mon. and Wed.-Thurs., noon-9pm Fri.-Sun.

$10-15), where a fusion of Indian and Mexican flavors includes a three-taco plate with posole, chorizo-and-beef, and tandoori chicken tacos.

Accommodations

Panguitch is the best place in greater Bryce Canyon to find an affordable motel room—there are more than a dozen older motor court lodgings, most quite basic but nicely maintained. Of these, the **Blue Pine Motel** (130 N. Main St., 435/676-2386, www. colorcountrymotel.com, $69-84) is one of the most attractive, with a friendly welcome and clean, well-furnished guest rooms, with microwaves and refrigerators in the guest rooms.

Another good midrange pick is the **Canyon Lodge Motel** (210 N. Main St., 435/676-8292 or 800/440-8292, www. canyonlodgemotel.com, $69-119), with clean, basic guest rooms plus a three-bed suite.

Along U.S. 89, the **New Western Motel** (180 E. Center St., 435/676-8876, http:// newbrycewesterninn.com, $89) has a swimming pool and a hot tub plus laundry facilities. Some guest rooms are in an older building, but all guest rooms have been recently refurbished.

Stay in one of the town's landmark redbrick homes: the tidy ★ **Red Brick Inn of Panguitch B&B** (161 N. 100 W., 435/690-1048 or 866/733-2745, www.redbrickinnutah. com, $130-160) has distinctive barnlike architecture and cozy bedrooms, including two adjoining bedrooms that share a bath—perfect for families. If you like B&Bs, this is definitely the best place in town to stay.

Cottonwood Meadow Lodge (milepost 123, U.S. 89, 435/676-8950, www. brycecanyoncabins.com, Apr.-Oct., $185-325, one-time cleaning fee in addition, 2-night minimum) is the exception to the modest-accommodations rule in the Panguitch area. This upscale lodge features four units, all with kitchen facilities: a bunkhouse, a log cabin dating from the 1860s, a three-bedroom farmhouse, and an attractively rehabbed barn that sleeps six. It's about 15 minutes from town and about 20 minutes from Bryce Canyon

National Park. Ranch animals are available for visits, and the Sevier River runs through the property, located two miles south of Highway 12 on U.S. 89.

CAMPGROUNDS

Hitch-N-Post Campground (420 N. Main St., 435/676-2436, www.hitchnpostrv.com, year-round) offers spaces for tents ($20) and RVs ($32-36) and has showers and a laundry room. The **Panguitch KOA Campground** (555 S. Main St., 435/676-2225, Apr.-Oct., $28 tents, $40-42 RVs, $53 cabins, $109-129 deluxe walled tents) on the road to Panguitch Lake includes a pool, a recreation room, laundry, and showers. The closest public campground is in **Red Canyon** (Hwy. 12, 435/676-2676, $18).

Information and Services

Contact **Bryce Canyon Country** (55 S. Main St., 435/676-1160 or 800/444-6689, www.brycecanyoncountry.com) for information on Panguitch and the nearby area. The **Powell Ranger District Office** (225 E. Center St., 435/676-9300, 8am-4:30pm Mon.-Fri.) of the Dixie National Forest has information on campgrounds, hiking trails, fishing, and scenic drives in the forest and canyons surrounding Bryce Canyon National Park.

Panguitch has a **post office** (65 N. 100 W.). **Garfield Memorial Hospital** (200 N. 400 E., hospital 435/676-8811, clinic 435/676-8811) is the main hospital in this part of the state.

Getting There

Panguitch is on U.S. 89, 7 miles (11.3 km) north from Bryce Junction (U.S. 89 and Hwy. 12). From this junction, it's 11 miles (17.7 km) east on Highway 12 to Bryce Canyon National Park.

ALONG U.S. 89

If you're driving between Zion and Bryce, you'll probably follow this route, at least as far as Mount Carmel Junction. Head farther south to Kanab to find a wide selection of mostly inexpensive lodgings and access to the southwestern part of Grand Staircase-Escalante National Monument.

At Mount Carmel Junction, Highway 9 turns west from U.S. 89 to Zion National Park. A good place to stay here is the **Best Western East Zion Thunderbird Resort** (435/648-2203, www.bestwestern.com, $150), which features a nine-hole golf course, a pool, and large attractive guest rooms with balconies.

On Highway 9, just a few miles east of Zion National Park, are the very appealing log cabins and lodges of the **Zion Mountain Ranch** (E. Hwy. 9, 435/648-2555 or 866/648-2555, www.zmr.com, $192-795). The cabins all have king beds and private baths plus microwaves and fridges; family lodges offer two or three bedrooms. The setting is great, with expansive views, a buffalo herd, and a decent on-site restaurant, the Bison Grill. Horseback riding and other outdoor recreation is offered.

KANAB AND VICINITY

Striking scenery surrounds this small town in Utah's far south. The Vermilion Cliffs to the west and east glow with a fiery intensity at sunrise and sunset. Streams have cut splendid canyons into surrounding plateaus. The Paiutes called the spot *kanab,* meaning "place of the willows," and the trees still grow along Kanab Creek. Mormon pioneers arrived in the mid-1860s and tried to farm along the unpredictable creek. Irrigation difficulties culminated in the massive floods of 1883, which in just two days gouged a section of creek bed 40 feet below its previous level. Ranching proved better suited to this rugged and arid land.

Hollywood discovered this dramatic scenery in the 1920s and has filmed more than 150 movies and TV series here since. Famous films shot hereabouts include movies as varied as *My Friend Flicka, The Lone Ranger,* and *The Greatest Story Ever Told.* The TV series *Gunsmoke* and *F Troop* were also shot locally. Film crews have constructed several Western sets near Kanab but most are on private land and are difficult to visit.

While most park visitors see Kanab (pop. 4,300) as a handy stopover on trips to Bryce,

Zion, and Grand Canyon National Parks and the southern reaches of the Grand Staircase and Kaiporawits Plateau national monuments, In fact, the presence of several nicely refurbished motels, excellent choices for dining, and a pleasantly alternative vibe in town make this one of the nicest and most affordable places to stay in southwest Utah.

Best Friends Animal Sanctuary

Best Friends Animal Sanctuary (5001 Angel Canyon Rd., 435/644-2001, www.bestfriends.org, 8am-5pm daily, tours 8:30am, 10am, 1pm, and 2:30pm daily, free, reservations required), the largest no-kill animal shelter in the country, takes in unwanted or abused animals and provides whatever rehabilitation is possible. Giant octagonal doghouses are filled with animals no one else wants: former research animals, aggressive dogs, old dogs, sick dogs, and dogs who have been abused or neglected. There are also plenty of cats, rabbits, birds, pot-bellied pigs, and horses. Many animals are adopted out, but even the unadoptable ones are given homes for life, with plenty of care and attention from the sanctuary's roster of employees and volunteers.

The shelter's origins date back to the 1970s, when a group of animal lovers began trying to prevent unadoptable animals from being euthanized by rescuing animals that were about to be put to sleep by shelters, rehabilitating them as necessary, and finding them homes. In the early 1980s, this group of dedicated rescuers bought land in Angel Canyon just north of Kanab and, with their motley crew of unadoptable animals, established this sanctuary. Now more than 1,000 animals live here at any given time, and the shelter is the county's largest employer, with more than 200 staff members caring for the animals and the grounds.

But even the large staff can't take care of all of the animals' needs. The shelter's volunteers spend anywhere from a couple of days to a couple of months feeding, walking, petting, and cleaning up after the animals. Volunteers also give the animals the attention and socialization necessary for them to become good companions.

Best Friends runs two-hour-long tours several times a day. Call for reservations or to learn more about volunteering at the shelter. There's no charge for the tour, although donations are gladly accepted.

Squaw Trail

This well-graded trail provides a close look at the geology, plant life, and animals of the Vermilion Cliffs just north of town. Allow about an hour on the moderately difficult trail to reach the first overlook (2 miles/3.2 km round-trip with a 400-foot elevation gain) or 90 minutes to go all the way up (3 miles/4.8 km round-trip with an 800-foot elevation gain). Views to the south take in Kanab, Fredonia, Kanab Canyon, and the vast Kaibab Plateau. At the top, look north to see the White, Gray, and Pink Cliffs of the Grand Staircase. The trailhead is at the north end of 100 East near the city park. Pick up a trail guide at the information center; brochures may also be available at the trailhead or the BLM office. Bring water, and try to get a very early start in summer.

Moqui Cave

The natural **Moqui Cave** (U.S. 89, 5 miles/8 km north of Kanab, 435/644-8525, 9am-7pm Mon.-Sat. Memorial Day-Labor Day, 10am-4pm Mon.-Sat. Labor Day-Memorial Day, $5) has been turned into a roadside tourist attraction with a large collection of Native American artifacts. Most of the arrowheads, pottery, sandals, and burial items on display have been excavated locally. A diorama recreates an Ancestral Puebloan ruin located 5 miles (8 km) away in Cottonwood Wash. Fossils, rocks, and minerals are exhibited as well, including what's claimed to be one of the largest fluorescent mineral displays in the country. There's even a Prohibition-era speakeasy (not open for drinks). The collections and a gift shop are within a spacious cave that stays pleasantly cool even in the hottest weather.

Kanab Heritage Museum

The 1895 Queen Anne-style Victorian **Kanab Heritage House** (13 S. 100 E., 435/644-3966, www.kanabheritagemuseum.com, 10am-5pm Mon.-Fri. May-Sept., free) reflects the prosperity of two of Kanab's early Mormon residents. Henry Bowman built it, but he lived here only two years before going on a mission. He sold the property to Thomas Chamberlain, who led a busy life serving as a leader in the Mormons' United Order and caring for his 6 wives and 55 children. A guide will show you around the house and explain its architectural details. The town had no stores when the house was built, so each family grew its own vegetables and fruit.

Frontier Movie Town

The owners assembled this movie-set replica, **Frontier Movie Town** (297 W. Center St., 435/644-5337, 9am-11pm Apr.-Oct., free), in Kanab to show visitors a bit of Hollywood's Old West. Some of the buildings have seen actual use in past movies and TV shows. Many small exhibits display Western and movie memorabilia; there's a selection of Western costumes available for rent if you feel like getting gussied up as a cowboy or showgirl. Souvenir photos, a gift shop, a saloon, and chuck wagon dinners bring in the money.

Tours

Kanab is central to an amazing number of sights, and if you'd like the pros to handle the logistics of your visit, turn to **Dreamland Safari Tours** (435/644-5506, www.dreamlandtours.net). Dreamland offers a day tour of local sights that includes slots canyons hikes, petroglyphs, dinosaur tracks, and the Coral Pink Sand Dunes (8-9 hours, $210 adults, $105 children 15 and under).

Entertainment and Events

A unique Kanab event is the **Greyhound Gathering** (435/644-2903, www.

greyhoundgang.com, mid-May most years), when hundreds of greyhound owners and their dogs converge on the town. Events include a parade, a race, and a howl-in. The Greyhound Gang, a nonprofit organization dedicated to the rescue, rehabilitation, and adoption of former racing greyhounds, hosts the festival.

During the third week of May, Kanab is the center of activity for the **Amazing Earthfest** (435/644-3735, http://amazingearthfest.com), which celebrates land and life on the Colorado Plateau with lectures, workshops, and outdoor activities delving into the area's natural and human history. Most events are free.

If you're looking for authentic Western entertainment, the Redstone Theater (29 W. Center St., 435/644-8025, https://theredstonetheater.com, $20 adult, $10 12 and under, early April-Oct.) hosts the **Bar G Wranglers,** a musical troupe that puts on a traditional Western revue of music, dancing, corny jokes and rope tricks. It's all good fun and a nostalgic throwback to the era of cowboy films in Kanab's past.

Shopping

Find a good selection of books, camping gear, and clothing, along with a little coffee bar, at **Willow Canyon Outdoor** (263 S. 100 E., 435/644-8884, www.willowcanyon.com). **Terry's Camera Trading Co.** (19 W. Center St., 435/644-5981) deals in cameras and their needs, including repairs for film cameras, beyond what you would expect in a town of this size. The shop almost qualifies as an antique camera museum.

Denny's Wigwam (78 E. Center St., 435/644-2452, www.dennyswigwam.com) is a landmark Old West trading post with a broad selection of Western jewelry, cowboy hats and boots, and souvenirs.

Food

Start the day at ★ **Kanab Creek Bakery** (238 West Center St., 435/644-5689, https://kanabcreekbakery.com, 6:30am-5pm Tues.-Sun., breakfast $7-11), a European-style bakery café operated by a Belgium-born woman. The breads and pastries are thoroughly authentic, and you'll have the option of omelets or quiche for breakfast, or fresh sandwiches and crepes for lunch.

★ **Sego** (190 N. 300 W., 435/644-5680, www.segokanab.com, 6pm-10pm Mon.-Sat., $11-22) is a surprisingly good find in this little town. Located in the Canyon Boutique Hotel, you'll find a cutting-edge menu, with starters of artisanal toast or a pork belly and watermelon salad and seafood dishes such as shrimp with mango puree and mandarin orange salsa. Most of the dishes are small plates designed for sharing.

Another good bet is the ★ **Rocking V Café** (97 W. Center St., 435/644-8001, www.rockingvcafe.com, 11:30am-10pm Thurs.-Mon., dinner $17-48). The setting is casual, and the food has a modern Southwestern flair. Rocking V, which caters to vegans as well as steak-lovers, pays homage to the "slow food" movement and makes everything from scratch. Be sure to check out the art gallery upstairs.

Wild Thyme Café (198 S. 100 E., 435/644-2848, https://wildthymekanab.com, 11:30am-10pm, $11-29) focuses on Southwest and Cajun flavors, supported by the restaurant's home-grown greens and vegetables. Pistachio chicken with poblano cream is a standout. No liquor is served, confirm winter hours.

It's small and often crowded, but **Escobar's Mexican Restaurant** (373 E. 300 S., 435/644-3739, 11am-9:30pm daily, $11-20) is the place for a Mexican lunch or dinner. Travelers setting out into the national monuments from Kanab should note that this is the best place for many miles around to stock up on groceries. **Honey's Food Jubilee** (260 E. 300 S., 435/644-5877) is a good grocery store on the way out of town to the east.

Accommodations

While a number of new hotels from the major chains line the edge of town, Kanab is blessed with a number of carefully refurbished vintage motor court hotels to fit diverse tastes and budgets. They're fun and in easy walking distance of downtown's notable dining options. Reservations are a good idea during the busy summer months and during mid-May, when most rooms are occupied by greyhounds and their people. All of the motels and campgrounds are on U.S. 89, which follows 300 West, Center, 100 East, and 300 South through town.

Relive Kanab's Hollywood heyday at the **Parry Lodge** (89 E. Center St., 435/644-2601 or 800/748-4104, www.parrylodge.com, $129-159). Built during Kanab's glory days as a movie-making center, the Parry Lodge was where the stars and movie crews stayed; more than 80 years later, this is still a pleasantly old-fashioned place to spend the night, and it has lots of character. At the very least you'll want to stroll through the lobby, where lots of photos of the celebrities who once stayed here are displayed. There are many room types, including two-bedroom units, kitchen suites, a pool, and a breakfast buffet. Rooms come in a variety of ages and styles, starting with entry level units that are small and basic for budget travelers, and moving up to traditional motel rooms in the two-story building. To experience where John Wayne and Julie Newmar stayed, ask for Pool Units. North of Kanab, at Mount Carmel Junction, is the **Best Western East Zion Thunderbird Resort** (4530 State St., Mount Carmel, 435/648-2203, www.bestwestern.com, $157-179), with a pool, a nine-hole golf course, and a restaurant. This pleasant crossroads motel is convenient if you're heading to Zion or Bryce Canyon National Parks. All guest rooms have balconies or patios.

The **Best Western Red Hills Motel** (125 W. Center St., 435/644-2675 or 800/830-2675, www.bestwesternredhills.com, $179-199), right in the heart of downtown (don't worry, it's a pretty mellow downtown), has balcony rooms and a pool, and is within a short walk of restaurants.

★ **Canyons Lodge** (236 U.S. 89 N., 435/644-3069, www.canyonslodge.com,

$119-179) is an extensively renovated motel with pleasant log cabin-style guest rooms, all with fridges and microwaves, plus an outdoor pool and breakfast included. What was once a typical mom-and-pop motel is now a stylish place to stay, although most rooms are still relatively small, as you'd expect in an older property. Several rooms here are pet-friendly, and because it's a popular place for visitors to Best Friends Animal Sanctuary to stay, it's best to reserve in advance. Canyons Lodge is one of several properties in town that have been renovated by local hotel group Canyons Collection (www.thecanyonscollection.com).

Another offering from Canyons Collection, the **Quail Park Lodge** (125 U.S. 89 N., 435/215-1447, www.quailparklodge.com, $129-149), a tricked out and updated early 60s-era motel, with a well-thought-out combination of vintage kitsch (a.k.a. mid-century modern) and quality linens and toiletries. The motel has a pool and accepts pets. It also rents cruiser bicycles (free to guests).

Another Canyons Collection property, the ★ **Canyons Boutique Hotel** (190 N. 300 W., 435/644-8660, www.canyonshotel.com, $149-169), seems to have taken its color scheme from the nearby Coral Pink Sand Dunes, but the decor is actually pretty classy and the beds are comfy. The entire top floor is taken up by a three-bedroom penthouse, and most rooms have large spa bathtubs; breakfast is included for all guests.

Another stylish entry from Canyons Collections is **Flagstone Boutique Inn and Suites** (233 W. Center St. 435/644-2020 or 844/322-8824, www.theflagstoneinn.com, $159-189), a former 1940s motor lodge that's been updated with contemporary pizzazz. A number of rooms have full or partial kitchens, and are set up for extended stays, so daily maid service is not provided. The onsite Peekaboo Canyon Wood-fired Kitchen makes vegetarian and vegan pizza and other specialties (open for three meals daily). This is a perfect spot if you are hubbing out of Kanab during your parks' exploration.

Especially nice if you're traveling with a group that plans to spend several nights in Kanab are the **Kanab Garden Cottages** (various locations, 435/644-2020, www.kanabcottages.com, $378 for 2 nights). These beautifully furnished three- or four-bedroom houses can easily sleep up to eight and are pet-friendly and within walking distance of town.

Northwest of Kanab, just a few miles east of Zion National Park, are the very appealing log cabins and lodges of the **Zion Mountain Ranch** (E. Hwy. 9, 435/648-2555 or 866/648-2555, www.zmr.com, 2 person cabins starting at $239). The cabins all have king beds and private baths plus microwaves and fridges; family lodges offer two or three bedrooms; the larger lodges can sleep up to 12. The setting is great, with expansive views, a buffalo herd, and a decent on-site restaurant, the Buffalo Grill. Horseback riding and other outdoor recreation are offered. The lodging options are boggling; explore the selection online and then give the ranch a call to discuss all the alternatives.

CAMPGROUNDS

The campground at **Coral Pink Sand Dunes State Park** (reservations 435/648-2800 or 800/322-3770, www.stateparks.utah.gov, $20) has restrooms with showers, paved pull-through sites, and a dump station. It's a pleasant shady spot, but it can hum with ATV traffic. It's open year-round, but the water is shut off late October-Easter; winter campers must bring their own water. Reservations are recommended for the busy Memorial Day-Labor Day season. The campground is about 10 miles (16 km) due west of Kanab, but the two are not directly connected by road. Reach the campground by turning west off U.S. 89 about 8 miles (12.9 km) north of Kanab onto Hancock Road and following it 12 miles (19.3 km) to the campground. The route is well marked by signs.

Just north of the state park, the BLM maintains **Ponderosa Grove Campground** (no water, $5) on the north edge of the dunes.

From Kanab, head 8 miles (12.9 km) north on U.S. 89, turn west onto Hancock Road (between mileposts 72 and 73), and continue 7.3 (11.7 km) miles to the campground.

The **Kanab RV Corral** (483 S. 100 E., 435/644-5330, www.kanabrvcorral.com, year-round, $36-40) has RV sites (no tents) with hot showers, a pool, and laundry service. The **Hitch'n Post RV Park** (196 E. 300 S., 435/644-2142 or 800/458-3516, www.hitchnpostrvpark.com, May-Oct., $23 tents, $35 RVs, $35-40 cabins) has showers.

The **Crazy Horse Campark** (625 E. 300 S., 435/644-2782, https://crazyhorsecampark.com, mid-Apr.-late Oct., $20 tents, $30-35 RVs) has a pool, a store, a game room, and showers.

Information and Services

Staff members at the **Kane County Visitor Center** (78 S. 100 E., 435/644-5033, www.visitsouthernutah.com, 8am-7pm Mon.-Fri., 8am-5pm Sat.) offer literature and advice for services in Kanab and travel in Kane County. For information about the Grand Staircase and Kaiparowits Plateau national monuments, go to the **Kanab Visitor Center** (745 E. U.S. 89, Kanab, 435/644-1300, 8am-4:30pm daily) on the east edge of town.

Getting There

Kanab is 15 miles (24 km) south of Mount Carmel Junction on U.S. 89, a total of 40 miles (64 km) from Zion National Park and just 7 miles (11.3 km) north of the Arizona-Utah border. From here, U.S. 89 continues southeast, providing access to the southern reaches of the Grand Staircase and Kaiparowits Plateau national monuments and, 74 miles (119 km) later, Glen Canyon Dam at Page, Arizona.

CORAL PINK SAND DUNES STATE PARK

Churning air currents funneled by surrounding mountains have deposited huge sand dunes in this valley west of Kanab. The ever-changing dunes reach heights of several hundred feet and cover about 2,000 of the park's 3,700 acres. Different areas in **Coral Pink Sand Dunes State Park** (435/648-2800, reservations 800/322-3770, www.stateparks.utah.gov, day-use $8 per vehicle, camping $20) have been set aside for hiking, off-road vehicles, and camping.

From Kanab, the shortest route to the park is to go north 8 miles (12.9 km) on U.S. 89, turn left between mileposts 72 and 73, and go 9.3 miles (15 km) on the paved

Coral Pink Sand Dunes State Park

Hancock Road to its end, then turn left (south) and go 1 mile (1.6 km) on a paved road into the park. From the north, you can follow U.S. 89 for 3.5 miles (5.6 km) south of Mount Carmel Junction, then turn right (south) and go 11 miles (17.7 km) on a paved road. The back road from Cane Beds in Arizona has about 16 miles (26 km) of gravel and dirt with some sandy spots; ask a park ranger for current conditions.

The canyon country surrounding the park has good opportunities for hiking and off-road-vehicle travel; the Kanab visitors center can supply maps and information. Drivers with 4WD vehicles can turn south onto Sand Springs Road (1.5 miles/2.4 km east of Ponderosa Grove Campground) and go 1 mile (1.6 km) to Sand Springs and another 4 miles (6.4 km) to the South Fork Indian Canyon Pictograph Site, in a pretty canyon. Visitors may not enter the Kaibab-Paiute Indian Reservation, which is south across the Arizona state line, from this side.

St. George

Southern Utah's largest city lies between lazy bends of the Virgin River on one side and rocky hills of red sandstone on the other. The warm climate, dramatic setting, and many year-round recreation opportunities have helped make St. George (approximate pop. 80,000) the fastest-growing city in the state. Local boosters claim that this is where Utah's summer sun spends the winter. Although it has gained a reputation as a retirement haven, thanks in large part to its warm winter climate and its plethora of golf courses, the city itself won't have much appeal to most travelers. However, the city's abundance of hotels and a clutch of good restaurants in the old downtown core make it a handy place to begin or end your southern Utah adventure.

In 1861, more than 300 Mormon families in the Salt Lake City area answered the call to go south to start the Cotton Mission, of which St. George became the center (hence the frequent use of "Dixie" to describe the area). The settlers overcame great difficulties to farm and to build an attractive city in this remote desert. Brigham Young chose the city's name to honor George A. Smith, who had served as head of the Southern (Iron) Mission during the 1850s. The title "Saint" means simply that he was a Mormon—a Latter-day Saint. Visits to some of the historic sites will add to your appreciation of the city's past; ask for the brochure *St. George Historic Walking Tour* at the chamber of commerce.

SIGHTS
St. George Temple
Visible for miles, the gleaming white **St. George Temple** (250 E. 400 S., at 200 South, 435/673-5181) rises from landscaped grounds in the center of St. George. In 1871 enthusiastic Mormons from all over the territory gathered to erect the temple. Dedicated on April 6, 1877, the structure was the church's first sacred house of worship in the West. The St. George Temple is the oldest active Mormon temple in the world. It's constructed of stuccoed stone in a castellated Gothic Revival style; a cupola with a weather vane caps the structure. Sacred ceremonies take place inside, so no tours are offered, but you're welcome to visit the grounds to admire the architecture. The temple is especially impressive at night when it's lit up against the black sky. A **visitors center** (490 S. 300 E., 9am-9pm daily, free) on the northeast corner of the grounds has short films and videos introducing the LDS Church.

Brigham Young Winter Home
Late in life, Brigham Young sought relief from arthritis and other aches and pains by

St. George

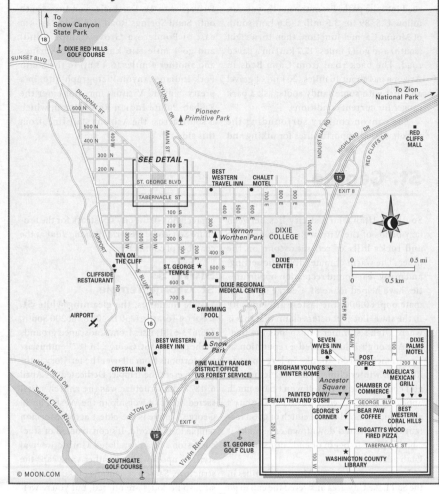

To
Snow Canyon
State Park

18

DIXIE RED HILLS
GOLF COURSE

SUNSET BLVD

DIAGONAL ST

600 N

500 N

400 N

300 N

200 N

400 W

SKYLINE

MAIN ST

DR

Pioneer
Primitive Park

SEE DETAIL

ST. GEORGE BLVD

TABERNACLE ST

100 S

200 S

300 S

400 S

500 S

600 S

700 S

300 W

200 W

100 W

100 E

200 E

300 E

400 E

500 E

600 E

700 E

800 E

900 E

1000 E

To Zion
National Park

INDUSTRIAL RD

HIGHLAND DR

RED CLIFFS DR

RED
CLIFFS
MALL

15

EXIT 8

BEST
WESTERN
TRAVEL INN

CHALET
MOTEL

Vernon
Worthen Park

DIXIE
COLLEGE

DIXIE
CENTER

DIXIE REGIONAL
MEDICAL CENTER

AIRPORT

RD

BLUFF ST

INN ON
THE CLIFF

ST. GEORGE
TEMPLE

CLIFFSIDE
RESTAURANT

SWIMMING
POOL

AIRPORT

18

900 S

BEST WESTERN
ABBEY INN

Snow
Park

INDIAN HILLS DR

CRYSTAL INN

PINE VALLEY RANGER
DISTRICT OFFICE
(US FOREST SERVICE)

Santa Clara River

HILTON DR

EXIT 6

15

Virgin River

ST. GEORGE
GOLF CLUB

SOUTHGATE
GOLF COURSE

© MOON.COM

RIVER RD

0   0.5 mi

0   0.5 km

SEVEN
WIVES INN
B&B

MAIN ST

100 E

DIXIE
PALMS
MOTEL

POST
OFFICE

200 N

BRIGHAM YOUNG'S
WINTER HOME

Ancestor
Square

ANGELICA'S
MEXICAN
GRILL

PAINTED PONY /
BENJA THAI AND SUSHI

CHAMBER OF
COMMERCE

ST. GEORGE BLVD

GEORGE'S
CORNER

BEAR PAW
COFFEE

BEST
WESTERN
CORAL HILLS

200 W

RIGGATTI'S WOOD
FIRED PIZZA

TABERNACLE ST

100 W

WASHINGTON COUNTY
LIBRARY

spending winters in Dixie's mild climate. This also gave him an opportunity to supervise more closely the affairs of the church here, especially construction of the temple. A telegraph line connected Young's house with Salt Lake City. He moved here late in 1873 and returned each winter until his death in 1877. The **Brigham Young Winter Home** (67 W. 200 N., 435/673-5181, 9am-dusk daily, free), a carefully restored adobe house, contains furnishings of the era, including some

that belonged to Young. Fruit and mulberry trees grow in the yard; mulberry leaves once fed the silkworms of the short-lived pioneer industry.

Jacob Hamblin Home

No one did more to extend the Mormons' southern settlements and keep peace with the Native Americans than Jacob Hamblin. He came west in 1850 with four children (his first wife refused to come) and settled in the Tooele area with wife number two. At Brigham Young's request, Hamblin moved south in 1856 and helped build the Santa Clara Fort. He built the present sandstone house, known as the **Jacob Hamblin Home** (Santa Clara Blvd. and Hamblin Dr., 435/673-5181, 9am-6:30pm Mon.-Sat., 1pm-6:30pm Sun., free), in the village of Santa Clara, 4 miles (6.4 km) northwest of St. George, after floods washed away the fort in 1862. Almost always on the move serving on missions, Hamblin had little time for home life. He moved to Kanab in 1870, then to Arizona and New Mexico. Even so, he had four wives and managed to father 24 children. The kitchen, work areas, and living rooms provide a good idea of what pioneer life was like.

St. George Art Museum

The **St. George Art Museum** (47 E. 200 N., 435/627-4525, www.sgcity.org/arts/artsfacilities/artmuseum, 10am-5pm Mon.-Sat., $3 adults, $1 ages 3-11), housed in a renovated beet-seed warehouse, is worth a visit both for its exhibits and its design. It's also a good place to get out of the sun for a couple of hours on a sweltering summer afternoon. The permanent collection has a strong regional emphasis; visiting shows often feature contemporary Western art. On Thursdays, the museum remains open until 8pm.

Dinosaur Trackways

Back in the early Jurassic, when the supercontinent of Pangaea was just beginning to break up, lakes covered this part of present-day Utah, and dinosaurs were becoming the earth's dominant vertebrates. Two sites southeast of St. George preserve dinosaur tracks from this era. Of the two, the more recently discovered site at Johnson Farm is more impressive and much easier to get to; indeed, it has been called one of the world's ten best dinosaur track sites. The Fort Pearce site is good if you're hankering for some back-road travel and scouting dino tracks and petroglyphs in remote washes.

★ **ST. GEORGE DINOSAUR DISCOVERY SITE AT JOHNSON FARM**

Tracks at the **Johnson Farm** (2180 E. Riverside Dr., 435/574-3466, www.utahdinosaurs.com, 10am-6pm daily, $6 adults, $3 ages 4-11) were discovered in 2000 by a retired optometrist. Since then, a vast number of tracks, including those of three species of theropods (meat-eating dinosaurs), and important trace fossils of pond scum, plants, invertebrates, and fish have also been uncovered. Excavation work is ongoing, and a visitors center provides a good look at some of the most exciting finds, including a wall-size slab of rock with footprints going to and fro. Also quite remarkable are the swim tracks, which settled a long-standing argument over whether dinosaurs actually swam.

The track site is on the outskirts of St. George, about two miles south of I-15 exit 10.

FORT PEARCE DINOSAUR TRACKS

A scenic back-road drive through the desert between St. George and Hurricane passes the ruins of Fort Pearce and more dinosaur tracks. Much of the road is unpaved and has rough and sandy spots, but it's usually suitable for cautious drivers in dry weather.

This group of tracks documents the passage of at least two different dinosaur species more than 200 million years ago. The well-preserved tracks in the Moenave Formation were made by a 20-foot-long herbivore weighing an estimated 8-10 tons and by a carnivore half as long. No remains of the dinosaurs themselves have been found here.

In 1861 ranchers arrived in Warner Valley to run cattle on the desert grasslands. Four years later, however, conflicts with Native Americans threatened to drive the settlers out. The Black Hawk War and periodic raids by Navajo made life precarious. Springs in Fort Pearce Wash—the only reliable water for many miles—proved the key to domination of the region. In December 1866, work began on a fort overlooking the springs. The stone walls stood about 8 feet high and were more than 30 feet long. No roof was ever added. Much of the fort and the adjacent corral, built in 1869, have survived to the present. Local cattle ranchers still use the springs for their herds. Petroglyphs can be seen in various places along the wash, including 0.25 mile (0.4 km) downstream from the fort along ledges on the north side of the wash.

To reach this somewhat remote site from St. George, head south on River Road, cross the Virgin River Bridge, and turn left onto 1450 South. Continue on the main road, bearing east through several 90-degree left and right turns. Turn left (east) onto a dirt road at the Fort Pearce sign and continue 5.6 miles (9 km) to a road that branches right along a small wash to the Fort Pearce parking lot. The dinosaur tracks are in a wash about 2 miles (3.2 km) farther down the road from Fort Pearce; a sign marks the parking area.

ENTERTAINMENT AND EVENTS

One of St. George's biggest annual events is the early October **St. George Marathon** (435/627-4500, www.stgeorgemarathon.com), which attracts about 4,000 runners from all over the United States. Also in October, the **Huntsman World Senior Games** (800/562-1268, www.seniorgames.net) presents a wide variety of Olympic-type competitions for seniors; you'll be amazed at the enthusiasm and ability on display. The city fills with triathletes in early May, when the **Ironman 70.3 St. George** (www.ironman.com) is held.

RECREATION
Golf

With over a dozen golf courses in the area, St. George enjoys a reputation as Utah's winter golf capital. Greens fees are highest in winter (the rates noted here) and drop by nearly 50 percent during the hot summer months. Red sandstone cliffs serve as the backdrop for **Dixie Red Hills** (1250 N. 645 W., 435/634-5852, www.stgeorgecitygolf.com, $20.50), the city's first golf course, built in the 1960s on the northwest edge of town; it's a nine-hole

par-34 municipal course. **Green Spring Golf Course** (588 N. Green Spring Dr., 435/673-7888, www.greenspringgolfcourse.com, $59), just west of I-15 exit 10 in the town of Washington, has 18 holes (par 71) and a reputation as one of the finest courses in Utah.

Professionals favor the cleverly designed **Sunbrook Golf Course** (2366 Sunbrook Dr., 435/634-5866, www.stgeorgecitygolf.com, $56) off Dixie Downs Road, between Green Valley and Santa Clara; it has 27 holes and is a par 72. The **St. George Golf Club** (2190 S. 1400 E., 435/634-5854, www.stgeorgecitygolf.com, $33) has a popular 18-hole, par-73 course south of town in Bloomington Hills. The **Southgate Golf Course** (1975 S. Tonaquint Dr., 435/627-4440, www.stgeorgecitygolf.com, $33), on the southwest edge of town, also has 18 holes. The adjacent Southgate Game Improvement Center (435/674-7728) can provide golfers with computerized golf-swing analyses plus plenty of indoor practice space and lots of balls.

Entrada (2511 W. Entrada Tr., 435/986-2200, www.golfentrada.com) is a newer 18-hole private course that's fast on its way to becoming St. George's most respected. The Johnny Miller-designed course is northwest of St. George at beautiful Snow Canyon and incorporates natural lava flows, rolling dunes, and arroyos (dry riverbeds) into its design. Guests at the Inn at Entrada can get a package deal to golf here (in peak winter season from around $255, including lodging for 2 and golf for 1). The 18-hole, par-72 **Sky Mountain** (1030 N. 2600 W., 435/635-7888, $66), northeast of St. George in nearby Hurricane, has a spectacular setting.

Mountain Biking

Mountain bikers in the know come to St. George for winter, early spring, and fall riding on single-track trails and slickrock that's just as good as what you'll find in Moab. One of Utah's most spectacular trails is **Gooseberry Mesa,** southeast of Hurricane—a challenging but fun ride with both slickrock and single-track. The **Green Valley Loop** starts at the

Green Valley Spa (1871 W. Canyon View Dr.) and is mostly advanced single-track.

Less intense biking can be found at **Snow Canyon State Park** (1002 Snow Canyon Dr., 435/628-2255, http://stateparks.utah.gov), where the paved 6-mile (9.7-km) Whiptail Trail and the 8-mile (12.9-km) gravel-and-sand West Canyon Road are open to bikes.

Parks

The outdoor public **swimming pool** (250 E. 700 S., 435/634-5867, Memorial Day-Labor Day) features a hydro slide. **Vernon Worthen Park** (400 E. 200 S.) offers shaded picnic tables, a playground, and tennis courts. **J. C. Snow Park** (400 E. 900 S.) has picnic tables, a playground, and a dog park, but little shade. **Pioneer Park** overlooks the city from the north. Set in desert country just off Skyline Drive, it's a less-developed park, with hiking trails and rock climbing.

Spa Resorts

St. George is home to two large spa resorts in gorgeous natural settings. The **Amira Resort and Spa** (1999 W. Canyon View Dr., 435/628-1370, https://amiraresort.com/, $229-279 room only, two-night spa packages with lodging from $645 pp) is a fitness, health, and beauty spa. Facilities include two pools, a fully equipped 1,500-square-foot gym with an array of fitness, wellness, and meditation classes as well as hiking and climbing in neighboring canyons. There's also a whole catalog of beauty and rejuvenation treatments, which may be included in a package deal or tacked on at extra cost, including massage, wraps, and aromatherapy as well as more spiritual renewals that include Native American healing methods. Guest rooms have their own fireplaces and private patios, and flank a park-like pool and garden area; in addition to hotel-style rooms are large one- and two-bedroom suites. Rates vary, with summer the least expensive time to visit.

Slightly less swanky, with more of an outdoorsy atmosphere, the ★ **Red Mountain Resort** (1275 E. Red Mountain Circle,

877/246-4453, http://redmountainresort.com, $205-285 room only) focuses more on outdoor adventure and fitness. It's located near Snow Canyon, and morning hikes in the beautiful state park are a great part of the routine. Facilities include numerous swimming and soaking pools, a fitness center and gym, a salon, a spa, and conference rooms, plus access to lots of hiking and biking trails. Packages, which include all meals, lodging, and use of most spa facilities and recreation, start at about $305 pp, with special deals often available online. Spa services, including massage, facials, body polishing, and aromatherapy, cost extra. In addition to hotel-style rooms, the resort offers a variety of suites, including some with two bedrooms and full kitchens.

FOOD

For a major recreation and retirement center, St. George is curiously lacking in unique places to eat. Almost every chain restaurant can be found here but don't expect a bevy of local fine-dining houses.

The best place to head for lunch or dinner is the old downtown area, known as Ancestor Square, at the intersection of St. George Boulevard and Main Street, where you'll find several blocks of locally owned restaurants and art galleries. The ★ **Painted Pony** (435/634-1700, www.painted-pony.com, 11:30am-10pm Mon.-Sat., 4pm-9pm Sun., $25-36) is a stylish restaurant where the kitchen puts Southwestern and, in some cases, Asian touches on American standards; try ratatouille raviolis with sweet corn sauce and smoked pepper coulis. Downstairs from the Painted Pony is another pretty good restaurant, **Benja Thai and Sushi** (435/628-9538, www.benjathai.com, 11:30am-10pm Mon.-Sat., $12-20), one of the very few Thai restaurants in southern Utah.

Also in the Ancestor Square complex, at the corner of St. George Boulevard and Main Street, is an actual pub, **George's Corner** (2 W. St. George Blvd., 435/216-7311, www.georgescorner.com, 7am-midnight daily,

$8-18). It's a little shocking to look in a window in the heart of downtown and see people gathered at a bar, but for many visitors, it's also a small joy. In addition to the bar area, George's Corner also has a family-friendly restaurant section featuring typical pub fare; breakfast is also served.

Just across St. George Boulevard from Ancestor Square, **Bear Paw Cafe** (75 N. Main St., 435/634-0126, 7am-3pm daily, $5-10) is a bright spot for coffee drinkers and anyone who wants a good breakfast; Belgian waffles are the house specialty. Next door, the deservedly popular **Rigatti's Wood Fired Pizza** (73 N. Main St., 435/674-9922, http://rigattis. com, 11am-8pm Mon.-Thurs., 11am-9pm Fri.-Sat., medium pizza $8-14) serves pizza and salad pizza (a little unusual, but pizza toppings are on top of lettuce rather than a pizza crust). Although the staff is friendly, the dining atmosphere is pretty basic; take your pizza to go.

Find excellent tacos at **Angelica's Mexican Grill** (101 E, St. George Blvd., 435/628-4399, www.irmitas.com, 11am-8pm Mon.-Thurs., 11am-9pm Fri.-Sat., about $6), an authentic Mexican restaurant near downtown. Also worth the drive is the **Cliffside Restaurant** (511 S. Airport Rd., 435/319-6005, www.cliffsiderestaurant.com, 11am-9pm Mon.-Thurs., 11am-10pm Fri.-Sat., $15-27), where the astounding views are nearly matched by the very good food (steaks, ribs, pizza and fresh fish).

ACCOMMODATIONS

St. George offers many places to stay and eat. Motel prices stay about the same year-round, although they may drop if business is slow in summer. Considering the popularity of this destination, prices are reasonable. Golfers should ask about golf-and-lodging packages. You'll find most lodgings along the busy I-15 business route of St. George Boulevard (exit 8) and Bluff Street (exit 6).

Under $100

Many of St. George's less expensive lodging choices are chains operating at exit 8 off I-15.

Near downtown, there are some decent, locally owned choices. The **Chalet Motel** (664 E. St. George Blvd., 435/628-6272, www.chaletmotelstgeorge.com, $74-85) offers fridges and microwaves, some efficiency kitchens in larger guest rooms, and a pool. ★ **Dixie Palms Motel** (185 E. St. George Blvd., 435/673-3531, www.dixiepalmsmotel. com, $56-67) is a classic old-fashioned courtyard motel on the main strip right downtown, with fridges and microwaves in the guest rooms. It's a top pick for budget travelers who won't be bothered by older furnishings (beds are fine) and small bathrooms. The Spanish-style **Best Western Travel Inn** (316 E. St. George Blvd., 435/673-4407 or 888/590-2835, www.stgeorgebestwestern.com, $81-96) is a relatively small motel with an outdoor pool, an indoor hot tub, and a pretty good free breakfast.

Over $100

Near the interstate's exit 4, the pet-friendly **La Quinta** (91 E. 2680 S., 435/674-2664 or 888/788-2457, www.laqstgeorge.com, $109-139) is a comfortable place to crash on the southern edge of town.

Just across from Brigham Young's winter home and a couple of blocks from Ancestor Square (and the city's best dining), the ★ **Seven Wives Inn Bed & Breakfast** (217 N. 100 W., 435/628-3737 or 800/600-3737, www.sevenwivesinn.com, $115-210) offers guest rooms in two historic homes, including one that served as a safe house for polygamists after the practice was banned in the 1880s, and a cute cottage. All guest rooms have private baths and are decorated with antiques. Children are welcome, and pets are permitted in the cottage. There's an outdoor pool, and in-room massages can be arranged.

Inn on the Cliff (511 S. Airport Rd., 435/216-5864, www.innonthecliff.com, $139-159) indeed perches over the city, with a good restaurant, great views and boutique-style amenities, including a pool, fitness center, and free breakfast box delivered to the room.

Note that weekend prices can be as much as $200 higher.

A particularly nice standard motel for golfers is the **Crystal Inn** (1450 S. Hilton Inn Dr., 435/688-7477 or 800/662-2525, www. crystalinns.com, $119-269). It's located on a golf course and has beautiful public areas and nicely appointed guest rooms. Facilities include a pool, a sauna, and private tennis courts.

Close to downtown is one of St. George's best: the **Best Western Coral Hills** (125 E. St. George Blvd., 435/673-4844 or 800/542-7733, www.coralhills.com, $165-219), a very attractive property with indoor and outdoor pools and two spas, an exercise room, and a complimentary continental breakfast. During the summer, prices drop by as much as $100!

Look for more motels at I-15's exit 6. Here you'll find St. George's third (and fanciest) Best Western, the **Best Western Plus Abbey Inn** (1129 S. Bluff St., 435/652-1234 or 888/222-3946, www.bwabbeyinn.com, $189-240); all guest rooms have microwaves and fridges. There's a small outdoor pool, an indoor spa, recreation and fitness facilities, and a hot breakfast included.

Golfers and those who want a bit of poshness should seriously consider the **Inn at Entrada** (2588 W. Sinagua Tr., 435/634-7100, www.innatentrada.com, $159-379), located near Snow Canyon State Park. A stay at the inn is the easiest way to gain access to the resort community's top-notch golf course. It's a lovely setting, lodging is in casitas, and there's a spa and restaurant on-site.

Campgrounds

The best camping in the area is at **Snow Canyon State Park** (435/628-2255 or 800/322-3770, www.stateparks.utah.gov, reservations at www.reserveamerica.com, necessary in spring, $9 reservation fee, $20 without hookups, $25 with hookups). Sites are in a pretty canyon and include showers; although RV sites are crammed together, tent sites are quite nice. From downtown St. George, go 12

miles north on Highway 18, then turn left and continue 2 miles (3.2 km).

The other public campgrounds in the area are **Quail Creek State Park** (435/879-2378, www.stateparks.utah.gov, reservations at www.reserveamerica.com, $15) and the BLM's **Red Cliffs Recreation Site** (435/688-3200, $15), both north of town off I-15 (take exit 16 when coming from the south for Quail Creek, exit 22 for Red Cliffs; for either place, take exit 23 when approaching from the north). Quail Creek is on a reservoir with little shade but is a good option if you have a boat. Red Cliffs is more scenic and has hiking trails, including one (Silver Reef) that leads to dinosaur tracks.

If you need a place to park an RV for the night right in town, **McArthur's Temple View RV Resort** (975 S. Main St., 435/673-6400 or 800/776-6410, www.templeviewrv. com, tents and RVs $42) is near the temple district but has little shade.

INFORMATION AND SERVICES

The **St. George Tourism Office** (20 N. Main St., Suite 105., 435/634-5747, www. visitstgeorge.com, 9am-5pm Mon.-Sat., can tell you about the sights, events, and services of southwestern Utah. Additional online sources of information are www.utahsdixie. com and www.utahstgeorge.com.

For information on fishing, hiking, and camping in the national forest, visit the **Dixie National Forest** office (196 E., Tabernacle St., 435/652-3100, www.fs.usda.gov/main/dixie, 8am-5pm Mon.-Fri.).

St. George has a **post office** (180 N. Main St., 435/673-3312), and the **Dixie Regional Medical Center** (544 S. 400 E., 435/688-4000) provides hospital care.

GETTING THERE

St. George's airport (SGU), located 5 miles (8 km) southeast of downtown, opened in early 2011. **Delta** (800/323-2323, www.delta.com), in partnership with **Skywest Airlines** (www. skywest.com), **American** (800/433-7300) and **United** (800/864-8331, www.ual.com) offer

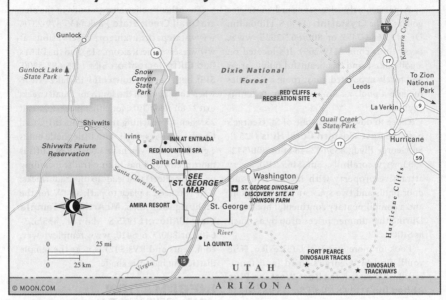

Vicinity of St. George

Gunlock

Gunlock Lake
State Park

Snow
Canyon
State
Park

Dixie National
Forest

RED CLIFFS
RECREATION SITE

Leeds

To Zion
National
Park

La Verkin

Shivwits

Ivins

INN AT ENTRADA

RED MOUNTAIN SPA

Santa Clara

Shivwits Paiute
Reservation

Santa Clara River

SEE
"ST. GEORGE"
MAP

Washington

ST. GEORGE DINOSAUR
DISCOVERY SITE AT
JOHNSON FARM

AMIRA RESORT

St. George

Quail Creek
State Park

Hurricane

Hurricane Cliffs

River

LA QUINTA

0   25 mi

0   25 km

Virgin

FORT PEARCE
DINOSAUR TRACKS

DINOSAUR
TRACKWAYS

UTAH

ARIZONA

© MOON.COM

several daily direct flights to and from Salt Lake City, Denver, Phoenix, and Los Angeles.

Several of the usual rental car companies operate from the St. George airport: **Budget** (435/673-6825), **Avis** (435/627-2002), and **Hertz** (435/652-9941).

It's an easy drive from Las Vegas to St. George (less than two hours), so travelers may want to consider flying into Vegas and renting a car there.

Greyhound (435/673-2933) buses depart from McDonald's (1235 S. Bluff St.) for Salt Lake City, Denver, Las Vegas, and other destinations. The **St. George Shuttle** (790 S. Bluff St., 435/628-8320 or 800/933-8320, www.stgshuttle.com) will take you to Las Vegas ($39) or the Salt Lake City airport ($60) in a 15-passenger van.

VICINITY OF ST. GEORGE

Some good scenic drives begin at St. George. Whether you're short on time or have all day, a good choice is the 24-mile (39-km) loop

through Snow Canyon State Park via Highway 18, the park road (Hwy. 300), and Santa Clara. In summer, the cool forests of the Pine Valley Mountains, 37 miles (60 km) northwest of town, are an especially attractive destination: You can make a 130-mile (209-km) drive with many possible side trips by circling the mountains on Highway 18, Highway 56, and I-15. Zion National Park, with its grandeur and color, is about 40 miles (64 km) northeast of St. George.

★ Snow Canyon State Park

North of St. George, **Snow Canyon State Park** (1002 N. Snow Canyon Rd., 435/628-2255, camping reservations 800/322-3770 or www.reserveamerica.com, day-use $6 per vehicle, camping $20-25) is a great place to explore and enjoy the desert scenery. Red-rock canyons, sand dunes, volcanoes, and lava flows have formed an incredible landscape. Walls of Navajo sandstone 50-750 feet high enclose 5-mile-long (8-km-long) Snow Canyon. Hiking trails lead into the backcountry for a closer look at the geology, flora, and fauna. Common plants are barrel, cholla, and prickly pear cacti, yucca, Mormon tea, shrub live oak, cliffrose, and cottonwood. Delicate wildflowers bloom mostly in the spring and autumn, following the wet seasons, but cacti and the sacred datura can flower in the heat of summer. Wildlife includes sidewinder and Great Basin rattlesnakes, Gila monsters, desert tortoises, kangaroo rats, squirrels, cottontails, kit foxes, coyotes, and mule deer. You may find some Native American rock art, arrowheads, bits of pottery, and ruins. Many of the place names in the park honor Mormon pioneers. Snow Canyon was named for Lorenzo and Erastus Snow, not for the rare snowfalls. Cooler months have the best weather; summers are too hot for comfortable hiking except in the early morning.

Highway 18 leads past an overlook on the rim of Snow Canyon and to the paved park road (Hwy. 300) that drops into the canyon and follows it to its mouth and the small town of Ivins. Snow Canyon is about 12 miles (19.3 km) northwest of St. George. It's reached either by Highway 18—the faster way—or via Santa Clara and Ivins.

HIKING
The **Hidden Piñon Trail** (also signed as Nature Trail) begins across the road from the campground entrance, then weaves among sandstone hills and lava flows to the Varnish Mountain Overlook above Snow Canyon. At the overlook, desert varnish on sandstone has turned the rock jet-black. The easy trail is 1.5 miles (2.4 km) round-trip and has a small elevation gain; some sections cross rough rocks and deep sand. It's an easy scramble from the overlook area to the canyon floor below. **West Canyon Trail** is the longest in the park; it begins near the stables (0.7 mile/1.1 km south of the campground) and goes northwest along an old road up Snow Canyon to West Canyon (you can also take cross-country hikes into other canyons passed on the way). The trail is 7 miles (11.3 km) round-trip with a small elevation gain. **Lava Tubes Trail** winds across

a lava field to an area of lava caves (1 mile/1.6 km round-trip). The caves formed when molten lava broke out of the partly cooled flow and left rooms and tunnels behind. Artifacts indicate that Native Americans took shelter in the chambers. The trailhead is 1.5 miles (2.4 km) north of the campground. The steep and strenuous **Volcano Trail** ascends a cinder cone northeast of Snow Canyon. The 1,000-year-old volcano is on the east side of Highway 18, 1 mile (1.6 km) north of the turnoff for Snow Canyon. Near the park entrance, the 0.5-mile (0.8-km) **Jenny's Canyon Trail** leads to a short slot canyon; this trail is closed mid-March-May.

Tuacahn Amphitheater
Tuacahn (1100 Tuacahn Dr., 800/746-9882, www.tuacahn.org, shows most Mon.-Sat. mid-June-mid-Oct., $29-91) is an outdoor amphitheater that seats 1,900 among 1,500-foot-high red-rock cliffs northwest of St. George. Tuacahn offers a three-show summer musical theater season; recent performances have included *The Hunchback of Notre Dame* and *Matilda the Musical.*

Tuacahn is also the place to catch a big concert with, say, Willie Nelson or a second-generation Osmond. On Saturday mornings, vendors set up for a crafts and food market. Between Thanksgiving and Christmas, Tuacahn hosts a free Festival of Lights. The amphitheater is northwest of St. George near the south entrance to Snow Canyon State Park.

Veyo
Warm-water springs feed a swimming pool in this pretty spot. The family-friendly **Veyo Resort** (435/574-2300, www.veyopool.com, noon-8pm daily May-Sept., $8.50 adults, $6.50 ages 14 and under) has picnic tables and a snack bar.

The resort has also developed a private rock-climbing area called **Crawdad Canyon.** For $8.50 (plus $8.50 Canyon Access Fee), climbers can scale the 80-foot basalt cliffs, with more than 250 bolted sport climbing routes rated from 5.6 to 5.13. Climbers (and other visitors) can also camp here ($25-30/tent).

Take the Veyo Pool Resort Road from Highway 18 southeast of town. The little village of Veyo is along the Santa Clara River, 19 miles northwest of St. George.

Mountain Meadows Massacre Historic Site

A short trip from Highway 18 west of the Pine Valley Mountains leads to the site of one of the darkest chapters of Mormon history. The pleasant valley had been a popular rest stop for pioneers about to cross the hot desert country to the west. In 1857 a California-bound wagon train whose members had already experienced trouble with Mormons in the region was attacked by an alliance of Mormons and local Native Americans. About 120 people in the wagon train died in the massacre. Only some small children too young to tell the story were spared. The closely knit Mormon community tried to cover up the incident and hindered federal attempts to apprehend the killers. Only John D. Lee, who was in charge of Indian affairs in southern Utah at the time, was ever brought to justice. After nearly 20 years and two trials, authorities took him back to this spot to be executed by firing squad. Many details of the massacre remain unknown. The major causes seem to have been a Mormon fear of invasion, aggressive Mormons and Native Americans, and poor communication between the Mormon leadership in Salt Lake City and southern Utah. Two monuments now mark the site of the tragedy. Take Highway 18 north and turn west onto a paved road between mileposts 31 and 32.

PINE VALLEY MOUNTAINS

A massive body of magma uncovered by erosion makes up the Pine Valley Mountains, located north of St. George between Highway 18 (to the west) and I-15 (to the east). Signal Peak (elev. 10,365 feet) tops the range, much

of which has been designated the Pine Valley Mountain Wilderness Area.

In 1856, pioneers established the town of Pine Valley (elev. 6,800 feet) to harvest the extensive forests and raise livestock. Lumber from Pine Valley helped build many southern Utah settlements and even went into Salt Lake City's great tabernacle organ. The town's picturesque white chapel was built in 1868 by Ebenezer Bryce, who later homesteaded at what's now Bryce Canyon National Park. Right near the chapel, the **Pine Valley Heritage Center** (100 E. Main St., 435/574-2463, 10am-6pm Mon.-Sat. Memorial Day-Labor Day) is run by the U.S. Forest Service and dispenses visitor information and sells books and maps.

Pine Valley Recreation Area

Three miles (4.8 km) past the town of Pine Valley are picnic areas, several popular **campgrounds**, and trails in Dixie National Forest (435/865-3700, www.fs.usda.gov). At Pine Valley Reservoir (2.3 miles/3.7 km up E. Pine Valley Rd., on the right), you can fish for rainbow and some brook trout; fishing is fair in the Santa Clara River upstream and downstream from the reservoir. About 0.5 mile (0.8 km) past the reservoir are several large streamside picnic areas.

The 50,000-acre Pine Valley Mountain Wilderness has the best scenery of the Pine Valley Mountains, but it can be seen only on foot or horseback. A network of trails from all directions leads into the wilderness. The road from Pine Valley provides access to the **Whipple trailhead** and **Brown's Point trailhead** on the east side of the wilderness area. Trails are usually open from mid-June into October. Several loops are possible, although most are too long for day hikes. **Whipple National Recreation Trail** is one of the most popular for both day and overnight trips; it ascends 2,100 vertical feet in 6 miles (9.7 km) to 35-mile-long (56-km-long) **Summit Trail,** which connects with many other trails. **Brown's Point Trail** also climbs to Summit Trail, but in 4 miles

(6.4 km). Strong hikers can use the Brown's Point and Summit Trails to reach the top of Signal Peak on a day hike; the last part of the climb is a rock-scramble. Generally, the trails from Pine Valley are signed and easy to follow; trails in other areas may not be maintained.

Red Cliffs National Conservation Area

Weather-sculpted cliffs of reddish-orange sandstone rise above this pretty spot. At **Red Cliffs National Conservation Area** (435/688-3200, www.blm.gov/ut, day-use $2), the seasonal Quail Creek emerges from a canyon, flows through the middle of the campground, then goes on to Quail Creek Reservoir 2 miles (3.2 km) away. **Desert Trail** starts on the left near the beginning of the campground loop and follows the creek 0.5 mile (0.8 km) into the canyon. Idyllic pools and graceful rock formations line the way. You'll need to do some wading to continue upstream past trail's end. A shorter (0.25 mile/0.4 km round-trip) but more rugged trail begins near the end of the campground loop. It crosses slickrock to Silver Reef Lookout Point, which yields a good panorama of the area, although you can't actually see Silver Reef ghost town. Take I-15 exit 22 or 23 for Leeds, go south 3 miles (4.8 km) on the frontage road, then turn west and go 1.7 miles (2.7 km) on a paved road. Long trailers and low-clearance cars may drag on dips at stream crossings.

The **Red Cliffs Campground** (435/688-3200, www.blm.gov/ut, $15) and a picnic area, at an elevation of 3,240 feet, have water and are open year-round; camping is most pleasant in spring and fall.

Silver Reef Ghost Town

This is probably Utah's most accessible ghost town. In about 1870, prospectors found rich silver deposits in the sandstone here, much to the surprise of mining experts, who thought such a combination impossible. The town grew up several years later and boomed 1878-1882. The population peaked at 1,500 and included a sizable Chinese community. Then a combination of lower silver prices, declining yields, and water in the mines forced the operations to close one by one, the last in 1891. Other attempts at mining have been made from time to time, including some uranium production in the 1950s and 1960s, but the town had died.

The **Wells Fargo Building,** which houses the visitors center (435/879-2254, 10am-5pm Mon. and Thurs.-Sat., $3), is now Silver Reef's main attraction. Built of stone in 1877, it looks as solid as ever and houses a small museum. Encroaching modern houses detract a bit from the setting, but the ghosts are still here. Stone walls and foundations peek out of the sagebrush. A short walk on the road past the building takes you to the ruins and tailings of the mills that once shook the town with their racket. From Leeds, take I-15 exit 22 or 23 and follow signs 1.3 miles (2.1 km) on a paved road.

Cedar City

Cedar City (approximate pop. 29,000), known for its scenic setting and its summertime Utah Shakespeare Festival, is a handy base for exploring a good chunk of southern Utah. Just east of town rise the high cliffs of the Markagunt Plateau—a land of panoramic views, colorful rock formations, desolate lava flows, extensive forests, and flower-filled meadows. Also on the Markagunt Plateau is the Cedar Breaks National Monument, an immense amphitheater eroded into the vividly hued underlying rock.

Within an easy day's drive are Zion National Park to the south and Bryce Canyon National Park and Grand Staircase-Escalante National Monument to the east. Cedar City is

Cedar City

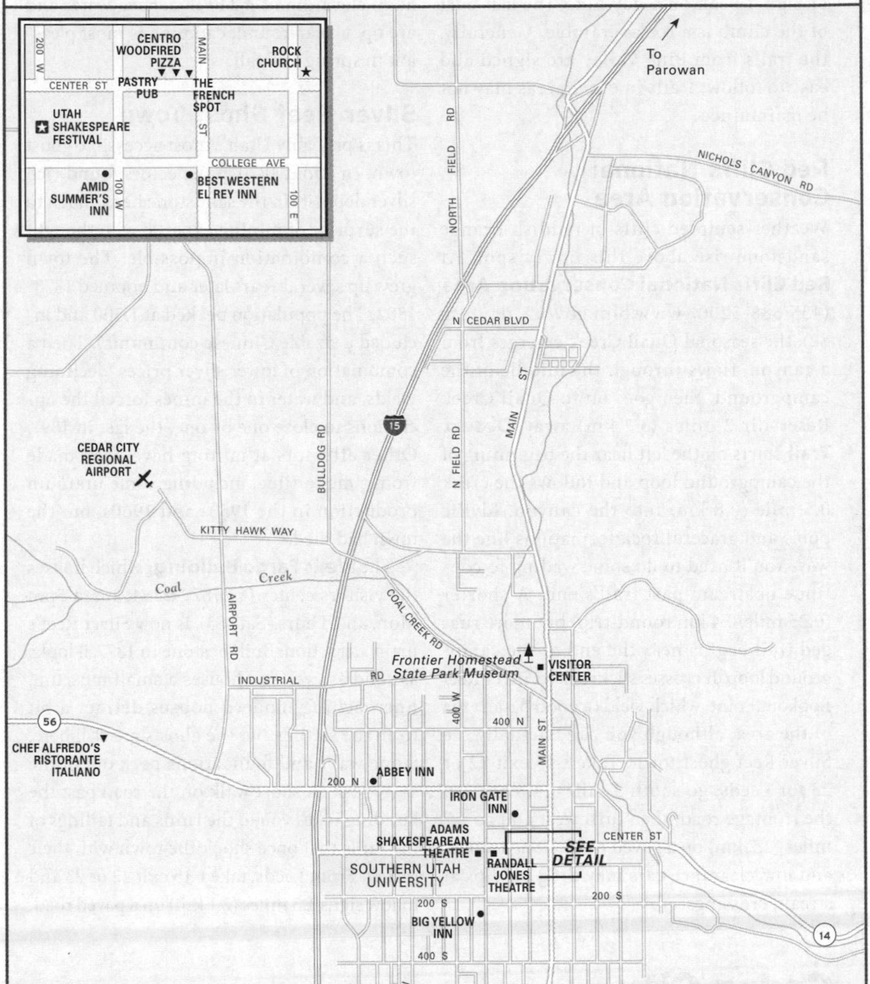
CENTRO WOODFIRED PIZZA
ROCK CHURCH
200 W
MAIN ST
CENTER ST
PASTRY PUB
THE FRENCH SPOT
UTAH SHAKESPEARE FESTIVAL
COLLEGE AVE
AMID SUMMER'S INN
100 W
BEST WESTERN EL REY INN
100 E
To Parowan
NORTH FIELD RD
NICHOLS CANYON RD
N CEDAR BLVD
MAIN ST
15
N FIELD RD
BULLDOG RD
CEDAR CITY REGIONAL AIRPORT
KITTY HAWK WAY
Coal Creek
COAL CREEK RD
AIRPORT RD
Frontier Homestead State Park Museum
VISITOR CENTER
INDUSTRIAL RD
56
CHEF ALFREDO'S RISTORANTE ITALIANO
400 W
400 N
MAIN ST
200 N
ABBEY INN
IRON GATE INN
ADAMS SHAKESPEAREAN THEATRE
SEE DETAIL
CENTER ST
SOUTHERN UTAH UNIVERSITY
RANDALL JONES THEATRE
200 S
200 S
BIG YELLOW INN
14
400 S
1100 W
800 W
300 W
600 S
300 E
800 S
MAIN ST
CROSS HOLLOW RD
0
0.5 mi
0.5 km
15
GREEN'S LAKE DR
© MOON.COM

just east of I-15, 52 miles (84 km) northeast of St. George and 253 miles (407 km) southwest of Salt Lake City; take I-15 exits 57, 59, or 62.

SIGHTS

Frontier Homestead State Park Museum

The in-town **Frontier Homestead State Park Museum** (635 N. Main St., 435/586-9290, https://frontierhomestead.org, 9am-6pm daily June-Aug., 9am-5pm Mon.-Sat., Sept.-May, $4) focuses on history rather than recreation. Cedar City was a center for iron mining and processing starting in 1850, when Brigham Young, hoping to increase Utah's self-sufficiency, sent workers to develop an "Iron Mission." The ironworks eventually became a private company, and although it never really prospered financially, the area has become Iron County. Here, indoor and outdoor exhibits focus on the iron foundry and other aspects of local history.

Rock Church

Depression-era residents needed a new Mormon Church building but lacked the money to build one. Undaunted, they set to work using local materials and came up with this beautiful structure, the **Rock Church** (75 E. Center St., 435/586-6759), composed of many different types of rocks. Skilled craftspeople made the metal lamps, carpets, western red cedar pews, and most other furnishings.

ENTERTAINMENT AND EVENTS

Although the Shakespeare Festival is better known, Cedar City's annual **Neil Simon Festival** (105 N. 100 E., 435/327-8673, www.simonfest.org, $25) is also quite popular. It runs mid-June-mid-August.

Utah athletes compete in the **Utah Summer Games** (435/865-8421, larryhmillerutahsummergames.org) through much of June; events, patterned after the Olympic games, begin with a torch relay and include track and field, 10K and marathon runs,

cycling, boxing, wrestling, basketball, tennis, soccer, karate, and swimming.

Everyone dresses up in period clothing in mid-July for the **Utah Midsummer Renaissance Faire** (www.umrf.net), with 16th-century entertainment, crafts, and food.

★ Utah Shakespeare Festival

Cedar City's lively **Shakespeare Festival** (435/586-7880, box office 435/586-7878 or 800/752-9849, www.bard.org) presents Shakespearean plays, contemporary theatre and musicals each summer season in the **Beverley Taylor Sorenson Center for the Arts** on the campus of Southern Utah University. This new theater complex opened in 2016 and boasts three performance areas, including the Engelstad Shakespeare Theatre, an open-air space reminiscent of Elizabethan theatres but with modern amenities and technology. The indoor Randall Jones Theatre presents the "Best of the Rest"—often recent Broadway hits, while the "black box" Eileen and Allen Anes Studio Theatre offers more experimental performances and seats only 200. A total of eight or nine plays are staged each season (late June-mid-Oct.).

Costumed actors stage the popular free Greenshow each evening (7pm Mon.-Sat. late June-Aug.) before the performances, with a variety of Elizabethan comedy skits, Punch-and-Judy shows, period dances, music, juggling, and other good-natured 16th-century fun. Backstage tours ($8) of the costume shop, makeup room, and stage show you how the festival works. At literary seminars each morning, actors and Shakespearean scholars discuss the previous night's play. Production seminars, held daily except Sunday, take a close look at acting, costumes, stage props, special effects, and other details of play production.

The Greenshow and seminars are free, but most plays are $36-75, and it's wise to purchase tickets well in advance; however, last-minute theatergoers can usually find tickets to something. The theaters are on the Southern Utah University campus near the corner of

Center Street and 300 West. Rain occasionally dampens the performances (the Elizabethan theater is open to the sky), and plays may move to a conventional theater next door, where the box office is located.

RECREATION

The main **City Park** (Main St. and 200 North) has picnic tables, a playground, and horseshoe courts. The **Municipal Swimming Pools** (401 W. Harding Ave., 435/586-2869) have indoor and outdoor areas and a hydrotube. From West Canyon Park (on 400 East, halfway between Center St. and 200 South), the paved **Coal Creek Walking and Biking Trail** leads 4 miles (6.4 km) up the desert canyon.

FOOD

Cedar City has a few good casual restaurants, though on a Sunday you may find yourself eating at the Subway. The brightest spot is ★ **Centro Woodfired Pizzeria** (50 W. Center St., 435/867-8123, 11am-10pm Mon.-Sat., $8-15), a stylish place with very good pizza (cooked to a char unless you specify otherwise), large salads, and a decent selection of beer and wine. It's a busy spot in the evening, especially when the Shakespeare Festival is in session, so plan accordingly.

Grind Coffeehouse (19 N. Main St., 435/867-3333, 7am-7pm Mon.-Sat., $5-8) has the best coffee in town and a good selection of sandwiches. The cavernous space isn't especially inviting in itself, but it does have the feeling of a community gathering place.

Nearby, **The French Spot** (5 N. Main St., 435/866-8587, www.thefrenchspotcafe.com, 10am-7pm Tues.-Thurs., 10am-9pm Fri.-Sat., 10am-2pm Sun., $7-25) is a sweet café run by a French pastry chef and his family. Stop in for an omelet, crepes, or a croissant; at dinner you can even get a steak.

At the **Pastry Pub** (86 W. Center St., 435/867-1400, www.cedarcitypastrypub.com, 7am-10pm Mon.-Sat., $6-9) you'll find pastries, good sandwiches, and coffee; although the atmosphere here is a bit fusty, it's a good place for lunch or a quick bite to eat before a play.

Chef Alfredo Ristorante Italiano (2313 W. 400 N., 435/586-2693, www.chefalfredos. com, 11am-2pm and 4pm-9pm Mon.-Fri., 4pm-9pm Sat.-Sun., $14-28) has a wide-ranging and well-executed Italian menu and an elegance that belies its location in a strip mall a ways from downtown. Come prepared for generous servings.

The Utah Shakespeare Festival takes place at an open-air theater-in-the-round.

ACCOMMODATIONS

During the Shakespeare Festival, Cedar City is a popular destination, so it's best to reserve a room at least a day or two in advance during the summer. There are two major concentrations of motels. Half a dozen large chain hotels cluster around the I-15 exits, together with lots of fast-food restaurants and strip malls. Downtown, along Main Street, are even more motels. You can easily walk from most of the downtown motels to the Shakespeare Festival. Many of Cedar City's B&Bs are also within a stroll of the festival grounds.

Note that the following prices are for the high summer festival season. Outside high season, expect rates to drop by about one-third.

Right downtown, the **El Rey Inn** (80 S. Main St., 435/586-6518 or 800/528-1234, http://www.elreyinncedarcity.com/, $116-140) is convenient and friendly, but hardly luxurious.

One of the best places to stay in Cedar City is the **Abbey Inn** (940 W. 200 N., 435/586-9966 or 800/325-5411, www.abbeyinncedar.com, $125-155), which has remodeled guest rooms, an indoor pool, and a good breakfast included.

Bed-and-breakfast inns and Shakespeare seem to go hand in hand. Near the festival, at the edge of the Southern Utah University campus, the ★ **Big Yellow Inn** (234 S. 300 W., 435/586-0960, www.bigyellowinn.com, $109-199) is easy to spot; it's yellow, full of antiques, and several of the guest rooms are in a house directly across the street from the main inn. The antiques-filled **Amid Summer's Inn** (140 S. 100 W., 435/589-2600, www.amidsummersinn.com, $109-189) has eight sumptuously decorated guest rooms in a restored 1930s cottage.

Enjoy some made-on-site wine at the **Iron Gate Inn** (100 N. 200 W., 435/867-0603, www.theirongateinn.com, $129-149), built in 1897, nicely remodeled in the early 2000s, and now home to one of Utah's very few wineries. Next door, a two-bedroom "carriage house" with a full kitchen goes for about $275.

Campgrounds

East of Cedar City on Highway 14 are a handful of campgrounds in the Dixie National Forest. The closest, **Cedar Canyon** (elev. 8,100 feet, 435/865-3200, www.fs.usda.gov/main/Dixie, Memorial Day-Labor Day, $17), is 12 miles (19.3 km) from town in a pretty canyon along Cow Creek.

Cedar City KOA (1121 N. Main St., 435/586-9872 or 800/562-9873, year-round, tents $30, RVs $55) has cabins ($57-68), showers, a playground, and a pool.

INFORMATION AND SERVICES

The **Cedar City Brian Head Tourism Bureau** (581 N. Main St., 435/586-5124 or 800/354-4849, www.visitcedarcity.com) is just south of Frontier Homestead State Park. The Dixie National Forest's **Cedar City Ranger District Office** (1789 N. Wedgewood Lane, 435/865-3700) has information on recreation and travel on the Markagunt Plateau. The **BLM's Cedar City District Office** (176 E. D. L. Sargent Dr., 435/865-3000) is just off Main Street on the north edge of town.

Valley View Medical Center (1303 N. Main St., 435/868-5000) provides hospital care. The **post office** is at 333 North Main Street.

GETTING THERE

Cedar City is just east of I-15, 52 miles northeast of St. George and 253 miles southwest of Salt Lake City; take I-15's exits 57, 59, or 62. **Delta** (800/221-1212, www.delta.com) has flights operated by SkyWest between the small **Cedar City Regional Airport** (CDC, 2560 Aviation Way, 435/867-9408) and Salt Lake City. Rent a car from **Avis** (435/867-9898) at the airport.

PAROWAN

Although just a small town, Parowan (pop. 2,829) is southern Utah's oldest community and the seat of Iron County. Highway 143 turns south from downtown to the Brian Head Ski Area, Cedar Breaks National Monument, and other scenic areas on the Markagunt Plateau. To the west is Utah's desert country. Accommodations in town offer a less expensive alternative to those in Brian Head. The **Iron County Fair** (www.ironcountyfair.net) presents a parade, rodeos, horse races, exhibits, and entertainment during the Labor Day holiday.

Stop by the **Parowan visitors center** (5 S. Main St., 435/477-8190, 10am-5pm Mon.-Sat.). Parowan is 18 miles (29 km) northeast of Cedar City and 14 miles (22.5 km) north of Brian Head; take I-15 exits 75 or 78.

Parowan Gap Petroglyphs

Native Americans have pecked many designs into the rocks at this pass 10.5 miles (16.9 km) northwest of Parowan. This impressive V-shaped notch in the rocky Red Hills is a landmark even today, and it clearly would have served as a route (and potential ambush site) for Native Americans and wildlife as they passed through this landscape. Perhaps the gap was an important site for hunting rituals. The rock art's meaning hasn't been deciphered, but it probably represents the thoughts of many different groups over the past 1,000 or more years. Geometric designs, snakes, lizards, mountain sheep, bear claws, and human figures are all still recognizable.

Parowan Gap may also have played a role in the early Native American calendar. On the summer solstice in late June, the year's longest day, the sun seems to set perfectly in the middle of the notch (if you're visiting in late June, join the small group of people who gather here to observe sunset). Researchers have discovered remains of rock cairns in the valley that align with the solstice sunset, leading them to postulate that Native Americans used the gap and the setting sun as part of their calendar system.

You can get here on a good gravel road from Parowan. Drive into town on Main Street, and turn west onto 400 North for 10.5 miles (16.9 km). Or, from Cedar City, go north on Main Street (or take I-15 exit 62), follow signs for Highway 130 north 13.5 miles (21.7,

and then turn right and go 2.5 miles (4 km) on a good gravel road (near milepost 19). You'll find an interpretive brochure and map at the BLM offices in Cedar City.

Food and Accommodations

There are not a lot of lodging options in Parowan. The **Mountain View Lodge** (625 W. 200 S., 435/263-0058, www.mountainviewlodge-parowan.com, $86-103) is surprisingly nice, with classy decor, including handmade wood furniture in the rooms, an indoor pool, and an on-site Chinese restaurant. To eat with the locals, head downtown to the homey **Parowan Cafe** (33 N. Main St., 435/477-3593, 7am-9pm daily, $6-17).

Tent campers should head a few miles out of town to the Markagunt Plateau.

THE MARKAGUNT PLATEAU

Markagunt is a Native American name for "highland of trees." The large, high plateau—much of the land is between 9,000 and 11,000 feet in elevation—consists mostly of gently rolling country, forests, and lakes. Black tongues of barren lava extend across some parts of the landscape. Cliffs at Cedar Breaks National Monument are the best-known feature of the plateau, but the land also drops away in the colorful pink cliffs farther southeast.

Two scenic byways cross this highly scenic area. The Markagunt Scenic Byway (Hwy. 14) climbs up a very dramatic cliff-lined canyon from Cedar City, reaching vista points over Zion National Park before dropping to Long Valley Junction on U.S. 89. The Brian Head-Panguitch Lake Scenic Byway, aka the Patchwork Parkway (Hwy. 143) departs from Parowan, climbing steeply up to lofty Brian Head with its ski and recreation area, past Panguitch Lake, and down to Panguitch in the Sevier Valley.

Popular activities on the Markagunt include fishing, hiking, mountain biking, downhill and cross-country skiing, and snowmobiling. Contact the **Cedar City Ranger**

The Markagunt Plateau

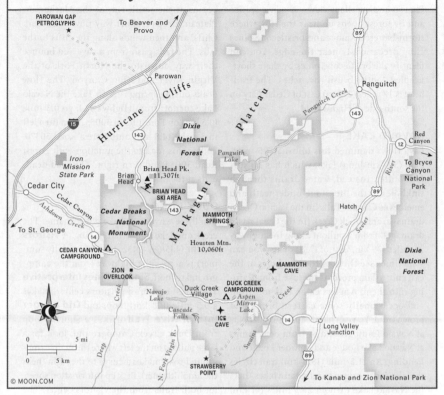

PAROWAN GAP
PETROGLYPHS ★

To Beaver and
Provo

89

Parowan

Cliffs

Panguitch

Panguitch Creek

143

15

Hurricane

143

Dixie
National
Forest

Plateau

Red
Canyon

12

Panguith
Lake

To Bryce
Canyon
National
Park

Iron
Mission
State Park

Brian Head Pk.
11,307ft

Brian
Head

BRIAN HEAD
SKI AREA

Cedar City

River

89

Hatch

Cedar Canyon

Ashdown Creek

Cedar Breaks
National
Monument

143

Markagunt

MAMMOTH
SPRINGS ★

Sevier River

To St. George

14

Housten Mtn.
10,060ft

CEDAR CANYON
CAMPGROUND

ZION
OVERLOOK ■

MAMMOTH
CAVE ✦

Dixie
National
Forest

Creek

Navajo
Lake

Duck Creek
Village

DUCK CREEK
CAMPGROUND
Aspen
Mirror
Lake

Creek

Cascade
Falls

ICE
CAVE ✦

14

Long Valley
Junction

0   5 mi

0   5 km

N. Fork Virgin R.

Deep

Swains

89

© MOON.COM

STRAWBERRY
POINT ✦

To Kanab and Zion National Park

District (1789 N. Wedgewood Lane, Cedar City, 435/865-3200) of the Dixie National Forest for information. In summer, volunteers or foresters staff the **visitors center** (435/682-2432) on Highway 14 opposite the Duck Creek Campground turnoff.

Markagunt Scenic Byway

Starting at Cedar City's eastern boundary, Markagunt Scenic Byway (Hwy. 14) plunges into a narrow canyon flanked by steep rock walls before climbing up to the top of the Markagunt Plateau. This is a very scenic route, passing dramatic rock cliffs and pink rock hoodoos that echo the formations at Zion and Bryce Canyon National Parks, but it's also a slow drive, especially if you get caught behind

a lumbering RV. The route also passes a number of wooded campgrounds and small mountain resorts, which are especially popular with snowmobilers and ATV riders (although cross-country skiing and mountain biking are tolerated). Because of their elevations (mostly 8,000-9,000 feet), these high mountain getaways are popular when the temperatures in the desert basin towns begin to bake. The route ends at U.S 89, the Long Valley Junction, 41 miles (66 km) from Cedar City.

At the **Zion Overlook,** a sweeping panorama takes in the deep canyons and monuments of Zion National Park to the south. Zion Overlook is 16.5 miles (26.6 km) east of Cedar City on the south side of the road.

The easy **Bristlecone Pine Trail**

(0.5-mile/0.8-km loop), graded for wheelchair access, leads to the rim of the Markagunt Plateau and excellent views. A dense spruce and fir forest opens up near the rim, where storm-battered limber and bristlecone pines cling precariously near the edge. You can identify the bristlecone pines by their short-needled "bottle brush" branches. The trailhead is 17 miles (27 km) east of Cedar City on the south side of Highway 14.

NAVAJO LAKE

Lava flows dammed this unusual 3.5-mile-long (5.6-km-long) lake, which has no surface outlet. Instead, water drains through sinkholes in the limestone underneath and emerges as Cascade Falls (in the Pacific Ocean drainage) and Duck Creek (in the Great Basin drainage). From a pullout along the highway 24 miles (39 km) east of Cedar City, you can sometimes see three of the sinkholes at the east end; a dam prevents the lake from draining into them. Anglers catch rainbow trout and occasionally some eastern brook and brown trout. You can hand-launch small boats at Navajo Campground or from boat ramps at Navajo Lake Lodge and Behmer Lodge and Landing. An 11.5-mile (18.5-km) trail circles the lake; it's also open to mountain bikes. Take the Navajo Lake turnoff, 25.5 miles (41 km) east of Cedar City, for the campgrounds, marina, and lodge along the south shore.

The **Virgin River Rim Trail** stretches about 38 miles (61 km) along the rim between Deer Haven Group Campground and Strawberry Point. Beautiful panoramas of Zion National Park and the headwaters of the Virgin River reward trail users. You can also reach it at Te-Ah Campground, from Navajo Lake via short spur trails (0.5-0.75 mile/0.8-1.2 km) and at the start of the Cascade Falls National Recreation Trail. The entire length is open to hikers and mountain bikers. Off-highway vehicles can use the section from Deer Haven to Te-Ah Campground.

Splendid views and a waterfall make the **Cascade Falls National Recreation Trail**

an exciting trip. The easy trail is 1.6 miles (2.6 km) round-trip with some ups and downs. It begins at the south rim of the Markagunt Plateau, drops a short way down the Pink Cliffs, and then winds along the cliffs to the falls. The falls gush from a cave and bounce their way down to the North Fork of the Virgin River and Zion Canyon. The flow peaks during spring runoff. Take the Navajo Lake turnoff from Highway 14, go 0.3 mile (0.5 km) on Forest Road 30053, then turn left in 3 miles (4.8 km) onto Forest Road 30370. Follow this road to the junction with Forest Road 30054 and turn right. The road dead-ends at the trailhead.

DUCK LAKE

You'll see why Duck Lake got its name. The creek and lake offer trout fishing. A **visitors center** (435/682-2432, 10am-5pm daily summer) is across the highway from the campground turnoff. **Singing Pines Interpretive Trail,** just east of the visitors center, makes a 0.5-mile (0.8-km) loop, and **Old Ranger Interpretive Trail** makes a shorter loop from Duck Creek Campground; look for a large pullout on the left where the main campground road makes a curve to the right (near the amphitheater). Pick up information sheets for both trails from the visitors center. The **Lost Hunter Trail** makes a 3-mile (4.8-km) loop from the same trailhead in Duck Creek Campground to the top of Duck Creek Bench; elevation gain is about 600 feet with many fine views. Turn north from Highway 14 at Duck Lake, about 28 miles (45 km) east of Cedar City.

Cool off inside the small **Ice Cave,** where the lava rock insulates ice throughout the summer. The road may be too rough for cars—ask about conditions at the visitors center. Turn south onto the dirt road beside the visitors center, keep left at the fork 0.2 mile (0.3 km) in, keep right at another fork 0.8 mile (1.3 km) farther, and continue 0.4 mile (0.6 km) to the cave at the end of the road; signs mark the way.

DUCK CREEK VILLAGE

Hollywood has used this area since the 1940s to film such productions as *How the West Was Won*, *My Friend Flicka*, and the *Daniel Boone* TV series. This handsome village—a collection of lodges, cabins, and log-built homes—is at the edge of a large meadow (elev. 8,400 feet) about 30 miles (48 km) east of Cedar City. The surrounding countryside is excellent for snowmobiling, a popular winter sport here. (Rentals are available at Pinewoods Resort, 435/682-2512.) Cross-country skiing is also good on meadow, forest, and bowl terrain. The snow season lasts about late November-late March.

Trout and scenic beauty attract visitors to pretty **Aspen Mirror Lake.** The turnoff (signed Movie Ranch Rd.) is on the north side of Highway 14, about midway between Duck Creek Campground and Duck Creek Village. Park and then walk the 0.25-mile (0.4-km) level trail.

STRAWBERRY POINT

A magnificent panorama takes in countless ridges, canyons, and mountains south of the Markagunt Plateau. You can spot Zion National Park and even the Arizona Strip from this lofty perch (elev. 9,016 feet). Erosion has cut delicate pinnacles and narrow canyons into the Pink Cliffs on either side below the viewpoint. Turn south from Highway 14 between mileposts 32 and 33 (32.5 miles/52 km east of Cedar City) onto a gravel road and go 9 miles (14.5 km) to its end. A 500-foot path continues to Strawberry Point. Take care near the edge—the rock is crumbly and there are no guardrails.

ACCOMMODATIONS

In Duck Creek Village, **Pinewoods Resort** (121 Duck Creek Ridge Rd., 435/682-2512, www.pinewoodsresort.com, lodge suites $195) offers accommodations ranging from motel rooms ($98-115), log lodges ($175) to a house that sleeps up to 15 ($345). The resort also has a coffee shop and a sit-down restaurant. **Duck Creek Village Inn** (Duck Creek Village,

435/682-2565, www.duckcreekvillageinn.com, May-Sept., $150-209) is a motel-B&B hybrid with pleasantly rustic rooms.

CAMPGROUNDS

All of the campgrounds in the area have water and a few sites for reservation (877/444-6777, www.recreation.gov, early June-Labor Day, $10 reservation fee, camping $17). Sites in the **Cedar Canyon Campground** (elev. 8,100 feet) are along Crow Creek among aspen, fir, and spruce in a pretty canyon setting, 12 miles (19.3 km) east of Cedar City on Highway 14. **Spruces** and **Navajo Campgrounds** are on Navajo Lake, where all of the spruce trees have been removed due to bark beetle infestations, leaving little shade. **Te-Ah Campground** is in an aspen grove 1.5 miles (2.4 km) west of Navajo Lake; expect cool nights at the 9,200-foot elevation.

Duck Creek Campground is north from Highway 14 at Duck Lake (elev. 8,600 feet).

Brian Head-Panguitch Lake Scenic Byway

Beginning in Parowan, Highway 143 very quickly climbs up to nearly 10,000 feet, ascending some of the steepest paved roads in Utah in the process (some of the grades here are 13 percent). The terrain changes from arid desert to pine forests to alpine aspen forests in just 14 miles (22.5 km).

At an elevation of 9,850 feet, Brian Head is the highest municipality in Utah, with a year-round population of about 100. Winter skiers like Brian Head for its abundant snow, challenging terrain, and good accommodations. Summer visitors come to enjoy the high country and to plunge down the slopes on mountain bikes. The beautiful colors of Cedar Breaks National Monument are just a few miles south. Panguitch Lake, to the east, receives high ratings for its excellent trout fishing.

BRIAN HEAD PEAK

You can drive all the way to Brian Head's 11,307-foot summit by car when the road is dry, usually July-October. Panoramas from the top take in much of southwestern Utah and beyond into Nevada and Arizona. Sheep graze the grassy slopes below. From Brian Head, follow Highway 143 about two miles south, then turn left (northeast) and go 3 miles (4.8 km) on a gravel road to the summit. The stone shelter here was built by the Civilian Conservation Corps in the 1930s.

BRIAN HEAD RESORT

Brian Head Resort (329 S. Hwy. 143, 435/677-2035, www.brianhead.com, weekend full-day $59 adults, $43 under age 13 and seniors, weekday $38 adults, $27 under age 13 and seniors, holiday $79 adults, $57 under age 13 and seniors) comes alive during the skiing season, late November-late April. While it's not Utah's most exciting ski area, it's a good place to bring a family, and lifts and a skier bridge make it easy to get between the two mountains of the main ski areas. Navajo Peak is good for beginners and families, and Giant Steps has more advanced runs. Lifts carry skiers up to elevations of 10,970 feet; the resort has 71 runs and 650 skiable acres, with a vertical drop of 1,320 feet from the lift and 1,707 feet from the top of Brian Head Peak. The resort also features three terrain parks as well as a tubing area.

Brian Head's second season is during the summer and fall, roughly June-September, when the area comes alive with mountain bikers taking advantage of great terrain and discounted accommodations. Brian Head Resort opens as a mountain bike park, complete with chairlift ($59 for a full-day bike lift pass) and trailhead shuttle services, bike wash, rentals, and repair services. They also supply free maps; preview the routes and print maps online at www.brianhead.com. Thrifty bikers can come away with some really good deals by shopping area hotels for mountain bike lodging packages, which combine a few days of lodging with lift tickets, shuttle service, and sometimes even food and bike

rentals. Mountain bike rentals are available from Brian Head Resort (866/930-1010, ext. 212, $35-60).

In addition to biking, the resort offers summer visitors the option of scenic lift rides ($12 adult, $8 children), a mini zip line ($12 for two runs) and an 18-hole disc golf course ($12).

FOOD AND ACCOMMODATIONS

Rates at Brian Head are moderate during the ski season, not nearly as high as at fancier ski resorts, and most places offer skiers package discounts. **Brian Head Condo Reservations** (435/677-2045 or 800/722-4742, www.brianheadcondoreservations. com) offers units near both the Giant Steps and Navajo Peak lifts in five large condo developments. Most units come with two bedrooms and two baths, a full kitchen, and a wood-burning fireplace. Prices for small studio condos start at about $85-175 in summer; during the ski season, expect to pay $115-300.

Cedar Breaks Lodge and Spa (223 Hunter Ridge Rd., 435/667-3000 or 888/438-2929, www.cedarbreakslodge.com, $95-165 summer, $110-221 winter) is at the base of Navajo Peak on the north (lower) side of town. All guest rooms come with jetted tubs, a refrigerator, in-room coffee, and cable TV; kitchens are available in some guest rooms. There's also an indoor pool, two hot tubs, a steam room, a sauna, a day spa, and a fitness center. Lodging choices range from hotel rooms to three-bedroom suites. The lodge offers a couple of dining rooms plus a comfortable lounge.

The fanciest lodging at Brian Head is the **Best Western Premier Brian Head** (314 Hunter Ridge Dr., 435/677-9000, www. bwpbrianheadhotel.com, $89-199 summer, $143-269 winter), with nicely decorated guest rooms, an on-site spa, an indoor pool, indoor and outdoor hot tubs, pool tables, and a fitness center. It's pet-friendly to boot. Hearty meals are available at the hotel's Grand Steakhouse (8am-11am, 5pm-10pm daily).

Cedar Breaks National Monument

Cedar Breaks (www.nps.gov/cebr, $5 pp, free for ages 15 and under) is much like Bryce Canyon, but it's on a different high plateau and lacks the crowds that flock to Bryce. Here, on the west edge of the Markagunt Plateau, a giant amphitheater 2,500 feet deep and more than 3 miles (4.8 km) across has been eroded into the stone. A fairyland of forms and colors appears below the rim. Ridges and pinnacles extend like buttresses from the steep cliffs. Cottony patches of clouds often drift through the craggy landscape. Traces of iron, manganese, and other minerals have tinted the normally white limestone a rainbow of warm hues. The intense colors blaze during sunsets and glow even on a cloudy day. Rock layers look much like those at Bryce Canyon National Park, but here they're 2,000 feet higher. Elevations range from 10,662 feet at the rim's highest point to 8,100 feet at Ashdown Creek. In the distance, beyond the amphitheater, are Cedar City and the desert's valleys and ranges. Dense forests broken by large alpine meadows cover the rolling plateau country away from the rim. More than 150 species of wildflowers brighten the meadows during summer; the colorful display peaks during the last two weeks in July, when the **Annual Wildflower Festival** (435/586-0787, www.nps.gov/cebr) takes place. Designated an **International Dark Sky Park,** Cedar Breaks is popular for **stargazing.** Star parties are held in the summer and winter seasons (www.nps.gov/cebr/star-parties.htm).

A 5-mile (8-km) scenic drive leads past four spectacular overlooks, each with a different perspective. Avoid overlooks and other exposed areas during thunderstorms, which are common on summer afternoons. Heavy snows close the road most of the year. You can drive in only from about late May until the first big snowstorm of fall, usually sometime in October. Winter visitors can come in on snowmobiles (unplowed roads only), skis, or snowshoes from Brian Head (2 miles north of the monument) or from Highway 14 (2.5 miles/4 km south).

VISITORS CENTER

A log cabin **visitors center** (435/586-0787 summer, 435/586-0787 winter, www.nps.gov/cebr, 9am-6pm daily late May-mid-Oct.) includes exhibits, an information desk, and a bookstore. The exhibits provide a good

Cedar Breaks National Monument

introduction to the Markagunt Plateau and identify local rocks, wildflowers, trees, animals, and birds. Staff members offer nature walks, geology talks, and campfire programs; see the schedules posted in the visitors center and at the campground. An **entrance fee** ($5 pp) is collected near the visitors center; there's no charge if you're just driving through the monument without stopping.

HIKING

Two easy trails near the rim provide an added appreciation of the geology and forests here. Allow extra time while on foot— it's easy to get out of breath at these high elevations. Regulations prohibit pets on the trails. **Spectra Point-Wasatch Rampart Trail** begins at the visitors center, then follows the rim along the south edge of the amphitheater to an overlook. The hike is 4 miles (6.4 km) round-trip with some ups and downs. Weather-beaten bristlecone pines grow at Spectra Point, about halfway down the trail.

Alpine Pond Trail forms a 2-mile (3.2-km) loop that drops below the rim into one of the few densely wooded areas of the amphitheater. The trail winds through enchanting forests of aspen, subalpine fir, and Engelmann spruce. You can cut the hiking distance in half with a car shuttle between the two trailheads or by taking a connector trail that joins the upper and lower parts of the loop near Alpine Pond. Begin from either Chessmen Ridge Overlook or the trailhead pullout, 1.1 miles (1.8 km) farther north. A trail guide is available at the start or at the visitors center.

CAMPGROUND

A small **campground** (reservations 877/444-6777, www.recreation.gov, mid-June-mid-Sept., has water, $18) is at 10,000 feet elevation. If you plan to visit in June or September, it's best to call ahead to check the campground's status; some years, its season is remarkably short. There's a picnic area near the campground.

GETTING THERE

Cedar Breaks National Monument is 24 miles (39 km) east of Cedar City, 17 miles (27 km) south of Parowan, 30 miles (48 km) southwest of Panguitch, and 27 miles (43 km) northwest of Long Valley Junction. Eighteen miles (29 km) east of Cedar City is the junction with Highway 148, which leads north to Cedar Breaks National Monument. The route climbs up to elevations well over 10,000 feet and is usually open late May-mid-October. The nearest accommodations and restaurants are 2 miles (3.2 km) north in Brian Head.

PANGUITCH LAKE AND VICINITY

This 1,250-acre reservoir is in a volcanic basin surrounded by forests and barren lava flows. The cool waters have a reputation for outstanding trout fishing, especially for rainbows. Resorts line the lakeshore. Many are venerable older fishing lodges with basic lodging in freestanding cabins; a couple are more upscale. Panguitch Lake is a popular site for resort homes.

Panguitch Lake is along Highway 143, about 16 miles (26 km) southwest of Panguitch and 14 miles (22.5 km) northeast of Cedar Breaks National Monument. The lake has public boat ramps on the south and north shores.

Mammoth Springs

Moss and luxuriant streamside vegetation surround the crystal-clear spring waters at this beautiful spot. Mammoth Springs is about 5.5 miles (8.9 km) south of Panguitch Lake. The last 2 miles (3.2 km) are on gravel Forest Road 068. A footbridge leads across the stream to the springs. See the Dixie National Forest map (available at the ranger district offices in Pine Valley and Cedar City) for details.

Mammoth Cave

Step a few feet underground to explore the inside of a lava flow. When this mass of lava began to cool, the molten interior burst through the surface and drained out through a network of tunnels. A cave-in revealed this section of tunnel, which has two levels. You can follow one of them through to another opening. The lower tunnel, with the large entrance, goes back about 0.25 mile (0.4 km). To explore beyond that or to check out other sections, you'll have to stoop or crawl. Bring at least two reliable, powerful flashlights; the caves are very dark. Mammoth Cave is about 14 miles (22.5 km) south of Panguitch Lake. Roads also lead in from Duck Creek on Highway 14 and Hatch on U.S. 89. You'll need a good map to navigate the back roads, although there are some signs for Mammoth Cave.

Food and Accommodations

Lodgings and campgrounds along Highway 143 are concentrated around Panguitch Lake, and there are a number of accommodations that serve Brian Head. **Bear Paw Fishing Resort** (905 S. Hwy. 143, 435/676-2650, www. fishbearpaw.com, late April-early Oct., $75-85) is on the east shore of Panguitch Lake and has lake-view cabins and a clientele composed mostly of anglers. There's also a small store, an on-site restaurant, a post office, and boat rentals.

Blue Springs Lodge (225 N. Shore Rd., 435/676-2277 or 800/987-5634, www. bluespringslodge.com, $95-105) is a ways from the lake but is convenient if you're passing through, as it's right on Highway 143; it comprises a line of modern log cabins with kitchens.

CAMPGROUNDS

The U.S. Forest Service has three campgrounds at Panguitch Lake (435/865-3200 or 877/444-6777, www.recreation.gov, June-Sept., $14-17). **Panguitch Lake North Campground,** on the southwest side of the lake, has developed sites in a ponderosa pine forest at an elevation of 8,400 feet. **Panguitch Lake South Campground** (no reservations), across the highway, is more suited for small rigs and tents. **White Bridge Campground,** elevation 7,900 feet, is along Panguitch Creek 4 miles (6.4 km) northeast of the lake.

The Escalante Region

South-central Utah is dominated by the Grand

Staircase-Escalante, Capitol Reef National Park, and the Glen Canyon National Recreation Area. While these public lands are not as famous as the brand-name national parks of southern Utah, they have much to offer those people who love the backcountry and solitude.

Grand Staircase-Escalante, established in 1996 as a national monument by President Bill Clinton, was modified by President Donald Trump in 2018. Trump's proclamation reduced the total size of the monument from 1.9 million acres to 1 million acres and divided it into three new national monuments.

Capitol Reef National Park is for the connoisseur of Utah backcountry—it may not be the first park you visit, but it's the one that you

Highlights

Look for ★ to find recommended sights, activities, dining, and lodging.

★ **Kodachrome Basin State Park:** Strange rock pillars are the attraction at this state park on the northwestern edge of Grand Staircase (page 302).

★ **Million-Dollar Road:** Although Highway 12 is spectacular for its entire length, this stretch between Escalante and Boulder was a real feat of engineering when it was built in 1935. Acrophobes should bring blinders (page 306).

★ **Anasazi State Park Museum:** The Ancestral Puebloan remains here date back 1,000 years. Tour village ruins, reconstructed sites, and an excellent museum (page 308).

★ **Dry Fork of Coyote Gulch:** This hike down into sinuous slot canyons requires a little bit of driving along the rugged Hole-in-the-Rock Road, but unlike many spectacular Escalante canyon treks, it's a moderate day hike (page 315).

★ **Calf Creek Recreation Area:** If your car won't make it down the bumpy dirt roads of Grand Staircase-Escalante, don't worry: Good hikes are just off Highway 12. Lower Calf Creek Falls is a classic (page 317).

★ **Capitol Gorge:** Here you'll find petroglyphs and incised names of Mormon pioneers. Go up a side trail to explore natural water pockets (page 342).

★ **Goblin Valley State Park:** Whether or not you find them spooky, the goblinlike spires at this state park are fun to explore (page 348).

will return to as you hone your enthusiasm for the desert outback. The rugged canyons leading to the Colorado River's Glen Canyon, which was once considered the equal of the Grand Canyon for drama and beauty, are now trapped beneath the waters of Lake Powell, a magnet for boating and water sports.

In addition to these federal parks, national monuments and recreation areas, there are a number of state parks. Kodachrome Basin State Park offers a colorful landscape dominated by towering sand pipes, a range of hiking trails, and an excellent campground. Goblin Valley State Park's easy hiking trails lead through a bizarre series of hoodoos, spires, and balancing rocks, many with wind-carved "eyes" that explain the area's supernatural moniker.

PLANNING YOUR TIME

Even the most casual travelers with a few hours to spare can enjoy traveling through this fantastic landscape of desert and rock.

Highway 12, which begins near Bryce Canyon National Park and continues along the wild canyon and slickrock country of the Grand Staircase-Escalante National Monument, is one of the most scenic roads in Utah. It's also worth spending a night along the road in Boulder, home of the Boulder Mountain Lodge and famed Hell's Backbone Grill.

If you have more time, plan to spend a couple of days exploring Escalante Canyons National Monument: perhaps a hike to Lower Calf Creek Falls and a day trip down Hole-in-the-Rock Road, with explorations of Devil's Garden and the slot canyons in the Dry Fork of Coyote Gulch. Allow at least a day to hike in Capitol Reef, which has many good day hikes, including the hike to water pockets in Capitol Gorge. In Glen Canyon National Recreation Area, the ultimate vacation is to rent a house-boat on Lake Powell, but if you're not ready to make that commitment, consider a ferry-boat ride across the reservoir between Halls Crossing and Bullfrog.

Grand Staircase-Escalante

Grand Staircase-Escalante (435/644-4600, www.ut.blm.gov/monument) contains a vast and wonderfully scenic collection of slick-rock canyon lands and desert, prehistoric village sites, Old West ranch land, arid plateaus, and miles of back roads linking stone arches, mesas, and abstract rock formations. It is the largest public land grouping designated as a national monument in the Lower 48.

Grand Staircase-Escalante includes three monuments. On the eastern third are the narrow wilderness canyons of the Escalante River and its tributaries, which are the new Escalante Canyons National Monument (242,836 acres). In the center of the monument is a vast swath of arid rangeland and canyons that's now the Kaiparowits Plateau National

Monument (551,034 acres). The western third of the monument edges up against the Gray, White, and Pink Cliffs of the Grand Staircase, and would become the Grand Staircase National Monument (209,993 acres). Critics of the revised monument status note that the boundaries of the new monuments have been drawn to remove protection from areas with rich coal seams and other mineral wealth. However, the original GSENM infrastructure is still in place and no change to public access to the monument's major recreational and scenic destinations is anticipated.

HISTORY

Ancestral Puebloan and Fremont people lived in the Escalante area about AD 1050-1200.

Previous: Coyote Gulch; Calf Creek Recreation Area; hiking in Coyote Gulch.

You can spot their petroglyphs, pictographs, artifacts, storage rooms, and village sites while you're hiking in the canyons of the Escalante River and its tributaries. High alcoves in canyon walls protect small stone granaries; check the floors of sandstone caves for things left behind—pieces of pottery, arrowheads, mats, sandals, and corncobs. (Federal laws prohibit removal of artifacts; please leave everything for the next person to enjoy.) You can visit an excavated Ancestral Puebloan village, along with a modern replica of the original, at Anasazi State Park, just north of Boulder.

The Southern Paiute people arrived in the 1500s and stayed until white settlers took over. The nomadic Paiute had few possessions and left little behind despite their long stay. Mormon colonists didn't learn about the Escalante region until 1866, when Captain James Andrus led his cavalry east from Kanab in pursuit of Paiutes. Reports of the expedition described the upper Escalante, which was named Potato Valley after the wild tubers growing there.

Major John Wesley Powell's expedition down the Green and Colorado Rivers in 1869 had failed to recognize the mouth of the Escalante River; it seemed too shallow and narrow to be a major tributary. In 1872 a detachment of Powell's second expedition, led by Almon H. Thompson and Frederick S. Dellenbaugh, stumbled across the Escalante on an overland journey. After some confusion they realized that an entire new river had been found, and they named it for Spanish explorer and priest Silvestre Vélez de Escalante. The elusive river was the last to be discovered in the contiguous United States. Mormon ranchers and farmers arrived in the upper valleys of the Escalante in 1876 from Panguitch and other towns to the west, not as part of a church-directed mission but simply in search of new and better land.

EXPLORING THE PARK

There is no entrance fee to visit **Grand Staircase-Escalante** (435/644-1200, www. ut.blm.gov/monument). Free permits are required for all overnight backcountry camping or backpacking. There is a fee to camp in the monument's three developed campgrounds.

Hikers in the Paria Wilderness area, which includes Paria Canyon and Coyote Buttes, are required to buy a permit, as are hikers at the Calf Creek Recreation Area.

It's best to have a travel strategy when visiting these huge national monuments. Just as important, especially for a visit of more than a couple of days, is a vehicle that can take on some rugged roads. (A Subaru wagon proved perfectly adequate in dry weather, but when the clay was wet and muddy, the back roads were virtually impassable in all but 4WD vehicles with significantly higher clearance than a station wagon.)

Only two paved roads pass through the monument, both on a west-east trajectory. Highway 12, on the northern boundary of the park, links Bryce Canyon and Capitol Reef National Parks with access to the Escalante canyons. This is one of the most scenic roads in Utah—in fact, *Car and Driver* magazine rates this route as one of the 10 most scenic in the United States. Its innumerable vistas and geologic curiosities will keep you on the edge of your seat. U.S. 89, which runs along the southern edge of the monument between Kanab and Lake Powell, is no scenery slouch either. It is also the access road for the North Rim of the Grand Canyon in Arizona.

Three fair-weather dirt roads, each with a network of side roads and trails, cut through the rugged heart of the monuments, linking the two paved roads. Before heading out on these back roads, check with a visitors center for conditions; high-clearance vehicles are recommended.

VISITORS CENTERS

The monuments' **administrative headquarters** (669 S. U.S. 89A, Kanab, 435/644-1200, www.ut.blm.gov/monument, 8am-4:30pm Mon.-Fri.) is about 15 miles (24 km) from the southwestern edge of the monument in Kanab, but the regional visitors

The Escalante Region

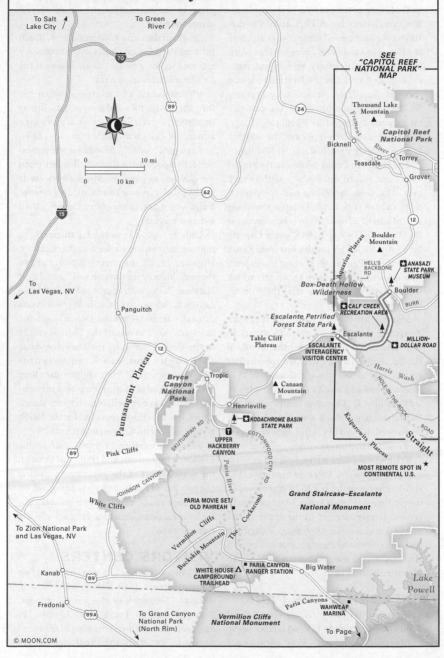

To Salt Lake City

To Green River

70

SEE "CAPITOL REEF NATIONAL PARK" MAP

89

24

Thousand Lake Mountain ▲

Capitol Reef National Park

Bicknell

Fremont River

Torrey

Teasdale

Grover

62

12

Aquarius Plateau

Boulder Mountain ▲

★ ANASAZI STATE PARK MUSEUM

HELL'S BACKBONE RD

To Las Vegas, NV

15

Box-Death Hollow Wilderness

Boulder

BURR

★ CALF CREEK RECREATION AREA

Panguitch

Escalante Petrified Forest State Park ▲

Escalante

MILLION-DOLLAR ROAD ★

Table Cliff Plateau

ESCALANTE INTERAGENCY VISITOR CENTER

Harris Wash

Tropic

12

Bryce Canyon National Park

▲ Canaan Mountain

Kaiparowits Plateau

HOLE-IN-THE-ROCK ROAD

Straight

Paunsaugunt Plateau

Henrieville

★ KODACHROME BASIN STATE PARK

SKUTUMPAH RD

COTTONWOOD CYN RD

UPPER HACKBERRY CANYON

MOST REMOTE SPOT IN CONTINENTAL U.S. ★

Pink Cliffs

89

JOHNSON CANYON

White Cliffs

Paria River

The Cockscomb

PARIA MOVIE SET/ OLD PAHREAH ■

Grand Staircase–Escalante

National Monument

To Zion National Park and Las Vegas, NV

Vermilion Cliffs

Buckskin Mountain

Kanab

89

WHITE HOUSE CAMPGROUND/ TRAILHEAD ▲

■ PARIA CANYON RANGER STATION

Big Water

Lake Powell

Fredonia

89A

To Grand Canyon National Park (North Rim)

Vermilion Cliffs National Monument

Paria Canyons

WAHWEAP MARINA

To Page

© MOON.COM

0   10 mi

0   10 km

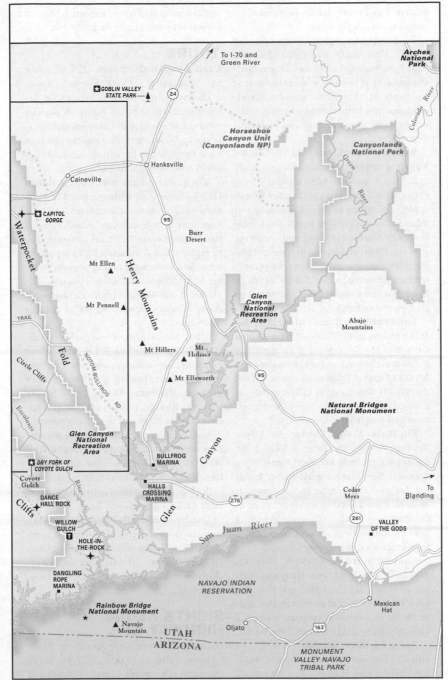

To I-70 and
Green River

Arches
National
Park

★ GOBLIN VALLEY
STATE PARK

24

Horseshoe
Canyon Unit
(Canyonlands NP)

Canyonlands
National Park

Hanksville

Caineville

Colorado River

Green River

★ CAPITOL
GORGE

Waterpocket

Burr
Desert

Mt Ellen ▲

Henry Mountains

Mt Pennell ▲

Glen
Canyon
National
Recreation
Area

Abajo
Mountains

Fold

Circle Cliffs

Mt Hillers ▲

Mt
Holmes ▲

95

TRAIL

NOTOM-BULLFROG RD

Mt Ellsworth ▲

95

Natural Bridges
National Monument

Escalante

Glen Canyon
National
Recreation
Area

BULLFROG
MARINA

Glen Canyon

★ DRY FORK OF
COYOTE GULCH

Cedar
Mesa

To
Blanding

Coyote
Gulch

HALLS
CROSSING
MARINA

276

DANCE
HALL ROCK

River

261

Cliffs

WILLOW
GULCH

VALLEY
OF THE GODS

HOLE-IN-
THE-ROCK

San Juan River

DANGLING
ROPE
MARINA

NAVAJO INDIAN
RESERVATION

Rainbow Bridge
National Monument

Mexican
Hat

▲ Navajo
Mountain

UTAH

Oljato

163

ARIZONA

MONUMENT
VALLEY NAVAJO
TRIBAL PARK

centers, listed below, are the best places for practical travel information.

Escalante Interagency Visitor Center (755 W. Main St., Escalante, 435/826-5499, 8am-5:30pm daily) is housed in a sprawling building at the west end of the town of Escalante. Staff members are very knowledgeable and helpful, and exhibits focus on the monument's ecology and biological diversity.

Kanab Visitor Center (745 E. U.S. 89, Kanab, 435/644-1300, 8am-4:30pm daily mid-Mar.-mid-Nov., 8am-4:30pm Mon.-Fri. mid-Nov.-mid-Mar.) is the place to stop if you're planning to drive Cottonwood or Johnson Canyon and Skutumpah Roads from the south. Staff can give you updates on the road conditions and suggest driving and hiking strategies. A walk-in lottery for permits to hike Coyote Buttes is held at 8:30am daily. Exhibits at this visitors center concentrate on geology and archaeology.

Cannonville Visitor Center (10 Center St., Cannonville, 435/826-5640, 8am-4:30pm daily mid-Mar.-mid-Nov.) is an attractive building at the north end of Cottonwood and Johnson Canyon-Skutumpah Roads. Even if the office is closed, stop by to look at the outdoor exhibits, which depict the different cultures that have lived in the area.

Big Water Visitor Center (100 Upper Revolution Way, Big Water, 435/675-3200, 8:30am-4:30pm daily Apr.-Oct., 8am-4:30pm Tues.-Sat. Nov.-Mar.), a spiral-shaped building designed to resemble an ammonite, is home to a small but distinctive collection of dinosaur bones and a wild mural depicting late Cretaceous life in the area. Stop here to learn about local paleontology.

Anasazi State Park (460 N. Hwy. 12, Boulder, 435/335-7382, www.stateparks.utah. gov, 9am-5pm daily mid-Mar.-mid-Nov., $5) has a ranger on duty at an information desk inside the museum. The museum is worth a visit, so don't be stingy with your five bucks!

Paria Contact Station (U.S. 89, 44 miles/71 km east of Kanab, 435/644-4628, 8am-4:30pm mid-Mar.-mid-Nov.) is a small visitors center, but it's an important stop for anyone planning to hike Paria Canyon.

TOURS

Utah Canyon Outdoors (325 W. Main St., Escalante, 435/826-4967, www. utahcanyonoutdoors.com) focuses on day hikes (full-day $120-140 pp), with popular trips to less crowded slot canyons and riparian areas. It also offers hiker shuttles and runs a good gear shop in the salmon-colored building in downtown Escalante.

The guides at **Excursions of Escalante** (125 E. Main St., Escalante, 800/839-7567, www.excursionsofescalante.com) lead trips into more remote canyons, including some that require some technical canyoneering to explore, and some multiday backpacking trips. Straightforward hiking trips ($155 pp) are also offered, either cross-country (easiest) or in slot canyons (more challenging). A day of basic canyoneering ($170) includes instruction.

Many local outfitters use pack animals. With **Escape Goats** (435/826-4652, www. escalantecanyonguides.com), you can hike with goats (and a friendly, goat-loving human guide) into canyons. This is a good bet for families with kids. A variety of hikes are available; full-day hikes start at $110 per person.

Saddle up for day rides or horse-packing trips with **Hells Backbone Ranch and Trail** (435/335-7581, www.bouldermountaintrails. com, $60-75 for 1.5-2-hour ride), located next to the Boulder Mountain Guest Ranch up the Hells Backbone/Salt Gulch Road.

Boulder-based **Earth Tours** (435/691-1241, www.earth-tours.com) offers guided hikes ($120 pp) as well as back-roads driving tours ($125) of the area. Most trips are led by a geologist with a wide-ranging interest in natural history.

SIGHTS ALONG HIGHWAY 12

Highway 12 runs west-east from Bryce Canyon National Park and Tropic along the north edge of the Grand Staircase and

Geology of the Grand Staircase

This desert landscape once sat at the verge of a vast inland sea. About 300 million years ago, sandy dunes rose hundreds of feet above the waves, then sank below sea level and were covered by water. Thick layers of sediment built up one on top of the other, turning the sand dunes to stone. During the last 50 million years, powerful forces within the earth slowly pushed the entire region 1 mile (1.6 km) upward. The ancestral Colorado River began to carve the deep gorges seen today near Glen Canyon. In turn, the tributaries of the Colorado River, such as the Escalante River, were also forced to trench deeper and deeper in order to drain their watershed.

The most characteristic rocks in the monument are the ancient dunes, turned to stone called slickrock, which make up many of the sheer canyon cliffs, arches, and spires of the region. Delicate cross-bedded lines of the former dunes add grace to these features. Forces within the restless plateau have also buckled and folded rock layers into great reefs as long as 100 miles (161 km). Weathering then carved them into rainbow-hued rock monuments. The aptly named Cockscomb, visible from Cottonwood Canyon Road, which cuts through the center of Grand Staircase-Escalante, is an example of these massive rock wrinkles.

Kaiparowits Plateau monuments to the town of Escalante, where the route cuts through Escalante Canyons monument to Boulder. Stop at the **Cannonville Visitor Center** (10 Center St., Cannonville, 435/826-5640, 8am-4:30pm daily mid-Mar.-mid-Nov.) for information about back-road conditions and hikes in the western parts of the monuments. Two backcountry roads depart from Cannonville and lead to remote corners of the monuments-Johnson Canyon/ Skutumpah Road.

The northern end of this route is in Cannonville; its southern terminus is at U.S. 89 just east of Kanab (46 miles/74 km one-way). From the northernmost stretch of this road, Bryce Canyon rises to the west; about 6 miles (9.7 km) from the southern end and off to the east on private land (look from the road, don't trespass) is the set from the TV show *Gunsmoke*.

The unpaved portions of the road are rough and rutted in places, and after rains, the bentonite soils that make up the roadbed turn to goo. In good weather, cars with good clearance can usually make the journey. The road follows the Pink and White Cliff terraces of the Grand Staircase, with access to some excellent and comparatively undersubscribed hiking trails. Several steep slot canyons make for excellent canyoneering. The best views (and the worst roads) are in the northernmost

20 miles (32 km) or so, above Lick Wash. Much of the rest of the way is rangeland, so watch for cattle grazing by the roadway. The lower 16 miles (26 km) of Johnson Canyon Road are paved.

Cottonwood Canyon Scenic Back Road

This 49-mile (79-km) route also connects Cannonville with U.S. 89, but it passes through quite different terrain and landscapes. One of the most scenic backcountry routes in the monument, the Cottonwood Canyon Road not only offers access to dramatic Grosvenor Arch, it also passes along the Cockscomb, a soaring buckle of rock that divides the Grand Staircase and the Kaiparowits Plateau. Cottonwood Creek, which this road parallels, is a normally dry streambed that cuts through the angular rock beds of the Cockscomb. Several excellent hikes lead into the canyons and narrows, where the Paria River, Hackberry Canyon, and Cottonwood Creek all meet, about 20 miles (32 km) south of Cannonville.

Check at the Cannonville or Big Water Visitor Center for information about road conditions. Although the road is sometimes passable for cars, several road crossings are susceptible to washouts after rainstorms, and the northern portion is impassable even to

4WD vehicles when wet because of the extremely unctuous nature of the roadbed. Check conditions before setting out if you plan to go beyond Grosvenor Arch.

★ Kodachrome Basin State Park

Although it's located in a basin southeast of Bryce, **Kodachrome Basin State Park** (435/679-8562, http://stateparks.utah.gov, 6am-10pm daily, day-use $8), is well worth a visit. Here you'll see not only colorful cliffs but also strange-looking rock pillars that occur nowhere else in the world. Sixty-seven rock pillars (here called sand pipes) found in and near the park range in height from 6 feet to nearly 170 feet. One theory of their origin is that earthquakes caused sediments deep underground to be churned up by water under high pressure. The particles of calcite, quartz, feldspar, and clay in the sand pipes came from underlying rock formations, and the pipes appeared when the surrounding rock eroded away. Most of the other rocks visible in the park are Entrada sandstone: The lower orange layer is the Gunsight Butte Member, and the white layer with orange bands is the Cannonville Member.

Signs name some of the rock features. Big Stoney, the phallus-shaped sand pipe overlooking the campground, is so explicit that it doesn't need a sign. The article "Motoring into Escalante Land," by Jack Breed, in the September 1949 issue of *National Geographic*, brought attention to the scenery and earned the area the name Kodachrome Flat, for the then-experimental Kodak film used by the expedition. The park also offers several good half-day hiking trails and a host of shorter hikes.

CAMPING

The state park has two **campgrounds** (435/679-8562, reservations 800/322-3770 or www.reserveamerica.com, year-round). The **Basin Campground** ($20 tents, $30 RVs with hookups) is in a natural amphitheater at an elevation of 5,800 feet. It has restrooms, showers, and a dump station. During the winter, restrooms and showers may close, but pit toilets are available. The campground usually has space except on summer holidays. The smaller **Bryce View Campground** ($20) is more primitive, and, not surprisingly, has good views of Bryce Canyon. In addition, at the park's Oasis group camping site are two new bunkhouse camping cabins that sleep six (bring your own bedding; no running

Grosvenor Arch

water, bathrooms and showers adjacent, $105 a night).

GETTING THERE

To reach the park, drive to Cannonville and follow signs for 9 miles (14.5 km) along paved Cottonwood Canyon Road. Adventurous drivers can also approach the park from U.S. 89 to the south via Cottonwood Canyon Road (35 miles/56 km) or Skutumpah Road through Bull Valley Gorge and Johnson Canyon (48 miles/77 km). These routes may be impassable in wet weather but are generally OK in dry weather for cars with good clearance.

Grosvenor Arch

Just 1 mile (1.6 km) off Cottonwood Canyon Road, a side road leads to the magnificent Grosvenor Arch. It takes a little bit of effort to get here (the 10-mile dirt road from the turnoff to Kodachrome Basin State Park to the arch can be bumpy and should be avoided in wet weather), so a visit to the arch can take on the qualities of a pilgrimage. There are actually two arches here, which is a pretty rare occurrence for such erosion-formed structures; their position, jutting like flying buttresses out of a soaring cliff, is also quite stunning. The larger of the two openings is 99 feet across. A 1949 National Geographic Society expedition named the double arch in honor of the society's president. The turnoff is 10 miles (16 km) from the Kodachrome Basin State Park turnoff and 29 miles (47 km) from U.S. 89.

Escalante Petrified Forest State Park

The pleasant **Escalante Petrified Forest State Park** (435/826-4466, http://stateparks. utah.gov, 7am-10pm daily summer, 8am-10pm daily winter, day-use $8, camping $19-25), just northwest of the town of Escalante, offers camping, boating, fishing, picnicking, hiking, a visitors center with displays of petrified wood and dinosaur bones, and a chance to see petrified wood along the trails. Rivers of 140 million years ago carried trees

to the site of present-day Escalante and buried them in sand and gravel. Burial prevented decay as crystals of silicon dioxide gradually replaced the wood cells. Mineral impurities added a rainbow of colors to the trees as they turned to stone. Weathering has exposed this petrified wood and the water-worn pebbles and sand of the Morrison Formation. For a look at some colorful petrified wood, follow the **Petrified Forest Trail** from the campground up a hillside wooded with piñon pine and juniper. At the top of the 240-foot-high ridge, continue on a loop trail to the petrified wood; allow 45-60 minutes for the 1-mile (1.6-km) round-trip hike. The steep **Rainbow Loop Trail** (0.75 mile/1.2 km) branches off the Petrified Forest Trail to more areas of petrified wood.

The **campground** (reservations 800/322-3770, www.reserveamerica.com, year-round, $20) offers drinking water, flush toilets, showers, and RV hookups ($28). The adjacent 139-acre Wide Hollow Reservoir offers fishing, boating, and bird-watching. The park is 1.5 miles (2.4 km) west of Escalante on Highway 12, then 0.7 mile (1.1 km) north on a gravel road.

Escalante

The town of Escalante, 38 miles (61 km) east of Bryce Canyon and 23 miles (37 km) south of Boulder, offers all visitor services and is the headquarters for explorations of the Escalante River canyons. The **Escalante Interagency Visitor Center** (755 W. Main St., 435/826-5499, 8am-5:30 daily) provides information on local hikes and road conditions.

Smokey Mountain Road

From Escalante, it's 78 miles (126 km) south to U.S. 89 at Big Water, just shy of Lake Powell, along Smokey Mountain Road. This road is rougher than other cross-monument roads. Be sure to check on conditions before setting out; 4WD vehicles are required. As this route passes across the Kaiparowits Plateau, the landscape is bleak and arid. Then the road drops precipitously down onto a bench

where side roads lead through badlands to Lake Powell beaches. Big Water is 19 miles (31 km) from Page, Arizona, and 57 miles (92 km) from Kanab.

Hole-in-the-Rock Road

The building of this road by determined Mormons was one of the great epics in the colonization of the West. Church leaders organized the Hole-in-the-Rock Expedition to settle the wildlands around the San Juan River of southeastern Utah, believing that a Mormon presence would aid in converting the Native Americans there and prevent non-Mormons from moving in. In 1878, the Parowan Stake issued the first call for a colonizing mission to the San Juan, even before a site had been selected.

Preparations and surveys took place the following year as the 236 men, women, and children received their calls. Food, seed, farming and building tools, 200 horses, and more than 1,000 head of cattle would be taken along. Planners ruled out lengthy routes through northern Arizona or eastern Utah in favor of a straight shot via Escalante that would cut the distance in half. The expedition set off in fall 1879, convinced that they were part of a divine mission.

Hints of trouble to come filtered back from the group as they discovered the Colorado River crossing to be far more difficult than first believed. Lack of springs along the way added to their worries. From their start at Escalante, road builders progressed rapidly for the first 50 miles (81 km), then slowly over rugged slickrock for the final 6 miles (9.7 km) to Hole-in-the-Rock. A sheer 45-foot drop below this narrow notch was followed by almost 1 mile (1.6 km) of extremely steep slickrock to the Colorado River. The route looked impossible, but three crews of workers armed with picks and blasting powder worked simultaneously to widen

the notch and construct a precarious wagon road down to the river and up the cliffs on the other side.

The job took six weeks. Miraculously, all of the people, animals, and wagons made it down and were ferried across the Colorado River without a serious accident. Canyons and other obstacles continued to block the way as the weary group pressed on. Only after six months of exhausting travel did they stop at the present-day site of Bluff on the San Juan River.

Today, on a journey from Escalante, you can experience a bit of the same adventure the pioneers knew. Except for scattered signs of ranching, the land remains unchanged. If the road is dry, vehicles with good clearance can drive to within a short distance of Hole-in-the-Rock. The rough conditions encountered past Dance Hall Rock require more clearance than most cars have. Bring sufficient gas, food, and water for the entire 124-mile (200-km) round-trip from Escalante; there are no services along this route.

SIGHTS

Metate Arch and other rock sculptures decorate **Devil's Garden,** 12.5 miles (20.1 km) down Hole-in-the-Rock Road. Turn west and go 0.3 mile (0.5 km) at the sign to the parking area; you can't really see the "garden" from the road. Red- and cream-colored sandstone formations sit atop pedestals or tilt at crazy angles. Delicate bedding lines run through the rocks. There are no trails or markers—just wander around at your whim. The Bureau of Land Management (BLM) has provided picnic tables, grills, and outhouses for day use. No overnight camping is permitted at Devil's Garden.

Dance Hall Rock (38 miles/61 km down Hole-in-the-Rock Rd.) jumped to the fiddle music and lively steps of the expedition members in 1879. Its natural amphitheater has a relatively smooth floor and made a perfect gathering spot when the Hole-in-the-Rock group had to wait three weeks at nearby Fortymile Spring for roadwork to be

1: sandpipe in Kodachrome Basin State Park; **2:** barren and harsh land around Escalante; **3:** hoodoos at Devil's Garden

completed ahead. Dance Hall Rock is an enjoyable place to explore and only a short walk from the parking area. Solution holes, left from water dissolving in the rock, pockmark the sandstone structure.

At road's end (57 miles/92 km from Hwy. 12), continue on foot across slickrock to the notch and views of the blue waters of Lake Powell below. Rockslides have made the descent impossible for vehicles, but hikers can scramble down to the lake and back in about one hour. The elevation change is 600 feet. The 0.5-mile (0.8-km) round-trip is strenuous. After a steep descent over boulders, look for the steps of Uncle Ben's Dugway at the base of the notch; below it, the grade is gentler. Drill holes in the rock once held oak stakes against which logs, brush, and earth supported the outer wagon wheels. The inner wheels followed a narrow rut 4-6 inches deep. About two-thirds of the route down is now under water, although the most impressive roadwork can still be seen.

GETTING THERE
The turnoff from Highway 12 is 5 miles (8 km) east of Escalante. In addition to rewarding you with scenic views, Hole-in-the-Rock Road passes many side drainages of the Escalante River to the east and some remote country of the Kaiparowits Plateau high above to the west. Staff at the information center just west of Escalante can give current road conditions and suggest hikes.

Boynton Overlook and the Hundred Hands Pictograph
Be sure to pull off Highway 12 at the unsigned **Boynton Overlook** (at the Escalante River bridge, 14 miles (22.5 km) east of Escalante) and scan the walls on the far side of the Escalante River, for the Hundred Hands pictograph (binoculars help immensely). For a closer look, hike 0.5 mile (0.8 km) up from the trailhead parking area just at the bottom of the hill, at the Escalante River crossing. Rather than hike along the river, go up above the house (don't stray

onto fenced-in private property), scramble up the face of the first cliff, and follow faint trails and rock cairns across the bench. (It's easiest if you've located the pictographs first from the overlook; this entire hike is just 1 mile/1.6 km round-trip.) The Hundred Hands are high up on a cliff face that's larger than the one you scrambled up. Follow the cliff to the right, where pictographs of goats are lower on the wall.

Back down at river level, head downstream a few hundred yards and look up to the left to see the Ancestral Puebloan ruins known as the Moki House.

Calf Creek Recreation Area
Located 15.5 miles (25 km) east of Escalante, stunning **Calf Creek Recreation Area** (day-use $5 per vehicle) offers the most accessible glimpse of what canyon country is all about. The trailhead to 126-foot **Lower Calf Creek Falls** is here, and you should definitely make plans for the half-day hike, especially if you have no time for further exploration of this magical landscape. Otherwise, stop here to picnic in the shade of willows and cottonwoods. This is also the most convenient and attractive **campsite** (water available, $15) for dozens of miles.

★ Million-Dollar Road
Highway 12 between Escalante and Boulder was completed in 1935 by workers from the Civilian Conservation Corps. The cost was a budget-busting $1 million. Before then, mules carried supplies and mail across this wilderness of slickrock and narrow canyons. The section of Highway 12 between Calf Creek and Boulder is extraordinarily scenic—even jaded travelers used to the wonders of Utah will have to pull over and ogle the views from the **Hog's Back,** where the road crests a fin of rock above the canyons of the Escalante. Be here for sunset on a clear evening and you'll have a memory to carry for the rest of your life.

1: Boynton Overlook; **2:** Burr Trail Road

Boulder

Boulder is a tiny community in a lovely location at the base of Boulder Mountain, where the alpine air mixes with the desert breezes. The single best lodging choice in the Escalante region—the Boulder Mountain Lodge—is here, so plan accordingly.

★ Anasazi State Park Museum

At the excellent **Anasazi State Park Museum** (Hwy. 12, 1 mile/1.6 km north of Boulder, 435/335-7308, http://stateparks. utah.gov, 8am-6pm daily Mar.-Oct., 8am-6pm daily Mar.-Oct., 8am-4pm daily Nov.-Feb., $5 pp), indoor exhibits and an outdoor excavated village site and pueblo replica provide a look into the life of these ancient people. The Ancestral Puebloans stayed here for 50-75 years sometime between AD 1050 and 1200. They grew corn, beans, and squash in fields nearby. The village population peaked at about 200, with an estimated 40-50 dwellings. Why the Ancestral Puebloans left or where they went isn't known for sure, but a fire swept through much of the village before the Ancestral Puebloans abandoned it. Perhaps they burned the village on purpose, knowing they would move on. University of Utah students and faculty excavated the village, known as the Coombs Site, in 1958-1959. You can view pottery, ax heads, arrow points, and other tools found at the site in the museum, along with delicate items like sandals and basketry that came from more protected sites elsewhere. You can see video programs on the Ancestral Puebloan people and modern Native American peoples on request.

The self-guided tour of the ruins begins behind the museum. You'll see a whole range of Ancestral Puebloan building styles—a pit house, masonry walls, jacal walls (mud reinforced by sticks), and combinations of masonry and jacal. Replicas of habitation and storage rooms behind the museum show complete construction details.

Fuel up for your museum tour at the food truck parked out front.

Burr Trail Road

Burr Trail Road, originally a cattle trail blazed by stockman John Atlantic Burr, extends from the town of Boulder on Highway 12 to the Notom-Bullfrog Road, which runs between Highway 24 near the eastern entrance to Capitol Reef National Park and Bullfrog Marina on Lake Powell, off Highway 276. Starting at Boulder, the road is paved until the boundary between the Grand Staircase-Escalante and Capitol Reef National Park (31 miles/50 km), where the route traverses the Circle Cliffs, as well as spectacular canyon areas such as Long Canyon and the Gulch. As the route meets the Waterpocket Fold in Capitol Reef National Park, a breathtaking set of switchbacks drop some 800 feet in just 0.5 mile (0.8 km). These switchbacks are not considered suitable for RVs or vehicles towing trailers. The unpaved sections of the road may be impassable in poor weather. Visitors should inquire about road and weather conditions before setting out. Also inquire about hiking trails that depart from side roads. Burr Trail Road joins Notom-Bullfrog Road just before it exits Capitol Reef National Park.

SIGHTS ALONG U.S. 89

In this region, U.S. 89 runs between Kanab in the west to the Utah-Arizona border in the Glen Canyon National Recreation Area. From Kanab to Page, Arizona, at the Colorado River's Glen Canyon Dam, is 80 miles (129 km).

Johnson Canyon Road

Eight miles (12.9 km) east of Kanab, Johnson Canyon Road heads north in Grand Staircase National Monnument before joining Skutumpah Road and Glendale Bench Road. This road system links up with several more remote backcountry roads in the Grand Staircase and Kaiparowits monuments, and eventually leads to Cannonville along Highway 12. From U.S. 89, Johnson Canyon Road is paved for its initial miles. The road passes an abandoned movie set, where parts of the TV series *Gunsmoke* were filmed, climbs up through the scenic Vermilion and then the White Cliffs of the Grand Staircase. The road eventually passes over Skutumpah Terrace, a rather featureless plateau covered with scrub.

Paria Canyon and Vermilion Cliffs National Monument

Paria Canyon—a set of magnificent slot canyons that drain from Utah down through northern Arizona to the Grand Canyon—is the focus of popular multiday canyoneering expeditions. Paria Canyon and 293,000 acres of surrounding desert grasslands are now protected as Vermilion Cliffs National Monument (www.blm.gov). Although the monument spreads south from the Utah-Arizona border, access to the monument's most famous sites is from back roads in Utah. In addition to the long Paria Canyon backpacking route, some shorter but strenuous day hikes explore this area. For more information, contact the **Kanab Visitor Center** (745 E. U.S. 89, Kanab, 435/644-4680, 8am-4:30pm daily mid-Mar.-mid-Nov., 8am-4:30pm Mon.-Fri. mid-Nov.-mid-Mar.) or stop at the **Paria Contact Station** (U.S. 89, 44 miles/71 km east of Kanab, 435/644-4628, 8am-4:30pm mid-Mar.-mid-Nov.), www.blm.gov), near milepost 21 on U.S. 89.

Cottonwood Canyon Road

A few miles east of the Paria Contact Station (milepost 21 on U.S. 89), Cottonwood Canyon Road leads north. The unpaved road's lower portions, usually passable with a car in dry weather, pass through scenic landscapes as the road pushes north. The route climbs up across a barren plateau before dropping down to the Paria River. Several good hikes lead from roadside trailheads into steep side canyons. The route continues north along the Cockscomb, a long wrinkle of rock ridges that runs north and south across the desert. At the northern end of this route are Grosvenor Arch, Kodachrome Basin State Park, and Highway 12 at Canyonville (46 miles/74 km).

Big Water and Smokey Mountain Road

At the little crossroads of Big Water, **a BLM visittor center** (100 Upper Revolution Way, Big Water, 435/675-3200, 8:30am-4:30pm daily Apr.-Oct., 8am-4:30pm Tues.-Sat. Nov.-Mar.) serves the needs of travelers to the monument and to Glen Canyon National Recreation Area (NRA), which is immediately adjacent to this area. The visitors center is definitely worth a stop—it houses bones from a 75-million-year-old, 30-foot-long duck-billed dinosaur. The backbone bearing tooth marks from a tyrannosaur and the 13-foot-long dinosaur tail are especially impressive.

Joining U.S. 89 at Big Water is Smokey Mountain Road. This long and rugged road links Big Water to Highway 12 at Escalante, 78 miles (126 km) north. The southern portions of the route pass through Glen Canyon NRA, and side roads lead to remote beaches and flooded canyons. The original *Planet of the Apes* was filmed here, before the area was inundated by Lake Powell.

From Big Water, it's 19 miles (31 km) to Page, Arizona, on U.S. 89.

HIKING

The monuments of Grand Staircase-Escalante preserves some of the best long-distance hiking trails in the American Southwest, but it also has shorter trails for travelers who want to sample the wonderful slot canyons and backcountry without venturing too far afield. Be sure to check at local visitors centers for road and trail conditions, and to get up-to-date maps. Many of the following hikes require extensive travel on backcountry roads, which can be impassable after rains and rough the rest of the time. In summer, these trails are hot and exposed: Always carry plenty of water and sunscreen, and wear a hat.

Hiking the **Escalante River Canyon** is recognized worldwide as one of the great wilderness treks. Most people devote 4-6 days to exploring these slickrock canyons, which involve frequent scrambling (if not rock climbing), stream fording (if not swimming), and

THE ESCALANTE REGION
GRAND STAIRCASE-ESCALANTE

Walk Softly

Only great care and awareness can preserve the pristine canyons of the Escalante. You can help if you pack out all trash, avoid trampling on the fragile cryptobiotic soils (dark areas of symbiotic algae and fungus on the sand), travel in groups of 12 or fewer, don't disturb Native American artifacts, and protect wildlife by leaving your dogs at home. Most important, pack out human waste in areas where that's required, and otherwise bury it well away from water sources, trails, and camping areas. Unless there's a fire hazard, burn toilet paper to aid decomposition. Campfires in developed or designated campgrounds are allowed only in fire grates, fire pits, or fire pans. Wood collection in these areas is not permitted. The use of backpacking stoves is recommended by the National Park Service and the Bureau of Land Management. Visitors are encouraged to maximize efforts to leave no trace of their passage in the area.

Leave No Trace Inc. (www.lnt.org) is a national organization dedicated to awareness, appreciation, and respect for our wildlands. The organization also promotes education about environmentally responsible outdoor recreation.

exhausting detours around rockfalls and log-jams. Some day hikes are possible along the Escalante River drainage. Hikers without a week to spare can sample the landscape along the Dry Fork Coyote Gulch Trail, which links two fascinating and beautifully constricted slot canyons.

Paria Canyon is another famed long-distance slickrock canyon hike that covers 37 miles (60 km) between the border of Utah and the edge of the Colorado River's Marble Canyon. Several long day hikes leave from trailheads on the Paria Plateau, along the border with Arizona.

Other areas with developed hiking trails include the Skutumpah Road area and Cottonwood Canyon, in the Kaiparowits Plateau National Monument. Otherwise, hiking in the monuments is mostly on unmarked routes. Although the monuments are developing more day-hiking options, the rangers also encourage hardy adventurers to consider extended hikes across the rugged and primitive outback, beyond the busy canyon corridors. Contact one of the visitors centers and ask for help from the rangers to plan a hiking adventure where there are no trails.

Johnson Canyon/ Skutumpah Road

The northern portions of this road pass through the White Cliffs area of the Grand Staircase, and several steep and narrow canyons are trenched into these terraces. Rough hiking trails explore these slot canyons. The **Willis Creek Narrows** trailhead is 9 miles (14.5 km) south of Cannonville along Skutumpah Road. The relatively easy trail follows a small stream as it etches a deep and narrow gorge through the Navajo sandstone. From the parking area, where Skutumpah Road crosses Willis Wash, walk downstream along the wash. Follow the streambed, which quickly descends between slickrock walls. The canyon is at times no more than 6-10 feet across, while the walls rise 200-300 feet. The trail follows the usually dry streambed through the canyon for nearly 2.5 miles (4 km). To return, backtrack up the canyon.

Approximately 1.5 miles (2.4 km) farther south on Skutumpah Road, a narrow bridge vaults over **Bull Valley Gorge.** Like the Willis Creek Narrows, this is a steep and narrow cleft in the slickrock; however, scrambling along the canyon bottom is a greater challenge, part of the reward for which is viewing a wrecked automobile wedged between the canyon walls. From the bridge, walk upstream along a faint trail on the north side of the crevice until the walls are low enough to scramble down. From here, the canyon deepens quickly, and you'll have to negotiate several dry falls along the way (a rope will come in handy). When you reach the area below the bridge, look up to see a 1950s-era pickup truck trapped between the canyon walls. Three men died in this 1954 mishap; their bodies were recovered, but the pickup was left in place. The canyon continues another mile (1.6 km) from this point; there is no loop trail out of the canyon, so turn back when you've seen enough.

Twenty miles (32 km) south of Cannonville, Skutumpah Road crosses **Lick Wash,** from which trails lead downstream into slot canyons to a remote arroyo (dry riverbed) surrounded by rock-topped mesas. One of these lofty perches contains a preserve of now-rare native grasses. Although this area can be reached on a day hike, this is also a good place to base a multiday camping trip. The trail starts just below the road crossing on Lick Wash and follows the usually dry streambed as it plunges down into a narrow slot canyon. The canyon bottom is mostly level and easy to hike. After 1 mile (1.6 km), the canyon begins to widen, and after 4 miles (6.4 km), Lick Wash joins Park Wash, a larger desert canyon.

Looming above this canyon junction are mesas topped with deep sandstone terraces that are part of the White Cliffs of the Grand Staircase. Rising to the east is **No Mans Mesa,** skirted on all sides by steep-sided cliffs. The 1,788 acres atop the mesa were grazed by goats for six months in the 1920s, but before or since have never been grazed by herbivores. This pristine grassland is protected by the BLM as an Area of Critical Environmental Concern. Hardy hikers can scramble up a steep trail—used by the aforementioned goats—to visit this wilderness preserve. The ascent of No Mans Mesa is best considered an overnight trip from the Lick Wash trailhead.

Cottonwood Canyon Road

The northerly portions of this route pass by **Kodachrome Basin State Park,** with a fine selection of hiking trails through colorful rock formations. The short **Nature Trail** introduces the park's ecology. The **Panorama Trail** loops through a highly scenic valley with sand pipes and colorful rocks; the easy trail is

3 miles (4.8 km) round-trip and takes about two hours. **Angel's Palace Trail** begins just east of the group campground and makes a 0.75-mile (1.2 km) loop with fine views; the elevation gain is about 300 feet. The **Grand Parade Trail** makes a 1.5-mile (2.4 km) loop with good views of rock pinnacles; begin from the concession stand or group campground. **Eagles View Trail,** a historic cattle trail, climbs nearly 1,000 vertical feet up steep cliffs above the campground, then drops into Henrieville, 2 miles (3.2 km) away; the highest overlook is a steep 0.5-mile (0.8 km) ascent from the campground. **Shakespeare Arch Trail** is a 0.5-mile (0.8 km) round-trip hike to a natural arch; access the trailhead by a signed dirt road.

Continue south on Cottonwood Canyon Road for 7.5 miles (12 km) from the state park to the crossing of Round Valley Draw. From here, turn south onto BLM Road 422 toward **Hackberry Canyon.** Hikers can travel the 22-mile (35-km) length of this scenic canyon in three days or make day hikes from either end of the trail. The lower canyon meets Cottonwood Canyon at an elevation of 4,700 feet just above the mouth of the Paria River. Cottonwood Canyon Road provides access to both ends. A small spring-fed stream flows down the lower half of Hackberry. Many side canyons invite exploration. One of them, Sam Pollock Canyon, is on the west about 4.5 miles (7.2 km) upstream from the junction of Hackberry and Cottonwood Canyons; follow it 1.75 miles (2.8 km) up to **Sam Pollock Arch** (60 feet high and 70 feet wide). Available topographic maps include the metric 1:100,000 Smoky Mountain or the 7.5-minute Slickrock Bench and Calico Peak.

The confluence of the Paria, Hackberry, and Cottonwood Canyons provides the backdrop to an excellent, although strenuous, day hike. The **Box of the Paria River** involves some steep climbs up rocky slopes as it traverses a tongue of slickrock between the mouth of the Hackberry and Paria Canyons. The route then follows the Paria River through its "box," or cliff-sided canyon, in the Cockscomb formation. The trail returns to the trailhead by following Cottonwood Canyon upstream to the trailhead. The round-trip hike is about 7 miles (11.3 km) long. Inquire at visitors centers for maps and about conditions.

Although not as well-known as the lower canyon, the **Upper Paria River Canyon** has some beautiful scenery and offers many side canyons to explore. The Paria is west of both Hackberry and Cottonwood Canyons. Access to the upper end is from the Skutumpah or Cottonwood Canyon Road near Kodachrome Basin State Park (elev. about 5,900 feet). The usual lower entry is from near Pahreah ghost town (elev. 4,720 feet); turn north and go 6 miles from U.S. 89 between mileposts 30 and 31 and continue past the Pahreah movie set to road's end. (The clay road surface is very slippery when wet but is OK for cars when dry.) The upper canyon is about 25 miles (40 km) long, and the hike takes 3-4 days, allowing some time to explore side canyons. You can find water at springs along the main canyon and in many side canyons (purify it first); try not to use water from the river itself as it may contain chemical pollution. Topo maps are the metric 1:100,000 Kanab and Smoky Mountain or the 7.5-minute Cannonville, Bull Valley Gorge, Deer Range Point, and Calico Peak.

The Escalante River

The maze of canyons that drain the Escalante River presents exceptional hiking opportunities. You'll find everything from easy day hikes to challenging backpacking treks. The Escalante's canyon begins just downstream from the town of Escalante and ends at Lake Powell about 85 miles (137 km) beyond. In all this distance, only one road (Hwy. 12) bridges the river. Many side canyons provide additional access to the Escalante and most are as beautiful as the main gorge. The river system covers such a large area that you can find solitude even in spring, the busiest hiking season. The many eastern canyons remain virtually untouched.

The Escalante canyons preserve some of the quiet beauty once found in Glen Canyon, which is now lost under the waters of Lake Powell. Prehistoric Ancestral Puebloan and Fremont peoples have left ruins, petroglyphs, pictographs, and artifacts in many locations. These archaeological resources are protected by federal law; don't collect or disturb them.

Before setting out, visit the rangers at the information center on the west edge of Escalante for the required free permit to backpack overnight in the Escalante Canyons National Monument and to check on the latest trail and road conditions. Restrictions on group size may be in force on some of the more popular trails. You can also obtain topographic maps and literature that show trailheads, mileages, and other information that may be useful. Some of the more popular trailheads have self-registration stations for permits.

The best times for a visit are early March-early June and mid-September-early November. Summertime trips are possible, but be prepared for higher temperatures and greater flash flood danger in narrow canyons. Travel along the Escalante River involves frequent crossings, and there's always water in the main canyon, usually ankle- or knee-deep. Pools in the Narrows between Scorpion Gulch and Stevens Canyon can be up to chest-deep in spots (which you can bypass), but that's the exception. Occasional springs, some tributaries, and the river itself provide drinking water. Always purify the water first; the BLM warns of the unpleasant disease giardiasis, which is caused by the invisible giardia protozoan. Don't forget insect repellent—mosquitoes and deer flies seek out hikers in late spring and summer. Long-sleeved shirts and long pants also discourage biting insects and protect against the brush.

For guided day hikes and hiking shuttles into the Escalante canyons, contact **Utah Canyon Outdoors** (325 W. Main St., Escalante, 435/826-4967, www.utahcanyonoutdoors.com.

ESCALANTE CANYON TRAILHEADS

The many approaches to the area allow all sorts of trips. Besides the road access at Escalante and the Highway 12 bridge, hikers can reach the Escalante River through western side canyons from Hole-in-the-Rock Road or eastern side canyons from Burr Trail Road. The western-canyon trailheads on Hole-in-the-Rock Road can more easily be reached by car, thus facilitating vehicle shuttles. To reach eastern-canyon trailheads, with the exceptions of Deer Creek and the Gulch on Burr Trail Road, you'll need lots of time and, if the road is wet, a 4WD vehicle. Carry water for these more remote canyons; with the exception of Deer Creek, they're usually dry.

ESCALANTE TO HIGHWAY 12 BRIDGE

This first section of canyon offers easy walking and stunning canyon scenery. Tributaries and sandstone caves invite exploration. You'll find good camping areas all along. Usually the river here is only ankle-deep. This 15-mile (24-km) hike begins either by entering Escalante River at the bridge next to the sawmill or going 1 mile (1.6 km) east of town on Highway 12 and turning north past the cemetery (visible from the highway). Almost immediately, the river knifes its way through the massive cliffs of the Escalante Monocline, leaving the broad valley of the upper river behind. Although there is no maintained trail along this stretch of the east-flowing river, it's relatively easy to pick your way along the riverbank.

Death Hollow, which is far prettier than the name suggests, comes into the Escalante from the north after 7.5 miles (12 km). Several good swimming holes carved in rock are a short hike upstream from the Escalante; watch for poison ivy among the greenery. Continue farther up Death Hollow to see more pools, little waterfalls, and outstanding canyon scenery. You can bypass some pools, but some you'll have to swim—bring a little inflatable boat, air mattress, or waterproof bag to ferry packs.

Sand Creek, on the Escalante's north side 4.5 miles (7.2 km) downstream from Death Hollow, is also worth exploring; deep pools begin a short way up from the mouth. After another 0.5 miles (0.8 km) down the Escalante, a natural arch appears high on the canyon wall. Then the Escalante Natural Bridge comes into view about 0.5 miles (0.8 km) farther, just 2 miles (3.2 km) from Highway 12 bridge. In fact, Escalante Natural Bridge makes a good day-hike destination upstream from the highway.

HIGHWAY 12 BRIDGE TO HARRIS WASH

This is where many long-distance trekkers begin their exploration of the Escalante canyons. In this 26.5-mile (43 km) section, the Escalante Canyon offers a varied show: In places the walls close in to make constricted narrows, at other places they step back to form great valleys. Side canyons filled with lush greenery and sparkling streams contrast with dry washes of desert, yet all can be fun to explore. A good hike of 4-6 days begins at the highway bridge, goes down the Escalante to Harris Wash, then up Harris to a trailhead off Hole-in-the-Rock Road (37 miles/60 km total).

From the Highway 12 bridge parking area, a trail leads to the river. Canyon access goes through private property; cross the river at the posted signs to avoid barking dogs at the ranch just downstream. **Phipps Wash** comes in from the south (right side) after 1.5 miles (2.4 km) and several more river crossings. Turn up its wide mouth 0.5 mile (0.8 km) to see Maverick Bridge in a drainage to the right. To reach Phipps Arch, continue another 0.75 mile (1.2 km) up the main wash, turn left into a box canyon, and scramble up the left side (see the 7.5-minute Calf Creek topo map).

Bowington (Boynton) Arch is an attraction of a north side canyon known locally as Deer Creek. Look for this small canyon on the left one mile beyond Phipps Wash and take it one mile past three deep pools, then turn left and go a short way into a tributary canyon.

In 1878, gunfire resolved a quarrel between local ranchers John Boynton and Washington Phipps. Phipps was killed, but both their names live on.

Waters of **Boulder Creek** come rushing into the Escalante from the north in the next major side canyon, 5.75 miles (9.3 km) below the Highway 12 bridge. The creek, along with its Dry Hollow and Deer Creek tributaries, provides good canyon walking; deep areas may require swimming or climbing up on the plateau. (You could also start down Deer Creek from Burr Trail Road, where they meet 6.5 miles (10.5 km) southeast of Boulder at a primitive BLM campground. Starting at the campground, follow Deer Creek 7.5 miles (12 km) to Boulder Creek, then go 3.5 miles (5.6 km) down Boulder Creek to the Escalante.) Deer and Boulder Creeks have water year-round.

High, sheer walls of Navajo sandstone constrict the Escalante River in a narrow channel below Boulder Creek, but the canyon widens again above the **Gulch** tributary, 14 miles (22.5 km) below the highway bridge. Hikers can head up the Gulch on a day hike.

Alternatively, descend the Gulch from Burr Trail Road to join the Escalante Canyon at this point (the Gulch trailhead is 10.8 miles southeast of Boulder). The hike from the road down to the Escalante is 12.5 miles (20.1 km), but there's one difficult spot: A 12-foot waterfall in a section of narrows about halfway down has to be bypassed. When Rudi Lambrechtse, author of *Hiking the Escalante,* tried friction climbing around the falls and the pool at their base, he fell 12 feet and broke his foot. That meant a painful three-day hobble out. Instead of taking the risk, Rudi recommends backtracking about 300 feet from the falls and friction climbing out from a small alcove in the west wall (look for a cairn on the ledge above). Climb up Brigham Tea Bench, walk south, then look for cairns leading back east to the narrows, and descend to the streambed (a rope helps to lower packs in a small chimney section).

Most springs along the Escalante are

difficult to spot. One that's easy to find is in the first south bend after the Gulch; water comes straight out of the rock a few feet above the river. The Escalante Canyon becomes wider as the river lazily meanders along. Hikers can cut off some of the bends by walking in the open desert between canyon walls and riverside willow thickets. A bend cut off by the river itself loops to the north just before **Horse Canyon,** 3 miles (4.8 km) below the Gulch. Along with its tributaries **Death Hollow** and **Wolverine Creek,** Horse Canyon drains the Circle Cliffs to the northeast. Floods in these mostly dry streambeds wash down pieces of black petrified wood. (Vehicles with good clearance can reach the upper sections of all three canyons from a loop road off Burr Trail Road.) Horse and Wolverine Creek Canyons offer good easy-to-moderate hiking, but if you really want a challenge, try Death Hollow (sometimes called "Little Death Hollow" to distinguish it from the larger one near Hell's Backbone Road). Starting from the Escalante River, go about 2 miles (3.2 km) up Horse Canyon and turn right into Death Hollow; rugged scrambling over boulders takes you back into a long section of twisting narrows. Carry water for Upper Horse Canyon and its tributaries; Lower Horse Canyon usually has water.

About 3.5 miles (5.6 km) down the Escalante from Horse Canyon, you enter Glen Canyon NRA and come to Sheffield Bend, a large, grassy field on the right. Only a chimney remains from Sam Sheffield's old homestead. Two grand amphitheaters lie beyond the clearing and up a stiff climb in loose sand. Over the next 5.5 river miles (8.9 km) to Silver Falls Creek, you'll pass long bends, dry side canyons, and a huge slope of sand on the right canyon wall. Don't look for any silver waterfalls in **Silver Falls Creek**—the name comes from streaks of shiny desert varnish on the cliffs. You can approach Upper Silver Falls Creek by a rough road from Burr Trail Road, but a car shuttle between here and any of the trailheads on the west side of the Escalante River would take all day. Most hikers visit this drainage on a day hike from the river. Carry water with you.

When the Hole-in-the-Rock route proved so difficult, pioneers figured there had to be a better way to the San Juan Mission. Their new wagon road descended Harris Wash to the Escalante River, climbed part of Silver Falls Creek, crossed the Circle Cliffs, descended Muley Twist Canyon in the Waterpocket Fold, then followed Hall's Creek to Halls Crossing on the Colorado River. Charles Hall operated a ferry there 1881-1884. Old maps show a jeep road through Harris Wash and Silver Falls Creek Canyons, used before the National Park Service closed off the Glen Canyon NRA section. Harris Wash is just 0.5 mile (0.8 km) downstream and across the Escalante from Silver Falls Creek.

HARRIS WASH

Clear shallow water glides down this gem of a canyon. High cliffs streaked with desert varnish are deeply undercut and support lush hanging gardens. Harris Wash (10.25 miles/16.5 km one-way from trailhead to river) provides a beautiful route to the Escalante River, but it can also be a destination in itself; tributaries and caves invite exploration along the way. The sand and gravel streambed makes for easy walking. Reach the trailhead from Highway 12 by turning south and going 10.8 miles (17.4 km) on Hole-in-the-Rock Road, then turning left to go 6.3 miles (10.1 km) on a dirt road (keep left at the fork near the end). Don't be dismayed by the drab appearance of upper Harris Wash. The canyon and creek appear a few miles downstream.

★ DRY FORK OF COYOTE GULCH

Twenty-six miles (42 km) south on the Hole-in-the-Rock Road is a series of narrow, scenic, and exciting-to-explore slot canyons reached by a moderate day hike. The canyons feed into the Dry Fork of Coyote Gulch, reached from the Dry Fork trailhead. These three enchanting canyons are named

Peek-a-boo, Spooky, and **Brimstone.** Exploring these slot canyons requires basic canyoneering or scrambling skills. From the trailhead parking lot, follow cairns down into the sandy bottom of Dry Fork Coyote Gulch. The slot canyons all enter the gulch from the north; watch for cairns and trails because the openings can be difficult to notice. The slots sometimes contain deep pools of water; choke stones and pour-offs can make access difficult. No loop trail links the three slot canyons; follow each until the canyon becomes too narrow to continue, and then come back out. To make a full circuit of these canyons requires about 3.5 miles (5.6 km) of hiking. Because they are relatively accessible, these canyons draw a crowd. Get an early start and remember to pack your garbage out!

COYOTE GULCH

Coyote Gulch has received more publicity than other areas of the Escalante, and you're more likely to meet other hikers here. Two arches, a natural bridge, graceful sculpturing of the streambed and canyon walls, deep undercuts, and a cascading creek make a visit well worthwhile. The best route in starts where Hole-in-the-Rock Road crosses Hurricane Wash, 34.7 miles (56 km) south of Highway 12. It's 12.5 miles (20.1 km) one-way from the trailhead to the river, and the hike is moderately strenuous. For the first mile you follow the dry, sandy wash without even a hint of being in a canyon. Water doesn't appear for 3 more miles. You'll reach Coyote Gulch, which has water, 5.25 miles (8.4 km) from the trailhead. Another way into Coyote Gulch begins at the Red Well trailhead; it's 31.5 miles (51 km) south on Hole-in-the-Rock Road, then 1.5 miles (2.4 km) east (keep left at the fork). A start from Red Well adds 0.75 mile (1.2 km) more to the hike than the Hurricane Wash route, but it is also less crowded.

In some seasons, Lake Powell comes within 1 mile (1.6 km) of Coyote Gulch, and it occasionally floods the canyon mouth. Coyote can stay flooded for several weeks, depending on the release flow of Glen

Canyon Dam and water volume coming in. The river and lake don't have a pretty meeting place—quicksand and dead trees are found here. Logjams make it difficult to travel in from the lake by boat.

★ Calf Creek Recreation Area

For many people, the hike to **Lower Calf Creek Falls** ($5 permit) is the highlight of their first trip to the Escalante area. It's the dazzling enticement that brings people back for longer and more remote hiking trips. From the trailhead and park just off Highway 12, 15.5 miles (25 km) east of Escalante, the trail winds between high cliffs of Navajo sandstone streaked with desert varnish, where you'll see beaver ponds, Native American ruins and pictographs, and the misty 126-foot-high Lower Calf Creek Falls. A brochure available at the trailhead next to the campground identifies many of the desert and riparian plant species along the way. The round-trip is 5.5 miles (8.9 km) with only a slight gain in elevation; bring water and perhaps lunch. Summer temperatures can soar, but the falls and the crystal-clear pool beneath stay cool. Sheer cliffs block travel farther upstream.

Calf Creek Campground (Mar.-late Oct., $15), near the road, has 13 sites and drinking water.

Paria Canyon and Vermilion Cliffs

The wild and twisting canyons of the Paria River and its tributaries offer a memorable experience for skilled hikers. Silt-laden waters have sculpted the colorful canyon walls, revealing 200 million years of geologic history. *Paria* means "muddy water" in the Paiute language. You enter the 2,000-foot-deep gorge of the Paria in southern Utah, then hike 37 miles (60 km) downstream to Lee's Ferry in Arizona, where the Paria empties into the Colorado River. A handful of shorter but

1: Escalante River; 2: Dry Fork of Coyote Gulch; 3: Lower Calf Creek Falls; 4: biking the Burr Trail Road

rugged day hikes lead to superb scenery and geologic curiosities.

Ancient petroglyphs and campsites show that Southwestern Native Americans traveled the Paria more than 700 years ago. They hunted mule deer and bighorn sheep while using the broad lower end of the canyon to grow corn, beans, and squash. The Dominguez-Escalante Expedition stopped at the mouth of the Paria in 1776, and they were the first nonnatives to see the river. John D. Lee and three companions traveled through the canyon in 1871 to bring a herd of cattle from the Pahreah settlement to Lee's Ferry. After Lee began a Colorado River ferry service in 1872, he and others farmed the lower Paria Canyon. Prospectors came here to search for gold, uranium, and other minerals, but much of the canyon remained unexplored. In the late 1960s, the BLM organized a small expedition whose research led to protection of the canyon as a primitive area. The Arizona Wilderness Act of 1984 designated Paria Canyon a wilderness, along with parts of the Paria Plateau and Vermilion Cliffs. In 2000, Vermilion Cliffs National Monument was created.

The **Paria Contact Station,** (435/644-4628, 8am-4:30pm mid-Mar.-mid-Nov.) is in Utah, 44 miles (71 km) east of Kanab on U.S. 89 near milepost 21. It's on the south side of the highway, just east of the Paria River. Self-serve day-use permits ($5) are required for hiking in Paria Canyon and to visit other sites in Vermilion Cliffs National Monument.

PARIA CANYON

Allow 4-6 days to hike Paria Canyon because of the many river crossings and because you'll want to make side trips up some of the tributary canyons. The hike is considered moderately difficult. Hikers should have enough backpacking experience to be self-sufficient, because help may be days away. Flash floods can race through the canyon, especially July-September. Rangers close the Paria if they think a danger exists. Because the upper end has the narrowest passages (between miles 4.2 and 9.0/6.8 and 14.5 km), rangers require that all hikers start here in order to have up-to-date weather information.

The actual trailhead is 2 miles (3.2 km) south of the contact station on a dirt road near a campground and old homestead site called White House Ruins. The exit trailhead is in Arizona at Lonely Dell Ranch of Lee's Ferry, 44 miles (71 km) southwest of Page via U.S. 89 and U.S. 89A (or 98 miles/158 km southeast of Kanab on U.S. 89A).

Permits to hike the canyon are $5 per person per day. Backpackers should get a permit at the contact station or online (www.blm.gov/programs/recreation/permits-and-passes/lotteries-and-permit-systems/arizona/paria-canyon, reserve in advance), but day hikers can just register and pay the fee at the trailhead. The visitors center and the office both provide weather forecasts and brochures with a map and hiking information. The visitors center always has the weather forecast posted at an outdoor information kiosk.

The hike requires a 150-mile (242-km) round-trip car shuttle. For a list of shuttle services, ask at the **Paria Contact Station** (U.S. 89, 44 miles/71 km east of Kanab, 435/644-4628, 8am-4:30pm mid-Mar.-mid-Nov.) or Kanab BLM Office. Expect to pay about $200 for this service.

All visitors need to take special care to minimize their impact on this beautiful canyon. Check the BLM *Visitor Use Regulations* for the Paria before you go. Regulations include no campfires in the Paria and its tributaries, a pack-in, pack-out policy, and a requirement that latrines be made at least 100 feet away from river and campsite locations. Also, remember to take some plastic bags to carry out toilet paper; the stuff lasts years and years in this desert climate. You don't want to haunt future hikers with TP flowers.

The Paria contact station recommends a maximum group size of 6; regulations specify a 10-person limit. No more than 20 people per day can enter the canyon for overnight trips. The best times to travel along the Paria are about mid-March-June and October-November. May, especially Memorial Day weekend, tends to be crowded. Winter hikers often complain of painfully cold feet. Wear (or bring) shoes suitable for frequent wading. You can get good drinking water from springs along the way (see the BLM hiking brochure for locations); it's best not to use the river water because of possible chemical pollution from farms and ranches upstream. Normally the river is only ankle-deep, but in spring or after rainy spells, it can become waist-deep. During thunderstorms, water levels can rise to more than 20 feet in the Paria Narrows, so heed weather warnings. Quicksand, which is most prevalent after flooding, is more a nuisance than a danger—usually it's just knee-deep. Many hikers carry a walking stick to probe the opaque waters for good crossing places.

WRATHER CANYON ARCH

One of Arizona's largest natural arches is about 1 mile (1.6 km) up this side canyon of the Paria. The massive structure has a 200-foot span. Turn right (southwest) at mile 20.6 on the Paria hike. The mouth of Wrather Canyon and other points along the Paria are unsigned; follow your map.

BUCKSKIN GULCH AND WIRE PASS

Buckskin Gulch is an amazing tributary of the Paria, with convoluted walls reaching hundreds of feet high, although the canyon narrows to as little as four feet in width. In places, the walls block out so much light that it's like walking in a cave. Be very careful to avoid times of flash-flood danger. Hiking this 20-mile-long (32-km-long) gulch can be strenuous, with rough terrain, deep pools of water, and logjams and rock jams that may require the use of ropes. Conditions vary considerably from one year to the next.

Day hikers can get a taste of this incredible canyon country by driving to the Wire Pass trailhead, 8.5 bumpy miles (13.7 km) down BLM Road 700 (also called Rock House Valley Rd.), between mileposts 25 and 26, about 37 miles (60 km) east of Kanab. From the trailhead, a relatively easy trail leads into **Wire Pass,** a narrow side canyon that joins Buckskin Gulch. The 3.5-mile (5.6-km) in-and-out round-trip travels the length of Wire Pass to its confluence with Buckskin Gulch. From here, you can explore this exceptionally narrow canyon or follow Buckskin Gulch to its appointment with Paria Canyon (12.5 miles/20.1 km).

For the full experience of Buckskin Gulch, long-distance hikers can begin at the Buckskin Gulch trailhead, 4.5 miles (7.2 km) south of U.S. 89 off BLM Road 700. From here, it's 16.3 miles (26 km) one-way to Paria Canyon. Hikers can continue down the Paria or turn upstream and hike 6 miles (9.7 km) to exit at the White House trailhead near the contact station. Regulations mandate that you pack your waste out of this area.

Hiking permits ($6 pp per day) are required; backpackers should get an overnight permit ($5) at the contact station, but day hikers can simply register and pay the fee at the trailhead.

COYOTE BUTTES

You've probably seen photos of these dramatic rock formations: towering sand dunes frozen into rock. These much-photographed buttes are located on the Paria Plateau, just south of Wire Pass. Access is strictly controlled, and you can only enter the area with advance reservations and by permit. The number of people allowed into the area is also strictly limited; however, the permit process, fees, and restrictions are exactly the same as for Paria Canyon.

Advance permits ($5-7) are required for day use and are available online and at the **Paria Contact Station** (U.S. 89, 44 miles (71 km) east of Kanab, no phone, call 435/644-1200 for current hours, which vary mid-Mar.-mid-Nov.); no overnight camping is allowed. Group size is limited to no more than six people. Dogs are allowed but require their

own $5 permits. All trash must be packed out, and campfires are not allowed. See the Vermilion Cliffs Monument website (www.blm.gov/programs/recreation/permits-and-passes/lotteries-and-permit-systems/arizona/coyote-buttes) for complete information and to obtain permits.

The BLM has divided the area into Coyote North and Coyote South. The Wave—the most photographed of the buttes—is in Coyote North, so this region is the most popular (and easiest to reach from the Wire Pass trailhead); BLM staff will give you a map and directions when you get your permit. After the trailhead, you're on your own, because the wilderness lacks signs. Permits are more difficult to obtain in spring and fall—the best times to visit—and on weekends. The fragile sandstone can break if climbed on, so it's important to stay on existing hiking routes and wear soft-soled footwear.

MOUNTAIN BIKING

Mountain bikes are allowed on all roads in the monument but not on hiking trails. Mountain bikers are not allowed to travel cross-country off roads or to make their own routes across slickrock; however, there are hundreds of miles of primitive roads in the monument, with dozens of loop routes available for cyclists on multiday trips. In addition to following the scenic **Burr Trail** from Boulder to the Waterpocket Fold in Capitol Reef National Park, cyclists can loop off this route and follow the Circle Cliffs-Wolverine Trail. This 45-mile (72-km) loop traverses the headwaters of several massive canyons as they plunge to meet the Escalante River.

Hole-in-the-Rock Road is mostly a one-way-in, one-way-out affair, but cyclists can follow side roads to hiking trailheads and big vistas over the Escalante canyons. Popular side roads include a 10-mile round-trip road to the area known as Egypt, and the Fifty Mile Bench Road, a 27-mile (43-km) loop from Hole-in-the-Rock Road that explores the terrain above Glen Canyon. Left Hand

Collet Road, a rough jeep trail that a mountain bike can bounce through easily enough, links Hole-in-the-Rock Road with the Smokey Mountain Road system, with links to both Escalante in the north and Big Water in the south.

Other popular routes in the **Big Water area** include the Nipple Butte loop and the steep loop around Smoky Butte and Smoky Hollow, with views over Lake Powell. **Cottonwood Canyon Road,** which runs between U.S. 89 and Cannonville, is another long back road with access to a network of less-traveled trails.

Request more information on mountain biking from the visitors centers. They have handouts and maps and can help cyclists plan backcountry bike adventures. This country is remote and primitive, so cyclists must carry everything they are likely to need. Also, there are no clean water sources in the monument, so cyclists must transport all drinking water or be prepared to purify it.

4WD EXPLORATION

Without a mountain bike or a pair of hiking boots, the best way to explore the backcountry of these monuments is with a 4WD high-clearance vehicle; however, the scale of the landscape, the primitive quality of many of the roads, and the extreme weather conditions common in the desert mean that you shouldn't head into the backcountry unless you are confident in your skills as a mechanic and driver. Choose roads that match your vehicle's capacity and your driving ability and you should be OK. Some roads that appear on maps are slowly going back to nature: Rather than close some roads, park officials are letting the desert reclaim them. Other roads are being closed, so it's best to check on access and road conditions before setting out. Remember that many of the roads in the monument are very slow going. If you've got somewhere to be in a hurry, these corrugated, boulder-dodging roads may not get you there in time. Be sure to take plenty of water—not only for drinking but also for overheated radiators. It's also wise to carry wooden planks or old carpet scraps for help in gaining traction should your wheels become mired in the sand.

RAFTING

Most of the year, shallow water and rocks make boat travel impossible on the Escalante River, but for two or three weeks during spring runoff, which peaks in mid-May-early June, river levels rise high enough to be passable. (In some years there may not be enough water in any season.) Contact the **Escalante Interagency Visitor Center** (755 W. Main St., Escalante, 435/826-5499, 8am-5:30pm daily) for ideas on when to hit the river at its highest. Shallow draft and maneuverability are essential, so inflatable canoes or kayaks work best (also because they are easier to carry out at trip's end or if water levels drop too low for floating). Not recommended are rafts (too wide and bulky) and hard-shelled kayaks and canoes (they get banged up on the many rocks). The usual launch is the Highway 12 bridge; Coyote Gulch—a 13-mile (21-km) hike—is a good spot to get out, as are Crack in the Wall (a 2.75-mile/4.4 km hike on steep sand from the junction of Coyote and Escalante Canyons to the Forty-Mile Ridge trailhead; 4WD vehicle needed; rope required to negotiate the vessel over the canyon rim) and Hole-in-the-Rock (a 600-foot ascent over boulders; rope suggested). You could also arrange for a friend to pick you up by boat from Halls Crossing or Bullfrog Marina. River boaters must obtain a free backcountry permit from either the BLM or the National Park Service.

OUTFITTERS

There aren't many places to shop for gear in this remote area. The most centrally located shops are in the town of Escalante, where you'll find **Utah Canyon Outdoors** (325 W. Main St., Escalante, 435/826-4967, www.utahcanyonoutdoors.com), which stocks books, maps, and some outdoor gear. Right across the street, **Escalante Outfitters** (310 W. Main St., Escalante, 435/826-4266, www.escalanteoutfitters.com) has a little bit of everything, including a small liquor store, and is a good place to pick up a warm jacket or a stylish tank top.

Another shop with a good selection of clothing and gear is in Kanab. **Willow Canyon Outdoor** (263 S. 100 E., Kanab, 435/644-8884 www.willowcanyon.com) also serves good coffee and has an excellent bookshop.

Escalante

Escalante (elev. 5,813 feet) is a natural hub for exploration of the Kaiporowits Plateau and Escalante Canyons national monuments. Even if you don't have the time or the inclination to explore the rugged canyon country that the monument protects, you'll discover incredible scenery just by traveling Highway 12 through Escalante country.

At first glance, Escalante looks like a town that time has passed by. Just fewer than 1,000 people live here, in addition to the resident cows, horses, and chickens that you'll meet just one block off Main Street. Yet this little community is the biggest place for scores of miles around and a center for ranchers and travelers. Escalante has the neatly laid-out streets and trim little houses typical of Mormon settlements.

FOOD

Escalante Outfitters (310 W. Main St., 435/826-4266, www.escalanteoutfitters.com, 8am-9pm daily), runs a little café that's a reliable place to eat in this little town. It serves espresso, sandwiches, handmade pizza ($17-25), and microbrew beer. The smoked trout plate ($14) is a special treat.

Stock up on food for the trail or the road at the **Escalante Mercantile and Natural Grocery** (210 W. Main St., 435/826-4114, 9am-7pm Mon.-Sat., 10am-5pm Sun. Mar.-Oct.). You know you need some fresh fruit by now, and you can also pick up excellent pre-made sandwiches ($8, made by a local baker, who also supplies muffins and scones) and bottled iced tea, juice, or kombucha.

Nemo's Drive Thru (40 E. Main St.,

435/826-4500, 11am-6pm daily, $8-13) is the perfect place to refuel after a long hike. The tiny restaurant doesn't look too impressive from the street, but the food is far better than what you'll find at most small-town burger joints. In addition to regular burgers, they serve veggie burgers, fish and chips, sweet potato fries, and good milk shakes.

As close as you'll get to fine dining in Escalante is the ★ **Circle D Eatery** (485 W. Main St., 435/826-4125, www.escalantecircledeatery.com, 7:30am-9pm Wed.-Mon., 5pm-9pm Tues., $10-24), which offers local open-range beef and a variety of house-smoked meats and cheeses. Steaks are dependably outstanding, as are the smoked brisket and the rainbow trout baked on a bed of peppers and onions.

The only true bar on the entire length of Hwy. 12 (at least according to Utah's arcane liquor laws) is **4th West Pub,** 425 West Main Street, 435/826-4525, 5pm-midnight daily, $8-12). The food is simple—sandwiches, wraps, salads—but good, and you don't need to go through contortions just to get a cocktail.

East of town, **Kiva Koffeehouse** (Hwy. 12, milepost 73.86, 435/826-4550, www.kivakoffeehouse.com, 8:30am-4:30pm Wed.-Mon. Apr.-Oct., $6-12) is worth a stop for a latte or for a simple lunch of delicious Southwestern-style food, much of it organic, and for a look at the view.

ACCOMMODATIONS

Accommodations in Escalante range from simple to luxurious, but add a hefty 13.3 percent room tax to the listed rates.

Escalante and Vicinity

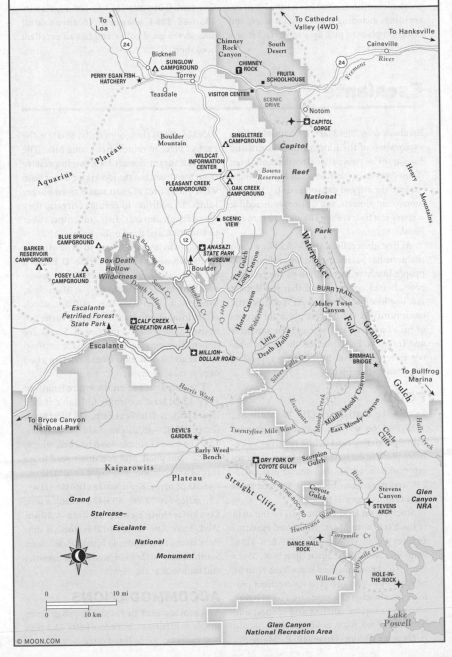

To Loa

24

Bicknell

SUNGLOW CAMPGROUND

Torrey

PERRY EGAN FISH HATCHERY

Teasdale

Chimney Rock Canyon

CHIMNEY ROCK

VISITOR CENTER

South Desert

To Cathedral Valley (4WD)

To Hanksville

Caineville

24

Fremont River

FRUITA SCHOOLHOUSE

SCENIC DRIVE

Notom

CAPITOL GORGE

Boulder Mountain

SINGLETREE CAMPGROUND

WILDCAT INFORMATION CENTER

PLEASANT CREEK CAMPGROUND

OAK CREEK CAMPGROUND

Bowns Reservoir

Capitol

Reef

National

Aquarius

Plateau

SCENIC VIEW

12

ANASAZI STATE PARK MUSEUM

Boulder

The Gulch

Long Canyon

Creek

Wolverine

Park

Waterpocket

BURR TRAIL

Muley Twist Canyon

BLUE SPRUCE CAMPGROUND

BARKER RESERVOIR CAMPGROUND

POSEY LAKE CAMPGROUND

HELL'S BACKBONE RD.

Box-Death Hollow Wilderness

Death Hollow

Sand Cr.

Boulder Cr.

Deer Cr.

Horse Canyon

Escalante Petrified Forest State Park

CALF CREEK RECREATION AREA

Escalante

MILLION-DOLLAR ROAD

Little Death Hollow

Silver Falls Cr.

BRIMHALL BRIDGE

Fold

Grand

To Bullfrog Marina

Gulch

Harris Wash

Escalante

Moody Creek

Middle Moody Canyon

East Moody Canyon

Circle Cliffs

Halls Creek

To Bryce Canyon National Park

DEVIL'S GARDEN

Twentyfive Mile Wash

Early Weed Bench

Kaiparowits

Plateau

DRY FORK OF COYOTE GULCH

HOLE-IN-THE-ROCK RD.

Scorpion Gulch

Straight Cliffs

Coyote Gulch

River

Stevens Canyon

STEVENS ARCH

Glen Canyon NRA

Grand

Staircase–

Escalante

National

Monument

Hurricane Wash

DANCE HALL ROCK

Fortymile Cr.

Fiftymile Cr.

Willow Cr.

HOLE-IN-THE-ROCK

Glen Canyon National Recreation Area

Lake Powell

0   10 mi
0   10 km

© MOON.COM

$50-100

The seven small but comfy log cabins at ★ **Escalante Outfitters** (310 W. Main St., 435/826-4266, www.escalanteoutfitters.com, $55) share men's and women's bathhouses and a common grassy area. A larger ADA-accessible cabin with bath ($150) sleeps four. Tucked behind the store, which also houses a casual pizza and espresso restaurant and a tiny liquor store, these cabins are convenient to all the action the town has to offer and include wireless internet access. If you'd rather sleep in your own tent, camping is permitted on the lawn ($16), which is sheltered from the street. Dogs are permitted for $10 in the cabins and are free if they stay in your tent.

On the west edge of town, the **Circle D Motel** (475 W. Main St., 435/826-4297, www.escalantecircledmotel.com, $80-115) reaches out to bicyclists and hikers with clean, basic guest rooms. Pets are welcome in some guest rooms; a restaurant is part of the complex.

The **Prospector Inn** (380 W. Main St., 435/826-4653, $79) is a large motor lodge near the center of town; there's a restaurant and lounge on the premises. A remodeled motel with a fanciful Old West theme, the **Cowboy Country Inn** (75 S. 100 W., 435/826-4250, www.cowboycountryinn.com, $89-158) is half a block off the highway and offers seven rooms, ranging from a small "bunkhouse" with bunk beds to a two-bedroom suite.

Another pleasant and modern establishment is **Rainbow Country B&B** (586 E. 300 S., 435/826-4567 or 800/252-8824, www.bnbescalante.com, $89-125), with four guest rooms; guests have the use of a hot tub, a pool table, and a TV lounge.

$100-150

A little over a mile (1.6 km) west of town, you can't miss seeing the row of Airstream trailers and classic cars that make up the **Shooting Star RV Resort** (2020 W. Hwy. 12, 435/826-4440, www.shootingstar-rvresort.com, $129-149, two-night minimum). The eight trailers are all in great shape, each with its own take on retro interior design, and each with a small deck, gas grill, and air conditioning. If you're already pulling your own trailer (or packing a tent), the Shooting Star also has **campsites** ($25 tents or RVs). After you get set up in your accommodations, kick back and watch an outdoor movie from a classic car (Tues, Thurs, Sat. after sundown, $20 for a car to sit in).

Right in the center of town but tucked back away from the main drag, guest rooms at **Inn of Escalante** (280 W. Main St., 435/826-4890 or 866/826-4890, www.escalantebnb.com, $150-170) are some of the nicest in the area. The eight purpose-built B&B guest rooms are individually decorated—several have rather bold murals—and are separate from the main house.

A remodeled motel with a fanciful Old West theme, the **Cowboy Country Inn** (75 S. 100 W., 435/826-4250, www.cowboycountryinn.com, $105-165) is half a block off the highway and offers seven rooms, ranging from a small "bunkhouse" with bunk beds to a two-bedroom suite.

Over $150

Head east from Escalante on Highway 12 to the landmark Kiva Koffeehouse, a quirky hilltop restaurant just east of the Boynton Overlook high above the Escalante River, and its beautiful ★ **Kiva Kottage** (Hwy. 12, milepost 73.86, 435/826-4550, www.kivakoffeehouse.com, $200, breakfast included). The two spacious and beautifully decorated guest rooms each include a remarkable view of the surrounding country. With their grand views, fireplaces, and big, deep, jetted bathtubs, these rooms are wonderful places to relax after a day of exploring, and the absence of TVs makes it all the better. The Kiva is just above the spot where the Escalante River crosses Highway 12 and is a good base for hikers. You'll have to drive to Escalante or Boulder for dinner, though the rooms do have microwaves and refrigerators.

The ★ **Slot Canyons Inn B&B** (3680 W. Hwy. 12, 435/826-4901 or 866/889-8375, www.slotcanyonsinn.com, $175-225) is a newer, purpose-built lodging about 5 miles (8

1 SMOOTHIES!

PICNIC TO GO!
SANDWICHES
BLUEBERRI-WAFFLE
FRESH BAKED BREAD
COFFEE BREAKFAST BAR

ESCALANTE MERCANTILE
natural GROCERY

2

OUTFITTERS
CABINS *and*
CAMPGROUND

km) west of Escalante on a dramatically scenic 160-acre ranch. Although the structure has adobe-like features and blends into the rustic environment, the eight guest rooms are very comfortable and modern, some with patios and balconies. A spacious pioneer cabin has also been moved to the property and restored; it sleeps six ($312). There's even North Creek Grill (dinner 6pm-9pmTues.-Sat. May-Oct., pizzas $12-15, reservations recommended) so you don't have to drive into Escalante for your dinner. This is a very lovely place to stay— think of it not so much as a B&B (although breakfast is included in the rates) but as an exclusive small country inn.

In downtown Escalante ★ **Canyons B&B** (120 E. Main St., 435/826-4747, www. canyonsbnb.com, late Mar.-Nov., $165-200) is a modern three-bedroom "bunkhouse" that's been built behind an old farmhouse, which offers its own "lodge" room. There's nothing rustic about the guest rooms; all are attractively decorated and equipped with TV, telephones, and Wi-Fi. Minimum stay requirements may apply.

The newest and most upscale of Escalante's hotels is the **Canyon Country Lodge** (760E Hwy.12, 435/826-4545 or 844/367-3080, https://canyoncountrylodge.com, $199-219), just east of town. Rooms are large and nicely appointed, and an indoor pool and outdoor hot tub await.

If you're traveling with a family or group of friends, consider renting the architecturally striking, solar-heated **La Luz Desert Retreat** (680 W. 600 S., 888/305-4708, www.laluz.net, high season $210 for four people, plus $75 cleaning fee, seasonal two-night minimum stay requirements), in a private setting just south of town. The house, designed in the Usonian tradition of Frank Lloyd Wright, can sleep up to six.

Campgrounds
Escalante Petrified Forest State Park

1: Escalante Mercantile and Natural Grocery; **2:** Escalante Outfitters cabins with shared bathhouses

(435/826-4466, www.stateparks.utah.gov, reservations 800/322-3770, www.reserveamerica. com, year-round, $20 tents, $28 RVs), just northwest of the town of Escalante, is conveniently located and full of attractions of its own, most notably trails passing big chunks of petrified wood. Drinking water and showers are available, as are RV hookups.

In town, you can stay at **Canyons of the Escalante RV Park** (495 W. Main St., 435/826-4959 or 888/241-8785, www. canyonsofescalantervpark.com, Mar.-Nov. 15), which has simple and deluxe cabins ($45-69, the more expensive ones have half baths) and sites for tents ($18) and RVs ($29-39), plus showers and a coin laundry. **Shooting Star RV Resort** (2020 W. Hwy. 12, 435/826-4440, www.shootingstar-rvresort.com) also has spaces for tents and RVs ($35).

A couple miles north of town in a lovely grove of cottonwoods and junipers, ★ **Escalante Yurts** (1605 N. Pine Creek Rd., 435/826-4222 or 844/2009878, $225-325) offers glamping comforts in 450 to 900 square foot yurts (smaller yurts sleep up to four, the larger sleep seven). Each yurt has private bathrooms, high quality furnishings, and a private patio platform. Complimentary continental breakfast is included.

Calf Creek Campground (early Apr.-late Oct., $15) is in a pretty canyon 15.5 miles (25 km) east of Escalante on Highway 12. Lower Calf Creek Falls Trail (5.5 miles/8.9 km round-trip) begins at the campground and follows the creek upstream to the 126-foot-high falls.

INFORMATION AND SERVICES

The **Escalante Interagency Visitor Center** (755 W. Main St., 435/826-5499, 8am-5:30pm daily), on the west edge of town, has an information center for visitors to U.S. Forest Service, BLM, and National Park Service areas around Escalante; this is also one of the best spots for information on Grand Staircase-Escalante. Hikers or bikers headed for overnight trips in the monument system can obtain permits at the information center.

Kazan Memorial Clinic (65 N. Center St., 435/826-4374) offers medical care but is not open on the weekends. The nearest hospital is 70 miles (113 km) west in Panguitch.

GETTING THERE

Escalante is located on Highway 12, 38 miles (61 km) east of Bryce Canyon and 23 miles (37 km) south of Boulder. One caveat: Drive slowly through town; the local police seem to have a refined eye for out-of-towners exceeding the speed limit.

HELL'S BACKBONE

Hell's Backbone Scenic Drive

This scenic 38-mile (61-km) drive climbs high into the pine forests north of Escalante with excellent views of the distant Navajo, Fifty Mile, and Henry Mountains. The highlight, though, is the one-lane **Hell's Backbone Bridge,** which vaults a chasm between precipitous Death Hollow and Sand Creek Canyons. You'll want to stop here for photographs of the swallow-your-gum vistas and to quell your vertigo.

Hell's Backbone Road reaches an elevation of 9,200 feet on the slopes of Roger Peak before descending to a bridge 25 miles (40 km) from town. Mule teams used this narrow ridge, with sheer canyons on either side, as a route to Boulder until the 1930s. At that time, a bridge built by the Civilian Conservation Corps allowed the first vehicles to make the trip.

To reach Hell's Backbone Road from Escalante, turn north onto 300 East and follow the initially paved road out of town; the bridge is about 25 miles (40 km) from town. Alternatively, you can turn onto Hell's Backbone Road, 3 miles (4.8 km) south of Boulder on Highway 12. From this turnoff, the bridge is 13 miles (21 km).

Cars can usually manage the gravel and dirt road when it's dry. Snows and snowmelt, however, block the way until about late May. Check with the Interagency Visitor Center in Escalante for current conditions. Trails and rough dirt roads lead deeper into the backcountry to more vistas and fishing lakes.

Campgrounds

Amid aspens and ponderosa pines, Posey Lake (elevation 8,700 feet) is stocked with rainbow and brook trout. The adjacent **Posey Lake Campground** (www.fs.usda.gov/recarea/dixie, Memorial Day-Labor Day, $11) has drinking water. A hiking trail (2 miles/3.2 km round-trip) begins near space number 14 and climbs 400 feet to an old fire-lookout tower, with good views of the lake and surrounding country. Posey Lake is 14 miles (22.5 km) north of Escalante, and then 2 miles (3.2 km) west on a side road.

Blue Spruce Campground (www.fs.usda.gov/recarea/dixie, $9) is another pretty spot at an elevation of 7,860 feet, but it has only six sites. Anglers can try for pan-size trout in a nearby stream. The campground, surrounded by blue spruce, aspen, and ponderosa pine, has drinking water Memorial Day-Labor Day; go north 19 miles (31 km) from town, then turn left and drive 0.5 mile (0.8 km).

About 200 people live in this farming community at the base of Boulder Mountain. Ranchers began drifting in during the late 1870s, although not with the intent to form a town. By the mid-1890s, Boulder had established itself as a ranching and dairy center. Remote and hemmed in by canyons and mountains, Boulder remained one of the last communities in the country to rely on pack trains for transportation. Motor vehicles couldn't drive in until the 1930s. Today, Boulder is worth a visit to see an excavated Ancestral Puebloan village and the spectacular scenery along the way.

FOOD

The Boulder Mountain Lodge restaurant, ★ **Hell's Backbone Grill** (Hwy. 12, 435/335-7464, http://hellsbackbonegrill.com, 7:30am-2pm and 5pm-9pm daily mid-Mar.-Nov., $17-36, dinner reservations highly recommended) has gained something of a cult following across the West. Run by two American Buddhist women, supplied with vegetables from their own farm, and typically filled with well-heeled guests from Boulder Mountain Lodge, the restaurant has a menu that changes with the seasons, but you can count on finding chipotle-rubbed meat, outstanding meatloaf, tasty posole, and excellent desserts. Breakfast is every bit as good as dinner here.

For simpler but still very good fare, the **Burr Trail Grill** (10 N. Hwy. 12, 435/335-7432, 11:30am-9pm daily, late Mar.-Oct., $12-25) is at the intersection of Highway 12 and Burr Trail Road. The atmospheric dining room, sided with weathered wood planking and filled with whimsical art, Grand Staircase-Escalante visitors, and local families, offers sophisticated soup and sandwiches for lunch, and dinner main courses such as grilled pork loin, steaks, chicken, and trout, all with subtle Southwestern spicing.

Stop by **Magnolia's Street Food**

(460 N. Hwy. 12, 801/643-3510, https://magnoliasstreetfood.com, 9am-4pm Thurs.-Mon. Mar.-Nov., $4-10) for a breakfast burrito or some lunchtime tacos. It's a food truck parked outside the Anasazi State Park Museum.

ACCOMMODATIONS

You wouldn't expect to find one of Utah's nicest places to stay in tiny Boulder, but the ★ **Boulder Mountain Lodge** (Hwy. 12, 435/355-7460 or 800/556-3446, www.boulderutah.com, $140-325), along the highway right in town, offers the kinds of facilities and setting that make this one of the few destination lodgings in the state. The lodge's buildings are grouped around the edge of a private 15-acre pond that serves as an ad hoc wildlife refuge. You can sit on the deck or wander paths along the pond, watching and listening to the amazing variety of birds that make this spot their home. The guest rooms and suites are in handsome and modern Western-style lodges facing the pond; guest rooms are nicely decorated with quality furniture and bedding, and there's a central great room with a fireplace and library and a large outdoor hot tub. One of Utah's best restaurants, **Hell's Backbone Grill** (435/355-7460 or 800/556-3446, 7:30am-2pm and 5pm-9pm daily mid-Mar.-Nov.), is on the premises.

More modest but perfectly acceptable accommodations are available at **Pole's Place** (435/335-7422, www.boulderutah.com/polesplace, spring-fall, $85, no TV or Wi-Fi), across the road from Anasazi State Park. While you're there, drop into the motel's gift shop and chat with the owner about local history.

Cowboy up at the **Boulder Mountain Guest Ranch** (3621 Hells Backbone Rd., 435/355-7480, http://bouldermountainguestranch.com), 7 miles (11.3 km) from Boulder on Hell's Backbone Road. Guests have a choice of tepees with stone flooring and a queen bed or canvas-walled tents ($72-95), simple bunk rooms with shared baths ($85), and queen-bed guest rooms with private baths ($85-120) in the main lodge, or in freestanding cabins that can sleep up to 6 to 8 guests each ($200-245) with full kitchen facilities and private baths. Also in the lodge is the **Sweetwater Kitchen** (open April-Oct., 5:30pm-9:30 Thurs.-Tues., $12-22, reservations recommended), open to guests and nonguests alike. This is a good base for horseback trail rides; right next door is **Hell's Backbone Ranch and Trail** (435/335-7581, www.bouldermountaintrails.com, 1.5-2-hour ride $60-75).

Campgrounds

The best bet for tent campers is **Deer Creek Campground** (year-round, $10), 6.5 miles (10.5 km) from Boulder on Burr Trail Road; bring your own drinking water. During the summer, another alternative is to head north on Highway 12 up Boulder Mountain to a cluster of Fishlake National Forest campgrounds— **Singletree** (www.recreation.gov, $10), **Pleasant Creek** ($10), and **Oak Creek** ($10).

INFORMATION AND SERVICES

A good stop for visitor information is the **Anasazi State Park Museum** (460 N. Hwy. 12, 435/335-7308, http://stateparks.utah.gov, 8am-6pm daily Apr.-Oct., 9am-5pm Mon.-Sat. Nov.-Mar., $5 pp museum admission fee), where there's an info desk for Grand Staircase-Escalante. The two gas stations in Boulder sell groceries and snack food; at **Hills and Hollows Mini-Mart** (on the hill above Hwy. 12, 435/335-7349, hours vary but generally 9am-7pm), you'll find provisions as diverse as soy milk and organic cashews. Every other Friday night during the summer, Hills and Hollows fires up a wood oven to make pizzas and holds an acoustic music jam.

GETTING THERE

Take paved Highway 12 either through the canyon and slickrock country from Escalante or over the Aquarius Plateau from Torrey (near Capitol Reef National Park). Burr Trail Road connects Boulder with Capitol Reef National Park's southern district via the Waterpocket Fold and the Circle Cliffs. A fourth way in is from Escalante on the dirt Hell's Backbone Road, which comes out 3 miles (4.8 km) west of Boulder at Highway 12.

BOULDER MOUNTAIN SCENIC DRIVE

Highway 12 climbs high into forests of ponderosa pine, aspen, and fir on Boulder Mountain between the towns of Boulder and Torrey. Travel in winter is usually possible, although heavy snows can close the road. Viewpoints along the drive offer sweeping panoramas of Escalante Canyon country, the Circle Cliffs, the Waterpocket Fold, and the Henry Mountains. Hikers and anglers can explore the alpine country of Boulder Mountain and seek out the 90 or so trout-filled lakes. The Great Western Trail, which was built with ATVers in mind, runs over Boulder Mountain to the west of the highway. The Dixie National Forest map, available at the Escalante and Teasdale Ranger District Offices, shows the back roads, trails, and lakes.

Campgrounds

The U.S. Forest Service has three developed campgrounds about midway along Boulder Mountain Scenic Drive: **Oak Creek** (18 miles/29 km from Boulder, elev. 8,800 feet, $10), **Pleasant Creek** (19 miles/31 km from Boulder, elev. 8,600 feet, $10), and **Singletree** (24 miles/39 km from Boulder, elev. 8,200 feet, www.recreation. gov, $10)—the largest of the three and the best pick for larger RVs. The season runs about late May-mid-September with water available; the campgrounds may also be open in spring and fall without water. **Lower Bowns Reservoir** (elev. 7,000 feet) has primitive camping (no water, free) and fishing for rainbow and cutthroat trout; turn east and go 5 miles (8 km) on a rough dirt road (not recommended for cars) just south of Pleasant Creek Campground.

Contact the **Teasdale Ranger District Office** (138 S. Main St., Loa, 435/425-3702) for information about camping or recreation on Boulder Mountain.

Capitol Reef National Park

Although **Capitol Reef National Park** (435/425-3791, www.nps.gov/care, $15 per vehicle for travel on scenic drive, $7 cyclists and pedestrians) gets far less attention than the region's other national parks, it is a great place to visit, with excellent hiking and splendid scenery. Wonderfully sculpted rock layers in a rainbow of colors put on a fine show here. You'll find these same rocks throughout much of the Four Corners region, but their artistic variety has no equal outside Capitol Reef National Park. About 70 million years ago, gigantic forces within the earth began to uplift, squeeze, and fold more than a dozen rock formations into the central feature of the park today—the Waterpocket Fold, so named for the many small pools of water trapped by the tilted strata. Erosion has since carved spires, graceful curves, canyons, and arches. The Waterpocket Fold extends 100 miles (161 km) between Thousand Lake Mountain to the north and Lake Powell to the south. (Look for it if you ever fly south from Salt Lake City—we never really grasped its magnitude until we flew over it on the way to Mexico.) The most spectacular cliffs and rock formations of the Waterpocket Fold make up Capitol Reef, located north of Pleasant Creek and curving northwest across the Fremont River toward Thousand Lake Mountain. The reef was named by explorers who found the Waterpocket Fold a barrier to travel and likened it to a reef blocking passage on the ocean. One particular rounded sandstone hill reminded them of the Capitol dome in Washington DC.

Roads and hiking trails in the park provide access to the colorful rock layers and to the plants and wildlife that live here. You'll also see remnants of the area's long human history—petroglyphs and storage bins of the prehistoric Fremont people, a schoolhouse and other structures built by Mormon pioneers, and several small uranium mines from the 20th century. Legends tell of Butch Cassidy and other outlaw members of the Wild Bunch who hid out in these remote canyons in the 1890s.

Even travelers short on time will enjoy a quick look at visitors center exhibits and a drive on Highway 24 through an impressive cross section of Capitol Reef cut by the Fremont River. You can see more of the park on the Scenic Drive, a narrow paved road that heads south from the visitors center. The drive passes beneath spectacular cliffs of the reef and enters Grand Wash and Capitol Gorge Canyons; allow at least 1.5 hours for the 21-mile (34-km) round-trip and any side trips. The fair-weather Notom-Bullfrog Road (about half paved, with paved segments at both north and south ends) heads south along the other side of the reef for almost 70 miles (113 km), offering fine views of the Waterpocket Fold. Burr Trail Road (dirt inside the park) in the south actually climbs over the fold in a steep set of switchbacks, connecting Notom Road with Boulder. Only drivers with high-clearance vehicles can explore Cathedral Valley in the park's northern district. All of these roads provide access to viewpoints and hiking trails.

VISITORS CENTER

At the **visitors center** (Hwy. 24, 8am-6pm daily mid-May-Sept., 8am-4:30pm daily Oct.-May), start with the 15-minute film that introduces Capitol Reef's natural wonders and history. Rock samples and diagrams illustrate the park's geologic formations, and photos identify local plants and birds. Prehistoric Fremont artifacts on display include petroglyph replicas, sheepskin moccasins, pottery, basketry, stone knives, spear and arrow points, and bone jewelry. Other historical exhibits outline exploration and early Mormon settlement.

Hikers can pick up a map of trails that are

Capitol Reef National Park

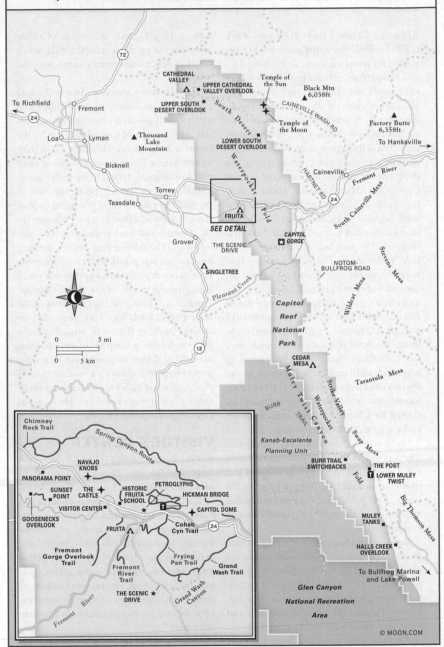

To Richfield

72

CATHEDRAL
VALLEY

Fremont

24

Loa

Lyman

Thousand
Lake
Mountain

Bicknell

Torrey

Teasdale

Grover

FRUITA

SEE DETAIL

Singletree

UPPER CATHEDRAL
VALLEY OVERLOOK

UPPER SOUTH
DESERT OVERLOOK

LOWER SOUTH
DESERT OVERLOOK

South Desert

Waterpocket Fold

THE SCENIC
DRIVE

Temple of
the Sun

Temple of
the Moon

Black Mtn
6,038ft

CAINEVILLE WASH RD

Caineville

HARTNET RD

24

Factory Butte
6,358ft

To Hanksville

Fremont River

South Caineville Mesa

CAPITOL
GORGE

NOTOM-
BULLFROG ROAD

Stevens Mesa

Pleasant Creek

Capitol
Reef
National
Park

Wildcat Mesa

CEDAR
MESA

Muley Twist Canyon

Waterpocket

Strike Valley

Tarantula Mesa

Swap Mesa

0   5 mi

0   5 km

12

BURR

BURR TRAIL

THE POST

BURR TRAIL
SWITCHBACKS

LOWER MULEY
TWIST

MULEY
TANKS

HALLS CREEK
OVERLOOK

Big Thomson Mesa

Kanab-Escalante
Planning Unit

Fold

To Bullfrog Marina
and Lake Powell

Glen Canyon

National Recreation

Area

© MOON.COM

Detail

Chimney
Rock Trail

Spring Canyon Route

NAVAJO
KNOBS

PANORAMA POINT

SUNSET
POINT

THE
CASTLE

HISTORIC
FRUITA
SCHOOL

PETROGLYPHS

HICKMAN BRIDGE

VISITOR CENTER

GOOSENECKS
OVERLOOK

FRUITA

CAPITOL DOME

Cohab
Cyn Trail

24

Fremont
Gorge Overlook
Trail

Fremont
River
Trail

THE SCENIC
DRIVE

Frying
Pan Trail

Grand
Wash Trail

Grand Wash Canyon

Fremont River

near the visitors center and of longer routes in the northern and southern areas of the park; naturalists will want the checklists of plants, birds, mammals, and other wildlife, while history buffs can learn more about the area's settlement and the founding of the park. Rangers offer talks, campfire programs, and other special events Easter-October; the bulletin board outside the visitors center lists what's going on. The visitors center is on Highway 24 at the turnoff for Fruita Campground and the Scenic Drive.

SIGHTS ALONG HIGHWAY 24

From the west, Highway 24 drops from the broad mountain valley near Torrey onto Sulphur Creek, with dramatic rock formations soaring into the horizon. A huge amphitheater of stone rings the basin, with formations such as Twin Rocks, Chimney Rock, and the Castle glowing in deep red and yellow tones. Ahead, the canyon narrows as the Fremont River slips between the cliffs to carve its chasm through Waterpocket Fold.

Panorama Point

Take in the incredible view from Panorama Point, 2.5 miles (4 km) west of the visitors center, on the south side of the highway. Follow signs south for 0.15 mile (0.24 km) to Panorama Point and views of Capitol Reef, the distant Henry Mountains to the east, and looming Boulder Mountain to the west. The large black basalt boulders were swept down from Boulder Mountain to the reef as part of giant debris flows between 8,000 and 200,000 years ago.

Goosenecks Overlook

On a gravel road 1 mile (1.6 km) south of Panorama Point are the Goosenecks of Sulphur Creek. A short trail leads to Goosenecks Overlook on the rim (elev. 6,400 feet) for dizzying views of the creek below. Canyon walls display shades of yellow, green, brown, and red. Another easy trail leads 0.3 mile (0.5 km) to **Sunset Point** and

panoramic views of the Capitol Reef cliffs and the distant Henry Mountains.

Historic Fruita School

Remnants of the pioneer community of Fruita stretch along the narrow Fremont River Canyon. The Fruita Schoolhouse is just east of the visitors center on the north side of Highway 24. Early settlers completed this one-room log structure, housing grades one through eight, in 1896. Mormon church meetings, dances, town meetings, elections, and other community gatherings took place here. A lack of students caused the school to close in 1941. Although the schoolhouse is locked, you can peer inside the windows and take photos.

Fremont Petroglyphs

Farther down the canyon, 1.2 miles (1.9 km) east of the visitors center on the north side of the highway are several panels of Fremont petroglyphs (watch for road signs and a parking area). Several mountain sheep and human figures with headdresses decorate the cliff. You can see more petroglyphs by walking to the left and right along the cliff face. Stay on the trail, and do not climb the talus slope.

Behunin Cabin

Behunin Cabin is 6.2 miles (10 km) east of the visitors center on the south side Highway 24. Elijah Cutlar Behunin used blocks of sandstone to build this cabin in about 1882. For several years, Behunin, his wife, and 11 of their 13 children shared this sturdy but quite small cabin (the kids slept outside). He moved on, though, when floods made life too difficult. A window allows a look inside the dirt-floored structure, but no furnishings remain.

THE SCENIC DRIVE

Turn south from Highway 24 at the visitors center to experience some of the reef's best scenery and to learn more about its geology. A quick tour of this 21-mile (34-km) out-and-back trip requires about 1.5 hours, but several hiking trails may tempt you to extend your stay. It's worth picking up a brochure at

The Orchards of Capitol Reef

Capitol Reef was one of the last places in the West to be seen by immigrant settlers. The first reports came in 1866 from a detachment of Mormon militia pursuing a group of Utes. In 1872, Professor Almon H. Thompson of the Powell Expedition led the first scientific exploration in the fold country and named several park features along the group's Pleasant Creek route. Mormons, expanding their network of settlements, arrived in the upper Fremont Valley in the late 1870s and spread downriver to Hanksville. Junction (renamed Fruita in 1902) and nearby Pleasant Creek (Sleeping Rainbow and Floral Ranch) were settled around 1880.

Floods, isolation, and transport difficulties forced many families to move on, especially downstream from Capitol Reef. Irrigation and hard work paid off with prosperous fruit orchards and the sobriquet "the Eden of Wayne County." The aptly named Fruita averaged about 10 families who grew alfalfa, sorghum (for syrup), vegetables, and a wide variety of fruit. Getting the produce to market required long and difficult journeys by wagon. The region remained one of the most isolated in Utah until after World War II.

Although Fruita's citizens have departed, the National Park Service still maintains the old orchards. They are lovely in late April, when the trees are in bloom beneath the towering canyon walls. Visitors are welcome to pick and carry away the cherries, apricots, peaches, pears, and apples during harvest seasons. Harvests begin in late June or early July and end in October. You'll be charged about the same as in commercial pick-your-own orchards.

the visitors center for descriptions of geology along the road. The Scenic Drive is paved, although side roads have gravel surfaces. Note that drivers must pay the $5 park entrance fee to travel this road.

Fruita

In the Fruita Historic District, you'll first pass orchards and several of Fruita's buildings. A **blacksmith shop** (0.7 mile/1.1 km from the visitors center, on the right) displays tools, harnesses, farm machinery, and Fruita's first tractor. The tractor didn't arrive until 1940, long after the rest of the country had modernized. In a recording, a rancher tells about living and working in Fruita. The nearby orchards and fields are still maintained using old-time farming techniques.

Ripple Rock Nature Center, just shy of 1 mile (1.6 km) south of the visitors center, has activities and exhibits for kids, many centering on pioneer life. Kids can also earn certification as junior rangers and junior geologists.

The **Gifford Farmhouse,** 1 mile (1.6 km)

south on the Scenic Drive, is typical of rural Utah farmhouses of the early 1900s. Cultural demonstrations and handmade baked goods (pie!) and gifts are available. A picnic area is just beyond; with fruit trees and grass, this is a pretty spot for lunch. A short trail crosses orchards and the Fremont River to the **Historic Fruita School.**

Grand Wash

The Scenic Drive leaves the Fremont River valley and climbs up a desert slope, with the rock walls of the Waterpocket Fold rising to the east. Turn east to explore Grand Wash, a dry channel etched through the sandstone. A dirt road follows the twisting gulch 1 mile (1.6 km), with sheer rock walls rising along the sandy streambed. At the road's end, an easy hiking trail follows the wash 2.5 miles (4 km) to its mouth along Highway 24.

Back on the paved Scenic Drive, continue south past Slickrock Divide, to where the rock lining the reef deepens into a ruby red and forms odd columns and spires that resemble statuary. Called the **Egyptian Temple,** this is one of the most striking and colorful areas along the road.

1: Fremont petroglyphs; **2:** Fruita orchards

Capitol Gorge

Capitol Gorge is at the end of the Scenic Drive, 10.7 miles (17.2 km) from the visitors center. Capitol Gorge is a dry canyon through Capitol Reef, much like Grand Wash. Believe it or not, narrow, twisting Capitol Gorge was the route of the main state highway through south-central Utah for 80 years. Mormon pioneers laboriously cleared a path so wagons could go through, a task they repeated every time flash floods rolled in a new set of boulders. Cars bounced their way down the canyon until 1962, when Highway 24 opened, but few traces of the old road remain today. Walking is easy along the gravel riverbed, but don't enter if storms threaten. An easy 1-mile (1.6 km) saunter down the gorge will take day hikers past petroglyphs and a "register" rock where pioneers carved their names.

Pleasant Creek Road

The Scenic Drive curves east toward Capitol Gorge and onto Pleasant Creek Road (turn right 8.3 miles/13.3 km from the visitors center), which continues south below the face of the reef. After 3 miles (4.8 km), the sometimes-rough dirt road passes Sleeping Rainbow-Floral Ranch (closed to the public) and ends at Pleasant Creek. A rugged 4WD road—South Draw Road—continues on the other side but is much too rough for cars. Floral Ranch dates back to the early years of settlement at Capitol Reef. In 1939 it became the Sleeping Rainbow Guest Ranch, from the translation of the Native American name for Waterpocket Fold. Now the ranch belongs to the park and is used as a field research station by students and faculty of Utah Valley University. Pleasant Creek's perennial waters begin high on Boulder Mountain to the west and cut a scenic canyon completely through Capitol Reef. Hikers can head downstream through the 3-mile-long (4.8-km-long) canyon and then return the way they went in, or they can continue another 3 miles (4.8 km) cross-country to Notom Road.

NORTH DISTRICT

Only the most adventurous travelers enter the remote canyons and desert country of the park's northern district. The few roads cannot be negotiated by 4WD vehicles, let alone ordinary cars, in wet weather. In good weather, high-clearance vehicles (good clearance is more important than four-wheel drive) can enter the region from the east, north, and west. The roads lead through stately sandstone monoliths of Cathedral Valley, volcanic remnants, badlands country, many low mesas, and vast sand flats. Foot travel allows closer inspection of these features or lengthy excursions into the canyons of Polk, Deep, and Spring Creeks, which cut deeply into the flanks of Thousand Lake Mountain.

Mountain bikers enjoy these challenging roads as well, but they must stay on established roads. Much of the north district is also good for horseback riding.

The district's two main roads—Hartnett Road and Cathedral Road (aka Caineville Wash Rd.)—combine with a short stretch of Highway 24 to form a loop, with a campground at their junction. **Cathedral Valley Campground's** five sites provide a place to stop for the night; rangers won't permit car camping elsewhere in the district. The campground is on the 4WD Cathedral Valley loop road about 36 miles (58 km) from the visitors center (from the park entrance, head 12 miles/19.3 km east on Highway 24 to milepost 91, turn north and ford the Fremont River, and then follow Hartnett Road about 24 miles/39 km to the campground); check on road conditions at the visitors center before heading out. The **Upper Cathedral Valley Trail,** just below the campground, is a 1-mile (1.6 km) walk offering excellent views of the Cathedrals. Backcountry hikers must have a permit and camp at least 0.5 mile (0.8 km) from the nearest road.

1: Chimney Rock; 2: North District; 3: Grand Wash

SOUTH DISTRICT
Notom-Bullfrog Road

Capitol Reef is only a small part of the Waterpocket Fold. By taking the Notom-Bullfrog Road, you'll see nearly 80 miles (129 km) of the fold's eastern side. This route crosses some of the younger geologic layers, such as those of the Morrison Formation, which form colorful hills. In other places, eroded layers of the Waterpocket Fold jut up at 70-degree angles. The Henry Mountains to the east and the many canyons on both sides of the road add to the memorable panoramas. The northernmost 10 miles (16 km) of the road has been paved, and about 25 miles (40 km) are paved on the southern end near Bullfrog, a settlement on the shores of Lake Powell. The rest of the road is dirt and gravel, and it can get pretty washboarded and bumpy. Most cars should have no trouble negotiating this road in good weather. Keep an eye on the weather before setting out, though; the dirt-and-gravel surface is usually OK for cars when dry but can be dangerous for any vehicle when wet. Sandy spots and washouts may present a problem for low-clearance vehicles; contact the visitors center to check current conditions. Have a full gas tank and carry extra water and food; no services are available between Highway 24 and Bullfrog Marina. Purchase a small guide to this area at the visitors center. Features and mileage along the drive from north to south include the following:

- **Mile 0.0:** The turnoff from Highway 24 is 9.2 miles (14.8 km) east of the visitors center and 30.2 miles (47 km) west of Hanksville (another turnoff from Highway 24 is 3 miles/4.8 km east).

- **Mile 4.1:** Notom Ranch is to the west; once a small town, Notom is now a private ranch.

- **Mile 8.1:** Burrow Wash; experienced hikers can explore the slot canyon upstream. A 2.5-mile (4-km) hike up the sandy wash leads to narrow slots.

- **Mile 9.3:** Cottonwood Wash; another

2.5-mile (4-km) trek along the wash to a slot canyon hike.

- **Mile 10.4:** Five Mile Wash; yet another sandy wash. Pavement ends.

- **Mile 13.3:** Sheets Gulch; a slot canyon is upstream here; the trail goes for 6.7 miles (10.8 km) and is sometimes done as an overnight (permit required).

- **Mile 14.4:** Oak Creek crossing.

- **Mile 20.0:** Entering Capitol Reef National Park; a small box has information sheets.

- **Mile 22.3:** Cedar Mesa Campground is to the west; the small five-site campground is surrounded by junipers and has fine views of the Waterpocket Fold and the Henry Mountains. Free sites have tables and grills; there's a pit toilet but no drinking water. Red Canyon Trail (5.6 miles/9 km roundtrip) begins here and heads west into a box canyon in the Waterpocket Fold.

- **Mile 26.0:** Bitter Creek Divide; streams to the north flow to the Fremont River; Halls Creek on the south side runs through Strike Valley to Lake Powell, 40 miles (64 km) away.

- **Mile 34.1:** Burr Trail Road Junction; turn west up the steep switchbacks to ascend the Waterpocket Fold and continue to Boulder and Highway 12 (36 miles/58 km). Burr Trail is the only road that actually crosses the top of the fold, and it's one of the most scenic in the park. Driving conditions are similar to the Notom-Bullfrog Road—OK for cars when dry. Pavement begins at the park boundary and continues to Boulder. Although paved, the Burr Trail still must be driven slowly because of its curves and potholes. The section of road through Long Canyon has especially pretty scenery.

- **Mile 36.0:** Surprise Canyon trailhead; the 2-mile (3.2-km) roundtrip hike into this narrow, usually shaded canyon takes 1-2 hours. This is your best bet for a shorter hike in this area of the park.

- **Mile 36.6:** Post Corral; a small trading

post here once served sheepherders and some cattle ranchers, but today this spot is just a reference point. Park here to hike to Headquarters Canyon (3.2 miles/5.1 km round-trip). A trailhead for Lower Muley Twist Canyon via Halls Creek is at the end of a 0.5-mile-long (0.8-km-long) road to the south.

- **Mile 37.5:** Leaving Capitol Reef National Park. Much of the road between here and Glen Canyon National Recreation Area has been paved.

- **Mile 45.5:** Road junction; turn right (south) to continue to Bullfrog Marina (25 miles/40 km) or go straight (east) for Starr Springs Campground (23 miles/37 km) in the Henry Mountains.

- **Mile 46.4:** The road to the right (west) goes to Halls Creek Overlook. This turn-off is poorly signed and easy to miss; look for it 0.9 mile (1.4 km) south of the previous junction.

- **Mile 49.0:** Colorful clay hills of deep red, cream, and gray rise beside the road. This clay turns to goo when wet, providing all the traction of axle grease.

- **Mile 54.0:** Beautiful panorama of countless mesas, mountains, and canyons; Lake Powell and Navajo Mountain can be seen to the south.

- **Mile 65.3:** Junction with paved Highway 276; turn left (north) for Hanksville (59 miles/95 km) or right (south) to Bullfrog Marina (5.2 miles/8.4 km).

- **Mile 70.5:** End at Bullfrog Marina in Glen Canyon National Recreation Area.

Lower Muley Twist Canyon

"So winding that it would twist a mule pulling a wagon," said an early visitor. This canyon has some of the best hiking in the southern district of the park. In the 1880s, Mormon pioneers used the canyon as part of a wagon route between Escalante and new settlements in southeastern Utah, replacing the even more difficult Hole-in-the-Rock route.

Unlike most canyons of the Waterpocket Fold, Muley Twist runs lengthwise along the crest for about 18 miles before finally turning east and leaving the fold. Hikers starting from Burr Trail Road can easily follow the twisting bends down to Halls Creek, 12 miles (19.3 km) away. Two trailheads and the Halls Creek route allow a variety of trips.

Start from Burr Trail Road near the top of the switchbacks (2.2 miles/3.5 km west of Notom-Bullfrog Rd.) and hike down the dry gravel streambed. After 4 miles (6.4 km), you have the option of returning the same way, taking the Cut Off route east 2.5 miles (4 km) to the Post Corral trailhead (off Notom-Bullfrog Rd.), or continuing 8 miles (12.9 km) down Lower Muley Twist Canyon to its end at Halls Creek. On reaching Halls Creek, turn left (north) and travel 5 miles (8 km) up the creek bed or the old jeep road beside it to the Post. This section of creek is in an open dry valley. With a car shuttle, the Post would be the end of a good two-day, 17-mile (27-km) hike, or you could loop back to Lower Muley Twist Canyon via the Cut Off route and hike back to Burr Trail Road for a 23.5-mile (38-km) trip. It's a good idea to check the weather beforehand and avoid the canyon if storms threaten.

Cream-colored sandstone cliffs lie atop the red Kayenta and Wingate Formations. Impressively deep undercuts have been carved into the lower canyon. Spring and fall offer the best conditions; summer temperatures can exceed 100°F. Elevations range from 5,640 feet at Burr Trail Road to 4,540 feet at the confluence with Halls Creek and 4,894 feet at the Post.

An information sheet is available at the visitors center, and the trailheads have a small map and route details. Topographic maps of Wagon Box Mesa, Mount Pennell, and Hall Mesa, and the 1:100,000-scale Escalante and Hite Crossing maps are sold at the visitors center. You'll also find this hike described in David Day's *Utah's Favorite Hiking Trails* and in the small spiral-bound *Explore Capitol Reef Trails* by the Capitol Reef Natural History Association, available at the visitors center. Carry all the water you'll need for the trip because natural sources are often dry or polluted.

Upper Muley Twist Canyon

This part of the canyon has plenty of scenery. Large and small natural arches along the way add to its beauty. Upper Muley Twist Road turns north off Burr Trail Road about 1 mile (1.6 km) west from the top of a set of switchbacks. Cars can usually go in 0.5 mile (0.8 km) to a trailhead parking area; high-clearance 4WD vehicles can head another 3 miles (4.8 km) up a wash to the end of the primitive road. Look for natural arches on the left along this last section. **Strike Valley Overlook Trail** (0.75 mile/1.2 km round-trip) begins at the end of the road and leads to a magnificent panorama of the Waterpocket Fold and beyond. Return to the canyon, where you can hike as far as 6.5 miles (10.5 km), to the head of Upper Muley Twist Canyon.

Two large arches are a short hike upstream; Saddle Arch is 1.7 miles (2.7 km) away. The **Rim Route** begins across from Saddle Arch, climbs the canyon wall, follows the rim (offering good views of Strike Valley and the Henry Mountains), and descends back into the canyon at a point just above the narrows, 4.75 miles (7.6 km) from the end of the road (the Rim Route is most easily followed in this direction). Proceed up-canyon to see several more arches. A narrow section of canyon beginning about 4 miles (6.4 km) from the end of the road must be bypassed to continue; look for rock cairns showing the way around to the right. Continuing up the canyon past the Rim Route sign will take you to several small drainages marking the upper end of Muley Twist Canyon. Climb a high tree-covered point on the west rim for great views; experienced hikers with a map can follow the rim back to Upper Muley Twist Road (no trail or markers on this route). Bring all the water you'll need; there are no reliable sources in Upper Muley Twist Canyon.

HIKING

Fifteen-day hike trails begin within a short drive of the visitors center. Of these, Grand Wash, Capitol Gorge, Sunset Point, and Goosenecks are easy. The others involve moderately strenuous climbs and travel over irregular slickrock. Signs and rock cairns mark the way, but it's all too easy to wander off if you don't pay attention to the route.

Although most hiking trails can easily be done in a day, backpackers and mountain hikers might want to try longer trips in Chimney Rock and Spring Canyons in the north or Muley Twist Canyon and Halls Creek in the south. Obtain the required backcountry permit (free) from a ranger and camp at least 0.5 mile (0.8 km) from the nearest maintained road or trail. Cairned routes like Chimney Rock Canyon, Muley Twist Canyon, and Halls Creek don't count as trails but are backcountry routes. Bring a stove for cooking; backcountry users are not permitted to build fires. Avoid camping or parking in washes at any time—torrents of mud and boulders can carry away everything.

Highway 24

Stop by the visitors center to pick up a map showing hiking trails and trail descriptions. These trailheads are along the main highway through the park and along the Fremont River. Note that the Grand Wash Trail cuts west through the reef to the Scenic Drive.

CHIMNEY ROCK TRAIL

The trailhead is 3 miles (4.8 km) west of the visitors center on the north side of the highway. Towering 660 feet above the highway, Chimney Rock is a fluted spire of dark red rock (the Moenkopi Formation) capped by a block of hard sandstone (Shinarump Member of the Chinle Formation). A 3.5-mile (5.6-km) loop trail ascends 540 vertical feet from the parking lot (elev. 6,100 feet) to a ridge overlooking Chimney Rock; allow 2.5 hours (4 km). Panoramic views take in the face of Capitol Reef. Petrified wood along the trail has been eroded from the Chinle Formation, the same rock layer found in Petrified Forest National Park in Arizona. It is illegal to take any of the petrified wood.

SPRING CANYON ROUTE

This moderately difficult hike begins at the top of the Chimney Rock Trail. The wonderfully eroded forms of Navajo sandstone present a continually changing exhibition. The riverbed is normally dry; allow about six hours for the 10-mile (16 km, one-way) trip from the Chimney Rock parking area to the Fremont River and Highway 24. (Some maps show all or part of this as Chimney Rock Canyon.) Check with rangers for the weather forecast before setting off because flash floods can be dangerous, and the Fremont River, which you must wade across, can rise quite high. Normally, the river runs less than knee-deep to Highway 24, 3.7 miles (6 km) east of the visitors center. With luck you'll have a car waiting for you. Summer hikers can beat the heat with a crack-of-dawn departure. Carry water; this section of canyon lacks a reliable source.

From the Chimney Rock parking area, hike Chimney Rock Trail to the top of the ridge and follow the signs for Chimney Rock Canyon. Enter the unnamed lead-in canyon and follow it downstream. A sign marks Chimney Rock Canyon, which is 2.5 miles (4 km) from the start. From this point, it's an additional 6.5 miles (10.5 km) downstream to reach the Fremont River. A section of narrows requires some rock-scrambling (bring a cord to lower backpacks), or the area can be bypassed on a narrow trail to the left above the narrows. Farther down, a natural arch high on the left marks the halfway point.

Upper Chimney Rock Canyon could be explored on an overnight trip. A spring (purify before drinking) is located in an alcove on the right side, about 1 mile (1.6 km) up Chimney Rock Canyon from the lead-in canyon. Wildlife uses this water source, so camp at least 0.25 mile (0.4 km) away. Chimney Rock Canyon, the longest in the park, begins high

on the slopes of Thousand Lake Mountain and descends nearly 15 miles (24 km) southeast to join the Fremont River.

SULPHUR CREEK ROUTE

This moderately difficult hike begins by following a wash across the highway from the Chimney Rock parking area, descending to Sulphur Creek, then heads down the narrow canyon to the visitors center. The trip is about 5.5 miles (8.9 km) one-way and takes 3-5 hours. Warm weather is the best time because you'll be wading in the normally shallow creek. Three small waterfalls can be bypassed fairly easily; two falls are just below the goosenecks, and the third is about 0.5 mile (0.8 km) before coming out at the visitors center. Carry water with you. The creek's name may be a mistake, because there's no sulfur along it; perhaps outcrops of yellow limonite caused the confusion. You can make an all-day 8-mile (12.9-km) hike in Sulphur Creek by starting where it crosses the highway between mileposts 72 and 73, 5 miles (8 km) west of the visitors center.

HICKMAN NATURAL BRIDGE TRAIL

The trailhead is 2 miles (3.2 km) east of the visitors center on the north side of the highway. The graceful Hickman Natural Bridge spans 133 feet across a small streambed. Numbered stops along the self-guided trail correspond to descriptions in a pamphlet available at the trailhead or visitors center. Starting from the parking area (elev. 5,320 feet), the trail follows the Fremont River's green banks a short distance before gaining 380 feet in the climb to the bridge. The last section of trail follows a dry wash shaded by cottonwood, juniper, and piñon pine trees. You'll pass under the bridge (eroded from the Kayenta Formation) at trail's end. Capitol Dome and other sculptured features of the Navajo sandstone surround the site. The 2 (3.2-km) round-trip hike takes about 90 minutes. Joseph Hickman served as principal of Wayne County High School and later in the state legislature during the 1920s; he and another local man, Ephraim Pectol, led efforts to promote Capitol Reef.

RIM OVERLOOK AND NAVAJO KNOBS

A splendid overlook 1,000 feet above Fruita beckons hikers up the Rim Overlook Trail. Take the Hickman Natural Bridge Trail 0.25 mile (0.4 km) from the parking area, then turn right and go 2 miles (3.2 km) at the signed fork. Allow 3.5 hours from the fork for this hike. Panoramic views take in the Fremont River valley below, the great cliffs of Capitol Reef above, the Henry Mountains to the southeast, and Boulder Mountain to the southwest.

Continue another 2.2 miles (3.5 km, and more than 500 feet higher) from the Rim Overlook to reach Navajo Knobs. Rock cairns lead the way over slickrock along the rim of the Waterpocket Fold. A magnificent panorama at trail's end takes in much of southeastern Utah.

COHAB CANYON AND FRYING PAN TRAILS

Park at the Hickman Natural Bridge trailhead, then walk across the highway bridge. This trail climbs Capitol Reef for fine views in all directions and a close look at the swirling lines in the Navajo sandstone. After 0.75 mile (1.2 km) and a 400-foot climb, you'll reach a trail fork: Keep right and go 1 mile (1.6 km) to stay on Cohab Canyon Trail and descend to Fruita Campground, or turn left onto Frying Pan Trail to Cassidy Arch (3.5 miles/5.6 km away) and Grand Wash (4 miles/6.4 km away). The trail from Cassidy Arch to Grand Wash is steep. All of these interconnecting trails offer many hiking possibilities, especially if you can arrange a car shuttle. For example, you could start up Cohab Canyon Trail from Highway 24, cross over the reef on Frying Pan Trail, make a side trip to Cassidy Arch, descend Cassidy Arch Trail to Grand Wash, walk down Grand Wash to Highway 24, then

walk (or car shuttle) 2.7 miles (4.3 km) along the highway back to the start (10.5 miles/16.9 km total).

Named for the polygamists (cohabitationists) who hid out here in the 1880s, Cohab is a pretty little canyon in the Wingate sandstone overlooking the campground. Mormon polygamists supposedly used the canyon to escape federal marshals during the 1880s. Hiking the Frying Pan Trail involves an additional 600 feet of climbing from either Cohab Canyon or Cassidy Arch Trail. Once atop Capitol Reef, the trail follows the gently rolling slickrock terrain.

GRAND WASH

The trailhead is 4.7 miles (7.6 km) east of the visitors center on the south side of the highway. One of only five canyons cutting completely through the reef, Grand Wash offers easy hiking and great scenery. There's no trail—just follow the dry gravel riverbed. Flash floods can occur during storms. Canyon walls of Navajo sandstone rise 800 feet above the floor and close in to as little as 20 feet in width. The Cassidy Arch trailhead is 2 miles away, and parking for Grand Wash from the Scenic Drive is 0.25 mile (0.4 km) farther.

The Scenic Drive

These hikes begin from trailheads along the Scenic Drive that turns south from the visitors center. You must pay the $5 park entrance fee to travel the Scenic Drive.

FREMONT GORGE OVERLOOK TRAIL

From the start at the Fruita blacksmith shop, the trail climbs a short distance, then crosses a lovely native prairie on Johnson Mesa and climbs steeply to the overlook about 1,000 feet above the Fremont River. The overlook is not a place for the acrophobe—even people who aren't ordinarily afraid of heights might find it a little daunting.

1: Hickman Natural Bridge; 2: Grand Wash; 3: Cassidy Arch; 4: Capitol Gorge

COHAB CANYON TRAIL

The Cohab Canyon trailhead is across the road from the Fruita Campground, 1.3 miles (2.1 km) from the visitors center. The trail follows steep switchbacks during the first 0.25 mile (0.4 km), then gentler grades to the top, 400 feet higher and 1 mile from the campground. You can take a short trail to viewpoints or continue 0.75 mile (1.2 km) down the other side of the ridge to Highway 24. Another option is to turn right at the top onto Frying Pan Trail to Cassidy Arch (3.5 miles/5.6 km one-way) and Grand Wash (4 miles/6 km one-way).

FREMONT RIVER TRAIL

From the trailhead near the amphitheater at the Fruita Campground, 1.3 miles (2.1 km) from the visitors center, the trail passes orchards along the Fremont River (elev. 5,350 feet), then begins the climb up sloping rock strata to a viewpoint on Miner's Mountain. Sweeping views take in Fruita, Boulder Mountain, and the reef. The round-trip distance of 2.5 miles (4 km) takes about 90 minutes; the elevation gain is 770 feet.

GRAND WASH ROAD

Grand Wash Road is a left turn off the Scenic Drive, 3.6 miles (5.8 km) from the visitors center. This side trip follows the twisting Grand Wash for 1 mile (1.6 km). At road's end, you can continue on foot 2.25 miles (3.6 km, one-way) through the canyon to its end at the Fremont River.

Cassidy Arch Trail begins near the end of Grand Wash Road. Energetic hikers will enjoy good views of Grand Wash, the great domes of Navajo sandstone, and the arch itself. The 3.5-mile (5.6-km) round-trip trail ascends the north wall of Grand Wash (Wingate and Kayenta Formations), then winds across slickrock of the Kayenta Formation to a vantage point close to the arch, also of Kayenta. Allow about three hours because the elevation gain is nearly 1,000 feet. The notorious outlaw Butch Cassidy may have traveled through Capitol Reef and seen this arch. Frying Pan Trail branches off Cassidy Arch Trail at the 1-mile (1.6-km) mark, then wends its way across 3 miles (4.8 km) of slickrock to Cohab Canyon.

OLD WAGON TRAIL

Wagon drivers once used this route as a shortcut between Grover and Capitol Gorge. Look for the trailhead 0.7 mile (1.1 km) south of Slickrock Divide, between Grand Wash and Capitol Gorge. The old trail crosses a wash to the west, then ascends steadily through piñon and juniper woodland on Miners Mountain. After 1.5 miles (2.4 km), the trail leaves the wagon road and goes north 0.5 mile (0.8 km) to a high knoll for the best views of the Capitol Reef area. The 4-mile (6.4 km, round-trip) hike climbs 1,000 feet.

★ CAPITOL GORGE

Follow the well-maintained dirt road to the parking area in Capitol Gorge to begin these hikes. The first mile (1.6 km) downstream is the most scenic: Fremont petroglyphs (in poor condition) appear on the left after 0.1 mile (0.2 km), narrows of Capitol Gorge close in at 0.3 mile (0.5 km), a "pioneer register" on the left at 0.5 mile (0.8 km) consists of names and dates of early travelers and ranchers scratched in the canyon wall, and natural water tanks on the left at 0.75 mile (1.2 km) are typical of those in the Waterpocket Fold. Hikers can continue another 3 miles (4.8 km) downstream to Notom Road.

The **Golden Throne Trail** also begins at the end of the Scenic Drive. Instead of heading down Capitol Gorge from the parking area, turn left up this trail for dramatic views of the reef and surrounding area. Golden Throne is a massive monolith of yellow-hued Navajo sandstone capped by a thin layer of red Carmel Formation. The 4-mile (6.4-km) round-trip trail climbs 1,100 feet in a steady grade to a viewpoint near the base of Golden Throne; allow four hours.

MOUNTAIN BIKING

Ditch the car and really get to know this country with a big loop tour. For a strenuous ride with steep grades, take the **Boulder Mountain Loop.** Start from Highway 24 near Capitol Reef, take the Notom-Bullfrog Road to Burr Trail Road, and then take Highway 12 over Boulder Mountain to Highway 24 and back to Capitol Reef. Carry plenty of water for the long dry section of Notom-Bullfrog and Burr Trail Roads, and be prepared for slow going over sandy sections of the Notom-Bullfrog Road. This is definitely the sort of trip that requires some touring experience and a decent level of training; Boulder Mountain is quite a haul. This route can run 80-125 (129-201 km) miles over several days.

In the remote northern section of the park, cyclists can ride the challenging **Cathedral Valley Loop.** The complete loop is more than 60 miles (97 km) long. Little water is available along the route, so it's best ridden in spring or fall, when temperatures are low. Access the loop on either Hartnett Road (11.7 miles/18.8 km east of the visitors center) or Caineville Wash Road (18.6 miles/30 km east of the visitors center). A small campground is located about 36 miles (58 km) into the loop.

Although the Scenic Drive doesn't have much of a shoulder, it's not a bad bicycling road, especially early in the morning before car traffic picks up. Dirt spur roads off the Scenic Drive lead up Grand Wash, into Capitol Gorge, and up South Draw to Pleasant Creek. Contact the visitors center for more information on these and other routes.

ROCK CLIMBING

Rock climbing is allowed in the park. Climbers should check with rangers to learn about restricted areas, but registration is voluntary. Permits are not required unless climbers plan to camp overnight. Climbers must use "clean" techniques (no pitons or bolts) and keep at least 100 feet from rock-art panels and prehistoric structures. Because of the abundance of prehistoric rock art found there, the rock wall north of Highway 24— between the Fruita School and the east end of Kreuger Orchard (mile 81.4)—is closed to

climbing. Other areas closed to climbing include Hickman Natural Bridge and all other arches and bridges, Temple of the Moon and Temple of the Sun, and Chimney Rock.

The hard, fractured sandstone of the Wingate Formation is better suited to climbing than the more crumbly Entrada sandstone. The rock is given to flaking, however, so climbers should use caution. Be sure that your chalk matches the color of the rock; white chalk is prohibited.

CAMPGROUNDS

Fruita Campground (year-round, $20), 1 mile (1.6 km) south of the visitors center on the Scenic Drive, has 71 sites for tents and RVs with drinking water and heated restrooms but no showers or hookups. November-April, campers must get their water from the visitors center. The surrounding orchards and lush grass make this an attractive spot. Most sites are reserveable through www.recreation.gov; $10 fee. Two campgrounds offer first-come, first-served primitive sites with no water. The five-site **Cedar Mesa Campground** (year-round, free) is in the park's southern district, just off the dirt Notom-Bullfrog Road; campers enjoy fine views of the Waterpocket Fold and the Henry Mountains. From the visitors center, go east 9.2 miles (14.8 km) on Highway 24, then turn right and go 22 miles (35 km) on Notom-Bullfrog Road (avoid this road if it's wet). **Cathedral Valley Campground** (year-round, free) serves the park's northern district; it has six sites near the Hartnett Junction, about 30 miles north of Highway 24. Take either Caineville Wash Road or Hartnett Road. Both roads are dirt and should be avoided when wet. Hartnett has a river ford.

If you're just looking for a place to park for the night, check out the public land east of the park boundary, off Highway 24. Areas on both sides of the highway (about 9 miles/14.5 km east of the visitors center) can be used for free primitive camping. Several Forest Service campgrounds are south of Torrey on Boulder Mountain, along Highway 12.

Backcountry camping is allowed in the

park; obtain a free backcountry permit at the visitors center.

GETTING THERE

Capitol Reef National Park flanks Highway 24, which is a major (by southern Utah standards) east-west road, roughly paralleling and south of I-70. Highway 24 does intersect I-70 at the town of Green River, which is north and east of the park; follow the road down through Hanksville to reach Capitol Reef. This is the quickest way to get from the Moab area to Capitol Reef.

Travelers coming from the Escalante should head north on Highway 12 toward the town of Boulder. (This is also the most scenic route from Zion and Bryce.) Twisty Highway 12 will take you over Boulder Mountain to Highway 24 at the town of Torrey; Capitol Reef is just 11 miles (17.7 km) east.

TORREY

Torrey (pop. 180) is an attractive little village with a real Western feel. Only 11 miles (17.7 km) west of the Capitol Reef National Park visitors center, at the junction of Highways 12 and 24, it's a friendly and convenient place to stay, with several excellent lodgings and a good restaurant.

Other little towns are along the Fremont River, which drains this steep-sided valley. Teasdale is a small community just 4 miles (6.4 km) west, situated in a grove of piñon pines. Bicknell, a small farm and ranch town, is 8 miles (12.9 km) west of Torrey.

The **Fremont River Ranger District** (138 S. Main St., Loa, 435/836-2800, www.fs.usda. gov/fishlake, 8am-4:30pm Mon.-Fri.) of the Fishlake National Forest has information about hiking, horseback riding, and road conditions in the northern and eastern parts of Boulder Mountain and the Aquarius Plateau.

Outfitters

You can rent mountain bikes at **Backcountry Outfitters** (875 E. Hwy. 24, 435/425-2010, www.ridethereef.com), which has a shop in a strip mall near the intersection of Highways

12 and 24; their main business is guiding people on hiking, canyoneering, 4WD, and horseback trips.

Hondoo Rivers and Trails (435/425-3519, www.hondoo.com), run by longtime locals, offers guided horseback riding adventures for multiday backcountry excursions; for a real treat, check out the inn-to-inn trail rides. They also provide, guided hiking tours and backpacking trips, jeep tours, and shuttle services.

Entertainment and Events

The **Entrada Institute** (www. entradainstitute.org), a nonprofit organization that seeks to further understanding and appreciation of the natural, historical, cultural, and scientific heritage of the Colorado Plateau, sponsors a cultural event as part of their **Saturday Sunset Series** (7:30pm Sat. late May-late Oct., usually free). Events range from talks by local ranchers on the cattle industry to musical performances. The institute is housed at the **Robber's Roost Bookstore** (185 W. Main St., 435/425-3265, www.robbersroostbooks.com, 8am-6pm daily spring-fall), which is a good place to visit any time of day.

Food

Torrey's restaurant of note is ★ **Cafe Diablo** (599 W. Main St., 435/425-3070, www. cafediablo.net, 3pm-9pm daily Apr.-Oct., dinner entrées $22-32). The specialty is zesty Southwestern cuisine, with excellent dishes like fire-roasted pork tenderloin, pomegranate- and chipotle-glazed ribs, and pumpkin-seed trout. This is one of the few places you can order free-range rattlesnake meat, cooked into crab cake-like patties. Because there aren't many restaurants this good in rural Utah, this place is worth a detour, though it must be said that it's not the place for a quiet romantic dinner—it's a high-volume, fast-paced, high-energy dining experience.

Another pleasant surprise in this small town is the **Capitol Reef Inn and Cafe** (360 W. Main St., 435/425-3271, www.

capitolreefinn.com, 7am-9pm daily, $9-19), where there's an emphasis on healthy and, when possible, locally grown food. It's easy to eat your veggies here—the 10-vegetable salad will make up for some of the less nutritious meals you've had on the road.

For something a little less elevated, try the burgers and milk shakes at **Slacker's Burger Joint** (165 E. Main St., 435/425-3710, 11am-7pm Mon.-Sat., $6-12), in the center of Torrey. The pastrami burger is rightfully famous, and an afternoon milk shake hits the spot after a day of hiking.

The best spot for coffee and breakfast is **Castle Rock Coffee & Candy** (685 E. Hwy. 24, 435/425-2100, www.castlerockcoffee.com, 7am-3pm daily, $3-8), tucked behind the Subway sandwich shop in a little strip mall near the intersection of Highways 12 and 24.

About 24 miles (39 km) east of the Capitol Reef visitors center, stop by the tiny ★ **Mesa Market** (milepost 102, Hwy. 24, Caineville, 435/487-9711, www.mesafarmmarket.com, 7am-7pm daily late Mar.-Oct.) for artisanal cheese and yogurt, sourdough bread baked in a wood-fired oven, and whatever produce is growing in the back 40. You won't find better picnic makings anywhere in southeastern Utah, and if he has a minute to spare, the owner will explain the sustainable nature of his farm and dairy.

Accommodations
$50-100

There are a few small bunkhouse cabins at the center of town, at the **Torrey Trading Post** (75 W. Main St., 435/425-3716, www.torreytradingpost.com, $50). These recently built, snug cabins aren't loaded with frills—the toilets and showers are in men's and women's bathhouses—but the price is right, pets are permitted, and there's a place to do laundry. In addition, a fully furnished studio cabin with a king bed, twin foldout bed, full bath and full kitchen is $105, and a fully furnished larger cabin that sleeps six, with two full baths and kitchen goes for $140.

The **Capitol Reef Inn and Cafe** (360 W.

Main St., 435/425-3271, www.capitolreefinn. com, spring-fall, $72) has homey motel rooms and a good café serving breakfast, lunch, and dinner. In the front yard, the motel's owner and his brother have built a kiva resembling those used by Native Americans. It's obviously a labor of love, and a pretty cool place to explore.

At the east end of Torrey, the **Rim Rock Inn** (2523 E. Hwy. 24, 435/425-3388 or 888/447-4676, www.therimrock.net, Mar.-Dec., $94-119) does indeed perch on a rim of red rock; it's just about as close as you can get to the park. The motel and its two restaurants are part of a 120-acre ranch, so the views are expansive.

In a grove of trees immediately behind downtown Torrey's old trading post and country store is **Austin's Chuck Wagon Lodge** (12 W. Main St., 435/425-3335 or 800/863-3288, www.austinschuckwagonmotel.com, Mar.-Dec., rooms $67-119, cabins $183), with guest rooms in an older motel ($61), a newer lodge-like building, or newer two-bedroom cabins. There's also a pool and a hot tub.

Just east of the nearby community of Teasdale, the **Cactus Hill Motel** (938 Birch Creek Road, Teasdale, 435/425-3578 or 800/507-2624, www.cactushillmotel.com, $65) is a small, simple motel on a family ranch.

$100-150

If you're looking for comfortable motel rooms with an outdoor pool and nice views, a good choice is the **Capitol Reef Resort** (2600 E. Hwy. 24, 435/425-3761, www.capitolreefresort. com, $149-189). If a motel room seems too tame, stay in an air-conditioned Conestoga wagons (sleeps six, $220, private bathroom a little walk away). Tepees ($269) and cabins ($259-309) are also available.

The lovely **SkyRidge Inn Bed and Breakfast** (950 W. Hwy. 24, 435/425-3775 or 877/824-1508, www.skyridgeinn.com, $125-162) is 1 mile (1.6 km) east of downtown Torrey. The modern inn has been decorated with high-quality Southwestern art and artifacts; all six guest rooms have private baths.

SkyRidge sits on a bluff amid 75 acres, and guests are invited to explore the land on foot or bike.

In a pretty setting 3 miles (4.8 km) south of town, **Cowboy Homestead Cabins** (Hwy. 12, 435/425-3414 or 888/854-5871, www.cowboyhomesteadcabins.com, $109-119) has attractive one- and two-bedroom cabins with private baths, kitchenettes, and outdoor gas barbecue grills.

In Teasdale, 4 miles (6.4 km) west of Torrey, **Pine Shadows** (125 S. 200 W., Teasdale, 435/425-3939 or 800/708-1223, www.pineshadowcabins.net, $109-164) offers spacious, modern cabins, equipped with two queen beds plus full baths and kitchens, in a piñon forest.

Muley Twist Inn (off 125 S., outside Teasdale, 435/425-3640 or 800/530-1038, www.muleytwistinn.com, $120-160), an elegantly decorated five-bedroom B&B, is on a 30-acre parcel with great views. One guest room is fully accessible to wheelchair users. It's another really wonderful place to come home to at the end of a day of driving or hiking.

Stay in a 1914 schoolhouse: The **Torrey Schoolhouse Bed and Breakfast** (150 N. Center St., 435/633-4643, www.torreyschoolhouse.com, Apr.-Oct., $125-160) has been renovated but retains many period touches and an old-fashioned atmosphere. Modern amenities include a shiatsu massage chair in every room, memory foam mattress toppers, flat-screen TVs, and a wheelchair-accessible suite.

$150-200

If you're looking for comfortable motel rooms with an outdoor pool and nice views, a good choice is the **Capitol Reef Resort** (2600 E. Hwy. 24, 435/425-3761, www.capitolreefresort.com, $169-209). If a motel room seems too tame, stay in an air-conditioned Conestoga wagons (sleeps six, $220), with private baths a little walk away. Teepees ($269) and cabins ($289-319) are also available.

The ★ **Lodge at Red River Ranch** (2900 W. Hwy. 24, 435/425-3322 or 800/205-6343, www.redriverranch.com, $179-260, two-night minimum) is between Bicknell and Torrey beneath towering cliffs of red sandstone on the banks of the Fremont River. This wood-beamed lodge sits on a 2,200-acre working ranch, but there's nothing rustic or unsophisticated about the accommodations. The three-story structure is built in the same grand architectural style as old-fashioned

Austin's Chuck Wagon Lodge offers a general store.

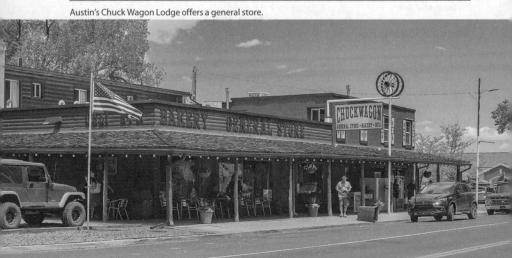

mountain lodges. The great room has a massive stone fireplace, cozy chairs and couches, and a splendid Old West atmosphere. There are 15 guest rooms, most decorated according to a theme, and all have private baths. Guests are welcome to wander ranch paths, fish for trout, or meander in the gardens and orchards. Breakfast and dinner are served in the lodge restaurant but are not included in the price of lodgings; box lunches can be ordered.

CAMPGROUNDS

Although most campers will try for a site at Capitol Reef National Park, the campground there does not take reservations and fills up quickly. Torrey has a couple of private campgrounds that cater to both RV and tent campers. Right in town, the **Sand Creek RV Park** (540 W. Hwy. 24, 435/425-3577, Mar.-Oct., $20 tents, $33-37 RVs, $39-60 camping cabins) has shaded tent spaces in a pleasant grassy field. Showers ($5 for nonguests) and laundry

facilities ($5 to wash and dry) are available. **Thousand Lakes RV Park** (1110 W. Hwy. 24, 1 mile/1.6 km west of Torrey, 435/425-3500 or 800/355-8995, www.thousandlakesrvpark.com, Apr.-late Oct., $20 tents, $41 RVs with full hookups) has showers, wireless Internet, a laundry room, and a store. Thousand Lakes also has cabins, ranging from spartan (no linens, $39) to deluxe (sleeps 6, linens provided, $109).

The U.S. Forest Service's **Sunglow Campground** (Forest Rd. 143, east of Bicknell, 435/836-2811, www.recreation.gov, open with water May-Oct., $8) is just east of Bicknell at an elevation of 7,200 feet. The surrounding red cliffs really light up at sunset, hence the name. Several other Forest Service campgrounds are on the slopes of Boulder Mountain along Highway 12 between Torrey and Boulder. These places are all above 8,600 feet and usually don't open until late May-early June.

East of Capitol Reef

Highway 24 follows the Fremont River east from Capitol Reef National Park to a junction at Hanksville; from there you can head north toward I-70 (the best route to Moab) or south, skirting the eastern edge of the Henry Mountains to the upper reaches of Lake Powell. Hanksville is a good place to gas up if you're exploring the remote Henry Mountains or the southern San Rafael Swell. Goblin Valley State Park is worth a visit, and it's a good place to camp.

HANKSVILLE

Even by Utah standards, tiny Hanksville (pop. just over 200) is pretty remote. Ebenezer Hanks and other Mormon settlers founded this out-of-the-way community in 1882 along the Fremont River, then known as the Dirty Devil River. The isolation attracted polygamists like Hanks and other fugitives from the law. Butch Cassidy and his gang found refuge

in the rugged canyon country of Robbers' Roost, east of town. Several houses and the old stone church on Center Street, one block south of the highway, survive from the 19th century.

Travelers exploring this scenic region find Hanksville a handy if lackluster stopover; Capitol Reef National Park is to the west, Lake Powell and the Henry Mountains to the south, the remote Maze District of Canyonlands National Park to the east, and Goblin Valley State Park to the north. Because Hanksville is a true crossroads, the few lodgings here are often booked up well in advance, so plan ahead.

Wolverton Mill

E. T. Wolverton built this ingenious mill during the 1920s at his gold-mining claims in the Henry Mountains. A 20-foot waterwheel, still perfectly balanced, powered ore-crushing machinery and a sawmill. Owners of claims at the mill's original site didn't like a steady stream of tourists coming through to see the mill, so it was moved to the BLM office at Hanksville. Drive south 0.5 mile (0.8 km) on 100 West to see the mill and some of its original interior mechanism.

Food

Hanksville's restaurants cluster at the south end of town; don't expect anything fancy. **Blondie's Eatery** (3 N. Hwy. 95, 435/542-3255, 7am-8pm daily, $5-10) is a casual sit-down place with chicken and burgers across from Whispering Sands Motel. **Stan's Burger Shack** (150 S. Hwy. 95, 435/542-3330, 7am-10pm daily, $5-9), at the Chevron station, is full of locals and a step up from the chains. The classiest spot for dinner is the **Slickrock Grill** (275 Hwy. 24, 435/542-3235, 7am-10pm daily, $9-28), with steaks, barbecue, and burgers.

Accommodations

Hanksville is a busy crossroads with just two lodging options, so rooms go fast. Book up in advance if your plans call for spending a night here, even though accommodations are pretty basic. At **Whispering Sands Motel** (90 S. Hwy. 95, 435/542-3238, $109-129) you'll have a choice of rooms in the motel or in "cabins" that look a lot like garden sheds. Never mind—by the time you arrive, you'll be glad to see them. The **Hanksville Inn** (280 E. 100 N., 435/542-3471, www.hanksvilleinn.com, $100) is the other option, also basic but serviceable.

It's also good to know about the **Rodeway Inn Capitol Reef,** 15 miles (24 km) west of Hanksville in Caineville (25 E. Hwy. 24, 435/456-9900, http://rodewayinncapitolreef. com, $120), another pleasant but standard lodging, but note that the nearest actual restaurant is in Hanksville. Fortunately, there's a small breakfast served; even better, the Mesa Market is nearby on the road to Capitol Reef National Park with excellent homemade bread and cheese.

In the center of town, the campground behind **Duke's Slickrock Grill** (435/542-3235 or 800/894-3242, mid-Mar.-Oct., $15 tents, $35 RVs) has showers and a laundry.

Information and Services

The **Bureau of Land Management** (435/542-3461, www.blm.gov) has a field station 0.5 mile (0.8 km) south of Highway 24 on 100 West, with information on road conditions, hiking, camping, and the buffalo herd in the Henry Mountains.

★ GOBLIN VALLEY STATE PARK

Thousands of rock formations, many with goblinlike "faces," inhabit this valley, now part of **Goblin Valley State Park** (435/564-8110, reservations 800/322-3770, www. reserveamerica.com, year-round, day-use $15 per vehicle, camping $30, yurts $100. All of these so-called goblins have weathered out of the Entrada Formation, here a soft red sandstone and even softer siltstone.

Carmel Canyon Trail (1.5-mile/2.4-km loop) begins at the northeast side of the parking lot at road's end, then drops down to the desert floor and a strange landscape of goblins, spires, and balanced rocks. Just wander around at your whim; this is a great place for the imagination. A 1.3-mile (2.1-km) trail connects the campground and the goblin-studded Carmel Canyon Trail. **Curtis Bench Trail** begins on the road between the parking lot and the campground and goes south to a viewpoint of the Henry Mountains; cairns mark the 1.5-mile (2.4 km, one-way) route.

The turnoff from Highway 24 for the state park is at milepost 137, which is 21 miles (34 km) north of Hanksville and 24 miles (39 km) south of I-70; follow the signs west 5 miles (8 km) on a paved road, then south 7 miles (11.3 km) on a gravel road.

Although there are off-road vehicle and motorcycle riding areas just west of the park, bicycling is limited to the park's roads. However, 12 miles (19.3 km) north, the **Temple Mountain Bike Trail** traverses old mining roads, ridges, and wash bottoms. Popular hikes near the state park include the

Little Wild Horse and Bell Canyons Loop, Chute and Crack Canyons Loop, and Wild Horse Canyon. The park is also a good base for exploring the **San Rafael Swell** area to the northwest.

Camping at Goblin Valley is a real treat; the late evening and early morning sun makes the sandstone spires glow. If you're not much of a camper, consider booking one of the park's two yurts. They're tucked back among the rock formations, and each is equipped with bunk beds and a futon, swamp cooler, and propane stove. There are only 26 camping sites, so it's best to reserve well in advance.

LITTLE WILD HORSE CANYON

West of Goblin Valley, Little Wild Horse is a good slot canyon hike for people without technical experience, though obstacles do require a little scrambling. Hike in as far as you like and turn around to exit or make a loop with Bell Canyon. Hiking is best in spring and fall; avoid the area when there's a chance of rain, which is often the case in August. Reach the trailhead by traveling south on Goblin Valley Road but turning west on Wild Horse Road before entering Goblin Valley State Park. The trailhead is about 6 miles (9.7 km) from the park.

HENRY MOUNTAINS

Great domes of intrusive igneous rock pushed into and deformed surrounding sedimentary layers about 70 million years ago. Erosion later uncovered the domes, revealing mountains towering 5,000 feet above the surrounding plateau. Mount Ellen's North Summit Ridge (elev. 11,522 feet) and Mount Pennell (elev. 11,320 feet) top the range. Scenic views and striking geologic features abound in and around the Henrys. Rock layers tilt dramatically in the Waterpocket Fold to the west and in the Pink Cliffs on the south side of Mount Hillers. Sheer cliffs of the Horn, between Mount Ellen and Mount Pennell, attract rock climbers.

The arid land and rugged canyons surrounding the Henry Mountains so discouraged early explorers and potential settlers that the range wasn't even named or described until 1869, when members of the Powell River Expedition sighted it.

Buffalo, brought to the Henrys from Yellowstone National Park in 1941, form one of the few free-roaming herds in the United States. They winter in the southwestern part of the mountains, then move higher as the snow melts.

Rough roads with panoramic views cross the range between the high peaks at Bull Creek, Pennellen, and Stanton Passes. Most driving routes are best suited for high-clearance vehicles. The road through Bull Creek Pass (elev. 10,485 feet) is snow-free only early July-late October. Rains, which peak in August, occasionally make travel difficult in late summer. Roads tend to be at their best after grading in autumn, just before the deer-hunting season. Travel at the lower elevations is possible all year, though spring and autumn have the most pleasant temperatures. Check in first with the BLM office in Hanksville before exploring the backcountry. Take precautions for desert travel, and have water, food, and extra clothing with you. The Henry Mountains remain a remote and little-traveled region.

Countless mountain and canyon hiking possibilities exist in the range; most routes go cross-country or follow old mining roads.

The only easily accessible campsites in the Henry Mountains are the BLM sites at **Starr Springs Campground** (elev. 6,300 feet, 435/542-3461, water Apr.-Nov.), off Highway 276 north of Ticaboo. The campground sits in an oak forest at the base of Mount Hillers. A good gravel road to Starr Springs Campground turns off Highway 276 near milepost 17 (23 miles/37 km north of Bullfrog and 43 miles/69 km south of Hanksville) and goes in 4 miles (6.4 km).

Lake Powell and Glen Canyon

Lake Powell is at the center of the **Glen Canyon National Recreation Area** (520/608-6404, www.nps.gov/glca, always open, $25 per vehicle, $20 per motorcycle, or $12 cyclists and pedestrians, no charge for passing through Page, Arizona, on U.S. 89), a vast preserve covering 1.25 million acres in Arizona and Utah. When the Glen Canyon Dam was completed in 1964, conservationists deplored the loss of the remote and beautiful Glen Canyon of the Colorado River beneath the lake's waters. In terms of beauty and sheer drama, Glen Canyon was considered the equal of the Grand Canyon. Today, we have only words, pictures, and memories to remind us of its wonders. On the other hand, the 186-mile-long (299-km-long) lake now provides easy access to an area most had not even known existed. Lake Powell is the second-largest artificial lake in the United States. Only Lake Mead, farther downstream, has a greater water storage capacity. Lake Powell, however, has three times more shoreline—1,960 miles (3,154 km)—and when full, it holds enough water to cover the state of Pennsylvania one foot deep. Just a handful of roads approach the lake, so access is basically limited to boats—bays and coves offer nearly limitless opportunities for exploration by boaters as well as long-distance hiking trails.

NATURAL BRIDGES TO BULLFROG MARINA BY FERRY

Eight miles (12.9 km) west of the entrance to Natural Bridges National Monument, travelers must make a decision: Continue on Highway 95 to cross the Colorado by bridge at Hite or follow Highway 276 to the Halls Crossing Marina and cross the river, at this point tamed by the Glen Canyon Dam and known as Lake Powell, by car ferry.

Obviously, the ferry is the more exotic choice, and both Halls Crossing and Bullfrog Marinas offer lodging and food, a relative scarcity in this remote area. Crossing the Colorado on the ferry also makes it easy to access **Bullfrog-Notom Road,** which climbs for 60 miles (97 km) through dramatic landscapes on its way to Capitol Reef National Park's otherwise remote Waterfold Pocket. The road ends at Notom, just 4 miles (6.4 km) from the eastern entrance to Capitol Reef National Park on Highway 24. Drivers can also turn west onto the Burr Trail and follow back roads to Boulder, near the Escalante River Canyon.

Halls Crossing and Bullfrog Ferry

At the junction of Highways 95 and 276, a large sign lists the departure times for the ferry; note that these may be different from the times listed in the widely circulated flyer or on the website. Confirm the departure times (435/684-3088, www.udot.utah.gov) before making the 42-mile (68-km) journey to Halls Crossing.

The crossing time for the 3-mile (4.8-km) trip from Halls Crossing to Bullfrog is 27 minutes. Fares are $25 for cars, which includes the driver and all passengers, $10 bicycles and foot passengers, and $15 motorcycles. Vehicles longer than 20 feet pay $1.50 per foot.

Ferry service runs late April-early October, and there's a trip every other hour daily beginning with the 8am boat from Halls Landing, which then leaves Bullfrog at 9am. In summer high season, the final ferry from Halls Crossing departs at 6pm, and the final ferry from Bullfrog departs at 7pm. The ferry does not run early October-late April.

If drought or downstream demand lowers the level of Lake Powell beyond a certain point, there may not be enough water for the ferry to operate. If this is the case, just about every park visitors center in southern Utah will post notices about the ferry's status.

Glen Canyon National Recreation Area

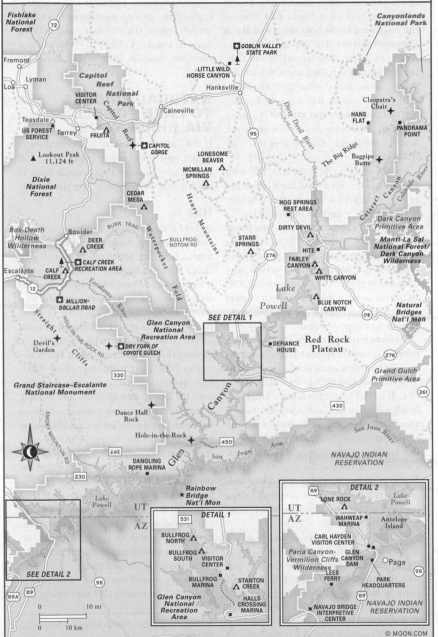

Fishlake
National
Forest
72

Fremont

Lyman

Loa

Teasdale

Torrey

Escalante

12

Box-Death
Hollow
Wilderness

Boulder

DEER
CREEK

CALF
CREEK

CALF CREEK
RECREATION AREA

MILLION-
DOLLAR ROAD

Devil's
Garden

Grand Staircase–Escalante
National Monument

Dance Hall
Rock

Hole-in-the-Rock

DANGLING
ROPE MARINA

Capitol
Reef
National
Park

VISITOR
CENTER

US FOREST
SERVICE

FRUITA

Lookout Peak
11,124 ft

Dixie
National
Forest

CEDAR
MESA

CAPITOL
GORGE

Cabinville

Caineville

Hanksville

GOBLIN VALLEY
STATE PARK

LITTLE WILD
HORSE CANYON

95

LONESOME
BEAVER

McMILLAN
SPRINGS

Henry Mountains

BURR TRAIL

BULLFROG-
NOTOM RD

STARR
SPRINGS

276

Lake

Powell

SEE DETAIL 1

Glen Canyon
National
Recreation Area

DRY FORK OF
COYOTE GULCH

330

DEFIANCE
HOUSE

Red Rock
Plateau

Dirty Devil River

The Big Ridge

Cleopatra's
Chair

HANS
FLAT

Bagpipe
Butte

HOG SPRINGS
REST AREA

DIRTY DEVIL

HITE

FARLEY
CANYON

WHITE CANYON

BLUE NOTCH
CANYON

Canyonlands
National Park

PANORAMA
POINT

Cataract Canyon

Colorado River

Dark Canyon
Primitive Area

Manti-La Sal
National Forest/
Dark Canyon
Wilderness

Natural
Bridges
Nat'l Mon

95

276

Grand Gulch
Primitive Area

261

430

San Juan River

NAVAJO INDIAN
RESERVATION

Rainbow
★ Bridge
Nat'l Mon

San Juan Arm

450

Glen Canyon

San Juan

230

Lake
Powell

SEE DETAIL 2

98

89A

89

UT

AZ

DETAIL 1

531

BULLFROG
NORTH

BULLFROG
SOUTH

VISITOR
CENTER

BULLFROG
MARINA

STANTON
CREEK

HALLS
CROSSING
MARINA

Glen Canyon
National
Recreation Area

DETAIL 2

89

LONE ROCK

UT

AZ

WAHWEAP
MARINA

Lake
Powell

Antelope
Island

CARL HAYDEN
VISITOR CENTER

Paria Canyon-
Vermilion Cliffs
Wilderness

GLEN
CANYON
DAM

LEES
FERRY

Page

98

PARK
HEADQUARTERS

89

NAVAJO BRIDGE
INTERPRETIVE
CENTER

NAVAJO INDIAN
RESERVATION

0   10 mi

0   10 km

© MOON.COM

Arriving at Halls Crossing by road, you'll first reach a small store offering three-bedroom units in trailer houses and an RV park. Continue for 0.5 mile (0.8 km) on the main road to the boat ramp and **Halls Crossing Marina** (435/684-2261). The marina has a larger store (groceries and fishing and boating supplies), tours to Rainbow Bridge, a boat-rental office (fishing, waterskiing, and houseboats), a gas dock, slips, and storage. The **ranger station** is nearby, although rangers are usually out on patrol; look for their vehicle in the area if the office is closed.

On the western side of the lake, **Bullfrog Marina** is more like a small town (albeit one run by Aramark), with a **visitors center** (435/684-7423, hours vary May-early Oct.), a clinic, stores, a service station, and a handsome hotel and restaurant. The marina rents boats ranging from kayaks ($50 per day) and paddleboards ($90 per day) to 12-person party boats ($800 per day) to houseboats ($2,370-10,200 per week), but for guided boat tours of Lake Powell, you'll have to go to the Wahweap Marina near Page, Arizona.

Defiance House Lodge (888/896-3829, www.lakepowell.com, $140-176) offers comfortable lake-view accommodations and the **Anasazi Restaurant** (7am-10pm daily April-Oct., $12-28). The front desk at the lodge also handles family units (well-equipped trailers, about $280 per night), an RV park ($46), and houseboat rentals (from $800 per day, three-day minimum). Showers, a laundry room, a convenience store, and a post office are at **Trailer Village.** Ask the visitors center staff or rangers for directions to primitive camping areas with vehicle access elsewhere along Bullfrog Bay.

Bullfrog Marina can be reached from the north via paved Highway 276. It is 40 miles (64 km) between Bullfrog and the junction with Highway 95. Ticaboo, 20 miles (32 km) north of Bullfrog, has another good lodging option. The **Ticaboo Lodge** (435/788-2110 or 800/842-2267, ticaboo.com, $107-129) is a hotel with a swimming pool, a restaurant, and

a service-station complex that pretty much constitutes all of Ticaboo.

For reservations and information regarding lodging, camping, tours, boating, and recreation at both Halls Crossing and Bullfrog Marina, contact **Lake Powell Resorts & Marinas** (888/896-3829, www.lakepowell. com).

NATURAL BRIDGES TO LAKE POWELL VIA HIGHWAY 95

If the Lake Powell ferry schedule doesn't match your travel plans, Highway 95 will quickly get you across the Colorado River to the junction with Highway 24 at Hanksville.

Hite

In 1883 Cass Hite came to Glen Canyon in search of gold. He found some at a place later named Hite City, which set off a small gold rush. Cass and a few of his relatives operated a small store and post office, which were the only services for many miles. Travelers who wanted to cross the Colorado River here had the difficult task of swimming their animals across. Arthur Chaffin, a later resident, put through the first road and opened a ferry service in 1946. The Chaffin Ferry served uranium prospectors and adventurous motorists until the lake backed up to the spot in 1964. A steel bridge now spans the Colorado River upstream from Hite Marina. Cass Hite's store and the ferry site are underwater about 5 miles (8 km) down the lake from Hite Marina.

Beyond Hite, on the tiny neck of land between the Colorado River Bridge and the Dirty Devil Bridge, an unmarked dirt road turns north. Called Hite Road, or Orange Cliffs Road, this long and rugged road eventually links up with backcountry routes—including the Flint Trail—in the Maze District of Canyonlands National Park.

The uppermost marina on Lake Powell, Hite is 141 lake miles (227 km) from Glen

1: Goblin Valley State Park; **2:** Wahweap Resort and Marina

Canyon Dam. It is hit hard when water levels drop in Lake Powell, which has been most of the time in recent years. When water is available, boats can continue up the lake to the mouth of Dark Canyon in Cataract Canyon at low water or into Canyonlands National Park at high water. During times of low water, the boat ramp is often high above the lake and the place is pretty desolate. Facilities include a small **store** with gas and a primitive **campground** (free) with no drinking water. Primitive camping is also available nearby, off Highway 95 at Dirty Devil, Farley Canyon, White Canyon, Blue Notch, and other locations. A **ranger station** (435/684-2457) is occasionally open; look for the ranger vehicle at other times.

PAGE, ARIZONA

Although the town of Page is hot, busy, and not particularly appealing, it is the largest community anywhere near Lake Powell, and it offers travelers a number of places to stay and eat. The town overlooks Lake Powell and Glen Canyon Dam.

The largest resort in the Glen Canyon National Recreation Area, **Wahweap Resort and Marina,** (100 Lakeshore Dr., 928/645-2433, www.lakepowell.com) is just 6 miles (9.7 km) northwest of Page off U.S. 89. Wahweap is a major center for all manner of watersports, including houseboats (from $3,900 for five days in high summer season; sleeps up to ten), to kayaks (from $50 per day) and paddleboards ($90 per day). Wahweap also offers an extensive range of boat tours and boat-assisted hiking, among other recreational activities. Wahweap's Lake Powell Resort, a hotel and restaurant complex, offers some of the most comfortable rooms in the area.

Tours

From Wahweap, board a tour boat to really see the special areas of Glen Canyon still visible from Lake Powell. A 1.5-hour tour (10:30am, 2:30pm, and 4:15pm daily Apr.-Oct., $47 adults, $32 children) into the mouth of 10-mile-long (16-km-long) **Antelope**

Canyon leaves from the Wahweap Marina (928/645-2433). During summer, a 6:15pm tour is added; in the winter, a 10:30am tour runs if there is sufficient demand. One of the most popular boat tours from Wahweap motors to **Rainbow Bridge National Monument** (Wahweap Marina, 928/645-2433, 7:30am daily April-mid-May and Sept.-Oct., 12:30pm mid-May-Aug., $122 adults, $77 children). This tour, which takes around six hours and includes a 1.25-mile (2-km) round trip hike, cruises 50 miles (81 km) of shorelines to reach Rainbow Bridge, one of the largest known natural bridges in the world, at 290 feet high and 275 feet. If the price seems too stiff, or the boat ride too tame, a couple of rugged 17-mile-long (27-km-long) trails leave from Page and travel across Navajo lands to the bridge. See the monument's website (www.nps.gov/rabr) for details on these trails.

Quite a different Antelope Canyon is the focus of a land-based tour to a famed slot canyon east of Page, beloved by multitudes of photographers seeking to capture the canyon's supple curves and pink-gold hues. Travel to Upper Antelope Canyon by truck with **Antelope Canyon Tours** (22 S. Lake Powell Blvd., 928/645-9102, www.antelopecanyon.com, $45-55). Tours last about 1.5 hours and run several times a day year round.

Food

If you've been traveling through remote rural Utah for a while, dipping into Page, Arizona, can seem like a gastronomic mecca. The **Ranch House Grill** (819 N. Navajo Dr., 928/645-1420, 6am-3pm daily, $7-15) serves breakfast all day plus sandwiches, burgers, steaks, and chops during the day. After a few days of abstemious travel in southern Utah, **Blue Wine Bar** (644 N. Navajo Dr., 928/608-0707, 6pm-11pm Tues.-Sat., $5-12) is a real treat. The tapas and small plates are excellent, as is the wine selection. In the same Dam Plaza complex, the stylish **Blue Buddha** (644 N. Navajo Dr., 928/608-0707, 5pm-9pm Tues.-Sat., $10-20) serves cocktails and Japanese food, including sushi, and the **Dam Bar and**

Grill (644 N. Navajo Dr., 928/645-2161, 5pm-11pm daily, $11-30) features steaks, barbecue, seafood, pasta, and sandwiches; it also has a sports bar. **Fiesta Mexicana** (125 S. Lake Powell Blvd., 928/645-4082, 11am-9pm daily, $9-15) is a busy but friendly little Mexican place (and here in Arizona, it's easy to get a margarita).

Accommodations

Nearly all Page motels are on or near Lake Powell Boulevard (U.S. 89L), a 3.25-mile (5.2-km) loop that branches off the main highway. Page is a busy place in summer, however, and a call ahead is a good idea if you don't want to chase around town looking for vacancies. Expect to pay top dollar for views of the lake. The summer rates listed here drop in winter (Nov.-Mar.).

In a way, the most appealing lodgings are in the small apartments-turned-motels on and around 8th Avenue, a quiet residential area two blocks off Lake Powell Boulevard. These apartments date back to 1958-1959, when they housed supervisors for the dam construction project. One such place is the **Lake Powell Motel** (750 S. Navajo Dr., 480/452-9895, www.powellmotel.net,

$99-159), a nicely remodeled place with standard motel rooms and stylish one- and two-bedroom apartments with kitchenettes. **Debbie's Hide A Way** (119 8th Ave., 928/645-1224, www.debbieshideaway.com, $99-179) is another place with a personal touch and a quiet garden in back; all guest rooms are suites with kitchens. Debbie's also has a two-bedroom apartment ($149) a couple of blocks from the motel.

If you prefer the standard comforts of chain motels, a quick search of hotel booking websites will reveal that Page has all the usual suspects, plus some upscale resorts if you're looking for luxury. **Courtyard Page** (600 Clubhouse Dr., 928/645-5000, www.marriott.com, $198-351) is a good option in a great setting, with views, a restaurant, a pool, a spa, an exercise room, and an adjacent 18-hole golf course.

If you want to play in the water, there's no better spot to spend the night than the **Lake Powell Resort** at Wahweap Resort (6 miles/9.7 km north of Page off U.S. 89 at 100 Lakeshore Dr., 928/645-2433, www.lakepowell.com, $208-244), with access to the lake recreation, tours and a lively drinking and dining scene out your front door.

Arches and Canyonlands

The Colorado River and its tributaries have carved extraordinary landscapes into the Colorado Plateau's vivid red and orange sandstone deposits that underlie southeastern Utah.

Intricate mazes of canyons, delicate arches, and massive rock monoliths make this region seem primordial at times and lunar at others. Two national parks—Arches and Canyonlands—preserve some of the most astounding of these landscapes, while state parks, national monuments, and recreation areas protect other sights of great interest and beauty. At every turn, the landscape invites exploration, offering solitude, ruins of prehistoric villages, wildlife, and dramatic records of geologic history.

Along with the drama of the landscape, outdoor recreation brings

Highlights

Look for ★ to find recommended sights, activities, dining, and lodging.

★ **Delicate Arch:** Rising directly from a slick-rock bluff, this is the most awe-inspiring of the national park's arches (page 390).

★ **Mesa Arch Trail:** It's a short, easy hike from the Canyonlands park highway to the Island in the Sky cliffs, where a rock window opens up at the very edge of the precipice—a soaring arch over the void (page 403).

★ **Grand View Point:** At the top of 1,000-foot cliffs is the most dramatic vista in all of Utah—see much of the state spread out beneath your feet (page 403).

★ **BLM Newspaper Rock Historical Monument:** The meaning of this ancient Native American rock art has been lost (perhaps some 2,000 years ago it was something like a newspaper?), but what remains is beautiful, mysterious, and oddly meaningful (page 405).

★ **Hovenweep National Monument:** Built around 900 years ago, the amazing Ancestral Puebloan ruins are mostly unexcavated and largely unvisited, which means that you can explore their mysteries on your own (page 425).

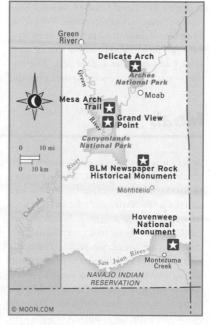

© MOON.COM

people to this corner of Utah. There are so many recreational options available here that plain old hiking almost seems passé. Moab is central for slickrock mountain biking, which brings people in from around the world to ride the area's red-rock cliffs and canyons. Another "sport" drawing legions of fans to the area is off-roading, or exploration of the canyon backcountry on four-wheel-drive (4WD) and all-terrain vehicles (ATVs). The huge surge of popularity for off-roading has the Bureau of Land Management (BLM), which governs much of the nonpark land in the area, considering restrictions on the number of people able to drive the backcountry, as the off-road vehicles are tearing up fragile ecosystems and causing other environmental damage.

PLANNING YOUR TIME

With two national parks and myriad public lands, the hiker, mountain biker, or lover of the outdoors could easily fill a week here with a diverse mix of recreation. Not everyone has that much time to spend, of course, but even more casual visitors should consider budgeting three days here. The national parks near Moab (Arches plus the Island in the Sky District of Canyonlands) will require a day to simply drive through, and the rest of Canyonlands and other national monuments in the extreme south (Hovenweep, Natural Bridges, Monument Valley) deserve at least a day. That leaves a single day to explore Moab itself, take a rafting trip down the Colorado River, or go on a hike or mountain bike ride.

As for timing, the rugged character of the canyon country causes many local variations in climate, as do extremes in elevation between cliff rims and canyon bottoms. Fall and spring are the most popular times to visit, as daytime temperatures are moderate. Real desert heat sets in late May-early June. Temperatures then soar into the 90s and 100s at midday, although the dry air makes the heat more bearable. Early morning is the choice time for summer travel. Autumn begins after late-summer rains end and lasts into November or even December; days are bright and sunny with ideal temperatures, but nights become cold. Winter lasts only about two months at the lower elevations. Light snow on the canyon walls adds new beauty to the rock layers, and winter can be a fine time for travel.

Moab

By far the largest town in southeastern Utah, Moab (pop. 5,100, elev. 4,025 feet) makes an excellent base for exploring Arches and Canyonlands National Parks and the surrounding canyon country. Moab is near the Colorado River in a green valley enclosed by high sandstone cliffs. The biblical Moab was a kingdom at the edge of Zion, and early Mormon settlers must have felt themselves at the edge of their world, too, being so isolated from Salt Lake City—the Mormon city of Zion. Moab's existence on the fringe of Mormon culture and the sizable non-Mormon population gave the town a unique character.

In recent years, Moab has become nearly synonymous with mountain biking. The slickrock canyon country seems made for exploration by bike, and people come from all over the world to pedal the backcountry. River trips on the Colorado River are nearly as popular, and a host of other outdoor recreational diversions—from horseback riding to 4WD jeep exploring to skydiving—combine to make Moab one of the most popular destinations in Utah.

Previous: Needles District; Delicate Arch; Hovenweep National Monument.

Arches and Canyonlands

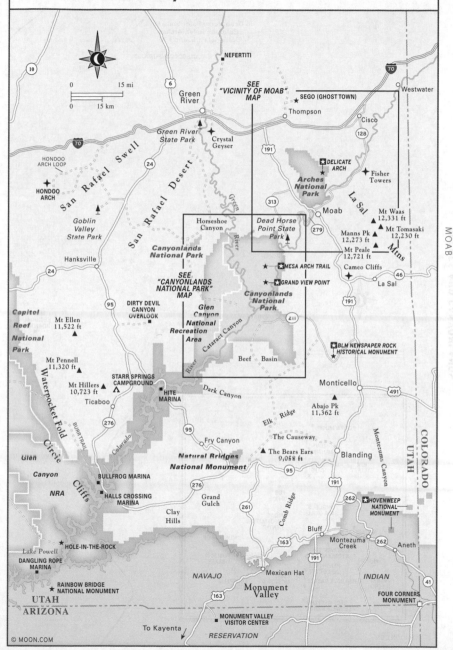

NEFERTITI

Green River

SEE
"VICINITY OF MOAB"
MAP

SEGO (GHOST TOWN)

Westwater

Thompson

Cisco

Green River
State Park

Crystal
Geyser

191

128

HONDOO
ARCH LOOP

24

DELICATE
ARCH

Fisher
Towers

HONDOO
ARCH

Arches
National
Park

La Sal

313

Moab

Mt Waas
12,331 ft

Goblin
Valley
State Park

Horseshoe
Canyon

Dead Horse
Point State
Park

279

Manns Pk
12,273 ft

Mt Tomasaki
12,230 ft

Hanksville

24

Canyonlands
National Park

River

MESA ARCH TRAIL

Mt Peale
12,721 ft

Cameo Cliffs

46

SEE
"CANYONLANDS
NATIONAL PARK"
MAP

GRAND VIEW POINT

La Sal

Capitol
Reef
National
Park

Mt Ellen
11,522 ft

95

DIRTY DEVIL
CANYON
OVERLOOK

Canyonlands
National
Park

Glen
Canyon
National
Recreation
Area

211

191

BLM NEWSPAPER ROCK
HISTORICAL MONUMENT

Cataract Canyon

Beef   Basin

Mt Pennell
11,320 ft

River

Waterpocket Fold

Mt Hillers
10,723 ft

STARR SPRINGS
CAMPGROUND

HITE
MARINA

Dark Canyon

Monticello

491

Ticaboo

276

Colorado

Abajo Pk
11,362 ft

95

Fry Canyon

Elk   Ridge

The Causeway

Glen

Circle

Canyon

NRA

Cliffs

BULLFROG MARINA

276

HALLS CROSSING
MARINA

Natural Bridges
National Monument

Grand
Gulch

261

The Bears Ears
9,058 ft

Blanding

191

Montezuma Canyon

COLORADO
UTAH

262

HOVENWEEP
NATIONAL
MONUMENT

Clay
Hills

Comb Ridge

Bluff

163

Montezuma
Creek

262

Aneth

Lake Powell

HOLE-IN-THE-ROCK

DANGLING ROPE
MARINA

191

RAINBOW BRIDGE
NATIONAL MONUMENT

UTAH

ARIZONA

NAVAJO

Mexican Hat

Monument
Valley

163

INDIAN

FOUR CORNERS
MONUMENT

41

To Kayenta

MONUMENT VALLEY
VISITOR CENTER

RESERVATION

0   15 mi
0   15 km

San Rafael Swell

San Rafael Desert

Green

La Sal
Mtns

Burr Trail

© MOON.COM

Moab

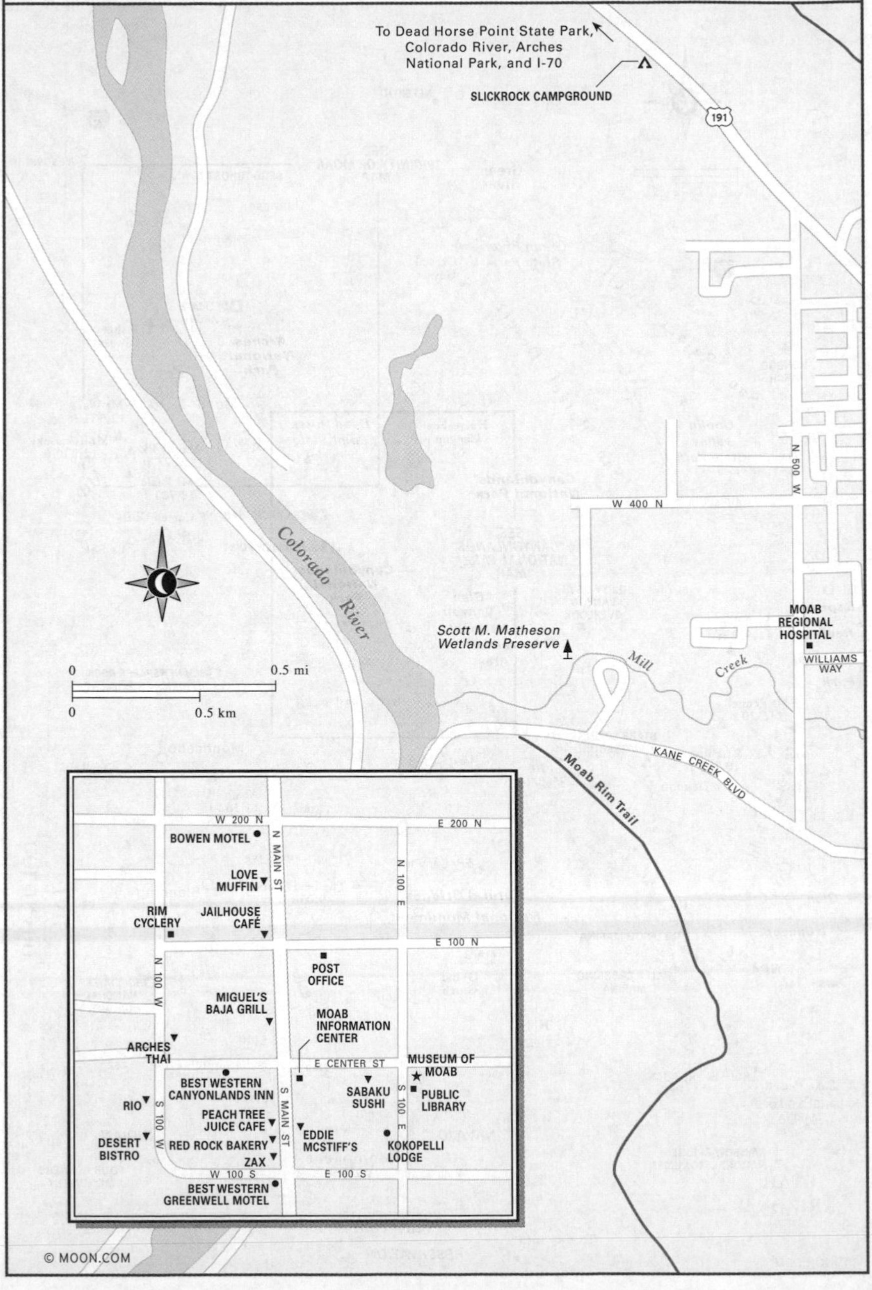

To Dead Horse Point State Park,
Colorado River, Arches
National Park, and I-70

SLICKROCK CAMPGROUND

191

Colorado River

W 400 N

N 500 W

MOAB
REGIONAL
HOSPITAL

WILLIAMS
WAY

*Scott M. Matheson
Wetlands Preserve*

Mill

Creek

KANE CREEK BLVD

Moab Rim Trail

| 0 | | 0.5 mi |
| 0 | | 0.5 km |

W 200 N

E 200 N

BOWEN MOTEL

N MAIN ST

N 100 E

LOVE
MUFFIN

RIM
CYCLERY

JAILHOUSE
CAFÉ

E 100 N

N 100 W

POST
OFFICE

MIGUEL'S
BAJA GRILL

MOAB
INFORMATION
CENTER

ARCHES
THAI

E CENTER ST

MUSEUM OF
MOAB

BEST WESTERN
CANYONLANDS INN

S MAIN ST

SABAKU
SUSHI

N 100 E

PUBLIC
LIBRARY

RIO

PEACH TREE
JUICE CAFE

S 100 W

DESERT
BISTRO

RED ROCK BAKERY
ZAX

EDDIE
MCSTIFF'S

KOKOPELLI
LODGE

W 100 S

E 100 S

BEST WESTERN
GREENWELL MOTEL

© MOON.COM

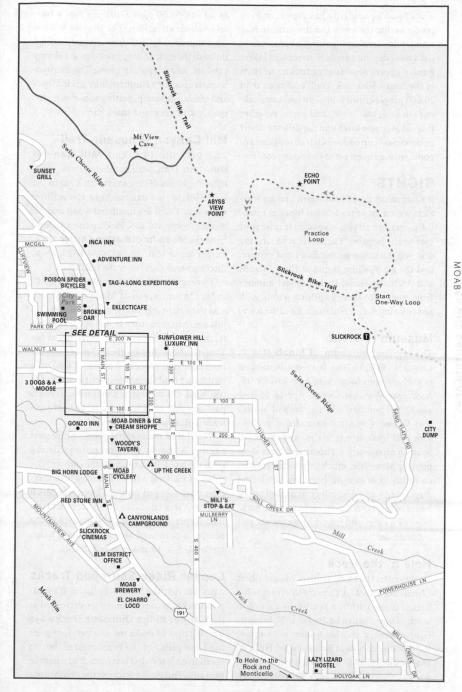

Slickrock Bike Trail

Mt View
Cave

Swiss Cheese Ridge

SUNSET
GRILL

ECHO
POINT

ABYSS
VIEW
POINT

Practice
Loop

MCGILL

INCA INN

CLIFFVIEW

ADVENTURE INN

Slickrock Bike Trail

POISON SPIDER
BICYCLES

TAG-A-LONG EXPEDITIONS

City
Park

N 100 W

EKLECTICAFE

Start
One-Way Loop

SWIMMING
POOL

BROKEN
OAR

PARK DR

SLICKROCK

SEE DETAIL

E 200 N

SUNFLOWER HILL
LUXURY INN

WALNUT LN

N MAIN ST

N 100 E

E 100 N

N 300 E

Swiss Cheese Ridge

3 DOGS & A
MOOSE

E CENTER ST

S 200 E

E 100 S

SAND FLATS RD

E 100 S

CITY
DUMP

GONZO INN

MOAB DINER & ICE
CREAM SHOPPE

S 300 E

E 200 S

TUSHER ST

WOODY'S
TAVERN

E 300 S

BIG HORN LODGE

S MAIN ST

MOAB
CYCLERY

UP THE CREEK

MILL CREEK DR

RED STONE INN

CANYONLANDS
CAMPGROUND

MILI'S
STOP & EAT

MULBERRY
LN

MOUNTAINVIEW AVE

SLICKROCK
CINEMAS

Mill

Creek

BLM DISTRICT
OFFICE

Moab Rim

MOAB
BREWERY

EL CHARRO
LOCO

191

POWERHOUSE LN

Pack

Creek

MILL CREEK DR

LAZY LIZARD
HOSTEL

To Hole 'n the
Rock and
Monticello

HOLYOAK LN

As Moab's popularity has grown, so have concerns that the town and the surrounding countryside are simply getting loved to death. On a busy day, hundreds of mountain bikers form queues to negotiate the trickier sections of the famed Slickrock Trail, and more than 20,000 people crowd into town on busy weekends to bike, hike, float, and party. Whether this old Mormon town and the delicate desert environment can endure such an onslaught of popularity is a question of increasing concern.

SIGHTS

It's fair to say that Moab doesn't tempt travelers with a lot of traditional tourism establishments, but all you have to do is raise your eyes to the horizon. The locale is so striking that you'll want to get outdoors and explore, and the astonishing sights of Canyonlands and Arches National Parks are just minutes from town. But there's nothing wrong with just enjoying the enthusiastic vibe of the town.

Museum of Moab

The regional **Museum of Moab** (118 E. Center St., 435/259-7985, www.moabmuseum. org, 10am-6pm Mon.-Sat., Apr. 15-Oct. 15, noon-5pm Mon.-Sat. Oct. 16-Apr. 14, $5 over age 17, $10 families) tells the story of Moab's and Grand County's past, from prehistoric and Ute artifacts to the explorations of Spanish missionaries. Photos and tools show pioneer Moab life, much of which centered on ranching or mining; here, too, you'll find displays of rocks and minerals as well as the bones of huge dinosaurs, including the backbone of a sauropod found by a rancher just outside town.

Hole n' the Rock

Twelve miles (19.3 km) south of Moab, Albert Christensen worked 12 years to excavate his dream home within a sandstone monolith south of town. When he died in 1957, his wife, Gladys, worked another 8 years to complete the 5,000-square-foot house, called **Hole n' the Rock** (11037 S. U.S. 191, 435/686-2250, www.theholeintherock.com, 9am-5pm daily,

$6 adults, $3.50 ages 5-10). It's now a full-on roadside attraction. The interior has notable touches like a 65-foot chimney drilled through the rock ceiling, paintings, taxidermy exhibits, and a lapidary room. The 14-room home is open for 12-minute-long guided tours and offers a gift shop, petting zoo, exotic animals, picnic area, and snack bar.

Mill Canyon Dinosaur Trail

The 0.5-mile (0.8 km) **Mill Canyon Dinosaur Trail,** with numbered stops, identifies the bones of dinosaurs that lived in the wet climate that existed here 150 million years ago. You'll see fossilized wood and dinosaur footprints, too. Pick up the brochure from the **Moab Information Center** (25 E. Center St., at Main St., 435/259-8825, www.discovermoab.com) or at the trailhead.

To reach the dinosaur bone site, drive 15 miles (24 km) north of Moab on U.S. 191, and then turn left (west) at an intersection just north of milepost 141. Cross the railroad tracks; after 0.6 miles (1 km), turn left at the Y intersection; after another 0.5 mile (0.8 km), turn right and proceed 0.6 mile (1 km) on a rough dirt road (impassable when wet) to the trailhead. On the way to the trailhead, you'll pass another trailhead where a short trail leads to dinosaur tracks.

You'll find many other points of interest nearby. A copper mill and tailings dating from the late 1800s are across the canyon. The ruins of Halfway Stage Station, where travelers once stopped on the Thompson-Moab run, are a short distance down the other road fork. Jeepers and mountain bikers explore the nearby Monitor and Merrimac Buttes; a sign just off U.S. 191 has a map and details.

Copper Ridge Sauropod Tracks

Apatosaurus, aka brontosaurus, and theropod tracks crisscross an ancient riverbed at the **Copper Ridge Dinosaur Trackways** site. It's easy to make out the two-foot-wide hind footprints of the brontosaurus, but its small front feet didn't leave much of a dent in the sand. Three-toed tracks of the carnivorous theropods, possibly allosaurus, are 8-15 inches long, and some show an irregular gait—perhaps indicating a limp.

The Copper Ridge tracks are 23 miles (37 km) north of Moab on U.S. 191; turn right (east) 0.75 mile (1.2 km) north of milepost 148. Cross the railroad tracks and turn south onto the dirt road, following signs 2 miles (3.2 km) to the tracks. It's a short walk to the trackway. A network of mountain bike trails, the Dino-Flow trails, can also be accessed from the parking area.

Moab Giants

If you (or your kids) want a more commercial take on the local dinosaurs, visit **Moab Giants** (112 W Hwy. 313, 435/355-0228, www.moabgiants.com, 10am-6pm daily, $16 adults, $14 seniors and teens 13-17, $12 children 4-12), where you can walk a well-executed 0.5-mile (0.8-km) trail alongside dinosaur replicas. Add $6 to your ticket price to visit a good museum with a focus on fossil footprints and catch a short 3D movie. This large complex is at the corner of U.S. 191 and the road to Dead Horse Point.

Dead Horse Point State Park

Just east of Canyonlands' Island in the Sky District and a short drive northwest of Moab is one of Utah's most spectacular state parks. At **Dead Horse Point State Park** (435/259-2614, www.stateparks.utah.gov, day-use $15 per vehicle, camping $30 tents, $99 yurt rental), the land drops away in sheer cliffs. Two thousand feet below, the Colorado River twists through a gooseneck on its long journey to the sea. The river and its tributaries have carved canyons that reveal a geologic layer cake of colorful rock formations. Even in a region of impressive views around nearly every corner, Dead Horse Point stands out for its exceptionally breathtaking panorama. You'll also see below you, along the Colorado River, the result of powerful underground forces: Salt, under pressure, has pushed up overlying rock layers into an anticline. This formation, the Shafer Dome, contains potash that is

being processed by the Moab Salt Plant. You can see the mine buildings, processing plant, and evaporation ponds (tinted blue to hasten evaporation).

A narrow neck of land only 30 yards wide connects the point with the rest of the plateau. Cowboys once herded wild horses onto the point, and then placed a fence across the neck to make a 40-acre corral. They chose the desirable animals from the herd and let the rest go. According to one tale, a group of horses left behind after such a roundup became confused by the geography of the point. They couldn't find their way off and circled repeatedly until they died of thirst within sight of the river below. You may also hear other stories of how the point got its name.

Besides the awe-inspiring views, the park also offers a **visitors center** (9am-5pm daily), a very popular campground, a picnic area, a group area, a nature trail, hiking trails, and great mountain biking on the **Intrepid Trail System.** Spectacularly scenic hiking trails run along the east and west rims of the peninsula-like park; hikers are also allowed on the Intrepid trails. Rangers lead hikes during the busy spring season and on some evenings during the summer, including monthly full-moon hikes. Whether you're visiting for the day or camping at Dead Horse Point, it's best to bring plenty of water; although water is available here, it is trucked in.

Dead Horse Point is easily reached by paved road, either as a destination itself or as a side trip on the way to the Island in the Sky District of Canyonlands National Park. From Moab, head northwest 9 miles (14.5 km) on U.S. 191, then turn left and travel 22 miles (35 km) on Highway 313. The drive along Highway 313 climbs through a scenic canyon and tops out on a ridge with panoramas of distant mesas, buttes, mountains, and canyons. Several rest areas are along the road.

SCENIC DRIVES

Each of the following routes is at least partly accessible to standard low-clearance highway vehicles. If you have a 4WD vehicle,

you'll have the option of additional off-road exploring.

You'll find detailed travel information on these and other places in Charles Wells's book *Guide to Moab, UT Backroads & 4-Wheel Drive Trails*, which, along with a good selection of maps, is available at the **Moab Information Center** (25 E. Center St., 435/259-8825, www.discovermoab.com). Staff at the info center usually know current road and trail conditions.

Utah Scenic Byway 279

Highway 279 goes downstream along the west side of the Colorado River Canyon on the other side of the river from Moab. Pavement extends 16 miles (26 km) past fine views, prehistoric rock art, arches, and hiking trails. A potash plant marks the end of the highway; a rough dirt road continues to Canyonlands National Park. From Moab, head north 3.5 miles (5.6 km) on U.S. 191, then turn left onto Highway 279. The highway enters the canyon at the "portal," 2.7 miles (4.3 km) from the turnoff. Towering sandstone cliffs rise on the right, and the Colorado River drifts along just below on the left.

Stop at a signed pullout on the left, 0.6 mile (1 km) past the canyon entrance, to see **Indian Ruins Viewpoint,** a small prehistoric Native American ruin tucked under a ledge across the river. The stone structure was probably used for food storage.

Groups of **petroglyphs** cover cliffs along the highway 5.2 miles (8.4 km) from U.S. 191, which is 0.7 mile (1.1 km) beyond milepost 11. Look across the river to see the Fickle Finger of Fate among the sandstone fins of Behind the Rocks. A petroglyph of a bear is 0.2 mile (0.3 km) farther down the highway. Archaeologists think that Fremonts and the later Utes did most of the artwork in this area.

A signed pullout on the right, 6.2 miles (10 km) from U.S. 191, points out **dinosaur tracks** and petroglyphs visible on rocks

above. Sighting tubes help locate the features. It's possible to hike up the steep hillside for a closer look.

Ten miles (16 km) west of the highway turnoff is the trailhead for the **Corona Arch Trail** (3 miles/4.8 km round-trip). The aptly named **Jug Handle Arch,** with an opening 46 feet high and 3 feet wide, is close to the road on the right, 13.6 miles (21.8 km) from U.S. 191. Ahead the canyon opens up where underground pressure from salt and potash has folded the rock layers into an anticline.

At the **Moab Salt Plant,** mining operations inject water underground to dissolve potash and other chemicals, then pump the solution to evaporation ponds. The ponds are dyed blue to hasten evaporation, which takes about a year. You can see these colorful solutions from Dead Horse Point and Anticline Overlook on the canyon rims.

High-clearance vehicles can continue on the unpaved road beyond the plant. The road passes through varied canyon country, with views overlooking the Colorado River. At a road junction in Canyonlands National Park's Island in the Sky District, you have a choice of turning left for the 100-mile White Rim Trail (4WD vehicles only past Musselman Arch), continuing up the steep switchbacks of the Shafer Trail Road (4WD vehicle recommended) to the paved park road, or returning the way you came.

Utah Scenic Byway 128

Highway 128 turns northeast from U.S. 191 just south of the Colorado River Bridge, 2 miles (3.2 km) north of Moab. This exceptionally scenic canyon route follows the Colorado for 30 miles (48 km) upstream before crossing at Dewey Bridge and turning north to I-70. The entire highway is paved. The Lions Park picnic area at the turnoff from U.S. 191 is a pleasant stopping place. Big Bend Recreation Site is another good spot 7.5 miles up Highway 128.

The rugged scenery along this stretch of the Colorado has been featured in many films (mostly Westerns, but also *Thelma & Louise*)

1: Dead Horse Point State Park; 2: The water at the Moab Salt Plant is dyed blue to hasten evaporation.

Rock Art Around Moab

The fertile valley around Moab has been home to humans for thousands of years. Prehistoric Fremont and Ancestral Puebloan people once lived and farmed in the bottoms of the canyons around Moab. Their rock art, granaries, and dwellings can still be seen here. Nomadic Utes had replaced the earlier groups by the time the first white settlers arrived. They left fewer signs of settlement but added their artistry to the area's rock-art panels. You don't need to travel far to see excellent examples of native pictographs and petroglyphs.

Sego Canyon: If you approach Moab along I-70, consider a side trip to one of the premier rock-art galleries in Utah. Sego Canyon is about 5 miles (8 km) north of I-70; take exit 187, the Thompson Springs exit. Drive through the slumbering little town and continue up the canyon behind it (BLM signs also point the way). A side road leads to a parking area where the canyon walls close in. Sego Canyon is a showcase of prehistoric rock art—it preserves rock drawings and images that are thousands of years old. The Barrier Canyon Style drawings may be 8,000 years old; the more recent Fremont Style images were created in the last 1,000 years. Compared to these ancient pictures, the Ute etchings are relatively recent: Experts speculate that they may have been drawn in the 1800s, when Ute villages still lined Sego Canyon. The newer petroglyphs and pictographs are more representational than the older ones. The ancient Barrier Canyon figures are typically horned ghostlike beings that look like aliens from early Hollywood sci-fi thrillers. The Fremont Style images depict stylized human figures made from geometric shapes; the crudest figures are the most recent. The Ute images are of bison and hunters on horseback.

Potash Road (Hwy. 279): From U.S. 191 just north of the Colorado River Bridge, take Highway 279 west along the river 5.2 miles (8.5 km) to these easily accessed petroglyphs. There's even a sign (Indian Writing) to guide you to them.

Golf Course Rock Art: Take U.S. 191 south to the Moab Golf Course, which is about 4 miles (6.4 km) from the corner of Main and Center Streets in downtown Moab. Turn left and proceed to Spanish Trail Road. Approximately 1 mile (1.6 km) past the fire station, turn right onto Westwater Drive. Proceed 0.5 mile (0.8 km) to a small pullout on the left side of the road. An area approximately 30 by 90 feet is covered with human and animal figures, including Moab Man and what is popularly referred to as the reindeer and sled.

Kane Creek Boulevard: Kane Creek Boulevard (south of downtown Moab; watch for the McDonald's) follows the Colorado River and leads to a number of excellent rock-art sites. From the junction with U.S. 191, turn west and proceed 0.8 mile (1.3 km) to the intersection of Kane Creek Boulevard and 500 West. Keep left and continue along Kane Creek Boulevard approximately 2.3 miles (3.7 km) to the mouth of Moon Flower Canyon. Along the rock cliff just beyond the canyon, you will see a rock-art panel behind a fence. Continue another 1.2 miles (1.9 km, 3.5 miles from 500 West) to another rock-art panel, where a huge rock surface streaked with desert varnish is covered with images of bighorn sheep, snakes, and human forms. For a unique rock-art image, continue on Kane Creek Boulevard past the cattle guard, where the road turns from pavement to graded gravel road. About 1.4 miles (2.3 km) from the cattle guard, just past the second sign for the Amasa Back trail, (5.5 miles/8.9 km from the intersection of Kane Creek Boulevard and 500 West), watch for two small pullouts. Down the slope from the road is a large boulder with rock art on all four sides. The most amazing image is of a woman giving birth.

Courthouse Wash: Although this site is located within Arches National Park, it is accessed from a parking lot off U.S. 191 just north of the Colorado River Bridge, 1 mile (1.6 km) north of Moab. A 0.5-mile (0.8-km) hike leads to the panel that is almost 19 feet high and 52 feet long. It has both pictographs and petroglyphs, with figures resembling ghostly humans, bighorn sheep, scorpions, and a large beaked bird. This panel, which was vandalized in 1980, was restored by the Park Service; restoration work revealed older images underneath the vandalized layer.

A *Rock Art Auto Tour* brochure is available at the Moab Information Center (25 E. Center St., at Main St., Moab, 435/259-8825, www.discovermoab.com, 8am-7pm Mon.-Sat., 9am-6pm Sun. mid-Mar.-Nov.).

and commercials. If you're intrigued, stop by the **Museum of Film,** housed in the lodge at Red Cliffs Ranch (435/259-2002 or 866/812-2002, www.redcliffslodge.com), a resort near the 14-mile (22.5-km) marker. Drop by anytime and browse free of charge.

The paved and scenic **La Sal Mountains Loop Road,** with viewpoints overlooking Castle Valley, Arches and Canyonlands National Parks, Moab Rim, and other scenic features, has its northern terminus at Castle Valley. From here, this route climbs high into the La Sals, then loops back to Moab. Vegetation along the drive runs the whole range from the cottonwoods, sage, and rabbitbrush of the desert to forests of aspen, fir, and spruce. The 62-mile (100-km) loop road can easily take a full day with stops for scenic overlooks, a picnic, and a bit of hiking or fishing. Because of the high elevations, the loop's season usually lasts May-October. Before venturing off the Loop Road, it's a good idea to check current back-road conditions with the Moab Information Center. You can also ask for a road log of sights and side roads. The turnoff from Highway 128 is 15.5 miles (25 km) up from U.S. 191.

A graded county road, **Onion Creek Road** turns southeast off Highway 128 about 20 miles (32 km) from U.S. 191 and heads up Onion Creek, crossing it many times. Avoid this route if storms threaten. The unpleasant-smelling creek contains poisonous arsenic and selenium. Colorful rock formations of dark red sandstone line the creek. After about 8 miles (12.9 km), the road climbs steeply out of Onion Creek to upper Fisher Valley and a junction with Kokopelli's Trail, which follows a jeep road over this part of its route.

One of the area's most striking sights are the Gothic spires of **Fisher Towers,** which soar as high as 900 feet above Professor Valley. Supposedly, the name Fisher is not that of a pioneer but a corruption of the geologic term *fissure*. In 1962, three climbers from Colorado made the first ascent of Titan Tower, the tallest of the three towers. The almost-vertical rock faces, overhanging bulges, and sections of rotten rock made for an exhausting 3.5 days of climbing (the party descended to the base for two of the nights). Their final descent from the summit took only six hours. In 2008, a slack-liner walked a rope strung between the two tallest towers, and visitors to the towers can frequently see climbers and occasionally slack-line walkers. The BLM has a small campground and picnic area nearby, and a hiking trail skirts the base of the three main

ARCHES AND CANYONLANDS
MOAB

Fisher Towers

towers. An unpaved road turns southeast off Highway 128 near milepost 21 (21 miles/34 km from U.S. 191) and continues 2 miles (3.2 km) to the picnic area.

The existing **Dewey Bridge,** 30 miles (48 km) up the highway, replaced a picturesque wood-and-steel suspension bridge built in 1916, which burned in 2008. Here, the BLM has built the Dewey Bridge Recreation Site, with a picnic area, a trailhead, a boat launch, and a small campground.

Upstream from Dewey Bridge are the wild rapids of **Westwater Canyon.** The Colorado River cut this narrow gorge into dark metamorphic rock. You can raft or kayak down the river in one day or a more leisurely two days; many local outfitters offer trips. Camping is limited to a single night. Unlike most desert rivers, this section of the Colorado also offers good river-running at low water levels in late summer-fall. Westwater Canyon's inner gorge, where boaters face their greatest challenge, is only about 3.5 miles (5.6 km) long; however, you can enjoy scenic sandstone canyons both upstream and downstream.

The rough 4WD **Top-of-the-World Road** climbs to an overlook with outstanding views of Fisher Towers, Fisher Valley, Onion Creek, and beyond. Pick up a map at the Moab Information Center (25 E. Center St., at Main St., 435/259-8825, www.discovermoab.com) to guide you to the rim. Elevation here is 6,800 feet, nearly 3,000 feet higher than the Colorado River.

Kane Creek Scenic Drive

Kane Creek Road heads downstream along the Colorado River on the same side as Moab. The four miles through the Colorado River Canyon are paved, followed by six miles of good dirt road through Kane Springs Canyon. This route also leads to the Matheson wetland preserve (a Nature Conservancy site at 934 W. Kane Creek Blvd.), great rock art, and several hiking trails and campgrounds, as well as some modern-day cave dwellings. People with high-clearance vehicles or mountain bikes can continue across Kane Springs

Creek to Hurrah Pass and an extensive network of 4WD trails. From Moab, drive south on Main Street (U.S. 191) for 1 mile (1.6 km), then turn right onto Kane Creek Boulevard, which becomes Kane Creek Road.

ENTERTAINMENT AND EVENTS
Nightlife

A lot of Moab's nightlife focuses on the well-loved **Eddie McStiff's** (57 S. Main St., 435/259-2337, www.eddiemcstiffs.com, 11:30am-close daily), right downtown, with abundant beers on draft, cocktails, two outdoor seating areas, and live music on a regular basis.

Woody's Tavern (221 S. Main St., 435/259-9323, www.woodystavernmoab.com, 2pm-1am Mon.-Sat., 11am-1am Sun.), a classic dive bar, has pool and live bands on the weekend—you may hear bluegrass, rock, or jam bands. **Club Rio** (2 S. 100 W., 435/259-2654, 11:30am-1am daily) is a sports bar with frequent live music and entertainment.

Come for some barbecue and stay for the blues (or vice versa; both are good) at **Blu Pig** (811 S. Main St., 435/259-3333, 11:30am-10pm daily).

For a more family-friendly evening out, cruise the Colorado with **Canyonlands by Night** (435/259-5261, www.canyonlandsbynight.com). The evening cruise ends with a sound-and-light presentation along the sandstone cliffs. Dinner packages are available; children under age four are not permitted, per Coast Guard regulations.

Festivals and Events

To find out about local happenings, contact the **Moab Information Center** (25 E. Center St., at Main St., 435/259-8825, www.discovermoab.com) or browse *Moab Happenings* (www.moabhappenings.com), available free around town or online. Unsurprisingly, Moab offers quite a few annual biking events. The **Moab Skinny Tire Festival,** held in mid-March, and the **Moab Century Tour,** held in late September or early

Vicinity of Moab

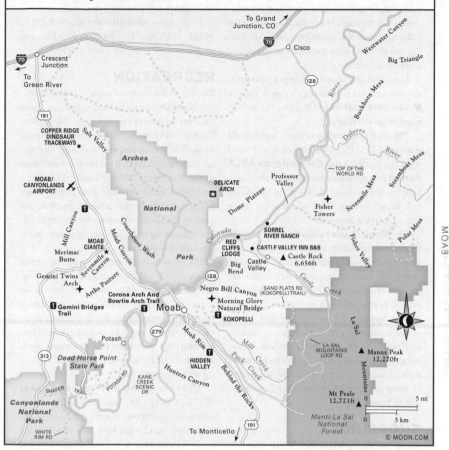

To Grand Junction, CO

Cisco

Crescent Junction

To Green River

Westwater Canyon

Big Triangle

Buckhorn Mesa

COPPER RIDGE DINOSAUR TRACKWAYS

Salt Valley

Arches

Dolores River

MOAB/ CANYONLANDS AIRPORT

National

DELICATE ARCH

Dome Plateau

TOP OF THE WORLD RD

Professor Valley

Steamboat Mesa

Sevenmile Mesa

Fisher Towers

Polar Mesa

Mill Canyon

MOAB GIANTS

Courthouse Wash

Moab Canyon

Park

Merimac Butte

Gemini Twins Arch

Sevenmile Canyon

Arths Pasture

Colorado

RED CLIFFS LODGE

Big Bend

SORREL RIVER RANCH

CASTLE VALLEY INN B&B

Castle Rock 6,656ft

Castle Valley

Fisher Valley

Castle Creek

Corona Arch And Bowtie Arch Trail

Gemini Bridges Trail

Moab

Negro Bill Canyon

Morning Glory Natural Bridge

KOKOPELLI

SAND FLATS RD (KOKOPELLI TRAIL)

La Sal Mountains

Potash

Dead Horse Point State Park

Moab Rim

Mill Creek

Pack Creek

HIDDEN VALLEY

Hunters Canyon

Behind the Rocks

LA SAL MOUNTAINS LOOP RD

Manns Peak 12,270ft

SHAFER TRAIL

POTASH RD

KANE CREEK SCENIC DR

Canyonlands National Park

WHITE RIM RD

To Monticello

Mt Peale 12,721ft

Manti-La Sal National Forest

0   5 mi
0   5 km

© MOON.COM

ARCHES AND CANYONLANDS

MOAB

October, are both supported road bike events that benefit the fight against cancer. For information on both, visit www.skinnytirefestival.com or call 435/260-8889. The bike demo event **OuterBike** (www.outerbike.com) is held in early April, and the **Moab Ho-Down Mountain Bike and Film Festival** (http://moabhodown.com) in late October offers both silly and endurance races, jump contests, skills camps and other fun events (costume party!), plus an evening of bike-themed films. Other major annual athletic events include a number of running events organized by **Mad**

Moose Events (www.madmooseevents.com). These include the **Canyonlands Half Marathon and Five Mile Run**, held the third Saturday in March, and a women's half-marathon held in early June, the **Thelma and Louise Half Marathon.** Moab's most popular annual event, more popular than anything celebrating two wheels, is the **Easter Jeep Safari** (www.rr4w.com), which is the Sturgis or Daytona Beach of recreational four-wheeling. Upward of 2,500 4WD vehicles (it's not exclusively for jeeps, although ATVs are not allowed) converge on Moab for ten day's worth of organized backcountry trail rides. Big Saturday (the day before Easter) is the climax of the event, when all participating vehicles parade through Moab. Plan well ahead for lodging if you are planning to visit Moab during this event, as hotel rooms are often booked a year in advance.

Memorial Day weekend brings artists, musicians, and art cars to the city park for the **Moab Arts Festival** (435/259-2742, www. moabartsfestival.org).

The dust is kicked up at the Spanish Trail Arena (3641 S. U.S. 191, just south of Moab) with the professional **Canyonlands PRCA Rodeo** (www.moabcanyonlandsrodeo.com), held the last weekend in May or first weekend in June, with a rodeo, a parade, a dance, horse racing, and a 4-H gymkhana.

The **Moab Music Festival** (435/259-7003, www.moabmusicfest.org) is first and foremost a classical chamber music festival, but every year a few jazz, bluegrass, or folk artists are included in the lineup. More than 30 artists are currently involved in the festival, held in late August and early September. Many of the concerts are held in dramatic outdoor settings. The **Moab Folk Festival** (www. moabfolkfestival.com) is the town's other big annual musical event, attracting top-notch acoustic performers to Moab the first weekend of November.

SHOPPING

Main Street, between 200 North and 200 South, has nearly a dozen galleries and gift shops selling T-shirts, outdoor apparel, Native American art, and other gifts. **Back of Beyond Books** (83 N. Main St., 435/259-5154, 9am-10pm daily) features an excellent selection of regional books and maps. Pick up those missing camping items at **Gearheads** (471 S. Main St., 435/259-4327, 8am-10pm daily spring-fall, shorter hours winter), an amazingly well-stocked outdoor store. If you're heading out to camp or hike in the desert, Gearheads is a good place to fill your water jugs with free filtered water.

Moab's largest grocery store, **City Market**

(425 S. Main St., 435/259-5181, 6am-11pm daily), is a good place to pick up supplies; it has a pharmacy and a gas station.

Stop by the **Moonflower Market** (39 E. 100 N., 435/259-5712, 9am-8pm daily) for natural-food groceries; it's a well-stocked store.

RECREATION

Moab is at the center of some of the most picturesque landscapes in North America. Even the least outdoorsy visitor will want to explore the river canyons, natural arches, and mesas. Mountain biking and river tours are the recreational activities that get the most attention in the Moab area, although hikers, climbers, and horseback riders also find plenty to do. If you're less physically adventurous, you can explore the landscape on scenic flights or follow old mining roads in a jeep to remote backcountry destinations.

It's easy to find outfitters and sporting goods rental operations in Moab; it's the largest business segment in town, and there's a remarkable cohesion to the town's operations. It seems that everyone markets everyone else's excursions and services, so just ask the closest outfitter for whatever service you need, and chances are excellent you'll get hooked up with what you want.

Make the **Moab Information Center** (25 E. Center St., 435/259-8825, www. discovermoab.com, 8am-7pm Mon.-Sat., 9am-6pm Sun.) your first stop in town; it's an excellent source for information about the area's recreational options. The center is staffed by representatives of the National Park Service, the BLM, the U.S. Forest Service, and the Canyonlands Field Institute; they can direct you to the adventure of your liking. The center also has literature, books, and maps for sale. BLM officials can point you to the developed and undeveloped designated campsites near the Moab Slickrock Bike Trail, Kane Creek, and along the Colorado River; you must use the designated sites in these areas.

Canyonlands Field Institute

1: Moab shops and galleries; 2: Hunter Canyon

(435/259-7750 or 800/860-5262, www. canyonlandsfieldinst.org) leads weekend day hikes mid-April-mid-October ($40-45, including transportation and park admission fees) at various locations near Moab; join one of these to really learn the area's natural history.

Hiking

Most of Moab's prime hiking trails require a short drive to trailheads; these routes are all picturesque.

KANE CREEK SCENIC DRIVE AND U.S. 191 SOUTH

The high cliffs just southwest of town provide fine views of the Moab Valley, highlands of Arches National Park, and the La Sal Mountains. The **Moab Rim Trail** turns off Kane Creek Boulevard 1.5 miles (2.4 km) downriver from Moab. The total driving distance from the junction of Main Street and Kane Creek Boulevard is 2.6 miles (4.2 km); look for the trailhead on the left, 0.1 mile (0.2 km) after a cattle guard.

You can see the sky through Little Arch across the river from the trailhead. Four-wheel-drive vehicles can also ascend the Moab Rim Trail, although the rough terrain is considered difficult for them; the first 200 yards will give drivers a feel for the difficulty. The trail climbs northeast 1.5 miles (2.4 km) along tilted rock strata of the Kayenta Formation to the top of the plateau. This hike is moderately difficult, with an elevation gain of 940 feet and good views nearly all the way. Once on top, hikers can follow jeep roads southeast to Hidden Valley Trail and descend on a hiking trail to U.S. 191 south of Moab—a 5.5-mile (8.9-km) one-way trip. Experienced hikers can also head south from the rim to Behind the Rocks, a fantastic maze of sandstone fins.

You'll see not only a "hidden valley" from the **Hidden Valley Trail** but also panoramas of the Moab area and Behind the Rocks. The moderately difficult trail ascends 500 feet in a series of switchbacks to a broad shelf below

the Moab Rim, then follows the shelf (hidden valley) to the northwest. It then crosses a low pass and follows a second shelf in the same direction. Near the end of the second shelf, the trail turns left to a divide, where you can see a portion of the remarkable fins of Behind the Rocks. This divide is 1 mile (1.6 km) from the start and 680 feet higher in elevation. The trail continues 0.3 mile (0.5 km) from the divide down to the end of the Moab Rim Trail, which is a jeep road and hiking trail. Instead of turning left to the divide, you can make a short side trip (no trail) to the right for views of Moab.

To reach the Hidden Valley trailhead, drive south 3 miles (4.8 km) on U.S. 191 from Moab, turn right, and go 0.4 mile (0.6 km) on Angel Rock Road to its end (the turnoff is just south of milepost 122), then turn right and go 0.3 mile (0.5 km) on Rimrock Lane.

A look at the topographic map will show that something strange is going on at the area called **Behind the Rocks.** Massive fins of Navajo sandstone 100-500 feet high, 50-200 feet thick, and up to 0.5 mile (0.8 km) long cover a large area. Narrow vertical cracks, sometimes only a few feet wide, separate the fins. Archaeological sites and several arches are in the area. The maze offers endless exploration routes. No maintained trails exist here, and some routes require technical climbing skills. If you get lost (which is very easy to do), remember that the fins are oriented east-west; the rim of the Colorado River Canyon is reached by going west, and Spanish Valley is reached by going east. Bring plenty of water, a topographic map (Moab 7.5-minute), and a compass. Access routes are Moab Rim and Hidden Valley Trails (from the north and east) and Pritchett Canyon (from the west and south). Although it is only a couple of miles from Moab, Behind the Rocks seems a world away.

Hikers along **Hunter Canyon** can see a rock arch and other rock formations in the canyon walls and the lush vegetation along the creek. Off-road vehicles have made tracks a short way up; beyond that you'll be walking mostly along the creek bed. Short sections of trail lead around thickets of tamarisk and other water-loving plants. Look for Hunters Arch on the right about 0.5 mile (0.8 km) up. Most of the water in Hunter Canyon comes from a deep pool surrounded by hanging gardens of maidenhair fern. A dry fall and a small natural bridge are above the pool. This pretty spot marks the hike's 3-mile (4.8-km) point and an elevation gain of 240 feet. To reach the trailhead from Moab, drive 8 miles (12.9 km) on Kane Creek Boulevard along the Colorado River and up Kane Creek Canyon. The road is asphalted where it fords Hunter Creek, but the asphalt is usually covered with dirt washed over it by the creek.

HIGHWAY 279

The **Portal Overlook Trail** switchbacks up a slope, then follows a sloping sandstone ledge of the Kayenta Formation to an overlook. A panorama takes in the Colorado River, Moab Valley, Arches National Park, and the La Sal Mountains. The hike is 1.5 miles (2.4 km, one-way) with an elevation gain of 980 feet. This trail is a twin of the Moab Rim Trail across the river. Begin from Jaycee Park Campground on the right, 3.8 miles (6.1 km) from the turnoff at U.S. 191; mulberry trees shade the attractive

spot. Expect to share this trail with many mountain bikers.

The 1.5-mile (2.4 km, one-way) **Corona Arch and Bowtie Arch Trail** leads across slickrock country to these impressive arches. You can't see them from the road, although a third arch—Pinto—is visible. The signed trailhead is on the right, 10 miles (16 km) from U.S. 191 (midway between mileposts 5 and 6); you'll see railroad tracks just beyond the trailhead. The trail climbs up from the parking area, crosses the tracks, and follows a bit of a jeep road and a small wash to an ancient gravel bar. Pinto (or Gold Bar) Arch stands to the left, although there's no trail to it. Follow cairns to Corona and Bowtie. Handrails and a ladder help in the few steep spots.

Despite being only a few hundred yards apart, each arch has a completely different character and history. Bowtie formed when a pothole in the cliffs above met a cave underneath. (It was called Paul Bunyan's Potty until that name was appropriated for an arch in Canyonlands National Park.) The hole is about 30 feet in diameter. Corona Arch, reminiscent of the larger Rainbow Bridge, eroded out of a sandstone fin. The graceful span is 140 feet long and 105 feet high. Both arches are composed of Navajo sandstone. If you

Corona Arch and Bowtie Arch Trail

have time for only one hike in the Moab area, this one is especially recommended.

HIGHWAY 128

Negro Bill Canyon is one of the most popular hiking destinations in the Moab area. The route follows a lively stream pooled by beavers and surrounded by abundant greenery and sheer canyon cliffs. The high point of the hike is **Morning Glory Natural Bridge,** the sixth-longest natural rock span in the country (243 feet). The trailhead is on the right just after crossing a concrete bridge 3 miles (4.8 km) from U.S. 191. A trail leads up-canyon, along the creek in some places, high on the banks in others.

To see Morning Glory Natural Bridge, head two miles up the main canyon to the second side canyon on the right, then follow a good side trail 0.5 mile (0.8 km) up to the long, slender bridge. The spring and small pool underneath keep the air cool even in summer; ferns, columbines, and poison ivy grow here. The elevation gain is 330 feet.

You can't miss the **Fisher Towers** as you drive Highway 128. These spires of dark red sandstone rise 900 feet above Professor Valley. You can hike around the base of these needle rocks on a trail accessed from the BLM picnic area. Titan, the third and highest rock tower, stands 1 mile (1.6 km) from the picnic area; a viewpoint overlooks Onion Creek 1.1 miles (2 km) farther along. Carry water for this moderately difficult hike.

Mountain Biking

The first mountain bikes came to Moab in 1982, when they were used to herd cattle. That didn't work out too well, but within a decade or so, Moab had become the West's most noted mountain biking destination. In addition to riding the famed and challenging slickrock trails (slickrock is the exposed sandstone that composes much of the land's surface here) that wind through astonishing desert landscapes, cyclists can pedal through alpine meadows in the La Sal Mountains or take nearly abandoned 4WD tracks into the surrounding backcountry. Beware: The most famous trails—like the Slickrock Bike Trail—are not for beginners. Other trails are better matched to the skills of novices.

It's a good idea to read up on Moab-area trails before planning a trip here (heaps of books and pamphlets are available). You can also hire an outfitter to teach you the special skills needed to mountain bike in slickrock country or join a guided tour. The Moab Information Center's website (www.discovermoab.com) also has good information about bike trails.

Most people come to Moab to mountain bike mid-March-late May, and then again in the fall mid-September-end of October. Unless you are an early riser, summer is simply too hot for extended bike touring in these desert canyons. Be prepared for crowds, especially in mid-March, during spring break. The Slickrock Bike Trail alone has been known to attract more than 150,000 riders per year.

If you've never biked on slickrock or in the desert, here are a few basic guidelines. Take care if venturing off a trail—it's a long way down some of the sheer cliff faces. A trail's steep slopes and sharp turns can be tricky, so a helmet is a must. Knee pads and riding gloves also protect from scrapes and bruises. Fat bald tires work best on the rock; partially deflated knobby tires do almost as well. Carry plenty of water—one gallon in summer, half a gallon in cooler months. Tiny plant associations, which live in fragile cryptobiotic soil, don't want you tearing through their homes; stay on the rock and avoid sandy areas.

MOAB BRAND TRAILS

The interconnected loops and spur trails (named for cattle brands that spell out M-O-A-B) here form a trail system with several options that are especially good for beginners or riders who are new to slickrock.

The 7-mile (11.3 km) **Bar-M** loop is easy and makes a good family ride, although you might share the packed-dirt trail with motor vehicles; try **Circle O** (no motor vehicles) for a good 3-mile (4.8 km) initiation to slickrock riding.

More experienced slickrock cyclists can find some challenges on the **Deadman's Ridge, Long Branch,** and **Killer-B** routes at the southern end of the trail system.

To reach the trailhead for all these rides, head about 8miles (12.9 km) north of town on U.S. 191 to the parking lot for the Bar M Chuckwagon (now closed), and park at the south end of its lot.

SLICKROCK BIKE TRAIL

Undulating slickrock in the Sand Flats Recreation Area just east of Moab challenges even the best mountain bike riders; this is not an area in which to learn riding skills. Originally, motorcyclists laid out this route, although now most riders rely on leg and lung power. The 1.7-mile (2.7-km) practice loop near the trail's beginning allows first-time visitors a chance to get a feel for the slickrock. The "trail" consists only of painted white lines. Riders following it have less chance of getting lost or finding themselves in hazardous areas. Plan on about five hours to do the 10.5-mile (16.9-km) main loop, and expect to do some walking.

Side trails lead to viewpoints overlooking Moab, the Colorado River, and arms of Negro Bill Canyon. Panoramas of the surrounding canyon country and the La Sal Mountains add to the pleasure of biking.

To reach the trailhead from Main Street in Moab, turn east and go 0.4 mile (0.6 km) on 300 South, turn right and go 0.1 mile (0.2 km) on 400 East, turn left (east) and go 0.5 mile (0.8 km) on Mill Creek Drive, then turn left and go 2.5 miles (4 km) on Sand Flats Road. The Sand Flats Recreation Area, where the trail is located, charges $5 for an automobile day pass, $2 for a bicycle or motorcycle. Camping ($15) is available, but there is no water. Bring plenty with you!

Farther up Sand Flats Road, the quite challenging, often rock-strewn **Porcupine Rim Trail** draws motorcyclists, jeeps, and mountain bikers; after about 11 miles (17.7 km), the trail becomes single-track, and four-wheelers drop out. The whole trail is about 15 miles (24 km) long.

GEMINI BRIDGES TRAIL

This 14-mile (22.5 km) one-way trail passes tremendous twin rock arches (the bridges) and the slickrock fins of the Wingate Formation, making this one of the most scenic of the Moab-area trails; it's also one of the more moderate trails in terms of necessary skill and fitness. The trail begins 12.5 miles (20.1 km) up Highway 313, just before the turnoff to Dead Horse Point State Park. It's a stiff 21-mile (34-km) uphill ride from Moab to reach the trailhead, so you may want to consider a shuttle. Several companies, including **Coyote Shuttle** (435/260-2097, $25), provide this service, enabling cyclists to concentrate on the fun, mostly downhill ride back toward Moab. The Gemini Bridges Trail, which is shared with motorcycles and 4WD vehicles, ends on U.S. 191 just north of town.

INTREPID TRAIL SYSTEM

Mountain bikers, including novices, should bring their rides to Dead Horse Point, where the Intrepid Trail System offers about 15 miles (24 km) of slickrock and sand single-track trails in three loops that range from a 1-mile (1.6-km) beginner's loop to a more challenging 9-mile (14.5-km) loop. All routes start at the visitors center and have great views into the canyon country. To reach Dead Horse Point State Park (435/259-2614, www.stateparks.utah.gov, $15) from Moab, take U.S. 191 9 miles (14.5 km) north, then turn west onto Highway 313 and follow it 22 miles (35 km) to the park entrance.

LOWER MONITOR AND MERRIMAC TRAIL

A good introduction to the varied terrains of the Moab area, the 7.5-mile (12 km) Lower Monitor and Merrimac Trail includes lots of slickrock riding and a bit of sand. Reach the trailhead by traveling 15 miles (24 km) north of Moab on U.S. 191 and turning west (left) onto Mill Canyon Road, just past milepost 141. Make sure to go on the lower trail, not the Monitor and Merrimac Jeep Trail. After your ride, explore the nearby Mill Canyon Dinosaur Trail (foot traffic only).

SOVEREIGN SINGLE-TRACK

Not every bike trail here is over slickrock; the challenging Sovereign single-track trail is good to ride in hot weather. The trail, which contains rocky technical sections, a bit of slickrock, and more flowing single-track, is shared with motorcycles. Several trailheads access this trail; a popular one is from Willow Springs Road. From Moab, travel 11 miles (17.7 km) north on U.S. 191 and turn right onto Willow Springs Road, then follow this sandy road 2.5 miles (4 km) to the trailhead. To best see the options, pick up a map at a local bike store.

KOKOPELLI'S TRAIL

Mountain bikers have linked together a 142-mile (229-km) series of back roads, paved roads, and bike trails through the magical canyons of eastern Utah and western Colorado. It's usually ridden from east to west, starting in Loma, Colorado, and passing Rabbit Valley, Cisco Boat Landing, Dewey Bridge, Fisher Valley, and Castle Valley before landing on Sand Flats Road in Moab. Lots of optional routes, access points, and campsites allow for many possibilities. This multiday trip requires a significant amount of advance planning; www.bikerpelli.com is a good place to start this process.

MOAB CANYON PATHWAY (ROAD BIKING)

Although the Moab area is great for biking, riding along busy U.S. 191 is no fun. The Moab Canyon Pathway starts at the pedestrian/bike bridge over the Colorado River on Highway 128 at the north end of town and closely parallels the highway north to Arches National Park. From the entrance to the park, the path, which is separated from the road, continues north, climbing to the junction of U.S. 191 and Highway 313, the road to Dead Horse Point State Park and Canyonlands' Island in the Sky District. From this intersection, the bike path is on a relatively wide shoulder; it's a 35-mile (56-km) ride to Canyonlands' Grand View Point, or a mere 24-mile (39-km) uphill chug to Dead Horse Point.

The paved route provides easy cycling access to the MOAB Brand mountain bike trails just off U.S. 191 and a more challenging ride to the Intrepid trails in Dead Horse Point State Park and the Gemini Bridges Trail, which starts just outside the park.

BIKE TOURS

Most of the bicycle rental shops in Moab offer daylong mountain bike excursions, while outfitters offer multiday tours that vary in price depending on the difficulty of the trail and the degree of comfort involved. The charge for these trips is usually around $200-250 per day, including food and shuttles. Be sure to inquire whether rates include bike rental.

Rim Tours (1233 S. U.S. 191, 435/259-5223 or 800/626-7335, https://rimtours.com) is a well-established local company offering several half-day (around $99 pp for 2-3 cyclists), full-day (around $125-150 pp for 2-3 cyclists), and multiday trips, including a five-day bike camping trip in Canyonlands' Maze District ($1,195). **Magpie Cycling** (800/546-4245, magpieadventures.com) is a small local business that runs day trips, which include instruction on mountain biking techniques and overnight rides, mostly in Canyonlands, including a three-day tour of the White Rim Trail ($875).

Western Spirit Cycling (478 Mill Creek Dr., 435/259-8732, www.westernspirit.com) offers mountain and road bike tours in the western United States, with about one-third of them in Utah. Moab-area trips include the White Rim, the Maze, and Kokopelli's Trail (five days, $1,260). Another Moab-based company with tours all over the West is **Escape Adventures** (local base at Moab Cyclery, 391 S. Main St., 435/259-7423 or 800/596-2953, www.escapeadventures.com), which leads multiday mountain biking trips, including a weekend tour of Moab's mountain bike trails (three days, $825 camping, $1,440 inn accommodations); some of the tours combine cycling with rafting, climbing, hiking, or plane rides.

RENTALS AND REPAIRS
Rim Cyclery (94 W. 100 N., 435/259-5333, www.rimcyclery.com, 8am-6pm daily) is Moab's oldest bike and outdoor gear store, offering both road and mountain bike sales, rentals, and service. Mountain bike rentals are also available at **Poison Spider Bicycles** (497 N. Main St., 435/259-7882 or 800/635-1792, www.poisonspiderbicycles.com, 8am-7pm daily spring and fall, 9am-6pm daily winter and summer) and **Chile Pepper** (702 S. Main St., 435/259-4688 or 888/677-4688, www.chilebikes.com, 8am-5pm daily). **Moab Cyclery** (391 S. Main St., 435/259-7423 or 800/559-1978, www.moabcyclery.com, 8am-6pm daily) offers rentals, tours, shuttles, and gear. Expect to pay about $45-80 per day to rent a mountain bike, a little less for a road bike. If you just want to tool around a bit, rent a basic townie for $20 at **Bike Fiend** (69 E. Center St., 435/315-0002, www.moabclassicbike.com, 8am-8pm daily).

SHUTTLE SERVICES
Several of the Moab area's best mountain bike trails are essentially one-way, and unless you want to cycle back the way you came, you'll need to arrange a shuttle service to pick you up and bring you back to Moab or your vehicle. Also, if you don't have a vehicle or a bike rack (available at most shops when you rent a bike), you will need to use a shuttle service to get to more distant trailheads. **Coyote Shuttle** (435/260-2097, www.coyoteshuttle.com) and **Porcupine Shuttle** (435/260-0896, http://poisonspiderbicycles.com/bike-shuttles/) both operate shuttle services; depending on distance, the usual fare is $20-30 per person. Both companies also shuttle hikers to trailheads and pick up rafters.

Rafting and Boating
Even a visitor with a tight schedule can get out and enjoy the canyon country on rafts and other watercraft. Outfitters offer both laid-back and exhilarating day trips, which usually require little advance planning. Longer multiday trips include gentle canoe paddles along the placid Green River and thrilling expeditions down the Colorado River.

You'll need to reserve well in advance for most of the longer trips because the BLM and the National Park Service limit trips through the backcountry, and space, especially in high season, is at a premium. Experienced rafters can also plan their own unguided trips, although you'll need a permit for all areas except for the daylong Fisher Towers float upstream from Moab.

The rafting season runs April-September, and jet boat tours run February-November. Most do-it-yourself river-runners obtain their permits by applying in January-February for a March drawing; the Moab Information Center's BLM ranger can advise on this process and provide the latest information about available cancellations.

RAFTING AND KAYAKING TRIPS
For most of the following trips, full-day rates include lunch and beverages, while part-day trips include just lemonade and soft drinks. On overnight trips you'll sleep in tents in backcountry campgrounds.

The **Colorado River** offers several exciting options. The most popular day run near Moab starts upstream near Fisher Towers and bounces through several moderate rapids on the way back to town. Full-day raft trips (about $70-80 pp adults) run from Fisher Towers to near Moab. Half-day trips ($50-55 pp adults) run over much the same stretch of river but don't include lunch.

Several outfitters offer guided **stand-up paddling** trips (about $75 for a half day) on quiet stretches of the Colorado River near the border of Arches National Park.

For a more adventurous rafting trip, the Colorado's rugged **Westwater Canyon** offers lots of white water and several Class III-IV rapids near the Utah-Colorado border. These long day trips are more expensive, typically around $170-200 per day. The Westwater Canyon is also often offered as part of multi-day adventure packages.

The **Cataract Canyon** section of the Colorado River, which begins south of the river's confluence with the Green River and extends to the backwater of Lake Powell, usually requires four days of rafting to complete. However, if you're in a hurry, some outfitters offer time-saving trips that motor rather than float through placid water and slow down only to shoot rapids, enabling these trips to conclude in as little as one day. This is the wildest white water in the Moab area, with big boiling Class III-IV rapids. Costs range $475-1,550, depending on what kind of craft, the number of days, and whether you fly, hike, or drive out at the end of the trip.

The **Green River** also offers Class II-III rafting and canoeing or kayaking opportunities, although they are milder than those on the Colorado. Trips on the Green make good family outings. Most trips require five days, leaving from the town of Green River, paddling through **Labyrinth Canyon** and taking out at Mineral Bottom, just before Canyonlands National Park. Costs range $950-1,250 for a five-day rafting trip.

RAFTING OR KAYAKING ON YOUR OWN

The Class II-III **Fisher Towers** section of the Colorado River is gentle enough for amateur rafters to negotiate on their own. A popular one-day raft trip with mild rapids begins from the Hittle Bottom Recreation Site (Hwy. 128, 23.5 miles/38 km north of Moab, near Fisher Towers) and ends 14 river miles (22.5 km) downstream at Takeout Beach (Hwy. 128, 10.3 miles/16.6 km north of U.S. 191). You can rent rafts and the mandatory life jackets in Moab, but you won't need a permit on this section of river.

Experienced white-water rafters run the Whitewater Canyon of the Colorado River on their own. Obtain permits ($10) by calling 435/259-7012 up to two months prior to launch date; it's important to plan well in advance. The usual put-in is at the Westwater Ranger Station 9 miles (14.5 km) south of I-70's exit 227; another option is the Loma boat launch in Colorado. A start at Loma adds a day or two to the trip along with the sights of Horsethief and Ruby Canyons. Normal takeout is at Cisco, although it's

kayaking the Colorado River near Moab

possible to continue 16 miles (26 km) on slow-moving water through open country to Dewey Bridge. **Canyon Voyages** (211 N. Main St., 435/315-4116 or 866/390-3994, www.canyonvoyages.com) and **Navtec Expeditions** (321 N. Main St., 435/259-7983 or 800/833-1278, www.navtec.com) are two local rafting companies that rent rafts (from $120 per day); Canyon Voyages also has kayaks ($55-70 per day), canoes ($40), and paddle boards ($58) for those who would rather organize their own river adventures.

RAFTING OUTFITTERS

Moab is full of river trip companies, and most offer a variety of day and multiday trips; in addition, many will combine raft trips with biking, horseback riding, hiking, or 4WD excursions. Check out the many websites at www.discovermoab.com/tour.htm. The list below includes major outfitters offering a variety of rafting options. Most of them lead trips to the main river destinations on the Colorado and Green Rivers as well as other rivers in Utah and the West. Red River Adventures runs trips in smaller self-paddled rafts and inflatable kayaks. Inquire about natural history or petroglyph tours if these specialty trips interest you.

- **Adrift Adventures** (378 N. Main St., 435/259-8594 or 800/874-4483, www.adrift.net)
- **Canyonlands Field Institute** (1320 S. Hwy. 191, 435/259-7750 or 800/860-5262, http://cfimoab.org)
- **Canyon Voyages** (211 N. Main St., 435/315-4116 or 866/390-3994www.canyonvoyages.com)
- **Moab Adventure Center** (225 S. Main St., 435/259-7019 or 866/904-1163, www.moabadventurecenter.com)
- **Navtec Expeditions** (321 N. Main St., 435/259-7983 or 800/833-1278, www.navtec.com)
- **Red River Adventures** (1140 S. Main

St., 435/259-4046 or 877/259-4046, www.redriveradventures.com)
- **Sheri Griffith Expeditions** (2231 S. Hwy. 191, 503/259-8229 or 800/332-2439, www.griffithexp.com)
- **Tag-A-Long Expeditions** (378 N. Main St., 435/259-8594 or 800/874-4483, www.tagalong.com)

CANOEING

Canoeists can also sample the calm waters of the Green River on multiday excursions with **Moab Rafting and Canoe Company** (420 Kane Creek Blvd., 435/259-7722, www.moab-rafting.com), which runs scheduled guided trips ($849 for a four-day trip) to four sections of the Green and to calmer stretches of the Colorado River. They also rent canoes (around $30-50 per day), including the necessary equipment.

Another good source for DIY canoe and kayak trips on the Green is **Tex's Riverways** (435/259-5101 or 877/662-2839, www.texsriverways.com), which specializes in rentals, shuttles, and support for self-guided trips.

JET BOAT AND MOTORBOAT

Guided jet boat excursions through Canyonlands National Park run $90 for a half-day trip. **Tag-A-Long Expeditions** (452 N. Main St., 435/259-8946 or 800/453-3292, www.tagalong.com) and **Adrift Adventures** (378 N. Main St., 435/259-8594 or 800/874-4483, www.adrift.net) both offer half-day trips and full-day combination jet boat-jeep excursions.

Canyonlands by Night & Day (435/259-5261 or 800/394-9978, www.canyonlandsbynight.com, Apr.-mid-Oct., $69 adults, $59 ages 4-12, includes dinner) tours leave at sunset in an open tour boat and go several miles upstream on the Colorado River; a guide points out canyon features. The sound and light show begins on the way back; music and historical narration accompany the play of lights on the canyon walls. Reservations are a good idea because the boat fills up fast. Daytime jet boat tours ($59-99 adults, $49-89 children) are longer—about four hours—and go a little farther. Trips depart from the Spanish mission-style office just north of Moab, across the Colorado River.

Air Tours

You'll have a bird's-eye view of southeastern Utah's incredible landscape from Moab's Canyonlands Field with **Redtail Aviation** (435/259-7421, www.redtailaviation.com). A short flight over Arches National Park is $79 per person; add Canyonlands and the rate is $179. Longer tours are also available, and flights operate year-round.

Skydiving

If you think the Arches and Canyonlands area looks dramatic from an airplane, imagine the excitement of parachuting into the desert landscape. **Skydive Moab** (Canyonlands Fields Airport, U.S. 191, 16 miles (26 km) north of Moab, 435/259-5867, www.skydivemoab.com) offers jumps for both first-time and experienced skydivers. First-timers receive 30 minutes of ground schooling, followed by a half-hour flight before a tandem parachute jump with an instructor from 10,000 feet. Tandem skydives, including instruction and equipment, start at $225. For experienced skydivers with their own equipment, jumps start at $18; equipment and parachutes are available for rent.

4WD Exploration

Road tours offer visitors a special opportunity to view unique canyon-country arches and spires, indigenous rock art, and wildlife. An interpretive brochure and map at the Moab Information Center (25 E. Center St., at Main St., 435/259-8825, www.discovermoab.com) outlines Moab-area 4WD trails: four rugged loop routes of 15-54 miles (24-87 km) through the desert that take 2.5-4 hours to drive. Those who left their trusty four-by-fours and off-road-driving skills at home can take an off-road jeep tour with a private operator. Most Moab outfitters offer jeep or Hummer tours, often in combination with rafting or hiking

options. The **Moab Adventure Center** (452 N. Main St., 435/259-7019 or 866/404-1163, www.moabadventurecenter.com) runs two-hour ($85 adults, $55 youths) and half-day ($175 adults, $125 youths) guided Hummer safaris. The Adventure Center, which can book you on any number of trips, can also arrange jeep rentals (from $230 per day).

Jeep and other 4WD-vehicle rentals are also available at a multitude of other Moab outfits, including **Twisted Jeep Rentals** (446 S. Main St., 435/259-0335, www.twistedjeeps.com), and **Cliffhanger Jeep Rentals** (40 W. Center St., 435/259-0889, www.cliffhangerjeeprental.com). Expect to pay at least $210 per day.

ATVs and Dirt Bikes

As an alternative to four-by-four touring in the backcountry, there's ATV and motorcycle dirt biking, typically but not exclusively geared toward youngsters and families. Although youths 8-15 years of age may operate an ATV, provided they possess an education certificate issued by Utah State Parks and Recreation or an equivalent certificate from their home state, parents should research ATV safety before agreeing to such an outing. Much of the public land surrounding Moab is open to ATV exploration, with many miles of unpaved roads and existing trails on which ATVs can travel. However, ATV and dirt bike riding is not allowed within either Arches or Canyonlands National Parks.

One particularly popular area for ATVs is **White Wash Sand Dunes,** with many miles of dirt roads in a strikingly scenic location 48 miles (77 km) northwest of Moab, reached by driving south 13 miles (21 km) from I-70 exit 175, just east of Green River. The dunes are interspersed with large cottonwood trees and bordered by red sandstone cliffs. In addition to the dunes, White Wash is a popular route around three sides of the dunes.

ATVs and dirt bikes are available from a number of Moab-area outfitters, including **High Point Hummer** (281 N. Main St., 435/259-2972 or 877/486-6833, www.

highpointhummer.com) and **Moab Tour Company** (543 N. Main St., 435/259-4080 or 877/725-7317, www.moabtourcompany.com). A half-day dirt bike or ATV rental starts at around $239.

Rock Climbing

Just outside town, the cliffs along Highway 279 and Fisher Towers attract rock climbers. For world-class crack climbing, head south to Indian Creek, near the Needles District of Canyonlands National Park.

Moab Desert Adventures (415 N. Main St., 435/260-2404 or 877/765-6622, www.moabdesertadventures.com) offers rock climbing and canyoneering lessons, both for beginners and experienced climbers; families are welcome. A half-day of basic climbing instruction is $175 for a private lesson; rates are lower for groups of 2-4 students. Head out for a climbing or canyoneering trip with **Moab Cliffs & Canyons** (253 N. Main St., 435/259-3317 or 877/641-5271, www.cliffsandcanyons.com). A day of climbing rock towers costs $365 for a private lesson and climb, $275 per person for two.

Moab has a couple of stores with rock climbing gear and informative staff: **Gearheads** (471 S. Main St., 435/259-4327, 8am-9pm daily) and **Pagan Mountaineering** (59 S. Main St., 435/259-1117, www.paganclimber.com, 8am-9pm daily).

Horseback Riding

Head up the Colorado River to the Fisher Towers area, where **Moab Horses** (Hauer Ranch, Hwy. 128, milepost 21, 435/259-8015, www.moabhorses.com, $8 half day for two or more ricdfx) runs guided trail rides. Also along Highway 128, **Red Cliffs Lodge** (Hwy. 128, milepost 14, 435/259-2002 or 866/812-2002, www.redcliffslodge.com) and **Sorrel River Ranch** (Hwy. 128, milepost 17, 435/259-4642 or 877/317-8244, www.sorrelriver.com) both offer trail rides.

Golf

The **Moab Golf Club** (2705 SE Bench Rd., 435/259-6488, www.moabcountryclub.com/golf, $50) is an 18-hole par-72 public course set in a well-watered oasis amid stunning redrock formations. To get there from Moab, go south 5 miles (8 km) on U.S. 191, turn left onto Spanish Trail Road and follow it 2 miles (3.2 km), then go right on Murphy Lane and follow it to Bench Road and the golf course.

Parks

The **city park** (181 W. 400 N.) has shaded picnic tables and a playground. It's also home to the **Moab Recreation and Aquatic Center** (374 Park Ave., 435/259-8226), a community center with indoor and outdoor swimming pools, a weight room, and group exercise classes.

Two miles (2 km) north of town, **Lions Park** (U.S. 191 and Hwy. 128) offers picnicking along the Colorado River, although ongoing bridge construction makes it less than peaceful. **Rotary Park** (Mill Creek Dr.) is family-oriented and has lots of activities for kids.

FOOD

Moab has the largest concentration of good restaurants in all of southern Utah; no matter what else the recreational craze has produced, it has certainly improved the food. Several Moab-area restaurants are closed for vacation in February, so call ahead if you're visiting in winter.

Casual Dining

Food isn't limited to muffins at **Love Muffin** (139 N. Main St., 435/259-6833, http://lovemuffincafe.com, 6:30am-1pm daily, $7-9), but if you decide to skip the breakfast burritos or tasty rainbow quinoa, the Burple Nurple muffin may be just what you need. While you're eating breakfast, order a muffuletta or barbecued tofu sandwich to pack along for lunch.

Another good option for a tasty but healthy breakfast or lunch is ★ **EklectiCafe** (352 N. Main St., 435/259-6896, 7am-2:30pm daily, $5-10), a charming and busy little café serving delicious organic and vegetarian dishes. For a more traditional breakfast, try the **Jailhouse Café** (101 N. Main St., 435/259-3900, 6:30am-noon Wed.-Mon., $8-11), a Moab classic.

Dense, chewy bagels and good sandwiches make the **Red Rock Bakery** (74 S. Main St., 435/259-5941, 7am-4pm daily, $3-7) worth a visit.

Peace Tree Juice Café (20 S. Main St., 435/259-0101, www.peacetreecafe.com, 7am-10pm daily, $9-28) is a great place for breakfast omelets and scrambles, and has a big menu of smoothies. At lunch and dinner you'll find everything from sandwiches, salads, wraps, and burgers to steak dinners. The Peace Tree is right in the heart of Moab and has a patio for outdoor dining.

Two Moab diners have an old-fashioned ambience and really good food. At the **Moab Diner & Ice Cream Shoppe** (189 S. Main St., 435/259-4006, http://moabdiner.com, 6am-9pm Mon.-Thurs., 6am-10pm Fri.-Sat., $7-15), the breakfasts are large, with a Southwestern green chili edge to much of the food. The house-made ice cream is delicious. Another spot with great burgers and shakes is ★ **Milt's Stop & Eat** (356 Millcreek Dr., 435/259-7424, www.miltsstopandeat.com, 11am-8pm Tues.-Sun., $5-8)—it's a local classic, and just the place to stop and sprawl under the big tree out front after a day of biking or hiking.

For good Mexican food in a friendly, unfussy strip mall setting, head south of downtown to tiny **El Charro Loco** (812 S. Main St., 435/355-0854, 11am-10pm daily, $7-20). Don't miss the pastries here; they're a special treat. (No alcohol.)

A more upscale Mexican restaurant is **Miguel's Baja Grill** (51 N. Main St., 435/259-6546, www.miguelsbajagrill.com, 5pm-10pm daily, $10-26) with well-prepared Baja-style seafood, including good fish tacos. It's a busy place, so make a reservation or be prepared to wait.

Zax (96 S. Main St., 435/259-6555, www.zaxmoab.com, 11am-10pm daily, $10-15) is a busy restaurant in the heart of downtown. If you're with kids, this might be the ticket for sandwiches, steaks, pasta, pizza, or salad. An all-you-can eat pizza, soup, and salad bar goes for $15.

Get away from high-volume assembly-line restaurants at **Sabaku Sushi** (90 E. Center St., 435/259-4455, www.sabakusushi.com, 5pm-9:30pm Tues.-Sun., rolls $6-16), which offers surprisingly good sushi with a few innovations (seared elk meat is featured in one roll). Arrive at 5pm for the sushi happy hour.

In a pretty building a block off the main drag, **Arches Thai** (60 N. 100 W., 435/355-0533, archesthai.com, 11am-9pm Wed.-Mon., $13-21) has surprisingly good Thai food. It's a pleasant place if you're not in a hurry.

The **Broken Oar** (53 W. 400 N., 435/259-3127, 11pm-9pm Mon.-Sat., $11-29) is just north of downtown in a large log building that looks like a ski lodge. In addition to burgers, pasta, and steaks, the restaurant offers a selection of meats from their smoker. The beer and wine menu veers toward local producers.

Brewpubs

After a hot day out on the trail, who can blame you for thinking about a cold brew and a hearty meal? Luckily, Moab has two excellent pubs to fill the bill. ★ **Eddie McStiff's** (57 S. Main St., 435/259-2337, www.eddiemcstiffs.com, 11:30am-close daily, $9-19) is an extremely popular place to sip a cool beer or a mojito, eat standard pub food (the pizza is a good bet), and meet other travelers; in good weather there's seating in a nice courtyard. You'd have to try hard not to have fun here.

There's more good beer and perhaps better food at the **Moab Brewery** (686 S. Main St., 435/259-6333, www.themoabbrewery.com, 11:30am-10pm Sun.-Thurs., 11:30am-11pm Fri.-Sat., $8-21), although it doesn't attract the kind of scene you'll find at Eddie McStiff's. The atmosphere is light and airy, and the food is good—steaks, sandwiches, burgers, and a wide selection of salads. Try the spinach salad with smoked salmon ($9) or prime rib ($19). There's deck seating when weather permits. Immediately next, the same folks now operate the Moab Distillery; though there's no tasting room, you can sample their gin and vodka in the brewery.

Fine Dining

The ★ **Desert Bistro** (36 S. 100 W., 435/259-0756, www.desertbistro.com, reservations recommended, dinner from 5pm-9:30pm daily, $22-50), a longtime favorite for regional fine dining. Its seasonal, sophisticated Southwest-meets-continental cuisine features local meats and game plus fresh fish and seafood. The patio dining is some of the nicest in Moab, and the indoor dining rooms are pretty and peaceful.

The **River Grill** (Sorrel River Ranch, Hwy. 128, 17 miles (27 km) northeast of Moab, 435/259-4642, www.sorrelriver.com, 7am-2pm and 6pm-9pm daily Apr.-Oct., 7am-10am and 6pm-9pm daily Nov.-Mar., $28-38) has a lovely dining room that overlooks spires of red rock and the dramatic cliffs of the Colorado River. The scenery is hard to top, and the food is good, with a focus on prime beef and continental specialties. Dinner reservations are strongly recommended.

The **Sunset Grill** (900 N. U.S. 191, 435/259-7146, www.moab-utah.com/sunsetgrill, 5pm-10pm Mon.-Sat., $14-24) is located in uranium king Charlie Steen's mansion, situated high above Moab, with million-dollar sweeping views of the valley. Choose from steaks, fresh seafood, and a selection of pasta dishes—what you'll remember is the road up here and the view. The grill now offers a free shuttle from most Moab locations; call 435/259-7777 to request a ride during regular restaurant hours.

ACCOMMODATIONS

A tourism destination for generations, Moab offers a wide variety of lodging choices, ranging from older motels to new upscale resorts. U.S. 191 is lined with all the usual chain motels, but we tend to go for the smaller local operations that are within walking distance of downtown restaurants and shopping, and that's mostly what you'll find listed here.

Check with hotel booking sites for chain motel rooms farther out of town.

Moab Property Management (435/259-5125 or 800/505-5343, www.moabutahlodging.com) can make bookings at area vacation homes, which include some relatively inexpensive apartments. Another handy tool is www.moab-utah.com, which has a complete listing of lodging websites for the Moab area.

The only time Moab isn't busy is in the dead of winter, November-February. At all other times, be sure to make reservations well in advance. Summer room rates are listed here; in winter, rates typically drop 40 percent and in the busy spring break season, they tend to rise, especially during Easter weekend, when jeepers fill the town.

Under $50

The **Lazy Lizard Hostel** (1213 S. U.S. 191, 435/259-6057, www.lazylizardhostel.com) costs just $11 (cash preferred) for simple dorm-style accommodations. To stay at this casual classic Moab lodging, you won't need a hostel membership, and all guests share access to a hot tub, a kitchen, a barbecue, a coin-operated laundry, and a common room with cable TV. Showers for nonguests ($3) and private guest rooms ($32-36 for 2 people) are also offered. Log cabins can sleep two ($41-43) to six ($58) people. If you're traveling in a large group, the hostel also offers a number of group houses that can sleep from 12 to 30 people under one roof. The Lazy Lizard is 1 mile (1.6 km) south of town, behind A-1 Storage; the turnoff is about 200 yards south of Moab Lanes.

$50-100

A reasonably priced motel that's simple, friendly, and noncorporate is the ★ **Kokopelli Lodge** (72 S. 100 E., 435/259-7615 or 800/505-5343, www.kokopellilodge.com, $74-94), offering small but colorful pet-friendly guest rooms and a convenient location one block off the main drag. Kokopelli also offers a number of cabins and condos at other locations around town if you're looking for a relatively inexpensive option with multiple beds and full kitchens.

$100-150

A couple of older but well-cared-for motels just north of downtown have guest rooms starting at about $125-140: the **Adventure Inn** (512 N. Main St., 435/662-2466 or 866/662-2466, www.adventureinnmoab.com) and the **Inca Inn** (570 N. Main St., 435/259-7261 or 866/462-2466, www.incainn.com), with a pool.

Another simple but quite adequate place is the **Bowen Motel** (169 N. Main St., 435/259-7132 or 800/874-5439, www.bowenmotel.com, $120-150), a homey motel with an outdoor pool. The Bowen offers a variety of room types, including three-bedroom family suites and a 1,800-square-foot three-bedroom house with full kitchen.

Also in the heart of town, but off the main drag and with a pool is the **Rustic Inn** (120 E. 100 S. 435/259-6477, www.moabrusticinn.com, $125). If you want something more spacious, try for one of the Rustic Inn's apartments; these are popular, so book well in advance.

A few blocks south of downtown, the **Red Stone Inn** (535 S. Main St., 435/259-3500 or 800/772-1972, www.moabredstone.com, $130-145) is a one-story, knotty-pine-sided motel; all guest rooms have efficiency kitchens. Other amenities include a bicycle maintenance area, a covered patio with a gas barbecue grill, a hot tub, and guest laundry. Motel guests have free access to the hotel pool next door at the Red Stone's sister property, the sprawling **Big Horn Lodge** (550 S. Main St., 435/259-6171 or 800/325-6171, www.moabbighorn.com, $130), which has similar knotty-pine guest rooms equipped with microwaves and fridges as well as a pool and a steak restaurant. Package deals for a guest room plus jeep tours, raft trips, and other activities are offered.

If you want seclusion in a quiet community 18 miles (29 km) east of Moab, stay at

the **Castle Valley Inn** (424 Amber Lane, Castle Valley, 435/259-6012 or 888/466-6012, www.castlevalleyinn.com, $135-245). The B&B-style inn adjoins a wildlife refuge in a stunning landscape of red-rock mesas and needle-pointed buttes. You can stay in one of the main house's five guest rooms or in one of the three bungalows with kitchens. Facilities include a hot tub. To reach Castle Valley Inn, follow Highway 128 east from Moab for 16 miles (26 km), turn south, and continue 2.3 miles (3.7 km) toward Castle Valley.

Over $150

The ★ **Best Western Canyonlands Inn** (16 S. Main St., 435/259-2300 or 800/649-5191, www.canyonlandsinn.com, $254-319) is at the heart of Moab, with suites, a pool, a fitness room and spa, a better-than-average complimentary breakfast, and a bike storage area. This property went through a major remodel just a few years back and is the best address in the downtown area if you're looking for upscale amenities.

At the heart of downtown Moab, **Best Western Greenwell Motel** (105 S. Main St., 435/259-6151 or 800/528-1234, www.bestwesternmoab.com, $214-234) has a pool, fitness facilities, an on-premises restaurant, and some kitchenettes.

One of the most interesting accommodations options in Moab is the ★ **Gonzo Inn** (100 W. 200 S., 435/259-2515 or 800/791-4044, www.gonzoinn.com, $199-249). With a look somewhere between an adobe inn and a postmodern warehouse, the Gonzo doesn't try to appear anything but hip. Expect large guest rooms with vibrant colors and modern decor, a pool, and a friendly welcome.

Located in a lovely and quiet residential area, the ★ **Sunflower Hill Luxury Inn** (185 N. 300 E., 435/259-2974 or 800/662-2786, www.sunflowerhill.com, $237-312) offers high-quality accommodations. Choose from a guest room in one of Moab's original farmhouses, a historic ranch house, or a garden cottage. All 12 guest rooms have private baths, air-conditioning, and queen beds; there are also two suites. Guests share access to an outdoor swimming pool and a hot tub, bike storage, patios, and large gardens. Children over age seven are welcome, and the place is open year-round.

Families or groups might want to rent a condo at **Moab Springs Ranch** (1266 N. U.S. 191, 435/259-7891 or 888/259-5759, www.moabspringsranch.com, $150-375, check website for full range of options), located on the north end of town on the site of Moab's oldest ranch. The townhomes have a parklike setting with a swimming pool and a hot tub, and they sleep up to 10. Book well in advance.

A cluster of four charming and pet-friendly cottages dubbed **3 Dogs & a Moose** (171 and 173 W. Center St., 435/260-1692, www.3dogsandamoosecottages.com) is just off the main drag. The two smaller cottages ($145-205) are perfect for couples, and the larger cottages ($295-325) sleep up to six.

A short drive from Moab along the Colorado River's red-rock canyon is the region's most upscale resort, the **Sorrel River Ranch** (Hwy. 128, 17 miles/27 km northeast of Moab, 435/259-4642 or 877/317-8244, www.sorrelriver.com, $499-615). The ranch sits on 240 acres in one of the most dramatic landscapes in the Moab area—just across the river from Arches National Park and beneath the soaring mesas of Castle Valley. Accommodations are in a series of beautifully furnished wooden lodges, all tastefully fitted with Old West-style furniture and kitchenettes. Horseback rides are offered into the arroyos behind the ranch, and kayaks and bicycles are available for rent. The ranch's restaurant, the **River Grill** (435/259-4642, 7am-2pm and 6pm-9pm daily Apr.-Oct., 7am-10am and 6pm-9pm daily Nov.-Mar., $31-48), has some of the best views in Utah.

Sharing a similar view of the Colorado River and Castle Valley but 3 miles (4.8 km) closer to Moab is the sprawling **Red Cliffs Lodge** (Hwy. 128, milepost 14, 435/259-2002 or 866/812-2002, www.redcliffslodge.com, $240), which houses guests in mini suites in the main lodge building and in a number of

riverside cabins that can sleep up to six ($340). The lodge offers the Cowboy Grill bar and restaurant, horseback rides, and mountain bike rentals and will arrange river raft trips. The lodge is also the headquarters for Castle Creek Winery and the site of the free Moab Museum of Film & Western Heritage, which displays a collection of movie memorabilia from Westerns filmed in the area.

Campgrounds

There are 26 BLM campgrounds (most $10-15) in the Moab area. Although these spots can't be reserved, sites are abundant enough that campers are rarely unable to get a site. The campgrounds are concentrated on the banks of the Colorado River—along Highway 128 toward Castle Valley, along Highway 279 toward the potash factory, and along Kane Creek Road—and at the Sand Flats Recreation Area near the Slickrock Bike Trail. Only a few of these campgrounds can handle large RVs, none have hookups, and few have piped water. For a full list of BLM campgrounds and facilities, visit www.discovermoab.com.

It's really easy and comfy to camp at ★ **Up the Creek** (210 E. 300 S., 435/260-1888, www.moabupthecreek.com, mid-Mar.-Oct., $25 for 1 person, $32 for 2, $40 for 3, $5 dogs), a walk-in, tents-only campground tucked into a residential neighborhood near downtown Moab. The shady campground, with a bathhouse and showers, picnic tables, and a few propane grills (campfires are prohibited), is right alongside a bike path.

RV parks cluster at the north and south ends of town. **Moab Valley RV Resort** (1773 N. U.S. 191, at Hwy. 128, 2 miles (3.2 km) north of Moab, 435/259-4469, www.moabvalleyrv.com, $34-48 tents, from $48 RVs) is open year-round; it has showers, a pool, a playground, and free wireless internet access. Pets are allowed only in RVs. Although this place is convenient to town and Arches, it is pretty close to a large ongoing environmental cleanup project involving removal of radioactive mine tailings (according to the Environmental Protection Agency, it's safe to camp here). **Moab KOA** (3225 S. U.S. 191, 435/259-6682 or 800/562-0372, http://moabkoa.com, Mar.-Nov., $37 tents, from $48 RVs with hookups, $96-175 cabins), barely off the highway 4 miles (6.4 km) south of town, has showers, a laundry room, a store, miniature golf, and a pool.

More convenient to downtown, **Canyonlands RV Resort and Campground** (555 S. Main St., 435/259-6848 or 800/522-6848, www.canyonlandsrv.com, $35-43 tents, 52-62 RVs, $697 cabins) is open year-round; it has showers, a laundry room, a store, a pool, and two-person air-conditioned cabins—bring your own bedding. One mile (1.6 km) north of Moab, **Slickrock Campground** (1301½ N. U.S. 191, 435/259-7660 or 800/448-8873, http://slickrockcampground.com, $29 tents or RVs without hookups, $4959 with hookups, $69 cabins with air-conditioning and heat but no bath or kitchen) remains open year-round; it has nice sites with some shade as well as showers, a store, an outdoor café, and a pool.

You'll also find campgrounds farther out at Arches and Canyonlands National Parks, Dead Horse Point State Park, Canyon Rims Recreation Area, and east of town in the cool La Sal Mountains.

For something a little less rugged, **Under Canvas Moab** (13748 N. U.S. 191, 801/895-3213, www.undercanvas.com/camps/moab, open mid-Mar.-Oct.) offers a luxury safari tent experience on 40 acres near the entrance to Arches National Park. Lodging is in a variety of large wall tents, some with private ensuite bathrooms, and all fitted with fine bedding and furniture. In other words, this isn't exactly roughing it. Tent accommodations that sleep four start at $249 per night, with modern plumbing and bathroom facilities in group shower houses. Adventure packages are also available that customize outdoor activities to your preferences, and also include three camp-cooked meals a day.

INFORMATION AND SERVICES
Information
Moab is a small town, and people are generally friendly. Between the excellent Moab Information Center and the county library—and the friendly advice of people in the street—you'll find it easy to assemble all the information you need to have a fine stay.

The **Moab Information Center** (25 E. Center St., 435/259-8825, www.discovermoab.com, 8am-7pm Mon.-Sat., 9am-6pm Sun.) is

An abundance of BLM campgrounds near Moab allows for free-form camping.

the place to start for nearly all local and area information. The National Park Service, the BLM, the U.S. Forest Service, the Grand County Travel Council, and the Canyonlands Natural History Association all are represented here. Visitors needing help from any of these agencies should start at the information center rather than at the agency offices. Free literature is available, the selection of books and maps for sale is large, and the staff is knowledgeable. The center's website is also well organized and packed with information.

The **BLM District Office** (82 E. Dogwood Ave., 435/259-2100, 7:45am-4:30pm Mon.-Fri.) is on the south side of town behind Comfort Suites. Some land-use maps are sold here, and this is the place to pick up river-running permits.

Services

The **Grand County Public Library** (257 E. Center St., 435/259-1111, 9am-8pm Mon.-Fri., 9am-5pm Sat.) is a good place for local history and general reading.

The **post office** (50 E. 100 N., 435/259-7427) is downtown. **Moab Regional Hospital** (450 W. Williams Way,

435/719-3500) provides medical care. For emergencies (ambulance, police, or fire), dial 911.

Dogs can spend a day or board at **Karen's Canine Campground** (435/259-7922) while their people hike the no-dog trails in Arches and Canyonlands.

GETTING THERE

SkyWest, associated with United Airlines (800/335-2247, www.united.com) provides daily scheduled air service between **Canyonlands Field** (CNY, U.S. 191, 16 miles/26 km north of Moab, 435/259-4849, www.moabairport.com) and Denver. Grand Junction, Colorado, is 120 miles (193 km) east of Moab via I-70 and has better air service; Salt Lake City is 240 miles (385 km) northwest of Moab.

Red Rock Express (435/260-0595, www.redrockexpress.com) runs shuttles between Moab and Canyonlands Field ($75 for up to four passengers). Red Rock Express shuttles also link Moab with the Salt Lake City and Grand Junction, Colorado, airports.

Enterprise (711 S. Main St., 435/259-8505, www.enterprise.com) rents cars at the airport.

Arches National Park

A concentration of rock arches of marvelous variety has formed within the maze of sandstone fins at **Arches National Park** (435/719-2299, www.nps.gov/arch, $25 per vehicle, $15 per motorcycle, $10 pedestrians and bicyclists), one of the most popular parks in the United States. Balanced rocks and tall spires add to the splendor. Paved roads and short hiking trails provide easy access to some of the more than 1,500 arches in the park. If you're short on time, a drive to the Windows Section (23.5 miles/38 km round-trip) affords a look at some of the largest and most spectacular arches. To visit all the stops and hike a few short trails would take all day.

Come prepared with a picnic lunch; there

are no accommodations and no restaurants inside the park.

Most of the early settlers and cowboys that passed through the Arches area paid little attention to the scenery. In 1923, however, a prospector by the name of Alexander Ringhoffer interested officials of the Rio Grande Railroad in the scenic attractions at what he called Devils Garden (now known as Klondike Bluffs). The railroad men liked the area and contacted Stephen Mather, who was the first director of the National Park Service. Mather started the political process that led to designating two small areas as a national monument in 1929, but Ringhoffer's Devils Garden wasn't included until later. The monument grew in size over the years and became Arches National Park in 1971. The park now comprises 76,519 acres—small enough to be appreciated in one day, yet large enough to warrant extensive exploration.

Thanks to unrelenting erosion, the arches themselves are constantly changing. Every so often there's a dramatic change, as there was during the summer of 2008 when Wall Arch, a 71-foot span on the Devils Garden Trail, collapsed.

VISITORS CENTER

The entrance to Arches is 5 miles (8 km) north of downtown Moab on U.S. 191. Located just past the park entrance booth, the expansive **visitors center** (7:30am-5pm daily Mar.-Oct., 8am-4:30pm daily Nov., 9am-4pm daily Dec.-Feb.) provides a good introduction to what you can expect ahead. Exhibits identify the rock layers, describe the geologic and human history, and illustrate some of the wildlife and plants of the park. A large outdoor plaza is a good place to troll for information after hours. A video runs regularly, and staff members are available to answer your questions, issue backcountry permits, and check you in for a ranger-led tour in the Fiery Furnace area of the park. Look for the posted list of special activities; rangers host campfire programs and lead a wide variety of guided walks April-September. You'll also find checklists, pamphlets, books, maps, posters, postcards, and film here for purchase. See the ranger for advice and the free backcountry permit required for overnight trips.

Desert bighorn sheep frequent the area around the visitors center and can sometimes be seen from U.S. 191 just south of the park entrance. A sheep crossing about 3 miles (4.8 km) north of the visitors center is also a good place to scan the steep talus slopes for these nimble animals.

If your plans include visiting Canyonlands National Park plus Hovenweep and Natural Bridges National Monuments, consider the Southeast Utah Parks Pass pass, which for $50 buys annual entry to all of these federal preserves. Purchase the pass at any of the park or national monument entrances.

SCENIC DRIVE

The 18-mile-long (29-km-long) scenic road through the park can be busy. Be sure to stop only in parking lots and designated pullouts. Watch out for others who are sightseeing in this popular park. The following are major points of interest.

Moab Fault

The park road begins a long but well-graded climb from the visitors center up the cliffs to the northeast. A pullout on the right after 1.1 miles (2 km) offers a good view of Moab Canyon and its geology. The rock layers on this side of the canyon have slipped down more than 2,600 feet in relation to the other side. Movement took place about six million years ago along the Moab Fault, which follows the canyon floor. Rock layers at the top of the far cliffs are nearly the same age as those at the bottom on this side. If you could stack the rocks of this side on top of rocks on the other side, you'd have a complete stratigraphic column of the Moab area—more than 150 million years' worth.

Park Avenue

The South Park Avenue overlook and trailhead are on the left 2.1 miles (3.4 km) from the visitors center. Great sandstone slabs form a skyline on each side of this dry wash. A trail goes north 1 mile (1.6 km) down the wash to the North Park Avenue trailhead (1.3 miles/2.1 km ahead by road). Arrange to be picked up there or backtrack to your starting point. The large rock monoliths of Courthouse Towers rise north of Park Avenue. Only a few small arches exist now, although major arches may have formed there in the past. One striking feature, visible from the road and the trail, is the group of sandstone towers forming the Three Gossips.

Balanced Rock

This gravity-defying formation is on the right,

Arches National Park

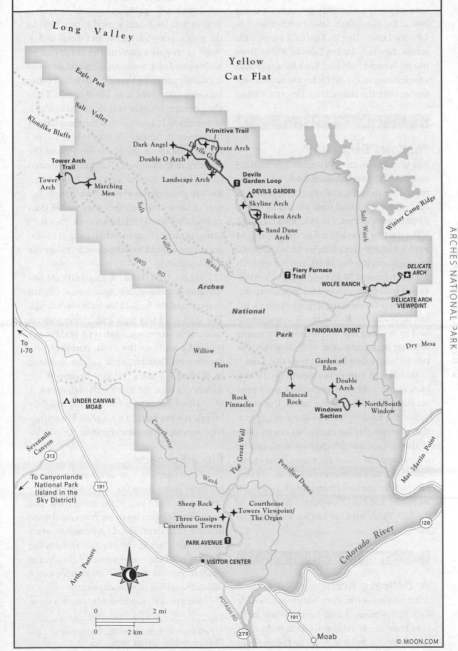

Long Valley

Yellow Cat Flat

Eagle Park

Salt Valley

Klondike Bluffs

Primitive Trail

Dark Angel — Private Arch
Devils Garden
Double O Arch

Tower Arch Trail

Tower Arch

Marching Men

Landscape Arch

Devils Garden Loop

DEVILS GARDEN

Skyline Arch

Broken Arch

Sand Dune Arch

Salt Valley Wash

Winter Camp Ridge

Salt Wash

4WD RD

Arches

Wash

Fiery Furnace Trail

WOLFE RANCH

DELICATE ARCH

DELICATE ARCH VIEWPOINT

National

Park

PANORAMA POINT

Dry Mesa

To I-70

Willow

Flats

Garden of Eden

Double Arch

UNDER CANVAS MOAB

Rock Pinnacles

Balanced Rock

Windows Section

North/South Window

Courthouse

Sevenmile Canyon

313

To Canyonlands National Park (Island in the Sky District)

191

The Great Wall

Wash

Petrified Dunes

Mat Martin Point

Sheep Rock

Three Gossips
Courthouse Towers

Courthouse Towers Viewpoint/ The Organ

128

PARK AVENUE

Colorado River

VISITOR CENTER

Arths Pasture

POTASH RD

0   2 mi

0   2 km

191

279

Moab

© MOON.COM

8.5 miles (13.7 km) from the visitors center. A boulder more than 55 feet high rests precariously atop a 73-foot pedestal. For a closer look at Balanced Rock, take the 0.3-mile (0.5-km) trail encircling it. There's a picnic area across the road. Author Edward Abbey lived in a trailer near Balanced Rock for a season as a park ranger in the 1950s; his journal became the basis for the classic book *Desert Solitaire*.

TOP EXPERIENCE

Windows Section

The Windows Section of Arches is located 2.5 miles (4 km) past Balanced Rock, on a paved road to the right. Short trails (0.25-1 mile/0.4-1.6 km one-way) lead from the road's end to some massive arches. The Windows trailhead is the start for North Window (an opening 51 feet high and 93 feet wide), South Window (66 feet high and 105 feet wide), and Turret Arch (64 feet high and 39 feet wide). Double Arch, a short walk from a second trailhead, is an unusual pair of arches; the larger opening—105 feet high and 163 feet wide—is best appreciated by walking inside. The smaller opening is 61 feet high and 60 feet wide. Together, the two arches frame a large opening overhead.

Garden of Eden Viewpoint, on the way back to the main road, promises a good panorama of Salt Valley to the north. Under the valley, the massive body of salt and gypsum that's responsible for the arches comes close to the surface. Far-off Delicate Arch can be seen across the valley on a sandstone ridge. Early nonnative visitors to the Garden of Eden saw rock formations resembling Adam (with an apple) and Eve. Two other viewpoints of the Salt Valley area are farther north on the main road.

TOP EXPERIENCE

★ Delicate Arch

A bit of pioneer history survives at Wolfe Ranch, 2.5 miles (4 km) north on the main road from the Windows junction (turn right and drive 1.8 miles/2.9 km to the parking

area). John Wesley Wolfe came to this spot in 1888, hoping the desert climate would provide relief for health problems related to a Civil War injury. He found a good spring high in the rocks, grass for cattle, and water in Salt Wash to irrigate a garden. The ranch that he built provided a home for him and some of his family for more than 20 years, and cattle ranchers later used it as a line ranch. Then sheepherders brought in their animals, which so overgrazed the range that the grass has yet to recover. A trail guide available at the entrance tells about the Wolfe family and the features of their ranch. The weather-beaten cabin built in 1906 still survives. A short trail leads to petroglyphs above Wolfe Ranch; figures of horses indicate that Utes, rather than earlier inhabitants, did the artwork. Park staff can give directions to other rock-art sites; great care should be taken not to touch the fragile artwork.

Delicate Arch stands in a magnificent setting atop gracefully curving slickrock. Distant canyons and the La Sal Mountains lie beyond. The span is 45 feet high and 33 feet wide. A moderately strenuous 3-mile (4.8 km) round-trip hike leads to the arch. Another perspective on Delicate Arch can be obtained by driving 1.2 miles (1.9 km) beyond Wolfe Ranch. Look for the small arch high above. A short wheelchair-accessible trail and a slightly longer, steeper trail (0.5 mile/0.8 km round-trip) provide views onto the arch.

Fiery Furnace

The Fiery Furnace Viewpoint and trailhead are three miles from the Wolfe Ranch junction, on the right side of the main road. The Fiery Furnace gets its name from sandstone fins that turn flaming red on occasions when thin cloud cover at the horizon reflects the warm light of sunrise or sunset. Actually, the shady recesses beneath the fins provide a cool respite from the hot summer sun.

Closely packed sandstone fins form a maze

1: Park Avenue; 2: Balanced Rock; 3: sunset at Delicate Arch; 4: Skyline Arch

of deep slots, with many arches and at least one natural bridge inside. Both for safety reasons and to reduce impact on this sensitive area, which harbors several species of rare plants, hikers are encouraged to join a ranger-led hike. The hike is moderately strenuous and involves steep ledges, squeezing through narrow cracks, a couple of jumps, and hoisting yourself up off the ground. There is no turning back once the hike starts, so make sure you're physically prepared and properly equipped.

Rangers offer two different guided hikes into the Fiery Furnace. (May.-Sept.) Ranger-led loop hikes are roughly three hours long and cover 2 miles/3.2 km ($16 adults, $8 ages 5-12), while ranger-led out-and-back hikes ($10 adults, $5 ages 5-12) are about 2.5 hours long and cover about 1.25 miles (2 km) of territory. Tours are offered both in the morning and in the afternoon; only the morning tours are reservable in advance. The afternoon tickets are only sold in person at the visitors center up to a week in advance.

Group size is limited to about 20 people, and children under age five are not allowed. An adult must accompany children 12 and under. Morning walks often fill weeks in advance. Make reservations for the morning hikes online at www.recreation.gov. To visit the Fiery Furnace without a ranger, visitors must obtain a permit at the visitors center ($6 adults, $3 ages 5-12). Several Moab outfitters also lead hikes into the Fiery Furnace; these cost considerably more, but there's usually space available.

Broken and Sand Dune Arches

The trailhead for these short walks is on the right side of the park road, 2.4 miles past the Fiery Furnace turnoff. The short **Broken Arch Trail** (1.2-2 miles/1.9-3.2 km round-trip) leads to small Sand Dune Arch (the opening is 8 feet high and 30 feet wide) tucked within fins. Another trail crosses a field to Broken Arch, which you can also see from the road. The opening is 43 feet high and 59 feet wide. Up close, you'll see that the arch isn't really broken. These arches can also be reached by trail near comfort station 3 at Devils Garden Campground. Low-growing canyon-lands biscuit root, found only in areas of Entrada sandstone, colonizes sand dunes. Hikers can protect the habitat of the biscuit root and other fragile plants by keeping to washes or rock surfaces.

Skyline Arch

Skyline Arch is on the right side of the park road, 1 mile past the Sand Dune-Broken Arch trailhead. In desert climates, erosion may proceed imperceptibly for centuries until a cataclysmic event happens. In 1940 a giant boulder fell from the opening of Skyline Arch, doubling the size of the arch in just seconds. The hole is now 45 feet high and 69 feet wide. The short **Skyline Arch Trail** (0.4 mile/0.6 km round-trip) leads to the base of the arch.

Devils Garden

The Devils Garden trailhead, picnic area, and campground are near the end of the main park road. Devils Garden offers fine scenery and more arches than any other section of the park. The hiking trail leads past large sandstone fins to Landscape and six other named arches. Carry water if the weather is hot or if you might want to continue past the one-mile point at Landscape Arch. Adventurous hikers could spend days exploring the maze of canyons among the fins.

Klondike Bluffs and Tower Arch

Relatively few visitors come to the spires, high bluffs, and fine arch in this northwestern section of the park. A fair-weather dirt road turns off the main drive 1.3 miles (2.1 km) before Devils Garden trailhead, winds down into Salt Valley, and heads northwest. After 7.5 miles (12 km), turn left on the road to Klondike Bluffs and proceed 1 mile to the Tower Arch trailhead. These roads may have washboards, but they are usually passable by cars in dry weather; don't drive on them if storms threaten. The trail to Tower Arch winds past the Marching Men and other rock formations (3 miles/4.8 km round-trip). Alexander Ringhoffer, who discovered the arch in 1922, carved an inscription on the south column. The area can also be fun to explore off-trail with a map and compass or a GPS receiver. Those with 4WD vehicles can drive close to the arch on a separate jeep road. Tower Arch has an opening 34 feet high by 92 feet wide. A tall monolith nearby gave the arch its name.

4WD Exploration

A rough road near Tower Arch in the Klondike Bluffs turns southeast past **Eye of the Whale Arch** in Herdina Park to Balanced Rock on the main park road, 10.8 miles (17.4 km) away. The road isn't particularly difficult for 4WD enthusiasts, although normal backcountry precautions should be taken. A steep sand hill north of Eye of the Whale Arch is difficult to climb for vehicles coming from Balanced Rock; it's better to drive from the Tower Arch area instead. (Trust us and don't try this road in a big pickup truck, even one with 4WD!)

HIKING

Established trails lead to many fine arches and overlooks that can't be seen from the road. You're free to wander cross-country too, but stay on rock or in washes to avoid damaging the fragile cryptobiotic soils. Wear good walking shoes with rubber soles for travel across slickrock. The summer sun can be especially harsh on the unprepared hiker—don't forget water, a hat, and sunscreen. The desert rule is to carry at least one gallon of water per person for an all-day hike. Take a map and compass for off-trail hiking. Be cautious on the slickrock; the soft sandstone can crumble easily. Also, remember that it's easier to go up a steep slickrock slope than it is to come back down.

You can reach almost any spot in the park on a day hike, although you'll also find some good overnight possibilities. Areas for longer trips include Courthouse Wash in the southern part of the park and Salt Wash in the eastern part. All backpacking is done off-trail. A backcountry permit must be obtained from a ranger before camping in the backcountry. Hiking regulations include no fires, no pets, and camping out of sight of any road (at least 1 mile/1.6 km away) or trail (at least 0.5 mile/0.8 km away) and at least 300 feet from a recognizable archaeological site or nonflowing water source.

Delicate Arch Trail

For those who are able, the hike to the base of Delicate Arch is one of the park's highlights. The round-trip distance is three miles with an elevation gain of 500 feet; carry water. Shortly after the trail's start at Wolfe Ranch, a spur trail leads to some petroglyphs depicting horses and their riders and a few bighorn sheep. Because of the horses, which didn't arrive in the area until the mid-1600s, these petroglyphs are believed to be the work of Ute people.

The first stretch of the main trail is broad, flat, and not especially scenic, except for a good display of spring wildflowers. After about half an hour of hiking, the trail climbs steeply up onto the slickrock and the views open up, spanning across the park to the La Sal Mountains in the distance.

Just before the end of the trail, walk up to a small arch for a framed view of the final destination. The classic photo of Delicate Arch is taken late in the afternoon when the sandstone glows with golden hues.

Fiery Furnace Trail

The Fiery Furnace area is open only to hikers with permits ($6 adults, $3 ages 5-12) or to those joining a ranger-led hike. During summer, rangers offer two daily hike options (May-Sept.). Ranger-led **loop hikes** are roughly three hours long and cover 1.5 miles ($16 adults, $8 ages 5-12), while ranger-led **out-and-back hikes** ($10 adults, $5 ages 5-12) are about 2.5 hours long and cover 1.25 miles (2 km) of territory. Tours are offered both in the morning and in the afternoon; only the morning tours are reservable in advance online at www.recreation.gov. The

1

2

afternoon tickets are only sold in person at the visitors center up to a week in advance. These hikes are popular and are often booked weeks in advance, so plan accordingly.

Hiking in the Fiery Furnace is not along a trail; hikers navigate a maze of narrow sandstone canyons. The route through the area is sometimes challenging, requiring hands-and-knees scrambling up cracks and ledges. Navigation is difficult: Route-finding can be tricky because what look like obvious paths often lead to dead ends. Drop-offs and ridges make straight-line travel impossible. It's easy to become disoriented. Even if you're an experienced hiker, the ranger-led hikes provide the best introduction to the Fiery Furnace.

If you're not able to get in on a ranger-led hike and aren't strapped for cash, several Moab outfitters, including **Canyonlands by Night and Day** (1861 N. U.S. 191, Moab, 435/259-5361 or 800/394-9978, www.canyonlandsbynight.com, $89 adults, $67 ages 5-15) offer guided tours in the Fiery Furnace.

Devils Garden Loop

A full tour of Devils Garden (7.2 miles/11.6 km round-trip, four hours) leads to eight named arches and a vacation's worth of scenic wonders. This is one of the park's most popular areas, with several shorter versions of the full loop hike that make the area accessible to nearly every hiker. Don't be shocked to find quite a crowd at the trailhead—it will most likely dissipate after the first two or three arches.

The first two arches are off a short side trail to the right. **Tunnel Arch** has a relatively symmetrical opening 22 feet high and 27 feet wide. The nearby **Pine Tree Arch** is named for a piñon pine that once grew inside; the arch has an opening 48 feet high and 46 feet wide. Continue on the main trail to **Landscape Arch,** which has an incredible 306-foot span (6 feet longer than a football field). This is one of the longest unsupported

rock spans in the world. The thin arch (106 feet high) looks ready to collapse at any moment. The distance from the trailhead to Landscape Arch is two miles round-trip, an easy one-hour walk.

The trail narrows past Landscape Arch and continues to the remains of **Wall Arch,** which collapsed in August 2008. A short side trail branches off to the left beyond the stubs of Wall Arch to **Partition Arch** and **Navajo Arch.** Partition was so named because a piece of rock divides the main opening from a smaller hole. Navajo Arch is a rock-shelter type; perhaps prehistoric Native Americans camped here. The main trail continues northwest and ends at **Double O Arch** (4 miles round-trip from the trailhead). Double O has a large, oval-shaped opening (45 feet high and 71 feet wide) and a smaller hole (9 feet high and 21 feet wide) underneath. **Dark Angel** is a distinctive rock pinnacle 0.25 mile (0.4 km) northwest; cairns mark the way. Another primitive trail loops back to Landscape Arch via Fin Canyon. This route goes through a different area of Devils Garden but adds about 1 mile to your trip (3 miles/4.8 km back to the trailhead instead of 2). Pay careful attention to the trail markers to keep on the correct route.

MOUNTAIN BIKING

Cyclists must stick to established roads in the park. There is no single-track or trail riding in the park. They also have to contend with heavy traffic on the narrow paved roads and dusty, washboard surfaces on the dirt roads. Beware of deep sand on the 4WD roads, traffic on the main park road, and summertime heat wherever you ride.

One good, not-too-hard ride is along the Willow Springs Road. Allow 2-3 hours for an out-and-back, starting from the Balanced Rock parking area and heading west.

Perhaps the best bet for relatively fit mountain bikers is the 24-mile (39 km) ride to Tower Arch and back. From the Devils Garden parking area, ride out the **Salt Valley Road** (which can be rough). After about 7.5

1: hiking the Fiery Furnace Trail; 2: Double O Arch

miles (12 km), turn left onto a jeep road that leads to the "back door" to Tower Arch.

Nearby, BLM and Canyonlands National Park areas offer world-class mountain biking.

ROCK CLIMBING

Rock climbers should stop by a kiosk outside the visitor center for a free permit (also available online at https://archespermits.nps. gov/). Groups are limited to five climbers and Balanced Rock, the "Arches Boulders," and all arches with openings greater than three feet are closed to climbing: Check at the visitors center or online for temporary closures (often due to nesting raptors). Slacklining and BASE jumping are prohibited in the park. There are still plenty of long-standing routes for advanced climbers to enjoy, although the rock in Arches is sandier and softer than in other areas around Moab.

Several additional climbing restrictions are in place. No new permanent climbing hardware may be installed in any fixed location. If an existing bolt or other hardware item is unsafe, it may be replaced. This effectively limits all technical climbing to existing routes or new routes not requiring placement of fixed anchors. Other restrictions are detailed on the park's website.

The most commonly climbed areas are along the sheer stone faces of **Park Avenue.** Another popular destination is **Owl Rock,** the small, owl-shaped tower located in the Windows Section of the park. For more information on climbing in Arches, consult *Desert Rock* by Eric Bjørnstad, or *High on Moab,* by Karl Kelley, or ask for advice at **Pagan Mountaineering** (59 S. Main St., Moab, 435/259-1117, www.paganclimber.com), a climbing and outdoor-gear store.

CAMPGROUND

Devils Garden Campground (elevation 5,355 feet, with water, year-round, $25) is near the end of the 18-mile (29-km) scenic drive. It's an excellent place to camp, with some sites tucked under rock formations and others offering great views, but it's extremely popular. The well-organized traveler must plan accordingly and reserve a site in advance for March-October. Reservations (www.recreation.gov) must be made no less than 4 days and no more than 240 days in advance. All campsites can be reserved, so during the busy spring, summer, and fall seasons, campers without reservations are pretty much out of luck. In winter, sites 1-24 are available as first-come, first-served. A camp host is on-site, and firewood

Devils Garden Campground

is available ($5), but there are no other services or amenities.

If you aren't able to score a coveted Arches campsite, all is not lost. There are many Bureau of Land Management (BLM) campsites within an easy drive of the park. Try the primitive BLM campgrounds on Highway 313, just west of U.S. 191 and on the way to Canyonlands National Park's Island in the Sky District. Another cluster of BLM campgrounds is along the Colorado River on

Highway 128, which runs northeast from U.S. 191 at the north end of Moab.

GETTING THERE

Arches National Park is 26 miles south of I-70 and 5 miles north of Moab, both off U.S. 191. If you're driving from Moab, allow 15 minutes to reach the park, as there is often slow-moving RV traffic along the route. If you're on a bike, a paved bike path parallels the highway between Moab and the park.

Canyonlands National Park

The canyon country puts on its supreme performance in this vast park, which spreads across 527 square miles. The deeply entrenched Colorado and Green Rivers meet in its heart, and then continue south, as the mighty Colorado, through tumultuous Cataract Canyon Rapids. The park is divided into four districts and a separate noncontiguous unit. The Colorado and Green Rivers form the River District and divide Canyonlands National Park into three other regions. Island in the Sky is north, between the rivers; the Maze is to the west; and Needles is to the east. The small Horseshoe Canyon Unit, farther to the west, preserves a canyon on Barrier Creek, a tributary of the Green River, in which astounding petroglyphs and ancient rock paintings are protected.

Each district has its own distinct character. No bridges or roads directly connect the three land districts and the Horseshoe Canyon Unit, so most visitors have to leave the park to go from one region to another. The huge park can be seen in many ways and on many levels. Paved roads reach a few areas, 4WD roads go to more places, and hiking trails reach still more, but much of the land shows no trace of human passage. To get the big picture, you can fly over this incredible complex of canyons on an air tour; however, only a river trip or a hike lets you experience the solitude and detail of the land.

The park can be visited in any season of the year, with spring and autumn the best choices. Summer temperatures can climb over 100°F; carrying and drinking lots of water becomes critical then (bring at least one gallon per person per day). Arm yourself with insect repellent late spring-midsummer. Winter days tend to be bright and sunny, although nighttime temperatures can dip into the teens or even below zero Fahrenheit. Winter visitors should inquire about travel conditions, as snow and ice occasionally close roads and trails at higher elevations.

EXPLORING THE PARK

There are four districts and a noncontiguous unit in the park, each affording great views, spectacular geology, a chance to see wildlife, and endless opportunities to explore. You won't find crowds or elaborate park facilities—most of Canyonlands remains a primitive backcountry park.

Admission to the park is $25 per vehicle, $15 per motorcycle, or $10 for bicyclists and pedestrians. In addition, fees are charged for backcountry camping, 4WD exploration, and river rafting. For information on the park, contact **Canyonlands National Park** (2282 SW Resource Blvd., Moab, 435/719-2313, www.nps.gov/cany).

Each of the land districts has a visitors center near the park entrance, but you may find it convenient to stop at the **Moab Information Center** (25 E. Center St., Moab, 435/259-8825, www.discovermoab.com, 8am-7pm Mon.-Sat., 9am-6pm Sun. mid-Mar.-Nov.). The centers have brochures, maps, and books as well as someone to answer your questions.

Island in the Sky District

Island in the Sky has paved roads on its top to impressive overlooks and to Upheaval Dome, a strange geologic feature. If you're short on time or don't want to make a rigorous backcountry trip, this district is the best choice. The "island," actually a large mesa, is much like Dead Horse Point on a giant scale; a narrow neck of land connects the north side with the "mainland." Hikers, mountain bikers, and those with suitable vehicles can drop off the Island in the Sky and descend about 1,300 feet to the White Rim 4WD Road, which follows cliffs of the White Rim around most of the island.

Needles District

Colorful rock spires prompted the name of the Needles District. Splendid canyons contain many arches, strange rock formations, and archaeological sites. Hikers enjoy day hikes and backpacking treks on the network of trails and routes within the district. Motorists with 4WD vehicles have their own challenging roads through canyons and other highly scenic areas. Reach overlooks and short trails from the paved scenic drive in the park. South of Moab, Highway 211 branches off U.S. 191, providing easy access to the Needles District.

Maze District

Few visitors make it over to the Maze District, some of the wildest country in the United States. Only the rivers and a handful of 4WD roads and hiking trails provide access. Experienced hikers can explore the "maze" of canyons on unmarked routes.

Horseshoe Canyon Unit

Horseshoe Canyon Unit, a detached section of Canyonlands National Park northwest of the Maze District, protects the Great Gallery, a group of pictographs left by prehistoric people.

River District

The River District includes long stretches of the Green and the Colorado Rivers. River-running provides one of the best ways to experience the inner depths of the park. Boaters can obtain helpful literature and advice from park rangers. Groups planning their own trip through Cataract Canyon need a river-running permit. Flat-water permits are also required, and there's a fee.

Backcountry Exploration

A complex system of fees is charged for backcountry camping, 4WD exploration, and river rafting. Except for the main campgrounds at Willow Flat (Island in the Sky) and Squaw Flat (Needles), you'll need a permit for backcountry camping. There is a $30 fee for a backpacking, biking, or 4WD overnight permit. Day-use permits (free, but limited in quantity) are required for vehicles, including motorcycles and bikes on the White Rim Road, Elephant Hill, and a couple of other areas. Each of the three major districts has a different policy for backcountry vehicle camping, so it's a good idea to make sure that you understand the details. Backcountry permits are also needed for any trips with horses or stock; check with a ranger for details.

It's possible to reserve a backcountry permit in advance; for spring and fall travel to popular areas like Island in the Sky's White Rim Trail or the Needles backcountry, this is an extremely good idea. Find application forms on the Canyonlands website (https://canypermits.nps.gov). Forms should be completed and returned at least two weeks in advance of your planned trip. Telephone reservations are not accepted.

Back-road travel is a popular method of exploring the park. Canyonlands National Park offers hundreds of miles of exceptionally scenic jeep roads, favorites both with mountain bikers and 4WD enthusiasts. Park regulations require all motorized vehicles to have proper registration and licensing for highway use, and ATVs are prohibited in the park; drivers must also be licensed. Normally you must have a vehicle with both 4WD and high clearance; it must also be maneuverable (large pickup trucks don't work for many places). It's essential for both motor vehicles and bicycles to stay on existing roads to prevent damage to the delicate desert vegetation. Carry tools, extra fuel, water, and food in case you break down in a remote area.

Before making a trip, drivers and cyclists should talk with a ranger to register and to check on current road conditions, which can change drastically from one day to the next. The rangers can also tell you where to seek help if you get stuck. Primitive campgrounds are provided on most of the roads, but you'll need a backcountry permit from a ranger. Books on backcountry exploration include Charles Wells's *Guide to Moab, UT Backroads & 4-Wheel Drive Trails,* which includes Canyonlands, and Damian Fagan and David Williams's *A Naturalist's Guide to the White Rim Trail.*

One more thing about backcountry travel in Canyonlands: You may need to pack your waste out of the backcountry. Because of the abundance of slickrock and the desert conditions, it's not always possible to dig a hole, and you can't just leave your waste on a rock until it decomposes (decomposition is a very slow process in these conditions). Check with the ranger when you pick up your backcountry permit for more information.

ISLAND IN THE SKY DISTRICT

Panoramic views from the "island" can be enjoyed from any point along the rim; you'll see much of the park and southeastern Utah. Short hiking trails lead to overlooks, Mesa Arch, Aztec Butte, Whale Rock, Upheaval Dome, and other features. Longer trails make steep, strenuous descents from the island to the White Rim 4WD Road below. Elevations

on the island average about 6,000 feet. Bring water for all hiking, camping, and travel on Island in the Sky. No services are available, except at the visitors center in emergencies (bottled water is sold).

Visitors Center

Stop here for information about Island in the Sky and to see exhibits on geology and history; books and maps are available for purchase. The **visitors center** (435/259-4712, 8am-6pm daily late Apr.-late-Sept., 8am-5pm early spring and fall, closed late Dec.-early Mar.) is located just before the neck crosses to Island in the Sky. From Moab, go northwest 10 miles (16 km) on U.S. 191, then turn left and drive 15 miles (24 km) on Highway 313 to the junction for Dead Horse Point State Park. From here, continue straight 7 miles (11.3 km). Many of the park's plants are grown and identified outside the visitors center; look also at the display of pressed plants inside the center.

Scenic Drive
SHAFER CANYON OVERLOOK

The Shafer Canyon Overlook is on the left of the park road, 0.5 mile (0.8 km) past the visitors center (just before crossing the neck). **Shafer Trail Viewpoint,** across the neck, provides another perspective 0.5 mile (0.8 km) farther. The neck is a narrow land bridge just wide enough for the road, and it's the only vehicle access to the 40-square-mile (64-square-mile) Island in the Sky. The overlooks have good views east down the canyon and the incredibly twisting **Shafer Trail Road.** Cattlemen Frank and John Schafer built the trail in the early 1900s to move stock to additional pastures (the *c* in their name was later dropped by mapmakers). Uranium prospectors upgraded the trail to a 4WD road during the 1950s so that they could reach their claims at the base of the cliffs. Today the Shafer Trail Road connects the mesa top with White Rim 4WD Road and Potash Road, 1,200 feet and 4 miles (6.4 km) below. High-clearance vehicles should be

Canyonlands National Park

SUNSET PASS

BAGPIPE BUTTE OVERLOOK

FLINT SHEEP

Orange Cliffs

FLINT TRAIL

North

Canyon Trail

Waterhole Flat

GOLDEN STAIRS

Elaterite Basin

Lake Powell

Colorado

Ernie's Country

Land of Standing Rocks

The Fins

MAZE OVERLOOK

Canyonlands National Park

River

DOLL HOUSE

MAZE DISTRICT

Cataract Canyon

Bobbys

Hole

NEEDLES

Spanish Bottom

Lower Red

Confluence

Bee f Basin

DISTRICT

CHESLER PARK

DEVILS KITCHEN

Lake Cyn Tr.

CONFLUENCE OVERLOOK

Druid Arch

Elephant

Canyon

ELEPHANT HILL

POTHOLE POINT

BIG SPRING CANYON OVERLOOK

COLORADO RIVER OVERLOOK

Big Spring Cyn Canyon

Squaw

Canyon

BIG SPRING CANYON SCENIC DRIVE

VISITOR CENTER

SLICKROCK

Lost Canyon

Peekaboo Trail

WOODEN SHOE OVERLOOK

SQUAW FLAT CAMPGROUND/TRAILHEAD

ROADSIDE RUIN

CAVE SPRING TRAIL

NEEDLES OUTPOST

To BLM NEWSPAPER ROCK HISTORICAL MONUMENT, Indian Creek, and Hwy 191

Salt Creek Canyon

Castle Arch

Angel Arch

Fortress Arch

Horse Canyon

Lavender Canyon

Davis Canyon

© MOON.COM

0   5 mi

0   5 km

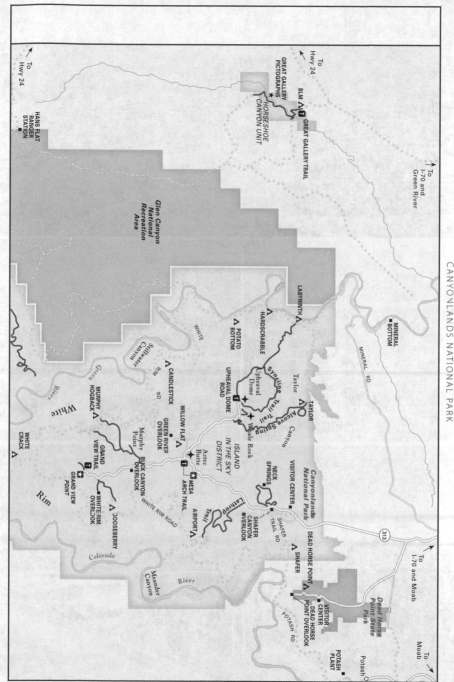

ARCHES AND CANYONLANDS

CANYONLANDS NATIONAL PARK

used on Shafer, preferably with four-wheel drive if you plan to climb up. Road conditions can vary considerably, so contact a ranger before starting out.

NECK SPRING TRAIL

This moderately difficult 5.8-mile (9.3 km) loop trail begins near the Shafer Canyon Overlook and heads down Taylor Canyon to Neck and Cabin Springs, formerly used by ranchers, then climbs back to Island in the Sky Road at a second trailhead 0.5 mile (0.8 km) south of the start. Water at the springs supports maidenhair ferns and other water-loving plants. Also watch for birds and wildlife attracted to this spot. Bring water with you, as the springs aren't suitable for drinking. The elevation change is 300 feet.

LATHROP TRAIL

The **Lathrop Trail** (13.6 miles/21.8 km to White Rim Rd., 21.6 miles/34 km to Colorado River, round-trip) is the only marked hiking route going all the way from Island in the Sky to the Colorado River. The trailhead is on the east side of the main road, 1.3 miles (2.1 km) past the neck. The first 2.5 miles (4 km) cross Gray's Pasture to the rim, and then the trail descends steeply, dropping 1,600 feet over the next 2.5 miles (4 km) to White Rim 4WD Road. Part of this section follows an old mining road past several abandoned mines, all relics of the uranium boom; don't enter the shafts, as they're in danger of collapse and may contain poisonous gases. From the mining area, the route descends through a wash to White Rim 4WD Road, follows the road a short distance south, and then goes down Lathrop Canyon Road to the Colorado River, another 4 miles with a descent of 500 feet. Total distance for the strenuous hike is 9 miles (14.5 km) one-way, with an elevation change of 2,100 feet. The trail has little shade and can be very hot.

1: Colorado River; **2:** Shafer Trail Road; **3:** Grand View Point; **4:** White Rim Road

★ MESA ARCH TRAIL

This easy trail leads to a dramatic arch that rises on the rim of a sheer 800-foot cliff. You'll marvel at how this arch has survived in its precarious location. The trailhead is on the left, 5.5 miles (8.9 km) from the neck. On the way, the road crosses the grasslands and scattered juniper trees of Gray's Pasture. Hiking distance is only 0.5 mile (0.8 km) round-trip (30 minutes) with an 80-foot elevation change. The arch, eroded from Navajo sandstone, frames views of rock formations below and the La Sal Mountains in the distance.

MURPHY LOOP

At the road junction just past the Mesa Arch trailhead are spectacular viewpoints. After 2.5 miles (4 km), a rough dirt road turns right and goes 1.7 miles (2.7 km) to Murphy Point. Hikers can take **Murphy Trail** (11-mile/17.7 km loop), which begins off the road to the point, to White Rim 4WD Road. This strenuous route forks partway down; one branch follows Murphy Hogback (a ridge) to Murphy Campground on the 4WD road, and the other branch follows a wash to the road 1 mile south of the campground. A loop hike along both branches has an elevation change of 1,100 feet.

★ GRAND VIEW POINT

A handy lunch stop, the **Grand View Picnic Area,** is 2.5 miles (4 km) along the main road past the Murphy Point turnoff. Two trails start here. **White Rim Overlook Trail** (1.8 miles/2.9 km round-trip) is an easy hike east along a peninsula to an overlook of Monument Basin and beyond. **Gooseberry Trail** (5.4 miles/8.7 km round-trip) drops off the mesa and descends some extremely steep grades to the White Rim 4WD Road just north of Gooseberry Campground; the strenuous trip takes up to four hours with an elevation change of 1,400 feet.

Continue 1 mile (1.6 km) on the main road past the picnic area to Grand View Point, perhaps the most spectacular panorama from

Island in the Sky. Monument Basin lies directly below, and countless canyons, the Colorado River, the Needles, and mountain ranges are in the distance. **Grand View Point Trail** (2 miles/3.2 km round-trip) continues past the end of the road for other vistas from the point, which is the southernmost tip of Island in the Sky.

GREEN RIVER OVERLOOK

The Green River Overlook is to the west of the main road junction; turn west and go 0.25 mile (0.4 km), then turn south and continue 1.5 miles (2.4 km) on an unpaved road to the overlook. Soda Springs Basin and a section of the Green River (deeply entrenched in Stillwater Canyon) can be seen below.

AZTEC BUTTE TRAIL

This trailhead is on the right 1 mile (1.6 km) northwest of the main road junction. Aztec Butte is one of the few areas at Island in the Sky with Native American ruins; shortage of water prevented permanent settlement. The easy trail (2 miles/3.2 km round-trip) climbs 200 vertical feet to the top of the butte in 0.5 mile (0.8 km) for a good panorama of the Island.

WHALE ROCK TRAIL

The Whale Rock trailhead is on the right of the park road, 4.4 miles (7 km) northwest of the road junction. An easy trail (1 mile/1.6 km round-trip) climbs this sandstone hump near the outer rim of Upheaval Dome for an ascent of 100 feet.

UPHEAVAL DOME

The park road ends 5.3 miles (8.5 km) northwest of the main road junction, providing a look at this geological curiosity. There's also a small **picnic area** here. The easy **Crater View Trail** (1.8 miles round-trip) leads to overlooks on the rim of Upheaval Dome: The first viewpoint is 0.8 mile (1.3 km) round-trip, the second one another mile farther. A fantastically deformed pile of rocks lies below, within a crater about 3 miles (4.8 km) across

and 1,200 feet deep. For many years, Upheaval Dome has kept geologists busy trying to figure out its origin. They once assumed that salt of the Paradox Formation pushed the rock layers upward to form the dome. Now, however, there is strong evidence that a meteorite impact caused the structure. The surrounding ring depression (caused by collapse) and the convergence of rock layers upward toward the center correspond precisely to known impact structures. Shatter cones and microscopic analysis also indicate an impact origin. When the meteorite struck, sometime in the last 150 million years, it formed a crater up to 5 miles (8 km) across. Erosion removed some of the overlying rock, perhaps as much as a vertical mile. The underlying salt may have played a role in uplifting the central section.

Energetic hikers can reach Upheaval Dome from the parking area at the overlook or from White Rim 4WD Road below. **Syncline Loop Trail** (8.3 miles/13.3 km round-trip) makes a strenuous circuit completely around Upheaval Dome; elevation change is 1,200 feet. The trail crosses Upheaval Dome Canyon about halfway around from the overlook; walk east 1.5 miles (2.4 km) up the canyon to enter the crater itself. This is the only nontechnical route into the center of the dome. A hike around Upheaval Dome with a side trip to the crater totals 11 miles (17.7 km); it's best done as an overnight trip. Carry plenty of water for the entire trip; this dry country can be very hot in summer. The Green River is the only reliable source of water. From near Upheaval Campsite on White Rim 4WD Road, you can hike 4 miles on **Upheaval Trail** through Upheaval Canyon to a junction with the Syncline Loop Trail, then another 1.5 miles (2.4 km) into the crater; elevation gain is about 600 feet.

White Rim Road

This driving adventure follows the White Rim 4WD Road below the sheer cliffs of Island in the Sky. A close look at the light-colored surface reveals ripple marks and cross-beds laid down near an ancient coastline. The plateau's east side is about 800 feet above the Colorado River. On the west side, the plateau meets the bank of the Green River.

Travel along the winding road presents a constantly changing panorama of rock, canyons, river, and sky. Keep an eye out for desert bighorn sheep. You'll see all three levels of Island in the Sky District, from the high plateaus to the White Rim to the rivers.

Only 4WD vehicles with high clearance can make the trip. With the proper vehicle, driving is mostly easy, but slow and winding; a few steep or rough sections have to be negotiated. The 100-mile (161-km) trip takes 2-3 days. Allow an extra day to travel all the road spurs.

Mountain bikers find this a great trip, too; most cyclists arrange an accompanying 4WD vehicle to carry water and camping gear. Primitive campgrounds along the way provide convenient stopping places. Both cyclists and 4WD drivers must obtain reservations and a backcountry permit ($30) for the White Rim campsites from the Island in the Sky visitors center. Find application forms on the Canyonlands website (https://canypermits.nps.gov); return the completed application at least two weeks in advance of your planned trip. Questions can be fielded via telephone (435/259-4351, 8am-12:30pm Mon.-Fri.), but no telephone reservations are accepted. Demand exceeds supply during the popular spring and autumn seasons, when you should make reservations as far in advance as possible. No services or developed water sources exist anywhere on the drive, so be sure to have plenty of fuel and water with some to spare. Access points are Shafer Trail Road (from near Island in the Sky) and Potash Road (Hwy. 279 from Moab) on the east and Mineral Bottom Road on the west. White Rim sandstone forms the distinctive plateau crossed on the drive.

Campground

There is only one developed campground in the Island in the Sky District. **Willow Flat Campground** on Murphy Point Road has only 12 sites ($15), available on a first-come, first-served basis; sites tend to fill up in all seasons except winter. No water or services are available.

Camping is available just outside the park at **Dead Horse Point State Park** (reservations 800/322-3770, www.reserveamerica.com, $25 plus $9 reservation fee), which is also very popular, so don't plan on getting a spot without reserving way ahead. There are also primitive Bureau of Land Management (BLM) campsites along Highway 313.

NEEDLES DISTRICT

The Needles District showcases some of the finest rock sculptures in Canyonlands National Park. Spires, arches, and monoliths appear in almost any direction you look. Prehistoric ruins and rock art exist in a greater variety and quantity than anywhere else in the park. Year-round springs and streams bring greenery to the desert. A paved road, several 4WD roads, and many hiking trails offer a variety of ways to explore the Needles.

The primary access road to Needles District, Highway 221, now passes through **Indian Creek National Monument,** designated in 2018 by President Donald Trump. This new monument is in the process of creating its management plan. For current information, contact the BLM office in Monticello (365 N. Main, 435/587-1500).

★ BLM Newspaper Rock Historical Monument

Although not in the park itself, Newspaper Rock is just 150 feet off Highway 211 on the way to the Needles District. At Newspaper Rock, a profusion of petroglyphs depict human figures, animals, birds, and abstract designs. These represent 2,000 years of human history during which archaic Native Americans as well as Ancestral Puebloan, Fremont, Paiute, Navajo, and Anglo travelers passed through Indian Creek Canyon. The patterns on the smooth sandstone rock face stand out clearly, thanks to a coating of dark desert varnish. A short nature trail introduces you to the area's desert and riparian vegetation.

Indian Creek

The splitter cracks in the rock walls around **Indian Creek** offer world-class rock climbing, with close to 1,000 routes. Most routes here are tough, 5.10 and above. Fall climbing is best, followed by early spring; summer afternoons are way too hot, and it's dangerous to climb after a rainstorm.

Climbers should track down a copy of *Indian Creek: A Climbing Guide,* by David Bloom, for details and lots of pictures. **Moab Desert Adventures** (415 N. Main St., Moab, 804/814-3872, www.moabdesertadventures. com) offers guided climbing at Indian Creek.

Indian Creek's climbing walls start on Highway 211, about 15 miles (24 km) west of U.S. 191, 3 miles (4.8 km) west of Newspaper Rock.

Needles and Anticline Overlooks

Although outside the park, these viewpoints atop the high mesa east of Canyonlands National Park offer magnificent panoramas of the surrounding area. Part of the BLM's **Canyon Rims Recreation Area** (www. blm.gov), these easily accessed overlooks provide the kind of awe-inspiring vistas over the Needles District that would otherwise require a hike in the park. The turnoff for both overlooks is at milepost 93 on U.S. 191, which is 32 miles (52 km) south of Moab and 7 miles (11.3 km) north of Highway 211. There are also two campgrounds along the access road.

For the Needles Overlook, follow the paved road 22 miles (35 km) west to its end (turn left at the junction 15 miles/24 km in). The BLM maintains a picnic area and interpretive exhibits here. A fence protects visitors from the sheer cliffs that drop off more than 1,000 feet. You can see much of Canyonlands National Park and southeastern Utah. Look south for the Six-shooter Peaks and the high country of the Abajo Mountains; southwest for the Needles (thousands of spires reaching for the

sky); west for the confluence area of the Green and Colorado Rivers, the Maze District, the Orange Cliffs, and the Henry Mountains; northwest for the lazy bends of the Colorado River Canyon and the sheer-walled mesas of Island in the Sky and Dead Horse Point; north for the Book Cliffs; and northeast for the La Sal Mountains. The changing shadows and colors of the canyon country make for a continuous show throughout the day.

For the Anticline Overlook, from Highway 191 head 15 miles (24 km) west to the junction with the Needles road, then turn right and drive 17 miles (27 km) north on a good gravel road to the fenced overlook at road's end. You'll be standing 1,600 feet above the Colorado River. The sweeping panorama over the canyons, the river (and the bright-blue evaporation ponds at the potash factory outside of Moab), and the twisted rocks of the Kane Creek Anticline is nearly as spectacular as that from Dead Horse Point, only 5.5 miles (8.9 km) west as the crow flies. Salt and other minerals of the Paradox Formation pushed up overlying rocks into the dome visible below. Down-cutting by the Colorado River has revealed the twisted rock layers. Look carefully at the northeast horizon to see an arch in the Windows Section of Arches National Park, 16 miles/26 km away.

The BLM operates two campgrounds in the Canyon Rims Recreation Area. **Hatch Point Campground** (10 sites, May-mid-Oct., $15) has a quiet and scenic mesa-top setting just off the road to the Anticline Overlook, about nine miles north of the road junction. Closer to the highway in a rock amphitheater is **Windwhistle Campground** (May-mid-Oct., $15); it's six miles west of U.S. 191 on the Needles Overlook road. Although both of these campgrounds supposedly have water, it wasn't evident when we visited.

Needles Outpost

The **Needles Outpost campground,** just

1: petroglyphs of Newspaper Rock; 2: Pothole Point Trail

outside the park boundary (435/979-4007, http://www.needlesoutpost.com, mid-Feb.-mid Dec., $20 tents or RVs, no hookups, $20 tents or RVs, no hookups) is a good place to stay if the campground in the park is full. A general store here has groceries, ice, gas, propane, showers ($3 campers, $6 noncampers), and basic camping supplies. Campsites have a fair amount of privacy and great views onto the park's spires. The turnoff from Highway 211 is 1 mile (1.6 km) before the Needles visitors center.

Visitors Center

Stop at the **visitors center** (west end of Hwy. 211, 435/259-4711, 8am-6pm spring and fall, 8am-5pm daily July-Aug.) for information on hiking, back roads, and other aspects of travel in the Needles, as well as backcountry permits (required for all overnight stays in the backcountry), and maps, brochures, and books. Take about 15 minutes to watch the film on the region's geology. When the office isn't open, you'll find information posted outside.

Scenic Drive

The main road runs 6.5 miles (10.5 km) past the visitors center to Big Spring Canyon Overlook. On the way, you can stop at several nature trails, turn off on 4WD roads, or take short spur roads to trailheads and Squaw Flat Campground.

Roadside Ruin (0.3 mile/0.5 km round-trip) is on the left, 0.4 mile (0.6 km) past the visitors center. A loop trail passes near a well-preserved granary left by Ancestral Puebloan people. A trail guide available at the start tells about the Ancestral Puebloans and the local plants.

Cave Spring Trail (0.6 mile/1 km round-trip) introduces the geology and ecology of the park and leads to an old cowboy line camp. Turn left 0.7 mile (1.1 km) past the visitors center and follow signs about 1 mile (1.6 km) to the trailhead. Pick up the brochure at the beginning. Follow the loop clockwise, crossing some slickrock; two ladders assist on the steep sections. Cowboys used the cave as a line

camp from the late 1800s until establishment of the park in 1964; the line camp is just 50 yards in from the trailhead.

A road to **Elephant Hill Trail** (6-11 miles/9.7-17.7 km round-trip) turns left 2.7 miles (4.3 km) past the ranger station. A picnic area is at the base of Elephant Hill, 3 miles (4.8 km) past the campground turnoff and on the scenic drive. Hiking trails lead into wonderful rock forms and canyons from both the campground and picnic area. Only experienced drivers in 4WD vehicles should continue past the picnic area up Elephant Hill.

Pothole Point Trail (0.6 mile/1 km round-trip) is on the left of the main road 5 miles (8 km) past the visitors center. Highlights of this loop hike are the many potholes dissolved in the Cedar Mesa sandstone. A brochure illustrates the fairy shrimp, tadpole shrimp, horsehair worms, snails, and other adaptable creatures that spring to life when rains fill the potholes. You'll also enjoy fine views of distant buttes from the trail.

Slickrock Trail (2.4 miles/3.9 km round-trip) begins on the right, 6.2 miles (10 km) past the visitors center. The loop trail takes you north to an overlook of the confluence of Big Spring and Little Spring Canyons. Hiking is easy and offers good panoramas.

Big Spring Canyon Overlook, 6.5 miles (10.5 km) past the visitors center, marks the end of the scenic drive but not the scenery. The **Confluence Overlook Trail** (11 miles/17.7 km round-trip) begins here and winds west to an overlook of the Green and Colorado Rivers.

Hiking

The Needles District has about 55 miles (89 km) of backcountry trails. Many interconnect to provide all sorts of day and overnight trips. Cairns mark the trails; signs point the way at junctions. You can normally find water in upper Elephant Canyon and canyons to the east in spring and early summer, though the remaining water often becomes stagnant by midsummer. Always ask the rangers about sources of water—don't depend on

Pothole Ecosystems

At Canyonlands it's easy to be in awe of the deep canyons and big desert rivers. But the little details of Canyonlands geology and ecology are pretty wonderful, too. Consider the potholes: shallow depressions dusted with wind-blown dirt. These holes, which range from less than an inch to several feet deep, fill after rainstorms and bring entire little ecosystems to life.

Pothole dwellers must be able to survive long periods of dryness and then pack as much living as possible into the short wet periods. Some creatures, like the tadpole shrimp, live for only a couple of weeks. Others, like the spadefoot toad, hatch from drought-resistant eggs when water is present, quickly pass through the critical tadpole stage, then move onto dry land, returning to mate and lay eggs in potholes.

Although pothole dwellers are tough enough to survive in a dormant form during the long dry spells, most are very sensitive to sudden water-chemistry changes, temperature changes, sediment input, being stepped on, and being splashed out onto dry land. Humans should never use pothole water for swimming, bathing, or drinking, as this can drastically change the salinity or pH of a pool. Organisms are unable to adapt to these human-generated changes, which occur suddenly, unlike slow natural changes. While the desert pothole ecosystems may seem unimportant, they act as an indicator of the health of the larger ecosystems in which they occur.

its availability. Treat water from all sources, including springs, before drinking. Chesler Park and other areas west of Elephant Canyon are very dry; bring all the water you'll need. Mosquitoes, gnats, and deer flies can be very pesky late spring-midsummer, especially in the wetter places—bring insect repellent. To plan your trip, obtain the small hiking map available from the visitors center, Trails Illustrated's *Needles District* map, or USGS topo maps.

CONFLUENCE OVERLOOK TRAIL

This 11-mile (17.7 km, round-trip) trail goes west 5.5 miles (8.9 km) from Big Spring Canyon Overlook (at the end of the scenic drive) to a fine viewpoint overlooking the Green and Colorado Rivers 1,000 feet below. You may see rafts in the water or bighorn sheep on the cliffs. The trail crosses Big Spring and Elephant Canyons and follows a jeep road for a short distance. Higher points have good views of the Needles to the south. Except for a few short steep sections, this trail is level and fairly easy. A very early start is recommended in summer, as there's little shade. Carry water even if you don't plan to go all the way—this enchanting country has lured many a hiker beyond his or her original goal.

SQUAW FLAT TRAILHEAD

The main trailhead is a short distance south of the campground and is reached by a separate signed road. You can also begin from a trailhead in the campground itself. **Squaw Canyon Trail** follows the canyon south. Intermittent water can often be found until late spring. You can take a connecting trail (Peekaboo, Lost Canyon, or Big Spring Canyon) or cross a slickrock pass to Elephant Canyon.

Peekaboo Trail (10 miles/16 km round-trip) winds southeast over rugged terrain, including some steep sections of slickrock (best avoided when wet, icy, or covered with snow). There's little shade; carry water. The trail follows Squaw Canyon, climbs over a pass to Lost Canyon, and then crosses more slickrock before descending to Peekaboo Campground on Salt Creek 4WD Road. Look for Ancestral Puebloan ruins on the way and rock art at the campground. A rockslide took out Peekaboo Spring, shown on some maps. Options on this trail include a turnoff south through Squaw Canyon or Lost Canyon to make a loop of 8.75 miles (14.1 km) or more.

Lost Canyon Trail (8.7 miles/14 km round-trip) is reached via Peekaboo or Squaw Canyon Trails and makes a loop with them.

Water supports abundant vegetation; you may need to wade. Most of the way is in the wash bottom, except for a section of slickrock to Squaw Canyon.

Big Spring Canyon Trail (7.5 miles/12 km round-trip) crosses an outcrop of slickrock from the trailhead, and then follows the canyon bottom to the head of the canyon. You can usually find intermittent water along the way except in summer. At canyon's end, a climb up steep slickrock (hazardous if covered by snow or ice) takes you to Squaw Canyon Trail and back to the trailhead. Another possibility is to turn southwest to the head of Squaw Canyon, then hike over a slickrock saddle to Elephant Canyon (10.5 miles/16.9 km round-trip).

ELEPHANT HILL TRAILHEAD

Three miles west of the campground turnoff is the picnic area and trailhead at the base of Elephant Hill. Sounds of racing engines and burning rubber can often be heard from above as vehicles attempt the difficult 4WD road that begins just past the picnic area. All of the following destinations can also be reached by trails from the Squaw Flat trailhead, although distances will be slightly greater.

Chesler Park is a favorite hiking destination. A lovely desert meadow contrasts with the red and white spires that gave the Needles District its name. An old cowboy line camp is on the west side of the rock island in the center of the park. **Chesler Park Trail** (6 miles/9.7 km round-trip) winds through sand and slickrock before ascending a small pass through the Needles to Chesler Park. Once inside, **Chesler Park Loop Trail** (11 miles/17.7 km round-trip) circles completely around the park. The loop includes the unusual 0.5-mile (0.8 km) **Joint Trail,** which follows the bottom of a very narrow crack. Camping in Chesler Park is restricted to certain areas; check with a ranger.

Druid Arch (11 miles/17.7 km round-trip) reminds many people of the massive stone slabs at Stonehenge, popularly associated with the druids, in southern England. The arch is a 15-mile (24-km) hike if you start at the Squaw Flat trailhead. Follow the Chesler Park Trail 2 miles (3.2 km) to Elephant Canyon, turn up the canyon 3.5 miles (5.6 km), and then climb 0.25 mile (0.4 km) to the arch. Upper Elephant Canyon has seasonal water, but the narrow canyon is closed to camping.

Lower Red Lake Canyon Trail (8-19 miles/12.9-31 km round-trip) provides access to Cataract Canyon of the Colorado River. This is a long, strenuous trip best suited for experienced hikers and completed in two days. Distance from the Elephant Hill trailhead is 19 miles (31 km) round-trip; you'll be walking on 4WD roads and trails. If you can drive Elephant Hill 4WD Road to the trail junction in Cyclone Canyon, the hike is only 8 miles (12.9 km) round-trip. The most difficult trail section is a steep talus slope that drops 700 vertical feet in 0.5 mile (0.8 km) into the lower canyon. Total elevation change is 1,000 feet. The canyon has little shade and lacks any water source above the river. Summer heat can make the trip grueling; temperatures tend to be 5-10 degrees hotter than on other Needles trails. The river level drops between midsummer and autumn, allowing hikers to go along the shore both downstream to see the rapids and upstream to the confluence. Undertows and strong currents make the river dangerous to cross.

UPPER SALT CREEK TRAIL

Several impressive arches and many inviting side canyons attract adventurous hikers to the extreme southeast corner of the park. This trail (12 miles/19.3 km round-trip) begins at the end of the 13.5-mile (21.7 km) 4WD road up Salt Creek, and then goes south up-canyon to Cottonwood Canyon-Beef Basin Road near Cathedral Butte, just outside the park boundary. The trail is nearly level except for a steep climb at the end. Water can usually be found. Some wading and bushwhacking may be necessary. The famous All American Man pictograph, shown on some topo maps (or ask a

1: Chesler Park; 2: Druid Arch

ranger), is in a cave a short way off to the east at about the midpoint of the trail; follow your map and unsigned paths to the cave, but don't climb in—it's dangerous to both you and the ruins and pictograph inside. Many more archaeological sites can be discovered near the trail; they're all fragile and need great care when visited.

4WD Exploration

A back-road tour allows you to see beautiful canyon scenery, arches, and Native American rock-art sites in the Needles District. Check with a ranger about special hazards before setting out. Also obtain a backcountry permit ($30 per vehicle) if you plan to use one of the backcountry campgrounds available along Salt Creek or in the area past Elephant Hill. Mountain bikers enjoy the challenge of going up Elephant Hill Road and the roads beyond. Colorado Overlook 4WD Road is good riding too, but Salt Creek and the other eastern canyons have too much loose sand.

SALT CREEK CANYON 4WD ROAD

Salt Creek Road begins near Cave Spring Trail, crosses sage flats for the next 2.5 miles (4 km), then heads deep into this spectacular canyon. Round-trip distance, including a side trip to 150-foot-high Angel Arch, is 26 miles (42 km). Agile hikers can follow a steep slickrock route into the window of Angel Arch. You can also explore side canyons of Salt Creek or take the Upper Salt Creek Trail; the All American Man pictograph (12 miles/19.3 km round-trip) makes a good day-hike destination. **Horse Canyon 4WD Road** (permit required) turns off to the left shortly before the mouth of Salt Canyon. Round-trip distance, including a side trip to Tower Ruin, is about 13 miles (21 km); other attractions include Paul Bunyan's Potty, Castle Arch, Fortress Arch, and side-canyon hiking. Salt and Horse Canyons can easily be driven in 4WD vehicles. Salt Canyon is frequently closed due to quicksand after flash floods in summer and shelf ice in winter.

DAVIS AND LAVENDER CANYONS

Four-wheel-drive roads enter Davis Canyon and Lavender Canyon (permit required) from Highway 211 east of the park boundary. Both canyons are accessed by Davis Canyon Road off Highway 211 and contain great scenery, arches, and Native American sites, and both are easily visited. Davis is about 20 miles (32 km) round-trip, and Lavender is about 26 miles (42 km) round-trip. Try to allow plenty of time in either canyon, as there is much to see and many inviting side canyons to hike. You can camp on BLM land just outside the park boundaries but not in the park itself.

COLORADO OVERLOOK 4WD ROAD

Colorado Overlook 4WD Road begins beside the visitors center and follows Salt Creek to Lower Jump Overlook. It then bounces across slickrock to a view of the Colorado River (upstream from the confluence). Driving is easy to moderate, although very rough the last 1.5 miles (2.4 km). The round-trip distance is 14 miles (22.5 km).

ELEPHANT HILL 4WD ROAD

Elephant Hill Road begins 3 miles (4.8 km) past the Squaw Flat Campground turnoff. Only experienced drivers with stout vehicles should attempt the extremely rough and steep climb up Elephant Hill; coming up the back side of Elephant Hill is even rougher. The loop is about 10 miles (16 km) round-trip. Connecting roads go to the Confluence Overlook trailhead (the viewpoint is 1 mile/1.6 km round-trip on foot), the Joint trailhead (Chesler Park is 2 miles/3.2 km round-trip on foot), and several canyons. Some road sections on the loop are one-way. The parallel canyons in this area are grabens caused by faulting, where a layer of salt has shifted deep underground. In addition to Elephant Hill, a few other difficult spots must be negotiated. This area can also be reached by a long route south of the park using Cottonwood Canyon-Beef Basin Road from Highway 211, about 60 miles (97 km) one-way. You'll enjoy spectacular vistas from the Abajo Highlands.

Two very steep descents from Pappys Pasture into Bobbys Hole effectively make this section one-way; travel from Elephant Hill up Bobbys Hole is possible but much more difficult than going the other way and may require hours of road building. The Bobbys Hole route may be impassable at times—ask about conditions at the BLM office in Monticello or at the Needles visitors center.

Campgrounds

The **Squaw Flat Campground** (year-round, has water, reservations for Loop A only Mar. 15-June 30 and Sept. 1-Oct. 31, $20), about six miles from the visitors center, has 26 sites, many snuggled under the slickrock. RVs must be less than 28 feet long. Rangers present evening programs at the campfire circle on loop A spring-autumn.

If you can't find a space at Squaw Flat, a common occurrence in spring and fall, the private campground at **Needles Outpost** (435/979-4007, www.canyonlandsneedlesoutpost.com, mid-Mar.-late Oct., $20 tents or RVs, no hookups, showers $3), just outside the park entrance, is a good alternative.

Nearby BLM land also offers a number of places to camp. A string of campsites along **Lockhart Basin Road** are convenient and inexpensive. Lockhart Basin Road heads north from Highway 211 about 5 miles (8 km) east of the entrance to the Needles District. **Hamburger Rock Campground** (no water, $6) is about 1 mile (1.6 km) up the road. North of Hamburger Rock, camping is dispersed, with many small (no water, free) campsites at turnoffs from the road. Not surprisingly, the road gets rougher the farther north you travel; beyond Indian Creek Falls it's best to have 4WD. These campsites are very popular with climbers who are here to scale the walls at Indian Creek.

There are two first-come, first-served campgrounds ($15) in the Canyon Rims Special Recreation Management Area (www.blm.gov). **Windwhistle Campground,** backed by cliffs to the south, has fine views to

the north and a nature trail; follow the main road from U.S. 191 for 6 miles (9.7 km) and turn left. At **Hatch Point Campground,** in a piñon-juniper woodland, you can enjoy views to the north. Go 24 miles (39 km) in on the paved and gravel roads toward Anticline Overlook, then turn right and continue for 1 mile (1.6 km). It's best to come supplied with water.

MAZE DISTRICT

Only adventurous and experienced travelers will want to visit this rugged land west of the Green and Colorado Rivers. Vehicle access wasn't even possible until 1957, when mineral-exploration roads first entered what later became Canyonlands National Park. Today, you'll need a high-clearance, low gear-range 4WD vehicle, a horse, or your own two feet to get around, and most visitors spend at least three days in the district. The National Park Service plans to keep this district in its remote and primitive condition. If you can't come overland, an airplane flight provides the only easy way to see the scenic features.

The names of erosional forms describe the landscape—Orange Cliffs, Golden Stairs, the Fins, Land of Standing Rocks, Lizard Rock, the Doll House, Chocolate Drops, the Maze, and Jasper Canyon. The many-fingered canyons of the Maze gave the district its name. Although not a true maze, these canyons give that impression. It is extremely important that you have a good map before entering this part of Canyonlands. National Geographic/Trails Illustrated makes a good one, called *Canyonlands National Park Maze District, NE Glen Canyon NRA.*

Getting to the Maze District

Dirt roads to the **Hans Flat Ranger Station** (435/259-2652, 8am-4:30pm daily) and Maze District branch off from Highway 24 (across from the Goblin Valley State Park turnoff) and Highway 95 (take the usually unmarked Hite-Orange Cliffs Road between the Dirty Devil and Hite Bridges at Lake Powell). The easiest way in is the graded 46-mile road from

Highway 24; it's fast, although sometimes badly corrugated. The 4WD Hite Road (also called Orange Cliffs Rd.) is longer, bumpier, and, for some drivers, tedious; it's 54 miles (87 km) from the turnoff at Highway 95 to the Hans Flat Ranger Station via the Flint Trail. All roads to the Maze District cross Glen Canyon National Recreation Area. From Highway 24, two-wheel-drive vehicles with good clearance can travel to Hans Flat Ranger Station and other areas near, but not actually in, the Maze District. From the ranger station it takes at least three hours of skillful four-wheeling to drive into the canyons of the Maze.

One other way of getting to the Maze District is by river. **Tex's Riverways** (435/259-5101 or 877/662-2839, www. texsriverways.com, about $135 pp) can arrange a jet boat shuttle on the Colorado River from Moab to the Spanish Bottom. After the two-hour boat ride, it's 1,260 vertical feet uphill in a little over one mile to the Doll House via the Spanish Bottom Trail.

Planning an Expedition

Maze District explorers need a backcountry permit ($30) for overnight trips. Note that a backcountry permit in this district is not a reservation. You may have to share a site, especially in the popular spring months. As in the rest of the park, only designated sites can be used for vehicle camping. You don't need a permit to camp in the adjacent Glen Canyon National Recreation Area (NRA) or on BLM land.

There are no developed sources of water in the Maze District. Hikers can obtain water from springs in some canyons (check with a ranger to find out which are flowing) or from the rivers; purify all water before drinking. The Maze District has nine camping areas (two at Maze Overlook, seven at Land of Standing Rocks), each with a 15-person, three-vehicle limit.

The National Geographic/Trails Illustrated topographic map of the Maze District describes and shows the few roads and trails here; some routes and springs are marked on it too. Agile hikers experienced in desert and canyon travel may want to take off on cross-country routes, which are either unmarked or lightly cairned.

Extra care and preparation must be undertaken for travel in both Glen Canyon NRA and the Maze. Always ask rangers beforehand for current conditions. Be sure to leave an itinerary with someone reliable who can contact the rangers if you're overdue returning. Unless the rangers know where to look for you in case of breakdown or accident, a rescue could take weeks.

North Point

Hans Flat Ranger Station, and this peninsula that reaches out to the east and north, are at an elevation of about 6,400 feet. Panoramas from North Point take in the vastness of Canyonlands, including the Maze, Needles, and Island in the Sky Districts. From **Millard Canyon Overlook,** just 0.9 mile (1.4 km) past the ranger station, you can see arches, Cleopatra's Chair, and features as distant as the La Sal Mountains and Book Cliffs. For the best views, drive out to Panorama Point, about 10.5 miles (16.9 km) one-way from the ranger station. A spur road to the left goes 2 miles (3.2 km) to Cleopatra's Chair, a massive sandstone monolith and area landmark. The trailhead for **North Trail Canyon** begins just down North Point Road (or 2.4 miles/3.9 km from the ranger station). Two-wheel-drive vehicles can usually reach this spot, where hikers can follow the trail down 7 miles (11.3 km, 1,000 feet elevation change) through the Orange Cliffs, follow 4WD roads 6 miles (9.7 km) to the Maze Overlook Trail, and then one more mile (1.6 km) into a canyon of the Maze. Because North Point belongs to the Glen Canyon NRA, you can camp on it without a permit.

Land of Standing Rocks

Here, in the heart of the Maze District, strange-shaped rock spires stand guard over myriad canyons. Camping areas offer scenic places to stay (permit required). Hikers have a choice of many ridge and canyon routes from the 4WD road, a trail to a confluence overlook, and a trail that descends to the Colorado River near Cataract Canyon. The well-named Chocolate Drops can be reached by a hiking route from the Wall near the beginning of the Land of Standing Rocks. A good day hike makes a loop from Chimney Rock to the Harvest Scene pictographs; take the ridge route (toward Petes Mesa) one direction and the canyon fork northwest of Chimney Rock the other. Follow your topo map through the canyons and the cairns between the canyons and ridge. Other routes from Chimney Rock lead to lower Jasper Canyon (no river access) or into Shot and Water Canyons and on to the Green River. Tall, rounded rock spires near the end of the road reminded early visitors of dolls, hence the name Doll House. The Doll House makes a delightful place to explore in itself, or you can head out on routes and trails. **Spanish Bottom Trail** (2.4 miles/3.9 km round-trip) begins here, then drops steeply to Spanish Bottom beside the Colorado River; a thin trail leads downstream into Cataract Canyon and the first of a long series of rapids. **Surprise Valley Overlook Trail** (3 miles/4.8 km round-trip) branches right off the Spanish Bottom Trail after about 300 feet and winds south past some dolls to a T-junction (turn right for views of Surprise Valley, Cataract Canyon, and beyond). The trail ends at some well-preserved granaries. The **Colorado-Green River Overlook Trail** (10 miles/16 km round-trip) heads north from the Doll House to a viewpoint of the confluence. See the area's Trails Illustrated map for routes, trails, and roads.

Getting to the Land of Standing Rocks takes some careful driving, especially on a 3-mile (4.8 km) stretch above Teapot Canyon. The many washes and small canyon crossings here make for slow going. Short-wheelbase vehicles have the easiest time, as usual. The turnoff for Land of Standing Rocks Road is 6.6 miles (10.6 km) from the junction at the bottom of the Flint Trail via a wash shortcut

(add about 3 miles/4.8 km if driving via the four-way intersection).

Hiking
MAZE OVERLOOK
This overlook is at the edge of the sinuous canyons of the Maze. You can stay at primitive camping areas (backcountry permit required) and enjoy the views. **Maze Overlook Trail** drops 1 mile (1.6 km) into the South Fork of Horse Canyon; a rope helps to lower packs in a difficult section. Once in the canyon, you can walk around to the Harvest Scene, a group of prehistoric pictographs, or do a variety of day hikes or backpack trips. These canyons have water in some places; check with the ranger when getting your permits. At least four routes connect with the 4WD road in Land of Standing Rocks (see the Trails Illustrated map). Hikers can also climb Petes Mesa from the canyons or head downstream to explore Horse Canyon (a dry fall blocks access to the Green River, however).

THE GOLDEN STAIRS
Hikers can descend this steep foot trail (four miles round-trip) to the Land of Standing Rocks Road in a fraction of the time it takes for drivers to follow roads. The trail offers good views of Ernies Country and the Fins but lacks shade or water. The upper trailhead is 2 miles (3.2 km) east from the road junction at the bottom of the Flint Trail.

SPANISH BOTTOM TRAIL
Just before the end of the Land of Standing Rocks Road, at the Doll House trailhead, Spanish Bottom Trail (2.4 miles/3.9 km round-trip) drops 1,260 vertical feet to Spanish Bottom beside the Colorado River. A thin trail leads downstream into Cataract Canyon and the first of a long series of rapids. If you've boated into the Maze District, you'll be taking this steep hike uphill.

4WD Exploration
The narrow, rough **Flint Trail 4WD Road** connects the Hans Flat area with the Maze

Overlook, Doll House, and other areas below. The road, driver, and vehicle should all be in good condition before driving it. Winter snow and mud close the road late December-March, as can rainstorms anytime. Check conditions first with a ranger. If you're starting from the top, stop at the signed overlook just before the descent to scout for vehicles headed up (the Flint Trail has very few places to pass). The top of the Flint Trail is 14 miles (22.5 km) south of Hans Flat Ranger Station; at the bottom, 2.8 nervous miles (4.5 km) later, you can turn left and continue 2 miles (3.2 km) to the Golden Stairs trailhead or 12.7 miles (20.4 km) to the Maze Overlook; keep straight and go 28 miles (45 km) to the Doll House or 39 miles (63 km) to Highway 95.

Campgrounds

The Maze District has nine camping areas (two at Maze Overlook, seven at Land of Standing Rocks) with a 15-person, three-vehicle limit. A $30 backcountry permit is needed to use these or for backpacking. Note that a backcountry permit in this district is not a reservation—you may have to share a site with someone else, especially in the popular spring months. Also, as in the rest of the park, only designated sites can be used for vehicle camping. You don't need a permit to camp in the Glen Canyon NRA or on BLM land.

HORSESHOE CANYON UNIT

TOP EXPERIENCE

This canyon contains exceptional prehistoric rock art in a separate section of Canyonlands National Park. Ghostly life-size pictographs in the Great Gallery provide an intriguing look into the past. Archaeologists think that the images had religious importance, although the meaning of the figures remains unknown. The Barrier Canyon Style of these drawings has been credited to an archaic Native American people beginning at least

1: Maze Overlook Trail; 2: Great Gallery

8,000 years ago and lasting until about AD 450. Horseshoe Canyon also contains rock art left by the subsequent Fremont and Ancestral Puebloan people. The relationship between the earlier and later prehistoric groups hasn't been determined.

Great Gallery

Horseshoe Canyon lies northwest of the Maze District. The easiest and most common way to reach Horseshoe Canyon is from the west on Highway 24. From Highway 24, turn east across from the Goblin Valley State Park turn-off, then continue east 30 miles (48 km) on a dirt road; keep left at the Hans Flat Ranger Station and Horseshoe Canyon turnoff 25 miles (40 km) in. From the rim, the trail descends 800 vertical feet in 1 mile (1.6 km) on an old jeep road, now closed to vehicles. At the canyon bottom, turn right and go 2 miles (3.2 km) upstream to the Great Gallery. The sandy canyon floor is mostly level; trees provide shade in some areas.

Horseshoe Canyon can also be reached via primitive roads from the east. A 4WD road goes north 21 miles (34 km) from Hans Flat Ranger Station and drops steeply into the canyon from the east side. The descent on this road is so rough that most people prefer to park on the rim and hike the last mile of road. A vehicle barricade prevents driving right up to the rock-art panel, but the 1.5-mile (2.4-km) walk is easy. A branch off the jeep road goes to the start of **Deadman's Trail** (1.5 miles/2.4 km one-way), which is less used and more difficult.

Look for other rock art along the canyon walls on the way to the Great Gallery. Take care not to touch any of the drawings; they're very fragile as well as irreplaceable. (The oil from your hands will remove the paint.) Horseshoe Canyon also offers pleasant scenery and spring wildflowers. Carry plenty of water. Neither camping nor pets are allowed in the canyon, but you can stay on the rim.

Call the **Hans Flat Ranger Station** (435/259-2652) to inquire about ranger-led hikes to the Great Gallery (Sat.-Sun. spring);

when staff are available, additional walks may be scheduled. In-shape hikers will have no trouble making the hike on their own, however.

RIVER DISTRICT
River-Running Above the Confluence

The Green and Colorado Rivers flow smoothly through their canyons above the confluence of the two rivers. Almost any shallow-draft boat can navigate these waters: Canoes, kayaks, rafts, and powerboats are commonly used. Any travel requires advance planning because of the remoteness of the canyons and the scarcity of river access points. No campgrounds, supplies, or other facilities exist past Moab on the Colorado River, or past the town of Green River on the Green. All river-runners must follow park regulations, which include the carrying of life jackets, use of a fire pan for fires, and packing out all garbage and solid human waste. The river flow on both the Colorado and the Green averages a gentle 2-4 mph (7-10 mph at high water). Boaters typically do 20 miles (32 km) a day in canoes and 15 miles (24 km) a day in rafts.

The Colorado has one modest rapid called the Slide, 1.5 miles (2.4 km) above the confluence, where rocks constrict the river to one-third of its normal width; the rapid is roughest during high water levels in May-June. This is the only difficulty on the 64 river miles (103 km) from Moab. Inexperienced canoeists and rafters may wish to portage around it. The most popular launch points on the Colorado River are the Moab Dock (just upstream from the U.S. 191 bridge near town) and the Potash Dock (17 miles/27 km downriver on Potash Rd./Hwy. 279).

On the Green River, boaters at low water need to watch for rocky areas at the mouth of Millard Canyon (33.5 miles/54 km above the confluence, where a rock bar extends across the river) and at the mouth of Horse Canyon (14.5 miles/23.3 km above the confluence, where a rock and gravel bar on the right leaves only a narrow channel on the left

side). The trip from the town of Green River through Labyrinth and Stillwater Canyons is 120 miles (193 km). Launch points include Green River State Park (in Green River) and Mineral Canyon (52 miles/84 km above the confluence; reached on a fair-weather road from Hwy. 313). Boaters who launch at Green River State Park will pass through Labyrinth Canyon; a free interagency permit is required for travel along this stretch of the river. Permits are available from the BLM office in Moab, the Canyonlands headquarters in Moab, Green River State Park, or the John Wesley Powell Museum in Green River. A permit can also be downloaded from the BLM website (www.blm.gov/ut).

No roads go to the confluence. The easiest return to civilization for nonmotorized craft is a pickup by jet boat from Moab by **Tex's Riverways** (435/259-5101, www.texsriverways.com) or **Tag-A-Long Tours** (800/453-3292, www.tagalong.com). A far more difficult way out is hiking either of two trails just above the Cataract Canyon Rapids to 4WD roads on the rim. Don't plan to attempt this unless you're a very strong hiker and have a packable watercraft.

National park rangers require that boaters above the confluence to obtain a backcountry permit ($30) either in person from the Moab National Park Service office (2282 SW Resource Blvd., Moab, 435/719-2313, 8am-4pm Mon.-Fri.) or via the Internet (http://canypermits.nps.gov) at least two weeks in advance.

Notes on boating the Green and Colorado Rivers are available on request from the National Park Service's Moab office (435/259-3911). Bill and Buzz Belknap's *Canyonlands River Guide* has river logs and maps pointing out items of interest on the Green River below the town of Green River and all of the Colorado River from the upper end of Westwater Canyon to Lake Powell.

River-Running Through Cataract Canyon

The Colorado River enters Cataract Canyon at

the confluence and picks up speed. The rapids begin 4 miles (6.4 km) downstream and extend for the next 14 miles (22.5 km) to Lake Powell. Especially in spring, the 26 or more rapids give a wild ride equal to the best in the Grand Canyon. The current zips along at up to 16 mph (26 km per hr) and forms waves more than seven feet high. When the excitement dies down, boaters have a 34-mile (55-km) trip across Lake Powell to Hite Marina; most people either carry a motor or arrange for a powerboat to pick them up. Because of the real hazards of running the rapids, the National Park Service requires boaters to have proper equipment and a permit ($30). Many people go on a commercial trip, where everything is taken care of by the operator. Private groups must contact the Canyonlands River Unit far in advance for permit details (435/259-3911, www.nps.gov/cany).

Southeast Utah

Although Arches and Canyonlands capture more attention, Utah's southeastern corner contains an incredible wealth of scenic and culturally significant sites. Consider rounding out your trip to this part of Utah with a tour of Ancestral Puebloan ruins, remote desert washes, soaring natural bridges, snowy mountain peaks, and deep river canyons.

MONTICELLO

This small Mormon town (pop. 2,000) is about 50 miles (81 km) south of Moab and pretty much its polar opposite. Quiet and relatively untouristed, it's the best place to stay if you're visiting the Needles District and don't want to camp. Monticello (mon-tuh-SELL-o) is at an elevation of 7,069 feet, just east of the Abajo Mountains, 46 miles (74 km) east of the entrance to the Needles District of Canyonlands National Park.

Food

Not only can you get a good cup of coffee and freshly made juice at **Peace Tree Juice Cafe** (516 N. Main St., 435/587-5063, 7am-10pm daily, $7-9), this is also the only place this side of Moab that you're likely to get a vegetarian Thai wrap sandwich (and it tastes really good).

Up the road at the Roughlock encampment, the **Line Camp** (U.S. 191, milepost 79.5, 435/587-2351, 5pm-8pm daily, $14-26) is a good steak house with sides of potatoes, beans, and salad as well as a big extra helping of Western atmosphere accompanying every meal. Beer is available at this restaurant, and you can bring your own wine (free corkage).

Accommodations

Monticello has a number of comfortable and affordable motels. The **Inn at the Canyons** (533 N. Main St., 435/587-2458, www.monticellocanyonlandsinn.com, $135-145) is nicely renovated and has an indoor pool, a pretty basic continental breakfast, and microwaves and fridges in the guest rooms. The **Monticello Inn** (164 E. Central St., 435/587-2274, www.themonticelloinn.com, $70-90) is a well-maintained older motel with a pleasant in-town setting and a few guest rooms that allow pets.

Eight miles north of town, the **Runnin' Iron Inn** (U.S. 191, milepost 79.5, 435/587-2351, http://canyonlandsbestkeptsecret.com, $65-84) is a small motel with an Old West ambience, fitting for its middle-of-nowhere location, which happens to be pretty convenient to the Needles District. If you don't need a luxurious guest room or a microwave and fridge, this is a fun place to stay. It's part of a faux-Western town called Roughlock, which also houses an RV park ($20) with tent sites ($20), a few camping cabins ($42) that have no bath or cooking facilities, and a steak house.

The local B&B, the **Grist Mill Inn** (64 S.

ARIZONA

To Kayenta

Grand Staircase-Escalante National Monument

RAINBOW BRIDGE NATIONAL MONUMENT

Lake Powell

Hole-in-the-Rock

Glen

Canyon

National

Recreation

Area

Colorado

BULLFROG BASIN MARINA

HALLS CROSSING MARINA

Capitol Reef National Park

Waterpocket Fold

BURR TRAIL

Mt Ellen 11,522 ft ▲

Henry

▲ Mt Pennell 11,320 ft

Mountains

276

Glen Canyon

River

Glen Canyon National Recreation Area

Fry Canyon

Hite

HITE CROSSING

Glen Canyon

95

Cataract Canyon

Dark

Canyon

Wilderness Area

Canyonlands National Park

BIG POCKET OVERLOOK

211

★ BLM NEWSPAPER ROCK HISTORICAL MONUMENT

Manti-La Sal

National

Forest

Abajo Mountains

Abajo Peak 11,360 ft ▲

191

Monticello

Natural Bridges National Monument

275

95

MULE CANYON RUIN

ARCH CANYON OVERLOOK

Arch Canyon

BUTLER WASH RUINS

Edge of the Cedars State Park

Blanding

191

Sun Juan

NAVAJO

GOULDING TRADING POST

Gouldings

163

MONUMENT VALLEY VISITOR CENTER

Monument

Valley

INDIAN

Goosenecks State Park

MULEY POINT OVERLOOK

Grand Gulch Primitive Area

276

Juan River

316

Mexican Hat

261

★ Valley of The Gods

Comb Ridge

RESERVATION

191

160

ST. CHRISTOPHER'S EPISCOPAL MISSION

Bluff

SAND ISLAND CAMPGROUND

FOURTEEN WINDOW RUIN

163

RECAPTURE POCKET

262

HATCH TRADING POST

CAJON RUINS ■

Montezuma Creek

Aneth

262

FOUR CORNERS MONUMENT

41

▟ HOVENWEEP NATIONAL MONUMENT

CUTTHROAT CASTLE

HACKBERRY AND HORSESHOE RUINS

★ HOLLY RUINS

SQUARE TOWER RUINS

491

COLORADO

NM

0   10 mi

0   10 km

300 E., 435/587-2597, www.oldgristmillinn. com, $97-149) is indeed housed in an old flour mill. But rest assured, you won't be sleeping under an old millstone; the seven guest rooms are all furnished in typical B&B fashion, and all have private baths and TVs. An additional four rooms are found in The Cottage, a separate but adjacent building; the inn also rents two large homes for groups.

Campgrounds

Campgrounds in the nearby Manti-La Sal National Forest include Buckboard and Dalton Springs (435/587-2041, $10). **Buckboard,** seven miles west of town on Blue Mountain Road (Forest Rd. 105), is at 8,600 feet in elevation, so it's not your best bet early in the spring. But when the rest of southeastern Utah swelters in the summer, this shady campground is perfect. **Dalton Springs** is along the same road, a couple of miles closer to town, at 8,200 feet. An abandoned ski area nearby is a good place for mountain biking.

Information and Services

Stop at the **Southeastern Utah Welcome Center** (216 S. Main St., 435/587-3401, http:// www.monticelloutah.org/, 9am-6pm daily Mar.-Oct., 9am-3pm Wed.-Sun. Nov.-Feb.) for information about southeastern Utah, including Canyonlands National Park.

The **San Juan Hospital** (364 W. 100 N., 435/587-2116) is friendly and small, and it's a good place to have any camping-related injuries repaired.

BLANDING

The largest town in San Juan County, Blanding (population 3,500, elevation 6,105 feet) is also a handy, if not exactly compelling, stop for travelers. The restaurant scene here is especially dire; if you're staying here, you might opt to picnic. Blanding is one of the few "dry" towns in Utah, meaning alcohol cannot be sold inside the municipality. In 2017, locals had a chance to vote to allow beer and wine sales in town for the first time in more than

80 years. Blanding overwhelmingly voted to keep the anti-alcohol restrictions in place. In this environment, few restaurants of note take root.

If you're heading east toward Hovenweep or west into the Cedar Mesa area, check your gas gauge; Blanding is a good place to gas up.

Edge of the Cedars State Park

One mile north of present-day Blanding, Ancestral Puebloan people built at least six groups of pueblo structures between AD 700 and 1220. The **Edge of the Cedars State Park Museum** (660 W. 400 N., 435/678-2238, www.stateparks.utah.gov, 9am-5pm Mon.-Sat., noon-4pm Sun., $5 adults, $3 children) features an excellent array of pottery, baskets, sandals, jewelry, and stone tools. The pottery collection on the second floor stands out for its rich variety of styles and decorative designs. This is the top museum in Utah if you're interested in the history and art of the Ancestral Puebloans, and serves as a marvelous introduction to the ruins at nearby Hovenweep National Monument. The museum also has exhibits and artifacts of the people who followed the Ancestral Puebloans—the Utes and Navajo and the early Anglo pioneers.

A short trail behind the museum leads past a ruin that has been excavated and partly restored to suggest the village's appearance when the Ancestral Puebloans lived here. You may enter the kiva by descending a ladder through the restored roof; the walls and interior features are original.

The Dinosaur Museum

The Dinosaur Museum (754 S. 200 W., 435/678-3454, www.dinosaur-museum.org, 9am-5pm Mon.-Sat. Apr. 15-Oct. 15, $3.50 adults, $2.50 seniors, $2 children) showcases the prehistoric plant and animal life of this corner of Utah. Exhibits include life-size models of dinosaurs (including the dino model used in the original *King Kong* movie) as well as fossils and skeletons. Don't miss the models of feathered dinosaurs.

Food

Blanding is not a center of gastronomy; in fact, restaurants seem to have trouble even staying open in this alcohol-free town. Only the fast-food joints are open on Sundays. Though **The Patio Drive In** (95 Grayson Pkwy., 435/678-2177, 10:30am-9pm Mon.-Sat., $7-10) has a big local reputation as a drive-in restaurant, there are also a handful of tables and booths in the diner. **The Homestead** (121 E. Center St., 435/678-3456, 9am-9:30pm Mon.-Sat., 4pm-9pm Sun., $11-30) is the local steak house, with typical American fare plus Navajo tacos.

Accommodations

With one exception, Blanding's motels are all pretty generic. That exception is **Stone Lizard Lodging** (88 W. Center St., 435/678-3323, www.stonelizardlodging.com, $114-165), an older motel with remodeled but homey guest rooms, including a two-bedroom suite ($149) and a good breakfast. The **Four Corners Inn** (131 E. Center St., 435/678-3257 or 800/574-3150, www.fourcornersinn.com, $76-85), which has a restaurant next door, a simple continental breakfast, and several pet-friendly rooms, is a fine enough place to spend a night.

CAMPGROUNDS

At the south edge of town, **Blue Mountain RV Park** (1930 S. Main St., 435/678-7840, www.bluemountainrvpark.com, $35 RVs) is also home to a trading post with some high-quality Native American rugs, jewelry, and baskets. Although tent campers are welcome at the RV park, **Devil's Canyon Campground** (reservations 877/444-6777, www.recreation.gov, $10, $9 reservation fee), at an elevation of 7,100 feet in the Manti-La Sal National Forest, is a better bet for tents. It has sites with water early May-late October (no water or fees off-season). A 0.25-mile (0.4-km) nature trail begins at the far end of the campground loop. From Blanding, go north 8 miles (12.9 km) on U.S. 191, then turn west onto a paved road for 1.3 miles (2.1 km); the turnoff from U.S. 191 is between mileposts 60 and 61.

BLUFF

Bluff, a sleepy community of about 300 inhabitants, is nestled in a striking physical location. In the past few years, Bluff has become a rather unlikely mecca for recreationists and escapees from urban congestion. The quality of lodging is better than that of almost any other town of this size in the state, and local

Edge of the Cedars State Park

outfitters make it easy to get out and enjoy the remarkable scenery hereabouts.

Bluff is the oldest non-Native American community in southeastern Utah; it was settled in 1880 by Mormon pioneers who had traveled the excruciatingly difficult Hole-in-the-Rock Road from the town of Escalante down into what's now Lake Powell. When the Mormon settlers finally got to the San Juan River valley, they founded **Bluff Fort,** which has been reconstructed at 550 East Black Locust Street (435/672-9995, 9am-5pm Mon.-Sat, free).

Spend an afternoon poking around local washes or examining a large pictograph panel, found along the cliff about 0.3 mile (0.5 km) downstream from the Sand Island Campground. The visitors center, located in the small fort museum, is worth a stop; the staff can give you detailed directions for good informal hikes in the nearby washes.

If you want a guided trip into the backcountry of southeastern Utah, **Far Out Expeditions** (425/672-2294, www.faroutexpeditions.com) is a local company with lots of experience leading day trips and overnights in the area. **Four Corners Adventures** (435/678-2628, www.riversandruins.com) leads half-day, full-day, and multiday trips to many of the destinations in southeastern Utah, with your choice of hiking, canyoneering, mountain biking, or 4WD touring.

Bluff is 100 miles (161 km) south of Moab and 22 miles (35 km) south of Blanding, both on U.S. 191. From Bluff, it's 22 miles (35 km) to Mexican Hat and 47 miles (76 km) to Monument Valley, both on U.S. 163.

Floating the San Juan River

From the high San Juan Mountains in southern Colorado, the San Juan River winds its way into New Mexico, enters Utah near Four Corners, and twists through spectacular canyons before ending at Lake Powell. Most boaters put in at Sand Island Campground near Bluff and take out at the

town of Mexican Hat, 30 river miles (48 km) downstream. This trip combines ancient Native American ruins, rock art, and a trip through Monument Upwarp and the Upper Canyon, with fast water for thrills (Class III rapids) and weirdly buckled geology to ponder. Longer trips continue on through the famous Goosenecks—the "entrenched meanders" carved thousands of feet below the desert surface—and through more Class III rapids on the way to Clay Hills Crossing or Paiute Farms (not always accessible) on Lake Powell. Allow at least four days for the full trip, though more time will allow for exploration of side canyons and visits to Ancestral Puebloan sites. Rafts, kayaks, and canoes can be used. The season usually lasts year-round because of adequate water flow from Navajo Reservoir upstream.

Several commercial river-running companies offer San Juan trips. If you go on your own, you should have river-running experience or be with someone who does. Private groups need to obtain permits ($10-30 pp) from the Bureau of Land Management's San Juan Resource Area office (435/587-1544, www.blm.gov/ut/st/en/fo/monticello.html); permits are issued through a preseason lottery (via www.recreation.gov), although boaters with flexible schedules can usually get permits close to their time of travel. Permit fees vary depending on how far you're floating.

Some people also like to run the river between Montezuma Creek and Sand Island, a leisurely trip of 20 river miles (32 km). The solitude often makes up for the lack of scenery. It's easy to get a river permit for this section because no use limits or fees apply.

If you're looking for a guided trip on the San Juan River, contact local **Wild Rivers Expeditions** (2625 S. Hwy. 191, 435/672-2244, www.riversandruins.com), which offers both day and multiday trips out of Bluff; trips run daily in summer, and only a day's notice is usually needed to join a float. Eight-hour, 26-mile (42-km) day excursions to Mexican Hat cost $175 adults,

$133 under age 13; motors may be used if the water level is low. This highly recommended trip includes lunch plus stops at Ancestral Puebloan ruins and rock-art panels.

Food

A longtime local hangout and a good place for a meal and a friendly vibe is the **Twin Rocks Cafe** (435/672-2341, www.twinrockscafe.com, 7am-9pm daily, $8-20), next to the trading post just below the impossible-to-miss Twin Rocks. Here you can dine on Navajo tacos (fry bread with chili) or Navajo pizza (fry bread with pizza toppings) as well as more standard fare. Be sure to visit the trading post for high-quality Native American crafts, many of them produced locally by Navajo artisans.

Settle in under the big cottonwood tree for a flame-grilled steak dinner at the **Cottonwood Steakhouse** (Main St. and 4th St. E., 435/672-2282, 5:30pm-9:30pm daily spring-fall, call for winter hours, $15-26). Dinners come with salad, beans, and potatoes; for $10, you can split an entrée with someone else and get full servings of side dishes. Indoor dining is also an option. Homemade pies are a specialty.

★ **Comb Ridge Eat and Drink** (680 S. U.S. 191, 435/485-5555, 8am-3pm and 5pm-9pm Tues.-Sun., $8-15), an artsy café housed in a historic trading post, has lots of character and surprisingly delicious food. Although the menu items are simple (burgers and pub grub), the quality is high. Where else in this part of Utah are you going to find an artisanal cheese plate? There are several good options for vegetarians here.

On the premises of the Desert Rose Inn find **Duke's** (701 W. Main St., 735/672-2303, http://www.desertroseinn.com/duke-s-bistro, 7am-11am and 5pm-9pm daily, $13-32), with very good burgers and steaks, an attractive dining room, and a lovely patio (but no alcohol).

Accommodations

Attractive ★ **Desert Rose Inn** (701 W. Main St., 735/672-2303 or 888/475-7673, www.desertroseinn.com, $169-199) is one of the nicest lodgings in this corner of the state. The large lodgelike log structure has two-story wraparound porches and guest rooms furnished with pine furniture, quilts, and Southwestern art. An additional wing has an indoor pool and spa, and a handsome restaurant has been added. At the edge

floating down the San Juan River

of the property are a number of handsome one-bedroom log cabins. This is definitely a class act.

Another classy place to stay is **La Posada Pintada,** 239 N. 7th E (Navajo Twins Drive), 435/459-2274, www.laposadapintada.com, $155-165), a stylish, recently built boutique inn with 11 spacious rooms (one a pioneer cabin) and serious breakfast buffet. This is a refined place: all rooms come with flat screen TVs, Wi-Fi, fridges and microwaves, private patios, large bathrooms and high-end linens and amenities.

Another great place to stay is **Recapture Lodge** (220 E. Main St., 435/672-2281, www. recapturelodge.com, $95). For many years the heart and soul of Bluff, the rustic, comfortable lodge is operated by longtime outfitters and the staff can help you plan an outdoor adventure. Besides guest rooms and kitchenettes, Recapture Lodge has trails out the back door, a swimming pool, a hot tub, and a coin laundry. The Recapture also rents a couple of fully equipped homes in Bluff for families and groups.

Kokopelli Inn Motel (160 E. Main St., 435/672-2322, www.kokoinnutah.com, $102-130), just next door to the Recapture, is a fine place to stay, though it pales in comparison to Bluff's more unique inns and lodges.

CAMPGROUNDS

Sand Island Recreation Area (435/587-1500, piped water, www.blm.gov, $15) is a BLM camping area along the San Juan River, 3 miles (4.8 km) south of town. Large cottonwood trees shade this pretty spot, but tenters need to watch for thorns in the grass. Riverrunners often put in at the campground, so it can be a busy place. Two RV parks are right in town: **Cadillac Ranch RV Park** (U.S. 191, 435/672-2262, www.cadillacranchrv.com, year-round, $30) is in the center of town, and **Cottonwood R.V. Park** (U.S. 191, 435/672-2287, http://cottonwoodrvpark.blogspot.com, Mar.-Nov. 15, $35) is at the west end of Bluff.

★ HOVENWEEP NATIONAL MONUMENT

The Ancestral Puebloans built many impressive masonry buildings during the early-mid-1200s, near the end of their 1,300-year stay in the area. A 25-year drought beginning in 1274 probably hastened their migration from this area. Several centuries of intensive farming, hunting, and woodcutting had already taken their toll on the land. Archaeologists believe the inhabitants retreated south in the late 1200s to sites in northwestern New Mexico and northeastern Arizona. The Ute word *hovenweep* means "deserted valley," an appropriate name for the lonely high desert country left behind. The Ancestral Puebloans at Hovenweep had much in common with the Mesa Verde culture, although the Dakota sandstone here doesn't form large alcoves suitable for cliff-dweller villages. Ruins at Hovenweep remain essentially unexcavated, awaiting the attention of future archaeologists.

The Ancestral Puebloan farmers had a keen interest in the seasons because of their need to know the best time for planting crops. Astronomical stations (alignments of walls, doorways, and tiny openings) allowed the sun priests to determine the equinoxes and solstices with an accuracy of 1-2 days. This precision also may have been necessary for a complex ceremonial calendar. Astronomical stations at Hovenweep have been discovered at Hovenweep Castle, at the Unit-type House at Square Tower Ruins, and at Cajon Ruins.

Hovenweep National Monument (970/562-4283, www.nps.gov/hove, free) protects six groups of villages left behind by the Ancestral Puebloans. The sites are near the Colorado border southeast of Blanding. The Square Tower Ruins Unit, where the visitors center is, has the greatest number of ruins and the most varied architecture. In fact, you can find all of the Hovenweep architectural styles here.

Visitors Center

The **visitors center** (970/562-4282, 5am-5pm daily Apr.-Oct., 9am-4pm daily Nov.-Mar.) has a few exhibits on the Ancestral Puebloan people and photos of local wildlife. A ranger will answer your questions, provide brochures and handouts about various aspects of the monument, and give directions for visiting the other ruin groups. There's also a small campground at the monument (no reservations, $10).

Square Tower Ruins

This extensive group of Ancestral Puebloan towers and dwellings lines the rim and slopes of Little Ruin Canyon, a short walk from the visitors center. Obtain a trail guide booklet from the visitors center; the booklet's map shows the several loop trails, and it has good descriptions of Ancestral Puebloan life and architecture and of the plants growing along the trail. You'll see towers (D-shaped, square, oval, and round), cliff dwellings, surface dwellings, storehouses, kivas, and rock art. Take care not to disturb the fragile ruins. Keep an eye out for the prairie rattlesnake, a subspecies of the western rattlesnake, which is active at night in summer and during the day in spring and fall. Stay on the trail—don't climb ruin walls or walk on rubble mounds.

Other Ruins

You'll need a map and directions from a ranger to find the other Hovenweep ruins, as they aren't signed. One group, the Goodman Point, near Cortez, Colorado, has relatively little to see except unexcavated mounds.

Holly Ruins is noted for its Great House, Holly Tower, and Tilted Tower. Most of Tilted Tower fell away after the boulder on which it sat shifted. Great piles of rubble mark the sites of structures built on loose ground. Look for remnants of farming terraces in the canyon below the Great House. A hiking trail connects the campground at Square Tower Ruins

with Holly Ruins; the route follows canyon bottoms and is about 8 miles (12.9 km) round-trip. Hikers could also continue to Horseshoe Ruins (1 mile/1.6 km farther) and Hackberry Ruins (0.3 mile/0.5 km beyond Horseshoe). All of these are just across the Colorado border and about 6 miles (9.7 km, one-way) by road from the visitors center.

Horseshoe Ruins and **Hackberry Ruins** are best reached by an easy trail (1 mile/1.6 km, round-trip) off the road to Holly Ruins. Horseshoe House, built in a horseshoe shape similar to Sun Temple at Mesa Verde, has exceptionally good masonry work. Archaeologists haven't determined the purpose of the structure. An alcove in the canyon below contains a spring and small shelter. A round tower nearby on the rim has a strategic view. Hackberry House has only one room still intact. Rubble piles and wall remnants abound in the area. The spring under an alcove here still has good flow and supports lush growths of hackberry and cottonwood trees along with smaller plants.

Cutthroat Castle Ruins were remote even in Ancestral Puebloan times. The ruins lie along an intermittent stream rather than at the head of a canyon like most other Hovenweep sites. Cutthroat Castle is a large multistory structure with both straight and curved walls. Three round towers stand nearby. Look for wall fragments and the circular depressions of kivas. High-clearance vehicles can go close to the ruins, about 11.5 miles (18.5 km, one-way) from the visitors center. Visitors with cars can drive to a trailhead and then walk to the ruins (1.5 miles/2.4 km round-trip on foot).

Cajon Ruins are at the head of a little canyon on Cajon Mesa on the Navajo Reservation in Utah, about 9 miles (14.5 km) southwest of the visitors center. The site has a commanding view across the San Juan Valley as far as Monument Valley. Buildings include a large multiroom structure, a round tower, and a tall square tower. An alcove just below has a spring and some rooms. Look for pictographs, petroglyphs, and grooves in rock (used for

1: Hovenweep National Monument; **2:** Ancestral Puebloan villages along Comb Wash

tool grinding). Farming terraces were located on the canyon's south side.

Getting There

One approach is from U.S. 191 between Blanding and Bluff; head east 9 miles (14.5 km) on Highway 262, continue straight 6 miles (9.7 km) on a small paved road to Hatch Trading Post, and then follow the signs for 16 miles (26 km). A good way in from Bluff is to go east 21 miles (34 km) on the paved road to Montezuma Creek and Aneth, then follow the signs north for 20 miles (32 km). A scenic 58-mile (93-km) route through Montezuma Canyon begins 5 miles (8 km) south of Monticello and follows unpaved roads to Hatch and on to Hovenweep; you can stop at the BLM's Three Turkey Ruin on the way. From Colorado, take a partly paved road west and north 41 miles (66 km) from U.S. 491 (the turnoff is 4 miles/6.4 km south of Cortez).

CEDAR MESA AREA

Just south of Blanding, Highway 95—here labeled Trail of the Ancients National Scenic Byway—heads west across a high plateau toward the Colorado River, traversing Comb Ridge, Cedar Mesa, and many canyons. This is remote country, so fill up with gas before leaving Blanding; you can't depend on finding gasoline until Hanksville, 122 miles (196 km) away. Hite and the other Lake Powell marinas do have gas and supplies, but their hours are limited.

Cedar Mesa and its canyons have an exceptionally large number of prehistoric Ancestral Puebloan sites. Several ruins are just off the highway, and hikers will discover many more

Cedar Mesa is also home to **Bears Ears Buttes,** two distinctive outcrops that are visible for miles across southeastern Utah. Native Americans in the area consider just about all of southeastern Utah to be a sacred place, and the Bears Ears have come to represent it. In 2016, 1.35 million acres in this part of the state was designated the Bears Ears National Monument by the Obama administration, to protect the cultural resources of local Native Americans. In 2018, the Trump administration shrank the monument by 85 percent, opening much of this land again to mineral and oil-and-gas extraction. In place of the original Bears Ears monument, the Trump administration designated two smaller monuments, the 71,896-acre **Indian Creek National Monument** and the 129,980-acre **Shash Jaa National Monument.**

If you would like to explore the Cedar Mesa and Bears Ears area, be sure to drop in at the BLM's **Kane Gulch Ranger Station** (435/587-1532, www.blm.gov, 8am-noon daily spring and fall), at the west end of Cedar Mesa, four miles south of Highway 95 on Highway 261. BLM staff issue the permits required to explore the Cedar Mesa backcountry for day-use ($2) and for overnight stays ($8 pp) in Grand Gulch, Fish Creek Canyon, and Owl Creek Canyon. The number of people permitted to camp at a given time is limited, so call ahead. BLM staff will also tell you about archaeological sites and their historic value, current hiking conditions, and where to find water. Cedar Mesa is managed for more primitive recreation, so hikers in the area should have good route-finding skills and come prepared with food and water. The ranger station sells maps but has no water.

If you'd rather leave the logistics to the professionals, the friendly folks at **Four Corner Adventures** (435/678-2628, www.riversandruins.com) offer multiday guided trips into the Cedar Mesa and Bears Ears area, and also offer rentals and support for personalized trips into this remote area.

Butler Wash Ruins

Well-preserved pueblo ruins left by the Ancestral Puebloans are tucked under an overhang across the wash. Find the trailhead on the north side of Highway 95, 11 miles (17.7 km) west of U.S. 191, between mileposts 111 and 112. Follow cairns for 0.5 mile (0.8 km) through juniper and piñon pine woodlands and across slickrock to the overlook, where you can see four kivas and several other structures. Parts have been reconstructed, but most of the site is about 900 years old.

Comb Ridge

Geologic forces have squeezed up the earth's crust in a long ridge running 80 miles (129 km) south from the Abajo Mountains into Arizona. Sheer cliffs plunge 800 feet into Comb Wash on the west side. Engineering the highway down these cliffs took considerable effort. A parking area near the top of the grade offers expansive panoramas across Comb Wash.

Arch Canyon

This tributary canyon of Comb Wash has spectacular scenery and many Native American ruins. Much of the canyon can be seen on a day hike, but 2-3 days are required to explore the upper reaches. The main streambeds usually have water, but purify it before drinking it. To reach the trailhead, turn north onto Comb Wash Road (between mileposts 107 and 108 on Hwy. 95) and go 2.5 miles (4 km) on the dirt road, past a house and a water tank, then park in a grove of cottonwood trees before a stream. The mouth of pretty Arch Canyon is just to the northwest (it's easy to miss). Look for a Native American ruin just up Arch Canyon on the right. More ruins are tucked under alcoves farther up-canyon; the canyon's three arches are past the 7-mile (11.3-km) point.

Arch Canyon Overlook

A road and a short trail to the rim of Arch Canyon provide a beautiful view into the depths. Turn north onto Texas Flat Road (County Rd. 263) from Highway 95, between mileposts 102 and 103, continue 4 miles (6.4 km), park just before the road begins a steep climb, and walk east on an old jeep road 0.25 mile (0.4 km) to the rim. This is a fine place for a picnic, although there are no facilities or guardrails. Texas Flat Road is dirt but passable when dry for cars with good clearance. Trucks can continue up the steep hill to other viewpoints of Arch and Texas Canyons.

Mule Canyon Ruin

Archaeologists have excavated and stabilized this Ancestral Puebloan village on the gentle slope of Mule Canyon's South Fork. A stone kiva, circular tower, and 12-room structure are all visible, and all were originally connected by tunnels. Cave Towers, 2 miles (3.2 km) southeast, would have been visible from the top of the tower here. Signs describe the ruins and periods of Ancestral Puebloan development. Turn north from Highway 95 between mileposts 101 and 102 and continue 0.3 mile (0.5 km) on a paved road. Hikers can explore other ruins in the North and South Forks of Mule Canyon; check with the Kane Gulch Ranger Station for advice and directions. You might see pieces of pottery and other artifacts in this area. Federal laws prohibit the removal of artifacts: Please leave every piece in place so that future visitors can enjoy the discovery, too. Be sure to have a BLM day-hiking permit when exploring this area.

Shash Jaa National Monument

This new national monument, established in 2018, protects 129,980 acres of striking geologic features, juniper forests, canyons, and a cultural, historic and prehistoric legacy that includes an abundance of early Native American historical artifacts, including a wealth of Ancestral Puebloan ruins and rock art. In addition to the Bears Ears Buttes area, Shash Jaa (which means Bears Ears in Navajo) also protects a long tail of land extending south along Comb Ridge to the San Juan River, another area also rich in ancient remains. The monument also includes two tiny satellite units that protect Doll House and Moon House ruins. Until the monument's management plan is put in place—probably sometime n 2019—access to these areas will remain as before. For recreational information on Shash Jaa, contact **Kane Gulch Ranger Station** (435/587-1532, www.blm.gov/visit/kane-gulch-ranger-station.)

Bears Ears National Monument: RIP

Bears Ears

The Bears Ears National Monument was established in 2016, in the waning weeks of the Obama administration; just over a year later, it was slashed by 85 percent of its acreage by the Trump administration, and divided into two much smaller national monuments.

The two new Utah national monuments are Indian Creek National Monument, which essentially adds an 71,896-acre eastern annex to the Needles unit of Canyonlands National Park (for instance, Newspaper Rock, famous for its petroglyphs, is now protected in the national monument). The second new national monument is 129,980-acre Shash Jaa National Monument, which protects the area that include Bears Ears Buttes, parts of Mule and Arch canyons, and the drainages of Comb Ridge, a sacred landscapes for many Indian tribes and an area rich in Ancestral Puebloan ruins and rock art. This redrawn monument notably eliminates the earlier designation's protections the for the Cedar Mesa area, an area rich in both Ancestral Puebloan remains—and uranium deposits.

The land in these two new national monuments is currently a mix of federal Forest Service, BLM, Utah state, and private land, and a management plan has yet to be worked out to administer these national monuments. Access to all current sites is expected to remain open in the meantime, though for specific questions contact the Kane Gulch Ranger Station (435/587-1532, www.blm.gov/visit/kane-gulch-ranger-station, the BLM field office in Monticello (365 North Main, 435/587-1510, https://www.blm.gov/programs/recreation/permits-and-passes/lotteries-and-permit-systems/utah/cedarmesa) or the Blanding Visitor Center (12 North Grayson Parkway, 435/678-3662, http://www.blanding-ut.gov/visitor-s-center.html).

NATURAL BRIDGES NATIONAL MONUMENT

Natural Bridges preserves some of the finest examples of natural stone architecture in the southwest. Streams in White Canyon and its tributaries cut deep canyons, and then floodwaters sculpted the bridges by gouging tunnels between closely spaced loops in the meandering canyons. You can distinguish a natural bridge from an arch because the bridge spans a streambed and was initially carved out of the rock by flowing water. In the monument, these bridges illustrate three different stages of development, from the massive, relatively newly formed Kachina Bridge to the middle-age Sipapu Bridge to the delicate and fragile span of Owachomo. All three natural bridges will continue to widen and eventually collapse under their own weight. A 9-mile (14.5 km) scenic drive has overlooks of the picturesque bridges, Ancestral Puebloan ruins, and the twisting canyons. You can follow short trails down from the rim to the base of each bridge or hike through all three bridges on a nine-mile (14.5-km) trail loop.

Natural Bridges National Monument (www.nps.gov/nabr, $10 per vehicle, $5 pedestrians, motorcyclists, and bicyclists) is 33 miles (53 km) west of Blanding and 91 miles (147 km) southeast of Hanksville, both on Hwy. 95. The route, which crosses the Colorado River at the Hite Bridge, is very picturesque and has been designated the Trail of the Ancients National Scenic Byway by the BLM.

Visitors Center

From the signed junction on Highway 95, it is 4.5 miles (7.2 km) on Highway 275 to the **visitors center** (435/692-1234, 9am-5pm daily April-mid-Oct., 9am-5pm mid-Oct.-March Thurs-Mon.), at an elevation of 6,505 feet. Exhibits and a short film introduce the people who once lived here, as well as the

area's geology, wildlife, and plants. Outside, labels identify native plants of the monument.

It's worth camping here—when the sun sets, Natural Bridges becomes one of the darkest places in the United States. In fact, the International Dark Sky Association named this the world's first dark-sky park. Come here for some serious stargazing!

Bridge View Drive

The 9-mile (14.5 km) drive begins its one-way loop just past the campground. You can stop for lunch at a picnic area. Allow about 90 minutes for a quick trip around. To make all the stops and do a bit of leisurely hiking will take most of a day.

Sipapu Bridge viewpoint is 2 miles (3.2 km) from the visitors center. The Hopi name refers to the gateway from which their ancestors entered this world from another world below. Sipapu Bridge has reached its mature, or middle-age, stage of development. The bridge is the largest in the monument and has a span of 268 feet and a height of 220 feet. Many people think Sipapu is the most magnificent of the bridges. Another view and a trail to the base of Sipapu are 0.8 mile (1.3 km) farther. The viewpoint is about halfway down on an easy trail; allow half an hour. A steeper

ARCHES AND CANYONLANDS
SOUTHEAST UTAH

Natural Bridges National Monument

and rougher trail branches off the viewpoint trail and winds down to the bottom of White Canyon, which is probably the best place to fully appreciate the bridge's size. The total round-trip distance is 1.2 miles (1.9 km), with an elevation change of 600 feet.

Horse Collar Ruin, built by the Ancestral Puebloans, looks as though it has been abandoned for just a few decades, not 800 years. A short trail leads to an overlook 3.1 miles (4.9 km) from the visitors center. The name comes from the shape of the doorway openings in two storage rooms. Hikers walking in the canyon between Sipapu and Kachina Bridges can scramble up a steep rock slope to the site. Like all ancient ruins, these are fragile and must not be touched or entered. Only with such care will future generations of visitors be able to admire the well-preserved structures. Other groups of Ancestral Puebloan dwellings can also be seen in or near the monument; ask a ranger for directions.

The **Kachina Bridge** viewpoint and trailhead are 5.1 miles (8.2 km) from the visitors center. The massive bridge has a span of 204 feet and a height of 210 feet. A trail, 1.5 miles (2.4 km) round-trip, leads to the canyon bottom next to the bridge; the elevation change is 650 feet. Look for pictographs near the base of the trail. Some of the figures resemble Hopi kachinas (spirits) and inspired the bridge's name. Armstrong Canyon joins White Canyon just downstream from the bridge; floods in each canyon abraded opposite sides of the rock fin that later became Kachina Bridge.

The **Owachomo Bridge** viewpoint and trailhead are 7.1 miles (11.4 km) from the visitors center. An easy walk leads to Owachomo's base—0.5 mile (0.8 km) round-trip with an elevation change of 180 feet. Graceful Owachomo spans 180 feet and is 106 feet high. Erosive forces have worn the venerable bridge to a thickness of only nine feet. Unlike the other two bridges, Owachomo spans a smaller tributary stream instead of a major canyon. Two streams played a role in the bridge's formation.

Floods coming down the larger Armstrong Canyon surged against a sandstone fin on one side while floods in a small side canyon wore away the rock on the other side. Eventually a hole formed, and waters flowing down the side canyon took the shorter route through the bridge. The word *owachomo* means "flat-rock mound" in the Hopi language; a large rock outcrop nearby inspired the name. Before construction of the present road, a trail winding down the opposite side of Armstrong Canyon provided the only access for monument visitors. The trail, little used now, connects with Highway 95.

Toward the end of the one-way loop drive, stop at the **Bears Ears Overlook** to see the twin mesas in the distance.

Bridge View Drive is always open during daylight hours, except after heavy snowstorms. A winter visit can be very enjoyable; ice or mud often closes the steep Sipapu and Kachina Trails, but the short trail to Owachomo Bridge usually stays open.

Vicinity of Natural Bridges National Monument
DARK CANYON

This magnificent canyon system is about 15 air (24 km) north of Natural Bridges National Monument. Dark Canyon, with its many tributaries, begins in the high country of Elk Ridge and extends west to Lake Powell in lower Cataract Canyon. Steep cliffs and the isolated location have protected the relatively pristine environment. The upper canyons tend to be wide with open areas and groves of Douglas fir and ponderosa pine. Creeks dry up after spring snowmelt, leaving only widely scattered springs as water sources for most of the year. Farther downstream, the canyon walls close in and the desert trees of piñon pine, juniper, and cottonwood take over. At its lower end, Dark Canyon has a year-round stream and deep plunge pools; cliffs tower more than 1,400 feet above the canyon floor. Springs and running water attract wildlife, including bighorn sheep, black bears, deer, mountain lions, coyotes, bobcats, ringtail cats, raccoons, foxes, and spotted skunks.

Experienced hikers come here for the solitude, wildlife, Ancestral Puebloan ruins, and varied canyon scenery. Although it's possible to visit Dark Canyon on a day hike, it takes several days to get a feel for this area. To explore the entire canyon and its major tributaries would take weeks.

The upper half of the canyon system is within Dark Canyon Wilderness, administered by the Manti-La Sal National Forest (435/587-2041, www.fs.usda.gov/mantilasal). The lower half of Dark Canyon is mostly BLM land.

The **Sundance Trail** is the most popular entry to lower Dark Canyon. The start of the trail can be reached on dirt roads that branch off Highway 95 southeast of the Hite Marina turnoff; this approach can be used year-round in dry weather. Cairns mark the trail, which drops 1,200 vertical feet in less than 1 mile (1.6 km) on a steep talus slope.

GRAND GULCH PRIMITIVE AREA

Within this twisting canyon system are some of the most captivating scenery and largest concentrations of Ancestral Puebloan ruins in southeastern Utah. The main canyon begins only about 6 miles (9.7 km) southeast of Natural Bridges National Monument. From an elevation of 6,400 feet, Grand Gulch cuts deeply into Cedar Mesa on a tortuous path southwest to the San Juan River, dropping 2,700 feet in about 53 miles (85 km). Sheer cliffs, alcoves, pinnacles, Ancestral Puebloan cliff dwellings, rock-art sites, arches, and a few natural bridges line Grand Gulch and its many tributaries.

From the Kane Gulch Ranger Station, a trail leads 4 miles (6.4 km) down Kane Gulch to the upper end of Grand Gulch, where a camping area is shaded by cottonwood trees. **Junction Ruin,** a cave dwelling, is visible from here, and less than 1 mile farther into Grand Gulch are more ruins and an arch.

Kane Gulch and Bullet Canyon provide access to the upper end of Grand Gulch from the east side. A popular loop hike using these canyons is 23 miles long (37 km, 3-4 days); arrange a 7.5-mile (12 km) car shuttle or hitch. Ask at the ranger station if a shuttle service is available. Collins Canyon, reached from the Collins Spring trailhead, leads into lower Grand Gulch from the west side. Hiking distance between the Kane Gulch and Collins Spring trailheads is 38 miles (61 km) one-way (5-7 days). A car shuttle of about 29 miles (47 km, including 8 miles/12.9 km of dirt road) is required. Be sure to visit the BLM's **Kane Gulch Ranger Station** (435/587-1532, www.blm.gov, 8am-noon daily spring and fall) or Monticello office for a permit and information. You must have a day-use ($2) or overnight camping permit ($8) to enter the area.

FISH CREEK AND OWL CREEK

Varied canyon scenery, year-round pools, Ancestral Puebloan ruins, and a magnificent natural arch make this an excellent hike. Fish Creek and its tributary Owl Creek are east of Grand Gulch on the other side of Highway 261. A 1.5-mile trail atop Cedar Mesa connects upper arms of the two creeks to make a 15.5-mile (25 km) loop. From the trailhead (elev. 6,160 feet), the path descends 1,400 vertical feet to the junction of the two creeks. Opinions differ as to which direction to begin the loop, but either way is fine. Owl Creek might be the better choice for a day hike because it's closer to the trailhead and has the added attractions of easily accessible ruins just 0.5 mile away and Nevill's Arch 3.5 miles farther (5.6 km, one-way). Contact the BLM's Kane Gulch Ranger Station or Monticello office for trail notes and current trail and water conditions. Permits cost $2 for day trips, $8 for overnight trips. Maps are essential for navigation because it's easy to get off the route in some places.

The canyons have been carved in Cedar Mesa sandstone, which forms many overhangs where the Ancestral Puebloans built cliff dwellings. Unfortunately, nearly all ruins sit high in the cliffs and can be hard to spot from the canyon bottoms (canyon depths average 500 feet). Binoculars come in handy for seeing the ruins, some of which are marked on the topo maps. Climbing equipment cannot be used to reach the ruins.

The turnoff for the trailhead is between mileposts 27 and 28 on Highway 261, 1 mile (1.6 km) south of Kane Gulch Ranger Station.

MEXICAN HAT

Spectacular geology surrounds this tiny community perched on the north bank of the San Juan River. Folded layers of red and gray rock stand out dramatically. Alhambra Rock, a jagged remnant of a volcano, marks the southern approach to Mexican Hat. Another rock, which looks just like an upside-down sombrero, gave Mexican Hat its name; you'll see this formation two miles north of town. The land has never proved useful for much except its scenery; farmers and ranchers thought it next to worthless. Stories of gold in the San Juan River brought a frenzy of prospecting in 1892-1893, but the mining proved mostly a bust. Oil, first struck by drillers in 1908, has brought mostly modest profits. The uranium mill across the river at Halchita gave a boost to the economy from 1956 until it closed in 1965. Mexican Hat now serves as a modest trade and tourism center. Monument Valley, Valley of the Gods Scenic Drive, Goosenecks State Park, and Grand Gulch Primitive Area are only short drives away. The shore near town can be a busy place in summer as river-runners on the San Juan put in, take out, or just stop for ice and beer.

Mexican Hat is 22 miles (35 km) west of Bluff and 25 miles (40 km) northeast of Monument Valley, both on U.S. 163.

Food and Accommodations

The **San Juan Inn and Trading Post** (435/683-2220 or 800/447-2022, www.sanjuaninn.net, $8124-140), at a dramatic location above the river just west of town, offers clean guest rooms without extras, a few yurts, Native American trade goods, and a restaurant, the **Olde Bridge Bar and Grill** (435/683-2322, 7am-10pm daily, $8-15), serving American, Mexican, and Navajo food. **Hat Rock Inn** (435/683-2221, www.hatrockinn.com, $144-159) offers the nicest guest rooms in town and a swimming pool. **Mexican Hat Lodge** (435/683-2222, www.mexicanhat.net, $84-160) offers guest rooms, a pool, and a fun but somewhat expensive restaurant (lunch and dinner daily) with grilled steaks and burgers.

CAMPGROUNDS

Valle's Trading Post and RV Park (435/683-2226, year-round, $32) has tent and RV sites with hookups. The camping area is pretty basic but great scenery surrounds it. The trading post offers crafts, groceries, showers, vehicle storage, and car shuttles. **Goosenecks State Park** has camping ($10) with great views but no amenities.

Vicinity of Mexican Hat
VALLEY OF THE GODS

Great sandstone monoliths, delicate spires, and long rock fins rise from the broad valley. This strange red-rock landscape resembles better-known Monument Valley but on a smaller scale. A 17-mile (27-km) dirt road winds through the spectacular scenery. Cars can usually travel the road at low speeds if the weather is dry (the road crosses washes). Allow 1-1.5 hours for the drive; it's studded with viewpoints, and you'll want to stop at all of them. The east end of the road connects with U.S. 163 at milepost 29 (7.5 miles/12 km northeast of Mexican Hat, 15 miles/24 km southwest of Bluff); the west end connects with Highway 261 just below the Moki Dugway switchbacks (4 miles/6 km north of Mexican Hat on U.S. 163, then 6.6 miles/10.6 km northwest on Hwy. 261).

1: The San Juan Inn and Trading Post; 2: Valley of the Gods; 3: Goosenecks State Park; 4: Monument Valley vista

If you're looking to really get away from it all, book a room at the **Valley of the Gods B&B** (970/749-1164, www.valleyofthegodsbandb.com, $140-165), a pretty Southwestern-style solar- and wind-powered ranch house (no TV!).

GOOSENECKS STATE PARK

The San Juan River winds through a series of incredibly tight bends 1,000 feet below. So closely spaced are the bends that the river takes 6 miles (9.7 km) to cover an air distance of only 1.5 miles (2.4 km). The bends and exposed rock layers form exquisitely graceful curves. Geologists know the site as a classic example of entrenched meanders caused by gradual uplift of a formerly level plain. Signs at the overlook explain the geologic history and identify the rock formations. **Goosenecks State Park** (435/678-2238, http://stateparks.utah.gov, $5 per vehicle) is an undeveloped area with a few picnic tables and vault toilets. A **campground** ($10) is available but has no water. From the junction of U.S. 163 and Highway 261, 4 miles (6.4 km) north of Mexican Hat, go 1 mile (1.6 km) northwest on Highway 261, then turn left and go 3 miles (4.8 km) on Highway 316 to its end.

MULEY POINT OVERLOOK

One of the great views in the Southwest is just a short drive from Goosenecks State Park and more than 1,000 feet higher in elevation. Although the view of the Goosenecks below is less dramatic than at the state park, the 6,200-foot elevation provides a magnificent panorama across the Navajo Reservation to Monument Valley and countless canyons and mountains. To get here, travel northwest 9 miles (14.5 km) on Highway 261 from the Goosenecks turnoff. At the top of the Moki Dugway switchbacks, turn left (southwest) and go 5.3 miles (8.5 km) on gravel County Road 241 (the turnoff may not be signed), and follow it toward the point. This road is not suitable for wet-weather travel.

MONUMENT VALLEY

Towering buttes, jagged pinnacles, and rippled sand dunes make this an otherworldly landscape. Changing colors and shifting shadows during the day add to the enchantment. Most of the natural monuments are remnants of sandstone eroded by wind and water. Agathla Peak and some lesser summits are roots of ancient volcanoes, which have dark rocks that contrast with the pale yellow sandstone of the other formations. The valley is at an elevation of 5,564 feet in the Upper Sonoran Life Zone; annual rainfall averages about 8.5 inches.

In 1863-1864, when Kit Carson was ravaging Canyon de Chelly in Arizona to round up the Navajo, Chief Hoskinini led his people to the safety and freedom of Monument Valley. Merrick Butte and Mitchell Mesa commemorate two miners who discovered rich silver deposits on their first trip to the valley in 1880. On their second trip, both were killed, reportedly shot by Paiutes. Hollywood movies made the splendor of Monument Valley known to the outside world. *Stagecoach*, filmed here in 1938 and directed by John Ford, became the first in a series of Westerns that has continued to the present. John Wayne and many other movie greats rode across these sands.

The Navajo Nation has preserved the valley as a park with a scenic drive, a visitors center, and a campground. From Mexican Hat, drive 22 miles (35 km) southwest on U.S. 163, turn left, and go 3.5 miles (5.6 km) to the visitors center. From Kayenta, go 24 miles (39 km) north on U.S. 163, turn right, and go 3.5 miles (5.6 km). At the junction of U.S. 163 is a village of outdoor market stalls and a modern complex of enclosed shops where you can stop to buy Navajo art and crafts.

Visitors Center

At the entrance to the **Monument Valley Navajo Tribal Park** is a visitors center (435/727-5874, http://www.navajonationparks.org/htm/

monumentvalley, 6am-8pm daily May-Sept., 8am-5pm daily Oct.-Apr., $20 per vehicle with up to four people, $6 pp for additional people in the same vehicle) with exhibits and crafts. This is a good place to get a list of Navajo tour guides to lead you on driving or hiking trips into the monument. Lots of folks along the road will also offer these services.

Tours

Take one of several guided tours leaving daily year-round from the visitors center to see sites such as a hogan, a cliff dwelling, and petroglyphs in areas beyond the self-guided drive. The trips last 1.5-4 hours and cost $55-100 per person. Guided horseback rides from near the visitors center cost around $90 for two hours; longer day and overnight trips can be arranged, too. If you'd like to hike in Monument Valley, you must hire a guide. Hiking tours of two hours to a full day or more can be arranged at the visitors center.

Monument Valley Drive

A 17-mile (27-km) **self-guided scenic drive** (6am-8pm daily May-Sept., 8am-4:30pm daily Oct.-Apr.) begins at the visitors center and loops through the heart of the valley. Overlooks provide sweeping views from different vantage points. The dirt road is normally OK for cautiously driven cars. Avoid stopping or you may get stuck in the loose sand that sometimes blows across the road. Allow 90 minutes for the drive. No hiking or driving is allowed off the signed route. Water and restrooms are available only at the visitors center.

Accommodations

Don't be surprised to find that lodgings at Monument Valley are expensive; they're also very popular, so be sure to book them well ahead.

The Navajo-owned ★ **View Hotel** (435/727-5555, www.monumentvalleyview.com, $269-410) provides the only lodging in Monument Valley Tribal Park. Views are

terrific from this stylish newer hotel; reserve a room well in advance. Secluded cabins ($2300-250) and camping ($20 tents, $40 RVs) are also available.

★ **Goulding's Lodge and Trading Post** (435/727-3231, www.gouldings.com, $213-393) is another great place to stay in the Monument Valley area. Harry Goulding and his wife, Leone (who was nicknamed "Mike"), opened this dramatically located trading post in 1924. It's a large complex tucked under the rimrocks 2 miles (3.2 km) west of the U.S. 163 Monument Valley turnoff, just north of the Arizona-Utah border. Modern motel rooms offer incredible views of Monument Valley. Guests can use a small indoor pool; meals are available in the dining room. A gift shop sells a wide range of souvenirs, books, and Native American crafts. The nearby store has groceries and gas pumps, a restaurant is open daily for all meals, and tours and horseback rides are available. The lodge stays open year-round, and rates drop in winter and early spring. Goulding's Museum, in the old trading post building, displays prehistoric and modern artifacts, movie photos, and memorabilia of the Goulding family. The Goulding's **campground** ($55 without hookups, $67 with hookups) is pleasant and well managed.

There are a handful of hotels about 30 minutes south in Kayenta, Arizona. The adobe-style **Hampton Inn** (U.S. 160, 520/697-3170 or 800/426-7866, $199) is the nicest place in town, and it's only a little more expensive than its Kayenta neighbors.

FOUR CORNERS MONUMENT

A concrete slab marks the point where Utah, Colorado, New Mexico, and Arizona meet. Five national parks and 18 national monuments are within a radius of 150 miles (242 km) from this point, and it's the only spot in the United States where you can put your finger on four states at once. More than 2,000 people a day are said to stop at the marker in the summer season. Average stay? Just 7-10 minutes. Native Americans, mostly Navajo, and perhaps some Ute and Pueblo people, set up dozens of crafts and refreshment booths in summer. Navajo Parks and Recreation collects a $5 per person fee.

Getting to the Four Corners from Bluff, the closest town in Utah, is a bit indirect.

Drive east from Bluff on Highway 162 for 13 miles (21 km), and at Montezuma Creek turn south onto Highway 406 (Tribal Route 35) and travel 20 miles (32 km) to Red Mesa, Arizona. Turn east onto U.S. 160 and drive 14 miles (22.5 km) to Teec Nos Pos, Arizona. The Four Corners Monument is 4 miles (6.4 km) north of Teec Nos Pos on U.S. 160.

Background

The Landscape

For many travelers, Utah's striking landforms and natural history provide the impetus for a visit to the state.

GEOGRAPHY

Utah's 84,990 square miles (136,778 km) place it 11th in size among the 50 states. The varied landscape is divided into three major physiographic provinces: the **Basin and Range Province** in the west; the **Middle Rocky Mountains Province** of the soaring Uinta, Wasatch, and Bear River Ranges in the north and northeast; and the **Colorado**

Plateau Province of canyons, mountains, and plateaus in the south.

Basin and Range Province

Rows of fault-block mountain ranges follow a north-south alignment in this province in the Great Basin, west of the Wasatch Range and the high plateaus. Most of the land is at elevations of 4,000-5,000 feet. Peaks in the Stansbury and Deep Creek Mountains rise more than 11,000 feet above sea level, creating "biological islands" inhabited by cool-climate plants and animals.

Erosion has worn down many of the ranges, forming large alluvial fans in adjacent basins. Many of these broad valleys lack effective drainage, and none have outlets to the ocean. Terraces mark the hills along the shore of prehistoric Lake Bonneville, which once covered most of this province. Few perennial streams originate in these rocky mountains, but rivers from eastern ranges end their voyages in Great Salt Lake, Sevier Lake, or barren silt-filled valleys.

Middle Rocky Mountains Province

The Wasatch Range and the Uinta Mountains, which form this province, provide some of the most dramatic alpine scenery in the state. In both mountainous areas, you'll find cirques, arêtes, horns, and glacial troughs carved by massive rivers of ice during periods of glaciation. Structurally, however, the ranges have little in common. The narrow Wasatch, one of the most rugged ranges in the country, runs north-south for about 200 miles (320 km) between the Idaho border and central Utah. Slippage along the still-active Wasatch Fault has resulted in a towering western face with few foothills. Most of Utah's ski resorts are in this area. The Uinta Mountains in the northeast corner of the state present a broad rise about 150 miles (242 km) west-east and 30 miles (48 km) across. Twenty-four peaks

exceed 13,000 feet, with Kings Peak (elev. 13,528 feet) the highest mountain in Utah. An estimated 1,400 tiny lakes dot the glacial moraines of the Uintas.

Colorado Plateau Province

World-famous for its scenery and geology, the Colorado Plateau covers nearly half of Utah. Elevations are mostly 3,000-6,000 feet, but some mountain peaks reach nearly 13,000 feet. The Uinta Basin forms the northern part of this vast complex of plateaus; it's bordered on the north by the Uinta Mountains and on the south by the Roan Cliffs. Although most of the basin terrain is gently rolling, the Green River and its tributaries have carved some spectacular canyons into the Roan and Book Cliffs. Farther south, the Green and Colorado Rivers have sculpted remarkable canyons, buttes, mesas, arches, and badlands.

Uplifts and foldings have formed such features as the San Rafael Swell, the Waterpocket Fold, and the Circle Cliffs. The rounded Abajo, Henry, La Sal, and Navajo Mountains are examples of intrusive rock—an igneous layer that is formed below the earth's surface and later exposed by erosion. The high plateaus in the Escalante region drop in a series of steps known as the Grand Staircase. Exposed layers range from the relatively young rocks of the Black Cliffs (lava flows) in the north to the increasingly older Pink Cliffs (Wasatch Formation), Gray Cliffs (Mancos Shale), White Cliffs (Navajo sandstone), and Vermilion Cliffs (Chinle and Wingate Formations) toward the south.

GEOLOGY

The land now contained in Utah began as undersea deposits when the North American continental plate sat near the equator, about 500 million years ago. The spectacular canyon country, now known as the Colorado Plateau, began as a basin of silt and sand deposits at the verge of a shallow sea. This basin sat on

---

The Colorado Plateau

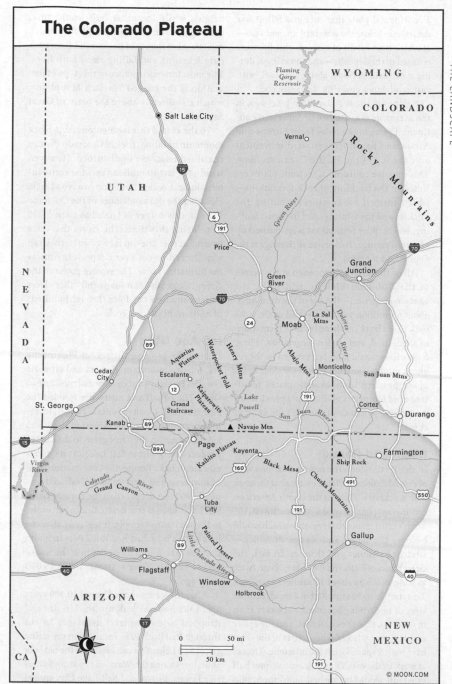

WYOMING

Flaming
Gorge
Reservoir

COLORADO

Salt Lake City

Vernal

Rocky Mountains

UTAH

15

Green River

6

191

Price

Grand
Junction

70

N
E
V
A
D
A

Green
River

70

24

Moab

La Sal
Mtns

Dolores River

Abajo Mtns

Monticello

San Juan Mtns

89

Aquarius
Plateau

Watepocket Fold

Henry Mtns

Cedar
City

Escalante

12

Kaiparowits
Plateau

Grand
Staircase

Lake
Powell

191

San Juan River

Cortez

Durango

St. George

Kanab

89

Navajo Mtn

15

89A

Page

Kaibito Plateau

Kayenta

Ship Rock

Farmington

Virgin
River

160

Black Mesa

Chuska Mountains

491

550

Colorado River

Grand Canyon

Tuba
City

191

Gallup

Williams

89

Painted Desert

Little Colorado River

40

Flagstaff

Winslow

Holbrook

40

ARIZONA

17

0   50 mi

0   50 km

NEW
MEXICO

CA

191

© MOON.COM

a continental plate that rose and fell; it was sometimes below the waters of ancient seas—at which time fossils of early marine life were encased in the deposits—and sometimes, during more arid periods, above sea level, with vast sand dunes covering the landscape.

Beginning about 200 million years ago, in the Mesozoic era, the North American continental plate broke away from Europe and Africa and began its westward movement over the top of the Pacific Ocean seafloor. This massive collision of tectonic plates resulted in the buckling of rock formations—which formed mountains, including the Rockies and the Uintas—and in thrust faulting, where older formations were pushed up and onto younger rocks; one such range is the Oquirrh Mountains.

All of this activity happened at the verges of the Colorado Plateau, which, by the Cretaceous period—the age of the dinosaurs, about 65 million years ago—had again sunk back to sea level, resulting in thick formations of sand, mud, and ancient vegetation. These formations would later be revealed in the region's mighty canyons and in the coal fields of northeastern Utah. In some places, fossilized mud footprints of dinosaurs provide unmistakable evidence of the era's far damper climate.

Basin and Range

In the Tertiary era, the new formations west of the old Colorado Plateau were shot through with volcanoes. Then, as the North American continental plate pivoted to the southwest, the earth's crust under this region—which would become the Basin and Range Province—stretched thinner and thinner. In fact, the Great Basin of Utah and Nevada is about twice as wide as it was about 18 million years ago. This stretching has resulted in a much thinner layer of underlying basement rock here than in other parts of the continent, and the entire area is riven by faults, where parts of the crust have pulled apart. Given the differential forces at work in the earth's mantle, sometimes half of a fault would be pushed up to mountain

heights while the other half would sink, causing a basin. The spectacular fault-block mountains of the Great Basin result from such parallel rising and falling along fault lines. The most famous instance of this type of formation is the rugged Wasatch Mountains, which rise directly above the basin of Great Salt Lake.

To the east of this momentous fault-block mountain building, the old Colorado Plateau remained relatively undisturbed. However, within the last 10 million years the entire intermountain region bowed up in a broad arch, elevating the old sandstones of the Colorado Plateau; this corner of Utah has risen 5,000 feet during this time. The rivers that once wound across the surface of eastern Utah were forced to cut ever deeper canyons as the formations rose. The erosive power of the Green, Colorado, San Juan, and other rivers and streams have cut down through hundreds of millions of years of rock.

Ice Age Utah

During the geologically recent Pleistocene era, ice-age mountain glaciers and climatic changes brought an abundance of moisture to Utah. The runoff and meltwater flooded the basins of fault-block mountain ranges, forming enormous lakes. The largest of these was Lake Bonneville, the name given to the ice-age predecessor of Great Salt Lake. At its greatest extent, Lake Bonneville covered nearly all of northern and west-central Utah and was nearly 900 feet deeper than the current Great Salt Lake. Even at that depth, finding an outlet to the sea was not simple. It was only after the lake waters breached Red Rock Pass in Idaho that the lake found an outlet into the Snake and Columbia River systems, about 16,000 years ago.

After the ice ages ended, about 10,000 years ago, Lake Bonneville diminished in size and dropped below the level necessary to cut through Red Rock Pass, resulting in the saline Great Salt Lake. You can easily see the old lake shorelines along the Wasatch Front, and cities like Logan, Provo, and Salt Lake City sprawl along these stair-step-like ledges. Much of the old lake bottom west of Salt Lake City is salt desert and extremely flat. In the Bonneville Salt Flats, the valley is so flat and unbroken that the curvature of the earth can be seen.

CLIMATE

Most of Utah is dry, with an average annual precipitation of about 12 inches. Precipitation varies greatly from place to place due to local topography and the irregularities of storm patterns. Deserts cover about 33 percent of the state; the driest areas are in the Great Basin, the Uinta Basin, and on the Colorado Plateau, where annual precipitation is around 5-10 inches. At the other extreme, the highest peaks of the Wasatch Range receive more than 50 inches of annual precipitation, most of it as snow.

Winter and Spring Weather Patterns

Periods of high-pressure systems broken by Pacific storm fronts shape most of Utah's winter weather. The high-pressure systems cause inversions when dense cold air flows down the snow-covered mountain slopes into the valleys, where it traps moisture and smoke. The blanket of fog or smog maintains even temperatures but is the bane of the Salt Lake City area. Skiers, however, enjoy bright sunny days and cold nights in the clear air of the mountain peaks. The blankets of stagnant air in the valleys are cleaned out when cold fronts roll in from the Pacific. When skies clear, the daily temperature range is much greater until the inversion process sets in again.

Most winter precipitation arrives as snow, which all regions of the state expect. Fronts originating over the Gulf of Alaska typically arrive every 6-7 days and trigger most of Utah's snowfall.

Summer and Fall Weather Patterns

During summer, the valleys still experience inversions of cold air on clear dry nights but with a much less pronounced effect than in winter. The canyon country in the south has higher daytime temperatures than do equivalent mountain elevations because there's no source of cold air in the canyons to replace the rising heated air. Also, canyon walls act as an oven, reflecting and trapping heat.

Thunderstorms are most common in summer, when moist warm air rises in billowing clouds. The storms, although they can produce heavy rains and hail, tend to be concentrated in small areas less than 3 miles (4.8 km) across. Southeastern Utah sees the first thunderstorms of the season, often in mid-June; by mid-July, these storms have spread across the entire state. They lose energy as autumn approaches, and by October they're supplanted by low-pressure systems at high altitudes and Pacific storm fronts, which can cause long periods of heavy precipitation. Hikers need to be aware that the highest mountain peaks can receive snow even in midsummer.

Storm Hazards

Rainwater runs quickly off the rocky desert surfaces and into gullies and canyons. Flash floods can sweep away anything in their path, including boulders, cars, and campsites. Do not camp or park in potential flash-flood areas. If you come to a section of flooded roadway—a common occurrence on desert roads after storms—wait until the water goes down before crossing (it shouldn't take long). Summer lightning causes forest and brush fires, posing a danger to hikers foolish enough to climb mountains when storms threaten.

ENVIRONMENTAL ISSUES

Like many other western states, Utah is deeply conflicted about environmental issues. One of the most conservative states in the nation, Utah has always been very business-oriented, especially toward the historic extractive industries such as mining, logging, and agriculture. Utah has also proved to be very friendly to the military; large portions of northwestern Utah are under Pentagon control as bases, weapons research areas, and munitions dumps.

On the other hand, tourism and high-tech industries are breathing life into Utah's economy. Tourism brings in 23.5 million visitors a year, making it the single largest employer in Utah. Wasatch Front cities are experiencing a phenomenal boom in population growth and new low-environmental-impact industry. A large part of the reason for this modern migration is Utah's quality of life—pristine wilderness and world-class outdoor recreation are available right out the back door. The interests of the tourism industry and new residents are often at odds with the interests of the state's traditional power base.

Redrawing Utah National Monuments

The 1.9 million acre Grand Staircase-Escalante National Monument (GSENM) was designated by President Bill Clinton in 1996; the 1.35 million acre Bears Ears National Monument was created by President Barack Obama in 2016. Both monuments were slashed in size and divided into smaller units in 2018, under the administration of President Donald Trump. The GSENM lost nearly half of its acreage, and is now divided into three units: the Grand Staircase, Kaiparowits Plateau and Escalante Canyons national monuments. Analysts quickly noted that the lands removed from national monument protection include areas known to be rich in coal deposits. The Bears Ears monument lost 85 percent of its land and was divided into two new monuments, Indian Creek and Shash Jaa. Commentators pointed out that some of the delisted land, particularly on Cedar Mesa, is rich in uranium deposits. A coalition of environmentalists, Indian tribes, and recreationalists haschallenged the delistings in court.

Water Use

The early Mormon pioneers came from well-watered New York and New England and the rich Midwestern prairies. When they arrived in Utah, they set about transforming the desert, following the scripture that says the desert will blossom as a rose. Brigham Young encouraged this endeavor, saying that God would change the climate, giving more water if the settlers worked to establish agriculture.

So the settlers planted fruit orchards, shade trees, and grass, turning the desert into an oasis. They built dams and created reservoirs. They dug canals, piping water from farther and farther away, turning the desert green.

According to a 2014 survey, Utah consumes more water per person than any state, despite having experienced many years of drought and being the second-driest state in the United States.

Water conservationists maintain that Utah residents, including state officials in charge of water-use policy, have not let go of 19th-century ideals about water development and conservation. The state's current goal is to cut water use by 25 percent over the next 50 years, which environmentalists see as incredibly wishy-washy.

Meanwhile, many individuals view the drought as a wake-up call and see water conservation and native-plant landscaping as the way of the new Utah pioneer.

ATV Overkill

All-terrain vehicles (ATVs), or off-road vehicles (ORVs), have gone from being the hobby of a small group of off-road enthusiasts to being one of the fastest growing recreational markets in the country, and these dune-buggies-on-steroids are having a huge impact on public lands. The scope of the issue is easy to measure. In 2000 there were 83,000 ORVs registered in Utah. By 2012 there were 200,000. In addition, the power and dexterity of these machines has greatly increased. Now essentially military-style assault machines that can climb near-vertical cliffs and clamber on any kind of terrain, ORVs are the new extreme sports toys of choice, and towns like Moab are now seeing more visitors coming to tear up the backcountry on ORVs than to mountain bike. The problem is that the ATVs are extremely destructive to the delicate natural environment of deserts and canyon lands, and the more powerful, roaring, exhaust-belching machines put even the most remote and isolated areas within reach of large numbers of people.

The Moab area, the San Rafael Swell near Hanksville, and the Vermillion Cliffs near Kanab are seeing unprecedented levels of ORV activity. Groups like the Southern Utah Wilderness Alliance (SUWA) have developed strategies to force the Bureau of Land Management to shoulder its responsibility for environmental stewardship of public land. For more information, see the SUWA website (www.suwa.org).

Plants and Animals

A wide variety of plants and animals find homes within Utah's great range of elevations (more than 11,000 feet). Regardless of the precipitation, the environment is harsh, and most plants and animals have had to adapt to endure the challenging climate.

PLANTS
Desert
In the southern Utah deserts near St. George, fewer than eight inches of rain fall yearly. Creosote bush dominates the plant life, although you're also likely to see rabbitbrush, snakeweed, blackbrush, saltbush, yuccas, and cacti. Joshua trees grow on some of the higher gravel benches. Flowering plants tend to bloom after winter or summer rains.

In the more temperate areas of the Great Basin, Uinta Basin, and canyon lands, shadscale—a plant resistant to both salt and drought—grows on the valley floors. Commonly growing with shadscale are grasses, annuals, Mormon tea, budsage, gray molley, and winterfat. In salty soils, more likely companions are greasewood, salt grass, and iodine bush. Nonalkaline soils, on the other hand, may have blackbrush as the dominant plant. Sagebrush, the most common shrub in Utah, thrives on higher terraces and in alluvial fans of nonalkaline soil. Grasses are commonly found mixed with sagebrush and may even dominate the landscape. Piñon pine and juniper, small trees often found together, can grow only where at least 12 inches of rain falls annually; the lower limit of their growth is sometimes called the arid timberline. In the Wasatch Range, scrub oaks often grow near junipers.

Mountain
As elevation rises and rainfall increases, you'll see growing numbers of ponderosa pines and chaparral in the forest. The chaparral association includes oak, maple, mountain mahogany, and sagebrush. Gambel oak, juniper, and Douglas fir commonly grow among the ponderosa pines in the Uintas and the high plateaus.

Douglas fir is the most common tree on the slopes of the Wasatch Range, the high plateaus, and the northern slopes of the Great Basin Ranges. In the Uintas, however, lodgepole pine dominates. Other trees include ponderosa pine, limber pine, white fir, blue spruce (Utah's state tree), and aspen.

Strong winds and a growing season of fewer than 120 days prevent trees from reaching their full size at higher elevations. Often gnarled and twisted, Engelmann spruce and subalpine fir grow in the cold heights over large areas of the Uintas and Wasatches. Limber and bristlecone pines live in the zone, too. Lakes and lush subalpine meadows are common.

Only grasses, mosses, sedges, and annuals can withstand the rugged conditions atop Utah's highest ranges. Freezing temperatures and snow can blast the mountain slopes even in midsummer.

Bark Beetles and the Death of Utah Forests

Drive a mountain road in Utah and you expect to see deep forests of pine and spruce as far as the eye can see. However, these forests may be a thing of the past. Ascend to a mountain pass today and you'll take in sweeping views of miles and miles of dead trees.

Since the early 2000s, forests in the western United States have been increasingly infested with small, native boring insects known collectively as bark beetles. These beetles live and reproduce in the inner bark of conifers, the tree layer responsible for providing moisture and nutrition to the tree. The beetles drill in through the tree's outer bark and, if present in sufficient numbers, destroy the life-giving inner bark as part of their reproductive cycle. The tree dies, and a new generation of bark beetles swarm on to other healthy trees. Essentially, there's a bark beetle species for each type of tree: the spruce beetle, the lodgepole pine beetle, the piñon pine beetle, and so on.

The bark beetle infestation is of epic proportions. In New Mexico, bark beetles have largely destroyed the piñon pine, the state tree. Ninety percent—tens of millions—of New Mexico's piñons are dead. In Utah, about 2.2 million acres of the state's 3.5 million acres of pine, fir, and spruce forests in the state are under attack by bark beetles, and entire forests are currently dead or dying. Especially hard hit is the north slope of the Uinta Mountains.

Of course, with millions of standing dead trees in the forests, the risk of wildfire is hugely amplified. Of practical concern to hikers and campers, these weakened trees can fall without warning; don't camp under red, dead trees.

Although bark beetles are native to western forests, a number of environmental factors and forest management practices have combined to create a bark beetle perfect storm. Climate change in the western United States has meant that bark beetle infestation is spreading faster and farther north; for the first time, Canadian forests above 60 degrees latitude are being decimated. Traditionally, bark beetles have a two-year reproductive cycle. In the past decade, warmer temperatures and longer seasons have instigated yearly reproductive cycles, and in some areas, bark beetles are reproducing twice a year, greatly increasing their numbers and broadening their area of attack.

Another factor in bark beetle infestation is the success of U.S. Forest Service fire suppression practices. Traditionally, wildfires cleared forests of mature trees, which were more affected by bark beetles than younger trees, and burned the colonies of bark beetles that existed. But the prevention of wildfires in the last half of the 20th century has had the effect of establishing thick conifer forests with abundant mature trees, perfect conditions to explode the bark beetle population.

One thing is certain: The iconic western forests that our generation has known won't be here for the next generation, if ever again. According to forest scientists, lodgepole pine forests will require 50-80 years to grow back, and spruce forests could take 150-350 years to recover. If climate change is indeed part of the problem, future replacement forests may not find the Utah mountains a hospitable home.

ANIMALS

Desert

Most desert animals retreat to a den or burrow during the heat of the day, when ground temperatures can reach 130°F. Look for wildlife in early morning, during late afternoon, or at night. You may see kangaroo rats, desert cottontails, black-tailed jackrabbits, striped and spotted skunks, kit foxes, ringtail cats, coyotes, bobcats, mountain lions, and several species of squirrels and mice. Birds include the native Gambel's quail, roadrunners, red-tailed hawks, great horned owls, cactus wrens, black-chinned and broad-tailed hummingbirds, and rufous-sided towhees. The desert tortoise lives here, too, but faces extinction in a losing battle with human activity, which has destroyed and fragmented its habitat.

The rare Gila monster, identified by its beadlike skin with black and yellow patterns, is found in the state's southwest corner. Sidewinder, Great Basin, and other western

Utah Vegetation Zones

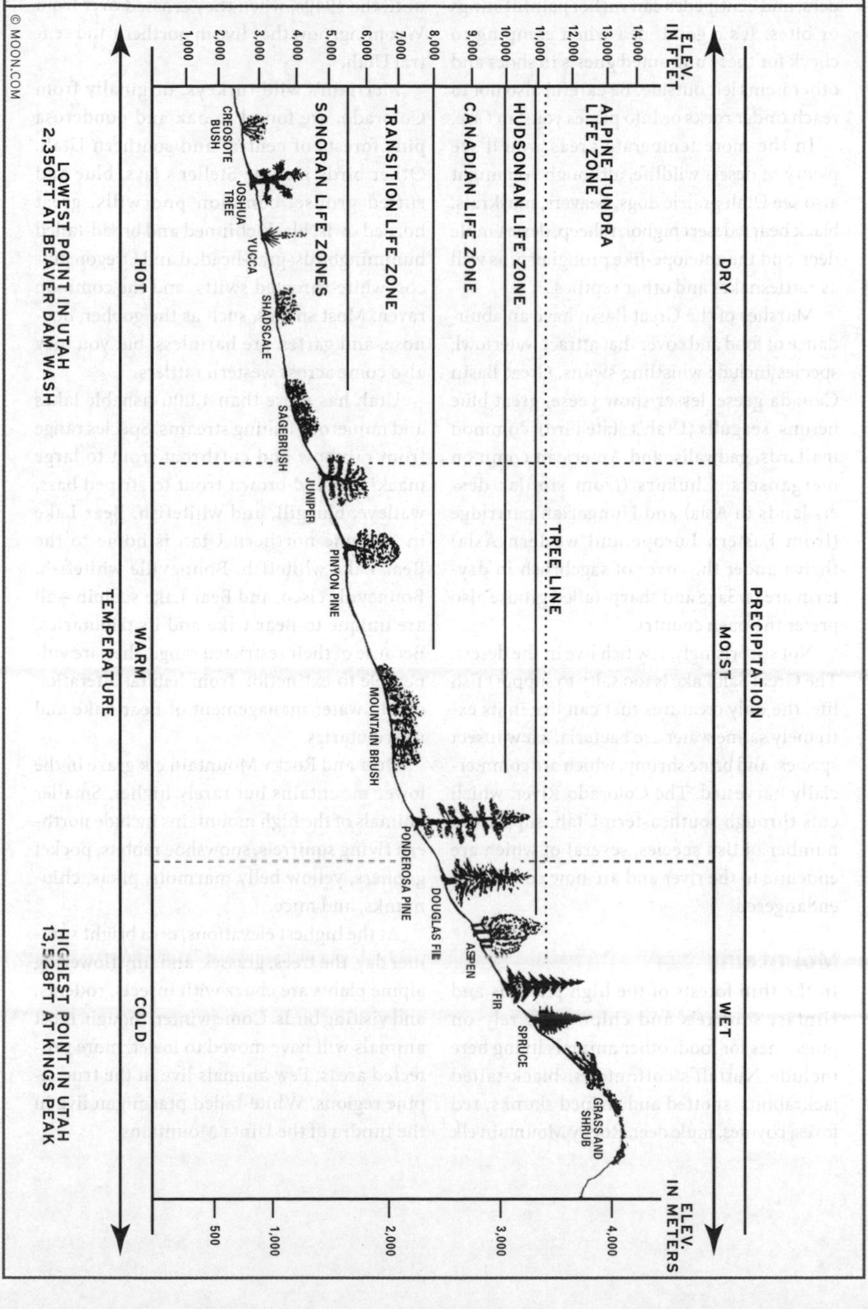

© MOON.COM

ELEV.
IN FEET

14,000
13,000
12,000
11,000
10,000
9,000
8,000
7,000
6,000
5,000
4,000
3,000
2,000
1,000

ALPINE TUNDRA
LIFE ZONE

HUDSONIAN LIFE ZONE

CANADIAN LIFE ZONE

TRANSITION LIFE ZONE

SONORAN LIFE ZONES

TREE LINE

CREOSOTE
BUSH

JOSHUA
TREE

YUCCA

SHADSCALE

SAGEBRUSH

JUNIPER

PINYON PINE

MOUNTAIN BRUSH

PONDEROSA PINE

DOUGLAS FIR

ASPEN

FIR

SPRUCE

GRASS AND
SHRUB

DRY   PRECIPITATION   MOIST   WET

HOT   TEMPERATURE   WARM   COLD

LOWEST POINT IN UTAH
2,350FT AT BEAVER DAM WASH

HIGHEST POINT IN UTAH
13,528FT AT KINGS PEAK

ELEV.
IN METERS

4,000

3,000

2,000

1,000

500

rattlesnakes are occasionally seen. Also watch for other poisonous creatures; scorpions, spiders, and centipedes can inflict painful stings or bites. It's a good idea when camping to check for these unwanted guests in shoes and other items left outside. Be careful also not to reach under rocks or into places you can't see.

In the more temperate areas, you'll see plenty of desert wildlife, although you might also see Utah prairie dogs, beavers, muskrats, black bears, desert bighorn sheep, desert mule deer, and the antelope-like pronghorn, as well as rattlesnakes and other reptiles.

Marshes of the Great Basin have an abundance of food and cover that attract waterfowl; species include whistling swans, Great Basin Canada geese, lesser snow geese, great blue herons, seagulls (Utah's state bird), common mallards, gadwalls, and American common mergansers. Chukars (from similar desert lands in Asia) and Hungarian partridge (from Eastern Europe and western Asia) thrive under the cover of sagebrush in dry-farm areas. Sage and sharp-tailed grouse also prefer the open country.

Not surprisingly, few fish live in the desert. The Great Salt Lake is too salty to support fish life; the only creatures that can live in its extremely saline water are bacteria, a few insect species, and brine shrimp, which are commercially harvested. The Colorado River, which cuts through southeastern Utah, supports a number of fish species, several of which are endemic to the river and are now considered endangered.

Mountain

In the thin forests of the high plateaus and Uintas, squirrels and chipmunks rely on pinecones for food; other animals living here include Nuttall's cottontails, black-tailed jackrabbits, spotted and striped skunks, red foxes, coyotes, mule deer, Rocky Mountain elk

(Utah's state mammal), moose, black bears, and mountain lions. Moose did not arrive until the 1940s, when they crossed over from Wyoming; now they live in northern and central Utah.

Merriam's wild turkeys, originally from Colorado, are found in oak and ponderosa pine forests of central and southern Utah. Other birds include Steller's jays, blue and ruffed grouse, common poorwills, great horned owls, black-chinned and broad-tailed hummingbirds, gray-headed and Oregon juncos, white-throated swifts, and the common raven. Most snakes, such as the gopher, hognose, and garter, are harmless, but you may also come across western rattlers.

Utah has more than 1,000 fishable lakes and numerous fishing streams. Species range from rainbow and cutthroat trout to large mackinaw and brown trout to striped bass, walleye, bluegill, and whitefish. Bear Lake in extreme northern Utah is home to the Bear Lake whitefish, Bonneville whitefish, Bonneville cisco, and Bear Lake sculpin—all are unique to Bear Lake and its tributaries. Because of their restricted range, they are vulnerable to extinction from habitat alteration due to water management of Bear Lake and its tributaries.

Deer and Rocky Mountain elk graze in the lower mountains but rarely higher. Smaller animals of the high mountains include northern flying squirrels, snowshoe rabbits, pocket gophers, yellow belly marmots, pikas, chipmunks, and mice.

At the highest elevations, on a bright summer day, the trees, grasses, and tiny flowering alpine plants are abuzz with insects, rodents, and visiting birds. Come winter, though, most animals will have moved to lower, more protected areas. Few animals live in the true alpine regions. White-tailed ptarmigan live in the tundra of the Uinta Mountains.

History

PRE-SETTLEMENT UTAH
Prehistory

Archaeologists have evidence that Paleo-Indians began to wander across the region that would become Utah about 15,000 years ago, hunting big game and gathering plant foods. The climate was probably cooler and wetter; food plants and game animals would have been more abundant than today. The early groups continued their primitive hunting and gathering despite climate changes and the extinction of many big-game species about 10,000 years ago.

The first tentative attempts at agriculture were introduced from the south about 2,000 years ago and brought about a slow transition to settled village life. The Fremont culture emerged in the northern part of the Colorado Plateau, the Ancestral Puebloans in the southern part. Although both groups developed crafts such as basketry, pottery, and jewelry, only the Ancestral Puebloans progressed to the construction of masonry buildings in their villages. Their corn, beans, and squash enabled them to be less reliant on migration and to construct year-round village sites. Thousands of stone dwellings, ceremonial kivas, and towers built by the Ancestral Puebloans still stand. Both groups also left behind intriguing rock art, either pecked into the surfaces (petroglyphs) or painted on (pictographs). The Ancestral Puebloans and the Fremont departed from this region about 800 years ago, perhaps because of drought, warfare, or disease. Some of the Ancestral Puebloans moved south and joined the Pueblo people of present-day Arizona and New Mexico. The fate of the Fremont people remains a mystery.

About the same time, perhaps by coincidence, the nomadic Shoshoni in the north and the Utes and Paiutes in the south moved through Utah; none of these groups seemed to have knowledge of their sophisticated predecessors. Relatives of the Athabaskans of western Canada, the seminomadic Navajo, wandered into New Mexico and Arizona between AD 1300 and 1500. These adaptable people learned agriculture, weaving, pottery, and other skills from their Pueblo neighbors and became expert horsepeople and sheepherders with livestock obtained from the Spanish.

The size of prehistoric populations has varied greatly in Utah. There were probably few inhabitants during the Archaic period (before AD 500) but many more during the time of the Ancestral Puebloan and Fremont cultures (AD 500-1250), rising to a peak of perhaps 500,000. Except for the Athabaskan-speaking Navajo, all of Utah's historic Native Americans spoke Shoshonian languages and had similar cultures.

Explorers and Colonizers

In 1776, Spanish explorers of the Dominguez-Escalante Expedition were the first Europeans to visit and describe the region during their unsuccessful attempt to find a route west to California. Utes guided the Spanish expedition through the Uinta Basin.

Retreating to New Mexico, the explorers encountered great difficulties in the canyons of southern Utah before finding a safe ford across the Colorado River. This spot, known as the Crossing of the Fathers, now lies under Lake Powell. Later explorers established the Old Spanish Trail through this area of Utah to connect New Mexico with California.

Adventurous mountain men seeking beaver pelts and other furs entered northern Utah in the mid-1820s. They explored the mountain ranges, the rivers, and Great Salt Lake and blazed most of the trails later used by wagon trains, the Pony Express, telegraph lines, and the railroads. By 1830, most of the mountain men had moved on to better trapping areas and left the land to the Native Americans;

Anasazi or Ancestral Puebloan?

As you travel through the Southwest, you may hear reference to the Anasazi, otherwise known as Ancestral Puebloans. The word *anasazi* is actually a Navajo term that archaeologists chose, thinking it meant "old people." A more literal translation is "enemy ancestors." For this reason, some consider the name inaccurate or even offensive. The terminology is in flux, and which name you hear depends on whom you're talking to or where you are. The National Park Service now uses the more descriptive term Ancestral Puebloan, and that's the term we've chosen to use in this book. These prehistoric people built masonry villages and eventually moved south to Arizona and New Mexico, where their descendants, such as the Acoma, Cochiti, Santa Clara, Taos, and Hopi Mesas, live in modern-day pueblos.

some, however, returned to guide government explorers and groups of pioneer settlers.

In 1843, John C. Frémont led one of his several government-sponsored scientific expeditions into Utah. Frémont determined the salinity of Great Salt Lake and laid to rest speculation that a river drained the lake into the Pacific Ocean. Two years later, he led a well-prepared group across the heart of the dreaded Great Salt Lake Desert, despite warnings from the local Native Americans that no one had crossed it and survived. His accounts of the region described not only the salty lake and barren deserts, but also the fertile valleys near the Wasatch Range. Mormon leaders planning a westward migration from Nauvoo, Illinois, carefully studied Frémont's reports.

Langsford Hastings, an ambitious politician, seized the opportunity to promote Frémont's desert route as a shortcut to California. Hastings had made the trip on horseback but failed to anticipate the problems of a wagon train. On this route in 1846, the Donner-Reed wagon train became so bogged down in the salt mud that many wagons were abandoned. Moreover, an 80-mile (129-km) stretch between water holes proved too far for many of the oxen, which died from dehydration. Today, motorists can cruise in comfort along I-80 on a similar route between Salt Lake City and Wendover.

Native Americans Versus Settlers

The Paiutes and Utes befriended and guided the early explorers and settlers, but troubles soon began for these and other groups when they saw their lands taken over by farmers and ranchers. None of the Native Americans proved a match for the white population, which eventually drove them from the most desirable lands and settled them on the state's five reservations.

The Navajo's habit of raiding neighboring communities and white settlements brought about their downfall. In 1863-1864 the U.S. Army rounded up all the Navajo they could find and forced the survivors on the Long Walk from Fort Defiance in northeastern Arizona to a bleak camp in eastern New Mexico. This internment was a dismal failure, and the Navajo were released four years later.

In 1868 the federal government "awarded" to the Navajo land that has since grown into a giant reservation spreading from northeastern Arizona into adjacent Utah and New Mexico.

THE MORMON MIGRATION
The Early LDS Church

At the time of his revelations, the founder of the Church of Jesus Christ of Latter-day Saints, Joseph Smith, worked as a farmer in the state of New York. In 1830, he and his followers founded the new religion and published the first edition of the Book of Mormon. But Smith's revelations evoked fear and anger in many of his neighbors, and in 1831 he and his new church moved to Kirtland, Ohio. They set to work building a temple for sacred ordinances, developing a missionary program, and recruiting new followers. Mormons also settled farther west in Missouri, where they made plans for a temple and a community of Zion.

Persecution by non-Mormons continued to mount in both Ohio and Missouri, fueled largely by the church's polygamist practices, the prosperity of its members, and the Latter-day Saint claim that it was the true church. Missourians disliked the Mormons' antislavery views as well. Violence by gangs of armed men eventually forced church members to flee for their lives.

The winter of 1838-1839 found Joseph Smith in jail on treason charges and many church members without homes or legal protection. The Missouri Mormons made their way east to Illinois, not knowing where else to go. Brigham Young, a member of the Council of the Twelve Apostles, directed this exodus, foreshadowing the much longer migration he would lead eight years later.

Nauvoo the Beautiful

The Mormons purchased a large tract of swampy land along the Mississippi River in Illinois and set to work draining swamps and building a city. Joseph Smith, allowed to escape from the Missouri jail, named the Mormons' new home Nauvoo—a Hebrew word for "the beautiful location." Despite extreme poverty and the inability to secure reparations for the losses they had suffered in Missouri, the Mormons succeeded in building an attractive city. A magnificent temple, begun in 1841, rose above Nauvoo. Despite their success, the Mormons continued to face virulent opposition from those who objected to their religion.

Smith, who had withstood tarring and feathering, among other punishments, met his death in 1844 at Carthage, Illinois. He had voluntarily surrendered to authorities to stand trial for treason, but a mob stormed the jail and killed Smith and his brother Hyrum in a hail of bullets. Opponents thought that the Mormons would disband on the death of their leader. When they did not, their crops and houses were destroyed and their livestock was driven off. Brigham Young, who succeeded Smith, realized the Mormons would never find peace in Illinois. He and other leaders began looking toward the vastness of the West. They hoped the remote Rocky Mountains would provide a sanctuary from mobs and politicians. Plans for departure from Nauvoo began in the autumn of 1845.

The Exodus

Attacks against Nauvoo's citizens made life so difficult that they had to evacuate the following February despite severe winter weather. Homes, businesses, the temple, and most personal possessions were left behind as the Saints crossed the Mississippi into Iowa. (Mobs later took over the town and desecrated the temple; not a single stone of the structure is in its original position today.) The group slowly pushed westward through the snow and mud. Faith, a spirit of sharing, and competent leadership enabled them to survive.

Brigham Young thought it best not to press on all the way to the Rocky Mountains that first year, so the group spent a second winter on the plains. Dugouts and log cabins housed more than 3,500 people at Winter Quarters, near present-day Omaha. By the early spring of 1847, the leaders had worked out plans for the rest of the journey. The Salt Lake Valley, an uninhabited and isolated region, would be their goal. Mountain men encountered on the journey gave discouraging descriptions of this place as a site for a major settlement. Samuel Brannan, a Mormon who had settled on the West Coast, rode east to meet Brigham Young and present glowing reports of California. But Young wouldn't be swayed from his original goal. On July 24, 1847, Young arrived at the edge of the Salt Lake Valley and announced, "This is the right place."

The City of Zion

The pioneers immediately set to work digging irrigation canals, planting crops, constructing a small fort, and laying out a city. Nearly 2,000 more immigrants arrived that same summer of 1847.

These early citizens had to be self-sufficient; the nearest cities lay 1,000 miles (1,610 km) away. Through trial and error, farmers learned techniques of irrigating and farming the desert land. The city continued to grow—immigrants poured in; tanneries, flour mills, blacksmith shops, stores, and other enterprises developed under church direction; residential neighborhoods sprang up; and workers commenced raising the religious structures that still dominate the area around Temple Square.

The Colonization of Utah

Soon other areas in Utah were colonized: In 1849-1850, Mormon leaders in Salt Lake City took the first steps in exploring the rest of the state when they sent an advance party led by Parley P. Pratt to southern Utah. Encouraging reports of rich iron ore west of Cedar Valley and of fertile land along the Virgin River convinced the Mormons to expand southward.

Calls went out for members to establish missions and to mine the iron ore and supply iron products needed for the expanding Mormon empire. In 1855, a successful experiment in growing cotton along Santa Clara Creek, near present-day St. George, aroused considerable interest among the Mormons. New settlements soon arose in the Virgin River Valley. However, poor roads hindered development of the cotton and iron industries, which mostly ended when cheaper products began arriving on the transcontinental railroad.

In the 1870s and early 1880s, the LDS Church sent out calls for members to colonize lands east of the Wasatch Plateau. Though at first the land looked harsh and barren, crops and orchards eventually prospered with irrigation.

An Agrarian Paradise

By the end of the 19th century, the small agricultural settlements in Utah—mostly free of non-Mormon influence—had by and large become the utopian religious communities envisioned by the religion's founders. Various tenets of the faith dictated nearly all aspects of life, from the width of the streets to social customs. Cultural homogeneity was greatly stressed; farmers and ranchers were discouraged from living on their land and encouraged instead to live in towns within range of the church. For a period, the church encouraged full-fledged communal and cooperative farm towns as the ideal social structure.

The Mormons were hardworking farmers and managed to convert an unyielding desert into a land of abundance. Streams were diverted into irrigation canals, and acres of orchards and fields blossomed. Little farm towns, all laid out with uniform street grids, were planted with trees and flowers; substantial homes of stone announced the prosperity of the LDS way of life.

The internal structure of the church—the ward (the parish) and stake (the diocese)—became the organizing principle of all religious and social life. Nearly all the social events of a small community were sponsored by the church. The overlap between church and civic authority was nearly complete.

The Road to Statehood

After many years of persecution, the early Latter-day Saints realized the importance of self-government. However, when the Mormon pioneers arrived in their new homeland of Zion, the land actually belonged to Mexico. But after victory in the Mexican War in 1848, the United States took possession of a vast territory in the American West, including the land that would become Utah.

The LDS Church quickly assessed the positive benefits that statehood would bring the new territory, and in 1849 a convention was called "to consider the political needs of the community." The convention created the proposed state of Deseret, which encompassed a great swath of the West, including all or parts of the current states of Utah, Nevada, Arizona, Wyoming, Colorado, New Mexico, Oregon, Idaho, and parts of southern California. The convention wrote a constitution, elected officials (Brigham Young was elected governor), and sent a delegate to the U.S. Congress. However, the House of Representatives declined to admit the delegate from Deseret, and the bid for statehood was effectively quashed. In fact, LDS-dominated Utah would find it exceedingly difficult to attain statehood. Nearly 50 years would pass before Utah would finally become a state.

The federal Senate did pass legislation naming Utah as a territory in 1850; however, a number of factors—especially the thorny cultural and moral issues surrounding polygamy—worked to exacerbate tensions between the new territory and the federal government.

In 1857-1858, the U.S. government sent a 2,500-man army to occupy Salt Lake City and remove Brigham Young from the governorship. Accompanying the army was Alfred Cummings, whom President Buchanan had selected as territorial governor. The army reached Salt Lake City to find it newly deserted, and Cummings assumed the governorship, ending—at least in theory—Utah's flirtation with theocracy. Cummings soon made peace with the Mormons, and residents returned to Salt Lake City.

Second and third attempts at statehood for Deseret were met with defeat in Washington and actually seemed to stir up anti-Mormon sentiment: Congress quickly passed legislation prohibiting polygamy in the territories. The same legislation also sought to unincorporate the LDS Church.

The building of the transcontinental railroad through Utah in the 1860s decreased Utah's isolation from the rest of the United States; however, greater contact with the outside world also meant increased Mormon-Gentile hostility. In 1874, Congress passed a bill effectively disenfranchising LDS-controlled district courts. In 1879, the U.S. Supreme Court upheld legislation that made the practice of plural marriage a criminal offense. Subsequent federal legislation made it illegal for polygamists to vote, hold public office, or serve on juries. The result

was persecution and pursuit of avowed polygamists, many of whom were forced into hiding or exile in Mexico. The federal government's anti-Mormon campaigns also had the effect of empowering the territory's non-Mormon minority far beyond its small power base.

In 1890, LDS president Wilford Woodruff issued the startling proclamation that henceforward he advised his brethren "to refrain from contracting any marriage forbidden by the law of the land." The new doctrine was published across the country, and while many doubted the proclamation's sincerity, it signaled a major shift in direction for the statehood movement. Finally, in 1894, Congress passed the Enabling Act, which set forth the steps Utah had to follow to achieve statehood (the act stipulated that the state constitution declare polygamy be banned forever). In 1896, President Cleveland proclaimed Utah the 45th state.

It's helpful to remember the long and rancorous disputes between Utah's LDS population and the federal government in the 19th century when trying to understand the state's fervid, ongoing antigovernment tendencies. In some ways, the state's anger over the establishment of the Grand Staircase-Escalante National Monument in 1996 is just an example of Utah's long memory of perceived past injustice.

MODERN TIMES

Utah's close-knit Mormon farm towns thrived from the late 19th century until the Great Depression years. The Dust Bowl years were particularly hard in Utah, as most farms were entirely dependent on irrigation, and the decade-long drought greatly reduced the flow of already scarce water. Communities quickly rebounded during World War II, especially as federal money poured into military camps like Wendover Air Base in the deserts west of Salt Lake City.

The designation of five national parks (beginning with Zion in 1919), two huge national recreation areas, and the erstwhile Grand

Staircase-Escalante National Monument (now the Grand Staircase, Kaiparowits Plateau and Escalante Canyons national monuments) has brought an ever-increasing stream of tourists to the state. Today, tourism is the state's largest industry, dwarfing such stalwarts as mining and lumber. In 2002, the Winter Olympics were held in the Salt Lake City area, and the world spotlight shone on the state as never before.

People and Culture

One of the oddest statistics about Utah is that it's the most urban state in the United States. According to the U.S. Census Bureau in 2015, 88.4 percent of Utah's nearly three million residents live in cities and towns, instead of unincorporated areas. To put it another way, 9 out of 10 Utahns live on 1 percent of the state's land (nearly all along the Wasatch Front).

A relatively young population, combined with the Mormons' emphasis on family life and clean living, has resulted in Utah having the highest birth rate and the second-lowest death rate in the country. Racially, the state largely reflects the northern European origins of Mormon pioneers; in 2010 the state was 84-89 percent white. The state's population includes Hispanics (10 percent), Pacific Islanders (7 percent), Native Americans (2.5 percent), Asians (2 percent), and African Americans (2.5 percent).

UTAH'S NATIVE AMERICANS

Shoshoni

Nomadic bands of Shoshoni lived in much of northern Utah, southern Idaho, and western Wyoming for thousands of years. Horses obtained from the Plains people—who had obtained them from the Spanish—allowed hunting parties to cover a large range. The great Chief Washakie led his people for 50 years and negotiated the Shoshoni treaties with the federal government. The Washakie Indian Reservation, near Plymouth in far northern Utah, belongs to the Northwestern band of Shoshoni, though few live there now. Headquarters are in Rock Springs, Wyoming, south of the large Wind River Indian Reservation.

Goshute (Gosiute)

This branch of the Western Shoshoni, more isolated than other Utah Native American groups, lived in the harsh Great Basin. They survived through intricate knowledge of the land and use of temporary shelters. These peaceful hunters and gatherers ate almost everything that they found—plants, birds, rodents, crickets, and other insects. Because the Goshute had to dig for much of their food, early explorers called the tribe Digger Indians. The newcomers couldn't believe these people survived in such a barren land of alkaline flats and sagebrush. Also known as the Newe, the Goshutes now live on the Skull Valley Indian Reservation in Tooele County and on the Goshute Indian Reservation along the Utah-Nevada border.

Ute

Several bands of Utes, or Núuci, ranged over large areas of central and eastern Utah and adjacent Colorado. Originally hunter-gatherers, they acquired horses in about 1800 and became skilled raiders. Customs adopted from Plains people included the use of rawhide, tepees, and the travois (a sled used to carry goods). The discovery of gold in southern Colorado and the pressures of farmers there and in Utah forced the Utes to move and renegotiate treaties many times. They now have the large Uintah and Ouray Indian Reservation in northeast Utah, the small White Mesa Indian Reservation in southeast Utah, and the Ute

Mountain Indian Reservation in southwest Colorado and northwest New Mexico.

Southern Paiute

Six of the 19 major bands of the Southern Paiutes, or Nuwuvi, lived along the Santa Clara, Beaver, and Virgin Rivers and in other parts of southwest Utah. Extended families hunted and gathered food together. Fishing and the cultivation of corn, beans, squash, and sunflowers supplemented the diet of most of the bands. Today, Utah's Paiutes have a tribal headquarters in Cedar City and scattered small parcels of reservation land. Southern Paiutes also live in southern Nevada and northern Arizona.

Navajo

Calling themselves Diné, the Navajo moved into the San Juan River area around 1600. They have proved exceptionally adaptable in learning new skills from other cultures: Many Navajo crafts, clothing, and religious practices have come from Native American, Spanish, and Anglo neighbors. The Navajo people were the first in the area to move away from a hunting and gathering lifestyle, relying instead on the farming and shepherding techniques they had learned from the Spanish. The Navajo have become one of the largest Native American groups in the country, occupying 16 million acres of exceptionally scenic land in southeast Utah and adjacent Arizona and New Mexico. The nation's headquarters is at Window Rock in Arizona.

THE MORMONS

If you're new to the Beehive State, you'll find plenty of opportunities to learn about Mormon history and religion. About 60 percent of Utah's population actively participates in the Church of Jesus Christ of Latter-day Saints; three-quarters of the population were born into the faith. Temple Square in Salt Lake City offers excellent tours and exhibits about the church. You'll also find many other visitors centers and historic sites scattered around the state.

Members believe that God's prophets have restored teachings of the true Christian church to the world "in these latter days." They believe their church presidents, starting with Joseph Smith, to be prophets of God, and they hold both the Bible and the Book of Mormon as the sacred word of God. The latter, they believe, was revealed to Joseph Smith from 1823 to 1830. The text tells of three migrations from the eastern hemisphere to the New World and the history of the people who lived in the Americas from about 600 BC to about AD 400. The book contains 239 chapters, which include teachings Christ gave in the Americas, prophecy, doctrines, and epic tales of the rise and fall of nations. It's regarded by the church as a valuable addition to the Bible—but not a replacement.

Membership in the LDS Church requires faith, a willingness to serve, tithing, and obedience to church authorities. The church emphasizes healthful living, moral conduct, secure family relationships, and a thoughtful approach to social service.

RELIGION

The Church of Jesus Christ of Latter-day Saints is by far the dominant religion in Utah; about 60 percent of the population belongs to the church. Most major Christian denominations are represented in midsize towns, and in Salt Lake City there are small Jewish and Islamic congregations as well.

Summer Music Festivals

Mormon Utah has a long musical history, dating back to the raising of Salt Lake City's tabernacle and its attendant choir in the 1860s until today, when outdoor music concerts and festivals form a backdrop to summer in all parts of Utah. Taking part in some of Utah's summer music festivals will add burnish to a trip otherwise dedicated to sunburned hiking or river-running in canyon country.

SALT LAKE CITY

The variety of live music available in Salt Lake City in the summer is prodigious. In addition to on-going music performances at the **tabernacle,** there is the LDS-sponsored **Concert Series at Temple Square,** concerts of classical and religious music, some of which take place outdoors.

The Roman Catholic Cathedral of the Madeleine presents the **Madeleine Arts and Humanities Program,** which offers classical music in a stunning 1909 place of worship.

For more modern music in an outdoor setting, head to **Gallivan Center** in the heart of downtown, where, in addition to free summer weekday noontime and Thursday evening concerts, there's a big-band dance on Tuesday evenings.

PARK CITY

During the summer, the **Utah Symphony** and other classical music performers grace the stage at Deer Valley's outdoor amphitheater.

The **Beethoven Festival Park City** brings classical music to the Park City area year-round, with an emphasis on concerts in July.

LOGAN

In summer, Logan is Utah's music festival center. This lovely small city in a verdant mountain valley plays host to the **Utah Festival Opera,** with fully staged professional operas in an intimate performing arts center that was once a movie palace and vaudeville hall (the season runs late June-early Aug.).

Another historic theater in Logan serves as home base for the **Old Lyric Repertory Company,** which produces musicals and other theatrical productions in June, July, and August.

SPRINGDALE

At the outdoor **O. C. Tanner Amphitheater,** you'll find a summertime series of concerts ranging from bluegrass, jazz, and folk to classical music.

ST. GEORGE

The **Tuacahn Amphitheater** was once devoted to uplifting Mormon-themed musicals. Now this dramatically located outdoor theater—amid 1,500-foot cliffs near St. George—features a July-December season of Broadway musicals and other music events.

MOAB

The **Moab Music Festival** offers concerts of classical chamber music, traditional music, vocal music, works of living composers, and jazz performed by acclaimed artists late August-mid-September. Performances take place in indoor and outdoor venues ranging from historic Star Hall in Moab to the banks of the Colorado River.

Outside the summer season, Moab offers the **Moab Folk Festival** in November.

The Arts

MUSIC

Generally speaking, Salt Lake City is the center of the state's arts scene. The state's Mormon heritage is reflected in the city's love of and support for fine music. The glittering Abravanel Concert Hall is home to the noted Utah Symphony, and the tabernacle at Temple Square is often filled with concerts and recitals. The famed Mormon Tabernacle Choir performs here, as do various other church-related music groups. Best of all, all performances at Temple Square are free, making this a great opportunity for travelers to soak up culture at a good price.

Salt Lake City is also the state's major venue for rock and alternative music. A number of lively clubs host both local bands and traveling acts from both coasts.

Come summer, there's fine music at more out-of-the-way places. Venues at Park City offer a full summer schedule ranging from rock concerts at the Park City Mountain Resort to the Utah Symphony at classy Deer Valley Resort and in the national parks. In Logan's sparkling Capitol Theatre, the Utah Festival Opera puts on a summer season of grand opera and classic musicals.

THEATER AND DANCE

Again, Salt Lake City is the center of things theatrical in Utah. Several year-round theatrical troupes dish up everything from Broadway musicals to serious plays like Tony Kushner's *Angels in America*.

In the summer, Cedar City's Utah Shakespeare Festival (www.bard.org) offers eight different plays performed by a professional repertory company. Both Shakespearean and contemporary plays are featured; the Bard's works are presented under the stars in an outdoor theater.

Salt Lake City supports a number of dance troupes. Ballet West performs a mix of classical and contemporary pieces, while the Ririe-Woodbury Dance Company has a more eclectic approach.

CINEMA

While you'll be able to see most first-run films and some art-house fare in Salt Lake City and, to a lesser extent, in smaller cities in Utah, the real cinematic event in Utah is the Sundance Film Festival, held every January in Park City. Founded by actor Robert Redford as a forum for little-seen documentary and independent films, the festival has grown into a major showcase of new high-quality cinema and now offers films in Salt Lake City as well. Make lodging and ticket reservations well in advance if you want to attend. For more information and email updates, visit the festival's website (www.sundance.org/festival).

MUSEUMS

Utah residents are very proud of their pioneer past, and nearly every community in the state has a Daughters of Utah Pioneers (DUP) museum, which recounts the story of local Mormon settlement. In fact, church history and state history are so closely interconnected that the primary state history museums are the various Temple Square institutions and the LDS-dominated Pioneer Memorial Museum.

Utah has a number of good museums dedicated to dinosaurs and other forms of ancient life. The area around Price and Vernal is rich in fossils, and both towns have good dinosaur museums; additionally, there are fossil digs with visitors centers at Dinosaur National Monument and at the Cleveland-Lloyd Dinosaur Quarry. The Museum of Ancient Life at Lehi's Thanksgiving Point has one of the largest collections of complete dinosaur skeletons in the country.

Ogden has converted its large and handsome railroad depot into a multi-museum complex with collections of minerals, fine art, firearms, and historic automobiles and train cars.

ART GALLERIES

Utah isn't exactly known for its fine-art collections, but the Utah Museum of Contemporary Art has a changing lineup of traveling shows that focus on regional artists. The universities in Salt Lake City, Provo, and Logan each have art galleries, and Ogden boasts the Myra Powell Art Gallery in the historic train depot. If you're looking for commercial art galleries, the state's richest pay dirt is in Park City. This resort town has more fine art galleries than Salt Lake City.

FESTIVALS AND EVENTS

Throughout Utah, the year's biggest summer event is **Pioneer Day** on July 24, with parades

and fireworks in almost every Utah community. It commemorates the day in 1847 when Brigham Young first saw the Salt Lake Valley and declared "This is the place."

To most of the outside world, the most followed event is January's **Sundance Film Festival,** in Park City, when you can see the best independent films shoulder to shoulder with the actors, directors, and press; tickets are hard to score, but it's possible. Likewise, be sure to book your room way in advance or be prepared for a long commute.

In June, the **Utah Shakespeare Festival** begins its summer-long run in Cedar City. July brings the **Utah Festival Opera** to Logan, and for six days in August the Bonneville Salt Flats are the site of **Speed Week,** when vehicles ranging from motorcycles to diesel trucks "shoot the salt."

Essentials

Transportation

Although Salt Lake City is well connected with the rest of the world and has a good public transportation system, to really explore the state, a car is the most realistic choice (although a case can be made for a bike and strong legs). However, if you're planning a winter trip with a focus on skiing the Wasatch ski areas, consider skipping the car rental and relying on shuttles or city buses.

GETTING THERE

Air

Salt Lake City is a hub for **Delta Airlines** (800/221-1212, www.delta.com), and all other major airlines have regular flights into **Salt Lake City International Airport** (SLC, 776 N. Terminal Dr., 801/575-2400, www.slcairport.com). The airport is an easy 7 miles (11.3 km) west of downtown, reached via I-80 or North Temple Street or by TRAX light rail service (www.rideuta.com).

If you're heading to southern Utah's parks, consider flying in to Las Vegas's **McCarran International Airport** (LAS, 5757 Wayne Newton Blvd., Las Vegas, Nevada, 702/261-5211, https://www.mccarran.com), which is served by all major airlines, often with cheaper airfares than you'll find to SLC.

Ogden and Provo also have small airports served by Allegiant.

Train

Amtrak (800/872-7245, www.amtrak.com) runs one passenger train across Utah daily in each direction. The *California Zephyr* runs between Oakland and Chicago via Salt Lake City, Provo, Helper, and Green River.

Bus

Greyhound (800/231-2222, www.greyhound.com) offers interstate service to Utah on its routes along I-15, I-70, and I-80.

RV

Many foreign travelers enter Utah in RVs, which they rent to drive on a tour of the western national parks. It takes more planning to line up a rental RV than a car, but there are plenty of agencies in Los Angeles, Phoenix, Las Vegas, and Salt Lake City able to do the job. Most travel agents can help, or you can contact the local travel office in the city of your departure.

In your travels around southern Utah, you'll probably see bright green mini-campers

(basically minivans that convert into campers. You can rent one of these **Jucy** campers (5895 Boulder Hwy Las Vegas, Nevada, 800/650-4180, www.jucyusa.com) in Las Vegas. In Salt Lake City, **Basecamper Vans** (423 W. 800 S., Salt Lake City, 801/949-3675, www.basecampervans.com) offers several lines of camper vans.

GETTING AROUND

Air

Regional airlines connect Salt Lake City with other communities in the state. Regular scheduled flights link SLC to/from St. George, Cedar City, and Moab.

Train

Amtrak (800/872-7245, www.amtrak.com) can get you to Green River, Helper, Provo, and Salt Lake City, but that's about all. Public transportation to other points of interest, such as the national parks, is notably absent.

Bus

Greyhound (800/231-2222, www.greyhound.com) provides bus service along Utah's interstate highways and U.S. 6 (between Green River and Provo), but these routes really don't get you close to the sorts of sights that most people come to Utah to see. The Wasatch Front area (from Provo to Ogden and from Salt Lake City out to Tooele) is served by the **Utah Transit Authority** (UTA, 801/287-4636, www.rideuta.com), a regional bus company with excellent service. Park City and other Salt Lake City ski areas are accessible via a number of ski-bus operations, some of which pick up at the airport.

Car

Public transportation serves cities and some towns but very few of the scenic, historic, and recreational areas. Unless you're on a tour, you really need your own transportation. Cars are easily rented in any large town, although the

Utah Driving Distances

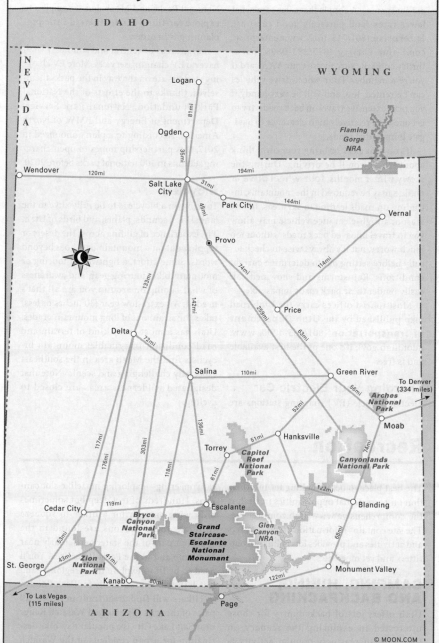

IDAHO

NEVADA

WYOMING

Logan

Ogden

118mi

35mi

Flaming
Gorge
NRA

Wendover   120mi   Salt Lake
City   31mi   194mi

45mi   Park City   144mi   Vernal

Provo

114mi

133mi   142mi   74mi   259mi   Price

63mi

Delta   72mi

Salina   110mi   Green River   56mi

To Denver
(334 miles)

Arches
National
Park

52mi

136mi   51mi   Hanksville   Moab

117mi   303mi   118mi   Torrey   Capitol
Reef
National
Park   74mi

Canyonlands
National
Park

61mi   122mi

176mi   Cedar City   119mi   Escalante   Blanding

Bryce
Canyon
National
Park   Glen
Canyon
NRA   88mi

53mi   St. George   43mi   Zion
National
Park   41mi   Grand
Staircase-
Escalante
National
Monumant   Monument Valley

Kanab   80mi   122mi

To Las Vegas
(115 miles)   Page

ARIZONA

© MOON.COM

Salt Lake City Airport offers by far the greatest selection, including all the major rental-car companies. A couple that offer somewhat lower rates (and perfectly good cars) are **Enterprise** (801/715-1617, www.enterprise.com) and **Thrifty** (877/283-0898, www.thrifty.com). Be sure to use your AAA card if you're a member. Four-wheel-drive vehicles can be rented, too, and will be very handy if you plan extensive travel on back roads; try to get one with relatively high clearance to navigate bumpy dirt roads.

If you rent a car or bring your own, think about where you'll be driving. During the snowy winter months, **four-wheel drive** or **chains** may be required in the mountains, including on roads leading to ski areas. In any season, a high-clearance vehicle may allow you to travel unpaved back roads without too much worry, but it's always wise to check locally before setting out to determine current conditions: Rainstorms and snowmelt can easily render these back roads impassable.

Most tourist offices carry the Utah road map published by the **Utah Department of Transportation** (801/965-4000, www.udot.utah.gov); it's one of the best available and is free.

Charging Your Electric Car

Electric vehicle (EV) charging stations are abundant in the Wasatch Valley, and present along I-15 and I-80 as well in Zion and Bryce National Parks and Moab, but if you plan to explore far-flung destinations, a little preplanning is in order.

Large areas of central and southeast Utah have no EV charging services. More EV charging stations are on the way in the parks themselves, thanks to the efforts of the National Park Foundation, National Park Service, Department of Energy and BMW of North America. According to a plan announced in 2017, this partnership hopes to open charging stations in 100 national parks before 2020.

Bicycle

Touring on a bicycle is to be fully alive to the land, skies, sounds, plants, and birds of Utah. The experience of gliding across the desert or topping out on a mountain pass goes beyond words. Some effort, a lightweight touring or mountain bike, touring gear, and awareness of what's going on around you are all that's needed. An extra-low gear (30 inches or less) takes the strain out of long mountain grades. Utah has almost every kind of terrain and road condition imaginable; mountain bicyclists find the Moab area in the southeast especially challenging and scenic. Note that designated wilderness areas are closed to cycling.

Recreation

The best place to begin looking for information on recreational opportunities in Utah is the comprehensive www.utah.com website. The site contains information on most sports and activities and provides lots of links to outfitters and yet more sites.

CAMPING, HIKING, AND BACKPACKING

Utah offers lots of backcountry for those interested in exploring the scenery on foot. One increasingly popular activity is canyoneering—exploring mazelike slot canyons. Hundreds of feet deep but sometimes only wide enough for a hiker to squeeze through, these canyons are found in the southern part of the state, particularly near Escalante and in the Paria River area. You'll need to be fit to explore these regions—and watch the weather carefully for flash floods.

Hikers will find great trails in almost all parts of the state. The rugged Wasatch Range near Salt Lake City is a popular day-hike destination for urban residents of the Wasatch

Front, while the lofty lake-filled Uintas in northeastern Utah are perfect for long-distance trips. Much of the canyon lands of southern and southeastern Utah are accessible only by foot; visits to remote Ancestral Puebloan ruins and petroglyphs reward the long-distance hiker.

Campers are in luck in Utah. The state has a highly developed network of campgrounds. During peak summer season, make reservations or arrive at your destination early.

FISHING

The Wasatch and Uinta Ranges are dotted with lakes and drained by streams that are rich in rainbow and cutthroat trout. Fly-fishing is a major sport in many mountain communities, and most towns have at least one fly shop and an outfitter anxious to take you out to a stream. Favorite fishing spots include Bear Lake, with good fishing for lake and cutthroat trout; Flaming Gorge Reservoir on the Green River, offering good fishing for lake trout, smallmouth bass, and kokanee salmon; and Lake Powell, with good fishing for catfish, striper, and bass.

GOLF

There are dozens of golf courses across Utah. Notable courses dot the Salt Lake City area and are also near Ogden, Logan, Provo, and Park City. The state's greatest concentration of courses, though, is in St. George, in the southern part of the state. Perhaps it's rhetorical to wonder which comes first, retirees or golf courses, but St. George's excellent courses amid magnificent red-rock formations certainly have contributed mightily to the town's reputation as a retirement haven.

MOUNTAIN BIKING

Mountain biking has done much to put Utah on the recreation map. Trails in the slick-rock canyon country near Moab attract more than 180,000 biking enthusiasts a year, and now nearly all corners of the state promote their old Forest Service or mining roads as a biking paradise. There's good info for planning bike trips at www.utah.com/bike, and excellent biking guidebooks are available from bookstores.

In general, Utah summers are too hot for mountain biking. The peak seasons in Moab are March-May and September-November.

RIVER-RUNNING

Rafting or canoeing Utah's rivers is another favorite activity for visitors and adventurers. The most notable float trip is down the Colorado River between Moab and the backwaters of Lake Powell. This multiday trip passes through Cataract Canyon, and for spectacular adventure it's second only to trips through the Grand Canyon. The Green and San Juan Rivers are also popular. For these trips, plan well in advance, as spaces are limited and demand more than outstrips availability. In towns like Moab, Green River, Vernal, and Bluff, numerous outfitters provide exciting day trips that can usually take people with only a day's notice.

ROCKHOUNDING

Utah is rich in curious stones, fossils, and gems. The lack of vegetation and the high level of erosion make rockhounding a relatively simple matter. One of the best places to plan a rock-hunting expedition is the Delta area, where you can explore for geodes, agates, garnets, and other treasures.

WINTER SPORTS

Skiing has always been excellent in the Wasatch Front ski areas near Salt Lake City and Park City, and since the 2002 Winter Olympics, the world knows about Utah's uncrowded slopes, which provide some of the best powder skiing in North America. If you've always wanted to ski or board Olympic-quality slopes, plan a trip to Utah: All the runs and facilities developed for the Olympics are still in place. For a good overview of Utah's ski areas and information on special package deals, check www.skiutah.com.

NATIONAL PARKS AND MONUMENTS

Utah is home to five major national parks, nearly a dozen national monuments, two national recreation areas, and one national historic site. Three of the crown jewels of the national park system—Zion, Arches, and Bryce Canyon—are here, as well as the less-traveled Capitol Reef and Canyonlands parks. Just across the border in Nevada is Great Basin National Park, and just south in Arizona is the Grand Canyon. These national park areas and national monuments are the state's largest attractions for visitors.

The parks are all open year-round, although spring and fall are the best times to visit—you'll avoid the heat and crowds of high summer. If you're planning on making the rounds of the Utah national parks, it's an excellent idea to purchase an America the Beautiful Pass ($80), which covers admission costs at national parks and other federal recreation sites.

STATE PARKS

Utah boasts 41 state parks, ranging from golf courses to fishing holes, from historic forts to Ancestral Puebloan ruins. Entry fees to state parks vary, but in general there's a $5-9 per vehicle day-use fee at the recreational parks. Many of these have campgrounds; you can make **reservations** (800/322-3770, www. reserveamerica.com, $9 reservation fee in addition to camping fee). For general information on Utah's state parks, contact **Utah State Parks** (801/538-7220, http://stateparks.utah.gov).

WILDERNESS TRAVEL

Utah has an abundance of designated wilderness areas, which are closed to mechanized vehicles (including mountain bikes) to protect both the environment and the experience of solitude. Most designated areas are within national forests or Bureau of Land Management lands, and many are free to visit without a permit; some have fees or require permits. The national parks and monuments require backcountry permits for overnight stays.

Travel Tips

WHAT TO PACK

Unless you want to return from Utah looking like a leather handbag, remember to use lots of **sunscreen.** Prepare for wide variations in temperature. Nights in the desert can be very chilly even when summer highs soar above 100°F.

There's little need to pack clothes to dress up. **Casual clothes** are acceptable nearly everywhere, although if you want to break out your $300 jeans, you'll feel good about doing it in Park City. If you're visiting **religious sites** in Salt Lake City or elsewhere, neat and modest casual clothing will be fine.

Alcohol presents another issue. If you want a drink, especially away from larger cities or in small towns near national parks, it may be easiest to pack your own—especially if you have discerning tastes. While drinking laws have relaxed tremendously and many restaurants in larger towns now offer a selection of alcoholic beverages (including good wine and Utah microbrews), Utah is not a drinking culture, to put it mildly.

Bring your cell phone, but don't count on reception in remote mountains or canyons.

INTERNATIONAL VISITORS
Entering the United States

Citizens of Canada must provide a passport to enter the United States. However, a visa is not required for Canadian citizens.

Citizens of 28 other countries can enter under a reciprocal visa-waiver program. These citizens can enter the United States for up to 90 days for tourism or business with a valid passport; however, no visa is required.

Say It Right!

The following place names are easy to mispronounce. Say it like a local!

- **Duchesne:** du-SHANE
- **Ephraim:** EE-from
- **Escalante:** es-kuh-LAN-tay
- **Hurricane:** HUR-ken
- **Kanab:** kuh-NAB
- **Lehi:** LEE-high
- **Manti:** MAN-tie
- **Moab:** Moe-AB
- **Monticello:** mon-ta-SELL-o
- **Nephi:** NEE-fi
- **Panguitch:** PAN-gwich
- **Tooele:** too-WILL-uh
- **Uinta:** you-IN-tuh
- **Weber:** WEE-ber

These countries include most of Western Europe, plus Japan, Australia, New Zealand, and Singapore. For a full list of reciprocal visa countries (and other late-breaking news for travelers to the United States), check out www.travel.state.gov. Visitors on this program who arrive by sea or air must show round-trip tickets back out of the United States dated within 90 days and must be able to present proof of financial solvency (credit cards are usually sufficient). If citizens of these countries are staying longer than 90 days, they must apply for and present a visa.

Citizens of countries not covered by the reciprocal visa program are required to present both a valid passport and a visa to enter the United States. These are obtained from U.S. embassies and consulates. These travelers are also required to offer proof of financial solvency and show a round-trip ticket out of the United States within the timeline of the visa.

Once in the United States, foreign visitors can travel freely among states without restrictions.

Customs

U.S. Customs allows each person over the age of 21 to bring one liter of liquor and 200 cigarettes into the country duty-free. Non-U.S. citizens can bring in $100 worth of gifts without paying duty. If you are carrying more than $10,000 in cash or traveler's checks, you are required to declare it.

Money and Currency Exchange

Except in Salt Lake City, there are few opportunities to exchange foreign currency or traveler's checks in non-U.S. funds at Utah banks or exchanges. Traveler's checks in U.S. dollars are accepted at face value in most businesses without additional transaction fees.

By far the best way to keep yourself in cash is by using bank, debit, or cash cards at ATMs (automated teller machines). Not only does withdrawing funds from your own home account save on fees, but you also often get a better rate of exchange. Nearly every town in Utah has an ATM. Most ATMs at banks require a small fee to dispense cash. Most grocery stores allow you to use a debit or cash card to purchase food, with the option of adding a cash withdrawal. These transactions are free to the withdrawer.

Credit cards are accepted nearly everywhere in Utah. The most common are Visa and MasterCard. American Express, Diners Club, and Discover are also used, although these aren't as ubiquitous.

ACCESS FOR TRAVELERS WITH DISABILITIES

Travelers with disabilities will find Utah quite progressive when it comes to accessibility issues, especially in Salt Lake City and the heavily traveled national parks in southern Utah. Most parks offer all-abilities trails, and many hotels advertise their fully accessible facilities. The **National Ability Center** (435/649-3991, www.discovernac.org), based in Park City, provides recreational opportunities for people of all ages and abilities, including a skiing program at nearby Park City Mountain Resort.

GAY AND LESBIAN TRAVELERS

Gay travelers will find Utah less welcoming to openly gay people than many of the surrounding western states. There's a gay scene of sorts in Salt Lake City, but very little sign of support elsewhere in the state. Salt Lake City's gay newspaper, Q (http://qsaltlake.com), is a good place to get a flavor for the Utah gay scene. Many of the support groups that do exist in the state are concerned with supporting gay and lesbian Mormons.

SENIOR TRAVELERS

The national and state parks, and Utah in general, are hospitable for senior travelers. The long-standing National Park Service-issued Golden Age Passport has been replaced by the America the Beautiful—National Parks and Federal Recreational Lands Senior Pass. This is a lifetime pass for U.S. citizens or permanent residents age 62 or older. The pass provides access to, and use of, federal parks and recreation sites that charge an entrance fee or standard amenity. The pass admits the pass holder and passengers in a noncommercial vehicle at per-vehicle fee areas, not to exceed four adults. The pass costs $80 and can only be obtained in person at the park. There is a similar discount program at Utah state parks.

CONDUCT AND CUSTOMS

If you've never traveled in Utah before, you may find that Utah residents don't initially seem as welcoming and outgoing as people in other western states. In many smaller towns, visitors from outside the community are a relatively new phenomenon, and not everyone in the state is anxious to have their towns turned into tourism or recreational meccas. The Mormons are very family- and community-oriented, and if certain individuals initially

seem insular and uninterested in travelers, don't take it as unfriendliness.

Mormons are also very orderly and socially conservative people. Brash displays of rudeness or use of foul language in public will not make you popular.

Alcohol and Nightlife

Observant Mormons don't drink alcoholic beverages, and state laws make purchasing alcohol relatively awkward. If going out for drinks and nightclubbing is part of your idea of entertainment, you'll find that only Salt Lake City, Park City, and Moab offer much in the way of clubs and nightspots. Most towns have a liquor store; outside of the Wasatch Front and Moab, don't expect casual restaurants to have liquor licenses.

Smoking

Smoking is taboo for observant Mormons, and as in many states, an Indoor Clean Air Act prohibits smoking in all public places (excluding taverns and private clubs). You're also not allowed to smoke on church grounds.

ACCOMMODATIONS

Utah is a major tourism destination, and you can plan on finding high-quality, reasonably priced motels and hotels in most cities and towns. Reservations are a good idea in major centers like Salt Lake City, Park City, and Moab, especially on weekends. Along the national parks loop, it can be tough to find a last-minute room in high season—be sure to book well in advance—off-season guest rooms are limited (some establishments are seasonal), so call ahead to make sure there's a room at the inn.

Hostels are available only in Salt Lake City, Park City, and Moab. They are open to travelers of all ages and don't require membership cards. You may need to provide your own sheets or sleeping bag. Utah also offers some comfortable bed-and-breakfast accommodations; contact the **Utah Travel Council** (800/200-1160, www.utah.com) for a general list of B&Bs.

Drinking Laws

Even though Utah's drinking laws have evolved recently, having a drink with your meal is easier in the major cities than in many other areas of the state. Access to alcohol in restaurants varies quite a bit from community to community, and some towns are practically "dry" (alcohol-free), at least in restaurants.

The state's liquor laws are rather confusing and peculiar, particularly if you're from Europe or U.S. states that have more open access to alcohol. A major change in liquor laws in 2010 did away with the private club requirement, under which you had to purchase a membership (temporary or yearly) in order to have a drink in a bar. However, it's worth knowing how Utah drinking laws work, because it's still a bit confusing. Several different kinds of establishments are licensed to sell alcoholic beverages.

Taverns, which include brewpubs, can sell only 3.2 percent beer (not wine, which is classed as hard liquor in Utah). You don't need to purchase food to have a beer in a tavern. With the exception of brewpubs, taverns are usually fairly derelict and not especially cheery places to hang out.

Licensed restaurants sell beer, wine, and hard liquor, but only with food orders. In Salt Lake City, Moab, and Park City, most restaurants have liquor licenses. In more out-of-the-way cities and towns, very few eating establishments offer alcohol.

Cocktail bars, lounges, live music venues, and nightclubs, which once operated on the private-club system, can now serve alcohol without asking for membership. However, some continue the income flow by demanding a cover charge for entry. Depending on which county you are in, you may still be required to order some food to have a drink.

Nearly all towns will have a state-owned **liquor store,** though they can be difficult to find, and 3.2 percent beer is available in most grocery stores and gas station minimarts. Many travelers find that carrying a bottle of your favorite beverage to your room is the easiest way to enjoy an evening drink. The state drinking age is 21.

Guest Ranches

Utah has fewer guest ranches than other western states, but some have sprung up here and there. Most are family ranches that take in guests during the summer. These tend to be authentic horse-powered operations, where you'll work alongside the family and stay in no-frills cabins or bunkhouses. Others are more upscale and offer a dude-ranch atmosphere with a number of recreational options.

Most guest ranches require minimum stays, and prices include all meals and lodging. Advance reservations are usually required. If you're contemplating staying at a guest ranch, be sure to ask specific questions about lodgings and work requirements. Expectations of the guest and host can vary widely. The Utah Travel Council can provide a full listing of Utah guest ranches.

Health and Safety

Utah has one of the lowest crime rates in the United States. Although parts of Salt Lake City look pretty scruffy, there's little reason to fear random violence unless you put yourself in unwise situations.

In emergencies, you can dial 911 throughout the state. Hospital emergency rooms offer the quickest help but cost more than a visit to a doctor's office or clinic.

DRIVING SAFETY

Summer heat in the desert puts an extra strain on both cars and drivers. It's worth double-checking your vehicle's cooling system, engine oil, transmission fluid, fan belts, and tires to make sure they are in top condition. Carry several gallons of water in case of a breakdown or radiator trouble. Never leave children or pets in a parked car during warm weather—temperatures inside can cause fatal heatstroke in minutes.

At times the desert has too much water, when late-summer storms frequently flood low spots in the road. Wait for the water level to subside before crossing.

Dust storms can completely block visibility but tend to be short-lived. During such storms, pull completely off the road, stop, and turn off your lights so as not to confuse other drivers.

If stranded, either on the desert or in the mountains, stay with your vehicle unless you're positive of where to go for help, then leave a note explaining your route and departure time. Airplanes can easily spot a stranded car (tie a piece of cloth to your antenna), but a person walking is more difficult to see. It's best to carry emergency supplies: blankets or sleeping bags, a first-aid kit, tools, jumper cables, a shovel, traction mats or chains, a flashlight, rain gear, water, food, and a can opener.

GIARDIA

Giardia, a protozoan that has become common in even the remotest mountain streams, is carried in animal or human waste that is deposited or washed into natural waters. When ingested, it begins reproducing, causing an intestinal sickness in the host that can become very serious and may require medical attention.

You can take precautions against giardia with a variety of chemicals and filtering methods or by boiling water before drinking it. The various chemical solutions on the market work in some applications, but because they need to be safe for human consumption, they are weak and ineffective against the protozoan in its cyst stage of life (when it encases itself in a hard shell). Filtering may eliminate giardia, but there are other water pests too small to be caught by most filters. The most effective way to eliminate such threats is to boil all suspect water. A few minutes at a rolling boil will kill giardia even in the cyst stage.

HANTAVIRUS

Hantavirus is an airborne infectious disease agent transmitted from rodents to humans when rodents shed hantavirus particles in their saliva, urine, and droppings and humans inhale infected particles. It is easiest for a human to contract hantavirus in a contained environment, such as a cabin infested with mouse droppings, where the virus-infected particles are not thoroughly dispersed.

Simply traveling to a place where the hantavirus is known to occur is not considered a risk factor. Camping, hiking, and other outdoor activities also pose low risk, especially if steps are taken to reduce rodent contact.

The very first symptoms can occur anywhere between five days and three weeks after infection. They almost always include fever, fatigue, and aching muscles (usually in the back, shoulders, or thighs) and other flu-like conditions. Other early symptoms may include headaches, dizziness, chills, and abdominal discomfort (such as vomiting, nausea, or diarrhea). These are shortly followed by intense coughing and shortness of breath. If you have these symptoms, seek medical help immediately. Untreated infections of hantavirus are almost always fatal.

HYPOTHERMIA

The greatest danger outdoors is one that can sneak up and kill with very little warning. Hypothermia—a lowering of the body's temperature below 95°F—causes disorientation, uncontrollable shivering, slurred speech, and drowsiness. The victim may not even realize what's wrong. Unless corrective action is taken immediately, hypothermia can lead to death. Hikers should therefore travel with companions and always carry wind and rain protection. Space blankets are lightweight and cheap and offer protection against the cold in emergencies. Remember that temperatures can plummet rapidly in Utah's dry climate—a drop of 40 degrees between day and night is common. Be especially careful at high elevations, where sunshine can quickly change into freezing rain or a blizzard. Simply falling into a mountain stream can also lead to hypothermia and death unless proper action is taken. If you're cold and tired, don't waste time: Seek shelter and build a fire, change into dry clothes, and drink warm liquids. If a victim isn't fully conscious, warm him or her by skin-to-skin contact in a sleeping bag. Try to keep the victim awake and offer plenty of warm liquids.

HEAT EXHAUSTION

Utah in summer is a very hot place. Be sure to use sunscreen, or else you risk having a very uncomfortable vacation. Heat exhaustion can also be a problem if you're hiking in the hot sun. Drink plenty of water; in midsummer try to get an early start if you're hiking in full sun.

Part of the attraction of Utah's vast wilderness backcountry is its remoteness. And if you're hiking in the canyon country in the southern part of the state, you'll spend most of your time hiking at the bottom of narrow and twisting canyons. It's easy to get lost, or at least disoriented. Always carry adequate and up-to-date maps and a compass (a GPS unit may not work in canyon country)—and know how to use them if you're heading off into the backcountry. Always plan a route. Planning usually saves time and effort. Tell someone (like a family member or a ranger) where you are going and when you'll be back, so they know where and when to start looking for you in case you get into trouble. Always take at least one other person with you: Do not venture into the desert alone. Parties of four people (or two vehicles) are ideal, because one person can stay with the person in trouble, while the other two escort each other to get help. It's a good idea to carry your cell phone in case you need to make an emergency call or send an email.

Thunderstorms can wash hikers away and bury them in the canyons and washes of the Southwest. Flash floods can happen almost any time of year but are most prevalent in the summer months. Before entering slot canyon areas like Paria or the Escalante Canyons, check with rangers or local authorities for weather reports. And while you're hiking, read and heed the clouds. Many washes and canyons drain large areas, with their headwaters many miles away. The dangerous part is that sometimes you just can't tell what's coming down the wash or canyon because of the vast number of acres that these canyons drain, and because the cliff walls are too high to see out to any storms that may be creating flood potential upstream. At any sign of a threat, get out of the canyon bottom—at least 60 vertical feet up—to avoid water and debris. Since many of these canyons are narrow, there are places where it's not possible to get out of the canyon on short notice. Never drive a vehicle into a flooded wash. Stop and wait for the water to recede, as it usually will within an hour.

WILDLIFE

Probably a greater threat to health are poisonous rattlesnakes and scorpions. When hiking or climbing in desert areas, never put your hand onto a ledge or into a hole that you can't see. Both are perfect lairs for snakes and scorpions. While snakebites are rarely fatal anymore, they're no fun either. If you are bitten, immobilize the affected area and seek immediate medical attention.

If you do much hiking and biking in the spring, there's a good chance you'll encounter ticks. While ticks in this part of the United States don't usually carry Lyme disease, there is a remote threat of Rocky Mountain spotted fever, spread by the wood tick. If a tick has bitten you, pull it off immediately. Grasp the tick's head parts (as close to your skin as possible) with tweezers and pull slowly and steadily. Do not attempt to remove ticks by burning them or coating them with anything. Removing a tick as soon as possible greatly reduces your chance of infection.

Utah is home to black bears, which aren't as menacing as their grizzly bear cousins. However, black bears weigh more than most humans and have far sharper claws and teeth. An encounter with a black bear is rarely fatal, but it's something to be avoided.

If you encounter a bear, give it plenty of room and try not to surprise it. Wearing a fragrance while in bear country isn't a good idea because it attracts bears, as do strong-smelling foods. Always store food items outside the tent, and if you're in bear territory, sleep well away from the cooking area. Waking up with a bear clawing at your tent is to be avoided. Hanging food in a bag from a tree is a longstanding and wise precaution. If a bear becomes aggressive, try to drop something that will divert its attention while you flee. If that isn't possible, the next best bet is to curl up into a ball, clasp your hands behind your neck, and play dead, even if the bear begins to bat you around. Taking precautions and having respect for bears will ensure not only your continued existence, but theirs as well.

In recent years, as humans have increasingly moved into mountain lion habitat (and as their numbers have increased), they have become a threat to humans, especially small children. Never leave children unattended in forests, and never allow them to lag far behind on a family hike. Nearly every summer, newspapers in the western states carry tragic stories of children stalked and killed by mountain lions, which are also known as cougars. Safety is in numbers.

Information and Services

MONEY

Prices of all services mentioned in this guide were current at press time. You're sure to find seasonal and long-term price changes, so please, don't use what's listed here to argue with the staff at a motel, campground, museum, airline, or other office.

Banks and ATMs

Cash machines (ATMs) are available throughout Utah, even in the smallest towns. It's hard to exchange foreign currency or travelers checks outside of central Salt Lake City, so foreign travelers should exchange all they'll need before setting out for rural parts of the state. Credit cards are generally accepted at most businesses.

Taxes

A sales tax, which varies from 5.95 to 8.1 percent, is added to most transactions on goods, food, and services. Additional room taxes are added; these vary by community and can be quite steep.

Tipping

It's customary to tip food and drink servers 15-20 percent; tips are almost never automatically added to the bill. Taxi drivers receive a 10-15 percent gratuity; bellhops get at least $1 a bag.

COMMUNICATIONS AND MEDIA

Normal post office hours are 8:30am-5pm Monday-Friday and sometimes 8:30am-noon Saturday. U.S. post offices sell stamps and postal money orders. Overnight express service is also available.

Utah has three area codes: 801 and 385 are the codes for the greater Salt Lake City area, which includes suburbs as far south as Provo and as far north as Ogden. The rest of the state has the area code 435.

Toll-free numbers in the United States have an 800, 888, 877, or 866 area code. To obtain directory assistance, dial 411.

Even in small towns, most hotels (and even most budget motels) offer wireless internet access.

Depending on your cellular provider, cell phone coverage can be very spotty in rural areas, and nonexistent in canyons.

MAPS AND VISITOR INFORMATION

General tourist literature and maps are available from the **Utah Travel Council** (800/200-1160, www.utah.com). Utah's many chambers of commerce also have free material and are happy to help with travel suggestions in their areas. (See the *Information* sections throughout this guide for contact information.) Also listed are national forest offices and other government agencies that have information on outdoor recreation in their areas.

The **Utah Department of Transportation** (801/965-4000, www.udot.utah.gov) prints and distributes a free, regularly updated map of Utah. Ask for it when you call for information or when you stop at a visitor information office. If you're planning on extensive backcountry exploration, be sure to ask locally about conditions. Backcountry enthusiasts or back-road explorers should also pick up Benchmark Maps' *Utah Road and Recreation Atlas.*

Obtain literature and the latest information on all of Utah's state parks from the **Utah State Parks and Recreation** office (801/538-7220 or 877/887-2757, http://stateparks.utah.gov). If you're planning a lot of state park visits, ask about the $75 annual state park pass. Reservations for campgrounds and some other services can be made at 800/322-3770 or www.reserveamerica.com; a reservation fee of $9 (online) or $10 (phone) applies.

Business Hours

In Utah, most commercial businesses are open 9am-6pm Monday-Saturday. The biggest surprise to many travelers is that nearly all businesses—and almost certainly those away from Salt Lake City, big recreational hubs, and the national parks—close on Sunday in Utah. Again, almost all businesses in Utah, including many restaurants, are closed on Sunday. This includes local public transportation. Even in Salt Lake City it can be difficult to find a place to eat on Sunday. Imagine how difficult it might be to find a bite to eat in, say, Monticello. If you're traveling outside the Wasatch Front on Sunday, ask your motel clerk if you'll be able to find a meal at your intended destination. Usually some gas stations along the interstates are open on Sunday, but in out-of-the-way places it's not guaranteed, so be sure to fill up on Saturday. Plan well ahead; it's easy to get stranded, hungry, and disappointed.

Note that most museums, recreation areas, and other attractions close on Thanksgiving, Christmas, New Year's Day, and other holidays. These closings are not always mentioned in the text, so call ahead to check.

WEIGHTS AND MEASURES
Time Zones

Utah is in the mountain time zone and goes

on daylight saving time (advanced one hour) March-November. Nevada is in the Pacific time zone, one hour earlier; all other bordering states are in the mountain time zone. An odd exception is Arizona, which stays on mountain standard time all year (except for the Navajo Reservation, which goes on daylight saving time to keep up with its Utah and New Mexico sections).

Electricity

As in all of the United States, electricity is 110 volts, 60 hertz. Plugs have either two flat prongs or two flat prongs plus one round prong. Older homes and hotels may only have two-prong outlets, and you may well be traveling with computers or appliances that have three-prong plugs. Ask your hotel or motel manager for an adapter; if necessary, you may need to buy a three-prong adapter, but the cost is small.

Resources

Suggested Reading

ARCHAEOLOGY

Lister, Robert, and Florence Lister. *Those Who Came Before*. Tucson: Southwest Parks and Monuments, 1993. A well-illustrated guide to the history, artifacts, and ruins of prehistoric Southwest Native Americans. The author also describes parks and monuments containing archaeological sites.

Simms, Steven R. *Traces of Fremont: Society and Rock Art in Ancient Utah*. Salt Lake City: University of Utah Press, 2010. Great photos accompany the text in this look into Fremont culture.

Slifer, Dennis. *Guide to Rock Art of the Utah Region: Sites with Public Access*. Albuquerque: University of New Mexico Press, 2000. The most complete guide to rock-art sites, with descriptions of more than 50 sites in the Four Corners region. Complete with maps and directions, and including an overview of rock-art styles and traditions.

GUIDEBOOKS AND TRAVEL

Benchmark Maps. *Utah Road & Recreation Atlas*. Medford, OR: Benchmark Maps, 2008. Shaded relief maps emphasize landforms, and recreational information is abundant. Use it to locate campgrounds, back roads, and major trailheads, though there's not enough detail to rely on it for hiking.

Huegel, Tony. *Utah Byways: 65 of Utah's Best Backcountry Drives*. Berkeley, CA: Wilderness Press, 2006. If you're looking for off-highway adventure, this is your guide. The book includes detailed directions, human and natural history, outstanding photography, full-page maps for each of the 65 routes, and an extensive how-to chapter for beginners.

Porter, Eliot. *The Place No One Knew: Glen Canyon on the Colorado*. San Francisco: Sierra Club Books, 2000. Beautiful color photos show a world now lost to the waters of Lake Powell. Thoughtful quotations from many individuals accompany the illustrations.

Roylance, Ward J. *Utah: A Guide to the State*. Layton, UT: Gibbs Smith Publishers, 1998. An updated version of the book published by the WPA Writers Program in 1941. Much of the original material and format have been preserved. The comprehensive introduction to Utah's people and history is followed by 11 tours of the state.

Stegner, Wallace, ed. *This Is Dinosaur: Echo Park Country and Its Magic Rivers*. Niwot, CO: Roberts Rinehart, 1985. Essays on this rugged land—its geology, dinosaurs, wildlife, Native Americans, explorers, riverrunning, and visiting Dinosaur National Monument.

Wells, Charles A. *Guide to Moab, UT Backroads & 4-Wheel Drive Trails*. Monument, CO: Funtreks Inc., 2008. Good descriptions and GPS waypoints for Moab-area four-wheelers.

Zwinger, Ann. *Wind in the Rock: The Canyonlands of Southeastern Utah*. Tucson: University of Arizona Press, 1986. Well-written accounts of hiking in the Grand Gulch and nearby canyons. The author tells of the area's history, archaeology, wildlife, and plants.

HISTORY AND CURRENT EVENTS

Bennet, Cynthia Larsen. *Roadside History of Utah*. Missoula, MT: Mountain Press Publishing, 1999. A very readable account of the state's history organized by driving tours. Full of great tales, yarns, and amazing human stories.

Krakauer, Jon. *Under the Banner of Heaven: A Story of Violent Faith*. New York: Doubleday Books, 2003. The story of two fundamentalist polygamous brothers who killed their sister-in-law and nephew upon receiving what they considered to be a message from God.

Stegner, Wallace. *Beyond the Hundredth Meridian: John Wesley Powell and the Second Opening of the West*. New York: Penguin Books, 1992 (first published in 1954). Stegner tells the story of Powell's wild rides down the Colorado River, then goes on to point out why the United States should have listened to what Powell had to say about the American Southwest.

MEMOIRS

Abbey, Edward. *Desert Solitaire*. New York: Ballantine Books, 1991. A meditation on the Red Rock Canyon country of Utah. Abbey brings his fiery prose to the service of the American outback, while excoriating the commercialization of the West.

Childs, Craig. *The Secret Knowledge of Water*. Boston: Back Bay Books, 2000. Childs looks for water in the desert, and finds plenty of it.

Meloy, Ellen. *Raven's Exile*. New York: Henry Holt and Company, 2003. Throughout a summer of Green River raft trips, Meloy reflects on the natural and human history of the area.

Williams, Terry Tempest. *Refuge: An Unnatural History of Family and Place*. New York: Vintage Books, 1992. A memoir of a family devastated by cancer (caused by federal government atomic testing), overlain with a natural history of birdlife along the Great Salt Lake. Haunting, deeply spiritual, and beautifully written.

NATURAL SCIENCES

Chronic, Halka. *Roadside Geology of Utah*. Missoula, MT: Mountain Press Publishing, 1990. Utah's geology as seen by following major roadways.

Fagan, Damian. *Canyon Country Wildflowers*. Helena, MT: Falcon Publishing, 1998. A comprehensive field guide to the diverse flora of the Four Corners area.

Williams, David. *A Naturalist's Guide to Canyon Country*. Helena, MT: Falcon Publishing, 2000. If you want to buy just one field guide, this is the one to get. It's well written, beautifully illustrated, and a delight to use.

RECREATION

Adkison, Ron. *Hiking Grand Staircase-Escalante & the Glen Canyon Region: A Guide to 59 of the Best Hiking Adventures in Southern Utah*. Helena, MT: Falcon Publishing, 2011. The vast Escalante-Glen Canyon area of southern Utah is nearly roadless, and hiking is about the only way you'll have a chance to visit these beautiful and austere canyons. This guide includes detailed information on 59 hikes, including Paria Canyon and Grand Gulch, in addition to the Grand Staircase-Escalante National Monument.

Allen, Steve. *Canyoneering: The San Rafael Swell*. Salt Lake City: University of Utah Press, 2000. Eight chapters each cover a different area of this exceptional, though little-known, canyon country. Trail and route descriptions cover adventures from easy rambles to challenging hikes. The author provides some climbing notes, too. Detailed road logs help you get there, whether by mountain bike, car, or truck.

Belknap, Buzz, and Loie Belknap Evans. *Belknap's Waterproof Dinosaur River Guide*. Evergreen, CO: Westwater Books, 2008. Topo maps show the canyons and points of interest along the Green and Yampa Rivers in Dinosaur National Monument of northeastern Utah and adjacent Colorado. Includes Lodore, Whirlpool, and Split Mountain Canyons of the Green River. The Belknaps' other river guides are also go-to guides.

Bjørnstad, Eric. *Desert Rock I: Rock Climbs in the National Parks*. Helena, MT: Falcon Publishing, 1996. One of several excellent climbing guides by one of Utah's most respected climbers. Also see Bjørnstad's *Rock Climbing Desert Rock IV: The Colorado Plateau Backcountry: Utah* for information on climbing outside Utah's national parks.

Brinkerhoff, Brian, and Greg Witt. *Best Easy Day Hikes Salt Lake City*. Helena, MT: Falcon Publishing, 2009. More than 20 short hikes in the Wasatch Front canyons near Salt Lake City.

Bromka, Gregg. *Mountain Biking Utah*. Helena, MT: Falcon Publishing, 1999. Detailed route descriptions of more than 100 rides, from the Salt Lake City area through Moab and Brian Head. Easy-to-use maps and elevation profiles included.

Crowell, David. *Mountain Biking Moab*. Helena, MT: Falcon Publishing, 2014. A handy guide to the many trails around Moab, from the most popular to the little explored, in a handy size: small enough to take on the bike with you.

Day, David. *Utah's Incredible Backcountry Trails*. Provo, UT: Rincon Publishing, 2006. Good selection of trips within Utah, with simple but very clear maps.

Green, Stewart M. *Rock Climbing Utah*. Helena, MT: Falcon Publishing, 2012. Comprehensive guide to climbing routes throughout the state. Route maps are superimposed over photographs to make sure climbers find the right route.

Kelsey, Michael R. *Canyon Hiking Guide to the Colorado Plateau: Non-Technical*. Provo, UT: Kelsey Publishing, 2006. A classic guide to hiking in southeastern Utah's canyon country. The author persists in using only the metric system, and the layout is a bit dense, but it's certainly comprehensive. Kelsey is also incredibly prolific—he has written many guides to the Southwest, and if you like this one, you should search for his others.

Lambrechtse, Rudi. *Hiking the Escalante*. Salt Lake City: Wasatch Publishers, 1999. An introduction to the history, geology, and natural history of the Escalante region in southern Utah, with descriptions of 42 hikes. Now out of print, but widely available used, this is still essential background reading for anyone considering canyoneering the Escalante.

Matson, Mike. *Moon Utah Camping*. Berkeley, CA: Avalon Travel, 2009. The best guide to public and private campgrounds across the state. A great resource if you're planning on doing any backcountry exploration.

Probst, Jeffrey. *Hiking Utah's High Uintas: 99 Day and Overnight Hikes.* Helena, MT: Falcon Publishing, 2006. Nearly 100 hiking trails, from easy to long-distance, and information on the area's 600 lakes.

Witt, Greg. *50 Best Hikes in Utah's National Parks*, Birmingham, AL: Wilderness Press, 2014. A veteran hiking guide shares his favorite routes in Utah's five national parks.

Internet Resources

NEWS

Deseret News
www.desnews.com
One of Salt Lake's major newspapers, the *Deseret News* has good regional and LDS coverage.

Salt Lake Tribune
www.sltrib.com
The *Salt Lake Tribune* is the state's newspaper of record.

Salt Lake City Weekly
www.cityweekly.net/
Salt Lake City's alternative weekly newspaper has online event listings and in-depth articles on city issues.

RECREATION

Desert USA
www.desertusa.com
Desert USA's Utah section discusses places to visit and what plants and animals you might meet there. Here's the best part of this site: you can find out what's in bloom at www.desertusa.com/wildflo/nv.html.

Federal Recreation Reservations
www.recreation.gov
If a campground is operated by the federal government, this is the place to make a reservation. You can expect to pay $9 for this convenience ($10 if you choose to use the phone to make the reservation).

National Park Service
www.nps.gov
The National Park Service offers pages for all their areas at this site, where a click-on map will take you to Utah's parks. You can also enter this URL followed by a slash and the first two letters of the first two words of the place (first four letters if there's just a one-word name); for example, www.nps.gov/brca takes you to Bryce Canyon National Park and www.nps.gov/zion leads to Zion National Park.

Reserve America
www.reserveamerica.com
Use this website to reserve campsites in state campgrounds. It costs a few extra bucks ($9 reservation fee) to reserve a campsite, but compare that with the cost of not being able to get a campsite and having to resort to a motel room.

U.S. Forest Service
www.fs.usda.gov/r4
Utah falls within U.S. Forest Service Region 4. From this site you can navigate to each of the national forests in Utah.

Utah State Parks
http://stateparks.utah.gov
The Utah State Parks website offers details on the large park system.

TRAVEL

Ghost Towns
www.ghosttowns.com/states/ut/ut.html
Histories and photos of Utah's loneliest towns.

Ski Utah
www.skiutah.com
If you're thinking snow, glide over to Ski Utah, where you'll also find summer activities at the ski resorts.

Utah Travel Council
www.utah.com
The Utah Travel Council is a one-stop shop for all sorts of information on Utah. It takes you around the state to sights, activities, events, and maps and offers links to local tourism offices. The accommodations listings are the most up-to-date source for current prices and options.

Visit Salt Lake City
www.visitsaltlake.com
Find the scoop on all aspects of visiting Salt Lake City, including accommodations (sometimes with special deals), events, and activities ranging from genealogical research to birdwatching. It's also a good place to find special deals on ski passes.

Index

XYZ

List of Maps

Photo Credits

Title page Photo: Kojihirano | Dreamstime.com;

page 2 © Fashionstock/123Rf; page 3 © Bill McRae; page 6 © (top left) Bill McRae; (top right) NPS/Chris Wonderly; (bottom) NPS/Neal Herbert; page 7 © (top) Alta Ski Area; (bottom left) Bill McRae; (bottom right) NPS/Neal Herbert; page 8 © (top) Anna Dudko | Dreamstime.com; page 9 © (top) Kan1234 | Dreamstime.com; (bottom left) NPS/Jonathan Fortner; (bottom right) Kwiktor | Dreamstime.com; page 10 © Dfikar | Dreamstime.com; page 12 © (top) Paul Levy; (bottom) Deer Valley Resort; page 13 © (top) Alexirina27000 | Dreamstime.com; (middle) NPS/Jacob W. Frank; (bottom) Maksershov | Dreamstime.com; page 14 © (top) Judy Jewell; (bottom) Bill McRae; page 15 © (top) Robert Cocquyt | Dreamstime.com; (bottom) NPS/Kirsten Kearse; page 16 © (bottom) Michael Gordon | Dreamstime.com; page 18 © (top) Jennifer Snarski; page 19 © Nyker1 | Dreamstime.com; Judy Jewell; page 20 © (top) NPS/Jacob W. Frank; page 21 © Bill McRae; Bill McRae; page 23 © (bottom) Jennifer Snarski; page 25 © (bottom) Judy Jewell; page 28 © (bottom) Robert Fullerton | Dreamstime.com; page 30 © Legacyimagesinc | Dreamstime.com; page 37 © (top left) Judy Jewell; (top right) Sainaniritu | Dreamstime.com; (bottom) Judy Jewell; page 45 © (top) Bill McRae; (bottom) Judy Jewell; page 59 © (top left) Judy Jewell; (top right) Judy Jewell; (bottom) Judy Jewell; page 65 © (top) Judy Jewell; (left middle) Judy Jewell; (right middle) Judy Jewell; (bottom) Judy Jewell; page 68 © Judy Jewell; page 81 © (top) Pureradiancephoto | Dreamstime.com; (bottom) Judy Jewell; page 85 © (top left) Judy Jewell; (top right) Judy Jewell; (bottom left) Judy Jewell; (bottom right) Judy Jewell; page 93 © Judy Jewell; page 95 © (top) Paul Levy; (bottom) Saltcityphotography | Dreamstime.com; page 99 © (top) Evan Lambson | Dreamstime.com; (bottom) Linda Bair | Dreamstime.com; page 106 © (top) Judy Jewell; (bottom) Judy Jewell; page 111 © Judy Jewell; page 116 © (top) Judy Jewell; (bottom) Alexander Gordeyev | Dreamstime.com; page 120 © (top) Judy Jewell; (bottom) Johnny Adolphson | Dreamstime.com; page 126 © Alta Ski Area; page 134 © (top left) Ritu Jethani | Dreamstime.com; (top right) Deer Valley Resort/Eric Schramm; (bottom) Judy Jewell; page 147 © (top) Judy Jewell; (bottom) Judy Jewell; page 153 © (top) Judy Jewell; (left middle)Judy Jewell; (right middle) Judy Jewell; (bottom) Judy Jewell; page 157 © Judy Jewell; page 163 © (top left) NPS; (top right) NPS; (bottom) Judy Jewell; page 169 © (top) Judy Jewell; (left middle) Alexstork | Dreamstime.com; (right middle)Judy Jewell; (bottom) Alexstork | Dreamstime.com; page 173 © Alan Mitchell | Dreamstime. com; page 178 © (top) Sandra Foyt | Dreamstime.com; (bottom) Judy Jewell; page 183 © Donald Fink | Dreamstime.com; page 190 © (top) Johnny Adolphson | Dreamstime.com; (bottom) Bill McRae; page 193 © Kim Lindvall | Dreamstime.com; page 201 © (top) Tristan Brynildsen | Dreamstime.com; (bottom) Irina Kozhemyakina | Dreamstime.com; page 205 © (top) Bill McRae; (bottom) Judy Jewell; page 207 © Galyna Andrushko | Dreamstime.com; page 216 © (top) Chris Curtis | Dreamstime.com; (bottom) Christina Felschen | Dreamstime.com; page 219 © Judy Jewell; page 221 © NPS/Marc Neidig; page 230 © (top) Bill McRae; (bottom) Bill McRae; page 236 © (top left) Robert Bohrer | Dreamstime.com; (top right) NPS/Marc Neidig; (bottom) Bill McRae; page 240 © NPS/Rendall Seely; page 252 © (top) Bill McRae; (bottom) Ekaterina Pokrovsky | Dreamstime.com; page 255 © (top) Venemama | Dreamstime.com; (bottom) Hikers On The Peekaboo Trail; page 262 © (top) Jennifer Snarski; (bottom) Bill McRae; page 270 © Bill McRae; page 284 © Utah Shakespeare Festival 2018/Karl Hugh; page 291 © Photosbyjam | Dreamstime.com; page 294 © Minnystock | Dreamstime.com; page 302 © James Phelps Jr | Dreamstime.com; page 304 © (top left) Bill McRae; (bottom) Kwiktor | Dreamstime.com; page 307 © (top) Bill McRae; (bottom) Larry Gevert | Dreamstime.com; page 316 © (top left) Bill McRae; (top right) Jennifer Snarski; (bottom left) Jaahnlieb | Dreamstime.com; (bottom right) Denniskoomen | Dreamstime.com; page 324 © (top) Bill McRae; (bottom) Bill McRae; page 332 © (top) Jeremy Christensen | Dreamstime.com; (bottom) Bill McRae; page 335 © (top left) Scott Prokop | Dreamstime.com; (top right) Bill McRae; (bottom) Björn Alberts | Dreamstime.com; page 341 © (top) James Phelps Jr | Dreamstime.com; (left middle)Bill McRae; (right middle)Pierre Leclerc | Dreamstime.com; (bottom) Frank Bach | Dreamstime.com; page 346 © Bill McRae; page 353 © (top) Anna Dudko | Dreamstime.com; (bottom) Bill McRae; page 356 © NPS/Neal Herbert; page 364 © (top) Bill McRae; (bottom) Bill McRae; page 367 © Philip Kononuk | Dreamstime. com; page 371 © (top) Bill McRae; (bottom) Kwiktor | Dreamstime.com; page 373 © Beatrice Preve | Dreamstime.com; page 378 © Cynthia Mccrary | Dreamstime.com; page 386 © Bill McRae; page 391 © (top) Bill McRae; (left middle) Bill McRae; (right middle) NPS/Jacob W. Frank; (bottom) NPS/Neal Herbert;

Travel with Moon in the Rockies, the Southwest, and Texas

MOON
ARIZONA
& THE GRAND CANYON
TIM HULL

MOON
AUSTIN
SAN ANTONIO &
THE HILL COUNTRY
JUSTIN MARLER

MOON
COLORADO
TERRI COOK

MOON
DENVER,
BOULDER &
COLORADO SPRINGS

MOON
IDAHO
JAMES P. KELLY

MOON
MONTANA
& WYOMING
CARTER G. WALKER

MOON
NEVADA
SCOTT SMITH

MOON
NEW
MEXICO

MOON
PHOENIX,
SCOTTSDALE
& SEDONA

MOON
SANTA FE, TAOS
& ALBUQUERQUE
STEVEN HORAK

MOON
TEXAS
ANDY RHODES

MOON
UTAH
With Zion, Bryce Canyon, Arches,
Capitol Reef & Canyonlands
National Parks
W. C. McRAE & JUDY JEWELL

Or go big and go abroad

MOON
TRIP OF A LIFETIME
ANGKOR WAT

MOON
FIJI

MOON
TRIP OF A LIFETIME
GALÁPAGOS
ISLANDS

MOON
TRIP OF A LIFETIME
MACHU
PICCHU

MOON
ROME,
FLORENCE
& VENICE

#TravelWithMoon

MAP SYMBOLS

═══ Expressway	○ City/Town	✈ Airport
─── Primary Road	◉ State Capital	✕ Airfield
─── Secondary Road	⊛ National Capital	▲ Mountain
------- Unpaved Road	★ Point of Interest	✦ Unique Natural Feature
─── Feature Trail	• Accommodation	≈ Waterfall
- - - Other Trail	▼ Restaurant/Bar	♠ Park
⋯⋯ Ferry	■ Other Location	▣ Trailhead
═══ Pedestrian Walkway	△ Campground	⛷ Skiing Area
▪▪▪ Stairs		

⌁ Golf Course	
℗ Parking Area	
⛾ Archaeological Site	
⛪ Church	
⛽ Gas Station	
🏔 Glacier	
▨ Mangrove	
⌇ Reef	
⌱ Swamp	

CONVERSION TABLES

$°C = (°F - 32) / 1.8$
$°F = (°C \times 1.8) + 32$
1 inch = 2.54 centimeters (cm)
1 foot = 0.304 meters (m)
1 yard = 0.914 meters
1 mile = 1.6093 kilometers (km)
1 km = 0.6214 miles
1 fathom = 1.8288 m
1 chain = 20.1168 m
1 furlong = 201.168 m
1 acre = 0.4047 hectares
1 sq km = 100 hectares
1 sq mile = 2.59 square km
1 ounce = 28.35 grams
1 pound = 0.4536 kilograms
1 short ton = 0.90718 metric ton
1 short ton = 2,000 pounds
1 long ton = 1.016 metric tons
1 long ton = 2,240 pounds
1 metric ton = 1,000 kilograms
1 quart = 0.94635 liters
1 US gallon = 3.7854 liters
1 Imperial gallon = 4.5459 liters
1 nautical mile = 1.852 km

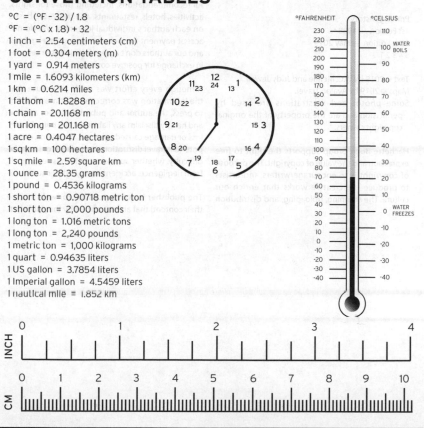

917.92
JEW

MOON UTAH
Avalon Travel
Hachette Book Group
1700 Fourth Street
Berkeley, CA 94710, USA
www.moon.com

Editor: Kimberly Ehart
Series Manager: Kathryn Ettinger
Copy Editor: Kelly Lydick
Graphics and Production Coordinator: Darren Alessi
Cover Design: Faceout Studios, Charles Brock
Moon Logo: Tim McGrath
Map Editor: Mike Morgenfeld
Cartographers: Austin Ehrhardt and Brian Shotwell
Proofreader: Anna Ho
Indexer: Greg Jewett

ISBN-13: 978-1-64049-360-5

Printing History
1st Edition — 1988
13th Edition — May 2019
5 4 3 2 1

Front cover photo: Totem Pole at dawn, Monument
    Valley © Peter Barritt / Alamy Stock Photo
Back cover photo: The Narrows, Zion National Park
    © Lukas Bischoff | Dreamstime.com

Printed in China by RR Donnelley